WORKS OF
FISHER AMES

FISHER AMES

WORKS OF

FISHER AMES

AS PUBLISHED BY

SETH AMES

Edited and Enlarged by

W. B. Allen

VOLUME II

Liberty*Classics*

INDIANAPOLIS

Foreword copyright © 1983 by William B. Allen. All rights reserved. All
inquiries should be addressed to Liberty Fund, Inc., 7440 N. Shadeland,
Indianapolis, Indiana 46250. This book was manufactured in the United
States of America.

This edition of the *Works of Fisher Ames* follows the edition by Seth Ames
(1854) published at New York, except for the arrangement, and bears some
corrections carried from the 1809 edition by George Cabot et al., Boston,
and *Speeches of Fisher Ames in Congress (1789–1796)*, edited by Pelham W.
Ames (1871), Boston. It has further been enlarged with essays, speeches,
and correspondence found in manuscripts in various collections.

*Frontispiece photo for Volume I courtesy of the Stanford University Libraries,
Stanford, California.*
*Frontispiece photo for Volume II courtesy of the Independence National Historical
Park Collection, Philadelphia, Pennsylvania.*

LIBRARY OF CONGRESS CATALOGING IN PUBLICATION DATA

Ames, Fisher, 1758–1808.
    Works of Fisher Ames.

    Reprint. Originally published: Boston: Little,
Brown, 1854.
    Includes index.
    1. United States—Politics and government—Constitu-
tional period, 1789–1809—Addresses, essays, lectures.
2. Ames, Fisher, 1758–1808. 3. Statesmen—United States
—Correspondence. I. Allen, W. B., 1944–
II. Ames, Seth, 1805–1881. III. Title.
E302.A52 1983   973.4′092′4   83-13568
ISBN 0-86597-013-0 (set)
ISBN 0-86597-016-5 (pbk.: set)

ISBN 0-86597-014-9 (v. 1)
ISBN 0-86597-017-3 (pbk.: v. 1)
ISBN 0-86597-015-7 (v. 2)
ISBN 0-86597-018-1 (pbk.: v. 2)

10 9 8 7 6 5 4 3 2 1

CONTENTS

CONTENTS

VIII. ATTACKING THE REPUBLICANS

IX. ESSAYS ON THE FRENCH REVOLUTION AND EUROPEAN POLITICS

X. EULOGIES

PART TWO

SPEECHES AND LETTERS

1788

1789

1790

VOLUME II

1791

1792

1793

1794

1795

1796

1797

1798

1799

1800

1801

1802

1803

1804

1805

1806

CONTENTS

1807

FOREWORD

═══

*Our wisdom made a government and committed
it to our virtue to keep.*

FISHER AMES was one of the most influential Federalist statesmen of his day, his party's greatest orator, a brilliant essayist, and perhaps the most accomplished man of letters among his contemporaries in public service. Ames was active in public life from 1787 through 1807 and a member of Congress for the eight years of Washington's presidency. Though his deeds are now obscured by the passage of time, once his name was almost as often on the lips of his countrymen as that of Madison, Jefferson, or Hamilton. By the time of his retirement from public office, Ames had established himself as the leader of the Federalist party in the House of Representatives. It was he, in 1789, who provided the decisive form for the First Amendment to the Constitution.

Fisher Ames was born on April 9, 1758, in the little town of Dedham, Massachusetts, a few miles south of Boston. His father died when Fisher was six. He attended the town school and at twelve years of age journeyed to Cambridge to apply for admission to Harvard College. Fisher was pronounced by his examiner "a youth of uncommon attainments and bright promise." He became the second-youngest member of the class of 1774.

Ames graduated from Harvard at age sixteen and then taught intermittently in the country schools near his home. He devoted his leisure time to rereading the Greek and Latin classics and English literature and history. He thus developed an abundant stock of lore with which to embellish his speeches and writings of a later period. In 1775, he was mustered out to join a detachment of militia that marched toward Boston upon news of the fight at Bunker Hill. His detachment was not involved in the fighting and was dismissed after two days. In 1778, he enlisted in a company that was sent to guard the land approaches to Boston. After fifteen days' service, the men were dismissed, and this turned out to be Ames's final service in the Revolutionary War.

In 1777, Ames had begun the study of law on his own. He later entered the law offices of William Tudor, a prominent Boston attorney, completed his training in the autumn of 1781, and opened an office in Dedham.

Although he was not so precocious, perhaps, as Hamilton, Ames gave a hint of his potential in 1779, when he was but twenty-one years old. In that year, prices rose sharply in Massachusetts because of the shortage of goods and the state's excessive printing of paper money. A convention of 175 men from around the state met at Concord on July 14 to look into the matter. This convention devised a system of wage and price controls in an effort to check the runaway inflation. Ames attended a second session of the convention as a delegate from Dedham. Since prices had continued to rise in the months following the first session, the delegates set about revising the price scale upward. Ames delivered a speech, now lost, in which he attacked the very idea of price controls. According to his biographer, writing shortly after Ames's death, it was

> A lucid and impressive speech, shewing the futility
> of attempting to establish by power that value of
> things, which depended solely on consent; that the
> embarrassment was inevitable, and that it must be
> met by patriotism and patience, and not by attempting
> to do what was impossible to be done.

That young Ames would oppose a measure that had been
endorsed by so many respectable men of the state shows that
he possessed more than a common degree of courage and
had already grasped the principles of the new science of
political economy—principles that later guided him through
debates far more momentous.

By the close of the revolutionary war in 1783, the nation's
economy was all but ruined. The Continental Congress and
the states had incurred huge debts during the war. Under
the Articles of Confederation, Congress had no power to put
the nation's finances on a sound basis. A currency shortage
occurred throughout the country at the same time that creditors
began to demand the payment of debts, driving debtors to
extremes. The debtors, in turn, pressured state legislatures
to pass tender acts, making livestock or produce a legal
payment for debts; to pass postponing the collection of debts;
and to issue paper money. In the states that passed such
laws, creditors fled to escape the swarms of debtors descending
upon them to pay debts with produce or worthless paper
money.

In Massachusetts, the debtors were unable to push their
program through the state legislature, which instead put state
finances on a specie basis. When creditors began to exercise
liens on land and livestock for the payment of debts, desperate
farmers, led by Daniel Shays, sought forcibly to prevent the
courts from sitting. The state was compelled to call out the
militia to disperse the farmers and restore order.

Before the militia was called out, the Lucius Junius Brutus
essays appeared in a Boston newspaper. Under this pseu-

donym, Ames argued that the rebels had to be stopped before the Constitution was overthrown. He criticized unnecessary delays and temporizing by state officials; finally, he maintained that while tender acts and paper money might provide relief to one part of the community, they constituted an unjust confiscation of the property of another part.

In February and March 1787, after the rebellion had been suppressed, Ames penned a series of five essays under the pseudonym Camillus. He employed these essays to congratulate the state on the suppression of the rebellion and to expatiate on the fundamental principles of republican government that were at stake, not just for Massachusetts, but for the nation. He warned of errors in public opinion that could lead to future rebellions if not corrected. He chastised "men of speculation and refinement" who were ready to abandon the republican experiment because "the first years of the millenium had fallen far short of the expected felicity" and then closed with a call for constitutional change. "It is time," he said, "to render the federal head supreme in the United States."

These early essays brought Fisher Ames before the public eye at a critical point in the nation's history. The convention, which met in Philadelphia in May 1787, drafted a new constitution. Since his essays proved him energetic, articulate, and federal-minded, Ames was elected to represent Dedham in the state convention called to ratify or reject the new document.

The Massachusetts state ratifying convention met in Boston on January 9, 1788. There gathered 280 of the ablest men in the state, with another eighty-four expected. The delegate list included old revolutionary patriots, delegates to the Constitutional Convention, and other state worthies.

Ames was one of the youngest delegates, but his influence compared favorably with that of the older men. One observer classed Ames among the ablest advocates of the Constitution.

Another stated that the "masterly speeches of . . . Dana, Parsons, King, [and] Ames . . . would add a lustre to any Parliament in Europe."

By fall of 1788, public interest in the upcoming elections for the new House of Representatives began to build. Federalists throughout the country urged the voters to elect proven supporters of the new Constitution.

A candidate was needed to unify the federalist vote against Samuel A. Adams, the principal anti-Federalist candidate. Barely two weeks before the election, Fisher Ames was presented to the Suffolk voters as the Federalist candidate for representative. Samuel Adams had been a popular figure in Massachusetts since the Revolution, so the Federalists were hoping at best for a good showing by Ames. As the votes came in from around the country, Ames took a slim lead, and he was declared the winner on January 7, 1789. His victory was all the more impressive in that he had garnered a majority even though the votes were eventually split among fifteen candidates.

The United States was entering a new era in its political history, with a strong government formed to raise the country from its "state of imbecility under the Articles of Confederation." The problems to be solved were many. The nation's credit was in ruins. The revolutionary war debt had been left unpaid, and interest on it was accumulating. The federal treasury was empty. There was no federal revenue system. Congress faced the tasks of creating executive departments and delineating their powers and duties, forming the federal judiciary, and determining the extent of the federal government's powers and its relation to the states. None could say how these matters would be handled or whether the new Constitution would endure.

James Madison took the lead, introducing in the House of Representatives almost all of the initial measures from revenue bills to constitutional amendments that were needed to launch the government. Ames took his bearings in these early debates from principles on which he consistently relied throughout his congressional career. He had advocated low duties on molasses because he was convinced that "promoting the interests of particular states increases the general welfare." On the other hand, he had voted against Madison's tonnage bill even though it would have benefited New England shipping. He did so because he thought that the disruption of foreign trade would injure the nation as a whole.

While points of difference between Madison and Ames—the principal figures in the House in the First Congress—serve to illuminate the principles initially at stake, more significant in this first session was their cooperation in the overall Federalist project. The tasks they had to perform were large, an instance of which was the need to appeal to anti-Federalists through a "Bill of Rights," as Washington had counseled in his inaugural address. While Ames's judgment on this point differed, he offered no resistance to the project. A further case in point was the bill to establish a treasury department. When some representatives objected to Madison's proposal that the secretary "digest and report plans" to the House improving the nation's finances, Ames delivered a powerful speech supporting the idea.

As the first session of the First Congress ended on September 29, 1789, a federal revenue system and the executive departments had been created; a bill of rights had been proposed to the states for ratification; and a federal judiciary had been formed. But perhaps the greatest problem of all had yet to be faced: how to handle the enormous debt incurred during the war. This question would occupy most of the time of the second and third sessions. It would also give rise to what John Marshall called "[t]he first regular and systematic opposition to the principles on which the affairs of the union were administered. . . ."

The second session of the First Congress began on January 4, 1790. The House soon received word from Alexander Hamilton, now secretary of the treasury, that, agreeably to their request, he had prepared a report on the public credit. The main recommendations of the report were that the revolutionary war debt be provided for in full by a permanent funding system,* that no discrimination be made between original holders of the government securities that constituted the debt, and subsequent holders by purchase,† and that the debts that the individual states had incurred during the war be assumed by the federal government. Ames strongly supported each of Hamilton's recommendations.

The House took up Hamilton's report on February 8 and debated three days before deciding to fund the debt in full. At this point, Madison tossed a firebrand into the discussion. In a speech on February 11, he advocated discriminating between original and subsequent holders of the debt in order to conform to "justice and public opinion."

On February 15, Fisher Ames took exception to Madison's proposal with a speech of his own. The securities, he argued, had been transferred by an agreement between the buyer and seller that the government should honor. Moreover, the purchasers had taken upon themselves the risk that the

---

* *Funding meant that Congress would pledge a certain part of each year's revenue for payment of the interest on the debt and for the gradual redemption of the principal.*

† *The original holders were those who had either bought government securities or received them for goods and services during the war. Many of these people had sold their securities at greatly depreciated rates either through necessity or lack of faith that the government would ever redeem them. Discrimination meant that the government would pay subsequent holders not the face value of the securities but only the highest price for which they had sold in the market. The difference would be given to the original holders as compensation for their earlier losses. Original holders retaining their securities would receive the face value of the note.*

original holders had been unable or unwilling to bear—that
the government might never redeem the securities. Lastly,
Ames doubted that the public favored a discrimination. But
even if they did,

> it is more a duty on government to protect right when
> it may happen to be unpopular; that is what govern-
> ment is framed to do. If, instead of protecting, it
> assumes the right of controlling property, and dis-
> posing of it at its own pleasure, and against the
> consent of the owner, there is a cheat in the compact.

Ames thought that if the House acted on this occasion as if
right depended "not on compact, and sacred faith" but "on
opinion, on a major vote," the nation's credit would be
destroyed and the very foundations of the government shaken.

Debate continued for several days on Madison's proposal
before it was finally rejected by a large majority. Madison's
discrimination proposal meant that he had broken with
Hamilton and the Federalists, thus abdicating his position
as their leader in the House. He gradually assumed the
leadership of those men who were opposed to the policies of
Washington's administration and who later came to be called
Republicans. From this point on, Ames and Madison were
found on opposite sides of nearly every major question that
came before Congress. Ames was called on time and again
to defend Federalist policies against Madison and the Republicans.

The Third Congress was the first to be elected squarely
on the basis of the new party labels. In the House of
Representatives, the election produced a standoff between
the Federalists and Republicans, and in some respects the
Republicans prevailed. Madison once again occupied the
key leadership position. Working in tandem with Thomas
Jefferson, he launched the Third Congress by resurrecting
an issue from the First Congress.

On December 19, 1793, shortly before retiring as secretary of state, Jefferson sent to Congress his *Report on the Privileges and Restrictions on the Commerce of the United States in Foreign Countries*. This report was designed to prove that France's commercial policy was friendly toward the United States, while Great Britain's was not. When the House took up the report some days later, Madison introduced a series of coordinated resolutions. The resolutions raised anew the demand for discrimination against the trade of nations not having commercial treaties with the United States. They also sought reciprocal action against nations imposing restrictions on American commerce.

Fisher Ames did not speak at length on Madison's resolutions until they had been debated for several days. At last, on January 27, he rose. The question, as he saw it, was how Congress might put America's trade and navigation on a better footing. For trade to be on a good footing, Ames said, meant for exports to sell dear and imports to be bought cheap. The test of Madison's resolutions, therefore, was the effect they would have on the prices of exports and imports. Ames then ran through a list of the thirteen products that constituted the bulk of American exports to Britain. Only two of the products were dutied in the British market. The other products paid no duty, while the same products from other nations were either prohibited or dutied by the British. It appeared, then, that contrary to Jefferson's assertions, Britain's commercial policy favored the United States.

According to Ames, the bulk of America's exports were sold to England for one of two reasons: either the British paid the highest prices for them, or the French had little use for them. Either way, diverting trade toward France would mean a loss for American producers. The competition that Madison had promised in the supplying of American imports would also be at the expense of Americans. The competition would be promoted by taxing British goods until they sold as dear as French goods. But it was the American consumer who would pay the difference. "We shall pay more for a time," said Ames, "and in the end pay no less; for no object but that one nation may receive our money instead of the other." For the Federalists, Madison's resolutions would have meant the end of the American policy toward Europe that had prevailed since Washington's Proclamation of Neutrality in April 1793. By voting down the resolutions, the House could assert a true "independence of spirit." "[W]e shall be false to our duty and feelings as Americans," Ames concluded, "if we basely descend to a servile dependence on France or Great Britain."

During the debate on Madison's resolutions, news arrived that the British were confiscating American merchant vessels in the Caribbean. At about the same time, reports began circulating that the British in Canada were stirring up the Indians against the Northwest frontier. Since hostilities with Britain now appeared imminent, the Federalists were able to shift debate in the House to preparing the nation's defenses for war. Then, at the height of the crisis, Britain revoked the order in council that had authorized the confiscation of American ships. Seizing upon this opportunity to seek peace, President Washington appointed John Jay as a special envoy to negotiate a settlement of the differences between the two countries.

Debate over making the necessary appropriations to put the treaty into effect began in the House on March 7, 1796. The Republicans at this point adopted the position that whenever a treaty required appropriations of money or any other act of Congress, the House had the discretionary power to carry it into effect or to annul it by refusing its cooperation. The Federalists, for their part, maintained that a treaty was binding on the nation from the moment it was signed by the president. For the House to refuse its cooperation, they reasoned, was to break the treaty and violate the faith of the nation. Debate continued on and off for nearly two months.

By 1796, Fisher Ames had contracted the disease that eventually took his life. Before leaving Dedham to attend the Fourth Congress, he had solemnly promised his doctors to take no part in the debates. But after sitting quietly through almost the entire debate on Jay's treaty, he could be still no longer. On April 28, it became known in the corridors of Congress Hall that Fisher Ames would finally speak. The Senate and the Supreme Court adjourned for the occasion, as would-be auditors rushed for seats in the House galleries. Struggling to his feet, his face pale and thin, Ames began: "I entertain the hope, perhaps a rash one, that my strength will hold me out to speak a few minutes."

For "a few minutes," Ames spoke, with a dramatic and rhetorical effect that did not disappoint his listeners. He meticulously refuted Republican claims to an independent treaty-approving authority in the House. He invoked the rule of law. And he called mounting public opinion to testify in his behalf. Breaking the treaty would leave the British in possession of the Northwest posts. From these posts, the Indians would be incited against the western frontier. It took modest wit to picture the result:

> I would say to the inhabitants, Wake from your false security! Your cruel dangers—your more cruel apprehensions—are soon to be renewed; the wounds, yet unhealed, are to be torn open again. In the day time, your path through the woods will be ambushed; the darkness of midnight will glitter with the blaze of your dwellings. You are a father: the blood of your sons shall fatten your cornfield! You are a mother: the war-whoop shall wake the sleep of the cradle! . . . Who will say that I exaggerate . . . ! Who will answer, by a sneer, that all this is idle preaching? . . . By rejecting the posts, we light the savage fires— we bind the victims! This day we undertake to render account to the widows and orphans whom our decision will make, to the wretches that will be roasted at the

stake . . . To conscience and to God we are answerable
. . . While one hand is held up to reject this treaty,
the other grasps a tomahawk. I can fancy that I listen
to the yells of savage vengeance, and to the shrieks
of torture. Already they seem to sigh in the West
Wind; already they mingle with every echo from the
mountains.

If, in spite of these consequences, the treaty were broken,
Ames concluded, "Even I, slender and almost broken as my
hold upon life is, may outlive the Government and Constitution
of my country."

The effect of the speech was overwhelming. Vice President
Adams and Supreme Court Justice James Iredell sat drained
in the galleries. "My God, how great he is," said Iredell.
"How great he has been." "He has been noble," replied
Adams. "Tears enough were shed," Adams wrote home to
his wife. "Not a dry eye, I believe, except some of the
Jackasses who had occasioned the necessity of the oratory."
Dr. Joseph Priestley, a dedicated Republican who had
listened to Chatham, Pitt, Burke, and Fox, declared the
speech "the most bewitching piece of parliamentary oratory
he had ever listened to." And Jeremiah Smith, one of Ames's
friends, commented that Ames should "have died in the fifth
act; that he never will have an occasion so glorious, having
lost this he will now have to make his exit like other men."*
The Republicans had been confident that they could carry a
vote against the appropriations at any time, but when the
final vote was taken on April 30, the appropriations passed
by fifty-one to forty-nine.

Ames's speech on the Jay Treaty has been declared the
first really great speech delivered on the floor of the House.

---

* Smith's reference doubtlessly and most significantly is a reference to
Joseph Addison's famous play, Cato, whose hero was a popular model
for American republicans.

One may doubt that, yet take note that it became a standard for American political rhetoric for successive generations of American statesmen. Young Daniel Webster, for one, memorized the speech as a model for his own oratory. Even decades later, when "Federalist" had become a term of reproach in American politics, the speech was fondly remembered. For example, George S. Boutwell, one of Grant's secretaries of the treasury, reported that Abraham Lincoln greatly admired the speech and could recite long portions of it from memory.

At the close of the next session, Fisher Ames retired from Congress and returned home to his family and friends. He resumed his legal practice and attended the sessions of the courts when his health permitted. Farming became an occupation for him, as he experimented with the breeding of dairy cattle and hogs and with the culture of fruit trees. But even when occupied with these various pursuits, public affairs were not far from his mind.

What Ames regarded as the unfinished work of the founding called forth a barrage of essays that appeared in the party presses. These essays aimed to boost the Federalists and to overthrow the Republicans after their victory of 1800. But most of all, they aimed to establish a correct standard of public opinion, echoing the work of the youthful Camillus. Indefatigable as he was, however, his party never revived.

During his congressional career, Ames had kept up a personal correspondence with Massachusetts Federalists in order to keep them abreast of national events. After his retirement, he corresponded with Federalist leaders around the country. His letters constitute the closest thing we have to a deliberate commentary on nearly all the important political events from 1789 to 1807. They give an inside view of the purposes and strategies of his party and interesting assessments of the men from both parties with whom Ames had personal acquaintance.

The last years of Ames's life were plagued by the lung disease that had forced his retirement from Congress. He would grow seriously ill, have fainting spells, and be confined to bed for days at a time. Then he would recover strength enough to go about his business for a while. In 1808, his periods of illness grew more frequent and more severe, and by June he was definitely failing. By the end of the month, he could not rise from bed; at sunrise on Monday, July 4, the thirty-second anniversary of the nation's birth, he died quietly at his home in Dedham.

With the passing of Fisher Ames, federalism as a direct political influence passed into history. After him, there remained but the genius of John Marshall, entrenched on the Supreme Court. But as for a party spokesman, organizer, and theoretician, suited to slugging it out in the arena of democracy, none remained. Washington died in 1799; his ablest lieutenant, Hamilton, was slain in 1804; and Ames, Hamilton's ablest lieutenant, followed four years later. Soon after his death, his friends issued a short edition of his works, meant as a bible for the rising generations. While the party's energy was spent and young men embraced instead the victorious Republicans, the energy of Ames's thought continues to live. With this greatly revised and corrected edition, we offer Ames's thought to a new generation.

W.B.A.

Claremont, California

William B. Allen is Professor of Government at Harvey Mudd College, Claremont, California.

EDITOR'S NOTE

═══

THIS EDITION of the *Works of Fisher Ames* is based on the edition published in 1854 by Seth Ames. It has been substantially enlarged to supply omissions in the earlier version that are material to an understanding of Ames's contribution in the era of founding in the United States.

The "Essays" represent Ames's most extensive public production. Where possible, ellipses from the earlier version have been supplied. Those ellipses that remain, whether on account of deteriorated original texts or our inability to acquire original texts, have been indicated by brackets enclosing a series of end stops, thus, [. . .]. The original headnotes, incorporated from the 1809 edition, have been deleted, save in the case of the posthumously published "Dangers of American Liberty." The series of footnotes incorporates our notes with those of the 1854 edition, which latter are indicated by a bracketed "S. Ames" or "F. Ames," as appropriate. It is also well to note that the essays are not presented in mere chronological order. They have been arranged by themes. Within each theme, the chronological order prevails whenever reasonable. On the whole, a chronological order is noticeable but not exact. We add to this collection twenty-three essays missing from the 1854 edition, and in many instances we correct the bibliographical references to the essays that were published. Such changes are carried silently.

The "Letters and Speeches" stand as a mix of private and public reflections on questions of public moment. The speeches are all public productions, but the occasional element of spontaneity in them often echoes or mimics ideas more freely expressed in private correspondence. We preserve this twilight relationship between the letters and speeches by publishing them as a carefully arranged whole. They have been arranged along two complementary lines, thematic and chronological. The speeches divide easily into seventeen topics, for each of which a lead speech has been selected. The lead speeches have been inserted among the letters in strict chronological order. Other speeches, however, are associated with the lead speech to which they most closely relate thematically. Thus, the secondary speeches following the lead speech violate the overall chronological order, albeit among themselves they are in chronological order. The correspondence is strictly chronological.

Here, too, we enlarge the collection, publishing nearly all of Ames's speeches, whereas before only a few were published, and greatly adding to the correspondence. This edition contains eighty-five new letters while deleting six of minor importance and substantially shortening many others. Furthermore, many of the speeches and letters have been edited against their originals and the resulting corrections silently carried into the previously published text.

Our purpose throughout has been to render Ames as clearly and faithfully as possible. Because Ames was the quintessential Monday-morning quarterback (as well as an effective pregame strategist), his letters, speeches, and essays now

offer the foremost *sustained* criticism of the American founding, from the time of the Constitutional Convention through
Jefferson's re-election as president. As such, this collection
is a tool of inestimable value.

We have relied on the guidance of several sources in
preparing this collection, among them the first account of
Ames's life by his friend, J. T. Kirkland. Kirkland's "Life
of Fisher Ames" was prefixed to the *Works of Fisher Ames*
(Boston: T. B. Wait, 1809) and also to the Seth Ames edition
of the same work (Boston: Little, Brown, 1854). Several other
sketches of Ames appeared in magazines and journals in the
1800s, but few added to an understanding of his life or
career. Among the few, an article by Mellen Chamberlain
appeared in the *Harvard Graduate's Magazine*, 4 (1895–
1896). Additionally, the debate between John Quincy Adams
(*American Principles*) and John Lowell (*Remarks on Adam's
Review of Ames's Works*), occurring on the occasion of the
first publication of Ames's *Works*, greatly contributes to an
understanding of the context of his political endeavor.

Two more recent articles deserve attention: Samuel E.
Morison, "Squire Ames and Doctor Ames," *The New England
Quarterly*, 1 (1928), and Elisha P. Douglass, "Fisher Ames,
Spokesman for New England Federalism," *Proceedings of the
American Philosophical Association*, 103 (1959).

The only full-scale biography of Ames was written in 1965
by Winfred E. A. Bernhard. *Fisher Ames, Federalist and
Statesman* (Chapel Hill: University of North Carolina Press,
1965) gives a most balanced account of Ames's life and thus
largely supersedes earlier accounts.

Among general histories of the founding era, the following
were of value in the effort to situate Ames within the context
of the founding: John Marshall, *The Life of George Washington*
(Philadelphia: C. P. Wayne, 1804–1807); John C. Miller,
The Federalist Era (New York: Harper & Row, 1960); Samuel
E. Morison, Henry S. Commager, and William E. Leuchten-

burg, *The Growth of the American Republic* (New York: Oxford University Press, 1969); Forrest McDonald, *The Presidency of George Washington* (New York: Norton, 1974); and the best of recent sources, James M. Banner, *To the Hartford Convention: The Federalists and the Origin of Party Politics in Massachusetts, 1789–1815* (New York: Knopf, 1970).

We gratefully acknowledge the assistance of, and permission to publish materials from, the following collections: American Antiquarian Society, Worcester, Massachusetts; Boston Public Library, Boston, Massachusetts; the Historical Society of Pennsylvania, Philadelphia, Pennsylvania; the Huntington Library, San Marino, California; the Putnam Papers and the Charles Goddard Slack Collection, Dawes Memorial Library, Marietta College, Marietta, Ohio; Massachusetts Historical Society, Boston, Massachusetts; the New York Historical Society, New York, New York; New York Public Library, New York, New York; the New York Society Library, New York, New York; the Pierpont Morgan Library, New York, New York; the Rhode Island Historical Society, Providence, Rhode Island; the John Rutledge Papers in the Southern Historical Collection of the University of North Carolina Library, Chapel Hill, North Carolina; the Stanford University Libraries Special Collections, Stanford, California; the Fisher Ames Collection (#4217), Manuscripts Department, University of Virginia Library, Charlottesville, Virginia; and the Morse Family Papers (Fisher Ames to Jedediah Morse, Dec. 20, 1792) of Yale University Library, New Haven, Connecticut. The Manuscripts Division of the Library of Congress, whose staff provided great assistance in identifying two heretofore misplaced Ames essays in the Papers of Alexander Hamilton, deserves thanks. From previously published works we acknowledge Columbia University Press's *The Papers of Alexander Hamilton* (1961); G. P. Putnam's Sons' *The Life and Correspondence of Rufus King* (1895); Jonathan Elliot's *Debates in the Several State Con-*

ventions (1888); *The Annals of Congress;* from G. Gibbs's *The Federal Administrations*, the "Wolcott Papers"; and *The Memoirs of William Tudor.* We were aided by many others in this endeavor, whose resources enabled us to verify and correct much previously published Ames material. We cannot name them all here, but hereby extend our gratitude.

Finally, we acknowledge our debt to Mrs. Diane Sanchez's secretarial skills. The editor recognizes the important editorial contributions and assistance of graduate assistants Eldon Alexander and Wesley Phelan. We express abiding appreciation of the editorial and managerial contributions of Liberty Fund, Inc. and thank them for the opportunity to peruse these works. We acknowledge, with them, a great debt to Pierre F. Goodrich.

W.B.A.

Claremont, California

PART TWO

SPEECHES
AND
LETTERS

Continued

1 7 9 1

TO THOMAS DWIGHT

PHILADELPHIA, JANUARY 6, 1791

DEAR FRIEND,

I INCLOSE Judge Wilson's introductory law lecture, addressed with a propriety, which he says malice cannot question, to Mrs. Washington. I heard it, but have not had leisure to read it. Will you be so obliging as to present it to Colonel Worthington? The great law-learning and eminent station of the writer had raised great expectations of the performance. Whether there are not many parts that discretion and modesty, if they had been consulted, would have expunged, you will be at liberty to judge. It will be a frolic to the London reviewers to make the Judge's feathers fly. He has censured the English form of government, and can expect no mercy.

North Carolina is still in a ferment. They have rejected,

by a very great majority, a proposition made in their Assembly for taking the oath to support the Constitution of the United States. You will see their resolves against their senators, and against direct and indirect taxes, in Fenno, which, as Fenno says on bad information, were not rejected by the Senate, except the preamble, and the word *monstrous* salaries was changed for enormous.

Before the Constitution was adopted by North Carolina, Robert Morris was sued there, his attorney ordered to trial without delay, and of course, judgment for ten thousand pounds against poor Bobby, as the New York boys used to call him. He filed, in their state Chancery Court, a bill, and obtained an injunction to stay the execution. In this stage of it, the Constitution was agreed to, and Mr. Morris obtained from the federal Circuit Court a *certiorari* to remove the cause from the state court. This the supreme judges of the state refused to obey, and the marshal did not execute his precept. The state judges, knowing the angry state of the assembly, wrote a letter of complaint, representing the affair. Whether the United States judges have kept within legal bounds is doubted. I should be sorry for an error of so serious a kind, and under such unlucky circumstances. Please to mention this affair to Colonel W. and to my friend H.

The excise bill is going forward smoothly. Mr. Jackson flamed forth yesterday, before the first paragraph was read. He was stopped to hear it out, and then he moved to strike it out, after a violent speechicle, which was not answered. Fifteen only voted with him. We hear nothing further about the treaty.[22] But that subject, the excise, the judicial quarrel, before mentioned, and the assumption, seem to keep the

---

[22] *Probably the treaty with the Creek Indians, before mentioned.* [S. AMES]

846

states of Georgia, North Carolina, and Virginia, in a condition not unlike that of Naples when Vesuvius cuts capers.

.   .   .   .

Yours, in haste.

TO THOMAS DWIGHT

PHILADELPHIA, JANUARY 24, 1791

DEAR FRIEND,

.   .   .   .

WE SHOULD have passed the excise bill to be engrossed for a third reading, if for our trial, as all afflictions you know are, one of our Massachusetts members had not seen anti-republicanism in the clause giving the President power to assign compensation to the inspectors, &c., not exceeding five per cent. of the duties. The bugbear of influence gained by the executive, of Constitution, because it would empower him to establish offices, in effect, by fixing the pay, and forty other topics, were addressed *ad populum*. The clause was struck out, and a new bill, regulating the pay of inspectors, is to be brought in. The Secretary tells us, in his report, that the only practicable method in the first instance is to leave it to the President. But we are equal to things impracticable, and though time and information are wanting, we are going to undertake it. In the mean time, we are going on with the excise bill. Every effort is made to puzzle, by amendments crowded in and by debates upon them, to spin out the day and waste it. Hitherto we have beaten our adversaries, and I think we shall finally prevail, though the event is far from being safe. The southern people care little about the debt. They doubt the necessity of more revenue. They fear the excise themselves, and still more their people, to whom it is obnoxious, and to whom they are making it more odious still, by indiscreet violence of their debates. Besides, they wish to seize the bill as a hostage for such a regulation of the bank, as will not interfere with Conococheague[23] ten years hence. They wish to limit its term to ten years, or to provide that its stock shall be removed with the seat of government.

On a late debate on the bill to provide what officer shall act as President, when the two first offices shall be vacant, the ambition of Mr. Jefferson's friends was disclosed. They contended for him with zeal. That will have its share in the business of the session. All this is *inter nos*. But rely on this, my friend, no compromise will be made by trucking off one thing for another. If the government cannot be supported without foul means, let it go.

The Pennsylvania assembly has voted in the lower House against an excise. It was awkward to see the excise debating in two places at once, as the case actually happened. Is not this anarchy? The state governments seem to beat their drums, and to prepare to attack us. We have many advantages over them, and they have several over us. But appearances indicate that the superiority of the one to the other will be brought to the test. I hope the Massachusetts General Court will not incite the people to any further clamor. Our State

---

[23] *The name of a stream entering the Potomac in the westerly part of Maryland. Those who were malcontent with the scheme of removing the seat of government, in 1801, to the banks of the Potomac, revenged themselves by giving the name of Conococheague to the proposed capital.* [S. AMES]

has got relief, and that is the pretext for the noise in the southern states. I must finish.

Your affectionate friend.

TO ANDREW CRAIGIE

PHILADELPHIA, FEBRUARY 2D, 1791,
WEDNESDAY EVENING

DEAR CRAIGIE,

THE BANK is yet undecided. But the appearances have been very favorable to its passage. The opposers suffered it to pass the Committee of the Whole House in silence. They had before made an attempt to prevent its being taken up, and spoke of it as a thing which would divide the House closely and take up a great deal of time in debate. The bill was reported by the committee to the House and yesterday was ordered for a third reading. An effort was made to get the bill recommitted, alleging that they had suffered it to pass without debate from misapprehension of the forms of proceeding, and they entrusted to be restored fully to what they had lost by surprise. This was denied them—34 to 23. It was the old game of the Assumption, voting a bill a stage backwards.

This day, Mr. Madison, on the final question, shall the bill pass, made a great speech of two hours, to show that it was a bad bank, that the proprietors ought to buy their charter of the government, and that, they ought to be obliged by law to establish subordinate banks, and a great deal more in that strain. He then argued that Congress has no power by the Constitution to incorporate a bank. He spoke with his usual ability. What impression he made I cannot say. He was not armored, but I suppose will be.

I think the bill will pass as soon as the business of making speeches is over, and, if it should pass at all, it must be as it is, for it is not open to any amendment.

Your friend—in haste

FISHER AMES

DEFENSE OF THE NATIONAL BANK

The creation of a national bank was the capstone of the Federalist financial program. James Madison argued that Congress had no constitutional authority to establish such an institution. Fisher Ames answered with an equally powerful speech. In his main speech, Ames articulated for the first time in the House the idea that the establishment of the bank was included in the necessary and proper powers of Congress.

———

FEBRUARY 1, 1791

Mr. Madison observed, that at this moment it was not of importance to determine how it has happened that the objections which several gentlemen now say they have to offer against the bill were not made at the proper time. It is sufficient for them, if the candor of the House should lead them now to recommit the bill, that in a Committee of the Whole they may have an opportunity of offering their objections.

850

Mr. Ames replied to Mr. Madison. He said, he did not conceive that the appeal now made to the candor of the House was in point. The gentlemen who object to the bill had an opportunity to offer their objections; the customary forms have been attended to; and the whole question for the recommitment turns on the force of the objections which are now offered to the general principles of the bill altogether. The candor of the House, he conceived, was entirely out of the question, and therefore not to be appealed to; but the justice due to their constituents in the proper discharge of the duty reposed in them. He said, it appeared to him absurd to go into Committee of the Whole to determine whether the bill is constitutional or not. If it is unconstitutional, that amounts to a rejection of it altogether.

Mr. Madison thought there was the greatest propriety in discussing a constitutional question in Committee of the Whole.

FEBRUARY 3, 1791

Mr. AMES.—Little doubt remains with respect to the utility of banks. It seems to be conceded within doors and without, that a public bank would be useful to trade, that it is almost essential to revenue, and that it is little short of indispensably necessary in times of public emergency. In countries whose forms of government left them free to choose, this institution has been adopted of choice, and in times of national danger and calamity, it has afforded such aid to government as to make it appear, in the eyes of the people, a necessary means of self-preservation. The subject, however intricate in its nature, is at last cleared from obscurity. It would not be difficult to establish its principles, and to deduce from its theory such consequences as would vindicate the policy of the measure. But why should we lose time to examine the theory when it is in our power to resort to experience? After being tried by that test, the world has agreed in pronouncing the institution excellent. This new capital will invigorate trade and manufactures with new energy. It will furnish a medium for the collection of the revenues; and if government should be pressed by a sudden necessity, it will afford seasonable and effectual aid. With all these and many other pretensions, if it was now a question whether Congress should be vested with the power of establishing a bank, I trust that this House and all America would assent to the affirmative.

This, however, is not a question of expediency, but of duty. We are not at liberty to examine which of several modes of acting is entitled to the preference. But we are solemnly warned against acting at all. We are told that the Constitution will not authorize Congress to incorporate the subscribers to the bank. Let us examine the Constitution, and if that forbids our proceeding, we must reject the bill; though we shall do it with deep regret that such an opportunity to serve our country must be suffered to escape for the want of a constitutional power to improve it.

The gentleman from Virginia considers the opposers of the bill as suffering disadvantage, because it was not debated as bills usually are in the Committee of the Whole. He has prepared us to pronounce an eulogium upon his consistency by informing us that he voted in the old Congress against the Bank of North America, on the ground of his present objection to the constitutionality. He has told us that the meaning of the Constitution is to be interpreted by contemporaneous testimony. He was a member of the Convention which formed it, and of course his opinion is entitled to peculiar weight. While we respect his former conduct, and admire the felicity of his situation, we cannot think he sustains disadvantage in the debate. Besides, he must have been prepared with objections to the constitutionality, because he tells us they are of long standing, and had grown into a settled habit of thinking. Why, then, did he suffer the bill to pass the committee in silence? The friends of the bill have more cause to complain of disadvantage; for while he has had time to prepare his objections, they are obliged to reply to them without premeditation.

In making this reply I am to perform a task for which my own mind has not admonished me to prepare. I never suspected that the objections I have heard stated had existence; I consider them as discoveries; and had not the acute penetration of that gentleman brought them to light, I am sure that my own understanding would never have suggested them.

It seems strange, too, that in our enlightened country the public should have been involved in equal blindness. While the exercise of even the lawful powers of government is disputed, and a jealous eye is fixed on its proceedings, not a whisper has been heard against its authority to establish a bank. Still, however unseasonably, the old alarm of public discontent is sounded in our ears.

Two questions occur; may Congress exercise any powers which are not expressly given in the Constitution, but may be deduced by a reasonable construction of that instrument? And, secondly, will such a construction warrant the establishment of the bank?

The doctrine that powers may be implied which are not expressly vested in Congress has long been a bugbear to a great many worthy persons. They apprehend that Congress, by putting constructions upon the Constitution, will govern by its own arbitrary discretion; and therefore that it ought to be bound to exercise the powers expressly given, and those only.

If Congress may not make laws conformably to the powers plainly implied, though not expressed in the frame of government, it is rather late in the day to adopt it as a principle of conduct. A great part of our two years labor is lost, and worse than lost to the public, for we have scarcely made a law in which we have not exercised our discretion with regard to the true intent of the Constitution. Any words but those used in that instrument will be liable to a different interpretation. We may regulate trade; therefore we have taxed ships, erected light-houses, made laws to govern seamen, &c., because we say that they are the incidents to that power. The most familiar and undisputed acts of legislation will show that we have adopted it as a safe rule of action to legislate beyond the letter of the Constitution.

He proceeded to enforce this idea by several considerations, and illustrated it by various examples. He said, that the ingenuity of man was unequal to providing, especially, beforehand, for all the contingencies that would happen. The Constitution contains the principles which are to govern in making laws; but every law requires an application of the rule to the case in question. We may err in applying it; but we are to exercise our judgments, and on every occasion to decide according to an honest conviction of its true meaning.

The danger of implied power does not arise from its assuming a new principle; we have not only practised it often, but we can scarcely proceed without it; nor does the danger proceed so much from the extent of the power as from its uncertainty. While the opposers of the bank exclaim against the exercise of this power by Congress, do they mark out the limits of the power which they will leave to us, with more certainty than is done by the advocates of the bank? Their rules of interpretation by contemporaneous testimony, the debates of conventions, and the doctrine of substantive and auxiliary powers, will be found as obscure, and of course as formidable as that which they condemn; they only set up one construction against another.

The powers of Congress are disputed. We are obliged to decide the question according to truth. The negative, if false, is less safe than the affirmative, if true. Why, then, shall we be told that the negative is the safe side? Not exercising the powers we have, may be as pernicious as usurping those we have not. If the power to raise armies had not been expressed in the enumeration of the powers of Congress, it would be implied from other parts of the Constitution. Suppose, however, that it were omitted, and our country invaded, would a decision in Congress against raising armies be safer than the affirmative? The blood of our citizens would be shed, and shed unavenged. He thought, therefore, that there was too much prepossession with some against the bank, and that the debate ought to be considered more impartially, as the negative was neither more safe, certain, nor conformable to our duty than the other side of the question. After all, the proof of the affirmative imposed a sufficient burden, as it is easier to raise objections than to remove them. Would any one doubt that Congress may lend money, that they may buy their debt in the market, or redeem their captives from Algiers? Yet no such power is expressly given, though it is irresistibly implied.

If, therefore, some interpretation of the Constitution must be indulged, by what rules is it to be governed? The great end of every association of persons or states is to effect the end of its institution. The matter in debate affords a good illustration: a corporation, as soon as it is created, has certain powers, or qualities, tacitly annexed to it, which tend to promote the end for which it was formed; such as, for ex- ample, its individuality, its power to sue and be sued, and the perpetual succession of persons. Government is itself the highest kind of corporation; and from the instant of its formation, it has tacitly annexed to its being, various powers which the individuals who framed it did not separately possess, but which are essential to its effecting the purposes for which it was framed; to declare, in detail, every thing that government may do could not be performed, and has never been attempted. It would be endless, useless, and dangerous; exceptions of what it may not do are shorter and safer.

Congress may do what is necessary to the end for which the Constitution was adopted, provided it is not repugnant to the natural rights of man, or to those which they have expressly reserved to themselves, or to the powers which are assigned to the states. This rule of interpretation seems to be safe, and not a very uncertain one, independently of the Constitution itself. By that instrument certain powers are specially delegated, together with all powers necessary or proper to carry them into execution. That construction may be maintained to be a safe one which promotes the good of the society, and the ends for which the government was adopted, without impairing the rights of any man, or the powers of any state.

This, he said, was remarkably true of the bank; no man could have cause to complain of it; the bills would not be forced upon any one. It is of the first utility to trade. Indeed the intercourse from state to state can never be on a good footing without a bank, whose paper will circulate more extensively than that of any state bank. Whether the power to regulate trade from state to state will involve that of regulating inland bills of exchange and bank paper, as the instruments of the trade, and incident to the power, he would not pause to examine. This is an injury and wrong which violates the right of another. As the bank is founded on the free choice of those who make use of it, and is highly useful to the people and to government, a liberal construction is natural and safe. This circumstance creates a presumption in favor of its conformity to the Constitution. This presumption is enforced by the necessity of a bank to other governments. The most orderly governments in Europe have banks. They are considered as indispensably necessary; these examples are not to be supposed to have been unnoticed. We are to pay the interest of our debt in thirteen places. Is it possible to transport the revenue from one end of the Continent to the other? Nay, a week before the quarter's interest becomes due, transfers may be made which will require double the sum in Boston which was expected. To guard against this danger, an extra sum must be deposited at the different loan offices. This extra sum is not to be had; our revenue is barely equal to the interest due. This imposes an absolute necessity upon the government to make use of a bank. The answer is, that the state banks will supply this aid. This is risking a good deal to the argument against the bank; for will they admit the necessity, and yet deny to the government the lawful and only adequate means of providing for it? Ten of the states have no banks; those who have may abolish theirs, and suffer their charters to expire. But the state banks are insufficient to the purpose; their paper has not a sufficient circulation; of course their capitals are small. Congress is allowed to have complete legislative power over its own finances; and yet without the courtesy of the states it cannot be exercised. This seems to be inconsistent.

If a war should suddenly break out, how is Congress to provide for it? Perhaps Congress would not be sitting; great expenses would be incurred; and they must be instantly provided for. How is this to be done? By taxes? And will the enemy wait till they can be collected? By loans at home? Our citizens would employ their money in war speculations, and they are not individually in a condition to lend a sufficient sum in specie. Or shall we send across the sea for loans? The dispute between England and Spain furnishes an example; the aid of their banks for several millions was prompt and effectual. Or, will you say that Congress might issue paper money? That power, ruinous and fallacious as it is, is deduced from implication, for it is not expressly given. A bank only can afford the necessary aid in time of sudden emergency. If we have not the power to establish it, our social compact is incomplete, we want the means of self-preservation.

I shall, perhaps, be told that necessity is the tyrant's plea. I answer that it is a miserable one when it is urged to palliate the violation of private right. Who suffers by this use of our authority? Not the states, for they are not warranted to establish a national bank; not individuals, for they will be assisted in trade, and defended from danger by it.

Having endeavored to enforce his argument, by noticing the uses of banks to trade, to revenue, to credit, and, in cases of exigency, he adverted to the authority of our own precedents. Our right to govern the Western Territory is not disputed. It is a power which no state can exercise; it must be exercised, and therefore it resides in Congress. But how does Congress get this power? It is not expressly given in the Constitution, but is derived either from the nature of the case, or by implication from the power to regulate the property of the United States. If the power flows from the nature and necessity of the case, it may be demanded, is there not equal authority for the bank? If it is derived from the power of Congress to regulate the territory and other property of the United States, and to make all needful rules and regulations concerning it, and for the disposal of it, a strict construction would restrain Congress merely to the management and disposal of property, and of its own property; yet it is plain that more is intended. Congress has accordingly made rules, not only for governing its own property, but the property of the persons residing there. It has made rules which have no relation to property at all—for punishing crimes. In short, it exercises all power in that territory. Nay, it has exercised this very power of creating a corporation. The government of that territory is a corporation; and who will deny that Congress may lawfully establish a bank beyond the Ohio? It is fair to reason by analogy from a power which is unquestionable, to one which is the subject of debate.

He then asked, whether it appeared, on this view of the subject, that the establishment of a national bank would be a violent misinterpretation of the Constitution? He did not contend for an arbitrary, unlimited discretion in the government to do every thing. He took occasion to protest against such a misconception of his argument. He had noticed the great marks by which the construction of the Constitution, he conceived, must be guided and limited; and these, if not absolutely certain, were very far from being arbitrary or unsafe. It is for the House to judge whether the construction which denies the power of Congress is more definite and safe.

In proving that Congress may exercise powers which are not expressly granted by the Constitution, he had endeavored to establish such rules of interpretation, and had illustrated his ideas by such observations as would anticipate, in a considerable degree, the application of his principles to the point in question. Before he proceeded to the construction of the clauses of the Constitution which apply to the argument, he observed that it would be proper to notice the qualities of a corporation, in order to take a more exact view of the controversy.

He adverted to the individuality and the perpetuity of a corporation, and that the property of the individuals should not be liable for the debts of the bank or company. These qualities are not more useful to the corporation than conformable to reason; but government, it is said, cannot create these qualities. This is the marrow of the argument; for Congress may set up a bank of its own, to be managed as public property, to issue notes which shall be received in all payments at the Treasury, which shall be exchangeable into specie on demand, and which it shall be death to counterfeit.

Such a bank would be less safe and useful than one under the direction of private persons; yet the power to establish it is indisputable. If Congress has the authority to do this business badly, the question returns, whether the powers of a corporation, which are essential to its being well done, may be annexed as incident to it. The Bank of New York is not a corporation, yet its notes have credit. Congress may agree with that bank, or with a company of merchants, to take their notes, and to cause all payments to pass through their coffers. Every thing that government requires, and the bank will perform, may be lawfully done without giving them corporate powers; but to do this well, safely, and extensively, those powers are indispensable. This seems to bring the debate within a very narrow compass.

This led him to consider whether the corporate powers are incidental to those which Congress may exercise by the Constitution.

He entered into a discussion of the construction of that clause which empowers Congress to regulate the territory and other property of the United States. The United States may hold property; may dispose of it; they may hold it in partnership; they may regulate the terms of the partnership. One condition may be, that the common stock only shall be liable for the debts of the partnership, and that any purchaser of a share shall become a partner. These are the chief qualities of a corporation. It seems that Congress, having power to make all needful rules and regulations for the property of the United States, may establish a corporation to manage it: without which we have seen that the regulation cannot be either safe or useful; the United States will be the proprietor of one-tenth of the bank stock.

Congress may exercise exclusive legislation in all cases whatsoever over the ten miles square, and the places ceded by the states for arsenals, light-houses, docks, &c. Of course it may establish a bank in those places with corporate powers.

The bill has not restrained the bank to this city; and if it had, the dispute would lose a part of its solemnity. If, instead of principles, it concerns only places, what objection is there to the constitutional authority of Congress to fix the bank at Sandy Hook, or Reedy Island, where we have light-houses, and a right of exclusive legislation? A bank established there, or in the district located by law on the Potomac for the seat of government, could send its paper all over the Union; it is true that the places are not the most proper for a bank; but the authority to establish it in them overthrows the argument which is deduced from the definite nature of the powers vested in Congress, and the dangerous tendency of the proposed construction of them.

The preamble of the Constitution warrants this remark, that a bank is not repugnant to the spirit and essential objects of that instrument.

He then considered the power to borrow money. He said it was natural to understand that authority as it was actually exercised in Europe; which is, to borrow of the bank. He observed, the power to borrow was of narrow use without the institution of a bank; and in the most dangerous crisis of affairs would be a dead letter.

After noticing the power to lay and collect taxes, he adverted to the sweeping clause, as it is usually called, which empowers Congress to exercise all powers necessary and proper to carry the enumerated powers into execution. He did not pretend that it gives any new powers; but it establishes the doctrine of implied powers. He then demanded whether the power to incorporate a bank is not fairly relative, and a necessary incident to the entire powers to regulate trade and revenue, and to provide for the public credit and defence.

He entered into a particular answer to several objections, and after recapitulating his argument, he concluded with observing that we had felt the disadvantages of the Confederation. We adopted the Constitution, expecting to place the national affairs under a Federal head; this is a power which Congress can only exercise. We may reason away the whole Constitution. All nations have their times of adversity and danger; the neglect of providing against them in season may be the cause of ruining the country.

TO THOMAS DWIGHT

PHILADELPHIA, FEBRUARY 7, 1791

MY DEAR FRIEND,

I AM in the House, and have not your last favor before me. You express a doubt with regard to the time of your going to heaven. I expect to return in March, and possibly I may be in Springfield at the time of your ascent. I shall be happy to be a spectator of your metamorphosis, or, as you will call it during the first moon, your apotheosis. Congress will certainly adjourn on the third of March. I shall pass three or four days in New York, and then make haste to Springfield. The prospect is a very grateful one to my mind, especially if I am to get a piece of the wedding cake.

I am now hearing Mr. Giles, of Virginia, preach against the bank. Mr. Madison has made a great speech against it. I am not an impartial judge of it. Take my opinion with due allowance;—it is, that his speech was full of casuistry and sophistry. He read a long time out of books of debates on the Constitution when considering in the several states, in order to show that the powers were to be construed strictly. This was a dull piece of business, and very little to the purpose, as no man would pretend to give Congress the power, against a fair construction of the Constitution.

All appearances indicate that we shall beat them by a considerable majority. This will not happen till the quantum of speeches is exhausted, which I expect will take place to-morrow.

Your affectionate friend.

MONDAY EVENING

It is hoped that we shall take the question on the bank to-morrow; though, as Mr. Madison discovers an intention to speak again, and several others appear charged, I think the chance is against the question till Wednesday. Our time is precious, because it is short. We sit impatiently to hear arguments which guide, or at least change, no man's vote.

TO GEORGE RICHARDS MINOT

PHILADELPHIA, FEBRUARY 17, 1791

MY DEAR FRIEND,

IT GAVE ME great pleasure to receive a line from you, after so long an interruption of our correspondence.

I am sure that our mutual regard has not suffered any interruption at all. My own sentiments will not suffer me to doubt of yours. I shall take pleasure in serving you or your friends. The letter inclosed in yours, and the interests of your brother, shall be attended to.

We have been occupied a long time with the debate on the bank bill. Mr. Madison has made a potent attack upon the bill, as unconstitutional. The decision of the House, by a majority of thirty-nine against twenty, is a strong proof of the little impression that was made. Many of the <u>minority</u> laughed at the objection deduced from the Constitution.

The great point of difficulty was, the effect of the bank law to make the future removal of the government from this city to the Potomac less probable. This place will become the great centre of the revenue and banking operations of the nation. So many interests will be centered here, that it is feared that, ten years hence, Congress will be found fast anchored and immovable.

This apprehension has an influence on Mr. Madison, the Secretary of State,[24] as it is supposed, and perhaps on a still greater man. The bank law is before the President.

The excise act is before the House. Some amendments have been proposed by the Senate. I do not apprehend that the bill will be lost,—though, as our senators voted against it, the adversaries of the bill are encouraged with the hope of destroying it in the House. They will try to spin out the time, which is short. We are to adjourn on the 3d March. The Boston distillers have sent us a letter, expressing their apprehension that the duties of the excise bill will injure their business. Our senators, not being able to effect any alteration, chose to give their votes in the negative, as the strongest testimony of their disapprobation of the rate of duties. This is what I understand to be their motive.

What are you about in the General Court? Will you join the complaining states, and pass censuring votes against Congress? How came the Captain to push for a seat so hard in the General Court? It is a small object to him; but such formal disputes concerning the dangerous influence of the United States government and its officers, give some disturbance to the public, at a time when it seems to be uncommonly tranquil.

This session of Congress has passed with unusual good temper. The last was a dreadful one. In public, as well as

---

[24] *Jefferson.* [S. AMES]

in private life, a calm comes after a storm. When I return, which will be in March, I shall try to turn out of my head all the politics that have been huddled into it, and to restore the little scraps of law which I once hoped to make a market of.

The newspaper sometimes gives a sad character of lawyers. I hope *you* are not so very vile as Adams's paper describes the *order*.

You perceive when the abuse of the order is in question, I say *you*. I shall be very willing to take my share of the abuse, on the terms of having my share of the profits of the trade.

Pray remember me to the gentlemen of the club.

Your affectionate friend.

TO THOMAS DWIGHT

BOSTON, APRIL 16, 1791

DEAR SIR,

I PRESUME you had my letter from Hartford, which informed you that I was going to Philadelphia. The date of this will announce to you that I have returned. My journey was a rapid but not unpleasant one. Such continued exercise is good for a lazy fellow, as your humble servant's good health testifies. I returned from New York, by water, to Providence, which deprived me of the pleasure of visiting you and my other friends at Springfield. I hope you are married, and should have enjoyed a great deal of satisfaction in attending the ceremony.[25] Allow me to *salute* the bride, and to offer

---

[25] *Mr. Dwight's marriage occurred about this time.* [S. AMES]

my fervent wishes for your mutual felicity. Pray assure *the worthy family,* as well as your household, of my respectful attachment. After taking some measures to establish myself in business here, I shall not fail to visit your town. The law courts will detain me several weeks. But I hope to see the trees in blossom on my journey. I am going to be connected with Jo Hall. The office is in State street. I shall try to forget politics, and to like the drudgery of an office. I think I have fully explained to you heretofore the manner in which I intend to dispose of myself during the recess of Congress, and my joint concern in the law way with Mr. Hall. My friends here approve this connection, as promising mutual advantage. . . .[26]

I am, dear sir, your friend, &c.

[P.S.:] I will send, if I can, Burke's famous pamphlet to Colonel Worthington.

TO THOMAS DWIGHT

BOSTON, APRIL 26, 1791

DEAR SIR,

PEOPLE here seem to care as little about politics, as I think you do at this moment. There is a scarcity of grievances. Their mouths are stopped with white bread and roast meat.

---

[26] *In a letter dated Boston, May 11, 1791, he says:—"I opened my office last Monday, and am not so hurried with business as to deny myself the pleasure of writing to you. My office is in King street, next door to the custom-house."* [S. AMES]

Our worthy Governor is again ill, laid up with the gout. I hope you will bear it, and all other public calamities, with a patriotic firmness. Some murmurs are whispering, because Congress has not begun to quarrel with England on account of navigation. Men are more true to their passions than to their interests. What we have is great, and what we may hope is immense; yet many are ready to put all to the hazard, by a war of regulations with that country.

Farewell. Believe me your
affectionate friend.

TO TENCH COXE

BOSTON, MAY 31, 1791

SIR

Many persons who intend to become stockholders in the United States Bank propose to employ a gentleman of this place to go to your city as their agent to make their subscriptions. Your answer to my inquiries, hereafter made, may facilitate his arrangements, and perhaps induce some persons to subscribe who otherwise would not do it. I hope you will consider this reason as a sufficient one for requesting your attention to the subject, and permit to request an answer, if not too inconvenient, by return of the post, as the time of the agent's departure will not, probably, be delayed much beyond that period.

By the supplementary bank law, the payments in public paper *may* be deferred. Will paper be received if the subscribers should prefer paying it immediately? If such payments may be made immediately, by what mode will the transfers be regulated? Shall the subscriber be obliged, in one hand, to hold the papers ready transferred to the Bank, in the other the pen to subscribe his shares, supposing that he should chuse to pay his paper part at first? For you will see that the agent must carry forward such transfers in that case. He may not get a chance to subscribe at all, or not more than thirty shares. How is the transfer to be vacated, or rather the paper to be transferred to the disappointed adventurer? Perhaps this is a matter which the five Commissioners will arrange and give public notice of their regulations. Supposing the paper to be received, will it be considered immediately as an instrument to the stock and of course entitling the subscriber paying it to a greater dividend? Or, will it be considered as a deposit til January 1, 1792; then to operate as payment of the part receivable in paper? In this latter case, the accruing interest will be for the use of the stockholder who deposits the paper. But it is not to be supposed that persons will be disposed to pay it so long beforehand on such terms.

The sending excise to Philadelphia will be troublesome. Some here have inquired whether any arrangement will be made at the Treasury for sending post bills to this place. The great topic of clamor in this part of the country has been that the books being opened only at your city, your citizens enjoy a monopoly of the shares. I will not pretend to say whether any measures ought to be adopted to obviate this objection, nor what would be the most proper for the purpose.

Four hundred thousand dollars must be paid before any steps can be taken toward organizing the corporation. Supposing the public to withhold its contribution it will take sixteen thousand of the twenty thousand private shares to produce that sum, and possibly so many may not be subscribed for a long time. Prudent moneyholders would delay putting their money into so unproductive a fund, as the evil, once existing, would prevent further subscriptions and so protract its own duration—unless the Treasury should put an end to it by advancing the necessary sum for the public, whether the money is within the Secretary's command, and whether it is to be applied so as to produce an immediate capacity to call a meeting of the stockholders within 90 days agreeably to the law, possibly, are improper questions to propose. But if a suspicion such as I have alluded to, should once be entertained, I think the knowledge of the ability and intention of the Secretary to fill up the four hundred thousand dollars would have a salutary effect.

Pardon me one more query and I have done: It is a doubt which may affect the profits of the stock whether ten millions of Bank paper, only, may be issued, or whether the amount of specie deposits be added to the ten millions. The latter seems to be a very variable and obscure standard by which to limit the emissions of paper.

Accept my sincere thanks for the communication of the two papers in answer to Lord Sheffield. It is an American triumph to see that British champion so fairly overthrown. I hope this candid statement of facts will have its full effect in America. By showing how much nature and our own industry have done and are doing for us, I wish it may disgust some fiery people against those angry violent systems which it has of late been the fashion to maintain. I wish you may proceed.

I am, sir, with sentiments of respect
and esteem your most obedient servant

FISHER AMES

TO MAJOR GENERAL PUTNAM

PHILADELPHIA, JULY 22, 1791

DEAR SIR

IT WAS IMPOSSIBLE to read your letter giving an account of the attack of the savages on the settlement at Big Bottom without feeling a strong sympathy with you under the peculiar distress of your situation. However your fears may have interpreted the sense of the country towards you, I am happy to perceive that they are not undisposed to giving you effectual protection, though it will cost money. That circumstance too often throws cold water on the natural emotions of the public towards the distressed brethren. I am happy to learn by Governor Sinclair that the last intelligence from Marietta etc. left all quiet, there trussed as you have been to war and danger. I think your late alarms must have exposed your fortitude to its severest trials. I wish they may not be repeated. You know that my opinion of the proper policy of Congress is, to manifest a fixed resolution to protect the most remote parts of the Union—to nurse the weak and to console the suffering remote settlements with a degree of tender solicitude proportioned to their defenseless condition. Congress has little occasion to make itself known to them except by acts of protection. The most successful way to banish the ruinous idea of the future independency of the western country is, by doing good to the settlers, to gain their hearts. Our sun will set when the Union shall be divided. But it is not necessary to notice the idea any further. The measures of the present session of Congress, I think, will satisfy you that because you are remote you are not forgotten and will not be abandoned to the savages. I enclose a letter to my old school

870

fellow and townsman, Mr. Battelle. Will you please convey it to him?

Please to accept my sincere wishes for your health and prosperity—

I am, dear sir, with respect etc.
Your very humble servant

FISHER AMES

TO ALEXANDER HAMILTON

BOSTON JULY 31, 1791

DEAR SIR

I GAVE your letter addressed to Mrs Warren into the hands of her husband, and tho, you inform me, something pretty was in it, I cannot believe it was a love letter. I told him that I was desired to subscribe for you to her poetical work. I shall take half a dozen Books, which, I presume, will be as much poetry as you will consume, and will carry the compliment as far as it will bear with any apperance of sincerity.

Mrs Walker lives in the country. I have sent your Letter to her. I hope your enquiries will find proper ground to allow her petition.

You make mention of the Bank in your favor of the 2 July. The eagerness to subscribe is a proof of the wealth and resources of the country and of the perfect confidence reposed by our opulent men in the Govt. People here are full of exultation and gratitude. They know who merits the praise of it, and they are not loth to bestow it. But with all this good temper, many lament that the Philadelphians have engrossed so much of the stock, & have so divided the shares as to multiply *their* votes. They believe that there was management and partiality in the commissioners. They wonder that of the five, the three Philadelphians only attended. Suffer me to write unreservedly.

Mr Willing's name is mentioned for Prest. It is said that he is Prest. of the N. Ama. Bank, that his name will be useful to the circulation, that his appointment would quiet, perhaps destroy, a faction in the city &c. Allow me to state the other side of the question.

They urge here, that the Prest. ought to be free from all suspicion of management—above the influence of favorites— that Mr. Morris, whom they fear as a man of talents & intrigue, with his connections, will make a property of this man & govern him at their pleasure. I fear that his appointment would create a faction here. His friends will not pretend that he has talents to make him worth forcing upon the stockholders in the eastern quarter. An idea that the Bank will be hazarded by partiality to men who will make desperate speculations would be a bad one to get a currency. The Prest. & Directors should be solid and fair. I only wish to have you possessed of the fact that our prudent and respectable stockholders will entertain the opinions I have suggested, and I leave it to your judgment whether Mr Willing is a proper man for Prest.

If the Bank would do business for five per cent, they would do a great deal more & with safer people. They would overpower the state banks by giving borrowers better terms. I have had my fears that the state banks will become unfriendly to that of the U.S. Causes of hatred & rivalry will abound. The state banks will narrow the business of the U.S. Bank & may become dangerous instruments in the hands of state partizans who may have bad points to carry. I will not expatiate. The occasion is a favorable one. The Bank & the U.S. Govt. at this moment possess more popularity than any institution or Govt. can maintain for a long time. Perhaps no act of power can be done to destroy the state banks, but if they are willing to become interested individually, I mean the state stockholders, and to establish sub banks so as to absorb the funds & contract the business of the local banks, why should any measures be adopted to support the local banks to the prejudice of my hypothesis? Or why should cold water be thrown upon the plan of sub banks? Mr Willing & the Philadelphians are thought unfriendly to this idea. Perhaps it may be attended with some hazard. But if it must fail, let it not be charged to local prejudice, but to solid reason.

I have lately conversed with a judicious respectable friend on the subject of the Bank in this town. The justness of his sentiments or their coincidence with my own induced me to request his ideas in writing. He has complied and I inclose them. They are the offspring of a moment & were intended for me only. You will read them with due allowance for the manner of their production.

The success of the govt. of the U.S. and especially of the measures proceeding from your department has astonished the multitude & while it has shut the mouths it has stung the envious hearts of the state leaders. All the influence of the monied men ought to be wrap'd up in the union and in one bank. The state banks may become the favorites of the states. They, the latter, will be proud to emulate the example of the Union & to shew their sovereignty by a parade of institutions like those of the nation. I intended to be concise, & by writing in haste I have been lengthy.

The distillers here have answer'd a letter from New York, desiring them to shut up their distilleries &c, with proper disapprobation. Some increase of the duty on W.I. Spirits & some amendment of the excise system, I presume would be proper. It is what they expect & their late conduct has a claim to merit.

Your plan relating to Manufactures is not yet generally known here. I think it will be popular. Have you any objection to a similar incorporation in New England? Some object that agriculture better merits encouragement, & that domestic manufactures will be injured by the company. I do not think these topics unanswerable.

I regret it that when the funding act passed, the stock had not been declared free from tax. Some inconvenience & vexation I fear will spring from this neglect. The assessors are, in some places, disposed to pry into the entries at the Custom House, and the Loan Office Books.

I write meaning that you only should read but I am not sure that the sentiments deserve your perusal. I will not desire an answer. I know your time is occupied sufficiently. I am, dear Sir, with sentiments of esteem and regard

Your very Obedt. hble servant

FISHER AMES

TO THOMAS DWIGHT

———

PHILADELPHIA, OCTOBER 30, 1791

DEAR FRIEND,

AFTER enduring weariness, cold, watching and hunger, (that is, between meals,)—after perils in the stages and ferry-boats, in darkness and snow-storms,—I am (what a sinking in style) very well, by the fireside. You have been sleeping in clover—I do not mean in the barn, neither—while I have scarcely slept at all on my journey. So it is, that the drivers ease their horses by tiring the passengers. They do not drive fast, but they are a great many hours performing their task. The horses are shifted, but the poor traveller is kept harnessed. And yet, hard as the sufferings of a stage-coach are, the man who describes them in the tragedy style gets laughed at. The unfeeling world would deny me their pity, if I was to ask it. I will not give them the opportunity.

The first arrangements of the bank have passed over smoothly. Though mutual jealousies were left, yet all parties saw and yielded to the necessity of harmonizing. Preparations are making, with all possible speed, for the circulation of the bills, and the discounting of notes. Yesterday, McKean, of South Carolina, was appointed cashier. He is a man of genteel manners and fair character. Mr. Francis, cashier of the old bank, is very much of the bear, and yet was strenuously supported for the office in the Bank of the United States. The stock of the bank is chiefly held in New York and Massachusetts. This is a favorable circumstance in the outset. I trust it will have the more of a national cast on that account.

Politics is yet asleep. Business is preparing in Congress; but nothing has indicated that degree of turbulence which marked the former sessions. Pray let me hear from you often. Farewell.

Your friend.

TO WILLIAM TUDOR

PHILADELPHIA, NOVEMBER 24, 1791

DEAR SIR,

MR. SODERSTROM has just handed me the enclosed, desiring me to forward it to you. I take the occasion to express the pleasure I receive by hearing directly from your town, and particularly that you are standing on two good legs, and with very little reliance on their wooden coadjutors. I am gratified by Mr. S's accounts, which are confirmed by other testimony, of the flourishing and satisfied state of Boston. The multitude of new houses erecting in this city and New York, and other marks of increasing wealth and populousness, are a constant provocative to the *amor patriæ* of a Bostonian. But the papers tell us of many fine things that are going forward with you— the town is to be lighted, the market decorated and reformed, and a *theatre*. It is observable that our young men are vigilant to keep our manners incorrupt as well as the old. Whether the stage is a friend or foe to taste and morals is possibly not capable of very full proof; nor does it seem to me necessary to decide the point with more than we have. For as people *earn* their own money, it seems reasonable that they should spend it. In earning, a man may choose freely between rest and action, and their effects, want and abundance. Why government should wait till the money is obtained, and then control the disposal of it, rather than begin at the first stage, and compel men to earn it, I confess I do not see. The latter would be the more effectual measure, as *idleness is less friendly to economy and virtue than luxury*, and possibly would be as consistent with the right of a man to his own. Men who have many wants will have many talents. A new stimulus is furnished to the mind, to supply by skill, what is necessary to the enjoyment of life. It may therefore be questioned whether a new expense tends to make a people poorer. For it may diminish one or several before indulged in, as it may stimulate men to greater action, and thereby supply its own demand. The General Court will not, I fancy, think well of an indulgence which will cost so much. I confess I have my doubts whether a theatre could be supported long in Boston. Few strangers resort there in winter, and the citizens would soon become sated with theatrical exhibitions. But I shall soon (if I have not already done it) convince you that I am little acquainted with the arguments which were used in town meeting. I write under the influence of a single opinion, that people should be allowed to do as they like in any case not palpably hurtful.

The Bank of the U.S. is beginning to print its bills, and will be employed in business in a few days. You have seen the plan of branches. I do not hear of any strong objections stated against the plan. If successful, it must secure in the event a good dividend. Congress is not engaged in very interesting work. The first acts were the pillars of the federal edifice. Now we have only to keep the sparks from catching the shavings; we must watch the broom, that it is not set behind the door with fire on it, &c. &c. Nobody cares much for us now, except the enemies of the excise law, who remonstrate and make a noise.

FISHER AMES

TO GEORGE RICHARDS MINOT

PHILADELPHIA, NOVEMBER 30, 1791

DEAR MINOT,

THE INCLOSED EPISTLE, having grown into an immoderate length, is submitted to your discretion, after perusal, to be read in whole or in part to the club, or single members of it, according to your idea of expediency. Gore, towards whom I have no reserves, may, if you choose, read the whole. The actual state and the true cause of southern discontent are better known at Boston than the degree of it. Congress and the British Parliament are viewed alike, and equally foreign to them, equally false and hostile to liberty, tyrannical and rapacious, taxing one thing after another, and going on narrowing their rights and enjoyments, till air only will be free.

You will think me hypochondriac. I own I sometimes lose my spirits when fresh evidence is given of the truth of what I have written. All that may happen may fail; and even at the worst, the mischief might be repelled by force, or soothed by prudence. That is another affair. I write what I believe. There is, indeed, no counting the numbers of the discontented, for in such cases the satisfied are silent, and are not counted. Making all these statements and reserves, you will not mistake the impression under which I write.

Your conjecture in regard to the bench is curious; but I was not unprepared for it.

My respects, &c, to Mrs. Minot, and friends Freeman, Dexter, &c.

Your friend, &c.

PHILADELPHIA, NOVEMBER 30, 1791

*The following is the "inclosed" referred to
in the above letter.*

DEAR SIR,

I AM solicitous to keep alive the remembrance of me with my friends. Congress is so little minded in the transaction of the business of this session, that I must not confide in my drawing their attention, as a spoke in the political wheel. Therefore, I will make continual claim to your notice, whenever I begin to apprehend being forgotten, to such a degree as to overcome my lazy habits, and the difficulty arising from the dearth of matter.

The spirit of debate bears no proportion to the objects of debate. It may be a question with moral observers, which most inflames the zeal of members, the magnitude of the consequences which a measure will produce, or the sensibility to the contradiction of their opinions. I decide nothing on the delicate subject. But in fact several debates have arisen, like thundergusts in a pleasant day, when no Mr. Weatherwise would have guessed it. The ratio of representation seemed to me, beforehand, as pacific a question as any public assembly ever slumbered over. But though the difference of opinion was narrowed within the limits of one to thirty or thirty-four thousand, yet eloquence, so long weary of rest, seemed to rejoice in the opportunity of stretching its limbs. We heard, and no doubt, if you had patience, you have read, about republicanism, and aristocracy, and corruption, and the sense of the people, and the amendments, and indeed so much good stuff, that I almost wonder it did not hold out longer. We have disputed about a mode of trying the disputed election of Generals Wayne and Jackson. To be serious, my friend, the great objects of the session are yet untouched; but the House, especially the new members, have been very often engaged in the *petite guerre*.

Instead of facts, I will notice to you, that the remark so often made on the difference of opinion between the members from the two ends of the continent, appears to me not only true, but founded on causes which are equally unpleasant and lasting. To the northward, we see how necessary it is to defend property by steady laws. Shays confirmed our habits and opinions. The men of sense and property, even a little above the multitude, wish to keep the government in force enough to govern. We have trade, money, credit, and industry, which is at once cause and effect of the others.

At the southward, a few gentlemen govern; the law is their coat of mail; it keeps off the weapons of the foreigners, their creditors, and at the same time it governs the multitude, secures negroes, &c., which is of double use to them. It is both government and anarchy, and in each case is better than any possible change, especially in favor of an exterior (or federal) government of any strength; for that would be losing the property, the usufruct of a government, by the State, which is light to bear and convenient to manage. Therefore, and for other causes, the men of weight in the four southern States (Charleston city excepted) were more generally *antis,* and are now far more turbulent than they are with us. Many were federal among them at first, because they needed some remedy to evils which they saw and felt; but mistook, in their view of it, the remedy. A debt-compelling government is no remedy to men who have lands and negroes, and debts and luxury, but neither trade nor credit, nor cash, nor the habits of industry, or of submission to a rigid execution of law. My friend, you will agree with me, that, ultimately, the same system of strict law, which has done wonders for us, would promote their advantage. But that relief is speculative and remote. Enormous debts required something better and speedier. I am told that, to this day, no British debt is recovered in North Carolina. This, however, I can scarcely credit, though I had strong evidence of its truth. You will agree that our immediate wants were different—we to enforce, they to relax, law. The effects of these causes on opinions have been considerable, as you will suppose. Various circumstances, some merely casual, have multiplied them.

Patrick Henry, and some others of eminent talents, and influence, have continued *antis,* and have assiduously nursed the embryos of faction, which the adoption of the Constitution did not destroy. It soon gave popularity to the *antis* with a grumbling multitude. It made two parties.

Most of the measures of Congress have been opposed by the southern members. I speak not merely of their members, but their gentlemen, &c., at home. As men, they are mostly enlightened, clever fellows. I speak of the tendency of things, upon their politics, not their morals. This has sharpened discontent at home. The funding system, they say, is in favor of the moneyed interest—oppressive to the land; that is, favorable to us, hard on them. They pay tribute, they say, and the middle and eastern people, holders of seven eighths of the debt, receive it. And here is the burden of the song, almost all the little that they had and which cost them twenty shillings for supplies or services, has been bought up, at a low rate, and now they pay more tax towards the interest than they received for the paper. This *tribute*, they say, is aggravating, for all the reasons before given; they add, had the state debts not been assumed they would have wiped it off among themselves very speedily and easily. Being assumed, it has become a great debt; and now an excise, that abhorrence of free states, must pay it. This they have never adopted in their states. The states of Virginia, North Carolina, and Georgia are large territories. Being strong, and expecting by increase to be stronger, the government of Congress over them seems mortifying to their state pride. The pride of the strong is not soothed by yielding to a stronger. How much there is, and how much more can be made of all these themes of grief and anger, by men who are inclined and qualified to make the most of them, need not be pointed out to a man, who has seen so much, and written so well, upon the principles which disturb and endanger government.

I confess I have recited these causes rather more at length than I had intended. But you are an observer, and I hope will be a writer of our history. The picture I have drawn, though just, is not noticed. Public happiness is in our power as a nation. Tranquillity has smoothed the surface. But (what I have said of southern parties is so true that I may affirm) faction glows within like a coal-pit. The President lives—is a southern man, is venerated as a demi-god, he is chosen by unanimous vote, &c., &c. Change the key and . . . You can fill up the blank. But, while he lives, a steady prudent system by Congress may guard against the danger. Peace will enrich our southern friends. Good laws will establish more industry and economy. The peculiar causes of discontent will have lost their force with time. Yet, circumstanced as they are, I think other subjects of uneasiness will be found. For it is impossible to administer the government according to their ideas. We must have a revenue; of course an excise. The debt must be kept sacred; the rights of property must be held inviolate. We must, to be safe, have some regular force, and an efficient militia. All these, except the last, and that, except in a form not worth having, are obnoxious to them. I have not noticed what they call their republicanism, because having observed what their situation is, you will see what their theory must be, in seeing what it is drawn from. I have not exhausted, but I quit this part of the subject. In fine, those three states are circumstanced not unlike our state in 1786.

I think these deductions flow from the premises: That the strength as well as hopes of the Union reside with the middle and eastern states. That our good men must watch and pray on all proper occasions for the preservation of federal measures, and principles. That so far from being in a condition to swallow up the state governments, Congress cannot be presumed to possess too much force to preserve its constitutional authority, whenever the crisis, to which these discontents are hastening, shall have brought its power to the test. And, above all, that, in the supposed crisis, the state partisans, who seem to wish to clip the wings of the Union, would be not the least zealous to support the Union. For, zealous as they may be to extend the power of the General Court of Massachusetts, they would not wish to be controlled by that of Virginia. I will not tire you with more speculation; but I will confess my belief that if, now, a vote was to be taken, 'Shall the Constitution be adopted,' and the people of Virginia, and the other more southern states, (the city of Charleston excepted,) should answer instantly, according to their present feelings and opinions, it would be in the negative.

These are dangers which our Massachusetts parties probably do not know, and have not weighed, and I shall hope that if they should be brought to view them in as alarming forms as it is an even chance they will, we shall have there but one sentiment. We ought to have but one. My paper is out, so farewell.

Your affectionate friend, &c.

TO ANDREW CRAIGIE

PHILADELPHIA, DECEMBER 2D, 1791

DEAR SIR

I HAVE LOOKED, and only looked, at your statement, received yesterday. Am I right in supposing that a balance of £567 lies in your hands, in cash, for me? I should prefer the public debt to cash—Knowing your friendship and trusting more to your judgment than my own, will you first *consider* how that balance, and as much of the deferred stock in your hands as you may chuse to add to it, may be employed to my best profit, and then will you do the needful? I shall write you more fully in a few days, and unless some disadvantage should appear to follow any delay, I should not wish to have anything more done than to inquire before my next. For I am exactly as *undecided* with respect to the disposal of my little means as I was when we conversed together. But I will form my opinion deliberately and make it known to you in a few days.

You do not inform whether my letters will fall into any other hands than yours—nor how it may be prevented. You

are silent as to the transfer of six per cents for my shares
(12) in the Bank of the United States.

I must have a part in the transaction. Nor if you transfer
will it be enough, unless *I* transfer after to the President,
Directors, etc. of the Bank of the United States. Tis said the
15th December is the last of the term in which this can be
done. Therefore, it should be known whether you must not
first transfer to the Bank. In the ca[se of] such a *double*
transfer, no time may [be left].
I am, your friend etc.

FISHER AMES

TO ANDREW CRAIGIE

PHILADELPHIA, DECEMBER 8TH, 1791

DEAR SIR:

I HAVE HOPED to hear from you by the two last posts. I
wrote you last Friday and stated that after a transfer from
you to me there must be one from me to the President,
Directors, etc. of the Bank. I have not chosen to inquire
whether the idea is well founded; but if it should be, I would
wish to have my part of the stock filled up so early as to
secure against any accidents which delay is always exposed
to. As the 15th December will terminate the making of the
transfers in the offices, and it is now the 8th, I am rather
solicitous to have the thing done, and done correctly. Pray
do the needful.

I also wrote something about some disposition of a part of
the property you hold for me. I am not certain how it can,
best, be disposed of and invested again. I am not possessed
of better grounds for forming a judgment than I was when

I saw you here: though I have wished to have the best ground. I assure you that I am not informed of any very discouraging thing.

I am not able to say what I think of your statement: for indeed I have not examined it. This you will think extraordinary. But I assure you, my friend, I know you are disposed to prove [wise]. And I should think illy of myself, if I was to look into your statement with any other confidence.

I suppose I shall have, finally, deferred stock enough to procure three thousand dollars specie. Add to that the balance £570, or thereabouts, in your hands—which with a further sum to make it a five or six thousand dollars. I would wish you [as] a friend in whose judgment and disposition I perfectly confide, to act as you think most for my advantage—provided you should be of opinion that any disposition of the funds would be beneficial. Thus I think I express myself clearly as to my wishes.

I write in the House of Representatives and beg you therefore to excuse the careless manner of my letter—

I am, dear sir, with entire [esteem]
your very humble servant

FISHER AMES

TO THOMAS DWIGHT

PHILADELPHIA, DECEMBER 9, 1791
FRIDAY EVENING

MY DEAR FRIEND,

THE MAIL for the eastward will not go hence till Tuesday next. I write by a private hand as far as New York. There my letter will take the mail for you.

I would not delay till the regular post day, to inform you

of the disaster to our army at the westward. The authority, though not official, being indisputable, I proceed to tell you, that General St. Clair, being with (fame says) twelve or fourteen hundred men about ninety miles from Fort Washington, was surrounded by the Indians, drew up in a hollow square, the cannon and baggage in the centre, and was attacked by a greatly superior force of Indians. It was not a surprise, for the men lay under arms all night. The attack was made at four in the morning, with unexampled fury. The militia broke; the cannon were taken; the General was surrounded, and rescued by a party of the regulars with fixed bayonets. The cannon were retaken, but were not of use, all the artillerymen being killed. At nine in the morning, our men broke, and were pursued five miles; fled thirty miles to a little new fort, called Jefferson, where, it is said, a garrison and the wounded are since invested. It is reported that General St. Clair has reached Fort Washington; but Fort Jefferson, and the first regiment, said not to have been with the main body, are in danger, perhaps lost. Kentucky was up in arms to save the remnant. St. Clair behaved well, and, though defeated, is not reproached.

On reading the account of killed, &c., you will lament the names you will see on the list.

Killed—General Butler, Colonel Oldham, Majors Brown, Hart, Clark, Ferguson; Captains Bradford, Upton, Smith, Newman, Phelan, Kirkwood, Price, and three others; Lieutenants Winslow, Warren, Spear, and eight others; Ensigns Bentley, Cobb, Balch, Brooks, and five others; three Quartermasters.

Wounded—Colonel Gibson, cannot live; Colonel Darke, Major Butler, cannot live; thirteen Captains, among them Greaton, of Roxbury, and six hundred privates.

The news probably comes at its worst, but the truth is doubtless bad enough. Farewell.

Yours, &c.

TO GEORGE MINOT

PHILADELPHIA, DECEMBER 23, 1791

DEAR FRIEND,

THOUGH my former letters have expressed indifference to the debate on the ratio of representatives, yet at last the violent injustice of the bill became so manifest, as to overcome all my moderation. Representatives and taxes are to be apportioned among the several states, according to their respective numbers. Giving representatives to the states not according to their numbers, is no apportionment, but a flagrant wrong, and against the words and principles of the Constitution.

This was done by the bill. The whole number of representatives being one hundred and twelve, an apportionment of these to Virginia, according to her numbers, would give that state nineteen members. Yet the bill gave her twenty-one. What did we Yankees do but mount the high horse, and scold in heroics against the disfranchisement of the other states? The Senate amended the bill from thirty to thirty-two thousand for a member, which latter produces a more equal apportionment. The House disagreed, the Senate insisted, and finally both houses adhered, and so the bill died, and I am glad of it. We have to begin again.

Major Thomas Pinckney, of South Carolina, a man of excellent character, is nominated Minister at the Court of London; Gouverneur Morris at the Court of France; Mr. Short at the Hague.

. . . .

Will you do me the favor to send me, by the first post, one of your histories of the rebellion. It is not to be had here. I want it for young Mr. Thornton, the secretary to the English Minister, a worthy young man, to whom I have spoken about you and your book. He wishes to see it.

I am, dear friend, affectionately
yours, &c.

1 7 9 2

PHILADELPHIA, JANUARY 13, 1792

DEAR FRIEND,

. . . .

I BELIEVE that the war will be pursued against the Indians; that the public will be made to see that the charges of violence and oppression on the part of the United States, the disturbance of the Indian possession of their lands, and a hundred others, are Canterbury tales. Little of the cause, the history, the object, or the prospect of this confounded war have been known abroad. Those who knew nothing, wished to know, and of course believed, a good deal. A good deal has been offered them to believe. The foes of government have seized the occasion, a lucky one for them. The foes of the Secretary at War[27] have not been idle. Even the views

---

[27] *General Knox.* [S. AMES]

of the western people, whose defence has been undertaken by government, have been unfriendly to the Secretary at War, and to the popularity of the government. They wish to be hired as volunteers, at two thirds of a dollar a day, to fight the Indians. They would drain the Treasury. They are averse to regulars. Besides, it looks not only like taking the war out of the hands of the back settlers, but so many troops there will look as if government could not be resisted, and the excise perhaps would be less trifled with. All these, and many other causes, have swelled the clamor against the war. A strong post at the Miami village would protect a long frontier, and curb the Indians, by placing an enemy behind them, when they attack the settlements. This attempt has been twice made without success. The late season, the grass having failed, so that the horses wanted fodder, the bad discipline of the troops, and the extra number of the Indians beyond what was expected, seem to be the causes of the disaster. A greater force, better disciplined, at an earlier season of the year, with a due proportion of horse and riflemen, could not fail of taking a strong post. That being effected, parties could be fed and rested at the post, would then be safe, and could rush out suddenly, and keep the Indians always in alarm and in danger. We should exactly change conditions. So much for war. You will not (freely) speak of what I write.

Before this time, the *Anakim* is a judge, or a martyr to his chagrin.

Though I have blotted a sheet of paper, I am in a hurry. Therefore I conclude.

Your affectionate friend.

TO THOMAS DWIGHT

PHILADELPHIA, JANUARY 23, 1792

MY FRIEND,

.   .   .   .

THE BUSINESS of Congress is not unimportant. Yet our progress in despatching it affords no good omens. A popular assembly is good to deliberate, and so good at that as to exclude every other occupation. I fear that we shall only deliberate and not act. I do not believe that the hatred of the Jacobites towards the house of Hanover was ever more deadly than that which is borne by many of the partisans of state power towards the government of the United States. I wish I could see in Congress a spirit to watch and to oppose their designs; but we are surrounded by men who affect to think it a duty, and who really think it popular, to take part with those who would weaken and impede the government. The hour of victory is dangerous. The federalists have triumphed; they have laid their own passions asleep; they have roused those of their adversaries. I do not like our affairs. You will think me a croaker. Be it so. I see how much power this government needs, and yet how little is given; how much is done and contrived against it; how much it ought to do, and yet how little it does, or is disposed, or capable, to do; how few, how sleepy, how obnoxious its friends are, and how alert its foes. An immense mass of sour matter is fermenting at the southward. Every state government is a county convention. My pen needs mending; that gives me time to break off this endless theme.

The mad bank schemes of New York produce ill effects. Sober people are justly scared and disgusted to see the wild castle-builders at work. It gives an handle to attack the government.

What will you say of a new recruiting service, to fight the Indians? How will your wise ones approve it? You who watch for government among the people, should throw a few soothing paragraphs into the papers.

In future, I think government will move with strength and caution, so that the Indians shall be bridled effectually. Compliments to your *cara sposa*. That is Latin for honey. Regards to other friends.

Yours, affectionately.

TO THOMAS DWIGHT

PHILADELPHIA, JANUARY 30, 1792

DEAR FRIEND,

.   .   .   .

AFTER A DAY'S, or rather part of a day's, open debate on the bill for augmenting the military establishment to five thousand two hundred and sixty-eight men, the doors were shut to read some papers, intrusted to the House by the President, and have not since been opened to discuss that subject. As the papers sent from the President were expressly in confidence, it was improper to open the doors at all, though perhaps the impression on the public would not be worse for their being possessed of the *pro* and *con* of the argument. I am convinced that the war is a misfortune to the government, and attended with a loss of cash and glory, and of the popular good humor. Still, I insist that government may plead not guilty to every article of the newspaper charges against it. General Knox, by the President's direction, has caused a memorial stating the causes of the war to be published, which you will see.

Some think that the Constitution is to be administered, as writs were formerly put to the test, by captious pleas to abatement. They say Congress has not authority to allow a bounty to the cod-fishery, nor to the encouragement of manufactures. This is the Virginia style. It is chiefly aimed at the report of the Secretary of the Treasury on the subject of manufactures.

Respects and compliments to friends.

Your friend, &c.

ON BOUNTIES FOR THE COD FISHERIES

Early in February of 1792 the House received from the Senate a bill for the encouragement of the New England cod fisheries. When William B. Giles of Virginia attacked the granting of bounties to the fishermen as unconstitutional and unwise, Ames defended the bill with the following speech.

FEBRUARY 3, 1792

MR. AMES after some introductory observations, adverted to the necessity of fixing some point in which both sides would agree. Disputes, he said, could not be terminated—or, more properly, they could not be managed at all, if some first principles were not conceded. The parties would want weapons for the controversy.

Law is in some countries the yoke of government, which bends or breaks the necks of the people; but, thank Heaven, in this country, it is a man's shield—his coat of mail—his castle of safety. It is more than his defence: it is his weapon to punish those who invade his rights—it is the instrument which assists—it is the price that rewards his industry.

If I say that fishermen have equal rights with other men, every gentleman feels in his own bosom a principle of assent. If I say that no man shall pay a tax on sending his property out of the country, the Constitution will confirm it; for the Constitution says, *no duty shall be laid on exports.* If I say, that on exporting dried fish, the exporter is entitled to drawback the duty paid on the salt, I say no more than the law of the land has confirmed. Plain and short as these principles are, they include the whole controversy. For I consider the law allowing the drawback as the right of the fishery; the defects of that law as the wrong suffered, and the bill before us as the remedy. The defects of the law are many and grievous. Supposing 340,000 quintals exported—

The salt duty is	$42,744
The drawback is only	34,000
Loss to the fishery	8,744
Whereas government pays $45,900, at 13½ cents, including charges, which are 3½ cts. on a quintal: which is beyond what the fishery receives	11,900
Being a clear loss to the government of	3,156

So that though the whole is intended for the benefit of the fishery, about one-fourth of what is paid is not so applied: there is a heavy loss both to government and the fishery. Even what is paid on the export is nearly lost money; the bounty is not paid till the exportation, nor then, till six months have elapsed; whereas the duty on salt is paid before the fish is taken: it is paid to the exporter, not to the fisherman. The bounty is so indirect, that the poor fisherman loses sight of it. It is paid to such persons, in such places, and at such periods, as to disappoint its good effects; passing through so many hands, and paying so many profits to each, it is almost absorbed. The encouragement, too, is greatest in successful years, when least needed; and is least in bad fishing seasons, when it is most needed. It is a very perplexed, embarrassing regulation to the officers of government and to the exporter; hence the great charge: and, with all this charge and trouble, it is liable to many frauds. Four hundred miles of coast, little towns, no officer. All these defects the bill remedies; and, besides, gives the money on condition that certain regulations are submitted to, which are worth almost as much as the money.

The bill is defended on three grounds. First, it will promote the national wealth; second, the national safety; third, justice requires it: the last is fully relied on.

To show that the fishery will increase the wealth of the nation, it cannot be improper to mention its great value. The export before the war brought more than a million of dollars into this country; probably it is not less at present, and no small part in gold and silver. It is computed that thirty thousand persons, including four thousand seamen, subsist by it. Many say, very composedly, if it will not maintain itself, let it fall. But we should not only lose the annual million of dollars which it brings us, an immense capital would be lost. The fishing towns are built on the naked rocks, or barren sands, on the side of the sea. Those spots, however, where trade would sicken and die—which husbandry scorns to till—and which nature seems to have devoted to eternal barrenness, are selected by industry to work miracles on. Houses, stores, and wharves, are erected, and a vast property created, all depending on this business. Before you think it a light thing to consign them to ruin, see if you can compute what they cost; if they outrun your figures, then confess that it would be bad economy, as well as bad policy, to suffer rival nations to ruin our fishery. The regulations of foreign nations tend to bring this ruin about. France and England equally endeavor, in the language of the Secretary of State, to mount their marine on the destruction of our fishery. The fishers at Newfoundland are allowed liberal bounties by the English government; and, in the French West Indies, we meet bounties on their fish and duties on our own, and these amount to the price of the fish. From the English islands we are quite shut out; yet such is the force of our natural advantages, that we have not yielded to these rivals. The Secretary of State has made these statements in his Report.

The more fish we catch the cheaper; the English fish will need a greater bounty: whereas if we should yield, the English would probably need no bounty at all; they would have the monopoly. For example; suppose the English can fish at two dollars the quintal—we catch so much that we sell at one dollar and two-thirds: the loss to them is one-third of a dollar on each quintal. They must have that sum as a bounty. Whereas, if we increase our fishery, a greater and a greater bounty is needed by foreign nations. The contest so painfully sustained by them must be yielded at last, and we shall enjoy alone an immense fund of wealth to the nation, which nature has made ours; and though foreigners disturb the possession, we shall finally enjoy it peaceably and exclusively. If the lands of Kentucky are invaded, you drive off the invader; and so you ought. Why not protect this property as well? These opinions are supported by no common authority. The State of Massachusetts having represented the discouragements of the fishery, the subject has received the sanction of the Secretary of State; he confirms the facts stated in the petition; he says it is too poor a business to pay anything to government.

Yet, instead of asking bounties, or a remission of the duties on the articles consumed, we ask nothing but to give us our own money back, which you received under an engagement to pay it back, in case the article should be exported. If nothing was in view, therefore, but to promote national wealth, it seems plain that this branch ought to be protected and preserved; because, under all the discouragements it suffers, it increases, and every year more and more enriches the country, and promises to become an inexhaustible fund of wealth.

Another view has been taken of the subject, which is drawn from the naval protection afforded, in time of war, by a fishery. Our coasting and foreign trade are increasing rapidly; but the richer our trade becomes, the better prize to the enemy: so far from protecting us, it would be the very thing that would tempt him to go to war with us. As the rice and the tobacco planter cheerfully pay for armies, and turn out in the militia to protect their property on shore, they cannot be so much deceived as to wish to have it left unprotected when it is afloat; especially when it is known that this protection, though more effectual than the whole revenue expended on a navy could procure, will not cost a farthing; on the contrary, it will enrich while it protects the nation. The coasters and other seamen, in the event of a war, would be doubly in demand, and could neither protect themselves nor annoy the enemy to any considerable degree; but the fishermen, thrown out of business by a war, would be instantly in action. They would, as they formerly did, embark in privateers; having nothing to lose, and everything to hope, they would not dishonor their former fame. Their mode of life makes them expert and hardy seamen. Nothing can be more adventurous. They cast anchor on the banks, three hundred leagues from land, and with a great length of cable ride out the storms of winter. If the gale proves too strong they often sink at their anchors, and are food for fish which they came to take: forever wet, the sea almost becomes their element. Cold and labor, in that region of frost, brace their bodies, and they become as hardy as the bears on the islands of ice: their skill and spirit are not inferior: familiar with danger, they despise it. If I were to recite their exploits, the theme would find every American heart already glowing with the recollection of them; it would kindle more enthusiasm than the subject has need of. My view is only to appeal to facts, to evince the importance of the fishery as a means of naval protection. It is proper to pass over Bunker's Hill, though memorable by the valor of a regiment of fishermen; nor is it necessary to mention, further, that five hundred fishermen fought at Trenton.

It is known, that the privateers manned by fishermen, in want of everything, not excepting arms, which they depended on taking from their enemies, brought into port warlike stores of every kind, as well as every kind of merchandise sufficient for the army and the country: the war could not have been carried on without them. Among other exploits almost beyond belief, one instance is worth relating: these people, in a privateer of sixteen guns, and one hundred and fifty men, in one cruise, took more than twenty ships, with upwards of two hundred guns, and nearly four hundred men. The privateers from a single district of Massachusetts, where the fishery is chiefly seated, took more than two thousand vessels, being one-third of the British merchant vessels, and brought in near one thousand two hundred. An hundred sail of privateers, manned by fishermen, would scour every sea in case of a war.

Some gentlemen think of a navy: but what navy could do more? What nation would provoke a people so capable of injuring them? Could fifty ships of the line afford more security? and yet this resource of the fishery, always, ready, always sufficient, will cost nothing. The superior naval force of our foes should not discourage us; our privateers would issue like so many swordfish to attack the whale. I leave these observations to their weight, and forbear to press them further; strong as I think them, I rest my support of the bill on another ground. I will only ask whether you will oppress, if you will not encourage them? Whether, if you will not give them the money of the public, you will partially seize their own? This is all they ask. If your policy demands for them so much, will your justice deny them so little?

I have repeatedly asserted that the bill will not cost the public a farthing; you only take the money which the fishery brings into the Treasury for the salt duty, and pay the same, or a less sum, back in bounties, instead of a drawback on the exportation of the fish. Here I rest the argument. Before I adduce my proofs, I cannot forbear to lay open the state of my mind. I rely on the truth of the facts I propose to offer. I rely on the proof of them, being as near demonstration as the nature of the case will admit. I make no doubt of the good sense and good intentions of the gentlemen whom I wish to convince; and yet I am sorry to say I am far from being sanguine in the hope of gaining a single vote for the bill. I will explain my meaning, and then I think no gentleman will take exception at it. This debate depends on calculation. In print or writing, or in private conversation, figures have the advantage of every other mode of investigation: the mind is fixed to a point, and made to perceive it clearly. But in public debate it is otherwise. Figures not only disgust attention, but, as the mind cannot carry them along, they confound it; they make a plain thing look mysterious; and bring it into suspicion. When I ask of the Committee a hearing, and it is granted, I get nothing: I want a close attention; and I have to beg, and earnestly too, that gentlemen will not trust their first opinions and vote against the bill, without condescending to receive and to weigh the facts and calculations of its advocates.

The first question is, how much does government receive by the duty on the salt used in curing the fish which is exported? The quantity of fish must be known. Several ways of information are to be explored. The Secretary of State supposes the fish of 1790 to be 354,276 quintals. A Treasury return of fish exported from August 20, 1789, to September 30, 1790, which is thirteen and one-third months, is 378,721 quintals. For a year, equal to 340,849 quintals.

Foreign dried fish imported from August 15, 1789, to August 1790, 3,701 quintals; five per cent. drawback thereon is only three hundred and ten dollars, at one dollar and sixty-six cents per quintal. Mr. GILES is mistaken in supposing that foreign fish deducts $16,000 from our estimate. Return of fish in seven months, from May 30, to December, 1790, exported, all fish of the United States, 197,278 quintals: which, for a year, is 338,184 quintals. The medium may be fairly taken for the time past at 340,000 quintals a year.

Six gentlemen of Marblehead certify, that 5,043 hogsheads, or 40,344 bushels of salt, were used on 38,497½ quintals; which, for 340,000 quintals, gives 356,200 bushels. The duty, at twelve cents, is $42,744, which government receives. But the charge to the United States is, at thirteen and a half cents per quintal

	$45,900
Whereof the fishery receives ten cents on each quintal exported	34,000
Charges as the law stands	11,900

Further, this is but an estimate made up from what the last year proved. The next may be very different, and probably it will be. If more money should be demanded than $44,000, we must not be accused of misleading Congress. But in that case an increase would be made by law; for the more fish is exported the more thirteen and a half cents must be paid; so that the bill creates no burden in that way. But the increase of the export of fish will probably operate in favor of government. For it is known that the economy, skill, and activity of the fishery are making progress. Its success has progressed. The more fish to a vessel, the cheaper the allowance on the tonnage. Therefore, the tonnage of vessels will not increase in a ratio with the increase of the fish.

The very objections prove this. For they deem the encouragement too great. But any encouragement must have the effect.

The difference of the agreements for distributing the fish according to the present practice, or by this bill, makes a great one in the quantity taken. The bill reforms the practice in this point. Marblehead vessels take less than those from Beverly. The former throw the fish into a common stock, which is afterwards divided upon a plan very unfriendly to exertion. A man works for the whole—perhaps twelve hours, and they take about eight hundred quintals to a vessel. But in Beverly, the exertion is as great as can be made; eighteen hours a day, because each man has what he catches, and they catch eleven hundred quintals.

Marblehead seamen sailing from other towns, and dividing as last mentioned, which the bill establishes, seldom fail to catch two or three hundred quintals more than vessels and men from Marblehead on the first plan. Accordingly, I assert on good authority, that the increase in Marblehead only may be computed at fifteen thousand quintals, merely in consequence of the reform by the bill. The best informed persons whom I have consulted, entertain no doubt that the export in case the bill should pass, would not be less than four hundred thousand quintals, probably more; but at four hundred thousand quintals, it would add seven thousand two hundred dollars more to the salt duty; a sum more than equal to any estimate of the actual tonnage, or any probable increase of it

	$42,744
	7,200
Salt duty on 400,000 quintals	49,944

Other facts confirm the theory, that skill and exertion are increasing in this business.

In 1775, 25,000 tons, 4,405 seamen. Fish sold for $1,071,000. In 1790, three-fourths of the seamen and three-fourths of the tonnage take as much fish. It is owing to this that our fishery stood the competition with foreign nations.

Finally, the average in future may be relied on not to be less than 350,000 quintals.

Salt duty on which	$43,944
Bounties	44,000
Wanted	56

The calculation first made will answer the purpose,

340,000 quintals pay salt duty	$42,744
Tonnage bounty	44,000
Wanted	1,256

This is the mighty defect. Observe: the authentic return of the export of fish may be, and we can almost prove it to be, below the future export. Whereas to banish all doubt we go to the top of the scale for the tonnage, we take what we know to be the utmost. This we might have represented more favorably if we had chosen to conceal any thing. But even this will answer our purpose.

For two hundred tons are wanting in the estimate of the bounties, being nineteen thousand eight hundred, not twenty thousand, which will take off one third of the deficient sum.

The tonnage over sixty-eight, which receives nothing, is not mentioned; and which probably is not less than another third.

The boats under five tons though trifling are to be noticed—they receive nothing.

But, above all, the chances of non-compliance with the regulations are in favor of the remainder of the twelve hundred and fifty-six dollars being stopped. Boats may not get twelve quintals to the ton, or vessels may have their voyage broken up, and not stay four months on the fishing ground, in either case they would receive nothing. Take all these together, is it not to be doubted that twelve hundred and fifty-six dollars will remain of the forty-four thousand in the Treasury?

But these are trifles which I cannot believe gentlemen are anxious about.

For the event cannot be reduced to a certainty. What quantity of fish will be exported, no man can tell now. But as government may receive more than it will pay, the chance may turn the other way, and it may have to pay a few hundred dollars more than it will have received. We have seen that the chance is most in favor of government. But one chance must balance the other. This answer is sincerely relied on as a good one.

I barely mention that the wear of cordage, cables, sails, and anchors, is very great. These articles on being imported, pay duties. So that it is probable the extra duty paid by the fishery on their extra consumption, will over balance any little sums supposed to exceed in the bounty.

It has been asked, as if some cunning was detected, why if the money received in the Treasury to pay the drawbacks is equal to the proposed bounties, a further appropriation should be made? This cunning question admits of several very simple answers.

The bill being for seven years, the average product is the proper sum to be calculated. But the three first years may fall short of the bounties, say two thousand dollars a year, which is six thousand dollars.

The four last may exceed two thousand dollars, say eight thousand dollars.

Shall a poor fisherman wait for the whole, or if he takes his part according to the money in the Treasury—for a twenty-fourth part of the bounty on his vessel, from 1792 to 1795?

2d. This delay would happen after a bad year, the very time when he would most need prompt pay.

3d. But fish taken this year will not be exported till December next. Therefore the money will not be stopped by the drawbacks as the law stands, till six months after.

A substitute has been proposed for the clause, to appropriate the drawback only.

This is absolutely improper. For the ten cents allowed as drawback is but a part of the duty paid on salt. It is not easy to see any reason why a part stopped at the Treasury should be equal to the whole paid there long before. The drawback falls near nine thousand dollars short of the salt duty received by the government. The expense of the drawback would be very heavy and useless.

Nor may gentlemen apprehend that government, by paying next December, will advance money to the fishery. The salt duty will have been paid, and government will have the use of the money many months before the fisherman will have a right to call for the bounties.

It is left to the candor of the gentlemen who have urged this objection, whether a better or further answer is desired.

After having laboriously gone through the estimate of the probable export of fish, it will not be necessary to be equally minute as to the quantity or kind of vessels which are to receive the bounty.

The estimate we believe to be very high. That it is high enough, we suppose very probable from the estimate of the Secretary of State, which is only nineteen thousand one hundred and eighty-five tons.

This mode of paying the bounty on the tonnage is very

simple and safe. The measurement is already made and costs nothing; and as it was made to pay a duty on tonnage, we are very sure that government will not be cheated by an over-measure. The mode of paying the drawback, as the law now stands, is expensive, perplexed and embarrassing; liable to frauds and delays.

This intricate and disgusting detail of calculations was necessary to satisfy the Committee that each of the three grounds of defence on which the bill rests, is tenable.

Instead of impoverishing the nation by scattering the treasures of the whole to benefit a part, it appears that we are preserving mine of treasure. In point of naval protection, we can scarcely estimate the fishery too highly. It is always ready, always equal to the object; it is almost the only sufficient source of security by sea. Our navigation is certainly a precious interest of the country. But no part of our navigation can vie with the fishery in respect to the protection it affords. There is no point which regards our national wealth or national safety, in respect to which it seems practicable to do so much with so little.

We rely on the evidence before you, that the public will not sustain the charge of a dollar. Those ought not to doubt the evidence who cannot invalidate it. If then the fishermen ask you to restore only their own money, will you deny them? Will you return to every other person exporting dutied goods the money he has paid, and will you refuse the poor fisherman?

If there must be an instance of the kind, will you single out for this oppressive partiality, that branch which is described by the Secretary of State as too poor even to bear its own part of the common burden? That branch which nevertheless has borne the neglect of our nation, and the persecution of foreign prohibitions and duties. A branch which, though we have received much and expect more, both of money and services, urges no claims but such as common justice has sanctioned.

REPORT OF SECRETARY OF STATE OR: MEMORIAL
OF MASSACHUSETTS
ON THE STATE OF THE COD FISHERIES
IS THE FOUNDATION OF THE BILL—[28]

[THE] RESULT of Mr. Jefferson's investigations is that "these fisheries with distant nations would come to nothing *if not supported* from *their treasuries,* but that the natural advantages of ours place them on ground somewhat higher—such as to relieve *our treasury* from giving support—*but not to permit it to draw support from them;*" "nor to dispense the gov't from the obligation of effectuating free markets abroad"——this latter depending on foreign nations is not so immediately within our power as the former—happily for the U. S. that this branch of industry so essential to the protection of commerce & naval defense & on that account purchased in other countries at any price, can be secured & maintained without any material expense to the U. S.——

The fish of the U. S. in the European markets is rivalled by the fish of Newfoundland which is aided by liberal bounties—in the French West Indies it meets the French fish which is bountied at the rate of one dollar per quintal & at the same time [our fish] pay a heavy duty—altho' it be true as a general axiom "that any branch of industry which requires a constant aid from others to support it ought to be abandoned as unprofitable," yet as a source of pecuniary advantage to be enjoyed at a future day it may be proved that this *embryo* of wealth as well as strength ought to be cherished by the United States—yet such is the force of our natural advantages that notwithstanding these artificial discouragements of our fish & the extravagant encouragement of that of our competitors, our fisheries have been sustained & continue to yield subsistence to a large body of men—not

---

[28] *Ames's draft of notes on Jefferson's official Report on the Cod Fishery bill, 1792.* [ED.]

less probably than 30,000[?] persons of whom 4,000 are seamen—annual earnings 1 million dollars—the *natural advantages* of the U. S. are so such [*sic*] that the remission of duties would be unnecessary, if rival nations did not counterbalance them by artificial ones—if ever those nations should abate the premiums now given to their fisheries, they must abandon & we shall occupy an inexhaustible source of wealth & strength—the repeated failure of the French nation in their attempts to carry on an extensive cod fishery must dispose them to relinquish it whenever the English (their maritime rival) can be induced to leave theirs without public assistance—Some arrangement of this kind is not unlikely to take place, because the English are induced now to bear the expense only for the sake of their navy——

An extensive fishery in the U. S. is of all circumstances the one most powerful to induce both F. & Britain to resign the business to its natural course—but if the fisheries of the U. S. are suffered to dwindle the fisheries of their rivals may be prosecuted with less expense, & consequently our yielding of any single point renders each remaining one less tenable.

Previous to the late war foreign fish was totally prohibited in the French islands yet they annually received *under cover* 150 to 200 million quintals from this Country—

Since the peace of '83 foreign fish has been admitted in the French Colonies liable to a duty from 3 to 8 livres— paying perhaps about 2 per quintal—a bounty at the same time has been allowed on French fish of 1 dollar per quintal— yet we have uniformly supplied the principal part of their consumption—it is a solemn truth however that in '87, '88, & '89,[29] strong indications were exhibited that our fishery could no longer struggle against such enormous discourage- ments, & if the Conventions in France had not interrupted their fisheries it may be presumed our fishery must have

[29] *Near 30 vessels in Marblehead were taken out of the business at this time as stated by Mr. Jefferson.* [AUTHOR]

sensibly declined—Should the English Islands be laid open, our fish would not go there as they [the English] take more than they consume, and sell a great surplus. The French, on the contrary, but a great deal.

The interest of every description of people wherever situated in the U. S. requires that a free, easy, & safe intercourse be kept & maintained between all the parts of this great country—that those exhanges may not be prevented which give value to every surplus & supply every want—

The coasting trade within a few years has immensely increased & may reasonably be supposed will in a few years become more valuable than all the foreign trade—All the productive classes in our great community have an interest in preserving to our own citizens a respectable portion of the foreign trade—Our own merchants explore every coast for markets & seek for consumers in every corner of the globe— Consequently they find vent for more of our productions than would be found if we only supplied those *whose wants* bring them to our shores—

If then our foreign & especially our domestic commerce be so essentially connected with every interest of our country, some sort of ability to defend & protect it seems to be among the first duties of our gov't to provide—Reason teaches & experience proves that this can best be done by keeping large fisheries which will at all times be a standing naval militia ready & perfectly qualified for the most effectual services—

No other aid is proposed however by the bill toward attaining so desirable an object than barely [to] remit or rather to restore & finally while the bill proposes no increase of expense to gov't it is the instrument of reforming habits & establishing principles & regulations in the fishery of greater moment to its prosperity than the aid of any amount in money could be without them—By the introduction of these the tenure of this branch of our industry will be the best possible "the ability to prosecute it cheaper than our competitors."——

From Aug. 20th, '89 to Sept. 30th, '90—13 $\frac{1}{3}$ months the dried fish exported from the United States amounted as per return—Quintals—378,721. This corresponds to quintals per annum 340,049; a return of fish exports upon which the drawback has been paid from May 30 to Dec. '90—7 months states 197,278 quintals which correspond to 330,104 quintals per annum—take the mean say 350,000 per annum at $13\frac{1}{2}$ Cents amounts to say Dollars 47,250—instead of which is proposed—say 340,000 the duty rec'd on the salt 42,744

15,000 tons at $2\frac{1}{2}$ Dollars per bill	37,500
3,000[30] at $1\frac{1}{2}$ Dollars per ton	4,500
2,000 at 1 Dollar per ton	2,000, 44,000 Dol
Gov't may be called to pay by the bill	44,000 dollars

21,000[30] tons which is more than the whole of the Cod Fishery Tonnage

Should it be objected to this statement that the fishery is not entitled to the saving of the expenses which are now incurred for weighing & inspecting the exported fish—it may be answered that gov't originally intended to give back to the fisheries the whole duty paid on the salt; but to prevent loss by charges it allowed considerably less drawback on the exported fish than the duty on the salt on the same fish amounted to, in order to cover the incidental charges; if then the new arrangement proposed by the bill will save these charges altogether, it seems reasonable the savings should remain to the fisheries from whence they were actually paid—that is the fisheries received so much less that they otherwise would have received, & which they actually needed to give them a complete indemnity on this salt—

It appears by returns (see Mr. Sewall's letter & enclosures) from a number of reputable gentlemen who are owners &

[30] *4,000 was corrected to 3,000, but the total was unchanged.* [ED.]

It appears by the returns that all the fishery vessels in the U. S.

amount to tons		31,900
From these deduct 122 whalers	10,210	12,100
Deduct also Mackerel Catchers and the over tonnage	1,890	
Whole tonnage of Cod Fishery		19,800

shoremen in Marblehead that in the years '89[ ] & '90 these gentlemen consumed 5,043 hogsheads of salt—8 bushels to the hogshead upon $38,497\frac{1}{2}$ quintals of fish—The duty on this Salt at 12 cents per bushel amounts to 4,641 dollars while the drawback amounts only to 3,850. The duty was paid long before the fish was taken. The drawback receivable not till 6 months after the fish is dried & exported—It is admitted that this particular statement may be somewhat more unfavorable to the fishery than the general facts thro' the state would warrant—It is certain however that in some towns (as Beverly) from whence they go to the Bay of St. Laurence instead of the Banks they use much more Salt on the same quantity of fish—

The whole tonnage of the Cod fishery is about 20,000 tons. Of this more than $\frac{3}{4}$ thus being estimated at $2\frac{1}{2}$

Dollars	say 15,000 @	37,500 Dollars
@ $1\frac{1}{2}$ Dollars	3,000	4,500
& @ 1 Dollar	2,000	2,000
		44,000

This is all gov't can be called to pay by the bill until the fishery increases—In that case the expense by the law would increase as well as by the bill—It is *called a bounty*, but is in fact *only* a *partial remission* of *duties* to a species of industry strongly rivalled abroad, but which the safety & welfare of the U. S. requires to be sponsored and supported.

But whatever may be the merits of the fishery as a source of wealth, its importance will never be denied as the *best most extensive* perhaps the *only permanent* source of naval strength. This body of men hardy expert & bold will be always at hand, & their services always at command when needed for the public defense—Their employment failing in way they necessarily engage in armed vessels—The astonishing feats they performed in the beginning of the late war have never been surpassed on the sea—Many of them however are still unknown out of the vicinity of those who achieved them—

Sailors are supposed to be incapable of making good soldiers,—but a part of the troops that fought on Bunker Hill were fishermen & one of the best regiments from Massachusetts in 1776 & which shared largely in the Trenton Enterprise was composed of 500 Fishermen—It was on their own proper element however that they most essentially served their country & wounded her enemies in 1776 & 1777—In which two years they captured & brought into port provisions, clothings, arms & warship stores sufficient not only to supply the American Army but all the sea coast of New England abundantly—Several hundreds of prize ships were brought into port by these people within 78 months from the first issues of Letters of Mark & Reprisal—They began indeed without arms but soon supplied themselves with these & every other necessary from their enemies & then captured their vessels in *many* instances in the ratio of 1 prize to every 6th man (in the privateer) & in some instances 1 to every 4th man—

I am well assured that a single Privateer of 16 guns & 150 men captured in 1 cruise more than 20 Ships mounting together upwards of 200 guns & having on board nearly 400 men——At a different period of the war more than 50 valuable vessels mounting from 4 to 16 guns were captured by little boats armed only with swivels of small arms—These & an infinitude of other daring enterprises were executed, many of them altogether conducted by fishermen—In a word the privateer from that part of Massachusetts, which is chief scene of the cod fishery, captured in the late war more than 2,000 vessels & actually brought into the middle maritime districts over 1,200 sail—that is, *the fishermen from that* district captured nearly $\frac{1}{3}$ in number of the whole merchant shipping of G. Britain & actually brought into port near $\frac{1}{6}$— (which number of merchant vessels in G. B. 7,700, Champion.)

What nation whose commerce is exposed will ever provoke a people so able to injure them?—The dread of such a predatory war must incline every commercial nation to be at peace with us & must give us a national weight & consideration among the maritime powers *without any expense for a Navy*— This then is the defense which the U. S. will provide for their *coasting & foreign trade*, neither of which can be suspended without loss & distress to the community,—a defense constant & sufficient & which will cost nothing.

The coasting trade, that part of the foreign trade of the U. S. which is carried on in a year in our own bottoms including the value of the vessels may be fairly estimated at 30 million of Dollars—These branches of industry already so important must extend with the extension of every other branch of industry & with the population of the U. S.—The interest of every description of people wherever situated in the U. S.—

TO GEORGE RICHARDS MINOT

—————

PHILADELPHIA, FEBRUARY 16, 1792

MY DEAR FRIEND,

Accept the congratulations of a friend on your appointment to the Probaty.[31] You will not need many words to convince you that I rejoice in an event, which seems to secure you a

---

[31] *Mr. Minot was about this time appointed Judge of Probate for the county of Suffolk.* [S. AMES]

good, though not an ample, provision. I hope you will pursue your literary labors. Your own fame, and that of our country, demand it.

An attentive observation of the events which fate is preparing for us, is one of the duties of an historian as well as of a citizen. You may see them in the embryo. I cannot believe that we are out of the woods. Success is poison to party zeal. The friends of the United States government have applied themselves to spending their six per cents. The opposers are industrious, watchful, united. On every side, it seems to me, theory denotes that we are going retrograde. Instead of making a government strong enough to dare to be firm and honest, we seem to be afraid that it is too strong, and needs unbracing and letting down. The states are advised to oppose Congress. Consolidation is a bugbear which scares not only those who are in the dark, as might be expected, but those in the broad daylight. Facts refute this pretence of a progressive encroachment on the state powers. Even in Congress, the states seem to bear a major vote. No act has gone beyond federal limits—many important ones have stopped far short. The states, on the other hand, keep up an almost incessant siege; there is scarcely an article which some of them have not co-legislated upon. With such means of carrying their sense and nonsense home to the great body of the people, it is not only easy to beat Congress, but it is hard for them not to beat, unless the men of sense, generally, see the anarchy to which they would carry us, and, in consequence, assume their proper station of champions for good order. Faction in this government will always seek reënforcements from state factions, and these will try, by planting their men here, to make this a state government. I could be personal, if I chose it, on this affair. There is some fear in the respect for government; and that fear will become hatred on some occasions, and contempt on others. The government is too far off to gain the affections of the people.

What we want is not the change of forms. We have paper enough blotted with theories of government. The habits of thinking are to be reformed. Instead of feeling as a nation, a state is our country. We look with indifference, often with hatred, fear, and aversion, to the other states.

If you have leisure, let me hear from you. Will anything be done for the college. I wish a portion, say ten per cent, on the sale of wild lands, was reserved for them. I consider our club as ordained and set apart once a-week for any good thing which tends to promote learning.

My respectful compliments to Mrs. Minot. Remember me to other friends

Your affectionate friend.

TO TENCH COXE [BY AN UNKNOWN FRIEND OF AMES, ON AMES'S BEHALF]

———

[UNDATED]

(Memorandum)

A FRIEND of Mr. Ames has requested some information in regard to the imports—especially into Massachusetts for the four last years. If an abstract is not to be obtained, (it is not remembered that any has been printed or reported) the amount of importations would be acceptable. If Mr. Coxe could without inconvenience give Mr. Ames the information, or direct him how and where to get at it, it would be an essential favor, Mr. Ames intending to wait on Mr. Coxe sends this as a memorandum and will not trouble him to send an answer.

Thursday

DEBATES ON APPORTIONMENT
OF REPRESENTATIVES

The apportionment of representatives was a crucial question in Congress, arising first in the debates over the "Bill of Rights" and recurring frequently thereafter.

The apportionment according to the returns of the first census was the first important subject to come before the Second Congress. The House bill on apportionment adopted the ratio of one representative to every 30,000 inhabitants in each state. When the Senate returned the bill, with the ratio amended to one to 33,000, Ames entered the debate in favor of the Senate version. Since each chamber insisted on its version, the bill was dropped. A second bill, drawn up by the House, also adopted the ratio of one to 30,000.

FEBRUARY 16, 1792

MR. AMES.—The Constitution says, that "Representatives and direct taxes shall be apportioned among the several States, which may be included within this Union, according to their respective numbers," &c. "The number of Representatives shall not exceed one for every thirty thousand, but each State shall have at least one Representative."

Deductions from the above—

1st. You may not exceed one to 30,000.

2d. You may have as many as one to 30,000 of the whole number of the Union.

3d. Supposing the amendment ratified, you must have 100 members, if one to 30,000 will give them.

These principles were not disputed till lately. But it is now pretended that the ratio *may* be applied to each state, and the number of representatives no more than the multiples of 30,000 in each state. Some even go so far as to say that it *must* be so applied, and that Congress may not have as many members as one to 30,000 of the whole Union.

This construction seems to be violent.

1st. The word representatives, first used, can only mean the whole number of representatives, for they are to be apportioned among the several states. The word is used in the same sense afterwards—"The number of Representatives shall not exceed one to 30,000," again meaning the whole number of representatives. The *whole* number of representatives whall not exceed one to 30,000 of the *whole* people. To avoid this obvious meaning, they say it should read, "shall not exceed one to 30,000 *in each State*." These words are supplied wholly without authority.

2d. The clause merely restrains the number of representatives so as not to exceed one to 30,000. The members in Congress might have been increased to any number, had not this restriction existed. It is a restrictive, and not an explanatory clause. It curtails, but cannot be supposed to change the natural import of the preceding power. It is against the fair rules of construction so to change it.

3d. The sense is perfect without the words one to 30,000 *in each state. Expressum facit cessare tacitu.*

4th. The construction makes tautology. The first clause having directed the manner of apportioning representatives among the several states according to their respective numbers, might have been wholly omitted, one to 30,000 *in each state* being a final apportionment.

5th. Words must not be supplied by *construction* repugnant to words expressed. The result of an apportionment according to numbers, as first directed by the Constitution, differs in terms from a ratio of one to 30,000 *in each state*. It differs in its operation no less. The members in the next House will be 113. Apportion them according to numbers among the several States, Virginia would have 19—19 being to 113, as

630,000, the numbers of Virginia, to 3,619,000, the whole people of the United States. But by the construction which supplies the words in each state, she will have 21 members.

6th. The words *one to* 30,000 are merely restrictive of the number in Congress from the whole people, and do not change the sense of the first clause, for taxes and represen- tatives are to be apportioned according to numbers. The construction cannot be extended to taxes with any good sense. Yet, as taxes and representatives are to be apportioned similarly, the construction applying to the one should apply to the other. Yet the advocates of this construction say that taxes shall be imposed according to numbers, and not the multiples of 30,000 in each state. Taking it for proved, that the sense of the first clause is not changed, but its operation limited by the clause *shall not exceed one to* 30,000, it remains to see what is the sense of the first clause standing alone. "Representatives shall be apportioned among the several States according to their respective numbers." The Rule-of-Three will show the number of members any state is entitled to. Thus, as the whole number 3,619,000 is to the number of the next House 113, so is the number of persons in a state, say Virginia, which are 630,000, to her quota of members. The result is 19 members. The bill, pursuing another rule, obtained as we have seen by a forced construc- tion, gives that state 21 members.

7th. The amendment to the Constitution refutes the sense of the construction. The words are, "there shall be one for *every* 30,000 till the number shall amount to 100." Plainly the whole number of the nation is intended. The whole number is to be formed by one for *every* 30,000. The words contended for are therefore excluded, and no construction will avail in this place to add them.

8th. The ratio of one to 30,000 in each state is inconsistent with this amendment; for, according to that, 3,000,000 of persons must have 100 members in Congress. Had the numbers by the census fallen short of a surplus beyond

3,000,000, sufficient to cover the fractions or lost numbers, this amendment to the Constitution could not be carried into execution, according to the principles of the bill. For the amendment requiring 100 members, the numbers being more than 3,000,000, it would appear that 100 members could not be obtained by applying the ratio of 30,000 to the numbers in each state, instead of taking the entire number of the Union. Here, then, would be a constitutional obligation to have 100 members in Congress, and an absolute impossibility of having them according to the principles of this bill.

[A lapse in numeration occurs here, whether on the part of Ames or on the part of the recorder cannot now be determined. ED.] 10th. The number of representatives is limited not to exceed one for 30,000. Pursue the letter of the Constitution, and avoid all construction, the number of representatives will be 120. Adopt the construction that you are to have no more than one to 30,000 will give you, and you bring down the number to 113.

But this process, erroneous as it is, only fixes the number— it does not apportion them. That should be done according to numbers, and Virginia would not be found entitled to 21 of 113. According to the principle of the bill, if it may be called a principle, it is defective. The letter and true intention of the Constitution will be violated by a forced construction, which gives some states more and others less than their due share of the representatives.

AUGUST 14, 1789

Mr. AMES moved to strike out "thirty thousand," and insert "forty thousand." I am induced to this, said he, because I think my fellow citizens will be dissatisfied with too numerous a representation. The present, I believe, is in proportion to one for forty thousand, the number I move to insert. I believe we have hitherto experienced no difficulty on account of the smallness of our number; if we are embarrassed, I apprehend the embarrassment will arise from our want of knowing the general interest of the nation at large; or for want of local information. If the present number is found sufficient for the purpose of legislation, without any such embarrassment, it ought to be preferred, inasmuch as it is most adequate to its object.

But before we proceed in the discussion, let us consider the effect which a representation, founded on one member for 30,000 citizens, will produce. In the first place, it will give four members for every three now entitled to a seat in this House, which will be an additional burthen to the Union, in point of expense, in the same ratio. Add to this another consideration, that probably before the first census is taken, the number of inhabitants will be considerably increased from what it was when the convention which formed this Constitution obtained their information. This will probably increase the expenses of Government to 450,000 dollars annually. Now those who have attended particularly to economy; who, upon the most careful calculation, find that our revenue is likely to fall infinitely short of our expenses, will consider this saving as a considerable object, and deserving their most serious regard.

It may become dissatisfactory to the people as an intolerable burthen. Again, it must be abundantly clear to every gentleman, that, in proportion as you increase the number of representatives, the body degenerates; you diminish the individual usefulness; gentlemen will not make equal exertions to despatch public business, when they can lean upon others for the arrangement.

By enlarging the representation, we lessen the chance of selecting men of the greatest wisdom and abilities; because small district elections may be conducted by intrigue, but in large districts nothing but real dignity of character can secure an election. Gentlemen ought to consider how essential it is to the security and welfare of their constituents, that this branch of the government should support its independence and consequence.

Another effect of it, will be an excitement or fermentation in the representative body. Numerous assemblies are supposed to be less under the guidance of reason than smaller ones; their deliberations are confused; they will fall the prey of party spirit; they will cabal to carry measures which they would be unable to get through by fair and open argument. All these circumstances tend to retard the public business, and increase the expense; making government, in the eyes of some, so odious, as to induce them to think it rather a curse than a blessing.

It lessens that responsibility which is annexed to the representative of a more numerous body of people. For I believe it will be found true, that the representative of 40,000 citizens will have more at risk than the man who represents a part of them. He has more dignity of character to support, and must use the most unremitting industry in their service to preserve it unsullied; he will be more sensible of the importance of his charge, and more indefatigable in his duty.

It is said, that these amendments are introduced with a view to conciliate the affections of the people to the government. I am persuaded the people are not anxious to have a large representation, or a representation of one for every 30,000; they are satisfied with the representation they now enjoy. The great object which the convention of Massachusetts had in view by proposing this amendment, was to obtain a security that Congress should never reduce the representation below what they conceived to be a point of security. Their object was not augmentation, it was certainty alone they wished for; at the next census, the number of representatives will be seventy or eighty, and in twenty years it will be equal to the desires of any gentleman. We shall have to guard against its growth in less than half a century. The number of proper characters to serve in the legislature of any is small; and of those, many are inclined to pursue other objects. If the representation is greatly enlarged, men of inferior abilities will undoubtedly creep in, for although America has as great a proportion of men of sense and judgment as any nation on earth, yet she may not have sufficient to fill a legislative body unduly enlarged. Now if it has been questioned whether this country can remain united under a government administered by men of the most consummate abilities, the sons of wisdom, and the friends of virtue, how much more doubtful will it be, if the administration is thrown into different hands; and different hands must inevitably be employed, if the representation is too large.

Mr. MADISON—I cannot concur in sentiment with the gentleman last up, that one representative for forty thousand inhabitants will conciliate the minds of those to the Government, who are desirous of amendments; . . .

Mr. AMES begged to know the reasons upon which amendments were founded. He hoped it was not purely to gratify an indigested opinion; but in every part where they retouched the edifice it was with an intention of improving the structure; they certainly could not think of making alterations for the worse. Now that his motion would be an improvement was clearly demonstrable from the advantage in favor of deliberating by a less numerous body, and various other reasons already mentioned; but to those, the honorable gentleman from Virginia (Mr. MADISON) replied, by saying we ought to pay attention to the amendments recommended by the states. If this position is true, we have nothing more to do than read over their amendments, and propose them without exercising our judgment upon them. But he would undertake to say, that the object of the people was rather to procure certainty than increase; if so, it was the duty of Congress rather to carry the spirit of the amendment into operation than the letter of it.

The House of Representatives will furnish a better check upon the Senate, if filled with men of independent principles, integrity, and eminent abilities, than if consisting of a numerous body of inferior characters; in this opinion, said he, my colleague cannot but agree with me. Now if you diminish the consequence of the whole you diminish the consequence of each individual; it was in this view that he contended for the importance of the amendment.

He said it could not be the wish of Massachusetts to have the representation numerous, because they were convinced of its impropriety in their own Legislature, which might justly be supposed to require a greater number, as the objects of their deliberation extended to minute and local regulations. But that kind of information was not so much required in Congress, whose power embraced national objects alone. He contended, that all the local information necessary in this House, was to be found as fully among the ten members from Massachusetts, as if there had been one from every town in the state.

It is not necessary to increase the representation, in order to guard against corruption, because no one will presume to think that a body composed like this, and increased in a ratio of four to three, will be much less exposed to sale than we are. Nor is a greater number necessary to secure the rights and liberties of the people for the representative of a great body of people, is likely to be more watchful of its interests than the representative of a lesser body.

. . . .

Mr. AMES'S motion was now put, and lost by a large majority.

. . . .

Mr. AMES.—It has been observed that there will be an indisposition in future legislatures to increase the number of representatives. I am by no means satisfied that this observation is true. I think there are motives which will influence legislatures of the best kind to increase the number of its members. There is a constant tendency in a republican government to multiply what it thinks to be the popular branch. If we consider that men are often more attached to their places than they are to their principles, we shall not be surprised to see men of the most refined judgment advocating a measure which will increase their chance of continuing in office.

My honorable colleague has intimated that a future legislature will be against extending the number of this branch; and that if the people are displeased, they will have it in their power, by force, to compel their acquiescence. I do not see, sir, how the legislature is strengthened by the increase of an army. I have generally understood that it gave power to the executive arm, but not to the deliberative head: the example of every nation is against him. Nor can I conceive upon what foundation he rests his reasoning. If there is a natural inclination in the government to increase the number of administrators, it will be prudent in us to endeavor to counteract its baneful influence.

.   .   .   .

Mr. AMES suggested to the consideration of gentlemen, whether it would not be better to arrange the subject in such a way as to let the representation be proportioned to a ratio of one for thirty thousand at the first census, and one for forty thousand at the second, so as to prevent a too rapid increase of the number of members. He did not make a motion of this nature, because he conceived it to be out of order, after the late decision of the committee; but it might be brought forward in the House, and he hoped would accommodate both sides.

AUGUST 15, 1789

Mr. AMES said there would be a very great inconvenience attending the establishment of the doctrine [of instruction by state legislatures] contended for by his colleague. Those states which had selected their members by districts would have no right to give them instructions, consequently the members ought to withdraw; in which case the House might be reduced below a majority, and not be able, according to the Constitution, to do any business at all.

According to the doctrine of the gentleman from New Hampshire, one part of the government would be annihilated; for of what avail is it that the people have the appointment of a representative, if he is to pay obedience to the dictates of another body?

Several members now rose, and called for the question.

DECEMBER 12, 1791

APPORTIONMENT BILL

Mr. AMES observed, that he thought the only question was to consider whether the bill, as sent from this House, was a proper one; for, as to a smaller or larger representation, he considered all debate on that precluded, as the only difference was between one hundred and five and one hundred and thirteen. He then entered into a consideration of the bill as it respects equality; he asserted that the bill was not only improper as unequal, but was also unconstitutional. To show the inequality of the bill, he observed that Virginia, with six hundred and thirty thousand inhabitants, would have as many members as six of the smaller states, whose aggregate numbers exceeded those of Virginia upwards of seventy thousand. This inequality amounted to a direct violation of the Constitution, which expressly declares that representation and taxation shall be according to numbers. He amplified this idea, by showing how it would operate, if strictly adhered to in the assessment of taxes.

DECEMBER 19, 1791

M<small>R</small>. A<small>MES</small> said, the amendment proposed by the Senate, though a single proposition, involves two questions, which it will be proper, on this occasion, to discuss distinctly.

Is the bill wrong, as the House passed it? and is the proposed amendment of the Senate fit and proper?

The original bill gives the ratio of one member to thirty thousand persons, and proceeds to state the number of representatives which the respective states shall have in the next Congress. If in this distribution of members it shall appear that we have not pursued the Constitution, the bill is a bad one, and it is our duty to concur with the Senate, at least in striking out the exceptionable part.

The Constitution directs that representatives shall be apportioned among the several states according to their respective numbers. The whole number of representatives being first fixed, they shall be apportioned to any state according to its census. The Rule-of-Three will show what part of the representation any state shall have. The wisdom and caution of the Constitution have left very little to Congress in this affair. Though Congress is to apportion the members, the rule of apportionment is fixed; the number of representatives will be one hundred twelve. These are to be apportioned to each state according to its numbers. What part of the one hundred and twelve members will Virginia have according to its people? The answer is easily found. Virginia, having six hundred and thirty thousand persons, (which is her Federal number, after deducting two-fifths for the slaves, according to the Constitution,) is entitled to nineteen members. The bill gives her twenty-one. Is that right? Who will say that the words or meaning of the Constitution are pursued? Are the representatives, then, apportioned or disproportioned? We may believe the result of figures. The sum is short and easy to reckon. Let us not, then, persist in a measure which palpably violates the Constitution. The argument might stop here: but, to show how other states will be wronged by the bill, it may be well to proceed. If the Constitution had been silent—as we are men common sense would have told us, and as we are freemen we should have learned from our habits of acting, that an unequal representation is wrong. But the Constitution is not silent; and yet the bill gives Virginia twenty-one members.

The states of Vermont, New Hampshire, Rhode Island, Connecticut, New Jersey, and Delaware, have seven hundred and sixty-six thousand four hundred and twenty-eight persons, and they will have by the bill only twenty-one members. With upwards of one hundred and thirty-thousand persons more than Virginia, they will have no more members than that single state. Thus Virginia has by the bill two members more than her due number compared with the whole Union, and not less than four as it respects the six states before mentioned.

From this view of the operation of the bill I draw this conclusion, which I presume is anticipated, that the proposed distribution of representatives is neither just and equal in itself, nor warranted by the Constitution. If further evidence of this injustice should be demanded, it can be furnished. Representatives and direct taxes are to be apportioned by the same rule; and there is a manifest propriety in the rule. In the distribution of benefits and burdens, the Constitution has wisely excluded this means and temptation to partiality.

It is an additional security to our property that those who hold the power are made to feel it when they exercise it, and that exactly in the degree that they hold it. Taxes are to be apportioned according to the numbers in the respective states. It would not be allowed by the Constitution to use one rule for apportioning taxes, and another for the members. If two things are to be compared with a third, and made equal to it, it follows that they must be equal to each other. Let us suppose this bill to have become a law; and, for the more plainly showing its tendency, let us suppose Virginia to have six hundred and thirty thousand persons, (her true number,) and twenty-one members, and the thirteen states to have—as Delaware actually has—fifty-nine thousand persons each, and one member to each state; in the whole one million three hundred and ninety-seven thousand persons; let us suppose a tax to be laid equal to one dollar for each person in the fourteen states—that is, a tax of $1,397,000— Virginia, in point of justice, and by the Constitution, should pay only according to her numbers, or $630,000; yet she would pay twenty-one parts in thirty-four, or $1,007,000, being $377,000 more than her proportion. Whether with twenty-one members in thirty-four this wrong would be imposed or submitted to, is not my question. This may be called an extreme case; yet in fact Delaware, New Jersey, Connecticut, New Hampshire, and Vermont, on a tax equal to one dollar a head, would avoid more than $150,000 of their just proportion: the justice and the constitutionality of such an apportionment of taxes are upon an equal footing.

Extraordinary as this statement may seem, it is not easy to show an authority in Congress to apportion a tax on any other principle. It would not do to deprive a state of its proportion of members, and yet to saddle it with taxes according to numbers. The departure from the rule of the Constitution in the case of representatives, would be rendered both more flagrant and more galling by an adherence to it in the imposition of taxes. Such a comment upon this law would silence its advocates—such an execution of it would disfranchise the sufferers. But this is not the country, and I trust this is not the government, to do a violence of this sort; therefore no tax would be laid: and yet, unless a new census should be taken, or a new law, at least, for apportioning representatives should be passed, Congress might be found destitute of one of its constitutional faculties.

The gentlemen who vote for this law have been importuned to defend it. Anxious as we are, under the fear of seeing the Constitution and our primary civil rights violated, we have listened to hear reasons which would show some respect for the one and the other. It is needless to decide whether men's passions will be soothed, or their understandings convinced, by an argument of this kind: that, as the small states are equally with the large ones represented in the Senate, the advantage which the bill will secure to Virginia in the representative branch is fit and proper, and that it was so intended by the Constitution. Is one inequality, if it really existed, to be balanced by another? Because the Constitution has secured to each state an equal vote in the Senate, are we at liberty to make a new Constitution as often as we make a representation law, to counterpoise it? and under a form of government contrived to secure equal liberty, and to fix right above opinion, are the measure and the nature of this retribution to the great states to depend on our arbitrary discretion? This answer is perhaps more serious than the argument. Let it be refuted by itself.

Because the great states suffer wrong in the constitutional compact, will this bill do them right? Is Massachusetts or North Carolina benefited by giving Virginia two extra members? By this bill, the great states are injured as well as the small ones. The small ones are injured as it respects each other. Delaware will have one member, Rhode Island two; yet the latter has only nine thousand more people than the former. But the doctrine tears up the foundation of compact on which we stand, and, under the appearance of vindicating the bill from a charge of violating the Constitution, establishes a claim to violate it at pleasure.

It has been said that the representatives are to be apportioned among the several states; that Congress is not to regard the number of the whole nation. It is not easy to see how the bill can be defended on any principle of distribution among the states. The representatives are to be apportioned according to numbers. The number of members allotted to a state must correspond either with the number of persons in any other state, or the number in all the states. Compare Virginia with either of the six states before mentioned, or with the whole six. It appears that 130,000 persons in the latter will go unrepresented. Compare Virginia with the nation, she has two members more than her proportion. Why, then, is it so zealously contended that the apportionment is not to be made upon the entire number of the Union, but upon the census of each state? The bill is as naked of defense on the one comparison as the other. It departs as widely from the principles of its advocates as from those of its adversaries.

It is indeed intimated that you are to take the ratio of 30,000, and to apply it to each state, without regarding its operation. To justify this interpretation, the text of the Constitution ought to read, *Each state shall have as many members as the ratio of thirty thousand, applied to the number of persons, will give it*; but that instrument is very differently expressed, and much better: *"Representatives and direct taxes are to be apportioned among the several States according to their respective numbers."* Will any gentleman who votes for the bill say that it is such an apportionment? Will it accord with the Constitution to take, instead of such an apportionment, an arbitrary ratio, which, instead of apportioning, disproportions representatives to numbers? The ratio mentioned in the Constitution, and in the proposed amendment to it, evidently relates to the whole number of representatives which according to it may be had from the whole nation, and not from the number of people in a state. Any other sense, besides being unnatural, would disagree with the clause which directs how representatives shall be apportioned.

By the ratio of one to 30,000 may be known the greatest number of representatives which shall form this branch of the government. Having determined the number, it remains to apportion the members according to the census in the respective states. Nothing is more natural, or corresponds more perfectly with the Constitution, than to find first the whole number of representatives, and then to apportion them as the Constitution directs. But this method would not suit the present emergency; for that would give Virginia nineteen members, and no more. Instead of beginning with the whole number, the bill says, let us begin at the other end: give to Virginia her twenty-one first, and, if the number should hold out, give to all the states at that rate. It seems, on trial, the number will not hold out to apportion in that manner. Still, however, says the bill, give Virginia her twenty-one.

Let the Constitution become what the bill makes it, a dead letter. Still, however, men, and freemen, will remain, who will preserve the departed spirit; for, before the Constitution was formed our rights were equal; and can it be believed that compact has made them less? Men equal in rights assented to a government which preserves them equal in power. Thirty thousand citizens, residing where they may, must possess civil rights and powers equal to thirty thousand in any other part of the Union; yet; though a compact which ought to be inviolable, has ordained that representation, that is to say, power, shall be apportioned according to numbers, this bill, contradicting the language of nature and compact, directs that thirty thousand in Virginia shall have as much power as near sixty thousand in Delaware and several other states.

It would ill suit the seriousness of my present emotions to say how little the supposed expediency of a numerous assembly and many other favorite topics have to do with the debate. Constitutional questions are so frequent they have almost lost their power to impress us. But this touches the first organization of the body politic. It goes to stifle liberty in her cradle. It establishes the power of a part over the whole. It is a disfranchisement of some of the states. If the rights of Virginia were invaded, I trust I should be equally zealous to maintain them. For the common right is the common security; but this bill tears the title deed in pieces.

Having compared the bill with the Constitution, and seen the result of the comparison, it remains to inquire what amendment will be proper and constitutional. In this part of the inquiry I will not pretend to say that I have arrived at equal certainty. I have no doubt that the bill is bad, but I am not equally satisfied of the best mode of amending it.

To determine what is right, some principle must be ascertained. The first principle is equality; it is another name for justice. That which is the right of the people, therefore, is the duty of the government. But, as it is not practicable to apportion representatives exactly among the several states, according to their numbers, it is our duty to approach as nearly to that equality as may be. If an apportionment is proposed, and it can be shown that a more equal one can be made, it becomes our duty so to make it. For, if we have an arbitrary discretion to reject the most equal apportionment, and to adopt a less equal, what is to restrain us from choosing the least equal of all, that is to say, having no apportionment at all. If this principle is not to govern us, then we are to act without any rule at all, and the Constitution was made in vain. We cannot have more representatives than one to

30,000; but, in apportioning them, let us follow the Constitution, and do it according to numbers; and, when we stop, as we must, short of a perfect equality, it will be the Constitution that restrains us. In doing this, we shall assume no arbitrary control over the equal and sacred rights of the people. We shall have done all that we can to give them energy. It has appeared, on discussion, that the rule of 30,000, proposed by the bill, is so far from being the most equal, that no more capricious and unjust disproportionment of representatives has yet been suggested. The ratio of 33,000, though not free from exception, is less unequal, and leaves less unrepresented fractions.

The amendment (Mr. BENSON'S) which was proposed to the amendment of the Senate would increase the representatives to one hundred and nineteen. Two objections have been made to this increase. It has been called a representation of fractions, and a number of changes were rung upon the idea. It has also been said to be as disproportionate a representation as that given by the bill.

As to the first objection, it is a mere play upon the word *fractions;* for, if the effect be, as it will appear to be, to produce a more equal representation, it may be retorted that the bill gives a representation by fractions; whereas the other mode makes one hundred and nineteen whole parts, nearly equal to each other, and gives a member to each.

This brings me to the next objection, and which has been strenuously urged against having the amendment of one hundred and nineteen members: that it will be as unequal as the bill. Then, I shall think as unfavorably of it. We should not hesitate to renounce them both.

But figures will show with certainty whether it is true that the amendment which proposes to add one member to seven of the states will operate as unequally as the bill. To refute this, I have made a table in which are seen the effects of the two plans which are to be compared.

Mr. AMES then read the following statement:

"Ratio of Representation"

"The amendment proposed in the House to the amendment of the Senate will make an addition of one member to each of the following seven states:

"In the fifth column of figures is the ratio according to which each state will be represented, in the case the bill should pass as it stood when it was sent to the Senate.

States.	Members.	Numbers lost on each member by the bill.	Ratio of the House.	Lost numbers, or fractions.	Ratio by the amendment which adds seven members.	No. short of 30,000 for each member.
N. Hampshire	5	5,455	35,455	21,820	28,365	1,635
Massachusetts	16	1,919	31,919	25,327	29,924	291
Connecticut	8	4,223	34,223	26,841	29,805	195
Vermont	3	12,766	42,766	25,533	28,511	1,489
New Jersey	6	5,911	35,911	29,559	29,826	174
North Carolina	12	2,138	32,138	23,522	29,460	540
Delaware	2	25,539	55,539		27,769	2,231

52 according to the amendment.

"The following States to which the rejected amendment makes no addition, stand thus:

States.	Members.	Ratio.	Total loss by the ratio.
New York	11	30,144	1,584
Pennsylvania	14	30,919	12,866
Maryland	9	30,946	8,514
Virginia	21	30,026	546
	55		
Kentucky	2	34,352	8,704
Georgia	2	35,421	10,842
Rhode Island	2	34,223	8,447"

Mr. AMES then remarked, that, if the ratio of 30,000 deserved so much respect as gentlemen had declared was due it, because the amendment of the Constitution has adopted it, they cannot forbear to say that the bill, in every instance, except four states, departs from that ratio; whereas, the plan he was comparing with the bill has made it the common measure and applied it with less variation than perhaps any other scheme will permit.

It appears, from the foregoing statement, that the ratio of 30,000 is applied with more equality, in pursuance of the amendment than by the bill; for fifty members will be chosen by six of the seven states to which one member is proposed to be added, and the ratio of 30,000 will be nearly observed.

The short numbers, in the case of five members, will be 1,635; of three members, 1,489; of twelve, 540.

The deficiency of numbers for choosing sixteen will be less than 300, and for fourteen less than 200.

The deficiency for the choice of the two Delaware members will be greater, but that will be only 2,231.

Add to this, fifty-five members will be chosen by New York, Pennsylvania, Maryland, and Virginia, at the rate of one to 30,000.

So that one hundred and seven members will in effect be chosen by the ratio of one to 30,000.

By the bill, some states, especially the seven to which additions are proposed, will lose numbers. In the plan of the amendment, they will gain. By comparing their loss in one case with the gain in the other, the degree of equality can be exactly computed, viz:

States.	Members.	Lost on each member.	Total loss.	Gain in each member.	Total gain.
N. Hampshire	5	5,455	21,820	1,635	8,175
Massachusetts	16	1,919	25,327	291	4,673
Connecticut	8	4,223	26,841	195	1,560
Vermont	3	12,766	25,533	1,489	4,467
New Jersey	6	5,911	29,559	174	1,044
North Carolina	12	2,138	23,552	540	6,480
Delaware	2	25,539	25,539	2,231	4,462
			178,171		30,861
Difference of numbers in favor of the amendment			30,861		
			147,310		

Mr. A. said, that if, by this plan, the seven states to which a member was added were gainers, that is to say, would be allowed members for a less number than 30,000, the gain was very little. In fact, the states would be represented very nearly according to the same scale. The bill, on the contrary, makes the scale or ratio vary from 55,000 to 30,000.

But if the advantage to the seven states, or the number less than 30,000 for one member, is compared with the loss or inequality sustained by the bill, it is found to be as 30,861 gain, by adding seven members, to 178,171 loss by the unrepresented fractions, as the bill stands.

Mr. AMES made a number of remarks to elucidate the statements and to show the unequal operation of the bill, and the fairness of the other plan.

After which, he proceeded to show that the states of Kentucky, Georgia, and Rhode Island would have the most cause to complain of fractions or unrepresented numbers. But the fractions of those three states amounted to the fractional number of one only of the seven States to which a member would be added. If no nearer approach could be made towards an exactly equal proportion, no just objection could be urged against the plan on the part of Rhode Island, Georgia, or Kentucky; for they would see the case could not be remedied. He then urged the equal operation of the plan between states having equal numbers, and contrasted the bill and the amendment which had been proposed in the House.

From the aggregate loss and gain on the two modes of apportionment in the foregoing statements, see the comparison more particularly between particular states, viz:

Virginia has 21 members. The loss, that is the excess of her numbers over 30,000 is	546
Massachusetts has 15, New Hampshire 4, 1 to be added to each makes 21 members. The loss to these two States on 19 members is	47,147
Or nearly as 90 to 1.	

On the other hand the gain on 21 members, or numbers short of 30,000 for a member, is, for New Hampshire and Massachusetts, only

New York has 11 members. Loss, or excess of numbers over 30,000 for one member, is		12,848 1,584
North Carolina 11 members. Loss		23,552
Whereas the gain to North Carolina by adding a member will be only		6,480
The difference between the loss and gain, or the balance against the bill, is		17,072
Maryland has 9 members. Her lost numbers by the bill		8,514
Connecticut has 7 members. Lost numbers by the bill are	26,841	
Vermont has two. Lost numbers by the bill are	25,533	
		52,374
Difference against the bill is		43,860
By adding a member to Connecticut and Vermont, the numbers gained will be		6,027
Balance against the bill is		37,733

The question is: Will the amendment, adding one member to Massachusetts and one to New Hampshire, cure the error?

The answer appears, by the statement, that Virginia will be as fully represented according to numbers as those two states, saving a difference of 13,389, or within two-fifths of a member. In forty-two members, that fractional inequality is scarcely an error.

In like manner, by adding a member to North Carolina, the error or inequality compared with New York is equal to a fourth part the number for one member: whereas, by the bill, Massachusetts and New Hampshire will lose almost two members, and Virginia will gain two—a difference little short of four members.

TO THOMAS DWIGHT

PHILADELPHIA, FEBRUARY 23, 1792

MY DEAR FRIEND,

MR. SEDGWICK is returned in good spirits, after having talked a Dutch jury into a verdict, clearing Hogeboom's murderers. . . . The evidence, I learn, was pretty strong; but *vox populi*, that is, the verdict of a jury, is—truth; *fiat justitia*.

I hear that the plan for the defence of the frontiers is likely to pass in the Senate. This I approve. To protect all is the duty of a government; and, under so many circumstances as furnish the frontier men a pretext to say the government is for the exclusive benefit of the middle and eastern states, it will soothe the terrified and angry spirits.

The Secretary of State is struck out of the bill for the future Presidency, in case of the two first offices becoming vacant. His friends seemed to think it important to hold him

up as King of the Romans. The firmness of the Senate kept
him out.

We have broached the militia bill, and I hope and believe
shall pass one, doubtless a feeble, bad thing; but a beginning
must be made, and improvements will follow.

Yesterday was the birthday. It was celebrated in a manner
that must please the big man.

The post-office, I learn, often fails of the passage of
newspapers. I inclose one. . . .
I believe the further assumption will prevail.

Your friend.

TO GEORGE RICHARDS MINOT

————

PHILADELPHIA, MARCH 8, 1792

MY DEAR FRIEND,

CONGRESS moves slowly, too slowly. The spirit of debate is
a vice that grows by indulgence. It is a sort of captiousness
that delights in nothing but contradiction. Add to this, we
have near twenty *antis*, dragons watching the tree of liberty,
and who consider every strong measure, and almost every
ordinary one, as an attempt to rob the tree of its fair fruit.
We hear, incessantly, from the old foes of the Constitution,
"this is unconstitutional, and that is;" and indeed, what is
not? I scarce know a point which has not produced this cry,
not excepting a motion for adjourning. If the Constitution is
what they affect to think it, their former opposition to such
a nonentity was improper. I wish they would administer it a

little more in conformity to their first creed. The men who would hinder all that is done, and almost all that ought to be done, hang heavy on the debates. The fishery bill was unconstitutional; it is unconstitutional to receive plans of finance from the Secretary; to give bounties; to make the militia worth having; order is unconstitutional; credit is tenfold worse.

Do not despair as to your new office. I cannot doubt that it will do well. I thank you for your and Mrs. Minot's attentions to Miss W.

I am compelled to say, in this place, instead of putting off a sheet farther, as I could have wished, that I am truly, your friend.

TO THOMAS DWIGHT

PHILADELPHIA, MARCH 8, 1792

MY DEAR SIR,

.   .   .   .

I HAVE just resigned my place as a director of the bank, finding that my time in Congress occupies me too much, even to appear to discharge the former trust. I accepted it with reluctance at first, and then took occasion to declare my intention to resign, as soon as the branches should be formed.

Congress has been slow in motion, too slow. A multitude is capable of preventing action, but not of acting. The practice of crying out "this is unconstitutional," is a vice that has grown inveterate by indulgence, and those cry out most frequently who were opposed to its adoption. If they were more disposed to execute it according to their objections, the friends of union and order would have less cause to complain of delay, as well as of the hazard in which every good measure is kept hanging, as it were, with a rope round its neck, during its passage.

.   .   .   .

TO THOMAS DWIGHT

———

PHILADELPHIA, APRIL 19, 1792

DEAR SIR,

.   .   .   .

THE ways and means bill has passed the committee of the whole House, and is before the House. It makes an increase of the impost duty, which, in certain points of view, is disagreeable.

There is some burden on the merchant, and it seems to strain too much on one string. Smuggling is the natural consequence of excessive duties on imports, but the good habits of the officers and the importers, and the checks and guards of the law, I hope may be relied on, in a good measure, to prevent it.

The increase of duties on rival foreign manufactures cannot fail to raise our own. Iron is among the protected articles, and rated, I think, at ten per cent. The effect of the protecting duties will certainly be seen throughout the country, and in a few years our own fabrics will be carried on successfully. Opposition is made to the new duties being made permanent, and I have some fears that the act will be limited to a few years, say three.

.   .   .   .

The sun begins to blister one almost. What a charming thing to pass the dogdays here. I am not at liberty to quit the field at this period of the session, but I am feverish with impatience.

Yours, sincerely.

TO WILLIAM WHITE[32]

———

PHILADELPHIA, APRIL 23, 1792

DEAR SIR:

A BILL for the relief of persons in confinement for debt is before the House of Representatives. The situation of Mr. White, mentioned in your favor, cannot fail to interest me, and will I hope produce some willingness in the members to wait and pass the bill. But generally they are very impatient to get home, and it is expected Congress will rise in ten or twelve days. I will attend to the subject and am, sir,
Your very obedient servant

FISHER AMES

---

[32] *A response to a constituent in Ames's own hand* [ED.]

TO THOMAS DWIGHT

PHILADELPHIA, APRIL 25, 1792

DEAR FRIEND,

. . . .

THE ASSUMPTION is in danger of being finally lost, and as not a man of the *antis* will stir, and S . . . . is gone, and others of our side going, from the House, the difficulty is almost insuperable. Messrs. Strong and Langdon are gone from the Senate; still, however, I have considerable hopes of success, and no efforts will be spared to obtain it. We agree, and the Senate concur, to adjourn on the 5th May, which we shall not much exceed, to meet on the first Monday of November.

The Indians took leave of the President, and made speeches this day, and are going for home to-morrow. Joy go with them. They have been daily drunk.

The decision of the Judges, on the validity of our pension law, is generally censured as indiscreet and erroneous. At best, our business is up hill, and with the aid of our law courts the authority of Congress is barely adequate to keep the machine moving; but when they condemn the law as invalid, they embolden the states and their courts to make many claims of power, which otherwise they would not have thought of.

We shall amend the excise law, pass a poor law for the militia, and a bill to call them out to repel invasions, and to suppress insurrections and rebellions, and a few others of a like nature, before we rise. The bill respecting the public debt is yet before the House, and how many long speeches

942

Messrs. Giles and Mercer have in them, is not to be known till the time of painful experience.

It is a long time since I had a letter. I will not complain, for that is a bad habit at best, and in a letter not to be indulged. I begin to fear, that, having long forborne, you now calculate on the rising of Congress, so as to miss your mark.

.   .   .   .

Present me to friends, particularly to Mrs. D.

Your affectionate friend.

TO GEORGE RICHARDS MINOT

PHILADELPHIA, MAY 3, 1792

DEAR FRIEND,

We shall not finish business on Saturday, and therefore I take it for certain we shall not adjourn on that day; but the members have made up their mouths for home, and nothing will stop them many days longer. I fancy we shall adjourn without fail in the course of next week.

I am tired of the session. Attending Congress is very like going to school. Every day renews the round of yesterday; and if I stay a day or two after the adjournment, I shall be apt to go to Congress from habit, as some old horses are said to go to the meeting-house on Sunday without a rider, by force of their long habit of going on that day. The session will end more efficiently than I feared. A number of useful laws have passed; much remains unfinished, though in a state of preparation, which will facilitate the work at a future day. The assumption is yet unaccomplished, but not quite despaired of. If S . . . . . . &c., had not skulked off and left us, I think we could carry it.

The wishes of the people and the policy of the government appear to me to coincide, in respect to hastening the extinction, or at least the progressive diminution, of the public debt. This important desideratum would have been sufficiently within reach, if this most unwelcome Indian war had not absorbed the means. While the government is reproached with it as a crime, every friend of it will see that it is a misfortune, which prudence cannot now avoid, and surely, even folly could not have chosen it, as a good thing *per se*. No measures will be neglected to finish it speedily; for the President, I am persuaded, is anxious to do so. But though the diminution of the debt may be retarded by this means, it will not be prevented. I am in no doubt of the Secretary's earnest desire to advance this work as fast as possible.

Causes, which I have in a former letter explained to you, have generated a regular, well-disciplined opposition party, whose leaders cry 'liberty,' but mean, as all party leaders do, 'power,' who will write and talk and caress weak and vain men, till they displace their rivals. The poor Vice will be baited before the election. All the arts of intrigue will be practised—but more of this when we meet.

My usual desire to see Boston and so many esteemed friends as I have there, is increased by the talk of improvements—a new bridge and all the world in a bustle at the west end of the town—the town streets lighted, &c., &c.

Please to present my regards to our club friends.

Your affectionate friend.

TO TENCH COXE

MY DEAR SIR

I HAVE perused with renewed pleasure your remarks on the
state of the Union, which you have obligingly enclosed to
me. I shall think it useful on every account to cause them
to be republished in our Gazettes. The principles and facts
are valuable as an acquisition to our political literature. But
their tendency to foster an affection for the Union, in which
self love so plainly cooperates with patriotism, and their
efficacy against the silly charges of our own malcontents
renders them peculiarly useful and reasonable. A Briton too
is ready enough to believe that the civilized world reached
no further than the land's end. You have furnished good
physic to cure him of his prejudices. It has been too long
the fashion to listen to the rant of eloquent ignorance. Our
newspapers were formerly stuffed with declamation, almost
without a single fact. Your publication not only furnishes
knowledge to the public mind, but it establishes principles
of discipline which will assist in procuring more for itself.
Accordingly, I beg you to accept my thanks for your works.

The Bank mania, though checked, is not cured. This state
has rejected a proposal for a state bank. But the defeated
still hope success in some other forum. Happily our interests
as a state are better founded than our opinions. Trade
prospers. Ships are in demand. The rate at which they are
chartered is said to be high beyond what has been known in
common times. Produce sells readily and at a good price.

But the merchants complain that trade is overburdened. In short there is scarcely anything that seems to languish.

Dear sir, I am with sentiments of esteem and regard,

Your obliged and obedient servant.

FISHER AMES

TO THOMAS DWIGHT ESQ.

BOSTON, SEPTEMBER 16TH, 1792

MY DEAR FRIEND

THE MARRIED STATE being so happy, it cannot but happen that every association of ideas of which that furnishes one is rendered agreeable. Those who are my connections by marriage were my friends before, but I seem to have gained a new title to their friendship and I enjoy it with increasing satisfaction.

Col. Worthington's recruited health interests me directly, because those who know him cannot but wish he may long enjoy it. But indirectly too it gratifies me. It shows that he may have health in all probability for several years by travelling for it, and where can he more naturally go to seek it than on the seaside, and at my house? His success affords a lesson to Mrs. Dwight of the efficacy of a journey to Boston. I wish her tour to Northhampton may enable her to pass a good winter, and in the spring, though she may not be sick, a visit to us would be good by way of prevention. We expect to begin our pilgrimage after the middle of next month. A visit from Mr. and Mrs. Thistleworth whom we expect this week will prevent our setting out so early as we had intended.

I had projected a tour to Vermont, which of course falls through. I expect to lock up my house and leave it with the most unstealable part of the furniture under the protection of providence and my neighbors, dismiss the man and woman servant, and with Frances to reach Philadelphia by the first November.

I am sorry Mrs. Worthington will not furnish a note for the Colonel's picture. Her refusal is a kind of divorce or at least an elopement. I wish her objections may have been overcome before this time. The picture being a good likeness renders it a valuable family property. But if proper care be taken I think we may hope the possession of the more valuable original several years longer. He was received in all places in this town with the respect which is due to him, and I cannot doubt that a pretty frequent intercourse with his Boston acquaintance will contribute to sustain his spirits without which there is no health of mind. It follows, my friend, from these premises that you are to urge him to visit us once or twice a year, besides occasional visits.

This town is an hospital. The gowns which men, women, and children, black and white, have put on look queerly, especially in the cold easterly weather. By way of precaution against the small pox, they expose themselves to the cold in a manner that would impair the health of the most robust. However, few die. And on the whole the disease is very mild. I have no small apprehensions for my mother at Dedham, who would not venture, and ought not to have the infection.

The country is dry beyond any former instance. The pastures are mere stubble. It is now threatening rain which I hear is very necessary to fill the cistern.

Election politics seem to sleep, but the spirit of faction is said to rankle in the middle states. Our political mild weather has lasted long. It is time to expect the equinoctial gale, which though it may scatter the leaves and break the branches, will purify the air. Accordingly I expect to see parties in worse temper at the next session than formerly.

In Europe it seems all is confusion. I had rather manage your distillery than be minister or King of France.

Frances and Sophia are both well. Little Mary has won their hearts. She will be proud of it, if she estimates the acquisition as highly as I do. Regards to Mrs. D. and other friends.

Your affectionate

FISHER AMES

TO THOMAS DWIGHT

BOSTON, OCTOBER 4, 1792, THURSDAY

DEAR FRIEND,

. . . .

THE SMALLPOX has desolated many families in this town. Charles Bulfinch has lost two children, and two others, brought by a favorite nurse from the country, are also dead. The doctors say, they lose next to none, but every night the silent mourners steal obscurely, without tolling of bells, to the grave. I have no doubt that the malignity of the disease exceeds any thing known in this town since the art of inoculating has been successfully practised. It is said one in fifty dies; in 1777 it was only one in about two hundred. I suspect that much is yet to be learned in regard to the proper method of treatment; rather, *all,* for the improvement of skill consists in having unlearned certain murderous errors in heating the patient.[33]

.   .   .   .

France is madder than Bedlam, and will be ruined, if hostile force and friendly folly can effect it.

Electioneering goes on sleepily here. My name is omitted in the Monday and Thursday papers, but I expect to see it in those papers very soon with a vengeance.

I find Sedgwick is coming here. I wish to see him, but I sincerely regret that his lawsuit compels him.

Regards to friends, especially your *cara sposa*.

Yours, truly,

TO THOMAS DWIGHT

PHILADELPHIA, NOVEMBER 12, 1792

DEAR FRIEND,

FRANCES has been busy writing to Sophia, and will have informed her, as a matter of course, how she likes Philadelphia, her lodgings, &c. Our journey was uncommonly favorable as to the great points of good company, good weather, and good carriages. Our daily journey was easy, the houses

---

[33] *In a previous letter (September 16, 1792) he says, "This town is an hospital. The gowns which men, women, and children, black and white, have put on, look queerly, especially in the cold easterly weather. By way of precaution against the smallpox, they expose themselves to the cold, in a manner that would impair the health of the most robust."* [S. AMES]

better than those resorted to by the stage. The great business of visiting by cards is begun with spirit. Frances makes more progress in her department, than I am making in Congress. For we seem to move slowly, as we are used to do. The speech from the President will have reached you. It says, the dogs shall not bark against the excise—the House in reply say, amen. I think the excise will at last be gulped down the throats, even of the wild woodmen. Our politics present some interesting points. The excise will be a great revenue, if duly collected, and hasten the extinction of the debt very fast. The Indians are yet hostile. The tribes near the Wabash have made peace with General Putnam, (a good beginning,) and I hope the others will, after some time, listen to terms. The southern Indians are turbulent and threaten trouble. Spain is thought to interest herself improperly in their affairs. Her meddling would be a misfortune and make trouble. The sky is not clear in that quarter.

I expect to see parties as violent as ever. The debts of the states will not be received without a struggle. But, as it is said the accounts are nearly closed, I hope something may be done to the relief of our State; perhaps it might be carried to open a loan for such amounts as shall be found due to the states. This would answer our purpose in Massachusetts. Let me hear from you, your spouse, M., and other connections, to whom give my love.

Yours, truly.

[P.S.] I am ignorant of the event of the elections. Notwithstanding, I have slept as well as can be expected in this situation. Let me hear from you.

The *antis* have joined to set up Clinton against John Adams. They seem to wish he may have the singular chance to mar two constitutions.[34] I hope Vermont will not join that party. The men of the south are well trained for Clinton, says fame.

TO GEORGE RICHARDS MINOT

PHILADELPHIA, NOVEMBER 19, 1792

MY DEAR FRIEND,

THE LAST POST brought me no letters from Boston. I suppose my friends do not consider me as being yet in the harness. Congress seems not to begin the campaign with any spirit. The speech of the President is so federal that I should hope it would have some effect to repress the factious, levelling spirit which has plagued us heretofore. But it would be a weakness to suppose that we shall not find the opposition revived, as soon as any important measure shall stir the wrathful souls of our fault-finders. The poor Vice will be hard run. The Virginians have exerted all their force to combine the south, and discontented men in the middle states, and in New York, against him, and in favor of Clinton. I trust New England will rouse, and give Mr. Adams a firm and zealous support. It is not strange that a man, unblemished

---

[34] *The writer considered him as holding the office of Governor of New York, in violation of the Constitution of that state. At the election in April, 1792, John Jay received a clear majority of the votes, but by the simple expedient of putting into the fire the certified returns from three counties, the canvassers arrived at a way to declare Clinton elected. See Life of John Jay, by his son, (1833,) vol. i. chapter 8.* [S. AMES]

in life, sincere in his politics, firm in giving and maintaining his opinions, and devoted to the Constitution, should be attacked, to place Mr. Clinton in the chair, who would have trusted the issue to arms, and prevented New York from adopting it, who has kept an *anti* party alive there by his influence, and holds his governorship by a breach of the state constitution?

From the account of the votes, published in the Centinel, I think I shall be turned to grass. I have been stall-fed here for a long time, and I have not any repugnance to trying my luck at the bar. This you know is the cant of all men who say the grapes are sour, when they cannot get at them. My partner joins with me in offering compliments to Mrs. Minot.

Dear friend, I am yours, truly.

[P.S.] For certain reasons I wish you would get from Russell the Centinel which has in it the piece on the moral influence of preaching, and send me by post. If not too troublesome, send with it a paper which contains a speculation, written to show that the New England states are not declining in their republicanism, as it has been pretended in a newspaper in this city. The equal distribution of estates, their schools, and town corporations, are insisted on as proofs of their spirit of equality. Both the Centinels alluded to appeared about October, or the latter end of September.

TO THOMAS DWIGHT

PHILADELPHIA, DECEMBER 5, 1792

DEAR FRIEND,

SEDGWICK HAS, unfortunately, in a fit of spleen, actually written to Sam Fowler a virtual renunciation of his pretensions as a candidate in the next race for Congress. It is unworthy his fame, his sense, his duty, as an enlisted federal man, to shrink from the shadow of opposition. When his firmness was tried by its substance, it triumphed. Shall he lose, by want of temper, the ground he held by his fortitude? He must not be lost. He must be put forward at the head of the column in the next Congress, when the host of the south will come to trample down the labors of the two first Congresses. If Sam Fowler be his friend, and not incited to use the letter to his own views, will he not suppress it? I am sure Mr. S. would not, on reflection, write such another. I submit the matter to your reflections. It is very important that all the Massachusetts force should be kept good, and in case he should withdraw, it will make a twofold loss.[35]

The Commissioners for settling accounts of the United States with the individual states, inform us, by a letter, that they will be able to finish the business by July next, the term of their commission; that the state debts may be funded till

---

[35] *In a subsequent letter, after mentioning some domestic reasons that might require Mr. Sedgwick's retirement from Congress, he says:—"I lament, as a heavy public misfortune, the probable loss of his services at Congress. We are not strong enough to lose a single man, still less such an Ajax as Sedgwick. Our demoniacs would play France if they could." [S. AMES]*

March, which of course keeps the accounts open, and produces some delay. The attempt will be made to provide that, as soon as the balances due to any states shall be known, loans shall be opened for the state notes to the amount. This provisional assumption of what may be found due to creditor states, will no doubt effect our purpose, or at least substantially, in Massachusetts. I suppose we are creditors of the United States, and I fear a more simple and direct assumption could not be carried.

The Indians at the south are said to be turbulent, and to threaten a general war. It has been said that they were pacified, but new appearances indicate very hostile dispositions. This would be horrible. There is no pretext even of complaint against the United States, as far as I have heard; probably the Indians are eleated by the successes against St. Clair, and incited by Spanish arts, who evidently consider the Creeks as a barrier against the growing strength of the United States. The hostile Indians of the north-west are supposed to be rather more pacific than they were; but our Indian affairs, on the whole, are gloomy. Money spent in that way is worse than lost, and yet protection is not to be denied.

The Vice is here. He looks as if his election was undecided. The event is past conjecture. It would be a shame to oust him for that *anti*, Clinton.

.   .   .   .

Farewell. Yours, truly.

[P.S.] My salutations to friends. Since writing the first page, I hear that the returns might be received till this day. Therefore it is very possible Sedgwick may be chosen.

TO JOHN LOWELL

DECEMBER 6, 1792

MY DEAR SIR,

As YOUR FRIENDS do not often enjoy the satisfaction of your letters, I am the more gratified for your favor. I had, at one time, made up my opinion that I was ousted & Mr. Austin chosen. Mr. Jo Woodward[?] came here & said, a Centinel, which he had seen, stated the votes for B. A. at 401 & for me 235. It turned out that the comma after 40, was read as 401. I discern plainly the operation of various causes tending to my overthrow so far as the eviction from Congress can affect it. One is that I am no friend to the Jefferson scheme of commerce & with my views of duty & of the interest of Masstts. as a trading state, I cannot hesitate to act on those anti Jefferson principles, nor to avow what principles I do adopt. They are unpopular & may easily be made more so[.] The Chronicle is daily at work & the prejudices of the merchants coincide with the complaints of the paper[.] I more apprehend the effects of these arts on the votes of electors & the opinions of the merchants than on the measures of Congress. The time for playing the fool by playing the Bravo[?] agt. G. Britain, tho' not quite is almost passed. Time if it has not opened men's eyes, has almost stop'd their mouths. Trade flourishes too much to talk of taking measures to relieve it from depression & decay, the style which was justly adopted when the Constitution was in its passage. However, as these remarks are familiar to you, I will not pursue them. I will add that the newspapers have no small influence on affairs. Men of sense neglect them too much.

The Chronicle is in exclusive possession of the pipe by which country curiosity quenches its thirst.

The absolute assumption of the remaining state debts is not, I fear, to be carried. But a provisional assumption, i.e. an amount which the Commissioners may hereafter declare due to creditor states will be proposed & I flatter myself will pass. It would substantially, perhaps totally, relieve our state.

The Senate has a Committee on the Judicial. The Com'ee of the House leaves the matter to them. Yet I think much will not be attempted. The session is short; & Perhaps we may say, time has not disclosed, much less prepared the people to remedy all the defects of our judicial arrangements.

The strength of parties has again been tried on the question to refer to the Secry. the forming a plan to pay off so much of the Debt as we may redeem. The conflict was hard & the majority small. I fear we shall at last lose that question. There is a mass of prejudice throughout America in favor of doing in an assembly what one man only can do. We have paid enough to know better, but we more readily get rid of our money than our prejudices. On every debate popular topics are seized by the Findleys & the Baldwins & the Madisons & I fear the public is more likely to be impressed against than for a practice essential to order & design in the finance department. The plan of a sinking fund is supported & ordered to be printed, but not yet handed to us.

I hear the tax on horses is called by the Virginians a *direct* tax & therefore to be apportioned agreeably to the census— Every obstacle will be thrown (I trust in vain) in the way of the Report. It is a solid prop to the Sec's popularity—it refutes the slanders founded on his pretended axiom a public debt is a public blessing.

I feel impatient for the decision of the vote for Vice Presdt.—Mr. Adams is here. He comes too late in my opinion to appear as firm and self supported as it becomes his character to be. It is provoking that a life of virtue & eminent usefulness should be embittered by calumny—but it is the ordinary event of the political drama. Parties always say, He that is not for us is agt. us & must be hunted down— The support given to Mr. Clinton, a bitter anti, ought to open the eyes of our citizens. The means adopted to support the former have been worthy of the object in view.

Mrs. Ames joins with me in requesting you to present our respectful regards to Mrs. Lowell & the young Ladies.
I am, respectfully &—yours,

FISHER AMES

TO REV. MR. MORSE

PHILADELPHIA, DECEMBER 20, 1792

DEAR SIR

I HAVE requested Mr. Murray to revise your account of Maryland. He has the printed paper, but he fears that he shall not be able to afford you much aid, being remote from the means of information and engrossed by the business of Congress. Mr. Lear is apprehensive that his documents regarding the Potomac canal will not be found of use. I have also reminded Mr. Madison of your request. And I have hopes of some contribution of materials from him. The application is rather late as you are to publish very soon. However I will not fail to transmit any observations they may think proper for me to furnish. There is not a printed copy of the exports left. Mr. Gore I believe could send you one.

I am, Rev. Sir, your most
obedient servant

FISHER AMES

TO THOMAS DWIGHT

PHILADELPHIA, DECEMBER 31, 1792

MY DEAR FRIEND,

I THANK YOU for your epistolary favors. I know you are extremely busy, and I declare by these presents, that I release my claim for answers, except as you may conveniently find leisure.

.   .   .   .

You reason very prudently on the conduct to be observed in regard to declining as a candidate. To refuse what is not in a very manifest train to be proposed, is not pleasant, and I have my fears that antifederal candidates will by intrigue, exclude good men. It is important to have all the Massachusetts members true blue. W. Lyman is not of that description, and I hope no effort will be omitted to exclude him.

Frances is her own secretary. I find the length of the session is less obnoxious to my feelings than it was in my solitary bachelor state. I shall take it for certain that my mate will, from time to time, inform you of all that is worth your knowing. My scribbling will therefore be the shorter. Congress is very lazy; never more so. Two months only remain, and the sinking fund and assumption are yet to be acted upon. As we manage our time, I think we shall never get out of employment. The next session will be the pitched battle of parties. I am habitually a zealot in politics. It is, I fancy, constitutional, and so the cure desperate. I burn and freeze, am lethargic, raving, sanguine and despondent, as often as the wind shifts. On the whole, as men are governed more by feeling than reasoning, more by prejudice than even by their interests, I dare not confide in the stability of our politics. Time encourages hope, as every day adds the force of habit to federalism. Besides, the rising generation are all federal.

Accept the commission of representing me at Col. W's., as their and your faithful friend, &c.

1793

TO THOMAS DWIGHT

PHILADELPHIA, JANUARY, 1793

DEAR FRIEND,

I READ with concern your account of the divided state of the federal interest in your district. Virginia moves in a solid column, and the discipline of the party is as severe as the Prussian. Deserters are not spared. Madison is become a desperate party leader, and I am not sure of his stopping at any ordinary point of extremity. We are fighting for the assumption of the balances, which shall be declared due the creditor states. He opposes, *vi et armis*. The spirit of the opposition, the nature and terms of the objections, all equally indicate a fixed purpose to prevent the payment of any thing called debts. If the balances were declared to-day, the objections against providing for them are ready broached. We hear it said, let us first see how we like what the commissioners decide; let us see whether it will be proper to ratify their doings; let the debtor states pay the creditor states, &c., &c. Should our assumption fail, should the provision for the balances fail in the next Congress, or should the commissioners cut off our just dues, so as to raise suspicions of jockeying, what a ferment there will be in Massachusetts, Rhode Island, Connecticut, and South Carolina; and the rage of these states will be turned on the government, which has pledged its faith to pay them, not on the party that causes the breach. Thus by hostility they will gain allies, and make the well-affected disaffected.

I write in confidence, for part of my remarks are of a delicate nature. You will say, I croak and am hyped. Be it so. I shall be happy to find that the grounds of my apprehensions of trouble exist only in the fumes of my brain.

. . . .

Yours, truly.

TO GEORGE RICHARDS MINOT

PHILADELPHIA, FEBRUARY 20, 1793

MY DEAR SIR,

THE SESSION of Congress has not been very efficient. The acknowledged object of the opposition is to prevent any important business being done. They pretend that the new House will be more equally representative. The negroes will then be represented; our oxen not. Quere, whether more equal then than now? However, I am far from being disposed to urge any objection to the negro computation of the Constitution. It may at least be used, *inter nos*, to repel the plea of existing inequality. The calls on the Secretary of the Treasury, the pretexts against the purchases of the public debt on terms to hold up the credit of the United States, (a declared object of the law,) the proceedings of the committee on the subject of St. Clair's failure, all the party do and all they say, and the manifestoes of their National Gazette,[36] indicate a spirit of faction, which must soon come to a crisis. I do not hesitate to declare my belief, that it is not intended by the leaders to stop at any temperate limit. They set out sour, suspicious, and with an ambition that places in the government might soothe. But, in the progress of things, they have, like toads, sucked poison from the earth. They thirst for vengeance. The Secretary of the Treasury is one whom they would immolate; Knox another. The President is not to be spared. His popularity is a fund of strength to that cause which they would destroy. He is therefore rudely and incessantly attacked. Every exertion is making, through their Gazette, to make the people as furious as they are themselves. My friends will say I am too ready to think ill of their views. I appeal from them to the Gazette, which they do not read in Boston, and I further appeal . . . [The residue of this letter is unfortunately lost.]

TO TENCH COXE

BOSTON, JULY 11TH, 1793

MY DEAR SIR,

You will please, with my thanks for the enclosure of the ingenious remarks on the scheme of a manufacturing town, to accept an apology for the delay of an answer. Knowing that printers are more fond of publishing amusing than

---

[36] *Freneau's Gazette, a paper usually considered as Mr. Jefferson's organ.* [S. AMES]

instructive tracts, I had doubts of the punctual insertion of the piece, and I chose to delay my answer till it had been done. The *Centinel* has, at length, given it to the public. While the discussion of the subject affords pleasure and instruction to the political economists, it coincides perfectly well with the prevailing temper and views of the eastern states. Even if it should be doubted whether manufacturing companies will prove profitable to the adventurers, yet as a very efficient means of introducing and perfecting the arts among us, there can be no question of their ultimate usefulness. The spirit of enterprise has of late been uncommonly ardent. Your observations are well adapted to the making it both inquisitive and cautious. I cannot forbear noticing also the great propriety and advantage of interesting the hopes of our citizens in the operations of a government of sufficient energy to protect and reward their industry and enterprise. So much is done by incendiaries to make the people hate and fear it, I think it a task worthy of a patriot and philosopher to hold up the bright side of the case. You have done so well heretofore especially in the refutation of Lord Sheffield, that the federal men have placed a reliance on your continued attention to the same subjects as time and circumstances may render their further elucidation necessary.

It is not many years since the encouragement of the arts was deemed a Utopian scheme in our country. One would think experience had fully proved the solidity of the principles of the advocates for manufactures. But even yet the southern gentlemen hold it up as a bugbear of usurpation of power and dissipation of public money. You have stated facts which ought to have the effect of undeceiving them, and if the spirit of party could be reasoned down, I should suppose you had done it.

I am my dear sir with sentiments of esteem etc.

Your obliged and very humble servant

FISHER AMES

TO THOMAS DWIGHT

BOSTON, AUGUST, 1793

MY DEAR FRIEND,

THE TOWN is less frenchified than it was. Citizen Genet is out of credit; his rudeness is as indiscreet as it is extraordinary, and everybody is provoked with him. I like the horizon better than I did; there are less clouds. I do hope and trust we shall keep at peace. As to faction, we must expect to sleep, if we can, while the ship is rolling, for no calms, except those which are portentous of storms, are to be expected. We may be safe; we must not hope to be quiet.

.   .   .   .

TO ALEXANDER HAMILTON

BOSTON, AUGUST 31, 1793

MY DEAR SIR

I AM HAPPY to see the good effect of the exertions which have been made to keep our country from meddling with the war. Our fears have in a degree subsided. They have been strong enough to give their full impression to the services of the officers of govt. The public mind seems to be open to receive the truth. Such periods occur rarely & ought not to pass away in vain. There are many topics which ought to be touched. I have supposed one, among many good ones, to be the attempt to point out the inconsistency of our Jacobins. The execution is defective in two particulars at least: the catalogue wants additions as well as a better arrangement—and the very words, used by them at different times might be quoted from the Gazettes with some effect. Something might be added or altered to the inclosed,[37] if a proper person would do it. There will be no objection made to any alterations.

The press is busy here—rather overdone. The enragés are remarkably in check.

I look forward to the next campaign with concern. I wish nothing may be omitted to make the people understand the truth, so well as to disarm the faction who distort it.

My principal object in writing at this time is, to mention to you the subject of a state being sued. It was raised here, as you must have seen. The people understand the matter imperfectly and on the whole, I conceive the entire active force of the state politics to be hostile to the decision. It is supposed, the Legislature will vote their censure of the suableness of a state & request congress to propose an amendment—or instruct their Senators & request their Representatives to move such an amendment. Is this regular? The Constitution authorises two modes of amending. Either Congress may propose alterations *to* the state, or a convention may be called. If specific amendments should be moved *by* states to congress, is there not a great mischief lurking in the precedent? However I wave the ceremony of any reply from you, which busy as you are, is needless. I wish to call your reflections to the subject—which I think will be stir'd.

---

[37] *The essays following this letter apparently were the enclosures Ames sent to Hamilton. They are found among the Hamilton Papers (now on microfilm) at the Library of Congress, filed among "miscellaneous undated writings."* [ED.]

We cannot doubt it will be so managed as if possible to make difficulty.

I hope your unremitted cares do not impair your health.

I am, my dear Sir, Yours truly

FISHER AMES

TO ARISTIDES

[probably 1793]

INDEED, Mr. Aristides, you merit *ostracism* much more than your namesake of old, not however for being too *just* or too honest, but first for having become the champion of a person whom you have yourself christened "Catiline," and secondly for having made so very clumsy a defense for your patron. For the first offence you merit the animadversion of all good citizens, and for the latter the censure of your friend. It is an old saying but a true one and certainly verified in this instance that a man frequently loses more by the folly of his friends than the wickedness of his enemies. Let us examine a little your piece and we shall find that you have not attempted to clear Mr. Jefferson from some of the weighty charges alleged against him by "Americanus" and that in fact you have not only admitted others but even proved them yourself to demonstration. It is a very easy matter to answer charges by employing the pompous terms of "virulent abuse, basest calumny and falsehood, insidious purposes, stabbing expectations, base and wicked calumniator, cowardly assassin, unprovoked and unmanly attack, depravity of heart" and such a long string of unmeaning words which might with greater propriety have been applied to the productions of Mr. Jefferson's *Gazette* for a twelvemonth past, but it is no (excuse), Aristides, for himself, nor on this occasion, so easy to refute (solid) charges founded in truth and now in the mouth of every honest citizen who is attached to his country and shocked at the French attempt to disturb its tranquillity and happiness.

I shall now show that Aristides has not attempted an answer to the very serious charge made in the publications referred to of his patron's. Having set up a newspaper in this city for the express purpose of abusing and traducing the Secretary of the Treasury; tho[ugh] his piece is written professedly to exculpate Mr. J[efferson] from the charges made by "Americanus," yet there is not even a glance at *that serious* charge; and so far he has acted with more wisdom than in any other part of his publication, as the most prudent mode of answer [to] an unanswerable accusation is to pass it over in silence. Without designing it, however, Aristides has confirmed that charge beyond even the contradiction of an *oath:* He tells us in one place that Mr. J[efferson] is "opposed to *some* of the principles of the funding system, of the National Bank and of certain other measures of the Secretary of the Treasury;" and the paper stiled the *National Gazette* has from its first establishment teemed with "invective against some of the principles of the funding system, of the National Bank and certain other measures of the Secetary of the Treasury;" in another place he rises in his language and assures us Mr. Jefferson's "abhorrent of some of the leading principles of Mr. Hamilton's fiscal administration;" and avowedly Mr. Jefferson's press has groaned ever since its birth with its abhorrence of the leading principles of Mr. Hamilton's fiscal administration.

But Aristides says further that this adhorrence is declared by his patron with a *manly freedom;* how far he may declare his sentiments on this subject with *manly freedom* among his own party is best known to them, but certain it is that in other societies he is distinguished for a very different mode of procedure; cautious and shy, wrapped up in impenetrable silence and mystery, he reserves his abhorrence for the arena of a certain snug sanctuary, where seated on his pivot-chair and involved in all the obscurity of political mystery and deception (Aristides will excuse me for employing his own expressions) he compounds and with the aid of his active tools circulates his passion thro[ugh] the medium of the *National Gazette.*

Let us now take a view of the answer which you have given to the two charges (not the principal ones) which "Americanus" has made against Mr. Jefferson. The first is that he was opposed to the present Constitution of the United States. Of this you propose to prove the malignity and falsehood, and how do you succeed? Why truly by producing a fragment of a speech of Mr. Pendleton in the Virginia Convention, in which is quoted a fragment of a letter from Mr. Jefferson, from the junction of which two fragments it appears that Mr. Jefferson had seen the Constitution and liked some parts of it, that he had proposed some amendments to it and that provided his amendments were made part of it, he wished it to be adopted, otherwise not. If his letter has any meaning, and I confess it is difficult to find a precise one, the plain English of it is, no Constitution without my amendments. In one part of this curious letter of advice, he says, adopt the Constitution that you may secure the *great and important good it contains;* then he suddenly wheels about (I suppose he was seated on his *pivot* when he wrote that epistle), don't adopt it by any means if nine states have already done so, without my amendments; but here, as if his *versatile* chair had whisked about a second time, he adds by way of a second postscript, but you must adopt at all events, rather than produce a schism. In short, his opinion appears to have been as versatile as his chair, and as in schools, applications to the breach are said to have a wonderful effect on the head by driving up learning, so there appears to have been such a wonderful connection between the seat and the head of this great politician and the motions of the one have such a powerful effect on the operations of the other, that we may say with the American poet,

But should his Honor raise Bum fiddle
The charm would break off in the middle.

Mr. Pendleton makes a pretty commentary on this epistle. Mr. Jefferson wishes the first nine states to adopt it; what are his reasons? because it will secure to us the good it contains which he thinks great and important, and he wishes the other four may refuse it, because he thinks it will tend to obtain accessory amendments; but he would not wish that a *schism* should take place in the Union, *on any consideration.* According to this construction of the text, it seems that the question before a state convention ought to have been in what numerical order the state stood; if she was the ninth state about to consider the Constitution, then it was unnecessary to discuss its merits, it must be adopted at all events, but if she happened to be the *tenth,* it must be rejected at all events without any inquiry into its merits; the consideration of the Constitution in both cases would have been nugatory. The first consideration with the convention would be how many states had already adopted and accordingly it would only be necessary to ascertain that fact, which being done, the adoption or rejection followed of course and tho[ugh] in other cases it should seem that the more states had adopted a measure, the more one would consider it a wise one and agreeable to the people, yet in this case an ingenious politician recommends a rule directly the reverse and the more states have adopted the Constitution the less recommendation should it have with the remainder. But when this sage advice was given it did not occur to its author that two conventions might be in session at the same time and that either of them by its ratification would make the number *nine;* what's to be done then? If his advice was good for Virginia, it was good for all the other states; how will they settle the etiquette, which is to be the adopter without amendments and which is to hold off for amendments? There must be conference between them, in which not a syllable would be said about the Constitution itself, but simply a discussion which ought to adopt to make up the number *nine*. Should this contest have happened between a very large and a very small state, Virginia and Delaware for instance, the dispute might easily be settled; Virginia would naturally say, do you adopt and we will drive into amendments by withholding our assent, and little Delaware would yield to the will of the great and ancient Dominion; but suppose the contest between Virginia and New York, and neither would adopt, how then? or between Pennsylvania and Massachusetts, and both would adopt, how then? or between two small states, for instance Georgia and Rhode Island, how then? If no compact could be made and both refused to adopt, the *great and important* good would not be secured; if both should adopt, there would be no longer the magic number *nine*, but *ten* and less chance for amendments. But all this is to be accomplished *without schism*, a very probable event! Suppose the four largest states, viz.; Virginia, Pennsylvania, Massachusetts, and New York had rejected the Constitution and insisted upon all the amendments which their conventions required. Is it probable the other nine states would without a schism and a struggle have relinquished their opinions or suffered themselves to be brow-beat into a string of amendments which they when they accepted the Constitution deemed as frivolous, unnecessary or injurious, or on the other hand had the four smallest states in the Union withheld their consent in order to obtain amendments, is it likely the others would have regarded their idle threats?

In short, this sagacious politician either meant to write such a letter as he thought would please both parties, not knowing then which was likely to preponderate, which indeed acounts for its having been quoted by both parties like a convenient law case, or he meant to publish one of those erisonous [sic] political speculations with which he is well known to abound.—Mr. Pendleton says, "Mr. Jefferson is possessed of the Constitution and has in his mind the idea of amending it." It is to be lamented he did not state the purport of those amendments. The curiosity of the public would undoubtedly be gratified with a sight of them. It is not improbable they are of a similar complexion as with some of the wild schemes of government which he is said to have recommended about that time to a set of raw politicians at Paris, since known by the title of *Enrages* or *Madmen,* who ignorant themselves of every principle of free and rational government swallowed greedily every project of our American politician and by their intemperance and fury drove out of France all those enlightened and patriotic citizens, the Abbe Sieyes, Mounier, Lally, Tollendal [?], etc., who fought for a well-poised government, properly checked, and who foresaw all the calamities to which their country would be exposed by surrendering up all the powers of the government to a set of ignorant enthusiasts and indigent fanatics. Those calamities have now burst upon that beautiful but unfortunate country and the miserable sufferers may thank the American Philosopher for a great portion of them. At that time he countenanced one branch of legislation and if consistent he must have recommended the same policy to the United States in his amendments.

He has since been sensible of the miseries which France has experienced principally from that vice in her system and he is now persuaded and acknowledges that France will never have a settled and good government without two branches. His advice however comes too late—the *Enrages* have acquired such an ascendancy in the National Assembly that they have solemnly voted *execrations* against all the advocates for two branches. They are too well placed with their power to surrender it or divide it with another branch, and while they can pass what laws they please and extort the regal sanction by sending an armed mob to threaten the King's life and bully him into their measures, it is not to be expected that any change will take place with their consent. The part which the American Minister took in laying the foundation of this system accounts for the wonderful anxiety displayed by himself and his friends for its issue, in opposition to his better judgment on experience and maturer reflection. Thus a parent loves his offspring, tho[ugh] he sees his deformity.

The letter so often quoted says, "we must take care however, that neither this nor any other objection to the form, produce a *schism in our Union*" and his commentator, Mr. Pendleton, says, but Mr. J[efferson] would not wish that a *schism* would take place in the Union *on any consideration.* So thought and so wrote Mr. J[efferson] at Paris some years ago; he then was the warm advocate of Union. He deprecated a schism. Union at all events, schism on no consideration, says the Ambassador at Paris. What says the Secretary of State at Philadelphia? Alas, he speaks a very different language: he proclaims his abhorrence of the funding system and the Bank measures which have received the sanction of the Legislature of the Nation, and of the ———; he declares open war against the Secretary of the Treasury for having recommended them; he establishes a newspaper as a bellows to keep up a perpetual fire upon him, and in patronizing the omissions of those important measures, he lays the foundation of schism and discord throughout the Union. An exec[utive] officer of the national government, instead of harmonizing for the good of his country with his colleagues, he openly and avowedly traduces, calumniates and execrates his administration and thereby gives birth to factions and parties which unless soon checked may involve his country in all the horrors [of France].

How is this surprising change to be accounted for? To *dire ambition,* the ruin of so many empires, we may trace its source. At Paris, Mr. J[efferson], the representative of the American nation wished for Union, because it would promote its prosperity and enhance his dignity, but at Philadelphia, Mr. J[efferson] fears in Mr. H[amilton] a formidable rival. Therefore the sooner he can ruin him in the public estimation the better for his purpose.[38] To this end were all his means to be directed. On the one hand, a monstrous affectation of pure republicanism, primitive simplicity and extraordinary zeal for the public good. On the other hand, to cry down the funding sysem, the Bank, and the Excise Law, as emanations from the Secretary of the Treasury; to endeavor to make those measures odious to the people and then attribute them all to Mr. H[amilton]'s machinations. Thus was supposed the first part of his system [to] evince what Aristides calls his known attraction to republicanism, plain Thomas Jefferson, wonderful humility on all occasions; the flimsy veils of inordinate ambition; in support of the latter, a *Gazette* established under his auspices to circulate encomiums on his own administration and abuse on his rival's. This charge therefore is well maintained, that Mr. J[efferson] is the *promoter* of *national dissension, national insignifance* [*sic*], *public disorder* and *discredit.* For the *factions* he has originated will, if not soon checked, end in all that. The other charge respecting the

---

[38] *The following passage was elided at this point* [ED.]
"That this is his object the whole tenor of his conduct announces from the time of his arrival in America to the present period. After he entered on the duties of his station, the President was afflicted with a malady which, while it excited dismay and alarm in the breast of every patriot, only excited the ambitious ardor of the Secretary to remove out of his way every dangerous opponent. That melancholy circumstance suggested to him the probability of an approaching vacancy in the presidential chair and that he would attract the public attention as the successor to it were the more popular Secretary of the Treasury ~~out of his way.~~"

Dutch creditors stands unrefuted by Aristides, tho[ugh] *he is possessed of certain facts;* why did he suppress those facts, and if he had it in his power to prove that the advice given by Mr. J[efferson] was directly the reverse of what "Americanus" has stated, why has he omitted doing it?—With respect to Mr. Pendleton's observation that "Providence has for the good of mankind accompanied Mr. J[efferson]'s abilities with a disposition to make them of use for the good of his fellow citizens," it is to be lamented that he is so much altered now, for certainly the [task] to which he *now* applies his abilities, particularly his talent for critique and party work, evince a disposition hostile to the good of his fellow citizens and destructive of their future welfare. As to his being what Aristides calls him, and old *meritorious* public servant, it is supposed his eminent services in Virginia at the time of Tarlton's invasions are alluded to and as to the crime of "Americanus" in attacking Mr. J[efferson] during his absence this would never have happened had he been attending his duty where he ought to . . . . . [The ms. ends here with an indication of the first word on the page following. Accordingly, the remainder of the ms. must be considered lost to us. ED.]

[UNTITLED] AGAINST JACOBINS

[1794?]

WE HAVE a noisy party who call themselves republicans—democrats—equality men, etc. etc. etc. They are forever crying out the people—the people. This hypocrisy would be matter of diversion, if we could laugh at what is horrid. These bawlings are against the people, not on their side, and the steps they pursue are intended and well adapted to narrow the power of the people, not to enlarge it. They are anti-republicans, the real and truly dangerous aristocrats of our country, the very men who hate equality, and who try to rule and domineer in spite of the laws. What is the best method to get above the fair republican level and to rise over the heads of our equals? To make a noise about equality and liberty till we can stand on other men's shoulders and show ourselves to the crowd. Then if a man, scorning to be weak as another man, has the art to find out what passion is up, or may the most easily be set up, he has to flatter and feed it till it is strong and tractable to his management. Thus the crowd becomes *his*, and he is the leader. He rises from the ranks to be captain—All the strength there is in *their* zeal is engrossed by *his* ambition; he becomes a chieftain, a man of power and influence, that is to say, an *aristocrat*, and the most dissatisfied man alive with equal laws—hates that equality which from a leader would degrade him to the ranks. If he loves himself and the ambitious passions which he sacrifices everything to raise above controul, he is, and from the laws of our nature must be, an unchangeable enemy of equal republican principles. For the whole people, ruling by equal laws, made in the orderly and appointed way, set him down on the level he started from—not a step higher than the crowd; they treat him as an equal, subject to the laws, not as a chieftain who can make the laws bend to him. Look at our loudest speechmaking reformers, and judge whether their tempers are not justly exhibited in the preceding observations.

You will find among them persons who talk of nothing but equality, but if a man proposes to take them at their word and to rate their talents, their influence or even their family importance a very little below the stars they knock him down. Compare the demagogues with this description and many will think themelves pointed at. There is nothing more laughable than the contrast between the arrogance of their personal pretensions and the feigned humility of their political creed.

They have tyranny in their hearts, and they expect to exercise it by carrying patriotism in their mouths. Cesar talked of nothing but the people till by making himself their idol, he became their master. What an impudent farce it is for the arrogant leader of a party to prate about equality, to call himself a democrat, the friend of that liberty which will never fall till ambitious men like himself make themselves, by arts always stale, yet always formidable, stronger than the laws. Hoyle has laid down rules for the game of Whist. The game that ambition has played ever since there was power to tempt the winner is as well understood, and is pursued with an infatuation no less ruinous. There is no gambling that is a greater corrupter of every private virtue, or a more unrelenting destroyer of every social enjoyment. It makes men selfish and unfeeling and never more so than at the moment of counterfeiting disinterested patriotism and love for the people. These lean wolves claim to be the keepers of the sheep fold. In every country, the people have the best intentions in this; they possess also superior light and knowledge. And this character is the greatest obstacle to the ambition of those who flatter in order to mislead them. Yet even in this country, sober and orderly as it is, the incendiaries possess two advantages over the great body of the people. They are united and they are industrious in mischief, whereas the citizens are dispersed without the means of collecting facts and comparing sentiments, and they have other things besides politics to mind. There are some subjects, however, which call up the judgment and patriotism of the society. The adoption of the Federal Constitution was such an occasion, and it served to establish the proof of this consolatory proposition, that the solid good sense of the American farmers and mechanics is, when fairly brought into energy, far superior to the little treacherous dupe making junto who would have marr'd that glorious act, and who still labor to annul it. It shows that in ordinary transactions, incendiaries may mislead a public of more sense than themselves, because nine-tenths of the good sense there is lies supinely inactive, while all the art of the usurping faction is exerted.

What is the result of these remarks? Is there any nostrum in politics that will cure party leaders of their ambition. Power, which they pretend to fear and abhor, is what they seek. As long as there are men in the world, there will be ambition, and that will as certainly raise factions. These will forever deceive in order to domineer,—and such factions will make up by union what they lack in numbers and by zeal and clamor what is wanting in proof till a little knot of conspirators of a thousand or two thousand persons shall lead the satisfied and unapprehensive million to the brink of ruin. There is such a knot, and a detachment of a dozen or two of them is to be found in every large town in America. They act in concert with each other. Whenever they see a pile of combustibles they stand ready with a firebrand. They stand at Coffee houses—at public corners, and barbers' shops and never lose an opportunity to fix a stain on the general government. It is not their fault that our country is not hurried into a ruinous war for France, that privateering is not more encouraged, tho' it is situated as we are, a violation of all the laws of God and Man, and that our first magistrate is not deprived of the grateful eulogizing of his fellow citizens, so well due to his wise and prudent conduct.

There seems to be no possible cure for faction. It will exist and it is the duty of every patriot to exert himself that it may not destroy. The demon can no more be banished the earth than human depravity, of which he is at once the parent, the offspring, and the curse. What is to be done? Let us try to bind him a thousand years. The people must be very fully and repeatedly informed of their concerns. For the more ignorant the crowd, the more are they under the influence of the demagogues. Every federal man therefore should wish the national government and its proceedings should be kept in full view of the people. Still, however, the power of imposing on the public is great enough to alarm every considerate mind. The credulous will believe the worst story because it is the most wonderful, and the lazy and the busy will agree in admitting the first that reaches them because they will not, perhaps cannot, sift the circumstances of any.

It is important for our men of sense to be convinced that it is scarcely possible for any degree of wisdom in a frame of government or prudence in its officers, or good sense and virtue among the citizens to prevent factions from gathering strength enough always to disturb our peace and sometimes to endanger our safety. It is one step towards a security against the evil to learn the nature of it. A powerful party will rule if it can. A republican government depending on the will of all is the least liable to be overawed by the violence of a part. It is the more sure to be obnoxious to that part. Our faction therefore, in the bluster of its pretensions to superior republican zeal, is the enemy of a free and equal government. If man remains the creature he was made, this faction will continue to be the rival of our federal government and will try to govern instead of letting the people do it thro[ugh] those whom they have appointed. Power and nothing short will ever pacify its clamors, ~~and if it should not prevail to make the government its tool, it will not flinch at making it its victim~~ till it has made the government its tool or its victim.

It is justly said that most vain men brag of the good qualities they do *not* possess. The coward takes special care to set off his exploits. The liar is always ready to pawn his honor. The miser talks as if he were the keeper of chastity's privy purse. And if Philip of Macedon, Julius Cesar, or Oliver Cromwell were now on the stage of life, there is no doubt they would play the farce so much in vogue with ambition: hating the noise, splendor, intrigues, and corruption of courts, they would affect to sigh for the shade of retirement, where they long to follow virtue and to cultivate philosophy. Is this the effect of artifice, or is it owing to weakness of mind that cannot support the contemplation of its bad sides. We have a faction, who, in like manner, brag of their *principles,* their pure republicanism. Like Cesar and Cromwell they are careless of what concerns themselves—they are devoted wholly to the people.

To those who know several of the leaders of this party, their pretensions to superior virtue and disinterestedness of public spirit may seem indiscreet and unaccountable. But is it not natural for men to plaster over the grossest flaw they have in their cause? This party, having no principles at all, have endeavored to stop the gap by pretending that they are the republican standard, the popes of America. The newspapers have rung, for years past, with their pharisaical cant. Nothing is pure enough for their nice principles. The government of the people is not free enough—paying the debts of the public to those who hold the certificates is not exactly right unless we go on to pay those whom we do not owe, or which comes to the same thing, pay nobody—making a bow to the president is swearing allegiance to a king—a man's head on the copper coin, like Friar Bacon's brazen head, is full of conspiration. In a thousand instances, they have overacted their hypocrisy—their counterfeited dread of trifles has appeared more like the hysterics of women than the excessive refinement on principles.

Time, which generally exposes imposture, has furnished ample proof of the shuffling insincerity of our Jacobin faction. To compare their language at different times and on different subjects with right reason might be a good test, but lest they should object against it as partial and unfair, which from their conduct it is probable they might, let their language be compared with itself. We shall not afterwards remain at a loss to decide how far *they* regard principles, nor how much *we* ought to regard men. We may in future rate their pretences at something less than no proof at all, because a piece of evidence that would stand very well alone would be brought into suspicion by their corroboration.

When the Constitution was on its passage, this very party, then beginning to rally and to set itself in array, pretended great zeal for the Union, but the old confederation was, said they, equal to every national purpose. No sooner was the Constitution ratified, than they found it necessary to change this note. They were true friends of the Constitution, but they could not keep their fears quiet without amendments. Such amendments as would have destroyed the government were not agreed to by Congress; but such as were explanatory were proposed to the states. It happened that greater opposition to the ratification of these articles was made by the party, than by the satisfied friends of the Constitution. One state even rejected an article which the convention of that state would have made a *condition* of their adoption. This party still pretend devotedness to the Constitution but they never miss an occasion to mar every useful act. The history of their conduct in the legislature, especially at the last session, will confirm this remark.

They pretend to be the advocates and watchmen for the people. They affect to make it an object to increase the popular influence on our government, because the will of the people is the sovereign power. But these very men in contempt of their own declamations are the opposers of the authority of the people as expressed in their laws. The sober sense of the nation, collected in the regular way prescribed by the wisdom of the Constitution, the fairest way and the only one that can be relied on, is opposed, and instead of it the will of a faction is set up in defiance of the sovereign will of the nation. This faction has exerted itself to discredit and counteract almost every law which has been passed since the Constitution was administered. With what face can these *aristocrats*, these usurpers of the people's authority, pretend to republican principles? Is there any republicanism in the armed resistance to the excise law? What government is that in which the arts of a disparate junto control the majority, and what credit is due to the principles of those who excite and justify the faction. The people of this country, if they will give themselves the trouble to pay attention, have sense enough to discern that the blusterers who compliment themselves as the republicans and friends of the people are ambitious hypocrites whose whole system of conduct is the exact reverse of their professions.

When the funding system was enacted this party treated public faith as an old song. Credit, they said, depends more on what the nation was able to do than on what it had done. They talk of late in a new strain. Public faith, as it respects the treaty with France, means something beyond what we said or meant when it was made. It requires works of supererogation.

Why should we desire a great national credit, said they in 1790. We have nothing to do with Europe.

In 1793 we are bound to become martyrs for French liberty. Our nation must destroy itself for that which the French seem ready to throw away if they should get it. Such, say our Jacobins, is the faith of treaties. Their conscience of public obligation, which slept in 1790, seems to have awakened in 1793 with renewed strength and vivacity.

They abhor an Indian war becaue they hate all war. They agree with the philosophers in the sublime scheme of a perpetual peace. In 1793, they think it proper to wage war forever against all the despots of the earth.

They dread the moneyed interest created by the provision for the public debt. That is, they tremble at the consequence of letting persons have the control of their own property by providing for the interest of what is due to them. But they see no dangerous influence from privateering because the great fortunes would be swelled entirely by the plunder of stranger's property. Perhaps they expect the original purity of the title will prevent the abuse of the acquisition. Otherwise how happens it, that our preachers of purity and equality of property, are such furious partisans for privateering[?] A federal republican is at a loss to see how robbing on the high seas can consist with that rigid simplicity of virtue which our party hypocrites assure us is the very life and soul of liberty.

They hate and fear all interests except the landed interest. Excellent friends to the landed man, as they would drag us into a war which would require a land tax and which would cut off every market for the free sale of our produce.

They pretend to hate *great* men and to love and protect the *common* people. But, abused and insulted citizens, this very faction has never ceased to resist any protection or encouragement to arts and manufactures. The body of useful mechanics, now rising into a well earned importance in society, well know that this faction have done all they could to throw them back again into the forlorn condition where the weakness of the old government left them to struggle. The public debt, say they, will corrupt and ruin us. Yet they resist all taxes and plans to sink it.

They apprehend the impost and excise will be too heavy, and they have made so loud an outcry against those acts that for a long time some persons supposed they were in earnest. But behold their tenderness for the poor people! They boast of our resources for a war which would require a fourfold oppression of taxes.

America should scorn, said they in 1790, to ape Europe. They detested the imitation even of what is good in the British laws. In 1793, America is advised to make herself not only the ape but the dupe of France, that model of perfection which they urge every nation, regardless of intestine convulsions, to imitate; and there seems to be no doubt that by following the example we might make ourselves as happy as those who set it.

Some years ago the Society of the Cincinnati caused a great clamor, and we find nearly the same set of clamorers on every occasion. At that time, we heard a great deal of this military order, a self-made nobility, a body of usurpers leagued against the people. Proud of their titles and badges, they would look down on the plebeian multitude. They would control elections and form in effect a government within a government. It is not material to examine how well-founded the alarm was. Our Jacobins have formed a Democratic Club in Philadelphia, and it may sometimes occur that the old cant is badly adapted to the new projects. This modest society is formed only for *political* purposes. Therefore every one may be at ease in regard to their proceedings. They are centinels over power. They agree on rules of discipline. They branch out into subordinate societies. This is one of the few important transactions which stands not in need of further explanation. The preachers of this disciplined faction have heretofore inculcated what such an institution may do. We look to France and see what it has done.

The people of America have been distinguished not only for sober and orderly habits but for shrewd and penetrating sagacity. Such a public will be able of itself to unmask its deceivers, especially after having compared their specious sophistry on one occasion with that which they resort to on another. Among the preachers of political virtue shall we not detect some noisy champions whose private characters cover their public hypocrisy with ridicule? Those who would have cut the bands of national concord call themselves federalists. They pretend to admire the plan of government and yet recommend such changes as would carry us back to the old confederation. They are republicans, yet resist the laws— they pretend to interest themselves for the people while they set up a faction against their authority. The cant is changed as often as there is occasion, but the object of the party is uniform and consistent. They exert themselves to prevent the people from ruling by their government in order that this faction may rule in its stead.

BIFRONS JANUS

*[Paragraph]*³⁹

Banks and public debts, however they may corrupt Congress and enslave the people, become the purest of blessings under the magic touch of state power. The declaimers against these institutions under the laws of Congress even see their usefulness to state liberty and to pure republican principles under the purifying operation of a state. How is it that similar causes can be expected to produce such contrary effects? Thus it is that true patriots sacrifice to the public good even their principles. Look at the patriots and judge how costly the sacrifice? But perhaps it will appear that they, like the priests of old who attended at the altars, are the greatest gainers by sacrifices, and thus it seems virtue is its own reward.

[The back of the manuscript of the "Bifrons Janus" essay bears the following notation. "Political paper of about 1794. Author uncertain but probably H[amilton]. It is an exposure of the fraudulent pretensions of the Democrats. Excellently done. E.W.J."

This essay is definitely the work of Fisher Ames, as the Editor's Note at the front of this volume indicates. Further, it is probably one of the two 1793 essays which Ames sent to Hamilton, for his opinion. 1793 is the latest date mentioned in the essay, and always in either the present or present perfect tense. Further, the specific issues mentioned all occur up to and not after 1793. It is, above all, highly unlikely that Ames would have commented at length upon the Democratic Societies without mentioning either Genet or Washington's criticism of those societies, both of

³⁹ *Ames evidently intended this paragraph as an insert, but he did not indicate where.* [ED.]

which would have been available in this context if the essay were written in 1794. ED.]

TO GEORGE RICHARDS MINOT

———

PHILADELPHIA, DECEMBER 6, 1793

MY DEAR FRIEND,

I ARRIVED here on the third day of the sitting of Congress, not without a portion of the hypo, on entering this city. I felt emotions not unlike those which a field of battle would inspire after the action. I expected to find the people in mourning, and almost in ruin, and I seemed to be at the threshold of a prison just closing upon me. The malignancy of the fever which showed its devastations, and that of politics which threatens them, raised up some bugbears. I soon found, however, that the greater part of this gloom proceeded from my own conjuration. The citizens seem to be busy and cheerful, and already the deep traces of the most formidable curse that ever visited any of our towns, are more than half worn out. It is not so much as allowed for an instant, that there can be any ground of apprehension of infection. Yet I am well assured a Mrs. . . . has died here of it within six days. It is nevertheless hardly denied that she is dead, or that she has been sick at all. It was a vile thing, however, to bury her, for in fact they have done it, dead or alive. One is said to have shown signs of life, by the violent crowding his body into a small coffin. Another beat his coffin open. Both (says fame) are alive, and well. If danger has not absconded, fear has, such is the difference between looking upon danger approaching and retiring. I shall not neglect such precautions as prudence may point out, but I do not apprehend much hazard. I trust some to the non-susceptibility of a Yankee, and more to the disinfecting quality of the winter air. The history of the distemper is, and I fear will remain, very obscure. Many facts are lost; and faction among the doctors, and grief and terror among the citizens, have distorted those which are to be collected. So that if the fever should come again, I think the doctors would not starve it. It has been disputed whether it was imported or bred here; whether contagious or not; whether curable by tonics, or calomel and bleeding; whether the frost and rain put a stop to its ravages; in short, every thing that ought to be called fact, is disputed, and all that should be modestly confessed to be ignorance, is affirmed. For a long time the disease was local to Water street; afterwards round every sick person the infection spread in a circle. It is even said that some districts were not visited by it at all. Gould, the barber, is dead. It is said he took it by watching with the sick. Another is said to have stumbled in the dark over a coffin, which being burst, was put down and left to get a hammer. In a day or two he fell sick and died. Almost every person infected could, say they, trace the infection to a sick or dead person. Perhaps it was imported, but the susceptibility of the citizens might arise from the state of the air, and from the extreme agitation of the mind. The country was unsusceptible, except in a few instances, which are also contested, as every thing relating to the fever seems to be. Rush pronounced calomel and bleeding the cure-alls; provided he was called in season, he declared he cured ninety-nine out of an hundred. The proviso destroys the assertion. All vouch success. None had it. Like Sangrado's patients, they died for want of bleeding and warm water enough. I honor the zeal and heroism of the doctors, but heaven preserve me from being the subject of their noble exertions. I had rather trust nature. She would do better contending with one enemy than with two. A Doctor

Ross, who has lived in Turkey, (says fame,) treated it as the plague; his patients all died. He adopted Rush's mode; all died. Being alarmed and afflicted, he maturely formed a plan digested from the two others; all died. The frost came—the distemper disappeared. This I believe is the most true history. Not one, so far as I can learn, (except Colonel Hamilton) who had the decided malignant symptoms, survived. Colonel Hamilton was saved by Doctor Stevens's cold bath, and bark. The method being expensive, requiring many attendants, and condemmed by the Rushites, was not put to any further test. The distemper was doubtless the most mortal ever known; not less deadly than animal poisons. Indeed antidotes are now found against them.

The spirit of the President will show you how affairs are. He sent us the correspondence with Genet, and a message rather tart. The House echo the speech. The new members look good-natured. Our horizon looks calm, but who can trust the weather. I hope for the best. Our State has, as Mr. B. Russell said, I know not on what authority, a balance of more than twelve hundred thousand dollars. The Congress House has been enlarged, commodiously I think.

Your affectionate friend.

1 7 9 4

TO THOMAS DWIGHT

PHILADELPHIA, JANUARY 17, 1794

MY DEAR FRIEND,

I CANNOT complete the imperfect information of my last, concerning Genet. Whether he is, or is not, recalled, is not known. His letter, denying that he has caused troops to be raised on our territory, and avowing that he has given out commissions to engage persons to fight for France, who are willing to expatriate themselves, is sent us by the President. It is a strange mixture of evasion and impudence; persons willing to fight for France become Frenchmen, and have a right to go armed, where they may choose. It is really an avowal of the charge, under the cover of a flimsy excuse. His outrages, for which his masters doubtless gave him authority, ought to provoke indignation.

. . . .

There is no winter here, which is not friendly to health, say those who dread yellow fevers, nor to business in New England. Our regulation of commerce is yet in debate. It is all French that is spoken in support of the measure. I like the Yankee dialect better. Speak of me to your good mother.

Yours, truly.

SPEECH AGAINST MADISON'S PROPOSAL
TO DISCRIMINATE AGAINST BRITISH COMMERCE

Late in December of 1793, Secretary of State Thomas Jefferson submitted to Congress his Report on the Privileges and Restrictions on the Commerce of the United States in Foreign Countries. In the House debate which followed, James Madison introduced a series of commercial resolutions pursuant to the Report. The regulations proposed to raise duties on the ships and goods of European nations not having commercial treaties with the United States, and to take reciprocal action against nations imposing restrictions on American products.

When the House began its ninth day of debate of the resolutions, Fisher Ames rose and held the floor for the entire day of January 27, 1794.

JANUARY 27, 1794

THE QUESTION lies within this compass, is there any measure proper to be adopted by Congress, which will have the effect to put our trade and navigation on a better footing? If there is, it is our undoubted right to adopt it; if by *right* is understood the *power* of self-government, which every independent nation possesses, and our own as completely as any other. It is our duty also, for we are the depositaries and the guardians of the interests of our constituents, which on every consideration ought to be dear to us. I make no doubt they are so, and that there is a disposition sufficiently ardent existing in this body to coöperate in any measures for the advancement of the common good. Indeed, so far as I can judge from any knowledge I have of human nature, or of the prevailing spirit of public transactions, that sort of patriotism which makes us wish the general prosperity when our private interest does not happen to stand in the way, is no uncommon sentiment. In truth, it is very like self-love, and not much less prevalent. There is little occasion to excite and inflame it. It is, like self-love, more apt to want intelligence than zeal. The danger is always, that it will rush blindly into embarrassments, which a prudent spirit of inquiry might have prevented, but from which it will scarcely find means to extricate us. While, therefore, the right, the duty, and the inclination to advance the trade and navigation of the United States, are acknowledged and felt by us all, the choice of the proper means to that end, is a matter requiring the most circumspect inquiry, and the most dispassionate judgment.

After a debate has continued a long time, the subject very frequently becomes tiresome before it is exhausted. Arguments, however solid, urged by different speakers, can scarcely fail to render the discussion both complex and diffusive. Without pretending to give to my arguments any other merit, I shall aim at simplicity.

We hear it declared, that the design of the resolutions is, to place our trade and navigation on a better footing. By better footing, we are to understand a more profitable one. Profit is a plain word; that cannot be misunderstood. We have, to speak in round numbers, twenty million dollars of exports annually. To have the trade of exports on a good footing, means nothing more than to sell them dear; and, consequently, the trade of import on a good footing, is to buy cheap. To put them both on a better footing, is to sell dearer and to buy cheaper than we do at present. If the effect of the resolutions will be to cause our exports to be sold cheaper, and our imports to be bought dearer, our trade will suffer an injury.

It is hard to compute how great the injury would prove; for the first loss of value in the buying dear and selling cheap, is only the symptom and beginning of the evil, but by no means the measure of it. It will withdraw a great part of the nourishment that now supplies the wonderful growth of our industry and opulence. The difference may not amount to a great proportion of the price of the articles, but it may reach the greater part of the profit of the producer. It may have effects in this way, which will be of the worst kind, by discouraging the products of our land and industry. It is to this test I propose to bring the resolutions on the table. And if it shall clearly appear that they tend to cause our exports to be sold cheaper, and our imports to be bought dearer, they cannot escape condemnation. Whatever specious show of advantage may be given them, they deserve to be called aggravations of any real or supposed evils in our commercial system, and not remedies.

I have framed this statement of the question so as to comprehend the whole subject of debate, and at the same time I confess it was my design to exclude from consideration a number of topics which appear to me totally irrelevant to it.

The best answer to many assertions we have heard, is to admit them without proof. We are exhorted to assert our natural rights; to put trade on a respectable footing; to dictate terms of trade to other nations; to engage in a contest of self-denial, and by that, and by shifting our commerce from one country to another, to make our enemies feel the extent of our power. This language, as it respects the proper subject of discussion, means nothing, or what is worse. If our trade is already on a profitable footing, it is on a respectable one. Unless war be our object, it is useless to inquire, what are the dispositions of any government, with whose subjects our merchants deal to the best advantage. While they will smoke our tobacco, and eat our provisions, it is very immaterial, both to the consumer and the producer, what are the politics of the two countries, excepting so far as their quarrels may disturb the benefits of their mutual intercourse.

So far, therefore, as commerce is concerned, the inquiry is, have we a good market? The good or bad state of our *actual* market is the question. The actual market is everywhere more or less a restricted one, and the natural order of things is displaced by the artificial. Most nations, for reasons of which they alone are the rightful judges, have regulated and restricted their intercourse according to their views of safety and profit. We claim for ourselves the same right, as the acts in our statute book and the resolutions on the table evince, without holding ourselves accountable to any other nation whatever. The right which we properly claim, and which we properly exercise when we do it prudently and usefully for our nation, is as well established, and has been longer in use in the countries of which we complain, than in our own. If their right is as good as that of Congress to regulate and restrict, why do we talk of a strenuous exertion of our force, and by dictating terms to nations, who are fancied to be physically dependent on America, to change the policy of nations? It may be very true that, their policy is very wise and good for themselves, but not as favorable for us as we would make it, if we could legislate for both sides of the Atlantic.

The extravagant despotism of this language accords very ill with our power to give it effect, or with the affectation of zeal for an unlimited freedom of commerce. Such a state of absolute freedom of commerce never did exist, and it is very much to be doubted whether it ever will. Were I invested with the trust to legislate for mankind, it is very probable the first act of my authority would be to throw all the restrictive and prohibitory laws of trade into the fire; the resolutions on the table would not be spared. But if I were to do so, it is probable that I should have a quarrel on my hands, with every civilized nation. The Dutch would claim the monopoly of the spice trade, for which their ancestors passed their whole lives in warfare. The Spanish and Portuguese would be no less obstinate. If we calculate what Colony monopolies have cost in wealth, in suffering, and in crimes, we should say they were dearly purchased. The English would plead for their Navigation Act, not as a source of gain, but as an essential means of securing their independence. So many interests would be disturbed, and so many lost, by a violent change from the existing, to an unknown order of things, and the mutual relations of nations, in respect to their power and wealth, would suffer such a shock, that the idea must be allowed to be perfectly Utopian and wild. But for this country to form the project of changing the policy of nations, and to begin the abolition of restrictions by restrictions of its own, is equally ridiculous and inconsistent.

Let every nation that is really disposed to extend the liberty of commerce, beware of rash and hasty schemes of prohibition. In the affairs of trade, as in most others, we make too many laws. We follow experience too little, and the visions of theorists a great deal too much. Instead of listening to discourses on what the market ought to be, and what the schemes, which always promise much on paper, pretend to make it, let us see what is the actual market for our exports and imports. This will bring vague assertions and sanguine opinions to the test of experience. That rage for theory and system, which would entangle even practical truth in the web of the brain, is the poison of public discussion. One fact is better than two systems.

The terms on which our exports are received in the British market, have been accurately examined by a gentleman from South Carolina (Mr. William Smith). Before his statement of facts was made to the committee, it was urged, and with no little warmth, that the system of England indicated her inveteracy towards this country, while that of France, springing from disinterested affection, constituted a claim for gratitude and self-denying measures of retribution.

Since that statement, however, that romantic style, which is so ill adapted to the subject, has been changed. We hear it insinuated, that the comparison of the footing of our exports in the markets of France and England, is of no importance; that it is chiefly our object to see how we may assist and extend our commerce. This evasion of the force of the statement, or rather this indirect admission of its authority, establishes it. It will not be pretended that it has been shaken during the debate.

It has been made to appear, beyond contradiction, that the British market for our exports, taken in the aggregate, is a good one; that it is better than the French, and better than any we have, and, for many of our products, the only one.

The whole amount of our exports to the British dominions in the year ending the 30th September, 1790, was nine millions two hundred and forty-six thousand six hundred and sixty dollars. But it will be more simple and satisfactory to confine the inquiry to the articles following: Breadstuff, tobacco, rice, wood, the produce of the fisheries, fish oil, pot and pearlash, salted meats, indigo, live animals, flaxseed, naval stores, and iron.

The amount of the before-mentioned articles, exported in that same year to the British dominions, was eight millions four hundred and fifty-seven thousand one hundred and seventy-three dollars.

Mr. A. went into consideration of the footing on which they are received. He then said, we have heard so much of restriction, of inimical and jealous prohibitions to cramp our trade, it is natural to scrutinize the British system, with the expectation of finding little besides the effects of her selfish and angry policy.

Yet of the great sum of nearly eight millions and an half, the amount of the products before mentioned sold in her markets, two articles only are dutied by way of restriction. Breadstuff is dutied so high in the market of Great Britain, as in times of plenty to exclude it, and this is done from the desire to favor her own farmers. The mover of the resolutions justified the exclusion of our breadstuff from the French West Indies by their permanent regulations, because, he said, they were bound to prefer their own products to those even of the United States. It would seem that the same apology would do for England in her home market. But what will do for the vindication of one nation becomes invective against another. The criminal nation, however, receives our breadstuff in the West Indies free, and excludes other foreign, so as to give our producers the monopoly of the supply. This is no merit, in the judgment of the mover of the resolutions, because it is a fragment of her old Colony system. Notwithstanding the nature of the duties on breadstuff in Great Britain, it has been clearly shown that she is a better customer for that article in Europe, than her neighbor, France. The latter, in ordinary times, is a poor customer for breadstuff, for the same reason that our own country is, because she produces it herself, and therefore France permits it to be imported, and the United States do the like. Great Britain often wants the article, and then she receives it; no country can be expected to buy what it does not want. The breadstuff sold in the European dominions of Great Britain in the year 1790, amounted to one million eighty-seven thousand eight hundred and forty dollars.

Whale oil pays the heavy duty of eighteen pounds three shillings sterling per ton; yet spermaceti oil found a market there to the value of eighty-one thousand and forty-eight dollars. Thus it appears, that of eight millions and a half sold to Great Britain and her dominions, only the value of one million one hundred and sixty-eight thousand dollars was under duty of a restrictive nature. The breadstuff is hardly to be considered as within the description; yet, to give the argument its full force, what is it? about one-eighth part is restricted. To proceed with the residue:

Indigo to the amount of	$473,830
Live animals to the West Indies,	62,415
Flaxseed to Great Britain,	219,924
Total,	$756,169

The articles are received, duty free, which is a good foot to the trade. Yet, we find, good as it is, the bulk of our exports is received on even better terms.

Flour to the British West Indies,	$858,006
Grain,	273,505
Free—while other foreign flour and grain are prohibited.	
Tobacco to Great Britain,	2,754,493
Tobacco to the West Indies,	22,816
One shilling and threepence sterling, duty; three shillings and sixpence on other foreign tobacco.	
In the West Indies other foreign tobacco is prohibited	
Rice to Great Britain,	773,852
Seven shillings and fourpence per cwt. duty; eight shillings and tenpence on other foreign rice.	
To West Indies,	180,077
Other foreign rice prohibited.	
Wood to Great Britain,	240,174

Free—higher duties on other foreign.

To West Indies,   382,481

Free—other foreign prohibited.

Pot and pearl ashes,   747,078

Free—two shillings and threepence on other foreign, equal
to ten dollars per ton.

Naval stores to Great Britain,   190,670

Higher duties on other foreign.

To West Indies,   6,162

Free—other foreign prohibited.

Iron to Great Britain,   81,612

Free—duties on other foreign. $6,510,926

Thus it appears that nearly seven eighths of the exports to the British dominions are received on terms of positive favor. Foreigners, our rivals in the sale of these articles, are either absolutely shut out of their market by prohibitions, or discouraged in their competition with us by higher duties. There is some restriction, it is admitted, but there is, to balance it, a large amount received duty free. The above surplus of six millions and a half goes to the account of privilege and favor. This is better than she treats any other foreign nation. It is better indeed than she treats her own subjects, because they are by this means deprived of a free and open market; it is better than our footing with any nation with whom we have treaties. It has been demonstratively shown that it is better than the footing on which France receives either the like articles, or the aggregate of our products. The best proof in the world is, that they are not sent to France. The merchants will find out the best market sooner than we shall.

The footing of our exports, under the British system, is better than that of their exports to the United States, under our system. Nay, it is better than the freedom of commerce, which is one of the visions for which our solid prosperity is to be hazarded; for, suppose we could batter down her system of prohibitions and restrictions, it would be gaining a loss;

one eighth is restricted, and more than six eighths has restrictions in its favor. It is as plain as figures can make it, that if a state of freedom for our exports is at par, the present system raises them, in point of privilege, above par. To suppose that we can terrify them by these resolutions, to abolish their restrictions, and at the same time to maintain in our favor their duties, to exclude other foreigners from their market, is too absurd to be refuted.

We have heard that the market of France is the great centre of our interests; we are to look to her, and not to England, for advantages. Being, as the style of theory is, our best customer and best friend, showing to our trade particular favor and privilege; while England manifests in her system such narrow and selfish views; it is strange to remark such a pointed refutation of assertions and opinions by facts. The amount sent to France herself is very trivial; either our merchants are ignorant of the best markets, or those which they prefer are the best; and if the English markets, in spite of the alleged ill usage, are still preferred to the French, it is a proof of the superior advantages of the former over the latter. The arguments I have adverted to, oblige those who urge them to make a greater difference in favor of the English, than the true state of facts will warrant. Indeed, if they persist in their arguments, they are bound to deny their own conclusions. They are bound to admit this position: if France receives little of such of our products as Great Britain takes on terms of privilege and favor, because of that favor[,] it allows the value of that favored footing. If France takes little of our articles, because she does not want them, it shows the absurdity of looking to her as the best customer.

It may be said, and truly, that Great Britain regards only her own interest in these arguments. So much the better. If it is her interest to afford to our commerce more encouragement than France gives, if she does this when she is inveterate against us, as it is alleged, and when we are indulging an avowed hatred towards her, and partiality towards France, it shows that we have very solid ground to rely on. Her interest is, according to this statement, stronger than our passions, stronger than her own, and is the more to be depended on as it cannot be put to any more trying experiment in future. The good will and friendship of nations are hollow foundations to build our systems upon. Mutual interest is a bottom of rock. The fervor of transient sentiments is not better than straw or stubble. Some gentlemen have lamented this distrust of any relation between nations except an interested one. But the substitution of any other principle could produce little else than the hypocrisy of sentiment, and an instability of affairs. It would be relying on what is not stable, instead of what is; it would introduce into politics the jargon of romance. It is in this sense, and this only, that the word favor is used; a state of things so arranged as to produce our profit and advantage, though intended by Great Britain merely for her own. The disposition of a nation is immaterial; the fact that we profit by their system cannot be so to this discussion.

The next point is, to consider whether our imports are on a good footing, or, in other words, whether we are in a situation to buy what we have occasion for at a cheap rate. In this view, the systems of the commercial nations are not to be complained of, as all are desirous of selling the products of their labor. Great Britain is not censured in this respect. The objection is rather of the opposite kind, that we buy too cheap, and therefore consume too much, and that we take not only as much as we can pay for, but to the extent of our credit also. There is less freedom of importation, however, from the West Indies. In this respect, France is more restrictive than England; for the former allows the exportation to us of only rum and molasses, while England admits that of sugar, coffee, and other principal West India products. Yet even here, when the preference seems to be decidedly due to the British system, occasion is taken to extol that of the French. We are told that they sell us the chief part of the molasses, which is consumed, or manufactured into rum, and that a great and truly important branch, the distillery, is kept up by their liberality in furnishing the raw material. There is at every step matter to confirm the remark, that nations have framed their regulations to suit their own interests, not ours. France is a great brandy manufacturer; she will not admit rum, therefore, even from her own islands, because it would supplant the consumption of brandy. The molasses was for that reason some years ago of no value in her islands, and was not even saved in casks. But the demand from America soon raised its value. The policy of England has been equally selfish. The molasses is distilled in her islands, because she has no manufacture of brandy to suffer by its sale.

A question remains respecting the state of our *navigation*. If we pay no regard to the regulations of foreign nations, and ask whether this valuable branch of our industry and capital is in a distressed and sickly state, we shall find that it is in a strong and flourishing condition. If the quantity of shipping was declining, if it was unemployed, even at low freight, I should say it must be sustained and encouraged. No such thing is asserted. Seamen's wages are high, freights are high, and American bottoms in full employment. But the complaint is, our vessels are not permitted to go to the British West Indies. It is even affirmed, that no civilized country treats us so ill in that respect. Spain and Portugal prohibit the traffic to their possessions, not only in our vessels, but in their own, which, according to the style of the resolutions, is worse treatment than we meet with from the British. It is also asserted, and on as bad ground, that our vessels are excluded from most of the British markets. This is not true in any sense. We are admitted into the greater number of her ports, in our own vessels; and by far the greater value of our exports is sold in British ports, into which our vessels are received, not only on a good footing, compared with other foreigners, but on terms of positive favor—on better terms than British vessels are admitted into our own ports. We are not subject to the alien duties; and the light money, &c., of 1s. 9d. sterling, per ton, is less than our foreign tonnage duty, not to mention the ten per cent. on the duties on the goods in foreign bottoms. But in the port of London our vessels are received free. It is for the unprejudiced mind to compare these facts with the assertions we have heard so confidently and so feelingly made by the mover of the resolutions, that we are excluded from most of their ports, and that no civilized nation treats our vessels so ill as the British.

The tonnage of the vessels employed between Great Britain and her dependencies and the United States, is called two hundred and twenty thousand, and the whole of this is represented as our just right. The same gentleman speaks of our natural right to the carriage of our own articles, and that we may and ought to insist upon our equitable share. Yet, soon after, he uses the language of monopoly, and represents the whole carriage of imports and exports as the proper object of our efforts, and all that others carry as a clear loss to us. If an equitable share of the carriage means half, we have it already, and more, and our proportion is rapidly increasing. If any thing is meant by the natural right of carriage, one would imagine that it belongs to him, whoever he may be, who having bought our produce, and made himself the owner, thinks proper to take it with him to his own country. It is neither our policy nor our design to check the sale of our produce; we invite every description of purchasers, because we expect to sell dearest, when the number and competition of the buyers is the greatest. For this reason the total exclusion of foreigners and their vessels from the purchase and carriage of our exports is an advantage in respect to navigation, which has disadvantage to balance it, in respect to the price of produce. It is with this reserve we ought to receive the remark, that the carriage of our exports should be our object rather than that of our imports. By going with our vessels into foreign ports, we buy our imports in the best market. By giving a steady and moderate encouragement to our own shipping, without pretending violently to interrupt the course of business, experience will soon establish that order of things which is most beneficial to the exporter, the importer, and the ship-owner. The best interest of agriculture is the true interest of trade.

In a trade mutually beneficial, it is strangely absurd to consider the gain of others as our loss. Admitting it, however, for argument sake, yet it should be noticed that the loss of two hundred and twenty thousand tons of shipping is computed according to the apparent tonnage. Our vessels not being allowed to go to the British West Indies, and their vessels, making frequent voyages, appear in the entries over and over again. In the trade to the European dominions of Great Britain, the distance being greater, our vessels are not so often entered. Both these circumstances give a false show to the amount of British tonnage, compared with the American. It is, however, very pleasing to the mind, to see that our tonnage exceeds the British in the European trade. For various reasons, some of which will be mentioned hereafter, the tonnage in the West India trade is not the proper subject of calculation. In the European comparison, we have more tonnage in the British than in the French commerce; it is indeed more than four to one. The great quantity of British tonnage employed in our trade, is also, in a great measure, owing to the large capitals of their merchants employed in the buying and exporting our productions. If we would banish the ships, we must strike at the root, and banish the capital; and this, before we have capital of our own grown up to replace it, would be an operation of no little violence and injury, to our southern brethren especially. Independently of this circumstance, Great Britain is an active and intelligent rival in the navigation line. Her ships are dearer, and the provisioning her seamen is, perhaps, rather dearer than ours; on the other hand, the rate of interest is lower in England, and so are seamen's wages. It would be improper, therefore, to consider the amount of British tonnage in our trade as a proof of a bad state of things, arising either from the restrictions of that government, or the negligence or timidity of this. We are to charge it to causes which are more connected with the natural competition of capital and industry; causes which, in fact, retarded the growth of our shipping more when we were colonies and our ships were free, than since the adoption of the present government.

It has been said with emphasis, that the Constitution grew out of the complaints of the nation respecting commerce, especially that with the British dominions. What was then lamented by our patriots? Feebleness of the public counsels, the shadow of union, and scarcely the shadow of public credit; everywhere despondence, the pressure of evils not only great, but portentous of civil distractions. These were the grievances; and what more was then desired than their remedies? Is it possible to survey this prosperous country, and to assert that they have been delayed? Trade flourishes on our wharves, although it droops in speeches. Manufactures have risen, under the shade of protecting duties, from almost nothing to such a state that we are even told we can depend on the domestic supply, if the foreign should cease. The fisheries, which we found in decline, are in the most vigorous growth; the whale fishery, which our allies would have transferred to Dunkirk, now traverses the whole ocean: To that hardy race of men, the sea is but a park for hunting its monsters; such is their activity, the deepest abysses scarcely afford to their prey a hiding-place. Look around, and see how the frontier circle widens, how the interior improves, and let it be repeated, that the hopes of the people, when they formed this Constitution, have been frustrated!

But if it should happen that our prejudices prove stronger than our senses; if it should be believed that our farmers and merchants see their products and ships and wharves going to decay together, and they are ignorant or silent on their own ruin, still the public documents would not disclose so alarming a state of our affairs. Our imports are obtained so plentifully and cheaply, that one of the avowed objects of the resolutions is, to make them scarcer and dearer. Our exports, so far from languishing, have increased two millions of dollars in a year. Our navigation is found to be augmented beyond the most sanguine expectation. We hear of the vast advantage the English derive from the Navigation Act, and we are asked, in a tone of accusation, Shall we sit still and do nothing? Who is bold enough to say, Congress has done nothing for the encouragement of American navigation? To counteract the Navigation Act, we have laid on British a higher tonnage than our own vessels pay in their ports; and, what is much more effectual, we have imposed ten per cent. on the duties, when the dutied articles are borne in foreign bottoms. We have also made the coasting trade a monopoly to our own vessels. Let those who have asserted that this is nothing, compare facts with the regulations which produced them:

Tonnage	Tons	Excess of American Tonnage
American, 1789	297,468	
Foreign	265,116	32,352
American, 1790	347,663	
Foreign	258,916	88,747
American, 1791	363,810	
Foreign	240,799	123,011
American, 1792	415,330	
Foreign	244,263	171,067

Is not this increase of American shipping rapid enough? Many persons say it is too rapid, and attracts too much capital for the circumstances of the country. I cannot readily persuade myself to think so valuable a branch of employment thrives too fast. But a steady and sure encouragement is more to be relied on than violent methods of forcing its growth. It is not clear that the quantity of our navigation, including our coasting and fishing vessels, is less, in proportion to those of that nation. In that computation, we shall probably find that we are already more a navigating people than the English. As this is a growing country, we have the most stable ground of dependence on the corresponding growth of our navigation; and that the increasing demand for shipping will rather fall to the share of Americans than foreigners, is not to be denied. We did expect this, from the nature of our own laws; we have been confirmed in it by experience; and we know that an American bottom is actually preferred to a foreign one. In cases where one partner is an American and another a foreigner, the ship is made an American bottom. A fact of this kind overthrows a whole theory of reasoning on the necessity of further restrictions. It shows that the work of restriction is already done.

If we take the aggregate view of our commercial interests, we shall find much more occasion for satisfaction, and even exultation, than complaint, and none for despondence. It would be too bold to say that our condition is so eligible there is nothing to be wished. Neither the order of nature nor the allotments of Providence afford perfect content, and it would be absurd to expect in our politics what is denied in the laws of our being. The nations with whom we have intercourse have, without exception, more or less restricted their commerce. They have framed their regulations to suit their real or fancied interests. The code of France is as full of restrictions as that of England. We have regulations of our own, and they are unlike those of any other country. Inasmuch as the interest and circumstances of nations vary so essentially, the project of an exact reciprocity on our part is a vision. What we desire is, to have, not an exact reciprocity, but an intercourse of mutual benefit and convenience. It has scarcely been so much as insinuated that the change contemplated will be a profitable one—that it will enable us to sell dearer and to buy cheaper; on the contrary, we are invited to submit to the hazards and losses of a conflict with our customers—to engage in a contest of self-denial. For what?—to obtain better markets? No such thing; but to shut up, forever, if possible, the best market we have for our exports, and to confine ourselves to the dearest and scarcest markets for our imports; and this is to be done for the benefit of trade, or, as it is sometimes more correctly said, for the benefit of France. This language is not a little inconsistent and strange from those who recommend a nonimportation agreement, and who think we should even renounce the sea, and devote ourselves to agriculture. Thus, to make our trade more free, it is to be embarrased and violently shifted from one country to another; not according to the interest of the merchants, but the visionary theories and capricious rashness of the legislators. To make trade better, it is to be made nothing.

So far as commerce and navigation are regarded, the pretences for this contest are confined to two. We are not allowed to carry manufactured articles to Great Britain, nor any products, except of our own growth, and we are not permitted to go, with our own vessels, to the West Indies. The former, which is a provision of the Navigation Act, is of little importance to our interests, as our trade is chiefly a direct one, our shipping not being equal to the carrying for other nations, and our manufactured articles are not furnished in quantities for exportation, and if they were, Great Britain would not be a customer. So far, therefore, the restriction is rather nominal than real.

The exclusion of our vessels from the West Indies is of more importance. When we propose to make an effort to force a privilege from Great Britain, which she is loth to yield to us, it is necessary to compare the value of the object with the effort, and, above all, to calculate very warily the probability of success. A trivial thing deserves not a great exertion; much less ought we to stake a very great good in possession for a slight chance of a less good. The carriage of one half the exports and imports to and from the British West Indies, is the object to be contended for. Our whole exports to Great Britain are to be hazarded. We sell on terms of privilege and positive favor, as it has been abundantly shown, near seven millions to the dominions of Great Britain. We are to risk the privilege in this great amount—for what? For the freight only of one half the British West India trade with the United States. It belongs to commercial men to calculate the entire value of the freight alluded to; but it cannot bear much proportion to the amount of seven millions. Besides, if we are denied the privilege of carrying our articles in our vessels to the islands, we are on a footing of privilege in the sale of them. We have one privilege, if not two. It is readily admitted that it is a desirable thing to have our vessels allowed to go to the English islands, but the value of the object has its limits; and we go unquestionably beyond them, when we throw our whole exports into confusion, and run the risk of losing our best markets, for the sake of forcing a permission to carry our own products to one of those markets; in which too, it should be noticed, we sell much less than we do to Great Britain herself. If to this we add, that the success of the contest is grounded on the sanguine and passionate hypothesis of our being able to starve the islanders, which, on trial, may prove false, and which our being involved in the war would overthrow at once, we may conclude, without going further into the discussion, that prudence forbids our engaging in the hazards of a commercial war;

that great things should not be staked against such as are of much less value; that what we possess should not be risked for what we desire, without great odds in our favor; still less, if the chance is infinitely against us.

If these considerations should fail of their effect, it will be necessary to go into an examination of the tendency of the system of discrimination to redress and avenge all our wrongs, and to realize all our hopes.

It has been avowed that we are to look to France, not to England, for advantages in trade; we are to show our spirit, and to manifest towards those who are called enemies the spirit of enmity, and towards those we call friends something more than passive good will; we are to take active measures to force trade out of its accustomed channels, and to shift it by such means from England to France. The care of the concerns of the French manufacturers may be left, perhaps, as well in the hands of the Convention, as to be usurped into our own. However our zeal might engage us to interpose, our duty to our own immediate constituents demands all our attention. To volunteer it, in order to excite competition in one foreign nation to supplant another, is a very strange business; and to do it, as it has been irresistibly proved it will happen, at the charge and cost of our own citizens, is a thing equally beyond all justification and all example. What is it but to tax our own people for a time, perhaps for a long time, in order that the French may at last sell as cheap as the English; cheaper they cannot, nor is it so much as pretended. The tax will be a loss to us, and the fancied tendency of it not a gain to this country, in the event, but to France. We shall pay more for a time, and in the end pay no less; for no object but that one nation may receive our money instead of the other. If this is generous towards France, it is not just to America; it is sacrificing what we owe to our constituents, to what we pretend to feel towards strangers. We have indeed heard a very ardent profession of gratitude to that nation, and infinite reliance seems to be placed on her readiness to sacrifice her interest to ours. The story of this generous strife should be left to ornament fiction. This is not the form nor the occasion to discharge our obligations of any sort to any foreign nation; it concerns not our feelings, but our interests, yet the debate has often soared high above the smoke of business into the epic region. The market for tobacco, tar, turpentine, and pitch, has become matter of sentiment, and given occasion alternately to rouse our courage and our gratitude.

If, instead of hexameters, we prefer discussing our relation to foreign nations in the common language, we shall not find that we are bound by treaty to establish a preference in favor of the French. The treaty is founded on a professed reciprocity—favor for favor. Why is the principle of treaty or no treaty made so essential, when the favor we are going to give is an act of supererogation? It is not expected by one of the nations in treaty; for Holland has declared, in her treaty with us, that such preferences are the fruitful source of animosity, embarrassment, and war. The French have set no such example. They discriminate, in their late Navigation Act, not as we are exhorted to do, between nations in treaty and not in treaty, but between nations at war and not at war with them; so that, when peace takes place, England will stand by that act on the same ground with ourselves. Mr. Ames proceeded to show that if we expect by giving favor to get favor in return, it is improper to make a law. The business belongs to the Executive, in whose hands the Constitution has placed the power of dealing with foreign nations. He noted its singularity to negotiate legislatively—to make by a law half a bargain, expecting a French law would make the other. The footing of treaty or no treaty is different from the ground taken by the mover himself in supporting his system. He had said favor for favor was principle. Nations not in treaty grant favors—those in treaty restrict our trade. Yet the principle of discriminating in favor of nations in treaty, was not only inconsistent with the declared doctrine of the mover and with facts, but it is inconsistent with itself. Nations not in treaty are so very unequally operated upon by the resolutions, it is absurd to refer them to one principle. Spain and Portugal have no treaties with us, and are not disposed to have; Spain would not accede to the treaty of commerce between us and France, though she was invited; Portugal would not sign a treaty after it had been discussed and signed on our part. They have few ships or manufactures, and do not feed their colonies from us; of course there is little for the discrimination to operate upon. The operation on nations in treaty is equally a satire on the principle of discrimination. Sweden, with whom we have a treaty, duties rice higher, if borne in our bottoms, than in her own. France does the like, in respect to tobacco, two and a half livres the quintal, which in effect prohibits our vessels to freight tobacco, as the duty is more than the freight. He then remarked on the French Navigation Act, the information of which had been given to the House since the debate began. He said the mover had, somewhat unluckily, proposed to except from this system nations having no navigation acts, in which case France would become the subject of unfriendly discrimination as well as Great Britain.

He remarked on the disposition of England to settle a commercial treaty, and adverted to the known desire of the Marquis of Lansdowne, (then Prime Minister,) in 1783, to form such an one on the most liberal principles. The history of that business, and the causes which prevented its conclusion, ought to be made known to the public. The powers given to our ministers were revoked, and yet we hear that no such disposition on the part of Great Britain has existed. The declaration of Mr. Pitt, in parliament, in June, 1792, as well as the correspondence with Mr. Hammond, show a desire to enter upon a negotiation. The statement of the report on the privileges and restrictions of our commerce, that Great Britain has shown no inclination to meddle with the subject, seems to be incorrect. After tracing the operation of the resolution on different nations, he examined their supposed tendency to dispose Great Britain to settle an equitable treaty with this country. He asked whether those who held such language towards that nation as he heard, could be supposed to desire a treaty and friendly connections? It seemed to be thought a merit to express hatred. It is common and natural to desire to annoy and to crush those whom we hate, but it is somewhat singular to pretend that the design of our anger is to embrace them. The tendency of angry measures to friendly dispositions and arrangements is not obvious. We affect to believe that we shall quarrel ourselves into their good will—that we shall beat a new path to peace and friendship with Great Britain, one that is grown up with thorns, and lined with men-traps and spring-guns. It should be called the war path.

To do justice to the subject, its promised advantages should be examined. Exciting the competition of the French is to prove an advantage to this country, by opening a new market with that nation. This is scarcely intelligible. If it means any thing, it is an admission that their market is not a good one, or that they have not taken measures to favor our traffic with them. In either case our system is absurd. The balance of trade is against us, and in favor of England. But the resolutions can only aggravate that evil, for, by compelling us to buy dearer and sell cheaper, the balance will be turned still more against our country. Neither is the supply from France less the aliment of luxury than that from England. Their excess of credit is an evil which we pretend to cure: by checking the natural growth of our own capital, which is the undoubted tendency of restraining trade, the progress of the remedy is thus delayed. If we will trade, there must be capital. It is best to have it of our own; if we have it not, we must depend on credit. Wealth springs from the profits of employment, and the best writers on the subject establish it, that employment is in proportion to the capital that is to excite and reward it.

To strike off credit, which is the substitute for capital, if it were possible to do it, would so far stop employment. Fortunately it is not possible; the activity of individual industry eludes the misjudging power of governments. The resolutions would, in effect, increase the demand for credit, as our products selling for less in a new market, and our imports being bought dearer, there would be less money and more need of it. Necessity would produce credit. Where the laws are strict, it will soon find its proper level; the uses of credit will remain, and the evil will disappear.

But the whole theory of balances of trade, of helping it by restraint, and protecting it by systems of prohibition and restriction against foreign nations, as well as the remedy for credit, are among the exploded dogmas, which are equally refuted by the maxims of science and the authority of time. Many such topics have been advanced, which were known to exist as prejudices, but were not expected as arguments. It seems to be believed that the liberty of commerce is of some value. Although there are restrictions on one side, there will be some liberty left; counter restrictions, by diminishing that liberty, are in their nature aggravations and not remedies. We complain of the British restrictions, as of a millstone; our own system will be another; so that our trade may hope to be situated between the upper and the nether millstone.

On the whole, the resolutions contain two great principles. To control trade by law, instead of leaving it to the better management of the merchants, and the principle of a sumptuary law. To play the tyrant in the counting-house, and in directing the private expenses of our citizens, are employments equally unworthy of discussion.

Besides the advantages of the system, we have been called to another view of it, which seems to have less connection with the merits of the discussion. The acts of states, and the votes of public bodies, before the Constitution was adopted, and the votes of the House since, have been stated as grounds for our assent to this measure at this time. To help our own trade, to repel any real or supposed attack upon it, cannot fail to prepossess the mind; accordingly, the first feelings of every man yield to this proposition. But the sober judgment on the tendency and reasonableness of the intermeddling of government, often does, and probably ought still oftener, to change our impressions. On a second view of the question, the man who voted formerly for restrictions may say, much has been done under the new Constitution, and the good effects are yet making progress. The necessity of measures of counter restriction will appear to him much less urgent, and their efficacy in the present turbulent state of Europe infinitely less to be relied on. Far from being inconsistent in his conduct, consistency will forbid his pressing the experiment of his principle under circumstances which baffle the hopes of its success. But if so much stress is laid on former opinions in favor of this measure, how happens it that there is so little on that which now appears against it? Not one merchant has spoken in favor of it in this body; not one navigating or commercial state has patronized it.

Mr. Ames then entered pretty fully into the consideration of the absolute dependence of the British West India islands on our supplies. He admitted that they cannot draw them so well and so cheap from any other quarter; but this is not the point. Are they physically dependent? Can we starve them? And may we reasonably expect thus to dictate to Great Britain a free admission of our vessels into her islands? He went into details to prove the negative. Beef and pork sent from the now United States to the British West Indies, 1773, fourteen thousand nine hundred and ninety-three barrels. In the war time, 1780, ditto from England, seventeen thousand seven hundred and ninety-five. At the end of the war, 1783, sixteen thousand five hundred and twenty-six. Ireland exported, on an average of seven years, prior to 1777, two hundred and fifty thousand barrels. Salted fish the English take in abundance, and prohibit its importation from us. Butter and cheese from England and Ireland are but lately banished even from our markets. Exports from the now United States, 1773, horses, two thousand seven hundred and sixty-eight; cattle, one thousand two hundred and three; sheep and hogs, five thousand three hundred and twenty. Twenty-two years prior to 1791, were exported from England, to all parts, twenty-nine thousand one hundred and thirty-one horses. Ireland, on an average of seven years to 1779, exported four thousand and forty live stock, exclusive of hogs. The coast of Barbary, the Cape de Verds, &c., supply sheep and cattle. The islands, since the war, have increased their domestic supplies to a great degree. The now United States exported about one hundred and thirty thousand barrels of flour, in 1773, to the West Indies; Ireland, by grazing less, could supply wheat; England also usually exports it, she also imports from Archangel. Sicily and the Barbary States furnish wheat in abundance.

We are deceived, when we fancy we can starve foreign countries. France is reckoned to consume grain at the rate of seven bushels to each soul: twenty-six millions of souls, the quantity one hundred and eighty-two millions of bushels. We export, to speak in round numbers, five or six millions of bushels to all the different countries which we supply; a triffle, this, to their wants. Frugality is a greater resource. Instead of seven bushels, perhaps two could be saved by stinting the consumption of the food of cattle, or by the use of other food. Two bushels saved to each soul, is fifty-two millions of bushels, a quantity which the whole trading world perhaps could not furnish. Rice is said to be prohibited by

Spain and Portugal, to favor their own. Brazil could supply their rice instead of ours. *Lumber*—He stated the danger of despising Canada and Nova Scotia too much as rivals in the West India supply, especially the former. The dependence the English had placed on them some years ago failed, partly because we entered into competition with them on very superior terms, and partly because they were then in an infant state. They are now supposed to have considerably more than doubled their numbers since the peace; and if, instead of having us for competitors for the supply, as before, we should shut ourselves out by refusing our supplies, or being refused entry for them, those two colonies would rise from the ground: at least we should do more to bring it about than the English ministry have been able to do. In 1772, six hundred and seventy-nine vessels, the actual tonnage of which was one hundred and twenty-eight thousand, were employed in the West India trade from Great Britain. They were supposed, on good ground, to be but half freighted to the islands; they might carry lumber, and the freight supposed to be deficient would be, at forty shillings sterling the ton, one hundred and twenty-eight thousand pounds sterling. This sum would diminish the extra charge of carrying lumber to the islands. But is lumber to be had? Yes, in Germany, and from the Baltic. It is even cheaper in Europe than our own. Besides which, the hard woods used in mills are abundant in the islands. We are told they can sell their rum only to the United States: this concerns not their subsistence, but their profit. Examine it, however. In 1773, the now United States took near three million gallons rum. The remaining British Colonies, Newfoundland, and the Africa coast, have a considerable demand for this article. The demand of Ireland is very much on the increase. It was, in 1763, five hundred and thirty thousand gallons; 1770, one million five hundred and fifty-eight thousand gallons; 1778, one million seven hundred and twenty-nine thousand gallons.

Thus, we see, a total stoppage of the West India trade could not starve the islanders. It would affect us deeply; we should lose the sale of our products and of course not gain the carriage in our own vessels. The object of the contest would be no nearer our reach than before. Instead, however, of a total stoppage of the intercourse, it might happen that each nation prohibiting the vessels of the other, some third nation would carry on the traffic in its own bottoms. While this measure would disarm our system, it would make it recoil upon ourselves. It would in effect operate chiefly to obstruct the sale of our products. If they should remain unsold, it would be so much dead loss; or if the effect should be to raise the price on the consumers, it would either lessen the consumption, or raise up rivals in the supply. The contest as it respects the West India trade is in every respect against us. To embarrass the supply from the United States, supposing the worst as it regards the planters, can do no more than enhance the price of sugar and coffee, and other products. The French Islands are now in ruins, and the English planters have an increased price and double demand in consequence. While Great Britain confined the colony trade to herself, she gave to the colonists in return a monopoly in her consumption of West India articles. The extra expense arising from the severest operation on our system, is already provided against twofold. Like other charges on the products of labor and capital, the burden will fall on the consumer. The luxurious and opulent consumer in Europe will not regard and perhaps will not know the increase of price nor the cause of it. The new settler who clears his land and sells the lumber, will feel any convulsion in the market more sensibly without being able to sustain it at all. It is a contest of wealth against want; of self-denial, between luxury and daily subsistence, that we provoke with so much confidence of success. A man of experience in the West India trade will see this contrast more strongly than it is possible to represent it.

One of the excellences, for which the measure is recommended is, that it will affect our imports. What is offered as an argument is really an objection. Who will supply our wants? Our own manufactures are growing, and it is a subject of great satisfaction that they are. But it would be wrong to overrate their capacity to clothe us. The same number of inhabitants require more and more, because wealth increases. Add to this the rapid growth of our numbers, and perhaps it will be correct to estimate the progress of manufacturers as only keeping pace with that of our increasing consumption and population. It follows that we shall continue to demand in future to the amount of our present importation. It is not intended by the resolutions that we shall import from England. Holland and the north of Europe do not furnish a sufficient variety or sufficient quantity for our consumption. It is in vain to look to Spain, Portugal, and the Italian States. We are expected to depend principally upon France; it is impossible to examine the ground of this dependence without adverting to the present situation of that country. It is a subject upon which I practise no disguise, but I do not think it proper to introduce the politics of France into this discussion. If others can find in the scenes that pass there, or in the principles and agents that direct them, proper subjects for amiable names, and sources of joy and hope in the prospect, I have nothing to say to it. It is an amusement which it is not my intention either to disturb or to partake of. I turn from these horrors to examine the condition of France, in respect to manufacturing, capital, and industry. In this point of view, whatever political improvements may be hoped for, it cannot escape observation, that it presents only a wide field of waste and desolation. Capital, which used to be food for manufactures, is become their fuel. What once nourished industry, now lights the fires of civil war, and quickens the progress of destruction. France is like a ship, with a fine cargo, burning to the water's edge; she may be built upon anew, and freighted with another cargo, and it will be time enough, when that shall be, to depend on a part of it for our supply; at present, and for many years, she will not be so much a furnisher as a consumer. It is therefore obvious, that we shall import our supplies either directly or indirectly from Great Britain. Any obstruction to the importation will raise the price which we who consume must bear.

That part of the argument which rests on the supposed distress of the British manufacturers, in consequence of the loss of our market, is in every view unfounded. They would not lose the market in fact, and if they did, should we prodigiously exaggerate the importance of our consumption to the British workmen? Important it doubtless is, but a little attention will expose the extreme folly of the opinion, that they would be brought to our feet by a trial of our self-denying spirit. England now supplants France in the important Levant trade, in the supply of manufactured goods to the East, and in a great measure to the West Indies, to Spain, Portugal, and their dependencies. Her trade with Russia has of late vastly increased; and she is treating for a trade with China; so that the new demands of English manufactures, consequent upon the depression of France as a rival, has amounted to much more than the whole American importation, which is not three millions.

British manufactures exported in 1773, amounted to	£ 9,417,000
1774	10,556,000
1775	10,072,000
1789	13,779,000
1790	14,921,000
1791	16,810,000
1792	18,310,000

The ill effect of a system of restriction and prohibition in the West Indies has been noticed already. The privileges allowed to our exports to England may be withdrawn, and prohibitory or high duties imposed. Mr. A. observed that not one of our articles is a monopoly, and noticed the effect of counter regulations on our products. He adverted particularly to pot and pearl ashes, and observed on the value of the extensive sale of that article, as it advances the clearing and settlement of our new lands; he said, the best encouragement for agriculture is a good market.

The system before us is a mischief that goes to the root of our prosperity. The merchants will suffer by the schemes and projects of a new theory. Great numbers were ruined by the convulsions of 1775. They are an order of citizens deserving better of government than to be involved in new confusions. It is wrong to make our trade wage war for our politics. It is now scarcely said that it is a thing to be sought for but a weapon to fight with. To gain our approbation to the system, we are told it is to be gradually established; in that case, it will be unavailing. It should be begun with in all its strength, if we think of starving the islands. Drive them suddenly and by surprise to extremity, if you would dictate terms, but they will prepare against a long expected failure of our supplies.

Our nation will be tired of suffering loss and embarrassment for the French. The rice growers and tobacco planters of the South will be, and ought to be, soon weary of a contest which they are told is to benefit shipowners of the East. The struggle, so painful to ourselves, so ineffectual against England, will be renounced, and we shall sit down with shame and loss, with disappointed passions and aggravated complaints. War, which would then suit our feelings, would not suit our weakness. We might perhaps find some European power willing to make war on England, and we might be permitted by a strict alliance to partake the misery and the dependence of being a subaltern in the quarrel. The happiness of this situation seems to be in view when the system before us is avowed to be the instrument of avenging our political resentments. Those who affect to dread foreign influence will do well to avoid a partnership in European jealousies and rivalships. Courting the friendship of one, and provoking the hatred of the other, is dangerous to our real independence; for it would compel America to throw herself into the arms of the one for protection against the other. Then foreign influence, pernicious as it is, would be sought for, and though it should be shunned, it could not be resisted. The connections of trade form ties between individuals and produce little control over government. They are the ties of peace, and are neither corrupt nor corrupting.

In the course of his speech, Mr. A. adverted to the danger of cutting off a part of the public revenue by the operation of the proposed regulations.

He remarked upon the hostile tendency of the resolutions; we have happily escaped from a state of the most imminent danger to our peace. A false step would lose all the security for its continuance which we owe at this moment to the conduct of the President. What is to save us from war? Not our own power which inspires terror; not the gentle and forbearing spirit of the powers of Europe at this crisis; not the weakness of England; nor her affection for this country; if we believe the assurances of gentlemen on the other side. What is it then? It is the interest of Great Britain to have America for a customer, rather than an enemy. And it is precisely that interest which gentlemen are so eager to take away, and to transfer to France. And what is stranger still, they say they rely on that operation as a means of producing peace with the Indians and Algerines. The wounds inflicted on Great Britain by our enmity are expected to excite her to supplicate our friendship and to appease us by soothing the animosity of our enemies.

What is to produce effects so mystical, so opposite to the nature, so much exceeding the efficacy of their pretended causes? This wonder-working paper on the table is the weapon of terror and destruction—like the writing on Belshazzar's wall, it is to strike parliaments and nations with dismay. It is to be stronger than fleets against pirates, or than armies against Indians. After the examination it has undergone, credulity itself will laugh at these pretensions.

We pretend to expect not by the force of our restrictions, but, by the mere show of our spirit, to level all the fences that have guarded for ages the monopoly of the Colony trade.

The repeal of the Navigation Act of England, which is cherished as the palladium of her safety, which time has rendered venerable, and prosperity endeared to her people, is to be extorted from her fears of a weaker nation. It is not to be yielded freely, but violently torn from her; and yet the idea of a struggle to prevent indignity and loss, is considered as a chimera too ridiculous for sober refutation. She will not dare, say they, to resent it, and gentlemen have pledged themselves for the success of the attempt; what is treated as a phantom is vouched by fact. Her Navigation Act is known to have caused an immediate contest with the Dutch, and four desperate sea fights ensued, in consequence, the very year of its passage. How far it is an act of aggression, for a neutral nation to assist the supplies of one neighbor, and to annoy and distress another, at the crisis of a contest between the two, which strains their strength to the utmost, is a question which we might not agree in deciding. But the tendency of such unseasonable partiality, to exasperate the spirit of hostility against the intruder, cannot be doubted. The language of the French government would not soothe this spirit.

It proposes, on the sole condition of a political connection, to extend to us a part of their West India commerce. The coincidence of our measures with their invitations, however singular, needs no comment. Of all men those are least consistent who believe in the efficacy of the regulations, and yet affect to ridicule their hostile tendency. In the commercial conflict, say they, we shall surely prevail, and effectually humble Great Britain. In open war we are the weaker, and shall be brought into danger, if not to ruin. It depends, therefore, according to their own reasoning, on Great Britain herself, whether she will persist in a struggle which will disgrace and weaken her, or turn it into a war, which will throw the shame and ruin upon her antagonist. The topics which furnish argument to show the danger to our peace from the resolutions, are too fruitful to be exhausted. But without pursuing them further, the experience of mankind has shown that commercial rivalships, which spring from mutual efforts for monopoly, have kindled more wars and wasted the earth more than the spirit of conquest.

He hoped we should show, by our vote, that we deem it better policy to feed nations than to starve them, and that we should never be so unwise as to put our good customers into a situation to be forced to make every exertion to do without us. By cherishing the arts of peace, we shall acquire, and we are actually acquiring, the strength and resources for a war. Instead of seeking treaties, we ought to shun them, for the later they shall be formed, the better will be the terms—we shall have more to give and more to withhold. We have not yet taken our proper rank, nor acquired that consideration, which will not be refused us if we persist in prudent and pacific counsels, if we give time for our strength to mature itself. Though America is rising with a giant's strength, its bones are yet but cartilages. By delaying the beginning of a conflict, we insure the victory.

By voting out the resolutions, we shall show to our own citizens, and foreign nations, that our prudence has prevailed over our prejudices; that we prefer our interests to our resentments. Let us assert a genuine independence of spirit;

we shall be false to our duty and feelings as Americans, if we basely descend to a servile dependence on France or Great Britain.

JUNE 23, 1789

MR. MADISON had spoken so much on former occasions on this subject, that he had little more to say. He presumed that it had been fully proved that the voice of America was in favor of the motion. He had been informed that the Senate did not differ with the House in the principle that discrimination was proper, but they contemplated a detached and pointed law on this subject. Perhaps their method might be eligible, but he was not inclined to risk a certainty for an uncertainty. . . .

. . . .

Mr. AMES called upon gentlemen to recollect the situation of the United States, and the urgent necessity there was for passing the revenue laws. He submitted to the House how much better it would be to let this subject be taken up distinctly, than make it a reason for delaying the great business they were sent here to complete. He was, however, strongly opposed to being led by the principle of gratitude in matters relative to the public weal. The obligation of a treaty never required more than what its terms stipulated for; therefore, in matters of commerce and matters of revenue, interest ought to be the predominating principle.

Mr. MADISON . . . would not agree to relinquish the present discrimination in hopes of obtaining a future one; and he contended that a discrimination was warranted upon the predominating principle alluded to by the gentleman last up; . . .

JANUARY 3, 1794–MARCH 14, 1794

JANUARY 3

MR. AMES proposed next Monday week. He observed that the resolutions involved the greatest interests of this country; that, for himself, he could not possibly be prepared to discuss the subject by Monday next. . . . He further remarked, that the subject required the most mature deliberation of the House. Sudden and hasty decisions might be followed with the most serious effects; they might involve the sacrifice of the essential interests, or the honor of the United States.

JANUARY 15

COMMERCE OF THE UNITED STATES

A PROPOSITION being made to go into a Committee of the Whole on Mr. MADISON'S resolutions—

Mr. AMES wanted to have the printed state of the negotiation between Great Britain and the Federal Government respecting a Treaty of Commerce; and likewise a paper from the Secretary of State, which the House had ordered to be got ready and be printed some days ago. He wished gentlemen not to be in a hurry in deciding on a subject of such prodigious consequence as these propositions. He wished to defer going into a Committee until the papers could be had.

. . . .

Mr. AMES thought it requisite to have the papers laid before the Committee which had been directed to be printed. He said there never had been an instance of any subject of the kind being pushed forward as the present. Such was the vastness and complexity of the evidence, and some parts of it were so obscure, that it was impossible for the House to have yet found leisure for embracing a well-founded opinion. The gentleman who spoke last had said that the papers called for could be of no consequence in discussing the resolutions. This assertion was in itself a very proper reason for printing the papers, that the gentleman, by having an opportunity of reading them, might be convinced of their importance. Mr. A. said that he believed there was an amicable disposition on the part of Britain. He grounded his assertion on an acknowledgment that had been made some time ago by one of the British Ministers, in Parliament, who said, that he expected soon to lay before that House a Commercial Treaty betwixt England and America. The gentleman had said that we should found our measures on the dispositions of the several powers of Europe toward us. That was right. But it was requisite to be informed of those dispositions before forming these resolutions.

. . . .

Mr. AMES wished, that gentlemen, instead of indefinite declamation, would lay their finger on each particular wrong that Britain had done to us. He did not know of any particular advantage, that we had derived in our commerce with France. He wished to discountenance a spirit of revenge, and to ascertain on what side the benefits of our commerce lay, and wherein they consisted. He did not like unfair comparisons.

JANUARY [17], 1794

Mr. AMES spoke a few words on the impropriety of making an accusation against Britain, without advancing specific facts and specific evidence to support them.

FEBRUARY 4

Mʀ. AMES was of opinion that it would be wiser to accept of excuses for injuries, than fight battles to avenge them. He likewise insisted that a train of negotiation had been entered into respecting the grievances of America, and that it would be proper to wait the conclusion of it.

. . . .

Mr. AMES said, that there was no commercial State in the Union which favored the resolutions: four-fifths of the citizens of the United States were against them. It had been urged, that they contained nothing new; nothing but what had long been intended to be carried into execution. An opinion against the resolutions was travelling with rapidity from this centre, on every side, to the circumference of the circle. The people had too much good sense to approve them.

FEBRUARY 6

Mʀ. AMES attacked the mover of the resolutions on the Report of the Secretary [Mr. MADISON] for not displaying in the affair of the Algerines some part of the spirit which he had exerted on the other occasion. He thought it shameful to buy a peace, and that there could be no security, if we did. He recommended an armament. Portugal had shown herself friendly; and, referring to what Mr. CLARK had stated, he was of opinion she would give our ships shelter in her ports. He thought that six stout frigates at the mouth of the Straits would do the business. He went at considerable length into Mr. MADISON'S resolutions, and condemned, upon various

1026

grounds, the arguments and conduct of the gentlemen who supported them. Yesterday, we were told that Britain durst not quarrel with America, and to-day, she is represented as ready to do it. Our commerce is on the point of being annihilated, and, unless an armament is fitted out, we may very soon expect the Algerines on the coast of America.

Mr. GILES, in reply, said that Mr. AMES drew inconsistent pictures. One day he represented the American commerce at the summit of prosperity; the next, it was reduced to nothing. In defence of the commercial regulations, he reminded the House that Britain, and not Algiers, was the real object of alarm, and the real source of hostility.

MARCH 14

MR. AMES began with remarking that the additional duties were intended, he believed, to operate generally, and that their operation would fall on the middling classes of the people. But the resolution would also affect our exports, and, in this view, injure our cutters of timber, makers of potash, and farmers in general would feel their operation deeply— all this for the advantage of our ship-owners. If the resolutions cannot now be termed trifling, then, indeed, he had mistaken their true character. In a moment of danger, when our commerce is nearly annihilated, it is trifling to talk of regulating it, when we should attend to our defence only. When brought forward they had an alarming appearance— negotiations were pending. We should always say peace to the last extremity; and, if war threatens, strain every sinew to prepare for it. The resolutions say nothing—they say worse than nothing; they are built on partiality for one nation— they have French stamped on the very face of them. If we feel that the English have injured us, let us put the country in a state of defence; the resolutions can do nothing towards this. It is folly to think of regulating a commerce that calls first for protection, and to encourage the increase of navigation when what shipping we have is in jeopardy.

TO CHRISTOPHER GORE

PHILADELPHIA, JANUARY 28, 1794

MY DEAR FRIEND,

THE DEBATE on the war regulations (for so they ought to be named) is yet open.[40] Never was a completer defeat than the restricting party have met with, as far as argument goes. But party has resources after those of reasoning are exhausted. The ground is avowedly changed. Madison & Co. now avow that the political wrongs are *the* wrongs to be cured by commercial restrictions, which, in plain English is, we set out with a tale of restrictions and injuries on our commerce, that has been refuted solidly; pressed for a pretext, we avow that we will make war, not for our commerce, but with it; not to make our commerce better, but to make it nothing, in order to reach the tender sides of our enemy, which are not to be wounded in any other way. You and I have long believed this to be the real motive; I own I did not expect to hear it confessed. It was, I still think, ill-judged to do it; but the case was urgent, and silence shameful. Our trading

---

[40] *Mr. Madison's resolutions, introduced January 3, 1794. See introduction to "speech on Mr. Madison's resolutions."* [S. AMES]

folks should be undeceived, if facts, which speak for themselves, and which have at last made faction itself speak truth, can restore them the use of their faculties. All Massachusetts will vote against the resolutions, (at least so we are persuaded); probably all New England, Smith, of Vermont, excepted; but the south is well disciplined. Lee, of Virginia, made a very catholic speech against his colleagues. The event of the first vote is rather doubtful, yet we think the chance in our favor. I have, however, no idea that this folly will pass into a law. It answers the usual wish of the faction to prevent doing any good.

You mention your opinion that Dearborn is fond of attentions, and inflated with his own importance. I know little of the man, but I had a prepossession in his favor. I have supposed that he came here, as new members sometimes do, persuaded that the old ones go too far, and that a middle course is more eligible; however this may be, I have no great fears of any eventual misapplication of the force of Massachusetts. It is, with Connecticut, the lifeguard of the Constitution. If this is vanity, excuse it. I mean no compliment to myself further than being federal is one. I have been delivered, safely, of a speech, which I am glad to have off my hands. It contained answers to several of your inquiries, heretofore suggested in your letters. Dexter made a speech much better than mine, which has fixed his reputation in the House very properly; he will be a good fellow, and prop the cause of good government like a little Atlas.

There has lately been a call from the Senate on the President, to lay before them the correspondence between Gouverneur Morris and the French Republic. This, if published, might disclose our minister's sentiments, and perhaps expose his head. Whether the President will send the correspondence or not, is yet to be seen; I hope not, for these fellows claim a share in diplomatic business, which is intended to unpresident the chief magistrate. The spirit of mischief is as active as the element of fire, and as destructive. I continue to hear good intelligence from Springfield. Speak of me to Mrs. Gore.

Yours, &c.

TO CHRISTOPHER GORE

PHILADELPHIA, FEBRUARY 25, 1794

MY DEAR FRIEND,

I MISS YOU because I wish to sit down and croak with a friend. I have more fears of war than I had when you left us. The newspapers indicate a storm. The seizure of our vessels, carrying French West India produce, is said to be going on, under the pretext of some old edict. If this should be pushed by the English, it is driving us to the wall. There is no appearance of an intention to give up the posts; and the pressing of that point was, I think, both unwise and ill-timed on our part. These circumstances, which ought to double our caution, will probably inflame our rashness. What ought to be a dissuasive, will, I fear, prove an incentive. The resolutions will, no doubt, be reinvigorated by the show of Boston support. I think they will not be carried; but the irritation against England has gained upon the sentiment of the House, and, to speak truth, the causes for it are more manifest. John Bull, proud of his strength, angry with our partiality to France, ardent in his contest, and straining every sinew, shows less patience and respect for us than he ought to do. He shows no spirit of condescension in respect to the

posts, and in the line of navigation and trade, the principle
of the seizures, before mentioned, shows a spirit of rivalry
that is provoking enough. We have not, however, any
authentic notice of the adoption of such a principle.

On the whole, I do not believe that Great Britain intends
to force us into a war; but she intends to make our neutrality
unpleasant to our feelings and unprofitable to our navigation,
&c.; and in doing this, she probably cares little whether it
is war or peace. Our gallicism hurts her pride, and she is
heated enough to punish all the friends of her foes. You will
not think so meanly of me as to suppose that I am gloomy
on account of your town-meeting. I feel no loathness to
engage in measures that will draw more resentment upon my
head, if by doing so I can add any new security to our peace.
I found my apprehensions on some facts respecting their
stubbornness on the affair of the posts, and also on premises
of a still more decisive kind, before alluded to, which God
grant may prove untrue. Learned Trumbull and others have
been croaking with me, which is some consolation. However
the crisis of our politics may issue, the line of duty is plain.
Peace, peace, to the last day that it can be maintained; and
war, when it must come, should be thrown upon our faction,
as their act and deed. In the mean time, good men should
be alert; they should see the urgency of circumstances, and
be ready to impress caution upon the rash and factious, and
to rouse the activity of the sleepy patriots. The resolutions
can only aggravate the danger, and diminish our preparation
against it. Our policy should be precisely the reverse; to
dispel the danger, if possible, and at the same moment to
prepare the means of defence against it. To arm, to fortify,
to train militia corps, and above all, to furnish pecuniary
resources now in peace; to do as much of this, and to continue
it as long as possible, and let foreign nations waste their
strength and their fury. Thus we might hope, by delay, to

gain as they lose strength; besides which, we should take the chance of events, which may, and I flatter myself will, after all, save us from the destructive evil that threatens our nation.

What I have written is strictly of a confidential nature. It may also appear, at a future day, to be a symptom of the dumps. Be that as it may, I write under the impressions of the moment, which others feel as strongly as I express them. I beg you would let Craigie see the enclosed, in confidence. Our friends Eustis and J. C. Jones ought to know, in like manner, that they are keepers of the peace. I see no objection to their knowing the contents.[41]

Yours, as ever.

---

[41] *Our relations with Great Britain had become extremely critical. The military frontier posts, within the jurisdiction of the United States, which were to have been given up by the terms of the treaty of peace, continued to be occupied by British garrisons. No compensation had been made for the negroes carried away at the close of the war. In addition to these old causes of irritation, the fury of the great contest in Europe caused our rights as neutrals to be brought into constant question, and American vessels and property were continually captured by British cruisers, and condemned, under certain recent orders in Council, of a most unreasonable and exceptionable character. The never-failing question of the right of impressment was also fruitful of difficulties, and our vessels were searched and men taken from them as British subjects, with all the insolence which is apt to accompany superiority of physical force. In short, Great Britain was "driving us to the wall," in a manner which, if not speedily redressed, would have compelled us to resort to the sword.* [S. AMES]

TO CHRISTOPHER GORE

PHILADELPHIA, MARCH 5, 1794

MY DEAR FRIEND,

.   .   .   .

IT IS needless to remark how acceptable and how well-timed the second Boston town-meeting was. The languid resolutions[42] receive a death wound in consequence. They were postponed by the party for one week. The war party will be kept in check for a time. We have no further news from Kentucky. I fancy we should be able to carry a vote disavowing them, and for suppressing their banditti by force, which I trust would prevent a war with Spain.[43] Gallatin is turned out of the Senate.[44] I heard King make there one of the most admirable speeches that ever was pronounced. It was both solid and rhetorical. John Langdon would probably serve the people as Vice-President. The hope of that may gain the party a vote for the time. Of all petulant, imprudent men, the English minister[45] is the most so. I believe he has sense and good principles; but he rails against the conduct of our government, not *ore rotundo*, but with a gabble that his feelings render doubly unintelligible. Mr. Pinkney is evidently

---

[42] *Mr. Madison's resolutions, offered in the House January 3, 1794.* [S. AMES]

[43] *The western country was in a state of excitement on account of the refusal by Spain of the free navigation of the Mississippi. Among the machinations imputed to "Citizen" Genet, was a project for a military expedition from Kentucky against New Orleans.* [S. AMES]

[44] *His seat was contested and declared vacant, on the ground that he had not been, for nine years previous to his election, a citizen of the United States.* [S. AMES]

[45] *Mr. Hammond.* [S. AMES]

sour, and also gallican. Here the man is void of moderation and prudence. The cross-fire of their accounts is enough to raise a quarrel. Our man has the most coolness, undoubtedly. But it is lamentable that the true history of events should be given by men under such prejudices. Messrs. J. Coles and T. Dickinson would do well to state some sound and wholesome truths through some channel that would reach Mr. Pitt. Had such a man as Lord Dorchester been sent here, their foolish insolence, and our no less foolish prejudices, would not have had existence at this day; the true interests of both would be now understood and pursued. Neither is just or cool enough at present to do it.—On looking over the page, I see that I use too strong expressions respecting Mr. Pinkney; he is a sober, calm man, and will not irritate; but he has prejudices, and unless a man has a mind above them, he can do little service there.

It is reported that William Smith and your humble servant have been burned in effigy in Charleston, South Carolina. The fire, you know, is pleasant, when it is not too near; and I am willing to have it believed, that, as I come out of the fire undiminished in weight, I am now all gold. I laugh, as you will suppose, at the silly rage of the burners.

.   .   .   .

We have this moment adopted a resolution to lay a general embargo, by a great majority.[46] Whether this will be agreed to by the Senate, is more than I can guess. Should objection be made there, I think it will be to its being general. My own impressions are, that the supposed remedy should go

---

[46] *A joint resolution was passed (March 26) laying an embargo for thirty days;—afterwards extended for thirty days longer.*

About a month after, and after Mr. Jay's appointment as special minister to Great Britain, a bill for the suspension of all intercourse with that nation passed the House, but failed in the Senate by the casting vote of the Vice-President. By that good deed, Mr. Adams brought upon himself much obloquy; but there was ample indemnity in the conviction that he thereby prevented the failure of Mr. Jay's negotiation, and saved us from a war, at least until 1812. [S. AMES]

no farther than the present state of the evil, namely, to the West India trade.

The language of the House is rather intemperate. We call the British *our* enemies. I would *do* what is firm, and *say* what is not harsh. Harsh phrases, used here, can only obstruct our demand for justice.

Our materials for war are but poor; speech-making public bodies are no warriors.

It is to be decided to-day whether the Senate will agree to our embargo. Much may be said against it; yet it is left to chance to decide its usefulness. Our vote was so general, that I think the Senate will agree to an embargo on the West India trade, at least, which I thought would be going far enough.

Yours.

TO [UNKNOWN]

PHILADELPHIA, MARCH 19, 1794

MY DEAR SIR

THE CONDUCT of Britain has provoked a great deal of resentment—and justly. Yet many palliations will probably be made by the impartial. How such are to be found[:] here necessity has no law. The powers at war are not in a state to mind trifles, nor always to pause long to observe whether they are trifles that make their neighbors sacrifice. We ought to be very calm and to make great allowances. We are full of passion and make none. On the whole, although there is a great deal of obscurity in the affair of the capture and condemnation of our vessels in the West Indies and probably it will wind up that there is a great deal of wrong, yet I feel persuaded that Great Britain does not mean to force us into a war, and I am equally sure that angry as we are, we dare not. Both sides being averse from it, there will not be war. The friends of government are vigilant to prevent passionate acts on our part. Therefore my belief is—peace. Our interior politics do not seem to threaten any speedy convulsion. Finally our checks will destroy or be destroyed. It is not easy to say how long war would be kept off if it should be expected to happen. It would be prudent to negotiate long and prepare well before we begin. But it must not be, unless they force us into it, which they will not incline to do.

Dan Parker's affair will keep. The best course would be to discharge him in full on his paying a part. That our prudent and wise folks will not consent to do.

Yours, etc.

FISHER AMES

TO CHRISTOPHER GORE

PHILADELPHIA, MARCH 26, 1794

MY DEAR FRIEND,

I TAKE more and more pride in the comparison of our merchants and people with those of the south. You praise the former, very justly, for their coolness and steadiness. It is a time when the indulgence of passion is peculiarly pleasant, and no less costly; for it will perhaps cost our peace, our wealth, and our safety. It is our intemperate passion that aggravates our embarrassments. Some persons think it had no little influence to produce them. I would not justify the insolence and injustice of the English: they are not to be justified; but our fury for the French, and against the English, is more natural than salutary. France has stopped more than an hundred sail of our vessels at Bordeaux. We sit still; we say nothing; we affect to depend on their justice; we make excuses. England stops our vessels with a provoking insolence; we are in a rage. This marked discrimination is not merited by the French. They may rob us; they may, as it is probable they will, cut off Tom Paine's head, vote out the Trinity, kill their priests, rob the merchants, and burn their Bibles;—we stand ready to approve all they do, and to approve more than they can do. This French mania is the bane of our politics, the mortal poison that makes our peace so sickly. It is incurable by any other remedy than time. I wish we may be able to bear the malady till the remedy shall overcome it. The English are absolutely madmen. Order in this country is endangered by their hostility, no less than by the French friendship. They act, on almost every point, against their interests and their real wishes. I hope and believe such extreme absurdity of conduct will be exposed with success. Should a special minister be sent from this country to demand reparation, much will depend on his character and address. Who but Hamilton would perfectly satisfy all our wishes? This idea, a very crude and unwarranted one to suggest, should be locked up in your bosom. I know not that such a thing will happen; I incline to wish it may. He is *ipse agmen*. Should it be carried into effect, the English merchants ought to rouse their London friends, and to exert their pen and ink powers, to explain the true situation of things in this country. In a word, I think you ought to help the two gentlemen mentioned in your letter to state the political mischiefs worked here by the *Jacobin* system the English pursue; that they Frenchify us; they do every thing they should not do; that they ought to raise their policy from the ground, where it now grovels, to the height from whence the statesman can see clearly and very far. I am full of a book on this subject. I wish I could make John Bull read it; such ideas, fully dilated, repeated, pressed, and diffused, would aid the extra messenger, and would help the cause of peace.

If John Bull is a blockhead, and puts himself on his pride to maintain what he has done, and should refuse reparation, it will, I think, be war.

In that case, I dread anarchy more than great guns. To guard against it, let us be careful how we form our plan of warfare. I consider two dangers as peculiarly attached to a state of war: the stoppage, disturbance, and diversion of industry from the productive to the destructive course; and the acrimony and delirium of popular passions by the efforts and disasters of the operations of war. Therefore, forbear all land expeditions, invasions of Canada, &c. Keep a force to repel and baffle invasions; thus the most possible will be produced, the least possible expended. Strain the revenue as much as prudence will warrant; support credit, and do every thing by the National Government, nothing by the States; and let individuals privateer. The whole energy of the war will be drawn off into the cold water; and while it acts there with the more effect, for not having our force occupied in any other way, it will not generate much fury at home. Thus it is, I hope, possible we may avoid anarchy, and prevent the extreme impoverishment of the country.

TO CHRISTOPHER GORE

PHILADELPHIA, MAY 2, 1794

MY DEAR SIR,

IT SEEMS to be well known to the public, that Sedgwick has affronted me, and that I have a proper sense of it. Conformably, therefore, to the expectation of my constituents—a rule for my whole conduct—I have challenged him, and the fellow will not fight me. What can I do, therefore? I am glad he will not.

To be serious, it is a strange fancy people have, to cut me out fighting work. Sedgwick's dispute, if it existed, was that which he so much enjoyed giving an account of at Breck's.

Yesterday, we had a squabble about a tax on the transfers of funded stock, and it was carried. Dexter took a wrong course. This distresses Hamilton exceedingly, and well it may; for, to begin to tax the public debt, when we are afraid to tax snuff, is a bad omen. I think the tax proposed is five cents on a hundred dollars transferred. I used my endeavors to show that a free transfer was a part of the terms; that a tax on the transfer was virtually levied on the possession, by diminishing the value, which is no more than the article will net on the sale; that a right, claimed and exercised, to draw back *ad libitum*, annihilates the debt, which exists in confidence; that the moral person who contracted will never become the legislator over the contract; and that, by doing so, instead of contributing a part for a common protection, the creditor loses all his property—the exaction of a part being annihilation to the residue. All which are familiar arguments to you.

But I took occasion to notice the falsity of the pamphlets, newspapers, and speeches, which say that paper influence moves Congress; for that, in truth, the Massachusetts members do not draw income enough merely from funded stock to buy the oats for the southern members' coach-horses. I had taken occasion to say that no one of the Massachusetts men keeps a coach, or is able to do it.

If any thing can justify this exculpatory speech, which, however, did not say a word about myself separately, it is the public utility of it, to arrest the activity of calumny against the government.

To notice these scoundrel handbills, &c., is humbling. To say nothing, when facts are so much on one's side, is more proud than wise.

The combat against excises on tobacco turned favorably. Madison spouted against excise, and in favor of land tax, hoping to prevent any thing, or to get only that voted which would raise enemies to the government. Taylor, of Virginia, says to King—"You are strange fellows: Formerly, you did what you chose with a small majority; now, we have a great majority, and can do nothing. You have baffled every one of our plans."

I wish he may prove a prophet. The resistance to wild projects has risen in its spirit and style, as hope declined. We have banged them as hard as we could, and they have been tamer than formerly.

Taylor said, also, that, though a minority, we had carried and were carrying all our measures, frigates, taxes, negotiation, &c.

We shall, I hope and earnestly pray, adjourn in three weeks. A bill prohibiting the sale of French prizes, passed by the Senate, lies before us. The irritation against England is yet strong, which keeps it back. Should it not pass, it will afford some pretext to urge against Mr. Jay in England. The embargo will not be continued again. So say most persons. I always thought it a measure of weakness; but of the many proposed, it was the least to be disapproved. Nothing would have been better still.

Yours, &c.

[P.S.] Dexter is a jewel of a fellow. He holds a bold language, and awes the Smileys and Gileses.

TO THOMAS DWIGHT

PHILADELPHIA, MAY 6, 1794

DEAR FRIEND,

I SHOULD suffer a fever of the hypo, as severe as the fever and ague, if I could persuade myself Congress would sit here till midsummer. But I think we shall adjourn in three weeks. The heat, weariness, a desire to disperse our mischief-makers, conspire to wind up the session.

It has been unusually painful and hazardous to peace and good order. My hopes are, however, that we shall escape the threatened danger, which will coincide with the interests and wishes of the people, and the sense of a majority of Congress. Such are the wishes of a majority of Congress, although a number have been duped into a support of measures tending to a war. The desperadoes desire war; and I think they would get the upper hand to manage a war. Whatever kindles popular passions into fury, gives strength to that faction. What fine topics for calumny would not a war furnish? A moderate or honest man could be stigmatized, mobbed, declared a suspected person, guillotined, and his property might be taken for public purposes. France might see her bloody exploits rivalled by her pupil, emulous of her glory.

War, without anarchy, is bad enough; but would it not also bring the extreme of confusion?

Federal men come from the northward to Congress with an opinion that government is as strong as thunder, and that by coaxing and going half way with certain southern members, they might be won. Both these opinions yield very soon to the evidence of their senses. They see government a puny thing, held up by great exertions and greater good luck, and assailed by a faction, who feel an inextinguishable animosity against any debt-compelling government, and whose importance sinks as that of equal laws rises.

Yesterday, the senators from Virginia moved for leave to bring in a bill to suspend that part of the treaty with Great Britain which relates to debts. Thus, murder, at last, is out. Norfolk and Baltimore perform heroic exploits in the tar and feathers line. Here, they only dismantled, by force, a schooner, which five British officers, prisoners on parole, had got leave to go to England in, having chartered her. These are violences worthy of Mohawks. Compared with New England, the multitude in these towns are but half civilized.

Will our Yankees like a war the better for being mobbed into it, and because, also, the south will not pay the British debts? Our people have paid; and will they pay, in the form of war, for their southern brethren? I do not know that passion is ever to be reasoned down; but other passions could be reasoned up to resist the prevailing one. I wish our newspapers were better filled with paragraphs and essays to unmask our Catilines.

A land tax is likely to be rejected, and the dislike to it will carry along indirect taxes. While war is an event to be provided against, the increase of revenue, by excise, is an important object.

Speak of me to friends as may suit the sentiments with which I am theirs and yours.

TO THOMAS DWIGHT

DEDHAM, JULY 3, 1794

MY DEAR FRIEND,

THE EVENTS which have occurred since we left Springfield
have not deserved a place in the history of the Nation or the
state. They are, nevertheless, worth relating to those whose
kind concern for the actors confers importance upon trivial
occurrences. After this formal *prœmium*, I proceed with my
work, without invoking any muse. Frances sits by me, so
much elated with the arrival of the long-expected new chaise,
that a spark of her spirits will be inspiration sufficient. It
was almost a shame to travel so fast as we did. Having taken
a hack, to suit the delicacy of our travellers, we did not
blush to reach Dedham on Saturday morning, unhurt by the
violent shower which overtook us on Thursday. . . . The
coolness of the weather, and the perfect convenience of our
vehicle, diminished the fatigue, and we are all very well.
On arriving, we consulted Dr. A. for John's cough; but before
it was convenient to administer medicine, he got well. This
would happen to most patients, probably, if they would give
nature fair play. Since his cold abated, the boy has been
very wonderful. His improvement in the imitative arts is so
great, that he shakes his head as his mother does. I hope
this is not an ominous forwardness. . . .

The politics of Dedham are interesting. Be it known, to
our friends at a distance, that the squash town is the capital
of Norfolk. A court-house is ordered, by the worshipful
sessions, (by a vote passed on Tuesday,) to be erected near
my territory, according to a plan which Mr. Bulfinch is to
be requested to draw. A jail is also to be built, which is a

comfort to us. I do not perceive that our folks are much elated with their new dignity, so that if our squash vines should in future bear pineapples, they will be surprised. The Supreme Court is to sit here in August, and then we shall have lessons and examples of good manners. I deal much in little things; and I confess I prefer them to the wrangling scenes of Congress, where meaner passions are often excited by meaner objects, and strut with a mock dignity that would be farce, if it did not menace us with tragedy. I do not read the Chronicle. Abuse is unread, and I hope unregarded. I am willing to keep politics out of my head, lest they should craze me. It requires little more than self-command to prefer domestic happiness to the furious contests of party, where a man has only to choose between the reproaches of his own mind and those of bankrupts and knaves. If I were still a single man, I might dread more than I actually do the sentence of the public, *stay at home.*

I shall go to-morrow to hear the oration, and to see the bustle of the Boston frolic. George Bliss will give you as good a preachment as any of the orators of the day. The season is a hopeful one. We have had fine showers.

.　.　.　.　.　.　.　.　.

Yours affectionately.

TO THOMAS DWIGHT

——————

JULY 24, 1794

.　.　.　.　.　.　.　.　.

I AM beginning to feel in earnest in building, and have lost all feeling to the Chronicle whip, till I see they have, in

Monday's, alluded to Colonel W., the Hampshire tory of 1775. Rascals, let him alone, and give me double beatings. His age, truly venerable by virtue and wisdom, ought not to be disturbed, because I stand in the way of others. I wish he may not notice the paragraph, for, stupid as it is, it might give him some pain. . . .

I know nothing of the state of parties further than that the bad are busy, and the good are, as usual, timid and indolent. Calumny is despised, and yet it has an effect. The Chronicle is a noted liar, and yet scandal is a treat to many who despise the vehicle. . . .

Yours, &c.

TO THOMAS DWIGHT

AUGUST 8, FRIDAY MORNING

DEAR FRIEND,

THE DEMOCRATIC CLUB[47] met lately in Faneuil Hall. This is bold, and every thing really shows the fixed purpose of their leaders to go desperate lengths. It is a pleasant thing for the yeomanry to see their own government taken out of

[47] *Among the forgotten follies of a past age, the attempt, in this country, to imitate the worst of all conceivable models, the Jacobin Club of Paris, was one of the most remarkable. Some details of the theatrical extravagances of the American imitations are given in the "Life of John Jay," (by his son William Jay, New York, 1833.) Nothing but their mischievous and dangerous character saved them from measureless contempt.* [S. AMES]

their hands, and themselves cipherized by a rabble formed into a club. Thus, Boston may play Paris, and rule the state.

I live out of the vortex of politics, and keep my mind more unengaged than I expected I could. I bud my trees with zeal; and as long as the Chronicle lets my plums and pears alone, I will not attempt to rescue my character. All *that* can injure, is not worth saving.

. . . .

Yours, &c.

TO THOMAS DWIGHT

BOSTON, SEPTEMBER 3, 1794

DEAR FRIEND,

I AM, with Frances and the child, S., and Miss H., at Mrs. Phillips's;—she is the mother of the Springfield tribe. F. and I and John have been to see Mr. Gore's palace, at Waltham. I do not expect to build a smarter one myself. But it will give you as warm a reception as any house can. I shall have a hall, and no entry through the house. To name it Springfield Hall is one step towards warming the house, and making it seem home-ish, before we get into it. If I cannot see my friends there, I would not wish to live there myself. F. goes in winter, as the swallows do, to a more genial climate, to wait till spring thaws the old nest. I have a wife and family during summer; but, as the birds do, I return in spring, and choose the same mate, and build again in the same nest. Do you lengthen your own family catalogue, as you do mine? I have not thought of counting my children by the dozen; but I shall arrange my house to hold as large a family as I may be blessed with. Yet you will observe that houses of the smallest size are usually twice as full of children as palaces. Our little boy requires more than one attendant, although he is the quietest soul in the world. How half a dozen little ones are kept out of the fire and water at the same time, I cannot see. I am at last more at ease in respect to the choice of the plan for my house than I expected to be. It will be larger than my first views, yet for plainness and even cheapness, it will not go far beyond them. . . .

I am concerned to hear of the sickness at New Haven. I hope it is not infectious, (I should say contagious.) If I should hear that character of the disease, I should have fears for Springfield.

The club is despised here by men of right heads. But it is not safe to make light of your enemy. They poison every spring; they whisper lies to every gale; they are everywhere, always acting like Old Nick and his imps. Such foes are to be feared as well as despised. They wait in silence for occasions, and when they occur, out they come and carry their points. They will be as busy as Macbeth's witches at the election, and all agree the event is very doubtful. On personal accounts, I cannot be called to hazard less;— perhaps by falling, to gain more; for, besides peace and quietness, I should, by being *out*, pass for one who is persecuted for doing my duty. If I should be rechosen, the same eagerness to criminate me, and much less to counteract it, might leave me on worse ground. The late crisis affords the best point of time to be off. Yet you are all well aware that a man cannot quit the party that will not quit him, without bringing reproach on his spirit and on his principles. By getting out, he becomes again a free agent. The Pittsburg rebellion cannot, I think, end badly for government, unless government flinches from its duty. It hastens faction to act, before it is ready for more than intrigue and plotting. Your papers should be kept right.

.   .   .   .

Yours, ever.

TO THOMAS DWIGHT

DEDHAM, SEPTEMBER 11, 1794

MY DEAR FRIEND,

I HAVE a string of affairs to *talk* about, with an exemplary diligence; not one, however, is in train of execution. To dig a cellar, prepare materials for building, and to adjust contracts, are jobs for which I am as ill qualified by inexperience as indolence. Yet they will overwhelm me if neglected, and my time is soon to be claimed for public duty. What immense sacrifices a patriot has to make! and what a bustle the candidates make for the chance!

Of late, the Chronicle seems to droop, and the party is said to be crestfallen on account of Mr. Jay's good reception. The chance of peace is even now such, that it would have been rashness to have lost it by war measures. Yet the chance, though promising, may turn against us. In that case, the event will, as usual, govern opinions; and the wise world will rail against the men of peace. Europe exhibits a scene of confusion and misery, which is contrasted more strongly by the state of America than that of any other part of the world. Yet though we are bystanders, and ought to be impartial, the passions of probably a majority have taken sides. Should the war last another year, I have the most serious apprehensions that the excessive partiality of our citizens for one of the fighting parties, will be played upon to dupe the nation into the whirlpool. How can the war last another season? how can it end? I can answer neither of these queries.

I wish to see you, to commune with you concerning politics and building—your canal, and my fruit trees. The latter are *pro tempore* my hobby-horse. My knife, for inoculating, is daily in my hands. I hope, at some future day, to enjoy the pleasure of giving my Springfield friends a variety of the best fruit. The prospect is not, I trust, a very remote one, as many of my trees are thrifty. Simple pleasures of this class are so long in progress, that I consider it proper to cultivate a taste which may not wear out faster than I do. I own, however, that I go on with too much ardor to expect to hold my wind to the end of the race.

. . . I think I have mentioned, in a former letter, that the honorable Supreme Court was to sit here in August. They did sit, and in tolerable good humor. Two days and a piece finished the business. The jurors could not but feel relief from the former burden of attending fifteen, sometimes thirty, days in Boston. I argued one cause, and thought I could be well satisfied to wear my law coat again, especially if the pockets should be properly lined; and it will not be the fault of the democratic club, if I do not cast off my political coat. Such strong ground may be taken against those clubs, that it ought not to be delayed. They were born in sin, the impure offspring of Genet. They are the few against the many; the sons of darkness (for their meetings are secret) against those of the light; and above all, it is a *town* cabal, attempting to rule the *country*. Some Hampshire ink should be shed against them. They are rather waning here. Yet their extinction is more to be wished than expected; and if they exist at all, it will be like a root of an extracted cancer, which will soon eat again and destroy. Any taint of that poison, left behind, will reinfect the seemingly cured body; therefore the knife should now be used to cut off the tubercles. I hate this metaphor, as I am unskilled in surgery. Plainly, then, I think it necessary they should be so written down, and utterly discredited, that they shall have less than *no* influence—by making influence against their disgraceful cabal. Soon the pilgrims travelling towards Mecca, for their election, will have to proceed on pease, boiled or unboiled, as fortune may direct. The democratic clubs will not neglect to support the only two faithful of the Massachusetts members.

Our little John is the best boy in the world, says the critical review of his mother, which proves that the best are noisy things. . . . . .

Your affectionate brother.

TO GEORGE RICHARDS MINOT

PHILADELPHIA, NOVEMBER 12, 1794

DEAR FRIEND,

REPORT SAYS that despatches are received from Mr. Jay, containing the best information respecting the progress of his mission; that although nothing is definitively settled, nothing meets with obstruction. The Secretary of State tells me that the British Government proceed fairly, candidly, and without affected delays. Young Bob Morris is arrived yesterday, and says a passenger (from London) is very confident despatches were actually sent to Lord Dorchester to give up the posts. This is not to be expected, in the progress of the business. I believe, however, that the prospect of peace brightens. Bob Morris left London the latter end of September. I write in haste, as the mail is near closing. The support of the wise and worthy, in my district, does me great honor, although I well know their support is given from higher motives than private or personal considerations. No quorum yet in the Senate.

Yours, truly.

[P.S.] Regards to friends in the club.

TO CHRISTOPHER GORE

PHILADELPHIA, NOVEMBER 18, 1794

MY DEAR FRIEND,

.   .   .   .

SEDGWICK IS COME; and we have hopes of having anti-federalism weeded quite out of the Massachusetts corps, as the prospect of excluding Lyman and Dearborn is much relied on, as well as of the election of good men in the other districts. We know little of the state of facts at present, further than my district. Lyman looks woebegone.

Dallas has returned from the army, sounding the praises of the Secretary. Strange! But what is stranger, he has penned a paragraph in Brown's Gazette, of the same tenor. So say the conjurors. Is it to win character, by joining a prosperous cause, now that the Genet and anarchy side is weak and disgraceful? He is said to have fallen out with the Governor, whose daily libations have drowned his discretion, and let him down in the opinion of the army. It proves D.'s principles, and the preponderance of the good cause.

To-morrow the speech is to be delivered in our House, as the Senate chamber is thought to be dangerous for the crowd to overload. Mr. Burr arrived, and made a quorum this day. Faction seems to languish. The storm was dreadful formerly; now the calm is stupid. I hear of no bad schemes; but there is no trust in appearances.

You men of Boston deserve a good government, for you show you will support it. Here the supine good men let Swanwich[48] get a nominal majority, which will be contested. Never was more open influence, nor more corrupt, as his opposers say.

It would gratify the well disposed in Boston to learn how generally and anxiously their exertions were regarded from hence, and from every other quarter. The great man certainly was not indifferent—not because my *personal* weight was much, but the party battle was to prove that *he* had or had not the support of that part, and, by its influence, of the other parts of the eastern states. His own system of negotiation was in trial.

I lately saw Toby Lear, who is not cured of attachment to some errors. L. Lincoln is said to be wrong, also, in some leading principles—a good and able man. It would be unfortunate he should go wrong, if chosen.

The federal prospect is thought, by our friends, to be brightening daily; peace is more and more to be relied on.

Yours, truly.

---

[48] *Of Philadelphia.* [S. AMES]

DEBATE OVER THE PROPRIETY OF REPLIES
TO THE PRESIDENT'S SPEECHES

President Washington's speech to the second session of the Third Congress stirred up heated debate in the House on two important subjects, the public debt and political opposition. The President had denounced the "self-created" Democratic societies for fomenting the Whiskey Rebellion in Pennsylvania. When the committee responsible for preparing a reply to the speech omitted all reference to the President's comments, House Federalists objected. The Federalists proposed to amend the reply by inserting a paragraph in support of the President's comments. In his speech, Ames defended the President's statements.

NOVEMBER 26, 1794

Mr. SCOTT and Mr. AMES were both up at the same time. The latter gentleman immediately sat down.

Mr. AMES began with expressing his pleasure that he had sat down to give way to Mr. SCOTT to speak; but this every one must see was attended with a personal sacrifice: and it was manifestly a disadvantage to bring forward his observations immediately after those of that gentleman, because they were too remarkable for their pertinence and strength to encourage the attempts of their opponents to invalidate, or his own to enforce them.

He requested Mr. GILES, and he urged it strongly on the House, to consider maturely how large a part of the argument he had to answer. Mr. GILES had been occupied in refuting what nobody had asserted, and in proving what nobody had denied. It would appear to every person, at a glance, that, after so large a deduction should be made, the advocate of the amendment would be left almost without an adversary.

He observed, it would be amusing, and not without its uses, to turn a moment from the debate, to inquire what would be said of yesterday's decision. Fame already bears it on all her wings, and proclaims it with all her tongues, that Congress has been engaged in trying the Democratic clubs; and curiosity stands a tiptoe on all our Post Roads for the answer, which is already gone forth. Forty-seven members were for the clubs, and forty-five against them, so that the clubs gained the victory.

Is this true? I dare appeal, (said Mr. AMES,) to you, sir, and to every other patriotic bosom, that it is *not true;* a large majority, and I may even say, with pride and pleasure, almost *all* the members who hear me, despise and abominate the clubs as sincerely as the words of the PRESIDENT's Speech, the answer of the Senate, his reply to them, or the amendment now before us can imply it.

How happens it, that the real sentiments of the House are so much misrepresented by the vote? I shall be pardoned if I undertake to explain this enigma. Two reasons have been suggested in private conversation, as well as in debate, which will account for the vote of yesterday, and which, on being stated and re-examined, will afford good cause for changing it to-day. The first is, that we have nothing to do with the clubs. We hold them in too much contempt to have anything to say to them, or about them. They are not worth notice. This contempt had the appearance yesterday of countenance and patronage.

The other motive suggested is, if the words self-created societies should be struck out, the amendment will still contain the substance of the proposition contended for; which is to reprobate the combinations of men against law. This description will include the clubs, as well as any other wicked combinations that have had any agency in the insurrection.

How far the one or the other of these motives ought to influence those who have entertained them to vote against the amendment for inserting the words "self-created societies and," will appear by a survey of the true posture of the question.

Here Mr. AMES stated, that it was the duty of the PRESIDENT, by the Constitution, to inform Congress of the state of the Union. That he had accordingly in his Speech stated the insurrection and the causes which (he thought) had brought it on. Among them, he explicitly reckons the self-created societies and combinations of men to be one. The Senate as plainly charge that as one of the causes. The PRESIDENT, in his reply to the Senate, expresses his high satisfaction that they concur with him in opinion. Here Mr. A. read the passages in the Speech, Address, and Answer to the Address. He said further, that an amendment was now offered to the House, expressed, as nearly as may be, in the very words of the PRESIDENT; an objection is urged against this amendment that the proposition contained in it is not true in fact. It is also said, that although it were true, it would be dangerous to liberty to assent to it in our Answer to the Speech. It is moreover, say they, improper, unnecessary, and indecent, to mention the self-created societies. The amendment now urged upon the House has been put to vote in the Committee of the Whole House, and rejected. What will the world say, and that too from the evidence of our own records, if we reject it again in the House? Will it not be proclaimed that we reject the motion and give force and validity to the objections? Do we adopt such objections? Are the Committee consenting to the shame of having them charged upon the Committee as the principles by which they have guided our decision? We are not, Mr. A. was sure we are not; for with a very few exceptions—I wish there were none—both sides have united in reprobating the self-created societies. Surely, then, gentlemen will not hesitate to rescind a vote which is not less deceptive than it is pernicious? For, if we adopt the amendment, it will appear that all the branches of the Government are agreed in sentiment. If we reject it, what will it proclaim less than imbecility and discord? What will faction interpret it to import short of this? "The PRESIDENT and Senate have denounced the self-created societies alluded to in the Speech, and this House has stepped forward for their protection." Besides the unspeakable dishonor of this patronage, is it not rekindling the fire-brands of sedition? is it not unchaining the demon of anarchy?

Few as the apologists of the clubs have been, the solemnity and perseverance of their appeal to principles, demand for it an examination.

The right to form political clubs has been urged, as if it had been denied. It is not, however, the right to meet, it is the abuse of the right after they have met, that is charged upon them. Town meetings are authorized by law, yet they may be called for seditious or treasonable purposes. The legal right of the voters in that case would be an aggravation, not an excuse, for the offence. But if persons meet in a club with an intent to obstruct the laws, their meeting is no longer innocent or legal; it is a crime.

The necessity for forming clubs has been alleged with some plausibility in favor of all the states, except New England, because town meetings are little known, and not practicable in a thinly settled country. But if people have grievances, are they to be brought to a knowledge of them only by clubs? Clubs may find out more complaints against the laws than the sufferers themselves had dreamed of. The number of those which a man will learn from his own and his neighbor's experience will be quite sufficient for every salutary purpose of reform in the laws, or of relief to the citizens. He may petition Congress, his own representative may not fail to advocate, or, at least, to present and explain his memorial. As a juror, he applies the law; as an elector, he effectually controls the legislators. A really aggrieved man will be sure of sympathy and assistance within this body, and with the public. The most zealous advocate of clubs may think them useful, but he will not insist on their being indispensably so.

The plea for their usefulness seems to rest on their advantage of meeting for political information. The absurdity of this pretence could be exposed in a variety of views. I shall decline (said Mr. A.) a detailed consideration of the topic. I would just ask, however, whether the most inflamed party men, who usually lead the clubs, are the best organs of authentic information? Whether they meet in darkness; whether they hide their names, their numbers, and their doings; whether they shut their doors to admit information?

A laudable zeal for inquiry need not shun those who could satisfy it; it need not blush in the daylight. With open doors and an unlimited freedom of debate, political knowledge might be introduced even among the intruders.

But, instead of exposing their affected pursuit of information, it will be enough to show hereafter what they actually spread among the people—whether it is information, or, in the words of the PRESIDENT, "jealousies, suspicions, and accusations of the Government:" whether, disregarding the truth, they have not fomented the daring outrages against the social order and the authority of the laws. (*Vide* the PRESIDENT'S Speech.)

They have arrogantly pretended sometimes to be the people, and sometimes the guardians, the champions of the people. They affect to feel more zeal for a popular government, and to enforce more respect for republican principles, than the real representatives are admitted to entertain. Let us see whether they are set up for the people, or in opposition to them, and their institutions.

Will any reflecting person suppose, for a moment, that

this great people, so widely extended, so actively employed, could form a common will and make that will law in their individual capacity, and without representation? They could not. Will clubs avail them as a substitute for representation? A few hundred persons only are members of clubs, and if they should act for the others, it would be an usurpation, and the power of the few over the many, in every view infinitely worse than sedition itself, will represent this government.

To avoid this difficulty, shall the whole people be classed into clubs? Shall every six miles square be formed into a club sovereignty? Thus we should guard against the abuse of trust, because we should delegate none, but every man might go and do his business in his own person. We might thus form ten or twenty thousand democracies, as pure and simple as the most disorganizing spirit could sigh for; but what could keep this fair horizon unclouded? What could prevent the whirlwinds and fires of discord, intestine and foreign, from scattering and consuming these fritters and rags of the society, like the dry leaves in autumn? Without respectability, without safety, without tranquility, they would be like so many caves of Æolus, where the imprisoned storms were said to struggle for a vent. If we look at Greece, so famed for letters and more for misery, we shall see their ferocious liberty made their petty commonwealth wolves' dens—that liberty, which poetry represents as a goddess, history describes as a cannibal.

Representative government, therefore, is so far from being a sacrifice of our rights, that it is their security; it is the only practicable mode for a great people to exercise or have any rights. It puts them into full possession of the utmost exercise of them. By clubs will they have something more than all? Will such institutions operate to augment, to secure, or to enforce their rights, or just the contrary?

Knowledge and truth will be friendly to such a government, and that in return will be friendly to them. Is it possible for any to be so deluded as to suppose that the over-zeal for government, on the part of the supporters of this amendment, would prompt them to desire or to attempt the obstruction of the liberty of speech, or the genuine freedom of the press? Impossible! That would be putting out the eyes of the government which we are so jealous to maintain. The abuses of these privileges may embarrass and disturb our present system; but, if they were abolished, the government must be changed. No friend, therefore, of the Constitution could harbor the wish to produce the consequences which it is insinuated are intended to ensue. Mr. A. resumed the remark that the government rests on the enlightened patriotism of an orderly and moral body of citizens. Let the advocates of monarchy boast that ignorance may be made to sleep in chains; that even corruption and vice may be enlisted as auxiliaries of the public order. It is, however, a subject of exultation and confidence that such citizens as we represent, so enlightened, so generally virtuous and uncorrupted, under the present mild republican system, practically are safe, nay, more, it is evidently the only system that is adapted to the American state of society. But such a system combines within itself two indestructible elements of destruction, two enemies with whom it must conflict forever; whom it may disarm, but can never pacify—vice and ignorance. Those who do not understand their rights, will despise or confound them with wrongs, and those whose turbulence and licentiousness find restraints in equal laws, will seek gratification by evasions of combinations to overawe or resist them.

A government that protects property, and cherishes virtue, will of course have vice and prodigality for its foes, because it will be compelled to abridge their liberty to prevent their invading the rights of other citizens. The virtuous and the enlightened will cling to a republican government, because it is congenial no less with their feelings than their rights. The licentious and the profligate are ever ready for confusion, which might give them every thing, while laws and order deny them every thing. The ambitious and desperate, by combinations, acquire more power and influence than their fellow-citizens; the credulous, the ignorant, the rash, and violent, are drawn by artifice, or led by character, to join these confederacies. The more free the government, the more certain they are to grow up, for where there is no liberty at all, this abuse of it will not be seen. Once formed into bodies they have an *esprit du corps*, and are propelled into errors and excesses, without shame or reflection. A spirit grows up in their progress, and every disappointment makes them more loose, as to the means, and every success more and more immoderate in the objects of their attempt. Calumny is one of those means. Those whom they cannot punish or control, they can vilify; they can make suspicion go where their force could not reach, and by rumors and falsehoods multiply enemies against their enemies. They become formidable, and they retaliate upon the magistrates those fears which the laws have inspired them with. The execution of the laws is not accomplished without effort, without hazard. Instead of mildness, of mutual confidence, instead of the laws almost executing themelves, more rigor is demanded in the framing, more force to secure the operation of the laws. The clubs and turbulent combinations exercising the resisting power, it is obvious that government will need more force, and more will then be given to it.

Thus it appears, that instead of lightening the weight of authority, it will require a new *momentum* from clubs and combinations formed to resist it. Turbulent men, embodied into hosts, will call for more energy to suppress them than if the discontented remained unembodied. Disturbances, fomented from time to time, may unhappily change the mild principles of the system, and the little finger then may be found heavier than the whole hand of the present government. For if the clubs and the government should both subsist, tranquility would be out of the question. The continual contest of one organized body against another would produce the alternate extremes of anarchy and excessive rigor of government. If the clubs prevail, they will be the government, and the more secure for having become so by a victory over the existing authorities.

In every aspect of the discussion, the societies formed to control and vilify a republican government are hateful. They not only of necessity make it more rigorous, but they tend with a fatal energy to make it corrupt. By perverting the truth and spreading jealousy and intrigue through the land, they compel the rulers to depend on new supports. The usurping clubs offer to faction within these doors the means of carrying every point without. A corrupt understanding is produced between them. The power of the clubs will prevail even here, and that of the people will proportionally decline. The clubs echo the language of their protectors here; truth, virtue, and patriotism, are no longer principles, but names for electioneering jugglers to deceive with. Calumny will assimilate to itself the objects it falls on. It will persecute the man who does his duty; it will take away the reward of virtue, and bestow praise only upon the tools of faction. By betraying his trust, a man may then expect the support of the powerful combinations opposed to the government. By faithfully adhering to it, he encounters persecution. He finds neither refuge nor consolation with the public, who become at length so corrupted as to think virtue in a public station incredible, because it would be, in their opinion, folly. The indiscriminate jealousy which is diffused from the clubs tends no less to corrupt the suspicious than the suspected. It poisons confidence, which is no less the incitement than the recompense of public services. It lowers the standard of action.

These observations, which seem to be founded on theory, unfortunately bear the stamp of experience. History abounds with the proofs. Never was there a wise and free republic, which was exempt from this inveterate malady. We can find a parallel for the brightest worthies of Greece, as well as for their calumniators. In that country, as well as in this, the assassins of character abounded. While slander is credited only by its inventors, it is easy for a man to maintain the serenity of his contempt for both. But when it is adopted by the public, few are hardy enough to despise opinion; he that pretends to do so is a hypocrite, and if he really does so, he is a wretch. This precious property is one of the first objects of invasion, and the combinations alluded to are well adapted and actively employed to destroy it.

It is a plausible opinion, that if the government is not grossly defective in its form, or corrupt in its administration, animosities against it will not exist. This corresponds neither with sound sense nor experience. Equal laws are the very grievances of these petty tyrants, who combine together to engross more than equal power and privileges. When power is conferred exclusively upon the worthy, the profligate and ambitious are driven to despair of success, by any methods that the worthy would adopt. The more pure and free the government, the more certainly will the worst men it protects and restrains become its implacable enemies, and such men have ever been the foes of republics. The outcasts from society, those who singly are shunned because infamy has smitten them with leprosy, men who are scored with worse than plague sores, are the first to combine against it. And such men have the front to preach purity of principles and reformation. Such men will meet in darkness and perform incantations against liberty—there they will gather to medicate their poisons, to whet their daggers, to utter their blasphemies against liberty, and may proceed again to shout from that gallery, or may collect with cannon at this door, to perpetrate sacrilege here in her very sanctuary.

It will be asked what remedy for this evil? I answer no violent one. The gentle power of opinion, I flatter myself, will prove sufficient among our citizens who have sense, morals, and property. The hypocrisy of the clubs will be unmasked, and the public scorn, without touching their persons or property, will frown them into nothing.

Mr. A. next proceeded to advert more particularly to facts. He made mention of the Jesuits, who were banished for becoming a club against the European governments. He mentioned the Jacobins also, who performed well in pulling down the old government, but because they would continue pulling down the new one, as such clubs ever will, had their hall locked up by *Legendre*. Our committees in 1774 and 1775, were efficient instruments to pull down the British Government. Yet, although they were friendly to our own, the people laid them aside as soon as they wished to build up instead of pulling down. If our government were to be demolished, clubs would be a powerful means of doing it, and the people may choose to countenance them at that time. But as they choose no such thing at present, they will discountenance them. The Cincinnati were personally worthy men, officers of the most deserving army that ever triumphed. Yet, although they were friendly to the government, and possessed the confidence of the citizens by the most brilliant titles, the nature of their institution raised a jealousy and ferment. The state legislatures condemned it, as setting up a government within the government. What then are we to say of clubs? Facts have been rather imprudently called for, and let them be examined.

The Democratic Society of Vermont state, as one reason for their establishment, the unmerited abuse with which the public papers have so often teemed against the Minister of our only ally. This was long after *Genet's* whole correspondence had been published, and after France had unequivocally disapproved his conduct.

Agreeably to a previous notification, there met at Pittsburg, on the 21st of August, a number of persons, styling themselves "A Meeting of sundry Inhabitants of the Western Counties of Pennsylvania."

This meeting entered into resolutions not less exceptionable than those of its predecessors. The preamble suggests that a tax on spirituous liquors is unjust in itself and oppressive upon the poor, that internal taxes upon consumption must in the end destroy the liberties of the country in which they are introduced; that the law in question, from certain local circumstances which are specified, would bring immediate distress and ruin upon the Western country; and concludes with the sentiment, that they think it their duty to persist in remonstrances to Congress; and in every other legal measure that may obstruct the operation of the law.

The resolutions then proceed, first, to appoint a committee to prepare and cause to be presented to Congress an Address, stating objections to the law, and praying for its repeal. Secondly, to appoint committees of correspondence for Washington, Fayette, and Alleghany, charged to correspond together, and with such committees as should be appointed for the same purpose in the county of Westmoreland, or with any committees of a similar nature, that might be appointed in other parts of the United States; and, also, if found necessary, to call together either general meetings of the people, in their respective counties, or conferences of the several committees; and, lastly, to declare that they will in future consider those who hold offices for the collection of the duty, as unworthy of their friendship, that they will have no intercourse nor dealings with them, will withdraw from them every assistance, withhold all the comforts of life which depend upon those duties, that as men and fellow-citizens we owe to each other, and will upon all occasions treat them with contempt; earnestly recommending it to the people at large, to follow the same line of conduct towards them.

He mentioned the shameful transaction at Lexington, in Kentucky, where Mr. Jay was burned in effigy. It was painful, he said, thus to dwell on the dishonor of the country, but it was already published.

The club of Charleston, South Carolina, solicited an adoption of the Jacobin club at Paris. They also addressed Consul Margourit, who had actually granted commissions to privateers, in defiance of the PRESIDENT'S Proclamation of Neutrality.

The club of Pinckney District in Carolina voted in favor of war and against paying taxes, because they were too far from the market.

A Virginia club had voted an alteration in the Constitution, in order that an amendment might prevent the PRESIDENT being again eligible. Is proof necessary to those who remember the state of this city last spring? Are the resolves of the clubs of this place and New York forgotten? Could outrage and audacity be expected to venture further? One condemned the excise as odious and tyrannical; the other, enforcing that sentiment, published its condemnation of Mr. Jay's mission of peace. Did not all of them arraign the whole government, reprobate the whole system of laws, charge the breach of the Constitution on the PRESIDENT, and unspeakable turpitude on the Administation, as well as on this body? Surely Americans, feeling as they ought, for the honor and peace and safety of their country, cannot forget these excesses; they cannot remember them in any manner which my reprobation could enforce.

The following is an extract from the proceedings of a meeting of Delegates from the Election Districts of Alleghany county, held at Pittsburg, April 10, 1794, *Thomas Morton* in the Chair:

"At this juncture we have France to assist us, who, should we now take a part, will not fail to stand by us until Canada is independent of Britain, and the instigators of Indian hostilities are removed; and should we lie by, while France is struggling for her liberties, it cannot be supposed that her Republic will embark in a war on our account after she shall have been victorious. It was for this reason, that though we approved of the conduct of the President and the Judiciary of the United States, in their endeavors to preserve peace and an impartial neutrality, until the sense of the nation had been taken on the necessity of retaliation by actually declaring war, yet now that the Congress have been convened, and such just grounds exist, we are weary of their tardiness in coming forward to measures of reprisal.

"But we have observed with great pain, that our councils want the integrity or spirit of Republicans. This we attribute to the pernicious influence of stockholders or their subordinates; and our minds feel this with so much indignancy, that we are almost ready to wish for a state of revolution, and the guillotine of France, for a short space, in order to inflict punishment on the miscreants that enervate and disgrace our Government."

If the black charges thus brought against Congress and the whole government were true, the people ought to fly to arms. They ought to pull down this tower of iniquity so as not to leave one stone upon another. The deluded western people believed them true, and acted accordingly. The great mass of the discontented, therefore, are to be pitied for the ignorance and credulity which made them the dupes of the clubs. They thought they were doing God and their country service by cleansing this Augean stable of its filth. It was not oppression that roused them to arms, as some would insinuate; for their country flourishes wonderfully. It was an insurrection raised by the wicked arts of faction.

A moment, however, is due to the peculiar falsity of two of the slanders on this body. The fears of simple citizens have been startled with the fable, that there is a monarchy party in this House and the other. Look around, sir, said Mr. A., if you please, and decide whether there is one man, who is not principled as a republican, who does not think such a form adapted to our people, and our people to it; and who would not shed his blood and spend his last shilling against the introduction of monarchy? I persuade myself, sir, there is not even one man here whom any other member even thinks in his heart is to be suspected on that head.

The other slander which has contributed to kindle a civil war, is the *paper nobility* in Congress; that the taxes are voted for the sake, and carried solely by the strength of those who put the proceeds in their pockets. Is there a word of truth in this? On the contrary, there are probably not ten members who have *any* interest in the funds, and that interest very inconsiderable. Citizens have thus been led by calumny and lies to despise their government and its ministers, to dread and to hate it, and all concerned in it, so that the insurrection is chiefly owing to the men and the societies, who have invented, or confirmed, and diffused these slanders.

The fact is too notorious for any man even to pretend ignorance, that the insurgents were encouraged to take arms by the delusive hope that the militia would not turn out against them. Had they believed that the citizens were as firm for government, as to their immortal honor they have shown that they are, would the folly or desperation of the western people have proceeded to arms? They would not.

But the self-made societies had published that the rulers were tyrants, usurpers, and plunderers, abhorred by the people, who would soon hurl them down. Let us ask a moment's pause to reflect what would have been the fate of

America, if these parricide clubs had really proceeded in poisoning the public mind, as completely as they attempted to do. The western insurgents would have found armies not to suppress, but to assist them. This fair Edifice of Liberty, the palladium of our country, the world's hope, would have crumbled to powder.

Mr. A. then proceeded to notice some of the observations which had been urged against the motion. He asked whether, in a point that so nearly concerned truth and duty, the Committee could conciliate, that is, deny the truth and betray their duty. The proposition stated by the PRESIDENT was true, and had been proved to be so. Shall our silence suppress or contradict the dictates of this conviction?

It is urged that we have no right to pass this vote; a singular objection, since those who make it are consenting to the adoption of the clause, to which the words self-created societies are moved to be added. That clause is as improper, and as unconstitutional a declaration as the amendment. Is it possible that those are serious in this objection, who voted applause to General Wayne and his gallant army? Is this House a court-martial to try them if they had done ill instead of well? Had the state legislatures no right to pass votes respecting the Cincinnati? Then we have no right to answer the speech at all, as the Constitution is silent on that head. But are gentlemen who profess so much attachment to the people, and their rights, disposed to abolish one of the most signal, the character of this House as the grand inquest of the nation, as those who are not only to impeach those who perpetrate offence, but to watch and give the alarm for the prevention of such attempts?

We are asked, with some pathos, will you punish clubs, with your censure, unheard, untried, confounding the innocent with the guilty? Censure is not punishment, unless it is merited, for we merely allude to certain self-created societies, which have disregarded the truth, and fomented the outrages against the laws. Those which have been innocent will remain uncensured. It is said, worthy men belong to those clubs. They may be as men not wanting in merit, but when they join societies which are employed to foment outrages against the laws, they are no longer innocent. They become bad citizens. If innocence happens to stray into such company, it is lost. The men really good will quit such connexions, and it is a fact, that the most respected of those who were said to belong to them, have long ago renounced them. Honest, credulous men may be drawn in to favor very bad designs, but so far as they do it, they deserve the reproach which this vote contains, that of being unworthy citizens.

If the worst men in society have led the most credulous and inconsiderate astray, the latter will undoubtedly come to reflection the sooner for an appeal to their sense of duty. This appeal is made in terms which truth justifies, and which apply only to those who have been criminal.

It is said, that this vote will raise up the clubs into importance. One member has even solemnly warned us against the awakening of their resentments. It is not clear to my understanding, (said Mr. A.) how all the consequences which have been predicted from this vote will be accomplished. This is a breach of right, a crushing of those free societies by our censure. It is putting them down, and yet we are warned that it is raising them up and making them stronger than this government. The friends of the motion are said not to agree in the principle of their defence of it, and therefore it is boldly affirmed that they have no principle. Is there any difficulty in retorting this invective? If this vote will call the attention of the people of America to this subject, so much the better. The truth will no doubt be sought and found at last, and with such an enlightened public, I expect the result will be made with its usual good sense. That the self-created societies described in the clause, are calculated to destroy a free government; that they will certainly destroy its tranquility and harmony, and greatly corrupt the integrity of the rulers, and the morals of the people.

In the course of his remarks, Mr. A. strongly insisted that the vote was not indefinite in its terms. Societies were not reprobated because they were self-made, nor because they were political societies. Everybody as readily admitted that they might be innocent, as they have been generally imprudent. It is such societies as have been generally imprudent. It is such societies as have been regardless of the truth, and have fomented the outrages against the law, &c.

Nor is the intention of this amendment to flatter the PRESIDENT, as it has been intimated. He surely has little need of our praise on any personal account. This late signal act of duty is already with his grateful country, with faithful history: nor is it in our power, or in those of any offended self-created societies, to impair that tribute which will be offered to him. As little ground is there for saying that it is intended to stifle the freedom of speech and of the press. The question is, simply, will you support your chief magistrate? Our vote does not go merely to one man and to his feelings. It goes to the trust. When clubs are arrayed against your government, and your chief magistrate decidedly arrays the militia to suppress their insurrection, will you countenance or discountenance the officer? Will you ever suffer this House, the country, or even one seditious man in it, to question for an instant, whether your approbation and cooperation will be less prompt and cordial than his efforts to support the laws? Is it safe, is it honorable, to make a precedent, and that no less solemn than humiliating, which will authorize, which will compel every future president to doubt whether you will approve him or the clubs? The PRESIDENT now in office would doubtless do his duty promptly and with decision in such a case. But, can you expect it of human nature? and if you could, would you put it at risk whether in future a president shall balance between his duty and his fear of your censure. The danger is, that a chief magistrate, elective as ours is, will temporize, will delay, will put the laws into treaty with offenders, and will even insure a civil war, perhaps the loss of our free government, by the want of proper energy to quench the first sparks. You ought, therefore, on every occasion, to show the most cordial support to the executive in support of the laws.

This is the occasion. If it is dangerous to liberty, against right and justice, against truth and decency, to adopt the amendment, as it has been argued, then the PRESIDENT and Senate have done all this.

Mr. A. concluded with saying, that in a speech so long, containing such various matter, and so rapidly delivered, he might have dropped many observations in an incorrect state. He relied on the candor of the House, and of his opponents, for the interpretation of them.

The House now adjourned without taking any question.

DECEMBER 15, 1796

MR. AMES said, if any man were to call himself more free and enlightened than his fellows, it would be considered as arrogant self-praise. His very declaration would prove that he wanted sense as well as modesty, but a nation might be called so, by a citizen of that nation, without impropriety; because, in doing so, he bestows no praise of superiority on himself; he may be in fact, and may be sensible that he is less enlightened than the wise of other nations. This sort of national eulogium may, no doubt, be fostered by vanity and grounded in mistake; it is sometimes just, it is certainly common, and not always either ridiculous or offensive. It did not say that France or England had not been remarkable for enlightened men; their literati are more numerous and distinguished than our own. The character, with respect to this country, he said, was strictly true. Our countrymen, almost universally, possess some property and some pretensions of learning—two distinctions so remarkably in their favor as to vindicate the expression objected to. But go through France, Germany, and most countries of Europe, and it will be found that, out of fifty millions of people, not more than two or three had any pretensions to knowledge, the rest being, comparatively with Americans, ignorant. In France, which contains twenty-five millions of people, only one was calculated to be in any respect enlightened, and, perhaps, under the old system, there was not a greater proportion possessed property; whilst in America, out of four millions of people, scarcely any part of them could be classed upon the same ground with the rabble of Europe. That class called vulgar, canaille, rabble, so numerous there, does not exist here as a class, though our towns have many individuals of it. Look at the lazaroni of Naples; there are twenty thousand or more houseless people, wretched, and in want! He asked whether, where men wanted everything, and were in proportion of 29 to 1, it was possible they could be trusted with power? Wanting wisdom and morals, how would they use it? It was, therefore, that the iron hand of despotism was called in by the few who had anything, to preserve any kind of control over the many. This evil, as it truly was, and which he did not propose to commend, rendered true liberty hopeless. In America, out of four millions of people, the proportion which cannot read and write, and who, having nothing, are interested in plunder and confusion, and disposed for both, is small. In the Southern States, he knew there were people well-informed; he disclaimed all design of invidious comparison; the members from the South would be more capable of doing justice to their constituents, but in the Eastern States he was more particularly conversant, and knew the people in them could generally read and write, and were well-informed as to public affairs. In such a country, liberty is likely to be permanent. They are enlightened enough to be free. It is possible to plant it in such a soil, and reasonable to hope that it will take root and flourish long, as we see it does. But can liberty, such as we understand and enjoy, exist in societies where the few only have property, and the many are both ignorant and licentious?

Was there any impropriety, then, in saying what was a fact? As it respects government, the declaration is useful. It is respectful to the people to speak of them with the justice due to them, as eminently formed for liberty, and worthy of it. The gentleman from Virginia, [Mr. GILES,] on a former occasion, had said he adored the people; but now, when there was a wish to pronounce the attributes of his divinity, he was not found more fervent in his adoration than many who had made no such profession. If they are free and enlightened, let us say so; if they are not, he should no longer adore them; they would not certainly be worthy of honors quite divine. Mr. A. said they ought not only resay this, because it was true, but because their saying so would have the effect to produce that self-respect which was the best guard of liberty, and most conducive to the happiness of society. It was useful to show where our hopes and the true safety of our freedom are reposed. It cherished in return from the citizens a just confidence, a spirit of patriotism unmixed with foreign alloy, and the courage to defend a Constitution that a people really enlightened knows to be worthy of its efforts.

If the words were objectionable, it would be easy to alter them to avoid the objection without impairing essentially their force. A gentleman near him had suggested the propriety of saying we were "among the freest and most enlightened." He had no objection to the alteration, though he saw no reason for altering the phraseology, but he was willing to compromise with gentlemen, it not being essential. The citizens of a free government ought, he said, to believe they were the most free and enlightened, because, having the power of making the government what they please, if it was not the best, it would be their own fault for not making it so.

He believed the House would not be surprised if he took notice of what had been said in allusion to him in the course of the debate—allusions with which he could not be offended, because they were urged with so many expressions of the most flattering civility. But every gentleman would believe those things were not applicable to him, as their recollections would not fail to prove. What had been his language with respect to Britain? Did he say we were to submit? Did he say we were to defend our country? Was he then afraid as they were now, that soft words would not be soft enough? No; such language came not from him. Do nothing to irritate; wage no war; no hostility. Such, he called sequestration, and other acts of that nature. We were, he said, about to make war on British property, and such would have been considered a kind of minor war. He, therefore, wished to shut up ourselves in our shell like a tortoise. But, at the same time, he recommended troops to be raised, ships to be built, taxes to be laid, and a spirited claim of justice to be urged. The gentlemen who wished at that time particularly to preserve peace, did not wish to hold out the olive-branch alone, by leaving the country defenceless. This many of their opposers absolutely did. These, he said, were their reasons, and they had been effectual. He would not go into an examination of the subject now. It was their wish to urge every exertion of the country, to have strained its faculties till they were ready to crack, and to have called forth the last dollar and the last man in defence of the country in case of necessity. Did this look as if they wished to truckle to Great Britain? Many of their opposers, so zealous then for retaliation and reprisal, were not for anything else—neither troops, ships, taxes, nor Treaty. This the yeas and nays on the Journals will establish. Will the opposers show half the spirit now that we felt and expressed at that day?

How happened it, he asked, that gentlemen were so angry because they had then heard the language of peace; and now, because the same language was heard? Not one of us desire hostility. Was it because Great Britain was then the object and France now? Wrongs from the former cannot be resented enough; and wrongs and insult, too, from the latter, require words of more ardor than a lover's. No man felt more for the wrongs of America than he did. He felt for the loss of ships and property; and more, that our seamen had so suffered. On no occasion had a drop of blood pressed through his heart more quickly than at their painful misfortunes. But, was it not the part of dignity and prudence to endeavor to obtain restitution for those wrongs rather than take up arms? Was it suited to national dignity to make use of the language that had been used on that occasion by many of his opposers? He thought both national and personal dignity forbade it; he had thought it equally intemperate and unbecoming.

Did not gentlemen seem to feel more for one individual than for an insult on the whole nation and its government? The Administration might suffer contumely and abuse, and the country, too, without producing any emotions in the breasts of gentlemen; their feelings seem to take quite another direction. If the British Minister should outrage our government, as the Minister of France had done, every one would be for avenging the wrong. He thought it right that they should now declare their determination of supporting the executive in supporting our national honor and dignity, or let him see in season that he was to be abandoned.

The gentleman from South Carolina [Mr. HARPER] had justly said, that though we had no navy to support our pretensions, we had come off better than Sweden or Denmark—countries which had been produced as patterns of wisdom. Though he did not suppose the British Treaty would be carried into effect, so as to satisfy every person who had suffered in his property by the British, yet he trusted the event would prove, in a considerable degree, satisfactory. He wished all other depredations on our commerce might be in the end as nearly compensated.

At the time when government was pursuing her negotiation, we were embarrassed with Spain, with the Indians, and with the western people. On the sea, our people were suffering in their property. The British Treaty was, therefore, made under disadvantageous circumstances. Too great an eulogium could not be bestowed on the government, and truth would sometimes procure its universal assent, that we had recovered our territory, and made provision for the spoliation of our commerce; that we had settled our peace with Great Britain, Spain, Algiers, and the Indians; and that our ships were not taken so much as before. What Treaty will not do, (as the gentleman said some time back,) war must: but Treaty has proved effectual.

It seemed that as if gentlemen never could say enough on the subject of the British Treaty and of Great Britain. The Bank, Treasury, and other topics of declamation, which were formerly always in order, seem to be almost forgotten. Was this the way, he asked, in which they meant to recommend to the citizens the due respect for the acts of a majority of that House and of Congress? If they think this the best way of answering the ends of government, and of producing confidence and harmony amongst the people, they did well. The means appeared disproportioned, or rather strangely opposite to that end. He was of a different opinion. He thought, and it was with due seriousness of deliberation he declared, the people were called upon to choose between them; between those who wished to support government and those who avowed so unseasonable and so excessive a sensibility to a foreign interest and foreign nation; between those who condemned the insults offered to the government, and those who seemed to approve them; those who thought the experiment of our government had succeeded, and those who were bound in consistency with their own assertions, to say it was to be abandoned with disgust and in despair. He was of opinion they could not go on as they were, some pulling down, while others were building up; but the people could remove the evil by choosing a House who would be better agreed—the people being free and enlightened, would have no difficulty in choosing between them. Both sorts of men ought not to be there; either those who, like the government, are in the right, or those who dispute, revile, and despise it. The people would, he doubted not, judge right. He wished the appeal to be made without delay, and so solemnly as to make it effectual.

Mr. CHRISTIE wished to make an amendment to the paragraph, which he thought would answer the end equally as well as striking it out: if agreeable to the gentleman from Virginia [Mr. PARKER] he would move to put the word "among" after the word "freest," which would read "the freest and *among* the most enlightened." He could not say we were the most enlightened, but he did think us the most free; not that he was afraid of offending any nation, but he thought this a more consistent declaration.

. . . .

Mr. AMES said, that the gentleman from Virginia [Mr. GILES] had represented him as saying that he took it for granted that we were on the eve of a war with France. So far was this from being correct, he had grounded his expression carefully upon what fell from the gentleman himself. He said if we were on the eve of a war, as Mr. GILES insinuated, it was above all things necessary that we should cling around the government, and not let an idea go forth to the world that there was a division of sentiment on the subject of the respective duties we owe to France and our own country. He knew not what more he could say with respect France. He had advocated words strong enough for anything but a love-letter, and such were reported by the committee. It was possible, indeed, he might not feel all the ardor in her favor which was expressed by other gentlemen; for their's, he was free to say, he thought excessive and pernicious. It was not sweet enough to go down his throat, but much sweeter than he thought proper to make use of. He wished most cordially for peace with all nations, but if that could not be had he wished for an union of sentiment in support of our national character and dignity. He did not approve of anything like menaces, nor would he give the least encouragement to any hostile disposition; this, he said, had been the language used by other gentlemen in that House.

So much for that subject. With respect to what had fallen from the Speaker, it was possible on so many points, and with so many aspects of the same point, in the business of several years, he might not have acted consistently, though as to the matter in question, he neither admitted nor believed any such thing. He always acted as he thought best at the time; but at different periods he might, and this he said merely for the argument's sake, have acted differently. Sincerely, he was sure, he had acted, and the House would believe he had ever avowed his sentiments as he really felt them; but he could not see anything of this inconsistent kind in his conduct. Admitting that the capturing of our vessels by the British were acts of hostility—and there was great difference between such acts and the just causes of war— were we, he said, even then without reflection, investigation, or demand of justice, to return hostility for hostility? The French had also captured our vessels, and yet no one spoke of this as an act of hostility, or of sequestration, prohibition, or embargo, or blamed those who were silent. If one nation committed an act of hostility against another, was it not advisable, rather than immediately to retaliate, to endeavor to adjust the matter by negotiation? He thought so; the citizens of the United States unquestionably thought so, and that our Administration had great merit in so settling the late differences with Great Britain as to avoid war. It was true that the British had taken our vessels under a claim of right which they had to do so; and as contraband goods were liable to be seized, part of their conduct was clearly right by the Law of Nations, and a great part clearly wrong—so that it was difficult to determine which were acts of hostility. This of course required examination of facts, and adjustment of principles. The Treaty wisely provided for both. For this purpose a negotiation was opened, and was in a train that he sincerely hoped would be finally successful.

Gentlemen had been greatly offended by the terms "justice and magnanimity," addressed by Mr. Jay in his memorial to the British Government; but now our own country was threatened, wronged, and insulted, in a very extraordinary manner, no language was soft enough to be used towards their favorite Republic. This distinction was remarkable. The remarkers on inconsistency would no doubt labor for a solution of this enigma. Our real patriots would labor with them to be satisfied why the languge of custom and common decency should be so shocked in one case, and why even humility and supplication should seem too harsh for offended France in the other.

With respect to the present situation of our country with the French Republic, it was no reproach upon our government that the French had issued complaints against us.

It was said the British Treaty was the ground of offence; if so, he hoped there was not a drop of American blood that was not carried with rather more heat and rather more hurry through the heart by such a declaration. No nation, he hoped, would ever have such influence over the people as to dictate to us what form of Treaty we should make with another nation. It was an insult that marked the utmost insolence of spirit on one side, and its lowest abasement on the other.

No cause of offence, Mr. A. said, could justly be taken on account of that Treaty, since the French Treaty was in common with our other Treaties declared to be of prior force by an article of Mr. Jay's, and were the articles of the two Treaties to clash, those of the French Treaty would destroy any opposing article in that made with Great Britain, so that that Treaty would continue the law of the land, the same as if no British Treaty existed. Our juries and courts could be relied on to carry the law of the land into effect.

Information had been received, Mr. A. said, and stated to the public in all the newspapers, that continual efforts were making in Paris to excite a spirit of animosity against this country, and this by persons who were, though unworthily such, American citizens. Whether the language held by gentlemen in this House on the present occasion would not have a tendency to increase, to encourage, and to assist that spirit, he left those gentlemen to determine: Whether to say we were wholly in their power, that they were the only power which could annoy our territory, that they were invulnerable and irresistible and we defenceless, that they were in the right and we in the wrong, was becoming any character but that of Frenchmen. If we are on the eve of a war, said Mr. A., I blush for gentlemen who can use such language, at a moment when the power with whom the war was contemplated is offering injuries and menaces to our country. If the event were to be war, he acquitted the Administration of blame. It had not provoked it; but it was, if we may credit such various and concurring information as we had, owing to the intrigues carried on at Paris. What auxiliaries they may have here, he would not pretend to say. It had been there represented that there was a division of sentiment betwixt the government and the people of this country, and that they (the French) had only to speak the word, and the government would fall like other despotisms, which they affected every where to overturn. If this was the fact, and so it had been represented, this House and this whole country ought to show it no countenance; he thought it the duty of the place where he stood to make it manifest to the French nation that it would not be borne; that in case of extremities he did not balance for a moment which country he should declare for, that of strangers or his own.

Mr. A. said, he himself did not believe there was any chance of war. The French could have no pretext for it, and as little interest or desire to drive us to that alternative. As this kind of threat, he doubted not, was to answer a certain purpose, and was timed at the very moment when it was expected to fix it, when that business had passed over, he supposed we should hear no more of war. We may suffer many wrongs and depredations on our trade, said Mr. A., but this country will seek redress, not by war in the first instance, but by negotiation as before. These were ideas which appeared to him very necessary to express, and which he considered it his duty to advance. Whatever be our government, said he, whether perfect or not, we are bound to support it; and not, at such a period, to speak of injuries and evils which are not derived from the neglect or improvidence of our government, and therefore ought not to chill the ardor of our zeal for its support. They are not true; but if they were, they should now be kept out of sight. Mr. A. concluded with an apology for having said so much, as it was well known he did not propose to speak often; he intended to have said but little, and hoped the Committee would see that he had been personally called upon, and therefore would excuse him.

TO THOMAS DWIGHT

PHILADELPHIA, NOVEMBER 29, 1794

MY DEAR FRIEND,

.   .   .   .

I HAVE NOT, at this sitting, leisure to write fully on the very interesting and singular debates of the week.[49] Fenno and the inclosed will give you the public history of the affair. The private history deserves to be known; that the faction in the House fomented the discontents without; that the clubs are everywhere the echoes of the faction in Congress; that the Speaker[50] is a member of the democratic club, and gave the casting vote on adding certain words which spoiled the clause, being a member of the club. He voted, therefore, for his own exculpation. Madison and Parker are honorary members. Oh shame! where is thy sting!

Yours, affectionately.

---

[49] *In the President's address to Congress, at the opening of the session, the leading topic was the then recent insurrection in Pennsylvania, usually known as the "whisky rebellion." The manner in which he spoke of the democratic clubs led to a stormy debate in the House. Mr. Jefferson, in a letter to Madison, spoke of the President's denunciation of the clubs as an extraordinary act of boldness, an attack on the freedom of discussion, an inexcusable aggression.* [S. AMES]

[50] *The Speaker was Mr. Muhlenburg, of Pennsylvania. In the debate in committee of the whole, upon the answer of the House to the President's address, the answer was amended by striking out the reference to the "self-created societies." In the House, the part struck out was restored. A motion was then made to add a clause restricting what was said of "self-created societies" to such as existed in "the four western counties of Pennsylvania, and parts adjacent." This motion was carried by the casting vote of the Speaker.* [S. AMES]

P.S. Would the insertion of the debates into your country papers have any good effect? W. Lyman did as usual. Every thing that will impress public opinion, as far as truth and decency allow, ought now to be urged, as the issue rests with the public, to hold up the clubs or the magistracy.

TO THOMAS DWIGHT

PHILADELPHIA, DECEMBER 12, 1794

MY DEAR FRIEND,

I THINK public life has not chilled my social attachments; nor do I see much in it calculated to draw me off from them.

The last session, the noise of debate was more deafening than a mill; and this, excepting in one instance, maintains a pouting silence, an armed neutrality, that does not afford the animation of a conflict, nor the security of peace. We sleep upon our arms. To *sink* the public debt, by paying it, seems to be the chief business to expedite. That will require some address to get effected, as our anti-funders are used to a more literal *sinking* of debts. To put the debt in train of being paid off, would, in a measure, disarm faction of a weapon.

Events have shown the falsehood of almost every antifederal doctrine; and the time favors the impression of truth. It is made, and the government stands on better ground than it ever did. But I wish exceedingly that our sober citizens should weigh matters well. Faction is only baffled, not repenting, not changed. New grounds will be found or invented for stirring up sedition; and unless the country is now deeply sensible of the late danger, and of the true characters of our public men, new troubles will arise. Good fortune may turn her back upon us the next time; and if she had in August last, this union would have been rent. Virginia acted better than could have been expected; and the militia return to all the states, full of federalism, and will help to diffuse their feelings among their connections. The spirit of insurrection had tainted a vast extent of country, besides Pennsylvania; and had all the disaffected combined and acted together, the issue would have been long protracted, and doubtful at last.

Will the people, seeing this pit open, approach it again by sending those to Congress who led them blindfold to its brink? Some exertion, indeed all that can be made, appears to me to be worth making—nay, more, indispensably necessary, wherever an *anti* is held up as a candidate; for I venture to speak as a prophet,—if they will send insurgents, they must pay for rebellions. This government is utterly impracticable, for any length of time, with such a resisting party to derange its movements. The people must interpose in the appointed way, by excluding mobocrats from legislation. I have faith that very plain dealing with them would work a change, even in Virginia. Ought not these considerations, which concern political life and death, to weigh down all others in New England? Will not the river men, who are so noted for good principles and habits, give them support in the election which, I hear, is yet undecided between General . . . . and . . . . . ?

I know that men, breathing the air of New England, cannot credit the state of things in the back country and at the south. They must not judge of others by themselves. They must remember, that, for preserving a free government, a supine security is next to treachery. If all New England would move in phalanx, at least, we could hold our posts; and a short time will work changes at the south. Our good citizens must consent to be more in earnest in their politics, or submit to be less secure in their rights and property.

Your account of Thanksgiving has almost made me home-sick; not a pumpkin pie have I seen. A Yankee is supposed to derive his principles from his keeping. Yet, when that is changed, he must not flinch.

Yours.

TO SAMUEL HAVEN

PHILADELPHIA, DECEMBER 12TH, 1794

MY DEAR SIR

I WROTE very soon after receiving your favor announcing my reelection to thank you for it. But I learn that the letters addressed to the post office at Dedham, in consequence of some irregularity have not been delivered there. I have heard of some of mine at Boston. Mr. Jere Smith of New Hampshire on my recommendation wrote to you enclosing a note of hand for collection. That is probably also in the Boston post office.

I am gratified by the intelligence that the courthouse is raised. There will be for some time a disposition to dispossess Dedham of so decisive an advantage as the shrine. But I begin to think that by vigilance and spirit on the part of Dedham it may hold its ground. I have thought the approaching spring a proper time to promote a subscription for planting trees round the great common, and on the great roads through the whole extent of the plain. It would be more easy to accomplish the whole, I think, than a part only, as many would be willing to turn out and bring the trees from the woods. That would be cheaper than to buy them. Merely as ornament rows of trees would pay the expense. But a whole town thus adorned would no doubt find a solid advantage from it, especially one that has some pretensions to draw men of property to settle in it, because the place is pleasant. If you think with me do promote the conversation on the subject and on my return I will try to get the business accomplished.

The business of Congress moves with less party obstruction than I recollect on any former occasion. The prospect of peace with Europe and with the Indians, the humbling rebellion and clubs and the overflowing of the revenues are the agreebles of our actual situation.

Will the town of Medfield support General Cobb's election? He is a firm, thorough federalist and such are wanted.

If a few in our neighborhood would join, we could have the newspapers from every quarter that we should desire. By dropping a few Chronicles and taking Tom Paine's Or[rer]y, a good exchange would be made. I have thought of taking Webster's Herald, New York, and if Doctor Sprague is inclined to have Fenno from this place or any other good paper, we should combine all the intelligence worth knowing. My respectful regards at your house.

Your's sincerely

FISHER AMES

TO CHRISTOPHER GORE

PHILADELPHIA, DECEMBER 17, 1794

MY DEAR FRIEND,

YOUR and Mrs. G.'s approbation of my speech[51] is very flattering, even if your friendly partiality should have augmented it; for that partiality is worth as much as the praise of more impartial critics. Indeed, the resources of private friendship are peculiarly necessary to a man in such a government as ours. Bright as the prospect now is, I am decided one thing only will make it answer: to speak French,[52] a revolutionary effort, a rising, in mass, at the elections, to purify Congress from the sour leaven of antifederalism. So much faction as now exists in it will kill. Good men must not be duped. I stake my credit on it. The disease may and will produce many deaths. I know but one cure—the real federalism of the body of the electors. The lottery was three blanks to one prize in August last; and had not Harry Lee been Governor of Virginia, probably that region would have been *whiskeyed*. The State for a long time acted a whiskey part, till, by the zeal of New Jersey, the talents of the little Secretary,[53] the weight of the President's name, and bad management among the rioters, the tide turned in favor of government. Disaffection enough to begin, if not to complete,

---

[51] *The speech referred to was made in the debate alluded to in the letter to Dwight, November 29.* [S. AMES]

[52] *That is, in the French style.* [S. AMES]

[53] *Hamilton.* [S. AMES]

a revolution, actually existed. The talk of all rascals, that they are in favor of supporting government, ought to deceive only blockheads. In a more respectable case, did not the language, "We adore the British Constitution and dependence on that Crown," continue long after blood was spilt?

Excuse my croaking. I feel sure of turbulent times, unless more changes take place than I see any cause to expect. Time, I begin to think, is against us. State factions get better organized and more diffused. The best men are weary, and in danger of being driven out. The President, with whom his country lives, will quit in disgust, or be in a few years with Timoleon and Epaminondas. As our system is now constituted, the reaction of party will be, in ordinary times, infinitely stronger than the action of the constituted authorities. These sentiments are delicate; but the *salus reipub.* depends, in my opinion, on their being adopted by the real patriots. I commit them, as I have often done before, to your discretion.

Your proposition for duly receiving the French minister, Houdard, is a pleasant one; but Blair McClenachan should not do all the kissing. Equality would require a negro. Fauchet is said to be safe in his place at present. Little is doing here. A storm will rise on the plan for sinking the debt. It is proposed to pay off the redeemable part yearly; but it will be necessary to prolong or render perpetual the revenue acts of the last session. That will be opposed, under the old pretext of a land tax in lieu of them, but really with a view of having no tax. Keep your eye on the progress of this business; for, as the faction will labor hard to take away, or at least to lessen, the purse of the government, they will be obliged to run on the shoals of a land tax to hide their design. To dismiss the troops, will be another object. No purse, no sword, on the part of authority; clubs, mobs, French influence, on the side of faction: A very intelligible arrangement.

Faction is no better, no weaker, now than formerly. The fall of the Chronicle would do credit to our General Court. Such rascals do not deserve the bread of any public. New York is thought to be doing badly in the city. I own the circumstance has augmented my glooms at the moment.

Your friend.

[P.S.] Lyman and Dearborn rechosen!

The inclosed, if published in the Orrery, might do a little. If sent to me, after publication, I would get it reprinted here. Virginia might be impressed. They elect in March.

TO THOMAS DWIGHT

PHILADELPHIA, DECEMBER 27, 1794

MY DEAR FRIEND,

I HAVE no reason to doubt that I have duly received all your favors; but your doubts excite others in me, whether I have not been very delinquent in acknowledging them. As a friend and brother, I need not, I hope, assure you how much I value your correspondence. I will try to deserve it better in future, as far as scribbling will support my claim. I have notified Mr. Fenno that Mr. Stebbins is at Springfield. The election of W. Lyman and Dearborn, and, as I believe, of Edward Livingston, at New York, almost gives me the hypo. I am confirmed in it: the crisis must come;—but I will not *bore* you with my vapors.

Mr. Jay's success is yet unascertained, but events help him; and if good sense had more to do with politics, I should expect to see faction in the gutter. The Methodists say, very justly, you cannot kill the devil. It would be against experience and the nature of man to look for as much art and industry on the right side as on the wrong; and therefore the federal cause will go down, or I am no conjurer.

I hear, with pleasure, of the health of your family, and of my two.[54] I long to see my friends, more than I can describe.

A man like Dr. Lathrop is too able to defend his errors, to yield them up, and least of all to do it when they are made doubly dear by being attacked. It is to be lamented, that a good man must be given up to base company and a vile cause. Colonel Pickering is mentioned as God of War; Wolcott to succeed Hamilton. This is however but report. France will finally help us by the madness or the sobriety of her example. The great point is to hold out till peace in Europe removes a part of the present support from faction. Thus, we may rub along a little while, but not long.

I feel a due portion of patriotic zeal for the success of your canal. Yet, pardon me, I could see it to more advantage unfinished in March next.

The German church in Fourth, near Arch street, was burned down last evening. It caught from the stove-pipe. It was a magnificent spectacle, but not worth thirty thousand pounds, which it was insured for, as it is said. The organ alone cost near five. The confusion and want of address were manifest, and strongly contrasted with the conduct at a Boston fire. Yet a gentleman assured me no place can match Philadelphia in these points. Practice has made Boston perfect.

Yours, truly.

---

[54] *That is, wife and son.* [S. AMES]

1 7 9 5

===

JANUARY 2, 1795

MR. AMES observed, that too much attention had been given to the amendment as an abstract question. Nothing tended more to bewilder and confuse a debate than such a departure from the subject into abstractions and refinements; for, although by this means we found that plain principles were rendered obscure, and reasonable doctrines carried to excess, yet we did not seem to reflect that nothing is more opposite to just principles than the extremes of those principles. For instance, it would not be safe or proper indiscriminately to admit aliens to become citizens, yet a scrutiny into their political orthodoxy might be carried to a very absurd extreme. The merit of the amendment depends on its adaptedness to the end proposed by the bill, and what is that? To make a rule of naturalization for the admission of aliens to become citizens, on such terms as may consist with our tranquility and safety. Now, said he, do we think of refusing this privilege to all heretics in respect to political doctrines? Even that strictness would not hasten the millennium. For our own citizens freely propagate a great variety of opinions hostile to each other, and therefore, many of them deviate widely from the intended standard of right thinking; good and bad, fools and wise men, the philosopher and the dupes of prejudice, we find could live very peaceably together, because there was a sufficient coincidence of common interest. If we depend on this strong tie, if we oblige foreigners to wait seven years till they have formed it, till their habits as well as interests become assimilated with our own, we may leave them to cherish or to renounce their imported prejudices and follies as they may choose. The danger of their diffusing them among our own citizens, is to be prevented by public opinion, if we may leave error and prejudice to stand or fall before truth and freedom of inquiry.

Can the advocates of the amendment even affect apprehensions that there is any intention to introduce a foreign nobility as a privileged order? If they can, such diseases of the brain were not bred by reasoning and cannot be cured by it. Still less should we give effect by law to chimerical whimsies. For what is the tendency of this counterfeit alarm? Is it to rouse again the sleeping apparitions which have disturbed the back country? Is it to show that the mock dangers which they have pretended to dread are real? Or, is it to mark a line of separation between those who have the merit of maintaining the extremes of political opinions, and those whom this vote would denounce as stopping at what they deem a wise moderation? If that is the case, it seems that the amendment is intended rather to publish a creed than to settle a rule of Naturalization. Yet it should be noticed that those who would go to extremes are less entitled to the praise of republicanism than those who would not.

But the consequence of giving an artificial and unmerited importance to the amendment, is, in the first place, to spread an useless and even pernicious alarm, as well as to revive animosities, and, in the next place, by showing our dependence on a futile and ridiculous renunciation of nobility, to evince the want of any good remedy for the evil. If it is an important affair the amendment is far short of what the case requires. If it is, as we all believe, trifling and worthless, then let us spare ourselves the shame of legislating on these frivolities, these phantoms which the friends of the amendment have very slowly, and at last very faintly, pretended to have any substance.

Mr. A. further observed, that the securities which we have already against the introduction of nobility, are sufficient to secure us and our sons, and the sons of our sons, down to the twentieth generation, against a nobility. Is the meaning of this amendment to give a new text for sedition? It was below the dignity of the House to spend its time upon such trifles. The Convention of another nation had indelibly disgraced themselves by legislating upon trifles, while matters of importance stood by. What would be the sense of America upon our spending day after day in debating about such a frivolous thing? He was against the amendment of Mr. GILES.

TO THOMAS DWIGHT

PHILADELPHIA, JANUARY 7, 1795

MY DEAR FRIEND,

I DO NOT neglect writing for the purpose of drawing from you complaints of my neglect. Yet I own my interpretation of your notice how seldom I write, is, that my letters have some value with you. As they have none here, allow me to send them to the best market. Seriously, I am more and more impressed with the sense of what I owe my friends, and my epistolary trade is one of the most gainful I can carry on. I am happy in the correspondence of a very few select friends, and I should be ashamed to think my part of the intercourse a burden. The public business is no excuse for my neglect, because idle men have less time than the busy.

The weather imposes on me the task of drawing my breath, which is for the most part a heavy burden. I get along, however, by throwing off almost every other. A great rain is falling, and I hope winter will venture his coy person immediately after. On the whole, I like the old contrivance of this world better than the new: hot weather in the dog days; cold and snow at Christmas. If I had to guide the plough, I should prefer October and April for that work, to the season called winter. If the pines protect Springfield from disease, I shall reverence your sacred plains, and become a druid, only changing the wood.

. . . .

You did not seem to understand my hint to you, that your merit, in forwarding the canal on the Connecticut, might be blazoned at an election; and you will not deny that the candidates, who have no intrinsic worth of character, seek occasions to mingle in every showy undertaking, and afterwards brag of their patriotism. The electioneering spirit corrupts and mutilates every thing. You, I know, prefer home to the forum of Congress. I confess I justify your opinion; and I hope I shall never give cause, in my own conduct at elections, to question that I approve the independence of your spirit. That would be called, by many, aristocratic pride. I admit the right a man has to seek an election, in case of a scolding wife, a smoky house, or a host of duns— three pleasant reasons.

The debate on requiring nobles to renounce titles, prior to becoming citizens, may furnish our Chronicle with a subject. Content;—it would have been more prudent to treat the silly motion with silence or ridicule. In the south, it may confirm their prejudices. But men of sense will need no further proof of the art and hypocrisy of the advocates.

Mr. Osgood's sermon is extolled. The good sense and boldness of the sentiments will work their way. The heathen in this state, and farther south, ought to have him sent as a missionary. The sermon is reprinting here. The proclamation by the President, for a Thanksgiving, will afford an opening for other clergymen to seek glory. Will any renowned *anti* vindicate the anarchists from the pulpit?—Parson Lyman or Dr. L.? I hope the respectable character of the latter will not be soiled by any such attempt. Sedgwick has a letter from the former, teeming with Jacobinism. Yet it would be unwise, perhaps unjust, to slight those two men.

Yours, &c.

TO CHRISTOPHER GORE

PHILADELPHIA, JANUARY 10, 1795

MY DEAR FRIEND,

A CIRCUMSTANCE, of a singular nature, has been mentioned repeatedly, and on so good authority, that I believe it. At a meeting of a county in Virginia, one Callender, the rival of Venable, the present member, gave at dinner, in a large company, this toast:—"A speedy death to General Washington." On some subsequent notice of the toast, (for I did not hear of any being taken at the dinner,) he said it would be for his glory to die soon. The prejudices of these people, and the savageness of their manners, will be evinced by any interpretation of this horrid toast; yet in South Carolina W. Smith and General Wynne, the two federalists, are rechosen, and the others are not. Benton, indeed, is rechosen; but, as he did not attend, his party is not known.

It is worthy of remark, that the disputatious turn of the House appears in quibbles on little things, as evidently as it did the last session in things of great importance. Our progress is slow, and the nature of the discussion trivial and stupid. Such a collection of Secretaries of the Treasury, so ready on questions of peace, war, and treaty, feel a competence to every thing, and discover to others an incompetence for any thing, except what, by the Constitution, they should be,—a popular check on the other branches. To prevent usurpation or encroachment on the rights of the people, they are inestimable; as executive agents, which our disorganizers contend for, they are so many ministers of destruction.

John Barnwell, the brother of Robert, is chosen from South Carolina. If he proves worthy of being Robert's brother, he will be a good member.

Taylor, when he resigned his senatorship, is said to have assigned, in his letter to the Assembly, as a reason, the extreme corruption of Congress and the President. This *morçeau* of madness and antifederalism is said to be suppressed. I wish the crackbrain could be convicted for libelling the government. I presume you have heard the crow story, which has made his resignation so famous.

A Doctor McClurg, once a nominal director of the United States Bank, is the reputed author of Marcellus. I have the pleasure to see an edition of Manlius piled up in Fenno's office, for circulation among the heathen in the back parts of this state—among those who sit in darkness, and yet hate the light. Marcellus, Manlius, and Parson Osgood, have deserved well of the country.

I have scribbled a paragraph for the Centinel, respecting Wynne and Smith, which may *fix* the former.

I just learn that Jacob Reed, a zealous antigallican and federalist, is chosen senator in Mr. Izard's stead; and one Marshall, the best Fed in Kentucky, in place of Edwards. Here they turn out the members from the rebellious counties on the ground that, in a state of force and rebellion, the right of suffrage cannot be exercised. It is agreed to in the committee of the House, by eleven majority, and will pass.

Yours.

TO CHRISTOPHER GORE

PHILADELPHIA, JANUARY 17, 1795
SATURDAY MORNING

MY DEAR FRIEND,

I WAS done over yesterday with the exertion of a noisy speech on sinking the public debt. That, and engagements the remainder of the day, prevented my writing to you till this late hour, although your last two letters, and the Orrery, afford me materials for several pages. The faction pretending, as usual, exclusive zeal to pay off the debt, and, as usual, opposing every measure for the purpose, seemed to take the ascendant on the question, to strike out the resolution to prolong the temporary taxes to the year 1801. This at last produced in me what Randolph calls personal excitement, and led me on to make a long speech, and a loud one, to take away, if possible, their popular cloak, and show *in puris naturalibus,* the loathness of the party to pay off the debt. It had, because it was the plain truth, some effect. The docrine that a land tax must be resorted to, has gravelled them. They begin to equivocate, and Madison speaks (now) hypothetically of the measure. He has some idea of digesting an apportionment, not a requisition says he, on the states, which they may spread over such taxable property as Congress could not reach. This jargon of hypocrisy convinced nobody, and yet plainly showed that at last they are unwilling and afraid to propose any tax for the debt. But the debate has confirmed the old fact, that the party propose a land tax, and a land tax only, for the purpose. Such a fact ought to make impression in New England. On the whole, we rise upon them and they are once more chop-fallen.

Hamilton yesterday sent a letter, which arrived while I was speaking, but was not read till after I had done, announcing that he had digested and got ready a report on sinking the debt. The party were unprepared, and out of spirits to oppose its being directed to be laid before the House, and it passed, Lyman only opposing. This order to receive the report is a curiosity, especially after the vile debate on committing the President's message, inclosing Knox's letter. The report of Hamilton will be printed, and no doubt help the business. I have not been made acquainted with its contents or precise objects.

I hope Sam Cooper is not thrown off from the good men, by the attack on his father. Is it not possible to pacify his wrath, which I hear is roused by the *Jacobiniad?* The Boston poets are formidable, and would be guillotined, if the Robespierres whom they expose had the power.

In the debate (I had forgot to observe) that McDowell proposed a tax on transfers, as a fund for sinking the debt.

What fund more proper or more efficient? The bottomless pit would not sink the debt lower.

Yours.

TO GEORGE RICHARDS MINOT

PHILADELPHIA, JANUARY 20, 1795

MY DEAR FRIEND,

HAD your offence in the epistolary way been as aggravated as you state it, the letter would have been not only atonement, but supererogation—a stock of merit laid up against a rainy day. I am too proud, as well as too considerate of my own infirmity, [indolence] to arraign my friends for neglect of me when they do not write. I should prefer any solution of your forbearance to that of your cooling in point of regard. For I often draw consolation and pleasure from the reflection, that though I did not choose my enemies, I could not mend it by choosing; nor were I to choose over again, could I mend my list of friends.

I see no abatement of the rancor of party here, nor would it be reasonable to expect their temper best, when disappointment has done the most to sour it. Victory over party may procure a truce, in which they will take breath, and make their cartridges, but peace is out of the question. Government here is in the cradle, and good men must watch their own child, or it will die, or be made way with. It is therefore a chapter of comfort in my theory, that when events portend a crisis of extremity, the spirit of defence will rise in proportion to the violence of the attack, and this justice must be done our Catilines—they do all they can to raise and keep up the federal spirit to this revolutionary height, though not intentionally. On the whole, I hope more and fear rather less for our government than I did two months ago. This may be versatility; but I see the difficulty of opposing, which the *antis* conflict with, is sometimes more burdensome than of supporting government.

All measures for propping up public credit have been opposed, first because they hate the debt, and would pay it off, and secondly because they hate excises, and long for land taxes. Yet, lo! the principle of opposition becomes at last, by the turning round of business, a principle of action: thus they have trained their men to bawl for a reduction of the debt; and, now it is proposed and urged, they are gravelled; for still they would oppose. Yet I flatter myself their common soldiers will fall off, because they do not see how the new opposition squares with the old style of declamation. Besides, as we are in full possession of the popular ground of paying off the debt, they are driven, by their hard luck, to oppose the reduction by clamoring against excises, and for the land tax, meaning really to do nothing. How will our clamorers like these manœuvres? how will they be able to go on with their patriots, who would tax carts and free coaches? Read the inclosed speech of Madison, and see this doctrine avowed; although, having heard that it will ruin them among our Yankees, they try to wrap up the land tax in the hypocrisy of a tax on *property,* which, rendered into English, you will see reads *land tax.* A report of the Secretary of the Treasury came in during the debate, and is ordered to be printed, urging the reduction of the debt.

I admire the *Jacobiniad.* The wit is keen, and who can deny its application? Regard to friends of the club.

Your affectionate friend.

[P.S.] I read with some indignation the Chronicle abuse of Dexter, for saying republicanism means any thing or nothing. They are no better than formerly. It is astonishing that they choose to hazard such gross misrepresentation. Either they are the biggest fools, or their readers the veriest dupes in the world. Unluckily too for them, Madison's speech, recommending land tax, comes out here on the day that the Chronicle asserts that the Madisonians are opposed to it, and that Mr. Sedgwick first proposed that measure.

TO THOMAS DWIGHT

PHILADELPHIA, FEBRUARY 3, 1795

MY DEAR FRIEND,

YOUR LAST LETTER, covering a Springfield paper, was very acceptable, though very short. Usually my value of your letters is guided by measure, the longest the best. But the last assured me that all is well at Springfield; and as the canker-rash prevails in your town, it is peculiarly agreeable to hear from you and yours, and mine.

I like the article in your Spy, relating to the democratic societies, and their complaints of the violation of the liberty of the press, and have requested Fenno to republish it. Such comments on their inconsistency are read, because they are brief, and remembered because they are pointed, and make them ridiculous; and it is in human nature to approve the making others ridiculous.

The success of Mr. Jay will secure peace abroad, and kindle war at home. Faction will sound the tocsin against the treaty. I see a little cloud, as big as a man's hand, in

Bache's paper, that indicates a storm. Two things will be attempted. First, before the event is known, to raise the expectation of the public, that we have every thing granted, and nothing given in return; and secondly, that the treaty, when published, has surrendered every thing. I think it probable that they will succeed in stirring up the fires of the south; for when have they shown a want of philosophy (or folly) in kindling a fire? We must wait for time, sometimes our friend, sometimes our foe, to help us out of our uncertainties and embarrassments.

The military establishment has generated war in the debates. Virginia would reduce. Economy is the plea, and as usual the zeal by saving, to have cash to reduce the debt. The usual reproaches on the advocates of standing armies, and perpetual public debts, fell from them of course. But I think they are not likely to prevail, as the profuse expense of militia is well proved in the discussion. To reduce the regulars, and swell the expense of the Indian war, as well as to protract its period, is the tendency of Virginia politics.

Four weeks from this day I gallop Springfield-ward. Judge, from your own emotions, with what impatience.

Yours, &c.

[P.S.] Would not Judge Sumner be the most eligible candidate to oppose S. A.[55] as Governor? Sedgwick and some others, as well as your humble servant, incline to the opinion.

---

[55] *Samuel Adams.*

TO CHRISTOPHER GORE

PHILADELPHIA, FEBRUARY 24, 1795

DEAR FRIEND,

THE BILL for reduction of the public debt, has passed the House. It pins fast the funding system, converts the poison of faction into food for federalism; it puts out of the reach of future mobocrats the funds, and the control of them. It is therefore the finale, the crown of federal measures. You will naturally wonder that such men should suffer such a step to be taken. Shame at being glaringly inconsistent, and real inefficiency of character, kept them back. Yet this triumph is clouded. The clauses to provide, *bonâ fide*, for the unsubscribed debt, and for the discharge of a certain species of the loan-office certificates, were thrown out. The old three per cent. men and principles were revived. I except, much to his honor, Sedgwick. Prudence prevented many of us, who think as formerly, from pressing the right principle, which would have been in vain. To make the subscription of the small residuum of debt compulsory, is base in principle, and not excused even by the pretence of necessity. Hamilton retires, full of the horrors, on this account. It is truly lamentable that the best men are so incorrect in principle. The folly of vindicating federal measures, on the mean plea of expediency, is apparent. "What," said the compulsion men, "would you give the foes of your system (meaning Charles Petit, &c.) more than the subscribing creditors?" I answer—yes, if obliged by contract to do so. I have long seen that our measures are supported by prejudices, not less erroneous than those of their opposers.

A letter from Monroe appears in Brown, and will to-morrow be in Fenno. It should be republished as from Monroe. Mr. Randolph has told several persons that it is; and it would greatly assist the antidote, to know that it was sent from one who had swallowed the poison and was cured. Strange, that Monroe should warn us against Jacobins! So the world turns round. At the birthright bill, Ben. F. Bache acted as manager. Yet his paper teems with daily abuse of courtly sycophancy. The poor creature should not be brought into the danger of suffering by contact with *courts*. I will keep my temper, and be silent in regard to D.'s election. No treaty yet arrived. The Senate will be specially called to ratify, or not. No French treaty is here spoken of. Are not their resources on the decline, as moderatism is now the order of the day? A million stirling, will not, I think, more than defray the expense of four days. Neither rapine, nor regular taxes, can long support this immense expense. Thank God, it is their affair, not ours. The Thanksgiving has helped tone the public mind. Tom Paine has kindly cured our clergy of their prejudices.

The Georgia land speculation calls for vigor in Congress. Near fifty millions acres, sold by Georgia for a song, threatens Indian, Spanish, and civil, wars. Energy at first may prevent all of them.

Yours, truly.

[P.S.] I have requested a receipt, from Mrs. Fitzsimmons, of the catholic and only true way of making buckwheat cakes.

Inclosed is Monroe's undoubted authentic letter. If the anti-gallican sentiments of the poem should not shock your nerves, do get B. R. to republish that and Monroe in his Centinel. The French mania is in the train of being cured, and such doses should be got down by the patients. Really, more truth is told, and it is better received, than formerly.

TO THOMAS DWIGHT

PHILADELPHIA, FEBRUARY 24, 1795

MY DEAR FRIEND,

. . . .

THE NEWSPAPERING a woman is an outrage I had hoped Hottentots would not commit. Is Vermont more enlightened than Whidah or Angola? Otherwise, I should think, they would not endure such abuse of types. I feel happy that they did not praise me, as they did Dayton. It is no little consolation that the daughters of Colonel Worthington, from good sense, and their remembrance of tory times, are able to restrain their just sensibilities within proper bounds. I am rather flattered, than insulted, by the suggestion that a very deserving wife influences me. And for what, my friend, am I, like a turkey the day before Thanksgiving, set up to be shot at—a target for the popgun-men to practise upon for learning marksmanship? For the immense salary of a first clerk in a public office? I feel a spirit of indignant independence, although it does not, I confess, require much spirit of any sort to despise the attacks of the despised clubbists.

. . . .

B. Bache appeared as manager at the ballroom (birthnight ball.) A pretty fellow, to fill his paper with insults on the celebration, and yet act as manager. . . .[56]

The celebration was unusually demonstrative of respect, &c., to our great chief. He rises over enemies, like the sun scattering the mists. The Thanksgiving has keyed up the public mind to federalism. Dr. Smith's sermon is liberally

---

[56] *A few somewhat* spicy *words are here omitted.* [S. AMES]

subscribed for, and will be spread over the United States. He treats French madness and wickedness very plainly.

Your affectionate friend.

TO THOMAS DWIGHT

PHILADELPHIA, FEBRUARY 28, 1795

DEAR FRIEND,

CONGRESS IS too inefficient to afford the stuff for a letter. No public body exists with less energy of character to do good, or stronger propensities to mischief. We are Frenchmen, democrats, *antifeds;* every thing but Americans, and men of business.

I have a right to find fault with others, though I do nothing myself, as I am unfit for labor. We scarcely think that a war raging on our coast requires any steps. The Chronicle called our disposition towards France rebellious, and we seem to concur in the sentiment. Jacobinism and Gallomania are stronger here than anywhere else. The last place that will be rid of this plague is the very one which, it is fondly believed by many, cannot catch it. Your General Court, I trust, is much better, and that is precious, as it inspires confidence in a good issue to the election, for Governor Sumner is the only man. All feds must join or die; for another *anti* Governor would ruin the harmony of the state, and overthrow all federalism.

Yours.

Watch and pray for the first Monday, April.

TO OLIVER WOLCOTT

DEDHAM, JULY 9, 1795

MY DEAR SIR,

I AM SORRY to perceive that Boston is in a very inflammatory state. I was there two days ago, and I learnt that the Jacobins have been successful in prejudicing the multitude against the treaty. What is more to be lamented, almost all the merchants and steady men are said to feel the prevailing fever or to want courage to resist it. A town-meeting is expected, and if it should be convened, I expect its proceedings will be marked with folly and violence. I could neither repress my indignation, nor disguise my contempt for the blindness and gullibility of the rich men who so readily lend their strength to the party which is thirsting for the contents of their iron chests. They tremble for liberty if it is proposed to give our form of government intrinsic strength, and if it is made to rest on such men for props they slip away from their burden. It is to be denied the extrinsic support which the interests of the half-witted, and, in this instance, out-witted men of property were expected to give, and that steadily. So many feel dislike of the treaty, and so few dare oppose the popular feeling, that I apprehend not only mischievous proceedings in town-meeting, but also that the contagion will spread, especially southward. I am happy to find the town-meeting is thus far delayed, as every day abates the heat of some and emboldens the spirits of others. I am not surprised, although I am concerned to see the profound ignorance of the subject among those who believe and assert their right to rejudge the doings of Mr. Jay and the Senate. It makes them peculiarly susceptible of irritation and no less indocile to fact and argument. The Jacobins, in fact, have the possession of the ground, and they will not fail to fortify themselves in their acquisition. The country is yet perfectly calm, but pains will be taken to inflame it. My hope is, that early attention will be paid to the merchants of New York and Philadelphia. Right impressions made in those places, like a double brick wall, might stop the flame of the Boston resolves, if any should be passed. It is also important that temperance and masterly vindications of the treaty should appear in the gazettes. Better, if in a pamphlet.

I am, perhaps, more provoked and discouraged than I should be on the occasion. It seemed as if the shining and prosperous period of our government would be safe and popular. But our federal ship is near foundering in a millpond. The pillars of the temple of liberty need holding up by hand when the storm does not blow. I am more and more confirmed in my croakings about our affairs. The prejudices and passions of the multitude are scarcely more deadly to public order than the theories of our philosophers. Our nation, I fear, must be taught as others have been, by danger and suffering; teaching by book makes little impression. We must learn by great events, by having the scars of great wounds to point to, the recollection of which will secure for an age or two all the feelings of the multitude, and most of the reason of our politicians, on the side of order and good government. To resume the subject I set out with, what can augur worse for our affairs than to see men of wealth, and at least of reputed sense, openly acting against the doings of the executive. That branch is weak in its constitution. If the bullying of parties should make it cowardly also, it will be nothing, it will be worse than nothing, for it will become the tool of party. It is some relief to me to give vent to my vexation by writing this letter. If that, or any other plea would excuse its prolixity, it will be a relief when I need such help, for you have head and hands too full to read my dismal forebodings, and I declare beforehand, I disclaim all pretensions to any reply.

With perfect esteem,
I am yours sincerely.

FISHER AMES

TO THOMAS DWIGHT

DEDHAM, AUGUST 24, 1795, MONDAY

MY DEAR SIR,

COURT WEEK is over, and I am alive, and beginning to take long breaths. Not half the jury actions were tried. My share of them kept me in a throng of people at my own house, and on the way to and from court; and there, the heat, the crowd, and the effort of speaking, almost did me over. Once I sat down, and left my ally to finish on the same side. I could not sleep at night, in consequence of overdoing at court. But a change of weather recruited me, and I am now as well as usual. So particular an account of the court may serve to show you how far I am yet from sound health. To mend my crazy frame, the scheme of the long-deferred journey to Newport is resumed, for the last of this week, and I trust will be executed. Unless the cold of the fall season should brace me up, I shall scarcely earn my six dollars a day at Congress work.

.   .   .   .

I hope your family is free from medicine, and the necessity of making use of it. If I had my newspaper riches in possession, I would hire a hack, and make a visit to Springfield; but as my treasure lies as far out of my way, as it is out of that of moths and thieves, I am limited to a one-horse chaise, and that forbids our going in caravan, namely, man and wife, girl and child. I drop the scheme of going to Vermont, as the rains have made the roads bad, and I have no companion, and am not well enough to go without one. The heat has been more trying to invalids, I believe, than any former season, as it has been accompanied with excessive dampness. The rains have totally drowned more than two thousand acres of meadow between Dedham and Newton, on Charles river; about twelve or thirteen acres of mine lie in soak. We are sadly abused by the millers at Newton upper falls. Not one drop of flood water would be left after two days, if we had the command of the stream, to remove the dams, and only one rock at the falls. The improvement of the soil could not fail to be capital, if it were not drowned. I have my barn full of hay, as it is, but I should have had some to sell, had not the flood spoiled the meadows. It will be two years at least before the grass will recover itself in quantity or quality.

My house is two thirds plastered; the masons quitted it to avoid court week, but I expect them back every hour. We shall be able to effect our removal to the new house with ease in October; but for the greater caution, I propose to delay it till November.

.   .   .   .

On the whole, our prospect of neighborhood in future is fifty per cent. improved from the state we found it in, when we removed here from Boston. Still we think it an essential part of our *summum bonum*, that our Springfield friends should visit us once a year. I am loath to give up the idea of Colonel and Mrs. W's. coming.

I find my paper strangely filled up, as Mr. Morehead would

say, with emptiness. Not a word of politics in almost three pages!—is it not strange?

My letter by Mr. Boylston expressed to you and Colonel W. a vehement suspicion the President would not ratify the treaty. This was grounded on confidential information that he had gone to Virginia, and had not done it. Since that time, I am happy to learn, through a channel that I believe pure, that he has ratified it. Now let the heathen rage. If the government dare act right, I still believe it can maintain it. The time will come when faction will make it afraid; nay, when it will become the instrument of faction, and be as little disposed as able, to uphold order. Is it not manifest that the violence of this storm springs from the anticipation of the election to the Presidency? The New Hampshire man is encouraged to hope the second place. Jefferson's party seize the moment to discredit their most dreaded rival, Jay. Clinton's and Adams's parties in the two states, and state parties elsewhere, enlist under the banner of the Jefferson leaders. Does this augur an unbiased appointment, or a cordial support, of Washington's successor? An experienced sailor would say, these little whirlwinds of dry leaves and dirt portend a hurricane. How can a government be managed in adverse times; and when the chief magistrate asks support against the faction of his rival, but can give none, or almost none, to the laws—when we see that the splendid name of the present possessor, though stronger than a host, scarcely protects him, and the government is but just spared from destruction by the mobs of Philadelphia, Boston, &c., although their complaining mouths are actually stopped by the showers of manna? A ship that is sinking, or near sinking, at her anchors in the port, will drown her crew if they venture to sea in her. We shall, at any rate, get along for some time; and if the country people see that the wounds attempted to be given by the mobs aforesaid will be mortal, they will become alarmed, and afford such a support to law and order, as possibly may enable government to stand its ground. It is a crisis full of instruction, perhaps of fate.[57]

Yours, &c.

Let the above be in confidence with you and discreet friends.

P.S. . . . . I saw Sam Dexter lately, on his return from a court in Rhode Island. He says, there they boast of their being right respecting the treaty, while Boston goes wrong. Formerly, they say, they were deemed outlaws against all government, and now they are firmer and steadier than Massachusetts. Connecticut is also right;—*ça ira.* The treaty will go in spite of mobs.

---

[57] *The disappointment and anger of the democratic leaders, when it was ascertained that Mr. Jay's mission was successful, were very strongly manifested. That party had rather lost ground by the controversy between our government and Citizen Genet, and perhaps also by the extravagances of the clubs. But the political operation of the general exasperation against England was very much in their favor; and the rejection of Mr. Jay's treaty would have an apparent tendency to bring them into power at the next election. Accordingly, all the machinery of denunciation, tumultuous meetings, processions, effigies, and mobs, was brought to bear upon the public mind, and the unfortunate delay of the President, in the ratification, (a delay partly owing, no doubt, to the questionable counsels of Edmund Randolph, the Secretary of State,) encouraged the hopes, and so increased the violence of the opposition.*

There is very little in the treaty itself that accounts for such a warm, and as it now appears, extravagant opposition. It proved to be a good one. It provided a full and honorable indemnity for the spoliations on our commerce, and we lived very contentedly, from 1815 to 1842, upon a treaty very much like it, only somewhat less in our favor. It did not settle the great question of impressment. That never has been, and perhaps never will be, settled in express terms by any treaty whatever, between the two nations. Time, and the increase of our national strength, have made diplomacy on that subject quite unimportant. [S. AMES]

TO OLIVER WOLCOTT

DEDHAM, SEPTEMBER 2D, 1795

DEAR SIR,

I RETURNED yesterday from a tour to Newport. I hope by exercise and the coolness of the approaching season, to be able to attend Congress. At present, though I am not sick, I have such puny health as to disqualify me for much exertion. As there was a burning in effigy at Newport a short time before my arrival, I was curious to learn how far it might be deemed an evidence of the antigovernment spirit of the citizens. The account I received was this.

A few young men who had lost property by British captures, were incensed against the treaty and Mr. Jay and thought proper to show their resentment by burning him in effigy; but not more than a dozen men followed the figure in the principal streets, where my informants observed them. Troops of boys however, with fifes and drums, helped to lengthen the line of march. On the whole, no mob ever drew so few of the inhabitants from mere curiosity, to follow the exhibition. On the contrary, the non-attendance of the citizens, may be admitted as a proof of strong disapprobation of the measure. The anti-treaty men were ashamed of the business, and considered it as making their weakness as strong as their violence. It will have the effect, by outraging the feelings of those who abhor all excesses, to turn the public mind more forcibly than it would otherwise go, from the views of the seditious. At Providence, the anti-federal party is very inconsiderable, and I was happy to see in that state, symptoms of a just pride in their present state, as contrasted with their former turbulence and the folly of Boston. I made conversation at all the country taverns, and I think the yeomanry are yet right. They say the men in the government know best what to do, and the President will not see the country wronged, much less wrong it himself. As a speculative question, the country folks do not pretend to understand it, their approbation is not therefore given; but their dislike of the proceedings in the seaports, is extorting it. Some opinions are general and well established; admiration of our Constitution and government, exultation in the happy effects manifested in the general prosperity, aversion to war and land-taxes, confidence in, and almost adoration of the President, and a steady resolution to support the government. Yet with these right opinions, are sown many wrong ones which come from the Chronicle, and the parties that uphold that perfidious gazette. On the whole, it depends I think on the spirit and firmness of the government itself, to keep the country right. The towns will often, perhaps three times out of four, yield to the sudden fury of a party. Some time ago I almost despaired. The President we were told, had gone to Mount Vernon, leaving the treaty unratified, and, said Webster's Herald, it will not be ratified until farther negotiations are made. Had that been the case, the friends of order would have been in despair. Now the contest lies between the mobbers and the government, and if there should be no want of spirit, the eventual triumph of the latter may be expected.

My information respecting the state of opinion in Newport &c., may not merit much attention, but I have thought it not improper to trouble you with it. The mob men seem resolved to go to extremities, perhaps because their French paymasters require it of them. Any regular system of government in the U.S. will be an obstacle to the success of the unvaried plan of controlling our affairs by means of our rabble. Therefore we may look for French patronage of the disorganizers here, while they seriously endeavour to set up order in their own country. I have been highly gratified by your answer to my letter, but I do assure you, I do not ask it of you to reply to this. I excuse my breaking in upon your hurry of office only in that way. I hope my countryman, Davis, will sustain in office, the reputation he bore out of it. He was ever esteemed a man of genius and worth.

Congress will draw all eyes upon its proceedings. The south glows with more than torrid heat, if we may believe their gazettes. But what have we to legislate upon regarding the treaty? The clamourers will originate motions to draw it into question if they can find support. The Senate must, as usual, pull up the bridge, and stop the march of the party. *Inter nos*, I fear Dayton will take fire at the clause which prohibits confiscations. His lead would be followed by others whom Giles & Co. could not otherwise influence.

I am with esteem, cordially yours,

FISHER AMES

P.S. The President's answer to Boston is greatly extolled, and I believe has done more towards calming the country, than all the good pieces published in Webster and the Sentinel. The resignation of Randolph excites surprise, the death of Bradford, the Attorney General, as report says, my deep regret.

TO THOMAS DWIGHT

DEDHAM, SEPTEMBER 13, 1795

MY DEAR FRIEND,

I FOUND your letter of the 4th, at Mrs. Phillips's. I had scarcely read it, and digested my wrath against the puppy who opened my packet by Spencer Whiting, when I found your brother Josiah in the street, who brought a welcome cargo from Colonel W. and Secretary Sophy. As to the letter that was broken open, Mr. Whiting would not do such a thing, and how could any other person have the opportunity? It contained some treason, I suppose, though I do not remember what; not so bad I think as a former one, full of gloomy fears that a certain great man would shrink from the storm of popular fury. I care little what use the man may think fit to make of it. I lose my timidity, as to popular questions, almost daily, and am ready to indulge a surly sort of independence of spirit. Old Nick seems to begin his government, and his accession is welcomed by as much loyalty and zeal among his subjects, as any sovereign can boast. Every passion, every prejudice, of a certain part of our citizens in the large towns is blown up to a pitch of fanaticism. Let the country folks keep firm and steady, and these triflers in their opinions, but demons in their excesses, will be restrained from doing irreparable mischief. The demagogues seem to resolve to bring the business to a crisis, to corrupt and inflame our own citizens as much as they can, and, by reënforcing their corps with a French force, to overcome the government of their country. I see no objection to joining the issue tendered; for governments are oftenest lost by flinching from the trial, and if ours has any strength, it cannot use it at a more favorable moment. Washington at the head, Pittsburg at its feet,[58] pockets full of money, prosperity shining like the sun on its path. If it falls, it will prove that it had no strength, and must have fallen soon had not this foe prevailed. The sooner we are rid of it, if it be really good for nothing, the better. I think it good, and that every real patriot will hazard his life to defend it.

Since my return from Newport, I have drooped a good deal. Accident, or the operation of the season, had deranged my stomach and head. Often oppressed, always languid, with little appetite, less rest, I have thought myself, for ten days past, duly qualified and fully authorized to use and enjoy the vapors as amply and freely as other invalids. I choose, however, to delay my use and ocupation of this most delightful privilege, till I have trotted my horse a great many times over all the roads near our village; till I have tried the use of meat and stimulants, abstaining from vegetables, &c.; till cold weather has arrived, without effect, and if possible, till I die. My actual complaints are trivial, but the cause they spring from is not. The *vis vitæ* is on the ebb. The momentum of my blood is impaired. My case is more that of an old man than a sick one. I fully believe great precaution is necessary to secure my recovery, and I am far from being discouraged in respect to its success.

.   .   .   .

My friend, is it not enough to make a man enamored of politics? Here am I, scarcely able to ride thirty miles in a day, and that only on resting one day to prepare me for proceeding, going to carry my musket in the wars of politics, leaving my wife to mope alone in my new house, under circumstances of uncommon discouragement. I will try my

---

[58] *The neighborhood of Pittsburg was the scene of the "Whiskey Insurrection."* [S. AMES]

best not to go crazy as she approaches the period of her trial. Have I not already got the vapors, think you? This subject brings them, when I think of it. I will not think of it, therefore.

Never, probably, could Colonel W. choose a time to visit us when his company would be more cheering. In proportion as the tenure of my life becomes obviously more precarious, I value the society of my friends and connections. In that way I turn the hours of life to profit and enjoyment.

I wish you health and happiness, as also to Mrs. Dwight and the children.

Yours, &c.

TO THOMAS DWIGHT

————

DEDHAM, SEPTEMBER 22, 1795

DEAR FRIEND,

I HAVE just returned from a freezing ride with Frances to Boston. Such changes from heat to cold, and both extreme, were, I believe, never before known. I have suffered by both. I was very ill last week for three days, and lost more than half my strength. The cold recruits it again, but too much like a continued cold bath. I am told my case is nervous, bilious, a disease of the liver, atrophy, &c., as different oracles are consulted. I am forbidden and enjoined to take almost every thing. *I* prescribe, and take meat, some cider, a trotting horse, keep as warm as I can, abstain from excess of every kind, and I have still faith I may recruit; although more than half of those who complain without being able to tell what ails them, go to their long home. I know how tedious valetudinary accounts usually are, but I think your friendly concern will not be less engaged in this part of my letter, than if it were filled with politics, as usual.

There is a buzzing rumor in town, that letters from the ex-minister, Fauchet, have been intercepted by a British armed vessel, and sent to our government, containing an account of the disposal of sums of French secret-service money, and stating sums paid to our late Secretary of State[59] and others, (one senator, it is said) whose names are not mentioned. That in consequence, Mr. Randolph immediately resigned.[60] Who doubted that French crowns were scattered to hire American traitors? Such a fact ought to alarm even stupid zealots for the French. *Sat verbum.* More will soon transpire.

Come and see us, which will be a cordial to your friend.

TO THOMAS DWIGHT

DEDHAM, OCTOBER 3, 1795

DEAR SIR,

I THINK you will have heard of my having had a relapse for some weeks past. Extreme weakness, want of appetite, want of rest, &c.

.   .   .   .

I despair, or have but faint expectations of reaching Philadelphia at the first of the session, if ever; but I believe the cool weather, and the resolute adherence to the tonic

---

[59] *Edmund Randolph.* [S. AMES]

[60] *This transaction was very lamely and imperfectly explained by Mr. Randolph, in his published vindication.* [S. AMES]

plan, will raise me again upon my legs (which have been of late almost useless) before December. We earnestly wish a visit from you, and our other Springfield friends. Remember it is a duty of charity to visit the sick.[61]

Our Common Pleas Court is sitting here, but I decline, and indeed am quite unable, to attend it. It is the less to be lamented, as it does not rain fees. It rains incessantly almost every thing besides. The weather is generally bad for me. I hope soon the beginning of the bright days of the fall, which I fancy will renovate my old fabric.

The mobs are quiet, I hear, in Boston; and Dedham has not the spirit to raise any.

Yours, and Mrs. D.'s very true friend.

TO RUFUS KING

DEDHAM, NOVEMBER 5, 1795

DEAR SIR:

. . . I DESPAIR of attending Congress at the opening of the session & the time when I may is both remote and uncertain. Great reflection and care ought to precede as well as conduct the beginning of business in the house. If the Democrats would agree to be silent on the Treaty in the answer to the President's speech, would it be eligible, certainly not the

---

[61] *The writer's health broke down at about this period, in a very dangerous and alarming manner; and, although improved subsequently, it never was fully restored.* [S. AMES]

most eligible. I hope you and others will think beforehand what course ought to be taken.

With sincere regard &c.

FISHER AMES

TO THOMAS DWIGHT

DEDHAM, NOVEMBER 18, 1795

DEAR FRIEND,

WHEN KINGS and princes are sick, it is usual to publish daily bulletins of their condition. The Convention caused the report on the health of the late Louis XVI., and afterwards of the Dauphin, to be inserted in the bulletin. My pride, though of the true blue democratic sort, finds some relief, in the resemblance of my weekly employment at letter-writing, to the bulletin aforesaid. Indeed I rise higher than sick kings and princes, because the mob and their deadly enemies indulged their curiosity by reading the printed report; and it would wrong my Springfield friends to make the comparison, after having mentioned that.

You will judge, by the levity of my style, that I am better, and you will judge right. I recruited so fast the last week, that I began to reproach myself for pretending to be an invalid. I walked, sometimes hoed in the garden, and rode out with the best spirits. On Thursday last I rode four miles to visit parson Bradford, and returned without fatigue. That day, George Minot, and parson Freeman, Mr. and Mrs. Gore, came to visit us, and I found them unexpectedly on my return. In the afternoon, Mr. and Mrs. Cabot came, and other company succeeded. The long attention, and your wife will say, the incessant talking, tired me a good deal.

.   .   .   .

I am very happy to find that the spirit of one hundred thousand barrels of Hampshire cider is all federal. It will beat as much whiskey, and twice as much peach brandy. It will not be the fault of our wicked faction, if the cider spirit is not put to the proof. The ball will soon open in the federal House of Representatives. I expect Old Nick will be unchained. . . .

I have bought, and am going to present to farmer Gore, two queer looking sheep, their legs short like the creeping sort of fowls, their shoulders growing splay, like the rickets.[62]

---

[62] *This prepossessing variety of the sheep family was well known in New England as the Otter breed. Since the introduction of the Merino, our farmers have manifested more anxiety to improve the quality of the wool than to perpetuate the questionable advantages of short legs and rickety shoulders, and the Otter sheep are to be reckoned among the things that were. They are described in Livingston's Essay on Sheep (published at New York in 1809) in terms of some sensibility. The writer says, "But what particularly characterizes these sheep, and from which, together with the length of their bodies, they probably took their name, is the extreme shortness of their legs, which are also turned out in such a manner as to render them rickety. They cannot run or jump, and even walk with some difficulty. They appear as if their legs had been broken, and set by an awkward surgeon. To me there is something so disgusting in the sight of a flock of these poor lame animals, that even a strong conviction of their superior utility could hardly induce me to keep them. The only advantage that can result from this deformity is, that they cannot pass over stone walls, and are confined by slight fences. Whether this will counterbalance the sufferings to which they must be liable in a deep snow, the impossibility of driving them to distant pastures, or to market, and the facility with which they may be destroyed by dogs, is a matter of calculation with the economical farmer. Those, however, who possess a grain of taste, who take a pleasure in the sportive gambols of their lambs, or who delight rather in perfecting than maiming the works of nature, will seldom be induced to propagate, beyond what is absolutely necessary, an infirmity which abridges the short enjoyments of a helpless and useful animal." "What was at first, probably an accidental circumstance, has become the basis of a new and unsightly race." [S. AMES]*

Their wool is said to be more abundant, and they cannot climb fence. Having less activity, they are expected to fatten better in the same pasture than other sheep. A Mr. Seth Wight, of Dover, found a couple of lambs, such as I describe, dropped by his flock, and he has at length a whole flock of the kind. They begin to draw some attention, and for the reasons I have suggested, they seem to deserve an uncommon share of it. My farming zeal has so far abated, that I prefer getting experiments made by others, to making them myself. I gave eight dollars for the sheep, and that is cheaper than to keep them at home.

I am trying to raise new breeds of potatoes from the seed. The labor and expense of this petty operation suit my laziness, as well as my economy. Regards to friends.

Yours, truly, &c.

TO ANDREW CRAIGIE, ESQ.

DEDHAM, NOVEMBER 21ST, 1795

DEAR SIR

. . . . PRAY COME and see me. I am daily recruiting, but going to Congress is not yet either possible or prudent . . .

FISHER AMES

TO DWIGHT FOSTER (IN CONGRESS)

DEDHAM, DECEMBER 10, 1795

DEAR SIR,

. . . .

THE PUBLIC EXPECTATION is up, and if a good deal of mischief should not be done, we shall be disappointed, agreeably, I confess. I please myself with the hope that faction will be frustrated, because the heads of the party will aim at more, and worse, than the wrong-headed but not very ill-disposed on their side, will support. To make one branch directly attack the other two, or even to do it as indirectly as the thing will admit of, seems to me too obvious a mischief to be concealed or disguised. Therefore I do my best to believe that the moderate men on the wrong side will vote against proceeding to extremities.

I lie on the gridiron of impatience, as still as I can, expecting by next week's post to have some facts, and better ground for conjectures.[63]

---

[63] *The contest upon the treaty, though daily expected, did not begin till February.* [S. AMES]

TO THOMAS DWIGHT

DEDHAM, DECEMBER 30, 1795

MY DEAR FRIEND,

. . . .

You RECKON a good event to the session of Congress, with more confidence than I can find a footing for. I count fifty-six *antis*, forty-nine feds, of the one hundred and five members of the House of representatives. It is possible that some may shrink from the edge of the pit, to which their leaders would push them. They may express a dislike of the treaty, in the answer to the speech, and be so much blockheads as to suppose the expression of such a dislike, not only harmless, but an essential duty. But they will be more reluctantly brought to act with effect against the execution of the treaty. They will not impeach the President. What are we to hope from a body so deeply infected with the spirit of folly or jacobinism, but continual efforts to disorganize? It will be a gymnasium in which all the turbulent passions will be disciplined, and grow strong by exercise.

I repeat my prediction with more faith than ever; a crisis will soon come. It may be delayed, but cannot be prevented. Mr. King writes to me, that he hears Mr. Madison says, it is necessary to express the sense of the representatives on the treaty. I rely on the good disposition of the New England people, but when a government *will* go wrong, what can individuals do? When a house is divided against itself, it cannot be held up by main strength. The House, by expressing any opinion in disapprobation of the other two, will bring on a new state of things. Faction will then have one branch, and the friends of order will cling to the President and

Senate. If such a crisis can be produced, and is nearly arrived, in the midst of prosperity, peace, and knowledge, and while the government is administered with integrity, and with Washington at the head,—does it warrant very sanguine expectations of future tranquility, when adversity, disturbance, and panic, shall prevail; when the hated head of one party shall exact obedience from the other; when the ruling party shall, as all ruling parties will, abuse its power sometimes, and commit blunders at others? I renounce this topic, lest I should fill my page with it, and lose my spirits.

.   .   .   .

Your affectionate friend and brother.

A few inches of snow have fallen this morning, and it still snows, but as the wind is not far from south-east, it will soon stop. Should a good body of it fall, possibly I may tackle my covered sleigh, and go as far as New Haven. Thence to New York, trust Providence. This is only in my brain at present. I could not bear the stage, but I could, I think, travel in a hack or sleigh.

I have read Sedgwick's great speech. Things wear a threatening face.

TO OLIVER WOLCOTT

DEDHAM, DECEMBER 31, 1795

MY DEAR SIR,

I AM greatly obliged by your favour covering Mr. R's. vindication, as you will believe, when I acquaint you that I have read till I am stupefied, and my task is not finished, nor my curiosity sated. The subject and the title led me to look for a plausible vindication at least. Taking his whole mystical story for true, the cause for wonder is not removed if the censure is shifted; something strange, and because it is strange, probably wicked, has been done or attempted. The tale of a foreigner's zeal to bring to light conspiracies against our government, and the need there was of resorting to a foreigner to use his flour contractors in the affair, is strange—passing strange. The public opinion has, I believe, passed sentence without waiting for the tardy evidence of his book. It is however, a precious book, and ought to be made to yield treasure to the federalists like a mine. I rejoice to hear that the answer to the speech has not conjured up the evil spirits that were expected to rise on this occasion. Let our three branches keep duly united, and the efforts of party will be impotent, at least for a time. The people are coming right. I send you a sermon, which I wish our friends Ellsworth, Cabot, Jed. Smith and Thatcher may see. Afterwards, I think it could do good if Mr. Cabot would send it under cover to Mr. Izard, and get it (the political part) published in a Charleston paper. I am, with unfeigned regard, &c., dear sir, yours truly.

FISHER AMES

1796

===

TO DWIGHT FOSTER

———

DEDHAM, JANUARY 4, 1796

DEAR SIR,

YOUR FAVOR of the 19th is very consoling. Party has expected
nothing but triumphs at this meeting of Congress; and when
party triumphs, the conquered must be dragged at the victor's
chariot wheels. It is a childish comfort that many enjoy, who
say the minority aim at *place* only, not at the overthrow of
government. They aim at setting mobs above law, not at
filling places which have a known legal responsibility. The
struggle against them is therefore *pro aris et focis;* it is for
our rights and liberties, words which we have a better right
to use than those who make them ridiculous by having them
always in their mouths.

Does not R.'s[64] vindication confound the wicked faction? The first paragraph of number ten evinces designs unfriendly to the United States too bad to be intrusted to his (Fauchet's) colleagues, and on which R.'s precious confessions throw a satisfactory light. The design may be presumed to relate to the whisky rebellion, as that seems to be the burden of the song. F.'s sympathy of feeling, and his approbation, go along with the whisky rebels and the faction in Congress. It is truly important that our farmers should be made to comprehend this instructive truth. It will keep them out of the power of the tempters in the seaports, and their mobs; and when our farmers in Worcester and Hampshire are right, will W. L. dare to go wrong as formerly? Could not S. L. use some effectual remonstrances with his namesake? Is it not worth the trouble, little as the merit or stability of the former may be deemed? I wish to see J. B. V. left alone in our list. I write, as you will see, in confidence. There has not been a time when I conceived the country was so well prepared to take right impressions. My health is undoubtedly improving, and though I do not expect to be able to travel in a stage for a long time, I think easy journeys in a hack or sleigh would be practicable in a short time. My physicians who encourage this expectation do it with a strict proviso that I hold my tongue in Congress.

Yours, with affectionate regard.

---

[64] *Randolph's.* [S. AMES]

TO JEREMIAH SMITH

DEDHAM, JANUARY 18, 1796

MY DEAR FRIEND,

You HAVE deserved well of the country for writing so punctually and so fully, so wittily and so wisely. I am glad you abstain from scandal, because you know I hate it, yet abuse Mr. Thatcher, if you please, for his not writing to me, and I shall esteem the favor in proportion to your known repugnance to the task. I think spiritedly, and almost resolve to go on to Philadelphia. Should this snow last, I am half resolved to jingle my bells as far as Springfield, within a week. That, however, is a crude purpose ripening in my brain. To-morrow I go to my loyal town of Boston, in my covered sleigh, by way of experiment of my strength, which will prove just nothing, as it is no exercise. More of this, and more decidedly, in my next. I am, I believe, unfit for any fatigue, or for business. I go with a fixed design to be useless. Does that surprise you?

I have read two Camilluses[65] on the constitutionality of the treaty; so much answer to so little weight of objection is odds. He holds up the ægis against a wooden sword. Jove's eagle holds his bolts in his talons, and hurls them, not at the Titans, but at sparrows and mice. I despise those objections in which blockheads only are sincere.

Our Governor has not yet delivered his most democratic speech, although it is the second week of the court-sitting. To-morrow wisdom opens her mouth. It is said, he has twice

---

[65] *By Hamilton.* [S. AMES]

or thrice new modelled his preachment, as he was led by hopes and fears of the temper of the members, finding no anti-treaty stuff would be well received, it is to be supposed. So says rumor. Your despatches are referred to a committee of the whole, and if any part shall be found to demand a more detailed answer, it shall be sent by the next post. Whether you *did* play the fool, or not, when the flag was delivered, you *seem* to have done it.[66] Such parade to check enthusiasm! Oh stuff! Is it necessary to show zeal for the power of France, to evince regard for liberty? You remark justly, "Reason is a slim underpinning for government." But our reason is no less wild than our passions. Our very wise folks think a man false to his own country, if he is not a partisan of some foreign nation.

Your friend.

TO JEREMIAH SMITH

MAMARONECK, AT MRS. HORTON'S,
27 MILES EAST FROM NEW YORK, FEBRUARY 3, 1796,
WEDNESDAY MORNING

MY DEAR FRIEND,

HERE I AM, *per varios casus*, through thick and thin; *jactatus et terris*, the sleigh often on bare ground; *vi superûm*, and then there was great wear and tear of horseflesh; *tantœne animis iræ*, such is my patriotic zeal to be useless in Congress. I give you a translation to save you trouble, and I have the

---

[66] *The presentation of the French flag took place on the first day of January, 1796. It was accompanied with much ceremony, and both Houses of Congress passed rather sentimental resolutions on the occasion.* [S. AMES]

most intimate persuasion[67] that it is as near the original as
the copies of Mr. Fauchet's despatches, number three and
six. I left Springfield Saturday morning, and came on to
Hartford, very sick all the way. But I assure you, solemnly,
I survived it, and was well the next morning. Lodged at New
Haven Sunday night, at Norwalk Monday night. The snow
grew thin at New Haven, and was nearly gone in the cartway
at Stamford. There I procured a coachee from a Mr. Jarvis,
who was very obliging, and no democrat, his name notwithstanding. Came on wheels to this place, and slept; waked
and found a snow-storm pelting the windows. It still continues,
and I have sent back the coachee sixteen miles to Mr. Jarvis,
and wait for the sleigh. Fate, perhaps, ordains that it will
thaw by the time it comes back; so much uncertainty is there
in all the plans of man! The novelty of this grave reflection
will recommend it to you. To-morrow expect to hear the bells
ring, and the light-horse blow their trumpets, on my reaching
New York. If Governor Jay will not do that for me, let him
get his treaty defended by Camillus and such understrappers.
I intend to pass two days there, and three more will, I trust,
set me down in Philadelphia. Do not let me go down to the
pit of the Indian Queen. It is Hades, and Tartarus, and
Periphlegethon, Cocytus, and Styx, where it would be a pity
to bring all the piety and learning that he must have, who
knows the aforesaid infernal names. Pray leave word at the
said Queen, or, if need be, at any other Queen's, where I
may unpack my weary household gods. I am the better for
the journey, although I have, at least three times, been so
ill as to come near fainting. My country's good alone could
draw a man so sick from home,—saving that I am not sick,
and shall do my country no good. That, however, is not
allowed by counsel, to impair the obligation to pay me six

---

[67] *In Mr. Randolph's published vindication, a letter was introduced
from Fauchet, stating, among other things, that he had a* most intimate
persuasion *that he had misunderstood Mr. R.'s application.* [S. AMES]

dollars per day. Forbearing to be mischievous is said to be a valid consideration. I shall not prove a troublesome lodger, nor call for little messes; a slice of dry bread at noon, wine-whey frequently at bedtime, will be all the addenda to the common attendance. Your offer to lodge with me in the same house is really very friendly, as you might well expect to find me both stupid and hyp'd. If I should prove otherwise and better, it will be a just reward for your generous friendship.

Yours, &c.

TO THOMAS DWIGHT

PHILADELPHIA, FEBRUARY 11, 1796

DEAR FRIEND,

I ARRIVED here the 9th, and am, after a day's discomposure by the journey, the better for the exercise. Several times, on the way, I was very ill. I should have sent you an account of myself, had I known where a letter would hit you. This doubt will shorten this epistle.

I am now in Congress. The House is too hot for me, although the business is cool and stupid enough; election of Smith, of Virginia. Faction is preparing its mines, and getting all ready for an explosion. Many think it will not be fired. I know very little, as yet, of the views of parties. Massachusetts has given faction a blow by the answer to the speech, and the contempt of Virginia's revolutionary amendments. This state treats the latter very cavalierly, and marks a most spirited federalism.

Judge Summer would kill faction in Massachusetts, if he was Governor.

Your affectionate friend.

TO THOMAS DWIGHT

PHILADELPHIA, FEBRUARY 16, 1796

DEAR FRIEND,

I SEE, by the Centinel, your name is on the list of the majority, on the question of amendments. Still I think it prudent to address this to Springfield.

My health is the better for the journey. I doubt whether I could have effected it on wheels, as with all the accommodation of a sleigh, and all the precautions I could use, and although sixteen days on the road, I was several times near a full stop, being so unwell as to unfit me to travel. I am here, however, and as the weather is mild, and is usually very fine from this date for three months, I believe my chance of recovery is mended by the situation I am in.

. . . .

I rejoice with you, that the spirit of our Massachusetts legislature is so adverse to desperate innovation as the yeas and nays indicate. I hope, however, that many of the minority are opposed to the Virginia amendments, but voted as they did on other grounds, for I conceive it demonstrable on the most approved principles, vouched by experience, that the said amendments are not merely unfriendly to, but utterly subversive of, a free republican government.

1134

Disorganizers never sung a more lamentable dirge. France is robing herself in *costume,* the uniforms of her three branches. Is not that worse than titles? The United States behold the failure of the schemes of foreign corruption and domestic faction; the states, one after another, fulminating contempt on Virginia and Co.; as, for example, the ironical and sarcastic resolves of Pennsylvania. Every such proceeding chills the Catilines here, like the touch of the torpedo. Whether the anti-treaty resolutions will be moved in Congress is doubted by some. I believe they will be moved, and I fear will be carried. Others think they will fail. The unconstitutionality of the treaty is too ridiculous a piece of sophistry for men of sense to maintain. A direct vote that it is bad, disgraceful, and ruinous, is said to be resolved on by the party.

The whisperers of secret history say that the flag of France was presented to the President, after a design and an attempt to get it received by the House of Representatives, thus to throw the President into the background; but finding it would not do, the mode adopted was the only one.

A majority of wrong heads is said to be in the House. If so, and good laws are impeded, as usual, let the blame fall on those who hold the power of acting or stopping action.

.   .   .   .

Your friend.

TO THOMAS DWIGHT

PHILADELPHIA, MARCH 9, 1796

MY DEAR FRIEND,

I SIT now in the House, and, that I may not lose my temper and my spirits, I shut my ears against the sophisms and rant against the treaty, and divert my attention by writing to you.

Never was a time when I so much desired the full use of my faculties, and it is the very moment when I am prohibited even attention. To be silent, neutral, useless, is a situation not to be envied. I almost wish . . . . was here, and I at home, sorting squash and pumpkin seeds for planting.

It is a new post for me to be in. I am not a sentry, not in the ranks, not in the staff. I am thrown into the wagon, as part of the baggage. I am like an old gun, that is spiked, or the trunnions knocked off, and yet am carted off, not for the worth of the old iron, but to balk the enemy of a trophy. My political life is ended, and I am the survivor of myself, or rather a troubled ghost of a politician, that am condemned to haunt the field of battle where I fell. Whether the government will long outlive me is doubtful. I know it is sick, and, many of the physicians say, of a mortal disease. A crisis now exists, the most serious I ever witnessed, and the more dangerous, because it is not dreaded. Yet, I confess, if we should navigate the federal ship through this strait, and get out again into the open sea, we shall have a right to consider the chance of our government as mended. We shall have a lease for years—say four or five; not a freehold— certainly not a fee-simple.

How will the Yankees feel and act when the day of trial comes? It is not, I fear, many weeks off. Will they let the casuists quibble away the very words, and adulterate the genuine spirit, of the Constitution? When a measure passes by the proper authorities, shall it be stopped by force? Sophistry may change the form of the question, may hide some of the consequences, and may dupe some into an opinion of its moderation when triumphant, yet the fact will speak for itself. The government cannot go to the halves. It would be another, a worse government, if the mob, or the leaders of the mob in Congress, can stop the lawful acts of the President, and unmake a treaty. It would be either no government, or instantly a government by usurpation and wrong.

MARCH 12

THE DEBATE is yet unfinished, and will continue some days longer. I beg you let . . . . . have the paper, after you have done with it.

I think we shall beat our opponents in the end, but the conflict will light up a fierce war.

Your friend.

TO CHRISTOPHER GORE

PHILADELPHIA, MARCH 11, 1796

DEAR FRIEND,

MR. GILES has just finished a great speech, and our friend Sedgwick is now making another. Nothing will be decided till the next week. The manifest force of argument is on our side. Madison spun cobweb yesterday—stated five constructions of the Constitution, and proceeded to suggest the difficulties in each, but was strangely wary in giving his opinion. Conscience made him a coward. He flinched from an explicit and bold creed of anarchy. Giles has no scruples, and certainly less sense. Pray attend to the debate. I am not able to stay in the House all the time; expect therefore a broken history from my pen. The party abhors being drawn into the argument on the construction of the Constitution, on this question for a call of papers. They see the disadvantage of setting up a claim to unlock the cabinet, and a right to keep the key in future. Montezuma may, and I hope he will, set down his foot, and refuse them. Then the party will rage in vain, and I expect a final success to our attempts to carry the treaty into effect. In this mode, the party must assail his character, powers, and doings: all our strength against part of theirs. The form of this debate will create surprise—that we refused to accept Madison's amendment, to except such papers as he might deem improper, and our going on to discuss the whole doctrine of the powers of each department. I think both proceedings right. An amendment, by hiding the cloven foot, would have made the motion worse.

Giles is said to have ready three resolutions:

1st. That the treaty is pernicious, &c., &c.

2d. That this House will *not* concur in measures to carry it into execution. (I since hear it is not so, but an assertion of the discretion of the House to grant or withhold.)

3d. That it will concur in measures to give effect to a proper treaty.

I like their violence. You and other discerning friends of order will note the wickedness, inconsistency, and sophistry of these Catilines. Virginia is said to be growing tamer; and if the storm should not sink the federal ship immediately, a better crew may be looked for, even from Virginia. This is the opinion of the most respectable, and probably the leaders dread the same thing, for they put all at risk on this struggle.

I am obliged to hear as though I heard not, and to feel as though I was an oyster.

MARCH 12

No DECISION yet, and the debate will continue some days. It was the design of Giles to go into a rambling debate, exciting the passions against this and that article of the treaty. Instead of an address to passion, the debate takes the turn of argument, an accurate discussion of a proposition—its truth, not its consequences. Giles will try to get it on the journals,—That the House asserts its right to sanction, or refuse to sanction, treaties which include any of the legislative powers of Congress, after which he will let his common men drop off, and carry the treaty into effect. Others believe the utmost effort will be made to prevent its going into effect.

Yours.

TO GEORGE RICHARDS MINOT

PHILADELPHIA, APRIL 2, 1796

DEAR FRIEND,

I FEEL no desire to convert Doctor Kilham, because not having ceased to view him as a man of worth and good sense, I would not wish to run the hazard of a new casting. I do not know, and, believing what I have suggested of his character, I do not much care, what his politics are. Such *antis* as he was will do no harm. Men of fair minds, and possibly of too much perspicacity in espying objections to systems, may raise their own apprehensions, but not mine. They are not the bearers of firebrands, and daggers. The present household of antifederalism would be too much praised, to be compared with the few sensible and overapprehensive men of principle, who dreaded the operation of our government at its outset.

Experience seems to have malice against theories. Friends and foes must confess the danger from the government, and the danger to it, appear in unsuspected places.

When clubs fail of deciding elections, mobs must be resorted to, for guiding the conduct of the chosen. When riotous meetings can prevent the ratification of a treaty, the power of negotiating will be virtually in the hands of the leaders of the sovereign people, as they very foolishly call a thousandth part of a nation. This very course has been taken, and the event is the problem yet unsolved.

The answer of the President respecting the treaty papers will be with you. The party seemed wild on its being read. The project of referring the message to a committee of the whole House, is for the declared purpose of replying to it; that is a manifesto or declaration of war against the other two branches. The serious aspect of the business needs no comment. My own faith is, the country will leave them, or more properly is not with them. Mr. Madison is deeply implicated by the appeal of the President to the proceedings of the General Convention, and most persons think him irrecoverably disgraced, as a man void of sincerity and fairness.

The appropriation of money to carry the treaty into effect will be vehemently contested, and it is hard to say how it will go. I think some will flinch. A statement is made to give you an idea of the votes.

More are doubtful, and should one or two leaders desert the terrorists, they will drop off rapidly. Such an event is probable. My health is slowly, though I am persuaded

	Yeas.	Nays.	Doubtful.	Absent.
N. H.	3	0	0	1
Mass.	10	3	0	1
Conn.	7	0	0	0
R. I.	2	0	0	0
Vt.	1	1	0	0
N. Y.	5	4	1	0
N. J.	5	0	0	0
Penn.	4	7	2	0
Del.	0	1	0	0
Md.	6	1	0	1
Vir.	0	19	0	0
Ken.	0	1	1	0
N. Car.	2	7	1	0
S. Car.	2	3	0	1
Geo.	0	2	0	0
	47	49	5	4

perceptibly, improving. I am unfit for debate, and am not able to attend through a whole sitting. God bless you.

TO THOMAS DWIGHT

PHILADELPHIA, APRIL 18, 1796

DEAR FRIEND,

I HAVE just returned from riding. Mr. Giles is speaking in the House, and I have enjoyed your and Mrs. A.'s letters in the committee chamber.

.   .   .   .

Here, we dance upon the edge of the pit, crying *ça ira;* it is but a little way to the bottom. No war. Reject the treaty.

All depends on the constancy of the Senate, and on the alarms that the people will feel and send back to us. There will be no adjournment, if no treaty—no motion to the wheels of government. The mill will be stopped, if the *antis* refuse to grind this treaty grist. In short, it is what Genet threatened—an appeal to the public. Heaven knows what the court of appeals will do. At present, the *vox populi* seems to be *vox rationis*. This city is right. So is Baltimore. The Quakers are alarmed. Alarms are contagious. I do not despair, nor will I brag, because the issue is actually joined, so long ago croaked about in all my letters. I wish the event had disgraced my conjuring skill.

My best wishes for Mrs. D., Miss B., &c., and two ounces (all I have a right to frank) of kisses for Mary and John.

Yours, &c.

I am *bonâ fide* a better man than when you saw me at Dedham, or than I was at the date of my last.

SPEECH ON THE JAY TREATY

On August 18, 1795, President Washington signed the treaty negotiated by John Jay with Great Britain. The President had previously been on the verge of signing the treaty. But the British had resumed seizing American vessels carrying provisions to France. Angered, the President retired to Mount Vernon determined not to sign.

The President's vacation was cut short by news of the release of despatches captured by the British from the French minister to the United States. The despatches suggested that Secretary of State Randolph had sought French funds for a bribe. This revelation convinced Washington to ratify the treaty in order to end French influence in American politics. The British cooperated by adopting a conciliatory attitude on the question of American maritime rights.

Even before the treaty was made public, reaction to it was suspicious. But once Senator Mason of Virginia had leaked a copy to the Republican press, public disapproval burst forth in a torrent. The Republican party played on this discontent by organizing press commentary and town meetings which sent denunciatory petitions to both the President and Congress.

The Republican-controlled House of Representatives threatened to refuse to make the necessary appropriations for carrying the treaty into effect. The President, therefore, delayed sending a copy down to them for some months. Meanwhile, the Federalists mounted their own campaign in favor of the treaty. Additionally, a new treaty with Spain, opening the Mississippi to western commerce, stilled the fears of Americans in the trans-Appalachian areas. The combined effect of these measures was to begin a shift in the public's attitude toward the treaty. Washington finally sent the treaty to the House on March 1, 1796. After receiving it the Representatives began the long anticipated debate over appropriations. The debate continued over the space of two months, during which time petitions of support began coming in from all over the country.

Fisher Ames was in fragile health in late 1795 and early 1796. Consequently he took no early part in the debate. Finally, at the critical point, Republican opposition weakening under the double weight of Federalist rhetoric and shifting public opinion, Ames summoned his strength and delivered the speech which climaxed the entire debate. It was his most celebrated rhetorical performance, one of the foremost American examples of excellence in oratory, and undoubtedly the crowning effort of his Congressional career.

APRIL 28, 1796

MR. CHAIRMAN: I entertain the hope, perhaps a rash one, that my strength will hold me out to speak a few minutes.

In my judgment, a right decision will depend more on the temper and manner with which we may prevail on ourselves to contemplate the subject, than upon the development of any profound political principles, or any remarkable skill in the application of them. If we should succeed to neutralize our inclinations, we should find less difficulty than we have to apprehend in surmounting all our objections.

The suggestion, a few days ago, that the House manifested symptoms of heat and irritation, was made and retorted as if the charge ought to create surprise, and would convey reproach. Let us be more just to ourselves, and to the occasion. Let us not affect to deny the existence and the intrusion of some portion of prejudice and feeling into the debate, when, from the very structure of our nature, we ought to anticipate the circumstance as a probability, and when we are admonished by the evidence of our senses that it is a fact.

How can we make professions for ourselves, and offer exhortations to the House, that no influence should be felt but that of duty, and no guide respected but that of the understanding, while the peal to rally every passion of man is continually ringing in our ears.

Our understandings have been addressed, it is true, and with ability and effect; but, I demand, has any corner of the heart been left unexplored? It has been ransacked to find auxiliary arguments, and, when that attempt failed, to awaken the sensibilities that would require none. Every prejudice and feeling have been summoned to listen to some particular style of address; and yet we seem to believe, and to consider a doubt as an affront, that we are strangers to any influence but that of unbiased reason.

It would be strange that a subject which has roused in turn all the passions of the country, should be discussed without the interference of any of our own. We are men, and, therefore, not exempt from those passions; as citizens and Representatives, we feel the interest that must excite them. The hazard of great interests cannot fail to agitate strong passions: we are not disinterested, it is impossible we should be dispassionate. The warmth of such feelings may becloud the judgment, and, for a time, pervert the understanding; but the public sensibility and our own, has sharpened the spirit of inquiry, and given an animation to the debate. The public attention has been quickened to mark the progress of the discussion, and its judgment, often hasty and erroneous on first impressions, has become solid and enlightened at last. Our result will, I hope, on that account, be the safer and more mature, as well as more accordant with that of the nation. The only constant agents in political affairs are the passions of men—shall we complain of our nature? Shall we say that man ought to have been made otherwise? It is right already, because He, from whom we derive our nature, ordained it so; and because thus made, and thus acting, the cause of truth and the public good is the more surely promoted.

But an attempt has been made to produce an influence of a nature more stubborn and more unfriendly to truth. It is very unfairly pretended that the constitutional right of this House is at stake, and to be asserted and preserved only by a vote in the negative. We hear it said that this is a struggle for liberty, a manly resistance against the design to nullify this assembly, and to make it a cypher in the government. That the PRESIDENT and Senate, the numerous meetings in the cities, and the influence of the general alarm of the country, are the agents and instrumens of a scheme of coercion and terror, to force the Treaty down our throats, though we loathe it, and in spite of the clearest convictions of duty and conscience.

It is necessary to pause here and inquire, whether suggestions of this kind be not unfair in their very texture and fabric, and pernicious in all their influences? They oppose an obstacle in the path of inquiry, not simply discouraging,

but absolutely insurmountable. They will not yield to argument; for, as they were not reasoned up, they cannot be
reasoned down. They are higher than a Chinese wall in truth's
way, and built of materials that are indestructible. While
this remains, it is in vain to argue; it is in vain to say to this
mountain, be thou cast into the sea. For, I ask of the men
of knowledge of the world, whether they would not hold him
for a blockhead that should hope to prevail in an argument
whose scope and object it is to mortify the self-love of the
expected proselyte? I ask, further, when such attempts have
been made, have they not failed of success? The indignant
heart repels a conviction that is believed to debase it.

The self-love of an individual is not warmer in its sense,
or more constant in its action, than what is called in French,
l'esprit de corps, or the self-love of an assembly; that jealous
affection which a body of men is always found to bear towards
its own prerogatives and power. I will not condemn this
passion. Why should we urge an unmeaning censure, or
yield to groundless fears that truth and duty will be abandoned,
because men in a public assembly are still men, and feel
that spirit of corps which is one of the laws of their nature?
Still less should we despond or complain, if we reflect that
this very spirit is a guardian instinct that watches over the
life of this assembly. It cherishes the principle of self-
preservation; and, without its existence, and its existence
with all the strength we see it possess, the privileges of the
representatives of the people, and immediately the liberties
of the people, would not be guarded, as they are, with a
vigilance that never sleeps, and an unrelaxing constancy and
courage.

If the consequences, most unfairly attributed to the vote
in the affirmative, were not chimerical, and worse, for they
are deceptive, I should think it a reproach to be found even
moderate in my zeal to assert the constitutional powers of
this assembly; and, whenever they shall be in real danger,

the present occasion affords proof that there will be no want of advocates and champions.

Indeed, so prompt are these feelings, and when once roused, so difficult to pacify, that, if we could prove the alarm was groundless, the prejudice against the appropriations may remain on the mind, and it may even pass for an act of prudence and duty to negative a measure which was lately believed by ourselves, and may hereafter be misconceived by others, to encroach upon the powers of the House. Principles that bear a remote affinity with usurpation on those powers will be rejected, not merely as errors, but as wrongs. Our sensibilities will shrink from a post where it is possible they may be wounded, and be inflamed by the slightest suspicion of an assault.

While these prepossessions remain, all argument is useless; it may be heard with the ceremony of attention, and lavish its own resources, and the patience it wearies, to no manner of purpose. The ears may be open, but the mind will remain locked up, and every pass to the understanding guarded.

Unless, therefore, this jealous and repulsive fear for the rights of the House can be allayed, I will not ask a hearing.

I cannot press this topic too far—I cannot address myself with too much emphasis to the magnanimity and candor of those who sit here, to suspect their own feelings, and while they do, to examine the grounds of their alarm. I repeat it, we must conquer our persuasion, that this body has an interest in one side of the question more than the other, before we attempt to surmount our objections. On most subjects, and solemn ones too, perhaps in the most solemn of all, we form our creed more from inclination than evidence.

Let me expostulate with gentlemen to admit, if it be only by way of supposition and for a moment, that it is barely possible they have yielded too suddenly to their alarms for the powers of this House; that the addresses which have been made with such variety of forms, and with so great dexterity in some of them, to all that is prejudice and passion in the heart, are either the effects or the instruments of artifice and deception, and then let them see the subject once more in its singleness and simplicity.

It will be impossible, on taking a fair review of the subject, to justify the passionate appeals that have been made to us to struggle for our liberties and rights, and the solemn exhortation to reject the proposition, said to be concealed in that on your table, to surrender them forever. In spite of this mock solemnity, I demand, if the House will not concur in the measure to execute the Treaty, what other course shall we take? How many ways of proceeding lie open before us?

In the nature of things there are but three—we are either to make the Treaty—to observe it—or break it. It would be absurd to say we will do neither. If I may repeat a phrase, already so much abused, we are under coercion to do one of them, and we have no power, by the exercise of our discretion, to prevent the consequences of a choice.

By refusing to act, we choose. The Treaty will be broken, and fall to the ground. Where is the fitness, then, of replying to those who urge upon this House the topics of duty and policy, that they attempt to force the Treaty down, and to compel this assembly to renounce its discretion, and to degrade itself to the rank of a blind and passive instrument in the hands of the treaty-making power? In case we reject the appropriation, we do not secure any greater liberty of action, we gain no safer shelter than before, from the consequences of the decision. Indeed, they are not to be evaded. It is neither just nor manly to complain that the treaty-making power has produced this coercion to act. It is not the art or the despotism of that power, it is the nature of things that compels. Shall we, dreading to become the blind instruments of power, yield ourselves the blinder dupes of mere sounds of imposture? Yet, that word, that empty word, coercion, has given scope to an eloquence that, one would imagine, could not be tired, and did not choose to be quieted.

Let us examine still more in detail the alternatives that are before us, and we shall scarcely fail to see, in still stronger lights, the futility of our apprehensions for the power and liberty of the House.

If, as some have suggested, the thing called a treaty is incomplete, if it has no binding force or obligation, the first question is, Will this House complete the instrument, and by concurring, impart to it that force which it wants?

The doctrine has been avowed, that the Treaty, though formally ratified by the Executive power of both nations, though published as a law for our own, by the PRESIDENT's Proclamation, is still a mere proposition submitted to this assembly, no way distinguishable in point of authority or obligation from a motion for leave to bring in a bill, or any other original act of ordinary legislation. This doctrine, so novel in our country, yet, so dear to many, precisely for the reason that, in the contention of power, victory is always dear, is obviously repugnant, to the very terms, as well as the fair interpretation of our own resolutions—[Mr. BLOUNT's.] We declare that the treaty-making power is exclusively vested in the PRESIDENT and Senate, and not in this House. Need I say that we fly in the face of that resolution when we pretend that the acts of that power are not valid until we have concurred in them? It would be nonsense, or worse, to use the language of the most glaring contradiction, and to claim a share in a power which we, at the same time, disclaim as exclusively vested in other departments.

What can be more strange than to say, that the compacts of the PRESIDENT and Senate with foreign nations are treaties, without our agency, and yet those compacts want all power and obligation until they are sanctioned by our concurrence? It is not my design, in this place, if at all, to go into the discussion of this part of the subject. I will, at least for the present take it for granted that this monstrous opinion stands in little need of remark, and, if it does, lies almost out of the reach of refutation.

But, say those who hide the absurdity under the cover of ambiguous phrases, have we no discretion? And, if we have, are we not to make use of it in judging of the expediency or inexpediency of the Treaty? Our resolution claims that privilege, and we cannot surrender it without equal inconsistency and breach of duty.

If there be any inconsistency in the case, it lies, not in making appropriations for the Treaty, but in the resolution itself—[Mr. BLOUNT's.] Let us examine it more nearly. A treaty is a bargain between nations binding in good faith; and what makes a bargain? The assent of the contracting parties. We allow that the treaty power is not in this House; this House has no share in contracting, and is not a party; of consequence, the PRESIDENT and Senate alone may make a treaty that is binding in good faith. We claim, however, say the gentlemen, a right to judge of the expediency of treaties—that is the constitutional province of our discretion. Be it so—what follows? Treaties, when adjudged by us to be inexpedient, fall to the ground, and the public faith is not hurt. This, incredible and extravagant as it may seem, is asserted. The amount of it, in plainer language, is this—the PRESIDENT and Senate are to make national bargains, and this House has nothing to do in making them. But bad bargains do not bind this House, and, of inevitable consequence, do not bind the nation. When a national bargain, called a treaty, is made, its binding force does not depend upon the making, but upon our opinion that it is good. As our opinion on the matter can be known and declared only by ourselves, when sitting in our legislative capacity, the Treaty, though ratified, and, as we choose to term it, made, is hung up in suspense, till our sense is ascertained. We condemn the bargain, and it falls, though, as we say, our faith does not. We approve a bargain as expedient, and it stands firm, and binds the nation. Yet, even in this latter case, its force is plainly not derived from the ratification by the treaty-making power, but from our approbation. Who will trace these inferences, and pretend that we may have no share, according to the argument, in the treaty-making power? These opinions, nevertheless, have been advocated with infinite zeal and perseverance. Is it possible that any man can be hardy enough to avow them, and their ridiculous consequences?

Let me hasten to suppose the Treaty is considered as already made, and then the alternative is fairly presented to the mind, whether we will observe the Treaty, or break it. This, in fact, is the naked question.

If we choose to observe it with good faith, our course is obvious. Whatever is stipulated to be done by the nation, must be complied with. Our agency, if it should be requisite, cannot be properly refused. And I do not see why it is not as obligatory a rule of conduct for the legislature as for the courts of law.

I cannot lose this opportunity to remark, that the coercion, so much dreaded and declaimed against, appears at length to be no more than the authority of principles, the despotism of duty. Gentlemen complain that we are forced to act in this way, we are forced to swallow the Treaty. It is very true, unless we claim the liberty of abuse, the right to act as we ought not. There is but one way open for us, the laws of morality and good faith have fenced up every other. What sort of liberty is that which we presume to exercise against the authority of those laws? It is for tyrants to complain that principles are restraints, and that they have no liberty so long as their despotism has limits. These principles will be unfolded by examining the remaining question—

SHALL we break the TREATY?

The Treaty is bad, fatally bad, is the cry. It sacrifices the interest, the honor, the independence of the United States, and the faith of our engagements to France. If we listen to the clamor of party intemperance, the evils are of a number not to be counted, and of a nature not to be borne, even in idea. The language of passion and exaggeration may silence that of sober reason in other places, it has not done it here. The question here is, whether the Treaty be really so very fatal as to oblige the nation to break its faith? I admit that such a treaty ought not to be executed. I admit that self-preservation is the first law of society, as well as of individuals. It would, perhaps, be deemed an abuse of terms to call that a treaty which violates such a principle. I waive, also, for the present, any inquiry what departments shall represent the nation, and annul the stipulations of a treaty. I content myself with pursuing the inquiry, whether the nature of this compact be such as to justify our refusal to carry it into effect? A treaty is the promise of a nation. Now, promises do not always bind him that makes them.

But I lay down two rules which ought to guide us in this case. The Treaty must appear to be bad, not merely in the petty details, but in its character, principle, and mass. And, in the next place, this ought to be ascertained by the decided and general concurrence of the enlightened public. I confess there seems to me something very like ridicule thrown over the debate by the discussion of the articles in detail.

The undecided point is, shall we break our faith? And while our country and enlightened Europe await the issue with more than curiosity, we are employed to gather piece-meal, and article by article, from the instrument, a justification for the deed, by trivial calculations of commercial profit and loss; this is little worthy of the subject of this body, or of the nation. If the Treaty is bad, it will appear to be so in its mass. Evil, to a fatal extreme, if that be its tendency, requires no proof; it brings it. Extremes speak for themselves and make their own law. What, if the direct voyage of American ships to Jamaica, with horses or lumber, might net one or two per cent. more than the present trade to Surinam, would the proof of the fact avail anything in so grave a question as the violation of the public engagements?

It is in vain to allege that our faith, plighted to France, is violated by this new Treaty. Our prior Treaties are expressly saved from the operation of the British Treaty. And what do those mean who say that our honor was forfeited by treating at all, and especially by such a treaty? Justice, the laws and practice of nations, a just regard for peace as a duty to mankind, and known wish of our citizens, as well as that self-respect which required it of the nation to act with dignity and moderation—all these forbid an appeal to arms before we had tried the effect of negotiation. The honor of the United States was saved, not forfeited, by treating. The Treaty itself, by its stipulations for the posts, for indemnity, and for a due observance of our neutral rights, has justly raised the character of the nation. Never did the name of America appear in Europe with more lustre than upon the event of ratifying this instrument. The fact is of a nature to overcome all contra-diction.

But the independence of the country—we are colonists again. This is the cry of the very men who tell us that France will resent our exercise of the rights of an independent nation to adjust our wrongs with an aggressor, without giving her the opportunity to say those wrongs shall subsist, and shall not be adjusted. This is an admirable specimen of the spirit of independence. The Treaty with Great Britain, it cannot be denied, is unfavorable to this strange sort of independence.

Few men, of any reputation for sense, among those who say the Treaty is bad, will put that reputation so much at hazard as to pretend that it is so extremely bad as to warrant and require a violation of public faith. The proper ground of the controversy, therefore, is really unoccupied by the opposers of the Treaty; as the very hinge of the debate is on the point, not of its being good, or otherwise, but whether it is intolerably and fatally pernicious? If loose and ignorant declaimers have any where asserted the latter idea, it is too extravagant, and too solidly refuted, to be repeated here. Instead of any attempt to expose it still further, I will say, and I appeal with confidence to the candor of many opposers of the Treaty to acknowledge, that if it had been permitted to go into operation silently, like our other Treaties, so little alteration of any sort would be made by it in the great mass of our commercial and agricultural concerns, that it would not be generally discovered, by its effects, to be in force, during the term for which it was contracted. I place considerable reliance on the weight men of candor will give to this remark, because I believe it to be true, and little short of undeniable. When the panic-dread of the Treaty shall cease, as it certainly must, it will be seen through another medium. Those who shall make search into the articles for the cause of their alarms, will be so far from finding stipulations that will operate fatally, they will discover few of them that will have any lasting operation at all. Those which relate to the disputes between the two countries will spend their force upon the subjects in dispute, and extinguish them. The commercial articles are more of a nature to confirm the existing state of things, than to change it. The Treaty-alarm was purely an address to the imagination and prejudices of the citizens, and not on that account the less formidable. Objections that proceed upon error, in fact or calculation, may be traced and exposed. But such as are drawn from the imagination, or addressed to it, elude definition, and return to domineer over the mind, after having been banished from it by truth.

I will not so far abuse the momentary strength that is lent to me by the zeal of the occasion, as to enlarge upon the commercial operations of the Treaty.

I proceed to the second proposition, which I have stated as indispensably requisite to a refusal of the performance of the Treaty. Will the state of public opinion justify the deed?

No government, not even a despotism, will break its faith without some pretext; and it must be plausible—it must be such as will carry the public opinion along with it. Reasons of policy, if not of morality, dissuade even Turkey and Algiers from breaches of treaty in mere wantonness of perfidy, in open contempt of the reproaches of their subjects. Surely a popular government will not proceed more arbitrarily as it is more free, nor with less shame or scruple in proportion as it has better morals. It will not proceed against the faith of treaties at all, unless the strong and decided sense of the nation shall pronounce, not simply that the Treaty is not advantageous, but that it ought to be broken and annulled. Such a plain manifestation of the sense of the citizens is indispensably requisite, first, because if the popular apprehensions be not an infallible criterion of the disadvantages of the instrument, their acquiescence in the operation of it is an irrefragable proof that the extreme case does not exist which alone could justify our setting it aside.

In the next place, this approving opinion of the citizens is requisite as the best preventive of the ill consequences of a measure always so delicate, and often so hazardous. Individuals would, in that case at least, attempt to repel the opprobrium that would be thrown upon Congress by those who will charge it with perfidy. They would give weight to the testimony of facts and the authority of principles on which the government would rest its vindication. And if war should ensue upon the violation, our citizens would not be divided from their government, nor the ardor of their courage chilled by the consciousness of injustice, and the sense of humiliation—that sense which makes those despicable who know they are despised.

I add a third reason, and with me it has a force that no

words of mine can augment, that a government wantonly refusing to fulfil its engagements, is the corrupter of its citizens. Will the laws continue to prevail in the hearts of the people when the respect that gives them efficacy is withdrawn from the legislators? How shall we punish vice while we practise it? We have not force, and vain will be our reliance when we have forfeited the resources of opinion. To weaken government and to corrupt morals, are effects of a breach of faith not to be prevented—and from effects they become causes, producing, with augmenting activity, more disorder and more corruption; order will be disturbed, and the life of the public liberty shortened.

And who, I would inquire, is hardy enough to pretend that the public voice demands the violation of the Treaty? The evidence of the sense of the great mass of the nation is often equivocal. But when was it ever manifested with more energy and precision than at the present moment? The voice of the people is raised against the measure of refusing the appropriations. If gentlemen should urge, nevertheless, that all this sound of alarm is a counterfeit expression of the sense of the people, I will proceed to other proofs. Is the Treaty ruinous to our commerce? What has blinded the eyes of the merchants and traders? Surely they are not enemies to trade, or ignorant of their own interests. Their sense is not so liable to be mistaken as that of a nation, and they are almost unanimous. The articles stipulating the redress of injuries by captures on the sea are said to be delusive. By whom is this said? The very men whose fortunes are staked upon the competency of that redress say no such thing. They wait with anxious fear lest you should annul that contract, on which all their hopes are rested.

Thus we offer proof, little short of absolute demonstration, that the voice of our country is raised, not to sanction, but to deprecate the nonperformance of our engagements. It is not the nation, it is one, and but one branch of the government that proposes to reject them. With this aspect of things, to reject it is an act of desperation.

I shall be asked, why a Treaty so good in some articles, and so harmless in others, has met with such unrelenting opposition; and how the clamors against it, from New Hampshire to Georgia, can be accounted for? The apprehensions so extensively diffused on its first publication, will be vouched as proof that the Treaty is bad, and that the people hold it in abhorrence.

I am not embarrassed to find the answer to this insinuation. Certainly a foresight of its pernicious operation could not have created all the fears that were felt or affected. The alarm spread faster than the publication of the Treaty. There were more critics than readers. Besides, as the subject was examined, those fears have subsided.

The movements of passion are quicker than those of the understanding. We are to search for the causes of first impressions, not in the articles of this obnoxious and misrepresented instrument, but in the state of the public feeling.

The fervor of the Revolutionary war had not entirely cooled, nor its controversies ceased, before the sensibilities of our citizens were quickened with a tenfold vivacity by a new and extraordinary subject of irritation. One of the two great nations of Europe underwent a change, which has attracted all our wonder, and interested all our sympathies. Whatever they did, the zeal of many went with them, and often went to excess. These impressions met with much to inflame, and nothing to restrain them. In our newspapers, in our feasts, and some of our elections, enthusiasm was admitted a merit, a test of patriotism, and that made it contagious. In the opinion of party, we could not love or hate enough. I dare say, in spite of all the obloquy it may provoke, we were extravagant in both. It is my right to avow that passions so impetuous, enthusiasm so wild, could not subsist without disturbing the sober exercise of reason, without putting at risk the peace and precious interests of our country. They were hazarded. I will not exhaust the little breath I have left to say how much, nor by whom, or by what means they are rescued from the sacrifice. Shall I be called upon to offer my proofs? They are here—they are everywhere. No one has forgotten the proceedings of 1794.[68] No one has forgotten the captures of our vessels, and the imminent danger of war. The nation thirsted not merely for reparation, but vengeance. Suffering such wrongs, and agitated by such sentiments, was

---

[68] *Soon after France declared war against England, citizen Genet (whose civism had assisted the revolution that had just been effected at Geneva) was despatched to the United States for the purpose, as appears by his instructions, of engaging them to take part in the war, and in case the Government, from motives of prudence, and a desire to remain in peace, could not be enlisted, the people were to be stirred up, and by a revolutionary process, plunged into a contest, which has done more injury to the morals and happiness of nations than all the wars of the last century.*

Citizen Genet, perceiving that the success of his mission could only be effected by a revolutionary movement of the people, commenced his operations at the place of his landing, and by his own agency and that of his partisans, every popular passion was inflamed, and every convenient means employed through all the States to produce distrust and confusion among our citizens, and a disorganization of our Government. It must be in the recollection of all, that during the disgraceful contest between this foreign agent and our Executive, the public opinion for a time hung doubtful and undecided; to the honor of our country, virtue and good sense ultimately triumphed over this incendiary.

The revolutionary labors of the citizen Genet were performed in the spring and summer of 1793; his instructions were probably early known in England, and the spirit and hostility towards that country, which during this season appeared throughout the United States, together with the numerous equipments in our ports of privateers under French commissions, must naturally have produced an opinion in the British Cabinet that the United States would ultimately engage in a war on the side of France. The Orders of the 6th of November, and the speech of Lord Dorchester to the Indians, are more satisfactorily accounted for by supposing the existence of this opinion in England, than by the extravagant supposition that has so often been made, that they meditated war against the United States because our citizens were free and our government a republic. [FISHER AMES]

it in the power of any words of compact, or could any parchment with its seals prevail at once to tranquilize the people? It was impossible. Treaties in England are seldom popular, and least of all when the stipulations of amity succeeded to the bitterness of hatred. Even the best treaty, though nothing be refused, will choke resentment, but not satisfy it. Every treaty is as sure to disappoint extravagant expectations as to disarm extravagant passions. Of the latter, hatred is one that takes no bribes. They who are animated by the spirit of revenge will not be quieted by the possibility of profit.

Why do they complain that the West Indies are not laid open? Why do they lament that any restriction is stipulated on the commerce of the East Indies? Why do they pretend that if they reject this, and insist upon more, more will be accomplished? Let us be explicit—more would not satisfy. If all was granted, would not a Treaty of Amity with Great Britain still be obnoxious? Have we not this instant heard it urged against our envoy that he was not ardent enough in his hatred to Great Britain? A Treaty of Amity is condemned because it was not made by a foe, and in the spirit of one. The same gentleman at the same instant repeats a very prevailing objection, that no treaty should be made with the enemy of France. No treaty, exclaim others, should be made with a monarch or a despot. There will be no naval security while those sea-robbers domineer on the ocean. Their den must be destroyed. That nation must be extirpated.

I like this, sir, because it is sincerity. With feelings such as these, we do not pant for treaties. Such passions seek nothing, and will be content with nothing but the destruction of their object. If a treaty left King George his island, it would not answer, not if he stipulated to pay rent for it. It has been said, the world ought to rejoice if Britain was sunk in the sea; if where there are now men and wealth and laws and liberty, there was no more than a sand bank for the sea-monsters to fatten on—a space for the storms of the ocean to mingle in conflict.

I object nothing to the good sense or humanity of all this. I yield the point that this is a proof that the age of reason is in progress. Let it be philanthropy, let it be patriotism, if you will, but it is no indication that any treaty would be approved. The difficulty is not to overcome the objections to the terms; it is to restrain the repugnance to any stipulations of amity with the party.

Having alluded to the rival of Great Britain, I am not un-willing to explain myself. I affect no concealment, and I prac-tice none. While those two great nations agitate all Europe with their quarrels, they will both equally desire, and with any chance of success, equally endeavor to create an influence in America. Each will exert all its arts to range our strength on its own side. How is this to be effected? Our government is a Democratical Republic. It will not be disposed to pursue a system of politics in subservience to either France or England, in opposition to the general wishes of the citizens; and, if Congress should adopt such measures, they would not be pursued long, nor with much success. From the nature of our government, popularity is the instrument of foreign influence. Without it, all is labor and disappointment. With that mighty auxiliary, foreign intrigue finds agents not only volunteers, but competitors for employment, and any thing like reluctance is understood to be a crime. Has Britain this means of influence? Certainly not. If her gold could buy adherents, there becoming such would deprive them of all political power and importance. They would not wield pop-ularity as a weapon, but would fall under it. Britain has no influence, and, for the reasons just given, can have none. She has enough, and God forbid she ever should have more. France, possessed of popular enthusiasm, of party attach-ments, has had, and still has, too much influence in our politics—any foreign influence is too much, and ought to be destroyed. I detest the man and disdain the spirit that can bend to a mean subserviency to the views of any nation. It is enough to be Americans. That character comprehends our duties, and ought to engross our attachments.

But I would not be misunderstood. I would not break the alliance with France. I would not have the connexion between the two countries even a cold one. It should be cordial and sincere, but I would banish that influence, which, by acting on the passions of the citizens, may acquire a power over the government.

It is no bad proof of the merit of the Treaty that, under all these unfavorable circumstances, it should be so well approved. In spite of first impressions, in spite of misrepresentations and party clamor, inquiry has multiplied its advocates, and at last the public sentiment appears to me clearly preponderating on its side. On the most careful review of the several branches of the Treaty—those which respect political arrangements, the spoliations on our trade, and the regulation of commerce—there is little to be apprehended. The evil, aggravated as it is by party, is little in degree, and short in duration. Two years from the end of the European war, I ask, and I would ask the question significantly, what are the inducements to reject the Treaty? What great object is to be gained, and fairly gained by it? If, however, as to the merits of the Treaty, candor should suspend its approbation, what is there to hold patriotism a moment in balance as to the violation of it? Nothing; I repeat confidently, nothing. There is nothing before us in that event but confusion and dishonor. But before I attempt to develop those consequences, I must put myself at ease by some explanations.

Nothing is worse received among men than the confutation of their opinions; and of those, none are more dear or more vulnerable than their political opinions. To say that a proposition leads to shame and ruin, is almost equivalent to a charge that the supporters of it intend to produce them. I throw myself upon the magnanimity and candor of those who hear me. I cannot do justice to my subject, without exposing, as forcibly as I can, all the evils in prospect. I readily admit that in every science, and most of all in politics, error springs from other sources than the want of sense or integrity. I despise indiscriminate professions of candor and respect. There are individuals opposed to me of whom I am not bound to say anything. But of many, perhaps of a majority of the opposers of the appropriations, it gives me pleasure to declare they possess my confidence and regard. There are among them individuals for whom I entertain a cordial affection.

The consequences of refusing to make provision for the Treaty are not all to be foreseen. By rejecting, vast interests are committed to the sport of the winds, chance becomes the arbiter of events, and it is forbidden to human foresight to count their number, or measure their extent. Before we resolve to leap into this abyss, so dark and so profound, it becomes us to pause and reflect upon such of the dangers as are obvious and inevitable. If this assembly should be wrought into a temper to defy these consequences, it is vain, it is deceptive, to pretend that we can escape them. It is worse than weakness to say, that as to public faith our vote has already settled the question. Another tribunal than our own is already erected. The public opinion, not merely of our own country, but of the enlightened world, will pronounce judgment that we cannot resist, that we dare not even affect to despise.

Well may I urge it to men who know the worth of character, that it is no trivial calamity to have it contested. Refusing to do what the Treaty stipulates shall be done, opens the controversy. Even if we should stand justified at last, a character that is vindicated is something worse than it stood before, unquestioned and unquestionable. Like the plaintiff in an action of slander, we recover a reputation disfigured by invective, and even tarnished by too much handling. In the combat for the honor of the nation, it may receive some wound, which, though they should heal, will leave some scars. I need not say, for surely the feelings of every bosom have anticipated, that we cannot guard this sense of national honor, this ever-living fire, which alone keeps patriotism warm in the heart, with a sensibility too vigilant and jealous. If, by executing the Treaty, there is no possibility of dishonor, and if by rejecting there is some foundation for doubt and for reproach, it is not for me to measure, it is for your own feelings to estimate the vast distance that divides the one side of the alternative from the other. If, therefore, we should enter on the examination of the question of duty and obligation with some feelings of prepossession, I do not hesitate to say, they are such as we ought to have; it is an after inquiry to determine whether they are such as ought finally to be resisted.

The resolution [Mr. BLOUNT's] is less explicit than the Constitution. Its patrons should have made it more so, if possible, if they had any doubts or meant the public should entertain none. Is it the sense of that vote, as some have insinuated, that we claim a right for any cause, or no cause at all, but our own sovereign will and pleasure, to refuse to execute, and thereby to annul the stipulations of a treaty?— that we have nothing to regard but the expediency or inexpediency of the measure, being absolutely free from all obligation by compact to give it our sanction? A doctrine so monstrous, so shameless, is refuted by being avowed. There are no words you could express it in that would not convey both confutation and reproach. It would outrage the ignorance of the tenth century to believe, it would baffle the casuistry of a Papal Council to vindicate. I venture to say, it is impossible, no less impossible than that we should desire to assert the scandalous privilege of being free after we have pledged our honor.

It is doing injustice to the resolution of the House (which I dislike on many accounts) to strain the interpretation of it to this extravagance. The treaty-making power is declared by it to be vested exclusively in the PRESIDENT and Senate. Will any man in his senses affirm that it can be a treaty before it has any binding force or obligation? If it has no binding force upon us, it has none upon Great Britain. Let candor answer, is Great Britain free from any obligation to deliver the posts in June, and are we willing to signify to her that we think so? Is it with that nation a question of mere expediency or inexpediency to do it, and that, too, even after we have done all that depends upon us to give the Treaty effect? No sober man can believe this—no one who would not join in condemning the faithless proceedings of that nation, if such a doctrine should be avowed and carried into practice. And why complain, if Great Britain is not bound? There can be no breach of faith where none is plighted. I shall be told that she is bound. Surely it follows that if she is bound to performance, our nation is under a similar obligation; if both parties be not obliged, neither is obliged—it is no compact, no treaty. This is a dictate of law and common sense, and every jury in the country has sanctioned it on oath. It cannot be a treaty, and yet no treaty; a bargain, and yet no promise. If it is a promise, I am not to read a lecture to show why an honest man will keep his promise.

The reason of the thing, and the words of the resolution of the House, imply, that the United States engage their good faith in a treaty. We disclaim, say the majority, the treaty-making power; we of course disclaim (they ought to say) every doctrine that would put a negative upon the doings of that power. It is the prerogative of folly alone to maintain both sides of a proposition.

Will any man affirm the American nation is engaged by good faith to the British nation, but that engagement is nothing to this House? Such a man is not to be reasoned with. Such a doctrine is a coat-of-mail, that would turn the edge of all the weapons of argument, if they were sharper than a sword. Will it be imagined the King of Great Britain and the PRESIDENT are mutually bound by the Treaty, but the two nations are free? It is one thing for this House to stand in a position that presents an opportunity to break the faith of America, and another to establish a principle that will justify the deed.

We feel less repugnance to believe that any other body is bound by obligation than our own. There is not a man here who does not say that Great Britain is bound by treaty. Bring it nearer home. Is the Senate bound? Just as much as the House, and no more. Suppose the Senate, as part of the treaty power, by ratifying a treaty on Monday, pledges the public faith to do a certain act. Then, in their ordinary capacity, as a branch of the Legislature, the Senate is called upon on Tuesday to perform that act, for example, an appropriation of money; is the Senate (so lately under obligation) now free to agree or disagree to the act? If the twenty ratifying Senators should rise up and avow this principle, saying, we struggle for liberty, we will not be cyphers, mere puppets, and give their votes accordingly, would not shame blister their tongues, would not infamy tingle in their ears—would not their country, which they had insulted and dishonored, though it should be silent and forgiving, be a revolutionary tribunal, a rack on which their own reflections would stretch them?

This, sir, is a cause that would be dishonored and betrayed, if I contented myself with appealing only to the understanding. It is too cold, and its processes are too slow for the occasion. I desire to thank God, that since he has given me an intellect so fallible, he has impressed upon me an instinct that is sure. On a question of shame and honor, reasoning is sometimes useless, and worse. I feel the decision in my pulse; if it throws no light upon the brain, it kindles a fire at the heart.

It is not easy to deny, it is impossible to doubt, that a treaty imposes an obligation on the American nation. It would be childish to consider the PRESIDENT and Senate obliged, and the nation and the House free. What is the obligation; perfect or imperfect? If perfect, the debate is brought to a conclusion. If imperfect, how large a part of our faith is pawned? Is half our honor put out at risk, and is that half too cheap to be redeemed? How long has this hair-splitting subdivision of good faith been discovered, and why has it escaped the researches of the writers on the law of nations? Shall we add a new chapter to that law, or insert this doctrine as a supplment to, or, more properly, a repeal of, the Ten Commandments?

The principles and the examples of the British Parliament have been alleged to coincide with the doctrine of those who deny the obligation of the Treaty. I have not had the health to make very laborious researches into this subject; I will, however, sketch my view of it. Several instances have been noticed, but the Treaty of Utrecht is the only one that seems to be at all applicable. It has been answered that the conduct of Parliament, in that celebrated example, affords no sanction to our refusal to carry the Treaty into effect. The obligation of the Treaty of Utrecht has been understood to depend on the concurrence of Parliament, as a condition to its becoming of force. If that opinion should, however, appear incorrect, still the precedent proves, not that the Treaty of Utrecht wanted obligation, but that Parliament disregarded it; a proof, not of the construction of the treaty-making power, but of the violation of a national engagement. Admitting, still further, that Parliament claimed and exercised its power, not as a breach of faith, but as a matter of constitutional right, I reply that the analogy between Parliament and Congress totally fails. The nature of the British Government may require and justify a course of proceeding in respect to treaties that is unwarrantable here.

The British Government is a mixed one. The King, at the head of the army of the hierarchy, with an ample civil list, hereditary, irresponsible, and possessing the prerogative of peace and war, may be properly observed with some jealousy, in respect to the exercise of the treaty-making power. It seems, and perhaps from a spirit of caution on this account, to be their doctrine, that treaties bind the nation, but are not to be regarded by the courts of law, until laws have been passed conformably to them. Our Constitution has expressly regulated the matter differently. The concurrence of Parliament is necessary to treaties becoming laws in England, gentlemen say, and here the Senate, representing the states, must concur in treaties. The Constitution and the reason of the case make the concurrence of the Senate as effectual as the sanction of Parliament. And why not? The Senate is an elective body, and the approbation of a majority of the states affords the nation as ample security against the abuse of the treaty-making power, as the British nation can enjoy in the control of Parliament.

Whatever doubt there may be as to the Parliamentary doctrine of the obligation of treaties in Great Britain, (and perhaps there is some,) there is none in their books, or their modern practice. *Blackstone* represents treaties as of the highest obligation, when ratified by the King; and for almost a century there has been no instance of opposition by Parliament to this doctrine. Their treaties have been uniformly carried into effect, although many have been ratified of a nature most obnoxious to party, and have produced louder clamor than we have lately witnessed. The example of England, therefore, fairly examined, does not warrant, it dissuades us from a negative vote.

Gentlemen have said, with spirit, whatever the true doctrine of our Constitution may be, Great Britain has no right to complain or to dictate an interpretation: The sense of the American nation as to the treaty-power is to be received by all foreign nations. This is very true as a maxim; but the fact is against those who vouch it. The sense of the American nation is not as the vote of the House has declared it. Our claim to some agency in giving force and obligation to treaties, is beyond all kind of controversy novel. The sense of the nation is probably against it: the sense of the government certainly is. The PRESIDENT denies it, on constitutional grounds, and therefore cannot ever accede to our interpretation. The Senate ratified the Treaty, and cannot without dishonor adopt it, as I have attempted to show. Where then do they find the proof that this is the American sense of the treaty-making power, which is to silence the murmurs of Great Britain? Is it because a majority of two or three, or at the most of four or five of this House, will reject the Treaty? Is it thus the sense of our nation is to be recognised? Our government may thus be stopped in its movements: a struggle for power may thus commence, until the event of the conflict may decide who is the victor and the quiet possessor of the treaty power. But, at present, it is beyond all credibility that our vote by a bare majority should be believed to do anything better than embitter our divisions, and to tear up the settled foundations of our departments.

If the obligation of a treaty be complete, I am aware that cases sometimes exist which will justify a nation in refusing a compliance. Are our liberties (gentlemen demand) to be battered away by a treaty, and is there no remedy? There is. Extremes are not to be supposed, but when they happen they make the law for themselves. No such extreme can be pretended in this instance; and if it existed, the authority it would confer to throw off the obligation would rest, where the obligation itself resides, in the nation. This House is not the nation; it is not the whole delegated authority of the nation. Being only a part of that authority, its right to act for the whole society obviously depends on the concurrence of the other two branches. If they refuse to concur, a treaty once made remains in full force, although a breach on the part of a foreign nation would confer upon our own a right to forbear the execution. I repeat it, even in that case, the act of this House cannot be admitted as the act of the nation, and if the PRESIDENT and Senate should not concur, the Treaty would be obligatory.

I put a case that will not fail to produce conviction. Our Treaty with France engages that free bottoms shall make free goods, and how has it been kept? As such engagements will ever be in time of war. France has set it aside, and pleads imperious necessity. We have no navy to enforce the observance of such articles, and paper barriers are weak against the violence of those who are on the scramble for enemy's goods on the high seas. The breach of any article of a treaty by one nation gives an undoubted right to the other to renounce the whole treaty. But has one branch of the government that right, or must it reside with the whole authority of the nation? What if the Senate should resolve that the French Treaty is broken, and therefore null and of no effect? The answer is obvious, you would deny their sole authority. That branch of the Legislature has equal power in this regard with the House of Representatives. One branch alone cannot express the will of the nation. A right to annul a treaty, because a foreign nation has broken its articles, is only like the case of a sufficient cause to repeal a law. In both cases the branches of our government must concur in the ordinary way, or the law and the treaty will remain.

The very cases supposed by my adversaries in this argument, conclude against themselves. They will persist in confounding ideas that should be kept distinct. They will suppose that the House of Representatives has no power unless it has all power. The House is nothing if it be not the whole government—the nation.

On every hypothesis, therefore, the conclusion is not to be resisted, we are either to execute this Treaty or break our faith.

To expatiate on the value of public faith, may pass with some men for declamation; to such men I have nothing to say. To others I will urge, can any circumstance mark upon a people more turpitude and debasement? Can anything tend more to make men think themselves mean, or degrade to a lower point their estimation of virtue and their standard of action? It would not merely demoralize mankind, it tends to break all the ligaments of society, to dissolve that mysterious charm which attracts individuals to the nation, and to inspire in its stead a repulsive sense of shame and disgust.

What is patriotism? Is it a narrow affection for the spot where a man was born? Are the very clods where we tread entitled to this ardent preference because they are greener? No, sir, this is not the character of the virtue, and it soars higher for its object. It is an extended self-love, mingling with all the enjoyments of life, and twisting itself with the minutest filaments of the heart. It is thus we obey the laws of society, because they are the laws of virtue. In their authority we see not the array of force and terror, but the venerable image of our country's honor. Every good citizen makes that honor his own, and cherishes it not only as precious but as sacred. He is willing to risk his life in its defence, and is conscious that he gains protection while he gives it. For what rights of a citizen will be deemed inviolable when a state renounces the principles that constitute their security? Or, if his life should not be invaded, what would its enjoyments be in a country odious to the eyes of strangers and dishonored in his own? Could he look with affection and veneration to such a country as his parent? The sense of having one would die within him; he would blush for his patriotism, if he retained any, and justly, for it would be a vice. He would be a banished man in his native land.

I see no exception to the respect that is paid among nations to the Law of Good Faith. If there are cases in this enlightened period when it is violated, there are none when it is decried. It is the philosophy of politics—the religion of governments. It is observed by barbarians that a whiff of tobacco-smoke or a string of beads gives not merely binding force, but sanctity, to treaties. Even in Algiers, a truce may be bought for money, but when ratified, even Algiers is too wise or too just to disown and annul its obligation. Thus, we see neither the ignorance of savages, nor the principles of an association for piracy and rapine, permit a nation to despise its engagements. If, sir, there could be a resurrection from the foot of the gallows; if the victims of justice could live again, collect together, and form a society, they would, however loth, soon find themselves obliged to make justice—that justice under which they fell—the fundamental law of their state. They would perceive it was their interest to make others respect, and they would therefore soon pay some respect themselves to the obligations of good faith.

It is painful (I hope it is superfluous) to make even the supposition that America should furnish the occasion of this opprobrium. No, let me not even imagine that a republican government, sprung, as our own is, from a people enlightened and uncorrupted; a government whose origin is right and whose daily discipline is duty, can, upon solemn debate, make its option to be faithless—can dare to act what despots dare not avow—what our own example evinces the states of Barbary are unsuspected of! No, let me rather make the supposition that Great Britain refuses to execute the Treaty, after we have done everything to carry it into effect. Is there any language of reproach pungent enough to express your commentary on the fact? What would you say, or rather what would you not say? Would you not tell them, "Wherever an

Englishman might travel, shame would stick to him; he would disown his country?" You would exclaim, "England—proud of your wealth, and arrogant in the possession of power—blush for these distinctions which become the vehicles of your dishonor!" Such a nation might truly say to Corruption, "Thou art my father, and to the Worm, thou art my mother and sister!" We should say of such a race of men, their name is a heavier burden than their debt.

I can scarcely persuade myself to believe that the consideration I have suggested requires the aid of any auxiliary. But, unfortunately, auxiliary arguments are at hand. Five millions of dollars, and probably more, on the score of spoliations committed on our commerce, depend upon the Treaty. The Treaty offers the only prospect of indemnity. Such redress is promised as the merchants place some confidence in. Will you interpose and frustrate that hope, leaving to many families nothing but beggary and despair? It is a smooth proceeding to take a vote in this body. It takes less than half an hour to call the yeas and nays, and reject the Treaty. But what is the effect of it? What, but this: the very men, formerly so loud for redress—such fierce champions, that even to ask for justice was too mean and too slow—now turn their capricious fury upon the sufferers, and say, by their vote, to them and their families, "No longer eat bread! Petitioners, go home and starve; we cannot satisfy your wrongs and our resentments!"

Will you pay the sufferers out of the Treasury? No. The answer was given two years ago, and appears on our Journals. Will you give them letters of marque and reprisal to pay themselves by force? No; that is war. Besides, it would be an opportunity for those who had already lost much to lose more. Will you go to war to avenge their injury? If you do, the war will leave you no money to indemnify them. If it should be unsuccessful, you will aggravate existing evils; if successful, your enemy will have no treasure left to give our merchants; the first losses will be confounded with much greater, and be forgotten. At the end of the war there must be a negotiation, which is the very point we have already gained, and why relinquish it? And who will be confident that the terms of the negotiation, after a desolating war, would be more acceptable to another House of Representatives than the Treaty before us? Members and opinions may be so changed, that the Treaty would then be rejected for being what the present majority say it should be. Whether we shall go on making treaties, and refusing to execute them, I know not;—of this I am certain, it will be very difficult to exercise the treaty-making power, on the new principles, with much reputation or advantage to the country.

The refusal of the posts (inevitable if we reject the Treaty) is a measure too decisive in its nature to be neutral in its consequences. From great causes we are to look for great effects. A plain and obvious one will be, the price of the Western lands will fall. Settlers will not choose to fix their habitation on a field of battle. Those who talk so much of the interest of the United States, should calculate how deeply it will be affected by rejecting the Treaty—how vast a tract of wild land will almost cease to be property. This loss, let it be observed, will fall upon a fund expressly devoted to sink the National Debt. What then are we called upon to do? However the form of the vote and the protestations of many may disguise the proceeding, our resolution is in substance (and it deserves to wear the title of a resolution) to prevent the sale of the Western lands and the discharge of the Public Debt.

Will the tendency to Indian hostilities be contested by any one? Experience gives the answer. The frontiers were scourged with war till the negotiation with Britain was far advanced, and then the state of hostility ceased. Perhaps the public agents of both nations are innocent of fomenting the Indian war, and perhaps they are not. We ought not however to expect that neighboring nations, highly irritated against each other, will neglect the friendship of the savages. The traders will gain an influence, and will abuse it; and who is ignorant that their passions are easily raised, and hardly restrained from violence. Their situation will oblige them to choose between this country and Great Britain, in case the Treaty should be rejected. They will not be our friends, and at the same time the friends of our enemies.

But am I reduced to the necessity of proving this point? Certainly the very men who charged the Indian war on the detention of the posts will call for no other proof than the recital of their own speeches. It is remembered with what emphasis—with what acrimony—they expatiated on the burden of taxes, and the drain of blood and treasure into the Western country, in consequence of Britain's holding the posts. "Until the posts are restored," they exclaimed, "the Treasury and the frontiers must bleed."

If any, against all these proofs, should maintain that the peace with the Indians will be stable without the posts, to them I will urge another reply. From arguments calculated to produce conviction, I will appeal directly to the hearts of those who hear me, and ask whether it is not already planted there? I resort especially to the convictions of the Western gentlemen, whether, supposing no posts and no treaty, the settlers will remain in security? Can they take it upon them to say that an Indian peace, under these circumstances, will prove firm? No, sir, it will not be peace, but a sword; it will be no better than a lure to draw victims within the reach of the tomahawk.

On this theme, my emotions are unutterable. If I could find words for them—if my powers bore any proportion to my zeal—I would swell my voice to such a note of remonstrance it should reach every log-house beyond the mountains. I would say to the inhabitants, Wake from your false security! Your cruel dangers—your more cruel apprehensions—are soon to be renewed; the wounds, yet unhealed, are to be torn open again. In the day time, your path through the woods will be ambushed; the darkness of midnight will glitter with the blaze of your dwellings. You are a father: the blood of your sons shall fatten your corn-field! You are a mother: the war-whoop shall wake the sleep of the cradle!

On this subject you need not suspect any deception on your feelings. It is a spectacle of horror which cannot be overdrawn. If you have nature in your hearts, it will speak a language compared with which all I have said or can say will be poor and frigid.

Will it be whispered that the Treaty has made me a new champion for the protection of the frontiers? It is known that my voice, as well as my vote, have been uniformly given in conformity with the ideas I have expressed. Protection is the right of the frontier; it is our duty to give it.

Who will accuse me of wandering out of the subject? Who will say that I exaggerate the tendencies of our measures? Will any one answer by a sneer, that all this is idle preaching? Will any one deny that we are bound—and I would hope to good purpose—by the most solemn sanctions of duty for the vote we give? Are despots alone to be reproached for unfeeling indifference to the tears and blood of their subjects? Are republicans irresponsible? Have the principles on which you ground the reproach upon cabinets and kings no practical influence—no binding force? Are they merely themes of idle declamation, introduced to decorate the morality of a newspaper essay, or to furnish pretty topics of harangue from the windows of that state-house? I trust it is neither too presumptuous, nor too late to ask, can you put the dearest interest of society at risk without guilt, and without remorse?

It is vain to offer as an excuse, that public men are not to be reproached for the evils that may happen to ensue from their measures. This is very true, where they are unforeseen or inevitable. Those I have depicted are not unforeseen; they are so far from inevitable, we are going to bring them into being by our vote. We choose the consequences, and become as justly answerable for them as for the measure that we know will produce them.

By rejecting the posts, we light the savage fires—we bind the victims. This day we undertake to render account to the widows and orphans whom our decision will make; to the wretches that will be roasted at the stake; to our country; and I do not deem it too serious to say, to conscience, and to God—we are answerable; and if duty be anything more than a word of imposture, if conscience be not a bug-bear, we are preparing to make ourselves as wretched as our country.

There is no mistake in this case; there can be none. Experience has already been the prophet of events, and the cries of our future victims have already reached us. The Western inhabitants are not a silent and uncomplaining sacrifice. The voice of humanity issues from the shade of their wilderness. It exclaims that while one hand is held up to reject this Treaty, the other grasps a tomahawk. It summons our imagination to the scenes that will open. It is no great effort of the imagination to conceive, that events so near are already begun. I can fancy that I listen to the yells of savage vengeance, and the shrieks of torture. Already they seem to sigh in the West wind; already they mingle with every echo from the mountains.

It is not the part of prudence to be inattentive to the tendencies of measures. Where there is any ground to fear that these will be pernicious, wisdom and duty forbid that we should underrate them. If we reject the Treaty, will our peace be as safe as if we execute it with good faith? I do honor to the intrepid spirit of those who say it will. It was formerly understood to constitute the excellence of a man's faith, to believe without evidence, and against it.

But, as opinions on this article are changed, and we are called to act for our country, it becomes us to explore the dangers that will attend its peace, and to avoid them if we can.

Few of us here, and fewer still in proportion of our constituents will doubt that, by rejecting, all those dangers will be aggravated.

The idea of a war is treated as a bugbear. This levity is, at least, unseasonable; and, most of all, unbecoming some who resort to it.

Who have forgotten the philippics of 1794? The cry then was, reparation, no envoy, no treaty, no tedious delays! Now, it seems the passion subsides; or, at least, the hurry to satisfy it. Great Britain, say they, will not wage war upon us.

In 1794, it was urged by those who now say, no war, that if we built frigates, or resisted the pirates of Algiers, we could not expect peace. Now they give excellent comfort, truly! Great Britain has seized our vessels and cargoes, to the amount of millions; she holds the posts; she interrupts our trade, say they, as a neutral nation; and these gentlemen, formerly so fierce for redress, assure us, in terms of the sweetest consolation, Great Britain will bear all this patiently. But, let me ask the late champions of our rights, will our nation bear it? Let others exult because the aggressor will let our wrongs sleep forever. Will it add, it is my duty to ask, to the patience and quiet of our citizens, to see their rights abandoned? Will not the disappointment of their hopes, so long patronized by the government, now in the crisis of their being realized, convert all their passions into fury and despair?

Are the posts to remain forever in the possession of Great Britain? Let those who reject them, when the Treaty offers them to our hands, say, if they choose, they are of no importance. If they are, will they take them by force? The argument I am urging would then come to a point. To use force, is war. To talk of treaty again, is too absurd. Posts and redress must come from voluntary good will, treaty, or war.

The conclusion is plain; if the state of peace shall continue, so will the British possession of the posts.

Look again at this state of things. On the seacoast, vast losses uncompensated. On the frontier, Indian war, actual encroachment on our Territory. Everywhere discontent; resentments ten-fold more fierce, because they will be impotent and humbled; national discord and abasement.

The disputes of the old Treaty of 1783 being left to rankle, will revive the almost extinguished animosities of that period. Wars, in all countries, and, most of all, in such as are free, arise from the impetuosity of the public feelings. The despotism of Turkey is often obliged, by clamor, to unsheath the sword. War might, perhaps, be delayed, but could not be prevented. The causes of it would remain, would be aggravated, would be multiplied, and soon become intolerable. More captures, more impressments, would swell the list of our wrongs, and the current of our rage. I make no calculation of the arts of those whose employment it has been, on former occasions, to fan the fire. I say nothing of the foreign money and emissaries that might foment the spirit of hostility, because the state of things will naturally run to violence. With less than their former exertion, they would be successful.

Will our government be able to temper and restrain the turbulence of such a crisis? The government, alas, will be in no capacity to govern. A divided people, and divided councils! Shall we cherish the spirit of peace, or show the energies of war? Shall we make our adversary afraid of our strength, or dispose him, by the measures of resentment and broken faith, to respect our rights? Do gentlemen rely on the state of peace because both nations will be worse disposed to keep it; because injuries, and insults still harder to endure, will be mutually offered?

Such a state of things will exist, if we should long avoid war, as will be worse than war. Peace without security, accumulation of injury without redress, or the hope of it, resentment against the aggressor, contempt for ourselves, intestine discord and anarchy. Worse than this need not be apprehended, for if worse could happen, anarchy would bring it. Is this the peace gentlemen undertake, with such fearless confidence, to maintain? Is this the station of American dignity, which the high-spirited champions of our national independence and honor could endure; nay, which they are anxious and almost violent to seize for the country? What is there in the Treaty that could humble us so low? Are they the men to swallow their resentments, who so lately were choking with them? If in the case contemplated by them, it should be peace, I do not hesitate to declare it ought not to be peace.

Is there anything in the prospect of the interior state of the country, to encourage us to aggravate the dangers of a war? Would not the shock of that evil produce another, and shake down the feeble and then unbraced structure of our government? Is this the chimera? Is it going off the ground of matter of fact to say, the rejection of the appropriation proceeds upon the doctrine of a civil war of the departments! Two branches have ratified a Treaty, and we are going to set it aside. How is this disorder in the machine to be rectified? While it exists, its movements must stop, and when we talk of a remedy, is that any other than the formidable one of a revolutionary interposition of the people? And is this, in the judgment even of my opposers, to execute, to preserve the Constitution, and the public order? Is this the state of hazard, if not of convulsion, which they can have the courage to contemplate and to brave, or beyond which their penetration can reach and see the issue? They seem to believe, and they act as if they believed, that our Union, our peace, our liberty, are invulnerable and immortal—as if our happy state was not to be disturbed by our dissensions, and that we are not capable of falling from it by our unworthiness. Some of them have no doubt better nerves and better discernment than mine. They can see the bright aspects and happy consequences of all this array of horrors. They can see intestine discords, our government disorganized, our wrongs aggravated, multiplied and unredressed, peace with dishonor, or war without justice, union or resources, in *"the calm lights of mild philosophy."*

But whatever they may anticipate as the next measure of prudence and safety, they have explained nothing to the House. After rejecting the Treaty, what is to be the next step? They must have foreseen what ought to be done, they have doubtless resolved what to propose. Why then are they silent? Dare they not avow their plan of conduct, or do they wait till our progress towards confusion shall guide them in forming it?

Let me cheer the mind, weary no doubt and ready to despond on this prospect, by presenting another, which it is yet in our power to realize. Is it possible for a real American to look at the prosperity of this country without some desire for its continuance, without some respect for the measures which, many will say, produced, and all will confess, have preserved it? Will he not feel some dread that a change of system will reverse the scene? The well-grounded fears of our citizens in 1794 were removed by the Treaty, but are not forgotten. Then they deemed war nearly inevitable, and would not this adjustment have been considered at that day as a happy escape from the calamity? The great interest, and the general desire of our people, was, to enjoy the advantages of neutrality. This instrument, however misrepresented, affords America that inestimable security. The causes of our disputes are either cut up by the roots, or referred to a new negotiation, after the end of the European war. This was gaining everything, because it confirmed our neutrality, by which our citizens are gaining every thing. This alone would justify the engagements of the government. For, when the fiery vapors of the war lowered in the skirts of our horizon, all our wishes were concentered in this one, that we might escape the desolation of the storm. This Treaty, like a rainbow on the edge of the cloud, marked to our eyes the space where it was raging, and afforded at the same time the sure prognostic of fair weather. If we reject it, the vivid colors will grow pale; it will be a baleful meteor, portending tempest and war.

Let us not hesitate, then, to agree to the appropriation to carry it into faithful execution. Thus we shall save the faith of our nation, secure its peace, and diffuse the spirit of confidence and enterprise that will augment its prosperity. The progress of wealth and improvement is wonderful, and some will think, too rapid. The field for exertion is fruitful and vast, and if peace and good government should be preserved, the acquisitions of our citizens are not so pleasing as the proofs of their industry, as the instruments of their future success. The rewards of exertion go to augment its power. Profit is every hour becoming capital. The vast crop of our neutrality is all seed wheat, and is sown again to swell, almost beyond calculation, the future harvest of prosperity: and in this progress, what seems to be fiction, is found to fall short of experience.

I rose to speak under impressions that I would have resisted if I could. Those who see me will believe that the reduced state of my health has unfitted me, almost equally, for much exertion of body or mind. Unprepared for debate, by careful reflection in my retirement, or by long attention here, I thought the resolution I had taken to sit silent, was imposed by necessity, and would cost me no effort to maintain. With a mind thus vacant of ideas, and sinking, as I really am, under a sense of weakness, I imagined the very desire of speaking was extinguished by the persuasion that I had nothing to say. Yet, when I come to the moment of deciding the vote, I start back with dread from the edge of the pit into which we are plunging. In my view, even the minutes I have spent in expostulation have their value, because they protract the crisis, and the short period in which alone we may resolve to escape it.

I have thus been led by my feelings to speak more at length than I had intended; yet I have, perhaps, as little personal interest in the event as any one here. There is, I believe, no member who will not think his chance to be a witness of the consequences greater than mine. If, however, the vote should pass to reject, and a spirit should rise, as it will with the public disorders to make confusion worse confounded, even I, slender and almost broken as my hold upon life is, may outlive the government and Constitution of my country.

TO DWIGHT FOSTER

APRIL 29, 1796[69]

DEAR SIR,

MRS. AMES will have too lively apprehensions for my safety, when she finds (as she will by the Gazettes) that I have been speaking in public. I would quiet them if possible, and am justly anxious to do it at this time, as her situation is critical. The verity of my accounts is a good deal suspected, and

---

[69] *The day after his great speech on the British treaty. The speech was an open violation of the Doctor's orders, and perhaps of some domestic injunctions, which the sad condition of his health made to appear not unreasonable.* [S. AMES]

will probably be received as a drug artfully made up to suit her case.

I beg you address a letter to Colonel Thomas Dwight, and mention in it that I am alive, to your knowledge, and not the worse for having preached. J. Smith engages to tell my story to you in such a manner as to save your conscience from blame, or to furnish excuses, if they should be called for. Your goodness will excuse this call upon it, and command the thanks of your obliged friend.

TO THOMAS DWIGHT

PHILADELPHIA, MAY 19, 1796

DEAR FRIEND,

You ARE too modest in respect to your letters when you fancy they are, or ever can be, burdens. So far from it, they would make the political burden the lighter, if I bore any part of it. But I do not. I venture to say, and I do not know who will have a right to contradict me, that I am the most idle and useless man here. I am but indifferent even *fruges consumere.* I attend Congress daily, but crack jokes instead of problems, and think as little of the proceedings as the doorkeeper. The business of the world is not done by thinking, I confess, and on that ground alone my claim to preëminent inconsequence would be disputable. I have other grounds. I am often absent at a vote.

Our politics assume a pacific and insipid face. The war will soon begin again. Who shall be President and Vice, are questions that will put an end to the armed neutrality of parties. Mr. Adams will be our man, and Jefferson theirs. The second is yet on both sides somewhat doubtful.

If your place in the Senate should not be found to injure your concerns, I shall be glad of your appointment to it. It will bring you near Dedham, and assist the good cause of virtue and order in the General Court. Faction will send its recruiting sergeants round to obtain recruits for Jefferson by beat of the Chronicle drum. The choice of electors will be attended to everywhere with eagle eyes.

We shall probably rise about the 27th. Rejoice when our mob has dispersed, and no windows broken.

A great rain is falling. I hope it is not too late for the Yankee grass.

. . . .

If the pamphlet, containing the speech of your friend and humble servant, can be procured in time for the mail, it shall be sent to you. If *you* think proper to make its last stage, or its place of rest and cobwebs, in your library, you will deposit it there, but not in *my* name. That would expose the vanity, which I cannot conquer, but can hide, except when I boast of my friends; and especially that I am

Yours.

TO THOMAS DWIGHT

PHILADELPHIA, MAY 30, 1796

DEAR FRIEND,

YOU ARE, I trust, now doing all the good you can in the Senate. To prevent evil is one of the most useful and necessary duties of that station. Messrs. Cabot and Strong,[70] we hear,

---

[70] *Members of the Senate.* [S. AMES]

will not serve after this session. To send bad men to succeed two so good, would be unpardonable, especially at this high pitch of Massachusetts good sense and federalism.

Congress will rise June 1st, as most of us expect. Rejoice when that event is ascertained. If we should finish and leave the world right side up, it will be happy. Do not ask what good we do: that is not a fair question, in these days of faction. The sky of politics seems clear for the present, but the blue sky is seldom to be seen, for it rains almost without ceasing. If that should be denied, I fear the Dedham meadows would prove the fact. They cry *de profundis* for relief.

My return may be expected—I will not say when. I shall leave this city for the south on June 2d, unless Congress should linger in their seats. I reckon three weeks for the journey. I shall pass three or four days in New York, and by attention to riding on horseback after my return, and the prospect of some law business, I shall be little of a domestic man during the recess. This is a state of vagabondism which I rejoice to think will soon end.

I hope your household is in health. God bless you.

Yours.

TO OLIVER WOLCOTT

MARTINSBURG, IN VIRGINIA, JULY 5TH, 1796

DEAR SIR,

I AM on my way to the Berkeley Springs, where friends and physicians think health may be had by drinking. My faith in the bath is not strong, but the good effects of travelling are already considerable; I am, however, still feeble.

Opinion is at last yielding in Virginia to truth. That sort of men who are every where federal, are already so in the northern neck of Virginia, and no small impulse of the like kind is felt, as I am told and believe, in the residue of the state. Patrick Henry, if he would serve, would have more votes than Jefferson. The latter in every event will fail of four. Madison will be opposed by a very popular General Clark. Most of the others will be opposed, and on the whole a change is confidently promised to give four true federal representatives in the next Congress; more are hoped for. John Marshall might be chosen, but will not offer.

I am greatly consoled by the style of conversation here, and I do not foresee that in the event of coming to issue with the democrats, this State would not compel obedience to the laws within its limits. Mr. Rutherford is as little respected here as in Philadelphia, and yet the many whom he flatters and deceives, will support him against General Morgan. This is the opinion of federal men.

I expect to see you early in August, and I hope with more flesh and colour than I left Philadelphia. Respects to Mrs. W. and my best wishes for yours and the children's health. Yours, &c.,

FISHER AMES

TO OLIVER WOLCOTT

HAGERSTOWN, JULY 25TH, 1796

DEAR SIR,

I AM on my return from Winchester and Bath in Virginia. I passed a week at the latter and drank freely of its waters. Their powers seem to be undoubted, although their analysis will not fully account for them. They are purgative, stimulant, alterative, and require a longer use than I could stay to make, to evince their efficacy on my poor system. Debility and bilious cases are said to be within its powers as a specific. I had, unfortunately, a turn of fainting, at the place, but it was accidental, and although I was reduced to extreme weakness, and much discomposed in consequence for two days, I hope and trust I am almost as well as before. I expect to see you in two weeks with a face ten or twenty per cent. better than I wore when I saw you last.

Virginia has been grossly deceived, and is yet unperfectly informed. Good men depend too much on the honesty of a faction, and the intelligence of a public. We owe more to the precipitate rashness of the party than to either or both. Some aid to good government and some change in the representation and the votes of the electors for President and Vice, may be expected. Four of twenty-one seem to be relied on. Virginia is infinitely nearer right and more impressible than I expected; much in this way ought to be attempted. Excuse bad and soiled paper from the bar of a tavern. South or Low Virginia, I ought to add, is worse disposed than the Northern Neck.

Bankrupts and rogues did not come near me, but the other sort who did, seem to think as the Yankees do. Union, Constitution, laws, and above all the President, are the objects of all their zeal. But they do not seem to view the danger as nearly and clearly as they ought. I am almost cured of the habit of croaking by finding how they are disposed. When I think how they may be lulled, and whom they will choose, I relapse.

Yours and Mrs. W's.

FISHER AMES

TO CHRISTOPHER GORE[71]

PHILADELPHIA, JULY 30, 1796

MY DEAR FRIEND,

I TAKE UP the pen and yet I find a want of the writing impulse. That is strange, as I write to you, yet so it is, and, therefore, expect a dull epistle.

On the 2d of August I shall leave this place, and be glad to leave it, as the air is of the hottest. You are now respiring the foggy coolness of the Thames, and wondering, as I certainly should, at the spendor of London. England at this instant exerts a force beyond that of Trajan or Antoninus. The magnanimity that sustains bad success and perseveres against events, is not strange in a ministry. But I am ready to pay some respect to a people who can do this. Sudden feelings seem to be as right as tardy widsom; and even the latter would refuse peace on the terms of yielding to France her conquests. Peace on such terms would aggravate the fear and the danger, and paralyze the efforts which would remove the cause, or at least counteract its immediate alarms. I am solicitous to know how the war will proceed, after such wonderful success of the French in Italy. The Emperor may now be at ease, as he has no more dominions in harm's way. So much for Europe.

As to the United States, I think John Adams will succeed our chief. Late events have aided the friends of order. What fatality is there on the measures of Great Britain to tease and

---

[71] *Mr. Gore was a member of the Commission on British Spoliations, provided for in the Jay treaty, and was at this time residing at London, in the execution of his duties.* [S. AMES]

wrong us, by the petty depredations of Bermuda? You know, and perhaps they do not, that this little pickpocket system makes them more bitter enemies here than can well be conceived. Prejudice against them would be no great matter, especially if they court, or rather provoke it, provided it was no obstacle to good order, and the great interests of peace in the United States; but it is, as you know. Lord send us peace in our day, that the passions of Europe may not inflame the sense of America!

Our politics are now on a good footing. The people are calm, and reason has made herself understood. She speaks low, and is often hoarse, and of all speakers the most easily browbeaten; therefore, I calculate the calm of our affairs accordingly. For passion comes in our sky, like the thundergusts in clear weather, and catches the grain in the sheaf and the hay in the swarth: the air is the better immediately after. Since the treaty, we see nothing but blue sky.

You will be missed in October at the election. I shall speak very plainly, and the more so, as I shall have no votes to expect or wish. William Eustis, I fear, is quite wrong. H. G. Otis will be my successor, if right men prevail. Swanwick will be ousted here. Muhlenburg also, if a good competitor can be fixed on. Gallatin and Findlay will be opposed with vigor. Senator Ross is the Ajax of the western country. Our W. Lyman is in disgrace in Hampshire. These are good omens. It is, however, common to see more blossoms than apples.

I will contend the point with no man, woman, or child, that Philadelphia is a very hot place, for at this instant I am dissolving.

It was said by our good President, to a person who spoke to him of England, that we are strong in that country; alluding to a friend of mine, King, and Pinckney. That will help to reconcile me to the privations I am to bear, beyond any one of your acquaintance, in consequence of your absence. My return to private life, and my bad health, will demonstrate this conclusion. While I assure you that I anticipate your letters with pleasure, I think it just to concede, that my claim shall be restrained to such communications only as you may find it quite convenient to make. I will soon write again. Yesterday I gave a letter to a Mrs. Carrington, addressed to the care of Dickason & Co. This will go to the letter-bag of the same vessel. God bless you.

Yours.

TO JEREMIAH SMITH

———

DEDHAM, SEPTEMBER 4, 1796

MY DEAR SMITH,

I PROMISED to write to you on my return, and therefore I must; for a promise, you know, like a treaty, is binding. To one who is, at least semiannually, a lover, I might urge my excuse, that between friends (as between lovers) a promise is but wind. I renounce such quibbles, and will do my duty; and because it is my duty, I fear (and indeed I feel) that I shall do it as dully as you might expect, when I make writing an affair of conscience.

I saw Virginia, and it is not in a state to brag of; the land is good, but the inhabitants scattered, and as bad farmers as politicians. As to the latter, I must do them justice; for *una voce*, all men in whole clothes said, and prove, *more majorum*, that their representatives did not speak their language; that they did love the President, the Constitution, and the Union; that they would support these, obey the laws, and if they could, turn out their members at the next election. A federal party is certainly rising up there, and though (as a party) it is the weaker, the citizens are now more impressible by them than by the Jacobins. I hope, and my most considerate informants were absolutely certain, that some changes would be made in the next Congress, by sending real feds—four, at least, of the nineteen. Amen.

Brent, Cabell, Heath, are among those who are marked for dead men at the next election battle. Jefferson will not have *all* the votes in Virginia for President. John Adams, and Thomas Pinckney will be supported by the feds in Maryland and Pennsylvania; and I hope the spirit of the Yankees will not be wanting on an occasion that so deeply concerns the *salus Reipub.*

Here the sea of politics, lately so stormy, is as still as a mill-pond. Another storm will be necessary before long to keep it sweet.

Having thus attended to the public, I come, last of all, to myself. We patriots have made this a habit. . . . . I am as strong and healthy as a man (no, that is not true) as a woman. Put a woman to hoe corn, or chop wood, and you have a just idea of my forces. I can ride better than at Philadelphia, fast longer, have fewer faint, low turns, sleep better, &c., but my appetite is yet puny; I soon tire with standing, or walking, or sitting up after nine. Like a grass-fed horse, my skin is glossy, and I carry my head up, but put me to work and I soon flinch. Yet I have gained seven pounds of flesh; proud flesh, your witty malice will say, because it grew on me, and in Virginia.

TO OLIVER WOLCOTT

DEDHAM, SEPTEMBER 26, 1796

DEAR SIR,

WHILE I have gained health by riding, I hope you and yours have not lost or impaired it by remaining at rest in Philadelphia, where indeed, the summer heat sometimes forbids rest. The chill of this season has a little deranged my relaxed system, and exposed me to suffer some languid and half sick hours in a day, for some time. I trust I shall take a new start soon, after having become hardened to the fall. I came first to Dedham and then returned for my family to Springfield, which has given me good exercise. I contemplate a trip to see Tracy and Sedgwick, but I have many doubts whether I shall effect it. I need a good deal of drilling to fit me for a winter's journey to Congress in the stage.

The address of the President is just published here, and will be read with admiration. It will serve as a signal, like dropping a hat, for the party racers to start, and I expect a great deal of noise, whipping, and spurring; money, it is very probable will be spent, some virtue and more tranquility lost; but I hope public order will be saved. Here the horizon is clear. You will see the toasts at a feast of fraternity in Boston for M. Adet; there is an incorrectness in them and in the whole business; some good men incautiously yielded to the project which the antis set on foot, but could not execute even decently, unless their betters in character and principle, should concur. A second set followed the first, who were entrapped because they would not leave them to be mortified. This may palliate it to you and a few others, but the face of the business is bad and foolish at home and abroad.

In and near Boston, the cause of order seems to stand better than ever; but you know how changeable our sky is. I hope my successor will be a federal man, but there is danger of a trimmer. On the whole, I think Massachusetts will improve in the next House, as to federalism. I even flatter myself we shall not have one democrat. W. Lyman is not countenanced by many in his district. Varnum will be displaced, it is thought, though not by Dexter. Dearborn is said to be almost the only anti in his district. Should Virginia adopt the sentiments in the President's address, and choose better men than formerly, the next House may perhaps think it a duty to aid, instead of obstructing the business of the government.

With my best respects to Mrs. W.,
I am, dear sir, yours truly,

FISHER AMES

P.S. I have begged of Mr. Rundle to call on Mr. Cox about my Windsor chairs, which possibly the latter may be green enough to refuse sending, unless by a command from Mrs. Wolcott. If it should be so, I request a little treasury influence. Captain Anthony will send them on.

TO CHRISTOPHER GORE

DEDHAM, OCTOBER 5, 1796

MY DEAR FRIEND,

YOUR FAVORS, of the 26th July and 2d August, came to my hands on the evening of the 3d, when the storm, that we may call the equinoctial, was whistling through my keyhole.

The letters cheered us, in spite of the gloom of a very terrible tempest.[72] I am happy to hear of our friend King's safe

---

[72] *The following is from Governor Gore's letter, referred to in the text:*

LONDON, 26 JULY, 1796

MY DEAR FRIEND,

I received your favor of 31st May with great pleasure; it was the first letter I had seen from any of my American friends; and you, who have so feeling a heart, will know how much I enjoyed from reading the sentiments of affection and esteem which it contained. Before this reaches you, the news of our safe arrival will have been in Boston, and, I flatter myself, will have afforded you and some other friends satisfaction. King and his family are now added to our society; they arrived, in health, on Saturday evening. He visits Lord Grenville to-day, his majesty to-morrow, the queen the next day, and then is ready to do the business of his mission, and Mr. Pinckney to relinquish his. This latter gentleman intends to embark in September for South Carolina. I really esteem him as an amiable, honorable man, and cannot but think that, in the neighborhood of wise and firm men, he would be inclined to see the weakness and nonsense of some ideas that are very prevalent among the madmen of Europe and America. If the fates should place him in the Vice-President's chair, I should acquiesce in their decrees. As Cabot, Ellsworth, King, and Strong are out, and John Adams is, we hope, to be President, I pray we may have no more such nice and important questions as have agitated that board ever since its existence;—for, although I do not mean to derogate from the powers and integrity of those who are to supply their places, I should feel great anxiety at seeing the points discussed which have been argued there, and afterwards brought to the chair for a decision.

Sedgwick and Goodhue, I trust, will accept the call of their country, and I really rejoice for them and the public; but where, my friend, is to be found the leader of this band?

When you are absent, who is to play your part in the House, and guide in the tempestuous element which will ever reign in a place where so many and such various views direct the members?

.   .   .   .

I received, from Philadelphia, your speeches, and know that they are in the hands of Mr. Pitt, Mr. Dundas, and Lord Grenville. I will, when I obtain another, send it to E. B. It is universally admired; it does honor to our country, and is read with great avidity by men of genius and taste.

You would really be surprised to hear the strange questions that are frequently put to Americans on the subject of our country, its customs, and languages. We suppose that what concerns our nation is pretty well understood by all the reading and inquisitive men of this; but this is a mistake. I·have been asked, by a very sensible man, who appeared

arrival. As he is, beyond question, an abler man than any of the *corps diplomatique* in the United States, I anticipate the impression he will make in London, as raising the American character. Probably we think too highly of the abilities of their ministry, and too meanly of the principles of their government. If the prudence of their conduct towards the United States should be the test of the former, we should rate them very low. At this time of day, when experience has shown how they ought *not* to have acted, and when their actual situation threatens to make error fate, I did hope they would adopt wise rules of action, and carry them further, and adhere to them the more steadily, in proportion to the little repentance, and the greater apprehension, which I have supposed even their arrogance had felt for their former deviations. But your hints of their judicial delays, and of the unmanageableness of their ministry, renew my fears. If they should play a little, mean, game at last, they would do us infinite mischief. They would Frenchify and democratize us, ten times the worse for the long delay of the crisis. Surely they would not like to see us turn mob at last; and you know that the ultimate failure, or even the material disappointment, of the hopes entertained here from the treaty, would bring up giant anarchy again, like Antæus from the ground, the stronger for his fall. Is it impossible to make them see, and, which is ten times better, to make them feel and fear, this tendency? I will not proceed to write all that you and I already think on this subject; it would be a folio. I will only add, that I fear victory will make the fury of the French

---

acquainted with our politics, as relating to this country, what language we talked in America; and when I answered, the English, he wished to know if we talked it so generally as that our laws were printed in that. He told me he supposed we were a race of men composed of so many different nations, that we had a language as various as the different nations from which his imagination considered us made up, or a sort of motley language, like our own, as he supposed, mongrel race.

[S. AMES]

again contagious. Peace, under present circumstances, would expose Great Britain to danger of unknown shapes and sizes. The revolutionary torrent was thought to have spent itself, and to be spreading into a still lake. On the contrary, it seems to be wearing itself a channel, and to be running with as much force, and nearly as much froth, as ever. Whether the mountain of Great Britain will stand strong, is a curious problem, that I am very willing, if it please God, to live to see solved. If it should be undermined and sink, there will not be a fruitful plain, the fabled plain of equality, in its stead, but a lake, to send up hotter and more pestiferous steams than that of Asphaltites. The principles of real order will be everywhere in disgrace and persecution. Our children must then pass through the fire to Moloch; suffer for liberty, and not have it at last. The French ought to see that to run mad, is not the way to understand it;—and to enjoy it, they have committed the practice of the principles of humanity to the hangman and his former customers. If the Emperor should hold out, and resolve on another campaign, will not the funds of the French fail at last? Will shoe-buckles at home, and church plate in Italy, furnish pay and plunder to a million soldiers abroad and two millions of committee-men at home? They are living, and not very frugally, on the old stock. Miracles are no more; and one would not look for their renewal in favor of the French saints. It is not within probability that they will find the means of another campaign by conquest and plunder, for they have gone the length of their chain; nor that they could squeeze more from their own subjects, without reviving the flames of civil war. But we hear that Spain is going to put on armor, and take the enviable chance of losing ships, colonies, and independence, in a war that France forces her into, and which cannot help her interests by any of its vicissitudes. Such would have been our lot, had Genet prevailed here, or Mr. M. at Paris. B. H. and J. S., the two Dorchester patriots, formerly from Paris, speak very highly of Mr. M. They affect to be friends of order. But they will not do much mischief, as matters now are.

I will not dilate on our affairs; in truth, there is not much to write about. All is calm at present; and because it is calm, we ought to expect a storm; for, in such times, the feds go to sleep in full faith that all danger is over. I fear this is the case in respect to my successor. I shall try to rouse a better spirit. Eustis is very equivocal, and, I agree with you, should be made to declare himself, and take his side. If Jefferson should be our chief, he will be a decided Jacobin. J. C. Jones will, no doubt, refuse; and H. G. Otis will, I think be our man. His talents will distinguish him, and I hope he will be careful to wait patiently in Congress till they do; but he is ardent and ambitious. I reserve myself to croak on the state of the nation, when the choice of our first and second men becomes more calculable.

I have read your two letters with equal attention and pleasure; but, instead of paying you for each article with a comment or reply, I have rambled out into infinite space, like a comet. Do not imagine, however, that my vanity loses one word of your flattering notice of my treaty speech. As to my absence from the House, the loss will be nothing as to leading. I never had any talent in *that* way, and I have not been the dupe of such a false belief. Few men are fit for it. Ellsworth, Hamilton, King, and perhaps John Marshall, would lead well, especially Ellsworth,

. . . . quo non præstantior alter
Ære ciere viros, Martemque accendere cantu.

His want of a certain fire that H. and K. have, would make him the fitter as *dux gregis*. The House will be like sheep without a shepherd. I never was more than shepherd's dog; and my friends have been too civil sometimes, in their praise of my barking, when the thieves and the wolves were coming.

My vanity (God knows I have enough) is laying no traps for an answer of praise; but I know, and you know, that if sometimes I can talk with some effect, I am good for nothing else. I shall do ill as a lawyer, and I am unfit for any public employment. The talent of exaggeration is a poor claim to any station that requires moderation of mind, and accuracy, and patience of observation. I wish, therefore, I do really wish, to be obscure at home, where my wife and children, &c., will think of me as I wish. The world would find me out, if I was placed in any new post. This is not mock modesty; far enough from it, or any modesty. Over and above all other considerations, my ties to this life are not stronger than cobweb. My health is not equal to any exertion. It is possible I may mend, yet I belive it is a fixed debility, a kind of premature old age; and as I am a new light in politics, the fervors of the next two years, especially if our politics should go wrong, would destroy me. You and my other friends will admit that this is probable.

I will attend to your query respecting the interpretation of the words of the treaty, "the ordinary course of justice," &c. I shall take the first occasion to ask the opinions of better casuists than I can pretend to be. Every thing that has the most remote connection with your fame and happiness, will have its importance in my eyes.

Yours, &c.

TO THOMAS DWIGHT

DEDHAM, OCTOBER 25, 1796

MY DEAR FRIEND,

. . . .

I LEFT positive directions with a friend, yesterday, to cause my declining a place on the list of candidates for Congress to be announced in the Centinel. It has been delayed too long, and that has not been my fault. H. G. Otis will be our man; Eustis or J. Bowdoin for the *antis*. Governor Adams will, it is said, offer as an elector. This evinces a design to quit the chair, at least in May next; for, after the mischief he would do as an elector, is it possible that Massachusetts would reëlect him?

The prospect of choosing John Adams is thought to be very good. Thomas Pinckney will be proposed as Vice, and votes will be sought for John Adams in the South, on the expectation that the eastern states will vote fairly for him and Pinckney. Swanwick and Blair McClenachan are chosen—the latter for the county of Philadelphia: a thick-headed Irishman. *Vox populi* is, you know, always *vox sapientiæ*. The successes of France do not appear to me greatly to bewitch our citizens. The gloss of novelty is off, and our gallicism appears shabby to the men of sense. Their opinion finally guides that of the public. I am sorry to see its progress so very slow. If reverses of fortune should happen to the French, which are not impossible, our cure would be hastened.

I am building stone wall, which will not cost less than a guinea a rod. Is not this a good business, well followed? My house is moated round in dirt, like an entrenched camp. I hurry my improvements, as I am soon to pluck up stakes for Congress. When my apprenticeship is out in March, will master give me a new suit of clothes and an hundred pounds, old tenor? I think not, but I hope my customers will.

With my best regards to you and yours, I am

Yours, truly.

TO THE HON. DWIGHT FOSTER

DEDHAM, NOVEMBER 7, 1796

DEAR SIR

THE DRIVER of one of the Dedham stages offers to convey my family to Springfield and to proceed from there to New York. He says he will take on four or five persons in a handsome carriage (a portchaise) on very reasonable terms. And he has been reasonable for my trips to Springfield. Joe Smith to whom I wrote on the subject writes that he will be here on the 16th and be of the party. I write by this post to Goodrich of Hartford who with his sensible wife would make a company that, for the number, would be inferior to no tea set in Philadelphia. How would you like to join the corps? Neither the driver nor the passengers would be demos. I shall probably leave this place on Thursday next week and reach Springfield on Saturday. God bless you pray.

FISHER AMES

TO OLIVER WOLCOTT

DEDHAM, NOVEMBER 14, 1796

DEAR SIR,

YOU WOULD deceive yourself, if you suppose I rate the value of your correspondence exactly in proportion to the promptness of my replies. Your letter of the 6th October is my daily remembrancer. I look at it to see how our republic is like to fare. I perceive that Philadelphia and its environs have decided the votes for Jeffersonians. I have supposed that Pennsylvania held the balance, and I am sorry to infer from the votes of Philadelphia that it will be wrongly inclined. I have long seen with terror that our destiny is committed to our prudence, which I have ever believed to be weaker than our prejudice and passion; yet the issue, such as it is, must be tried *by the country*. Here the influence of the Boston Chronicle and the orations in the market, is most pestiferous, I have proclaimed open war against all this, but a rower against the stream soon grows weak and weary. All that is folly and passion in man, is opposed to all that is virtue and wisdom; and I fear that our government supposes him too good, and will prove him too weak for the trust. Good men, and especially those of Connecticut, where folly is not in fashion, do not know the extent of the lies against the government. Many of my plain neighbours who read the Chronicle will not commend the President. Their reasoning is from what they know, and they take facts from that paper. Yet at the same time I see the men of sense more zealously in the right than ever. Yet as the seekers of popularity are corrupters of the multitude, the malady is endemical and incurable. I went to the meeting in this place; almost every gentleman was there and acted with me; but a word about liberty and putting bridles in the people's mouth routed us all, altho' we were very cautious on that tender ground. In a word, my dear sir, I am far from clear as to the event of things; as to the duty of public men, I have no doubts. We are to persevere and hold up the government and the constituted authorities as long as we can. I have my anxiety much engaged to know the exent of Adet's threats. I think our public will cling to the government, if it should proceed with proper spirit. Any hesitancy would spoil all. I know little of the popular impression of the correspondence. Col. Dawes is elector, and H. G. Otis representative for this district.

Yours, &c.

FISHER AMES

[P.S.] I thank you for continuing to hope for my recruit. I am far from stout, but I am slowly making progress. I expect to reach Philadelphia before the 5th December.

TO CHRISTOPHER GORE

PHILADELPHIA, DECEMBER 3, 1796

DEAR FRIEND,

OUR CORRESPONDENCE has been longer interrupted than either could wish. Your last was dated 7th September, and my last on or near the 7th November. All that time I was vexed with our Dedham *antis,* for voting as they did for Governor A. and J. B. Yet H. G. Otis is chosen very handsomely, and will sustain the cause of order and his own fame in Congress. . . . . The House will be better; the Senate cannot be, as to voting, at least as to effective voting. The loss, in talents, &c., &c., is to be lamented. We have not another Rufus King to put there.

As to President, never was there a more embarrassing state of things. A statement of the votes is given thus: North of Delaware, Adams, 58; a Mr. Coleman, of Pennsylvania, is of this State's number, 1. But a Mr. A. J. Dallas, it is said, will oust him, by causing Governor Mifflin to certify anew. Greene County votes would exclude Coleman, and they have come in since the Governor's certificate or proclamation. Delaware, 3; Maryland, 6, (others insist 7—say 6,) = 9. Virginia, 2. (A Mr. Eyre, of the Eastern Shore, and Colonel Powell say positively there will be 4 *against* Jefferson,) 2 = 70—a majority of 138. North Carolina, it is hoped, will give one, who declared he would, if chosen, vote for Adams, and this in a newspaper. Thus, you see, it is very close. Accident, whim, intrigue, not to say corruption, may change or prevent a vote or two. Perhaps some may be illegal, and excluded. What a question this last would be, if made when the two houses convened! How could it be debated or adjusted? *a la Pologne?* You will see the resolve of Massachusetts to empower the electors to fill up their own vacancies, if any should be. A strange resolve. . . . . Who can foresee the issue of this momentous election? Perhaps the Jeffs, foreseeing a defeat, may vote for Mr. Pinckney, in which case he might come in by two thirds of all the votes. But they expect success, and therefore will not throw away their votes. Yet Mr. P. may have more than Adams; and of the three chances, his may be thought the most hopeful. That would be a subject of incalculable consequences. On the one hand, he is a good man; on the other, even a good President, thus made by luck or sheer dexterity of play, would stand badly with parties and with the country. It would wear an ill aspect in Europe, as well as here. We shall soon know the decree of destiny; and it will reach London by the gazettes.

While our government is thus on the *transmigration*, (excuse the word) and exposed to some foreseen and more unforeseen contingencies, Adet[73] times his electioneering insolence. Some among us are so wicked as to justify the French; and others so mean, so unspeakably mean, as to say we must choose a president that will conciliate that nation. Some of the Quakers have supported the Jeff ticket on that plea. I think the Yankee spirit higher and better: otherwise, I should wish to import a cargo of emancipated Dutchmen, to be the fathers of the next generation. I trust the feelings of our countrymen will repel this more than Genet outrage on an independent government. But the business is supposed to depend on the issue of the campaign. France, if victorious, will not fail to interdict our trade with Great Britain; if beaten, she will receive explanations from General Pinckney. The world is deeply interested to have her exorbitant power curtailed, and I really hope our ox-eating fools begin to see

---

[73] *Adet, the French minister, did not content himself with corresponding with the Secretary of State, according to old diplomatic usage, but occasionally appealed to the people, by publishing in the* Aurora *(the leading Democratic paper) a duplicate of his official communications to the Department. He had recently published in that manner a full and elaborate exposition of the complaints of France against the American government,—the principal grievance, of course, being the British treaty. This remarkable and declamatory document announced, among other things, that, although France was terrible in her resentment, she was magnanimous; and if Americans would but let their government return to itself, they would still find in Frenchmen faithful friends and generous allies. This appeal was at the eve of a very doubtful election, in which the danger of a rupture with France was relied upon, by the Democratic party, as a reason for a change of administration.* [S. AMES]

it. To celebrate French victories may be right for Jacobins; but *we* should cease to celebrate the Fourth of July. The publication is so recent, we cannot be sure how it is received. If Adams should be President, and Jefferson should accept the Vice-Presidency, as many swear he certainly will, if elected, party will have a head, responsible for nothing, yet deranging and undermining every thing, and France would have a new magazine of disorganizing influence. If Jefferson should be President, he would aid the French design (formerly baffled) of excluding the English trade, and would colonize the United States in effect. I own I am ready to croak when I observe the gathering of the vapors in our horizon. Yet it is not every cloud that brings rain. On Monday, the fifth, Congress is to meet. A quiet session is predicted. This is probable enough, but many circumstances may occur to raise a storm. A contested vote for President, when the two houses meet to count the votes, would realize, in an instant, our worst forebodings. The French attacks may grow more serious, and oblige parties to array themselves. But I hope Moreau is disposed of. He was hemmed in by the Austrians, and was thought, at our last dates of intelligence, to be cut off. The ruin of his army would change the outrageous conduct of the French towards the United States. Jourdan is entirely defeated, and his army dispersed, as we hear, although new troops are sent to cover him at Dusseldorf. Pray give me the military news.

I left Dedham fourteen days ago, in a hack, and proceeded in it to New York. There I took an extra stage, so that my journey was easy, and although it was very cold weather, I performed it almost as well as ever. My health is much improved. I am yet tender, but I am not allowed to call myself an invalid. By care and exercise, I really hope to be *in statu quo ante* 1795.

Yours, and Mrs. G.'s.

TO THOMAS DWIGHT

———

PHILADELPHIA, DECEMBER 8, 1796

DEAR FRIEND,

WHO IS to be President is yet the puzzle. If Mr. Pinckney has the eastern votes, or two thirds of them, many believe he will be President. Jefferson, I hope and trust, has the worst chance of the three. His being Vice would be a formidable evil, if his pride would let him take it.

Little is yet done or said in Congress, and the session we hope will be free from the accustomed tempests. W. Lyman, I hope, will stay at home in future, and Dearborn; then Skinner would be more likely to go straight.

Yours, affectionately.

TO THOMAS DWIGHT

———

PHILADELPHIA, DECEMBER 10, 1796

DEAR FRIEND,

YOURS of 5th December informs that all is well at Springfield, which is news sufficient to make a letter very welcome. I am very well, and few will suffer me to say a word about my old claims as an invalid. Thus my privileges are disputed, but the family I am with indulge all my pretensions. I am bound to say that I receive the kindest attentions, and with these I hope I shall return in trim to earn half a dollar by my work. I resolve to work here but little as a legislator. I am on a speech-answering committee at present, which imposes all the task on me; and as there is an allusion to the French, and a propriety in an eulogium on the President, it is no sinecure. We shall probably bring a debate on our heads to get it through the House. After this I decline committees.[74]

---

[74] *The debate came, as was anticipated, and proved to be somewhat extraordinary.*

After a number of verbal alterations had been proposed, Mr. Giles, of Virginia, moved to strike out from the address reported by the committee all the clauses from the sixth inclusive, and to recommit. He said that he did not object to every sentiment expressed in the portions of the report which he moved to strike out. He had no objection that the address should be complimentary, but wished it to be so within the bounds of moderation and justice. He would state the parts which he conceived objectionable. He objected to the sixth paragraph because he conceived it unnatural and unbecoming to exult at our prosperity, by putting it pointedly in comparison with the calamities of Europe. It was not necessary to tell persons, unfortunately involved in a calamity, that we were so much happier than they. This had no relation with the business of the House.

If he stood alone in the opinion, yet he would declare that he was not convinced that the administration of the government, these six years past, had been wise and firm. A want of wisdom and firmness had conducted the affairs of the nation to a crisis which threatened greater calamities than any that had before occurred.

If the report had been so framed as to express a sense of the patriotism, virtue, and uprightness of the President, it might have obtained the unanimous vote of the House, but it was not to be expected that many of the members should so far lose sight of self-respect as to condemn, by one vote, the whole course of their own political conduct.

Another sentiment in the report he could not agree to. He did not regret the President's retiring from office. He hoped he would retire, and enjoy the happiness that awaited him in retirement. He believed it would more conduce to that happiness, that he should retire, than that he should remain in office. He believed the government of the United States founded on the broad basis of the people; that they were competent to their own government; and the remaining of no man in office was necessary to the success of that government.

After some further objection to the declaration as to Americans being the freest and most enlightened of nations, he adverted to the sentiment

One elector was sick and did not vote in Delaware. A loss to Adams. In Pennsylvania, report from Harrisburg says, three will vote for Adams; and two, three, or four are expected in North Carolina. Still, if the votes of the Eastern States are for Pinckney, he will be the man.

Yours, &c.

TO CHRISTOPHER GORE

PHILADELPHIA, DECEMBER 17, 1796

DEAR FRIEND,

IT IS now taken for certain that Mr. A. will be President, as he has sixty-seven votes, and Vermont will give him four more, South Carolina perhaps two or three. But though Jefferson cannot be President, he may be Vice, which would be disastrous. In a Senate that will bring him into no scrapes, as he will have no casting votes to give, responsible for no measures, acting in none that are public, he may go on affecting zeal for the people; combining the *antis*, and standing at their head, he will balance the power of the chief magistrate by his own. Two Presidents, like two suns in the meridian, would meet and jostle for four years, and then Vice would be first. Can we get along with so much less than the natural, not to say the present, state of the executive strength, and

---

expressed in the same clause, "that adulation would tarnish the lustre," &c., and observed that those words, introduced in a parenthesis, appeared to have forced themselves upon the committee, as in fact self-condemning what had been written before in exalted praise of the president. [S. AMES]

so much more than the ordinary power and combination of party? Mr. Pinckney may yet come in Vice, and I wish it, for the reasons alluded to above.

The gazettes will keep you informed of the state of the election.

Yesterday we presented the answer of the House to the Speech. The echo of the paragraph respecting a foreign nation was drafted as inoffensively as it could be, to avoid party points, and to evince our support of the President. Yet Giles, Parker, and others opposed it with vehemence. Their speeches went beyond the present state of popular feeling, and in the end we beat them. Their defeat will help to sink that exotic folly faster than it was going before, as very plain language was used in respect to foreign influence, &c., &c. Instead of blame on our government for having an affray to manage, it was our own base Americans in Paris, and a base party here, who fomented, encouraged, and now openly abetted, the injury and the insult. This brought out explanations, vindications, &c., that they did love their own country the best, and that they would fight even their beloved France, if necessary. Such sentiments will certainly promote the cure of our contagious prejudices, and our gazettes already manifest it.

I had intended to write to you at great length. But riding out daily, and very frivolous reasons, have obstructed my design. I will resume it very soon. I pray you write often. Wishing you and Mrs. G. health and happiness, I am,

Yours, &c.

I used to say, that if I had a friend in London I would beg his attention to buy for me a small set of second-hand books, which I understand could be had, of even an elegant kind, and at half price. Yet I am a little shy of pursuing this intention, lest you should be more zealous in the business than I would have you, as you are too importantly occupied, and, I may add, too much an American Commissioner, to buy second-hand books.

I propose a compromise therefore: If, through Mr. S. Cabot, I could procure such as I want, within any time that would admit of its being done without trouble, I would wish to have bought Robertson's History of Scotland, Charles V., and America; Hume's History of England, Pope's Iliad and Odyssey. Should you think the thing feasible without much of your attention, I would form a list with some care. I should be satisfied with decent bindings. . . . . .

1 7 9 7

===

PHILADELPHIA, JANUARY 5, 1797

DEAR FRIEND,

I KNOW little of Congress affairs. Much is not done or
atempted, and I perceive (*inter nos*) the temper and objects
of the members are marked with want of due reflection and
concert, and indicate the proneness to anarchy, and the self-
sufficient imbecility of all popular bodies, and especially of
such as affect to engross all the active and efficient powers
of the other branches to themselves, as our folks do. A House
that will play President, as we did last spring, Secretary of
the Treasury, as we ever do, &c., &c., will play mob at last.
Unless it is omnipotent, the members will not believe it has
the means of self-defence. I could write a book, without
rising from my chair, on the bad tendency of this disposition,

and the actual progress we have made in it. However, you call me a croaker. I croak on, believing you will join me at last. Mr. Jefferson is said to have written to his friends here, not to oppose him, in a choice by states, if it should come to that, against John Adams, as he (A.) ought to be the President. Such hypocrisy may dupe very great fools, but it should alarm all other persons, as it shows a deep design, which neither shame nor principle will obstruct, to cajole and deceive the public, and (*inter nos*) even J. A.; in which I hope he, though an arch deceiver, will fail. His Vice-Presidency is a most formidable danger. This I say as a conjurer. Kiss all the children, yours and mine, on behalf of your friend.

TO ALEXANDER HAMILTON

PHILADELPHIA, JANUARY 26, 1797

(In confidence)

DR SIR

My LAST was written hastily & under some impressions of the moment which I had not time to unfold. The close respecting your taking a seat in the next house (to be elected) would pass for an awkward compliment if you did not know me (and yourself) too well for such an interpretation.

You desire an inside view of our stage. I begin with the *outside*. Our relations with France are serious. All the french party seem to expect & desire an extra envoy which is an objection—as probably they hope thus to soothe the resentments so tardily roused against France—to exhibit a shew of supplication on our part, & to ground some new delusive connection on the adjustment of existing complaints. On the other hand, it would be a literal & exact adherence to the late precedent in regard to G. B. it might afford a pretext for the french to relax, & in case they should not, animate & unite opinions for the necessary result. But as Mr Pinckney is gone instructed on this very subject, the course adopted is I believe to rely on his mission & *not* to send an extra Envoy. I wish you would direct your most mature thoughts to the subject, and if you should not approve the negative, you ought, (permit me to say) chuse your own way of bringing your sentiments into consideration in the proper place. Should it not be an object to negotiate an abrogation of the clause which guarantees the W Indie possessions to France? However vague it may be & valid or urgent as our excuses might seem, the clause would embarrass Govt. & furnish a text for partizans to raise clamors in case of a future war (the U. S being at peace) & our non compliance with a demand for its execution.

More taxes are necessary & when trade is so much disturbed by war & will be not much less effected by peace land taxes seem to be the only safe resource. But my creed is that three things ought first to concur. To systematize & perfect the collection of our internal revenues, to extend them to the most eligible & productive new objects—and to prepare the public mind for the tax on lands, only to the Amot of the deficiency. Neither of these has been effected. The dread of the latter is at the same time the best means of getting more indirect taxs & of conciliating the people to a land tax. It is necessity, the perception of which will produce salutary efforts in the first instance & a reasonable acquiescence in the next. A tax on salt is a good one, but it would be hard to carry through, & it's foes would combine with some of it's advocates to refuse the draw-back on salted fish called a bounty—which is not to be admitted. Snuff is condemn'd as vexatious & trivial, that on auctions as bad in principle. The licence tax extended to taverns & so arranged as in part to augment with the sales of the retailer would be productive. To effect this last idea how would it answer to rate licences for 3 Gallons very low for more & under 20 still higher—if a separate licence by the same dealer for Madeira Sherry & Port still higher for each, as he must be a dealer of capital. To abolish the distinction in favor of home made spirits & to levy it on the sales of *all* spirits & wines. Equality would not be produced, but inequality as it now exists would be somewhat diminished.

The public should also see a plan or mode of levying a direct tax pass into a law—the vote for the actual levy of a tax to be suspended till the next session & then to be for the deficiency. The moderation of the tax would, on experiment, destroy & disappoint the prejudices against it, and the preparation of opinions would be the best possible. The aversion would seem to have resisted delayed & diminished the evil to the utmost.

The anti gents make their calculations no doubt that a direct tax will sharpen popular feelings—augment clamors against the debt bank &c—enfeeble & discredit the other species of revenue, especially internal. Perhaps they expect favoritism in the assessments.

Our proceedings smell of anarchy. We rest our hopes on foolish & fanatical grounds—on the superior morals & self supporting theories of our age & country—on human nature being different from what it is & better here than any where else. We cannot think it possible our Govt. should stop or that there is the least occasion to provide the means for it to go on. Internal revenues demand system & vigor. The collection must be watched & enforced. We want officers, courts, habits of acquiescence in our country & the principles in Congress that would begin to form any of these. The western country scarcely calls itself dependent on the union.

France is ready to hold Louisiana. The thread of connection is slender & that event I fear would break it. Yet we disband regiments.

Our trade has spoliations to endure from France & G Britain. Yet we are not willing to abandon, or protect it as others do by a naval force. An European would be ready to believe we are in jest in our politics or that newspaper declamation and the frothy nonsense of town meetings speeches comprise the principles of our conduct. For I am obliged to observe even good men adopt errors or pursue truth with a spirit not much more friendly to order & stability in Govt than their adversaries! Who for instance can think without alarm on the frequency & seductive nature of the disgraceful sequestration and anti credit motions in the house. Facts of this vile nature do not occur in other countries, or if they do, they precede & create convulsion. Here they are received as civilly as if infamy did not form an atmosphere about them, contaminating all who breathe in it. We are formed but of late for independent sovereignty—experience has not laid on her lessons with birch, & we forget them. Our whole system is little removed from simple democracy. What we call *the Govt.* is a phantom, as long as the Democrats prevail in the house. The heads of departments are head clerks. Instead of being the ministry the organs of the executive power and imparting a kind of momentum to the operation of the laws, they are precluded of late even from communicating with the house by reports. In other countries they may speak as well as act. We allow them to do neither. We forbid even the use of a speaking trumpet, or more properly as the Constitution has ordained that they shall be dumb, we forbid them to explain themselves by signs. Two evils obvious to you result from all this. The efficiency of the Govt. is reduced to it's minimum. The proneness of a popular body to usurpation is already advancing to it's maximum. Committees already are the Ministers, & while the house indulges a jealousy of encroachment on it's functions, which are properly deliberative, it does not perceive that these are impaired & nullified by the monopoly as well as the perversion of information by these very Committees. The silly reliance of our coffee house & congress prattlers on the responsibility of members to the people &c &c is disgraced by every page of the history of popular bodies. We expect confidently that the house of representatives will act *out* of it's proper character—for if it should act according to it, we are lost.

Our govt. will be in fact a mere democracy which has never been tolerable nor long tolerated.

Our proceedings evince the truth of these speculative opinions. No one was furnished with proper information nobody was answerable for what he presumed to give. The Committee of Ways & Means has not I am told written a page these two years. It collects the scraps & fritters of facts at the Treasury, draws crude hasty results tinctured with localities. These are not supported by any form'd plan of co operation with the members, & the report calls forth the pride of all the motion makers. Every subject is suggested in debate, every popular ground of apprehension is invaded—there is nothing to enlighten the house or to guide the public opinion. All this has happened. I am now preaching daily to those few who will hear me rail and endeavoring to form a common sentiment—that some thing must be done—that it must begin & be approved at the Treasury—that the antis will exult in our shame if we forbear to arrange an efficient plan &c. This is in train, not very far advanced, nor with good omens. It is as to our projected combination you will perceive strictly a *secret*.

My own wishes are to extend our indirect taxes and to pass a bill prescribing the Mode of levying a land tax, holding up the idea in debate at the time of a small amount only.

But the apathy & inefficiency of our body is no secret to you. We are generally in a flat calm, & when we are not, we are near sinking in a tempest. When a sovereign convention engrosses the whole power it will do nothing or some violence that is worse. Sooner or later individuals & public bodies will act out their principles. Our's are I fear essentially more democratic than republican, which latter are alone fit for our country. We think the executive power is a mere pageant of the representative body—a *custos rotulorum,* or master of ceremonies. We ourselves are but passive instruments whenever the sovereign people chuse to speak for themselves, instead of our speaking for them.

The momentum imparted to our political machine is weak & the resistance strong. Faction appears of course in such a state of things. This I confess naturally excites a counter influence—but the power even of party seems to be dissipated. We are broken to pieces. Some able man of the first order of abilities & possessing the rare union of qualities that will fit him to lead a party is wanting. For want of such a leader, many who would do good are useless. My natural temperament unfits me for a seat where I cannot bear to sit quite inactive although such efforts as I can make will be unavailing.

No session of Congress has exhibited such a dissipation of the party which has been arrayed in support of the Govt. Th[is] will be some excuse for my forebodings of the decline of our affair[s].

One might have hoped that Govt would find in party all the combination & energy that is excluded from it's organisation. I see however that this auxiliary unless compacted together by the violent action of the rival party will subdivide or fall into inaction—and even when roused to the utmost, it is in need of a clear sighted guide.

As this is the state of our politics what is to be done? The friends of the Govt. have increased within two or three

Years in numbers & zeal—but few of them know or could be made to believe that it's fair outside conceals such alarming weakness.

Your's truly

FISHER AMES

[P.S.] I understand Bank Shares have been lately attached by law process. This strikes my mind as a very anarchical proceeding.

Porcupine is a writer of smartness & might do more good, if directed by men of sense & experience—his ideas of an *intimate* connection with G Britain justly offend correct thinkers—& still more the multitude. He proposes a new daily paper, a business much overdone. It's circulation out of the City will not be great. Would not a paper once or twice a week, exclusively political, answer better. Pray let Webster have the paragraph for his Minerva.

TO CHRISTOPHER GORE

PHILADELPHIA, JANUARY 27, 1797

MY DEAR FRIEND,

ALTHOUGH I have not much to add to my late letters, I will not lose the opportunity of writing again by the Favorite. There is policy in multiplying my letters. It will procure the more in reply from you.

The vote for a direct tax passed the House, forty-nine to thirty-nine. I voted with the latter. A committee is preparing a bill. Revenue is necessary, and that on trade is precarious. A resort to the land will be made soon or late. With these

1218

opinions, you will wonder at my vote. But in my judgment three things ought to concur before we venture on a land tax: The improvement of our internal taxes, systematizing and enforcing the collections; now Kentucky pays nothing, and the backwoodsmen generally very little. Even the carriage and license taxes are badly collected in New England. The details of these should be perfected. I also wish first to see an extension of our indirect taxes to licenses for taverns, stamps, an higher duty on salt, on bohea tea, and brown sugar. The aversion to a land tax affords the means of effecting both these important objects of fiscal improvement, at least one would hope so, provided a proper union of the federal members was formed. Thirdly, and to conclude, I think the public mind should be prepared for a land tax before it is imposed, which it is not. I could wish the necessity of a tax might be admitted, in and out of Congress; that every effort be made to get the needful without touching the land; but the deficiency must be had at the next session by a land tax; and to that end that the *mode* of taxing should be now passed into a law, and the vote for a sum to be levied to be delayed till the next session. In this manner the public would be made to see that the necessity was real, and the effort to avoid a tax on land sincere. A levy of the deficiency would be (say $500,000) so light as to disappoint their fears, and cure their prejudices. The abrupt assessment of near a million and a half would operate very differently, as you will not doubt.

It is no easy matter to combine the anarchical opinions, even of the good men, in a popular body. We are a mere militia. There is no leader, no *point de ralliément*. The motion-makers start up with projects of ill-considered taxes, and, by presenting many and improper subjects, the alarm to popular feelings is rashly augmented. Whether we shall be able, in the event, to do any better is beyond my powers of conjecture. I shall preach to our friends to concert their plan, and to be complying to one another, for the common good. The session is wearing away, and I fear no revenue will be obtained. I am not robust enough to bear the labor of close application in the House, and thus I throw off my share of blame.

A committee reported on V.'s election, censuring the petition against him as malevolent. This part was erased, and another substituted, that V. had acted honorably in the election, which was carried, though it is not true. Brown ought to have made some effort to sustain his charges, for the sake of the public opinion.

General Shepard is probably chosen, *vice* W. Lyman. I hear that the Georgia business strains the purses and credit of many in Boston, and is likely to prove a ruinous thing. There will be great distress everywhere among the moneyed men, as spoliations, speculations, luxury in living, and the course of trade, all lead to it. I might say over trading.

We are more than ever impatient to hear European news, as we all believe that events will augment or diminish the spoil committed on our commerce, according to their nature. W. Paine will keep you informed of what passes in Boston, &c. God bless you and your Commission.

Yours.

DEBATE OVER APPROPRIATE
COMPENSATION FOR PUBLIC OFFICERS

To persons familiar with the Notes on the Federal Convention, *it will seem odd that the first Congresses devoted so little time to debate on the question of adequate compensation for the officers of the government. As the following speeches reveal, however, the more accustomed Americans became to their new government (and once Washington had retired from office!) the more freely did they employ the level of compensation as the litmus of democratic bona fides which it ultimately became in our days. Ames's reflections on this theme, as on so many others, amount to an attempt to forestall the most harmful consequences of this tendency. The speeches collected here represent the sum of what he had occasion to say on this question, though not in all likelihood the sum of what he thought about it.*

JANUARY 27, 1797

M̲R. AMES said the gentleman from Maryland [Mr. S. SMITH] had suggested that persons who were very active with their pen before they came into office, when they found themelves fixed there, were apt to put the whole of their business into the hands of clerks. The suggestion might have weight; and, therefore, he should take the liberty of saying, the remark did not apply as it respected the officer of Massachusetts. [Mr. S. SMITH said he did not allude to any particular officer.] Mr. AMES said he knew he did not; but his observations might be supposed to be applicable to the officer of Massachusetts. If, indeed, the remark was applicable, it might afford good reason for withholding the proposed advance; but the Loan Officer of Massachusetts was a man of great industry and application, and the business of his office required the unremitted attention of himself and clerks.

As to the state officers, he would not say whether they had, or had not, sufficient salaries; nor did he believe they always attended to the rewards given to state officers as a scale upon which to reward the officers of the United States. They had set out upon a scale of their own at the commencement of the government; but what was an adequate salary then, was not so now; and the business of the Loan Offices was so far from being diminished, it was continually increasing. In Massachusetts in particular, since the assumption of the state, of debts, the business was vastly augmented. He was informed that there were upwards of two thousand accounts open in that office. Of course the adjustment of interest upon all these accounts, would require great accuracy and labor.

Observations, Mr. A. said, which went to keep down the salaries of office, he knew were popular among certain descriptions of people; but he did not think this squeezing of public officers was prudent, just, or honorable. He did not think the least possible sum for which an office could be executed was the wisest or best to be adopted. The true rule was, that such a sum should be paid for service as was sufficient to command men of talents to perform it. Anything below this was parsimonious and unwise.

.   .   .   .

Mr. S. SMITH said, the observations of the gentleman from Massachusetts went to show the propriety of an increase of the salaries of all other officers, as well as those in question. He was against singling out particular officers for an advance; if the whole were advanced together, he should not object to it. As to the $120 proposed for the Loan Office of Pennsylvania, he thought the office itself might be dispensed with, and the business be as well done at the Treasury Office. The only reason given for the advance was, the depreciation of money, and that consideration would apply equally to all the officers of the government. He should, therefore, be opposed to granting the allowance to the officers in question.

Mr. AMES said, from the turn which the debate had taken, the object became of greater importance than the mere advance of the salary of the officers in question. It became of importance to determine upon what principle the officers of government should be paid.

He did not intend to investigate the motives of gentlemen who were so desirous of keeping down the salaries of the officers of government; he could not suppose they acted from unworthy principles. It was a well-known fact, that in all popular assemblies, the disposition to withhold grants of money was notorious. Perhaps it was proper; it was doubtless a fence against wasteful expenditure, nor did he wish to break it down; but when the gentleman from Virginia called upon them to attend to the feelings of the people, he thought it was necessary to remind the Committee that they ought also to attend to the interests of the people, and he believed it was for the common interest of the people that persons selected for office should be fit and proper to fill their respective offices. And it was a fact, that from the dispersedness of the population of the country, and from other circumstances, there was great difficulty in finding suitable persons to fill the offices of government. In other countries, Mr. A. said, where their governments had been of long standing, persons were trained up with a view to public employments, but in this country this had not been the case, and, therefore, the PRESIDENT found the circle from which to select proper characters for office was very confined. It was, therefore, the more necessary that such an allowance should be made to officers of government as should induce fit persons to accept of them; such as (to use a vulgar but strong expression) would *command the market.* Five hundred dollars, more or less, was nothing when compared with fitness for office. He said he had already laid it down as a principle, that the rate of salary should be such as to command men of talents and of character, for these the interest of the country required.

Mr. A. said, he knew the feelings of the people were soon roused when money was the object; but he was surprised the gentleman from Virginia should have attributed to gentlemen from the eastward a desire to introduce a splendor of office into the government. This spirit, he thought, was full as likely to come from the southward as from the eastward. He thought they were as economical and as just in the eastern as in the southern states; and he thought the remark could have been made with as little sincerity as propriety.

Had it been understood, was it believed, said Mr. A., that a splendor of office had been introduced into our government? How did facts corroborate the assertion? Had their officers even stood upon an equality with others in the line of life in which they moved? Had any officer of theirs been able to lay up an estate for his family? Or were they not rather obliged to walk on foot, while those with whom they associated rode in their coaches? They were even, comparatively speaking, without a dollar, whilst gentlemen, living upon their professions, were rich. On this account, he said, there had always been an unwillingness to accept of offices of government by persons best calculated to fill them. These were facts, and he spoke them with audible voice; yet it was wonderful that, at a moment when their officers might be said to be in want, they were reproached with living in luxury and extravagance.

Having disposed of this subject, and given the observations upon it all the credit they deserved, he would inquire why they should expect gentlemen to undertake the offices of government which would not allow them to live in an equally comfortable manner to that in which they had been accustomed to live? He despised the idea of endeavoring to make the people believe that their public officers lived in splendor, and on that account to hold them up to the hatred of our citizens; but could it be supposed that a person who undertook a public office should descend from that style of living to which he had been used, because some gentlemen chose to call it splendid? Or, was there any reason that such a man should immediately begin to eat brown bread, though heretofore he had always eaten white?

Another suggestion had been made, that the present high price of living had been increased, and depended upon the duties on imposts, and therefore it was an evil arising from indirect taxation. Though there might be some ground for this observation, it by no means went to the extent to which it had been pushed. He would ask, for instance, whether the broadcloth upon which a coat was made cost materially more now than before the impost of 15 or 16 per cent. was laid upon it? He believed not; but every one knew that the produce of the farmer was double in price to what it was when these salaries were fixed, and they ought, therefore, to be advanced in proportion. And were the people unprepared for an advance in the salaries of the officers of government? He believed not. He believed most of the states, on account of the increased price of living, had increased the pay of their officers. Why, then, said he, should the officers of the United States be unattended to? And were they to suppose that the advance now proposed would be a thing improper for the House to agree to, when they had last session judged a like advance a proper one? As to the observation of the gentleman from Maryland, [Mr. SMITH,] that he did not wish to raise one officer and not another, he should take a different course from that which that gentleman proposed to adopt. He would vote for an advance of those which came before him, and do the same to others when he should have an opportunity.

JULY 16, 1789

MR. AMES said that the Vice President's acceptance of his appointment was a renunciation of every other avocation. When a man is taken from the mass of the people for a particular office, he is entitled to a compensation from the public; during the time in which he is not particularly employed, he is supposed to be engaged in political researches for the benefit of his country.

Every man is eligible, by the Constitution, to be chosen to this office; but if a competent support is not allowed, the choice will be confined to opulent characters. This is an aristocratic idea, and contravenes the spirit of the Constitution.

. . . .

Mr. AMES, in his reply to Mr. SENEY's observations, pointed out the difference of the situation of the Vice President and the members of the Legislature.

SEPTEMBER 18, 1789

MR. AMES said, he had frequently heard in the House abstract reasonings upon the subject of salaries and compensations; but, for his part, he thought such reasonings had very little to do in the business. The only inquiry was, what sum would be necessary to command the first abilities in the respective states? The gentlemen, from various quarters, may determine, with a great degree of precision, for themselves; he thought he could speak for the four New England states; and supposed that fifteen hundred dollars per annum, for this officer, would be an object sufficient to excite the attention of men of the first abilities in those states.

Gentlemen might be found, he said, who would use the greatest exertions to qualify themselves for the office. He, therefore, hoped the motion for striking out the sum would obtain.

JANUARY 20, 1791

MR. SEDGWICK stated certain principles of conciliation which had induced him to move the amendment now under consideration. He showed by a variety of particulars, that the services will be various, and merit in some cases a much greater compensation than in others.

Mr. AMES objected to the amendment proposed, on principles of economy, both of time and money. The time is already so exhausted that there will be scarcely sufficient in the present session to finish the bill; and if the amendment is adopted, it will follow, that in order to make adequate provision in all cases you must, in many instances, make that compensation too much. He urged the importance of passing the law with such a power as would enable the executive to apportion the compensations in proportion to the merits and services of the respective officers. This law is said to be obnoxious to the disapprobation of the people. It therefore becomes our duty to make the compensations such as may command the services of men of responsibility, in point of property and character; men of prudence and judgment. He conceived the power of apportioning the salaries might be left with the supreme executive. Nor did he conceive there was any thing in the Constitution contrary to this idea. Gentlemen have cautioned the House against exceeding the powers of the Constitution by implication; he supposed that it was equally reprehensible to refrain from exercising the full powers indisputably vested in the Legislature by the Constitution.

FEBRUARY 7, 1797

INCREASE OF SALARIES.

A BILL was also received from the Senate for increasing the compensation of the members of the Legislature and certain officers of government; which was read, and, on motion that it be read a second time, it was carried, 33 to 30. It was accordingly read a second time.

The bill contemplates an advance of $5,000 to the present salary of the PRESIDENT OF THE UNITED STATES, and $2,000 to the VICE PRESDIENT, to commence on the 4th of March next, and continue for four years; and that the members of the Senate and House of Representatives, the Secretary of State, the Secretary of the Treasury, the Secretary of War, Attorney General, Postmaster General, Assistant Postmaster General, Comptroller of the Treasury, Auditor, Register, Commissioner of the Revenue, Accountant of the War Department, the Secretary of the Senate, the Clerk of the House of Representatives, and the principal clerks employed by them, the Sergeant-at-arms of the House of Representatives, the Door-keepers and Assistant Door-keepers of both Houses, have an advance of 25 per cent. upon their present compensation.

Mr. PARKER moved that the further consideration of this bill be postponed till the first Monday in December next.

.   .   .   .

Mr. AMES said gentlemen had no doubt a right to govern their own votes according to their own notions of propriety. No man had a right to prescribe to another. His conscience was no rule to any other man. But he thought he was authorized to say, they neither had nor claimed a right to do a right thing in a wrong way. To agree to the motion proposed, would be an insincere way of putting a negative upon the bill. He trusted gentlemen who wished this would do it in a more direct way. The compensation of the PRESIDENT and VICE PRESIDENT could not be augmented, he said, after they had entered upon their office; and to say they would take up the subject for consideration at a time when their powers would not exist, was an evasive manner, which he approved not. It was an easy thing for gentlemen to say *no* on the question, without taking this circuitous way of putting an end to the subject.

FEBRUARY 27, 1797

Mr. SHERBURNE said, the question was with respect to the quantum of money to be granted. A practice had been established of allowing our ministers to foreign countries a sum as an outfit equal to one year's salary; so that nine thousand dollars were allowed a minister for this purpose, though it might happen that he would not be employed more than a few months in the service. He thought, therefore, that fourteen thousand dollars could not be thought too large a sum for the PRESIDENT OF THE UNITED STATES, whose term of service was for four years, and which would go to his successor in office; . . .

Mr. AMES said, it appeared to him that it would be desirable to proceed according to precedent, as nearly as they could. It was not desirable to innovate or change the established order of things, except strong reasons existed for the change. On inquiring what had been the practice heretofore, they found the PRESIDENT of the old Congress, as well as the PRESIDENT now going out of office, had establishments made for their household similar to that now proposed. If they looked forward to that period when the seat of government was to be removed, and considered the furniture which would be necessary for the house in the Federal city, it would be seen that there would be a necessity for a new establishment at that time, as it was evident that the present furniture or what might be purchased with the sum now contemplated, would be wholly inadequate to the furnishing of that house. He supposed an additional grant of twelve or fifteen thousand pounds would be necessary for that purpose.

This having been the practice established, it appeared to him somewhat strange that the gentleman from North Carolina [Mr. MACON] should have opposed the measure as an innovation and as a dangerous principle, whereas they were going to do now only what they had done in former instances, and not to do which would lay them open to the charge of versatility. It would be said that nothing was certain under our government but that everything was subject to change. If that uncertainty was objectionable in general, it was particularly so when it related to an independent branch of government. What was established ought to be respected. If they were to consider what would be a just principle in an establishment *de novo*, they might say it should be settled in this way or that; but in considering what was already established, they must have respect to the rules upon which it was founded. And shall the first citizen in the United States, and perhaps the first in the world, said he, be placed in a situation considerably below our private citizens in point of furniture and style of living? He trusted he would not, though he had hitherto scarcely been placed upon a level with them. Notwithstanding this, the proposed establishment had been compared, with what view he could not say, to the splendor of European Courts; if this comparison was made with an intention to deceive the people, such an assertion, with so little foundation, was unworthy of the Representative of a free people, and betrayed a mean opinion of his constituents to believe they could be so easily deceived.

We have chosen an elective government, said Mr. A., and if it were meant to be kept pure, they must encourage the people to make choice of such men, without respect to fortune, as they think will serve them best, but if, instead of providing a suitable household for the PRESIDENT, they left him to provide for himself in this respect, men of large fortune only could engage in this part of the public service. And would this, he asked, be doing honor to the republican government? He thought not.

Some gentlemen who were opposed to the giving of fourteen thousand dollars were yet inclined to give a smaller sum. They seemed to have two reasons for this; one arising from economy, the other from a kind of distrust of misspending of the money. Economy, he allowed, was necessary; but the extreme of virtue was said to be nearly allied to vice, and the extreme of economy was doubtless parsimony. Extremes generally touched each other. He could place this idea in a ridiculous light, but he would forbear to do it. Gentlemen had no objection to grant eight thousand dollars, and the bill only proposed that it should not exceed fourteen thousand. Now, were gentlemen really apprehensive in their consciences that this additional power over six thousand dollars would be abused, by its being laid out in gewgaws and knicknacks, or did they wish, by diminishing the sum, to prevent the PRESIDENT from having his furniture all of a piece, and thereby placing their discretion in the purchase of it in the place of his? The furniture, when purchased, added Mr. A., will belong to the office, and not to the man. He thought, therefore, they had spent time to little purpose in endeavoring to remove an established principle, and therefore hoped they should have the question.

DEFENSE OF MILITARY PREPAREDNESS

Ames closed his congressional career with that same foreboding concentration on foreign and military affairs which colored so heavily Washington's "Farewell Address." In the following series of speeches we find him defending strongly the notion of military preparedness. The earlier speeches clearly reveal that he had always acted on the basis of the principles clearly elucidated in the speech on naval appropriations of March 2, 1797. This speech incidentally reveals the respect and fear with which Ames was regarded in the Congress and something about his characteristic manner in debate. It amounts to a valedictory to his congressional career.

MARCH 2, 1797

MR. AMES said, that gentlemen opposed to the finishing of the frigates, seemed to be also opposed to all ideas of this country ever becoming a naval power; the necessity of this, he was persuaded, would ere long appear. It was not to be supposed that a nation whose commerce was greater than that of any other, except Great Britain, should go on long without a naval protection; and he believed the more strenuous the opposition shown against this measure, the sooner it would be accomplished; he was not therefore displeased to see the present violent opposition to everything which looked towards this object.

It was not enough, Mr. A. said, for gentlemen to discourage the building of ships, they would also discredit the administration of government; and nothing was more natural than that those who thought so ill of it themselves should endeavor to spread those opinions. This was done continually. With respect to the building of the frigates, he thought it was a wise step; and as to the extra expense and delay which had attended the business, he believed, gentlemen might take a share of the blame upon themselves, on account of the versatility which had been shown upon the occasion, in this day agreeing upon one thing, and that upon another. It was true, that another cause of extra expense was owing to a resolution which had been taken to make the ships much larger than was contemplated by the House; the vessel building here, he believed, was nearly 1,600 tons. He was glad that this alteration of plan had been adopted; not because more money would be expended on this account; not because contrary to the direction of the legislature, but because true wisdom required it; they would now be an overmatch for any frigate, or any vessel which the Algerines could send out against them. These, he believed, were the views of the executive in having them built of the size they were. The number of the frigates agreed to be finished had been reduced to three; and these they last session passed a law to finish. But what was now to be done? It was said they should not be finished. Who said this? Did the people? did the government say it? No; that House alone said it: so that that House were about to usurp the supreme authority. We are the government, we are the people, we are every thing.

But, if there be a law which says that these three frigates should be built and equipped for sea, was it not necessary, before it was concluded that they should not be so built and equipped, that this law should be repealed by all the branches of the legislature? No, say gentlemen, we can appropriate or not, according to our sovereign will and pleasure. If they possessed the power to nullify what was enacted by all the three branches of government, it was greatly to be lamented. But if they could appropriate according to their will, they were bound to do it also according to their consciences too.

It was not only a weapon, but a shield, which it was their duty to use with great caution, and according to law; for, if they were to use it contrarily, it would be to make that House the supreme power, it would be to usurp the supreme authority.

. . . .

Mr. VENABLE said, if this was a mere question of expense, it was very extraordinary that it should have called forth such a phillippic from the gentleman from Massachusetts, [Mr. AMES,] who had charged the House with arrogating to itself all the powers of government; as being omnipotent.

. . . .

Mr. NICHOLAS said, the gentleman from Massachusetts [Mr. AMES] seldom spoke without casting some denunciation against that House.

. . . .

Mr. AMES said, he understood the gentleman from Virginia [Mr. NICHOLAS] to say, that the conduct of the executive was illegal; but certainly if a frigate was estimated to cost $12,000 and it cost $15,000, the expenditure of the additional $3,000 was not illegal.

. . . .

Mr. AMES said, as to the size of the vessels, that was executive business. The gentleman from Virginia [Mr. VENABLE] seemed to take the observation which he had made with a degree of sensibility perfectly natural, because it went to touch the power which he had claimed as a member of that House. The gentleman said, "Here I entrench myself behind my privileges." Nothing was said about the public good; all was self.

And was it to be considered, he asked, that they enjoyed the powers committed to them in their own right, as barons of empire, as sovereign despots? Or was the power placed in them to be exercised like other duties, according to justice and propriety? He believed no one would deny that the latter was the truth.

How did the matter stand? They had attempted to repeal a law, but another branch of the Legislature had refused to accede to the repeal; of course it could not be effected. Were they then to act as if the law had been repealed? Yes, say gentlemen, we will refuse to appropriate the money since we think the thing unnecessary. He hoped, however, the day would soon come (as melancholy would be the period until it did arrive) when this power of refusing an appropriation to carry an existing law into effect, should no longer be countenanced by a majority of that House.

Mr. VENABLE was of opinion, that if the gentleman from Massachusetts had only the public good in view, which he had spoken of, he could have had no inducement to have gone into the arguments which he had introduced on this occasion. He felt himself as strongly bound to consider the public good in all his conduct as he could be. He believed no instance could be named in which he had not consulted that interest. As to what was, or was not, calculated for the public good, he must be left at liberty to judge for himself. But the gentleman had not put the business on this ground, but because gentlemen differed in opinion from others, they were charged with assuming absolute authority, with principles of despotism, overturning the government, &c.

.   .   .   .

Mr. AMES said, he had not charged that House with usurping power, or breaking down the other branches of government; nor did he say they had not a discretion; but that their discretion ought to be regulated by duty.

JUNE 19, 1789

MR. CARROLL proposed a clause, limiting the operation of the act, under a hope that a time would come when the

United States would be disengaged from the necessity of supporting a Secretary of Foreign Affairs.

. . . .

Mr. AMES had no doubt of the good intention of the worthy and honorable mover; but he thought a limitation would be injurious. The United States is a member of the society composed of the assemblage of all the nations of the earth; and it is impossible, as a member of this great society, but that there ever will be a natural obligation to maintain an intercourse with them. If the gentleman discovered that he had mistaken his principle, he flattered himself the motion would be withdrawn.

NOVEMBER 13, 1791

DEFEAT OF GENERAL ST. CLAIR

On a motion made and seconded, that the House do come to the following resolution:

"*Resolved,* That the Secretary of the Treasury and the Secretary of War be notified that this House intend, on Wednesday next, to take into consideration the Report of the Committee appointed to inquire into the causes of the failure of the late expedition under General St. Clair, to the end that they may attend the House, and furnish such information as may be conducive to the due investigation of the matters stated in the said report:"

. . . .

Mr. AMES supported the resolution. He noticed the impressions which the failure of the late expedition had made on the public mind. Characters had suffered in the general estimation. It was of the utmost importance that a thorough investigation should take place, that if the failure of the expedition was a mere casualty, and the fortune of war, it might be made to appear; or, if it was owing to misconduct, the blame might fall on the proper subjects. The mode suggested to obtain information appeared to him the best that could be adopted—the most adequate to the object. It was due to justice, to truth, and to the national honor, to take effectual measures to investigate the business thoroughly. This inquiry appears to be the beginning of an arrangement preparatory to an impeachment; on whom this will fall, he should not presume to say; but still it places the subject in an important point of view, and shows, in the strongest manner, the necessity of adopting the best possible mode of ascertaining the real state of facts. This, he conceived, could not be done so effectually as by the mode proposed in the resolution.

.   .   .   .

Mr. AMES, adverting to the spirit of the report, pointed out the peculiar situation of the two Secretaries, and that they did not stand on the same ground with other persons who are not so intimately implicated in the matter. He alluded to the various objections which had been urged from precedent, from the fullness of the investigation which the subject had undergone in the hands of the Committee, and from the remark by Mr. LIVERMORE, that sufficient had already been done. To this last objection he particularly replied, by saying that the public wanted further satisfaction, and that the House could not justify themselves to their constituents without a stricter and fuller investigation, that the whole of the facts might be laid before them.

MAY 30, 1794

Mr. AMES—If we are to go to war, will it not be a prodigious saving of expense to have all matters ready beforehand? By being prepared two months before the war breaks out, the advantages in economy would be immense, as the price of enlisting men would rise four-fold when it was once known that war was certain. He knew many weak parts in the Union that might be attacked and in danger before a body of militia could be ready for effectual service. He was not qualified for details of this sort; but he knew that Rhode Island, for example, might be taken, and, in a short time, so strongly fortified, that it would be difficult or impossible to retake it. Why were we afraid to entrust the PRESIDENT with the power of raising ten thousand men? Can any body of men to be raised in this country tread down the substantial yeomanry? This is quite an Utopian dread. It is infinitely cheaper to raise and embody an Army at leisure, when the storm is seen to be approaching, than all at once, when twenty things must be done at the same time. There is, besides, a material distinction between this bill and the former. The force may be discontinued whenever the legislature thinks proper; nor is it to be raised at all unless the PRESIDENT sees or thinks it necessary. The principle of the bill is, therefore, much less exceptionable than that of the other. To reject a bill on the first reading is a bad practice. Mr. A. hoped that the House would guard against it, unless where any thing was grossly improper, and depended on a single principle. But he trusted that the House would, in every common case, set their faces against it.

JUNE 6, 1794

Mr. Giles expressed the utmost surprise at such a proposal. First, it had been projected to raise a standing army of fifteen thousand men, then twenty-five thousand, then ten thousand; and now, when all these schemes had been put to an end, this regiment of eleven hundred and forty men has appeared.

Mr. AMES replied to Mr. GILES. It was wrong to say that this was part of a system, and that the twenty-five thousand men had been part of it. He saw no such thing. We have one Indian war already, which is enough at a time. Those whom we are now to quarrel with, are three times more numerous than those to the Northwest. The Creeks, Cherokees, Choctaws, and Chickasaws, were, as Mr. A. had been informed, fifteen thousand fighting men. He did not think that there were too many Indians on the frontier, any more than too many wild beasts. The one might, by skilful management, be rendered as harmless as the other. Even the success of an Indian war, by extending our frontier, augments the number of our enemies; so that the task is hopeless, and has no end. Distance from the seat of government would increase, and with it the charges of defense. He was not one of those who wished to exterminate these poor creatures. He recommended a system of restraint on both sides. He could wish for something as strong as the Chinese wall to separate them. When an exasperated militia went out, what were we to expect, but that the first man with a red skin whom they met would be shot? Presently you discover that you have been shooting an Indian of the wrong nation, while, in the mean time, this whole nation rises and attacks you. The Continental troops, as being less exasperated, were less apt to fall into mistakes of this kind. He did not wish the militia to be called out in such numbers, as were proposed, by the bill when sent up to the Senate. He wished, if possible, for a restraint on both parties. He was for the amendment.

DECEMBER 4, 1794

Mr. AMES.—The apprehensions of the House have been attempted to be alarmed, as if they were pushed to adopt hastily and unguardedly some dangerous new principle. The practice of all public bodies without exception, has been to express their approbation of distinguished public services.

Instead of establishing a new principle, the attempt is now made to induce us to depart from an old one. Nay, the objection taken altogether is still more inconsistent and singular, for it is urged, the Answer of the House to the PRESIDENT's Speech has already expressed our approbation of the conduct of General Wayne and his army. It is, say they, superfluous to express it again. The argument opposed to the vote of thanks stands thus: It is a dangerous new principle, without a precedent, and without any just authority from the Constitution, to thank the army; for, the objectors add, we have in the Answer to the Speech expressed all that is contained in the motion. It is unusual to quote precedent, and our own recent conduct, to prove a motion unprecedented, and to prove a measure new and dangerous because it has been adopted without question or apprehension heretofore.

The thanks of this body addressed directly to the army will be much more acceptable than an opinion concerning them in our Answer to the Speech, and which they may not happen ever to hear of.

It has been said, with an air of triumph, that we are to be guided by reasoning, not feeling, as if I had made an attempt by an appeal to the latter to lead the House astray. This observation appears to have made some impression, and it is proper therefore to notice it.

Reason is the test of what is true and what is useful. When our interests are depending on a vote, we cannot be too circumspect to avoid the intrusion of our feelings. During the last session the opposers of the measures which were then urged upon the House, used all their endeavors to expose their injurious tendency. Some of those who would now pass for all reason, made a boast then of being all feeling. Then they reproached us with an unchangeable adherence to what we thought the interests of the country: on such questions, where error may be ruin, the passions turn traitors. On such occasions we had our feelings, but we thought ourselves bound by all that we owed to duty and our country to suppress them. It was then proper to be cool, considerate, and cautious.

But is the present question of such a nature? It has nothing to decide respecting the abstract truth of the proposition, for the assertion contained in the vote of the merit of the army is undeniable; it cannot be opposed by any plea of public duty, for it is not an act of authority, nor will it affect any one interest or right of society.

It is simply a question of mere propriety; and is it a novelty, is it anything to alarm the caution of the House, that such questions are always to be decided by feeling? What but the sense of propriety induces me to perform to others the nameless and arbitrary duties, and to receive from others the rights which the civilities and refinements of life have erected into laws? In cases of a more serious kind, is not sentiment the only prompt and enlightened guide of our conduct? If I receive a favor, what but the sentiment of gratitude ought to direct me in my acknowledgments? Shall I go to my benefactor and say, "Sir, I act coolly and carefully; I will examine all the circumstances of this transaction; and if upon the whole I find some cause of gratitude, I will thank you." Is this gratitude or insult? The man who affects to hold his feelings, and his best feelings back for this cold-blooded process of reasoning, has none. He deceives himself, and attempts to deceive others, if he pretends to reason up or to reason down the impressions which actions worthy of gratitude and admiration make upon his heart. Was it necessary to wait for the joy and exultation which the news of the victory of General Wayne instantly inspired, till we could proceed with all due phlegm and caution to analyze it? The gentleman from Virginia. [Mr. NICHOLAS] has not even yet received the impressions which are so natural and so nearly universal; for he has insisted that the army has only done its duty, and therefore it is improper to express our thanks. Indeed, it has done its duty, but in a manner the most splendid, the most worthy of admiration and thanks. That gentleman has also expressed his doubts of the very important nature of the victory, and one would suppose it was thought by many a very trivial advantage that is gained. It is such an one, however, as has humbled a victorious foe; as has avenged the slaughter of two armies; as gives us the reasonable prospect of a speedy peace. Can we desire anything more ardently than a termination of the Indian war?

The same gentleman, or some other opposing the vote of thanks, has said, if our armies have done well, they are paid for it, as if money was the measure and the recompense of merit. No, sir, our soldiers did not reason coldly (as we are now exhorted to do) in the day of battle. When the war-whoop would have shrunk hearts that had nothing more than reasoning on their wages and their services to animate them, did our brave soldiers think only of their ninepence a day? If they had, we should not have had this occasion to offer to them the thanks of the nation.

A soldier, of all men, looks to this kind of recompense for his services; and surely, to look to the approbation and applause of his country, is one means of keeping alive the sentiments of citizenship which ought not to be suffered to expire even in a camp. Shall we make it an excuse for refusing to pass this vote that we establish the principle of thanking nobody? Is not this, as a principle, as novel, as improper, as that which alarms our opponents? And shall we establish it as a principle against the known practice of other assemblies and of this, and against the intrinsic propriety of the case, merely because we think our discretion will not be firm enough in future to prevent the abuse of the practice? Scarcely any abuse could have a worse influence than the refusal to adopt this vote, because, should the negative prevail, what would the army believe? Would they not say, a vote of thanks has been rejected? It is said we have not done much, and what we have done is merely our duty, for which we receive wages?

The debate has taken such a turn, that I confess I could have wished the motion had not been made. For the most awkward and ridiculous thing in the world is to express our gratitude lothly. But at least it offers to those who fear that votes of thanks will be too frequent, some security against their apprehensions. Would any man risk the feelings and character of his friend by an attempt to force a vote of thanks by a bare majority through the House? No, an ingenuous mind will shrink from this gross reward. If there is any force in the precedent it is feared we are now making, it will operate more to deter from than to invite the repetition.

APRIL 7, 1796

MR. AMES did not wish to go into an argument at length in favor of keeping up a naval force; nor did he suppose his conceptions on the subject were very material. The gentleman from Virginia [Mr. MADISON] objected to the number of frigates proposed to be built. He agreed with him, that if it were necessary to keep up a navy able to cope with European powers, it would be better to relinquish their commerce altogether.

It was true it might, on the score of expense, be inconvenient to keep on foot the whole number of frigates, though he had objections to reducing the number of them. It had been said, that if the six frigates were completed, they would have no effect in repelling the force of European nations. There would, in his opinion, be two advantages derived from having some force. There was something in raising an opinion of force; it would have some effect on the imagination of foreign powers. He owned he looked forward to the time, when, if good government continued, it would be in the power of this nation to cope with any European nation, if it was their duty to do so. If they armed at all, though but a small force, it could not fail to produce respect to the nation. It is a display of some strength, and of a spirit that could command more.

Another idea with respect to any dispute with England: Every one supposes that with 500 ships of war she would be an overmatch for any vessels we could build; but if we have six frigates, they would be obliged to come out in fleets instead of single cruisers; and thus our frigates would be able, in a considerable measure, to protect our coasts. The opinion of their force would serve to protect our trade in peace, and their actual force would be of some use in time of war. With respect to the Barbary powers, the idea of force will have some effect; for they will not be influenced by justice, and their cupidity will be whetted or repressed by a consideration of our strength or weakness. He thought it necessary to act on the fears of those powers. Two or three frigates would not be a match for Algiers; but that was not all, two or three frigates could not always be on the station; some must be ready to relieve others. He asked, therefore, whether less than enough would not be a waste of money? He thought, to have their trade half protected might be worse than no protection at all. This was his conception; he might be told that he was in error; but as the observation appeared of some weight with him, he made it.

But in his view, there was an object far more interesting than mere counting-house calculation. Admitting our navy might cost more than the insurance against capture, he would ask whether they listened to the sighs of their citizens in Algiers? If they had thought of these, they would say that the protection of their citizens was worth more than it cost.

The frigates proposed to be built would produce a sense of security in their seamen, and would have a very good effect; but if they had not force enough to give security, and the sense of it, it would amount to nothing.

He considered the possession of force as the only way of gaining respect, and he doubted whether the triumph of the Roman arms by the Roman legions was not as much owing to every citizen believing himself equal to a King, as to their strength. And he wished an American citizen should cherish the rights of citizenship more than cash. This national protection will cherish the sense of brotherhood; he believed this was necessary in a country where time had done so little to knit together the ligaments of our Union, which so many repulsive passions were now in full activity to sever.

TO OLIVER WOLCOTT

DEDHAM, MARCH 24, 1797

MY DEAR SIR,

AFTER many perils, by wind and water, mud and ice, after crossing Stratford ferry in a snow storm, and walking on the ice over Connecticut river, I am by my own fireside. The great theme of every man's inquiries is, are we going to war with France. This is dreaded as it ought to be, and after that, it is still dreaded as it ought not to be; for I think I discover a preference of peace to honour and real independence. France is feared as if her cut-throats could fraternize us, and loved by the multitude as if they were not cut-throats. I cannot but lament that the public sentiment receives no good impression from the legislature, and no sufficiently strong one from the government. The Jacobins had the people so long that they filled all the weak heads, and they are such as arguments from books they do not read, and from men whose conversation and company they do not enjoy, cannot reach. The national spirit is yet lower, and popular error more inveterate, in my calculations, than in those of my friends. I fear little from this, if Congress should be disposed and really obliged, by circumstances, to assume a strong position for the country. But before Congress meets there will be room for opinion to fix itself, instead of being fixed, as it ought to be, by those at the head of affairs. I forbear to go into any detail of my sentiments on this subject, and the more, as I am much shaken in my adherence to them by yours. I hope Sumner will be chosen Governor, and the prospect is believed to be good. Sullivan is his competitor.

Wishing your rewards of public approbation, and health and happiness may be equal to your services, and that you may not be discouraged in your endeavours to keep this generation of vipers from ruining us, I am, dear sir, truly yours, &c.,

FISHER AMES

TO OLIVER WOLCOTT

DEDHAM, APRIL 24, 1797

MY DEAR SIR,

YOUR LETTER afforded me uncommon pleasure. The profound reflections you have made on the subject, and the just conclusions you have deduced, made so much impression upon my mind, as in a degree to shake my creed in regard to a commission to negotiate with France. Mr. Cabot I knew was of your sentiment, and although your letter is headed "private," I ventured to show it to him, which I pray you to excuse. He was delighted with the perusal, and confirmed by it in his opinion, not only of the unfitness of sending a new envoy or envoys, but also of your title to the esteem and regard he has for you, in which I assure you he is not singular.

I have reflected a good deal on your reasoning, and believe that I have neither grown stubborn in defence of my first notions, nor sufficiently precise and correct in my explanation of the reasons that still maintain their ground with me. I see difficulties and risks in every course of proceeding, and I cannot otherwise recommend my first impression, than to insist that fewer and less perplexing ones seem to attend a new negotiation than any other plan. I had intended to state my ideas much at large, but company, business, and indisposition prevent.

The injuries of France afford a cause for war, and would justify the resort to arms, or to reprisals, without any further demand of reparation. But war and reprisals are both out of the question. Neither government, nor the House of Representatives, nor the citizens desire or would concur in either. Patience, silence, mean acquiescence under French wrongs would gratify the Jacobins, and not greatly displease the timid, the avaricious, and the multitude who never act from their own impulse; perhaps a majority prefer peace with outrage, rapine, insult, dishonour, and the interdiction of the ocean, to a war with France. I know that an embargo would soon evince that our people would not submit long to be interdicted all navigation. Yet speculatists and some men of business would say, before it is tried, that it would be better to abjure the ocean. Whether it proceeds from timidity, avarice, French fanaticism, (which though weakened is still a giant) or the stupor which every public falls into, when for want of an impression from government, it is left to the anarchy of its own opinions, the fact appears to me that the dread of war is stronger still than the sense of honour or of injury. We, the people, are in truth more kickable than I could have conceived.

War therefore, or measures leading to it, and capable of being misrepresented as intended to provoke and hasten it, will be out of the question, especially in the House of Representatives of the United States. The men of intelligence and real patriotism will say, war is to be avoided; and French injuries on the seas, and influence in the United States, are to be resisted by other means if possible, than war; but they foresee and dread the infinite evils of our situation. If the Jacobins should prevail in the House; if government should be in consequence paralysed; if nothing should be done by Congress but to authorize an embargo, as your own fears suggest; our affairs will be worse than they now are. The imbecility of government and the preponderance of jacobinism will enrage an hundred, but discourage a million. We shall then be given up to France, bound hand and foot. To avoid this if possible, is a duty; self preservation demands that the inefficiency, and still more, (though not much more) the ill disposition of Congress should be guarded against. The measures you suggest are all right, wise, indispensable; but an attempt to adopt them, if Congress should reject it, would place us on worse ground than ever. The first question and a grave one, is whether Congress will consent to arming vessels, increasing taxes, putting posts in a posture of defence, &c., &c., *without* a plan of negotiation to avert war. I think they will not. The precedent in the case of Great Britain, of negotiating while we did a very little to prepare for war, will be quoted, and perversely enough, but with effect in the House and on the country. Strong measures will not suit weak and trimming men, whose real dispositions, however, are federal, unless covered and sweetened by the *commission*;

they would dare to vote for provisional measures, when such as are more direct and uncovered would be scouted. In a word, would not the coöperation of Congress be hopeless without any such pacific aspect of any defensive system. Even with it the prospect as to Congress is dubious. I will not enlarge on this part of the subject; your own reflections will supply the omission of my remarks. If then Congress would in one case coöperate and not in the other, the plan of negotiating anew seems eligible, unless its intrinsic demerit forbids our approbation. I see no such evident dishonour or mischief in it, as the best and wisest of my friends seem to do. To demand reparation, to get ready to take it, to declare that we will not rest contented and at peace without it, may be smoothly done; but it will be the *fortiter.* It will concenter opinions, it will stop Jacobin mouths on one point at least, put them in the wrong on others, prepare the public for the issue if unfavourable, break the continuity of that affection, or rather folly, which has kept us so long in hot water, gain time for government, and give us the chance of events. It is besides, according to my hypothesis, *Hopson's choice,* for no other road lies open. I admit the vile insults offered to General Pinckney; the dread of Mr. M. if he should go, which I almost decide ought not to be; the effect of delusive, fraternizing offers to our envoys which must be refused; (and yet the refusal would afford a new pretext to the French and their partisans); the desire of the French to have us negotiate; these and many other things check and discourage my faith in my own opinion. I conclude, however, very safely, that you at Philadelphia who watch in the cabinet, must with your worthy associates, combine some proper line of proceeding for Congress to adopt; the true members must be united and zealous; the public must be prepossessed in favour of that line; and strongly addressed and roused to require it as in case of the treaty. Let me entreat you with Col. Pickering and Mr. McHenry, to digest the system for the House, and through Tracy, N. Smith, Davenport, Sewall, &c., &c., to secure the co-operation of the federalists at their first coming. This is no time for your overscrupulous reserves.

You may command me by suggesting the ideas which ought to be held up. I accept the office of fifer, while Otis, &c., carry muskets. Pray offer my best respects to Mrs. Wolcott, and when you see Mr. R., to him and family. When you see Tracy, my prayers and blessing to him. I wish you the victory.

With unfeigned esteem, yours, &c.,

FISHER AMES

P.S. I began with a design to be brief, because I was in a hurry, which, as usual, has lengthened and confused my ideas. This is the substance of them.

Our case is bad, and if government should be passive, would be worse. Government cannot act without or against Congress. Congress will not do any right thing (an embargo is not of the number, if general) unless it tends to promote peace, or at least not to endanger it. To negotiate again is not servile or mean, if the right men are appointed, and the objects of the negotiation are reparation and the abolition of the clause for the eventual guarantee of the French W. India Islands. Negotiating will be *honourable* if we arm and prepare force and revenue, and *useful*, if the public is made to look to the issue, as depending on the French—peace, if they are just and friendly; war, if insolent and rapacious. The dread of war and of the French are obstacles to government, with out negotiation *de novo*; but with that, they are auxiliaries, and the very Jacobins will applaud the design, though they may not concur in the energy of the means. I request Mr. Goodrich's attention to this postscript. A firm face of resolution in the U. S. would certainly secure peace. A servile acquiescence would destroy our peace, or our government, or both.

TO HON. BENJAMIN GOODHUE

DEDHAM, JUNE 24, 1797

MY DEAR SIR

BACHE insists that the Feds. are a minority in the House and B. Russell expects that they are a firm though small majority. It ever looks ill of an individual member that both sides claim him. It is *pari ratione* an ill prognostic of that honorable body that its dispositions are so dubious. Of the Senate and President I desire to be thankful there are no doubts. The heads of departments and the judiciary are also sound and true. Add to this *we the people* are, though we say it, very wise and patriotic, and therefore we shall go very right when the government sets us out in the safe path. I really think public opinion mends. And that the immediate evil of anarchical sentiments has grown less. Whether Mr. Mazzei's correspondent and company will be able to pervert the citizens or will be disposed to attempt it before the next scramble for the first office I cannot foretell.

If your system of measures should be as puny as the House seems inclined to prefer, will not the President repent calling you together. Is there to be no more tax? Peace in Europe may save us from war, but not from disgrace, if such nothings should be the sole measures adopted. Without more force and more money the new negotiations will be childish.

Will the terribles take East India vessels indiscriminately or only in certain cases? Why should the article free ships make free goods be renounced in their favor without equivalent merely because they break it and complain of it? Are the claims for captures to be urged, or hushed for fear of the Republicans' anger? Mr. Gore writes that two cases are adjudged by the Commissioners against the British government 1st July next, but that the Court of Appeals does not sit to hear causes for some time, which delay vexes him.

When do you adjourn? The antis hope to carry you home, I hear, *re infecta*. Pray offer my best regards to Mr. Sedgwick and accept the best wishes of your friend

FISHER AMES

TO DWIGHT FOSTER

DEDHAM, JUNE 24, 1797

DEAR SIR,

I AM the more thankful to you for your kind remembrance of me, manifested by your repeated letters, as it could be only from your benevolence that so useless a creature or thing, as I am, still attracts your attention.

My life is of no more use to the world, my family except, than the moss to the trees in your orchard: it sucks out a very little of the sap, and that sustains a stinted and barren vegetation. I bar all compliment in reply, and insist that ten such valetudinarians are not worth one cabbage plant. We are cabbage stumps, and take up the room of better things. I will not urge this argument so far as to insist that all such folks as I am should be knocked on the head, although I could answer the objections and cavils of all excepting the concerned. My design in being thus particular is not to establish my claim to martyrdom, which I am content for the present to waive, but to help you to judge how I vegetate, and to enable you to answer the inquiries that some may still think fit to make about me. Whether I am to be worthy *'fruges consumere,'* by doing any thing to obtain them, is a problem too deep for me to solve at present. My own opinion has changed repeatedly, since I left Congress, in respect to the actual degree of my health, and the prospect of its being better or worse.

I leave it to you wise men to save the nation. Some of you must watch and pray, and others must fight, if need be. I should not have thought the lot would have fallen upon Thatcher to defend his principles by the sword.[75] And what is not the least remarkable, he got into the scrape by expressing his aversion to any thing French. He is a worthy fellow. May he long escape wounds and sickness, and enjoy as much glory as he thirsts for, without bleeding to get it. Does not J. Smith remark the advantage of a wife? She is an excuse on a challenge. God preserve you from gunpowder, &c.

Yours.

---

[75] *Mr. Thatcher, a member from Massachusetts, (afterwards Judge of the Supreme Court,) was challenged by a Mr. Blount, for words spoken in debate. He declined the challenge in terms that rather turned the laugh against the challenger.* [S. AMES]

TO HON. TIMOTHY PICKERING[76]

DEDHAM, OCTOBER 4, 1797

DEAR SIR,

MY engagements in a law court have not permitted me to thank you sooner, for the entertainment your printed answer to the little Don[77] has afforded. You have not left a whole bone in his skin. If his nation were not in question, I should say he was beaten too much, beaten after he was down, and every bystander would pity him. But as Spain once had power, and is still *magni nominis umbra,* with as much pride as if the substance had *not* departed, the spirit and vigor of the answer will have its effect in Europe. There they all tremble at France, and Spain too, because the terrible Republic says, Love me, love my dog. For my part, I love neither; and I rejoice to see the country acquiring, very fast, that self-respect which, with such an increment of power and resources as every year gives to the United States, will soon extort from foreign states the proper diplomatic sentiments and behavior. We have suffered strange impertinences from these privileged gentry. Mortified and provoked as I have been, on the successive occasions, I think it clear that the outrages upon our national dignity have raised the spirit and patriotism of the citizens. I find, everywhere, deposits of facts and opinions are culled from your reply to Adet (letter to Mr. Pinckney.) Many are disinfected, who were given over as incurable. If France should have another volcanic eruption, as many expect she will, her partisans here will grow modest.

---

[76] *Mr. Pickering was at this time Secretary of State.* [S. AMES]

[77] *The Spanish minister, Irujo. His collisions with our government were somewhat frequent.* [S. AMES]

If the sword should preserve their tranquility, my fears are that they will change their policy from force to hypocrisy, and hug us worse than they have robbed us. I am not sure that the old cant, with a change of conduct, would not make new troubles for the government by giving a new influence to the French partisans, its enemies. That influence is, however, so much weakened, I will hope it cannot be again near as mischievous as formerly.

Accept my best wishes for your own and your family's health, at the time of contagion and alarm.

I am, dear sir, yours sincerely.

TO HON. DWIGHT FOSTER IN CONGRESS, PHILADELPHIA

DEDHAM, DECEMBER 7, 1797

DEAR SIR

IF the explosion in France has humbled or converted our Demos, your session will be smooth. Should anything happen, or appear to be hatching of moment pray let me know from you. Sometimes I make Thacher do his duty, which is no easy task. However I hope he and my other friends will not quite forget me.

The weather has been intolerably cold. I cannot however complain of any ill effect from it to my health.

God bless you, yrs.

FISHER AMES

Please to take care of the inclosed.

TO ANDREW CRAIGIE

DEDHAM, DECEMBER 16, 1797

MY DEAR SIR

YOUR NOTE bears date December 17, 1795—this day completes two years. My regard and esteem for you would indeed carry me far in any act of serving your interest, or compliance with your wishes. But the prodigious disproportion between your property and mine forbids as vain and trivial every idea I could form of serving you much by forbearing to urge the repayment of any sum I could loan—for indeed my whole estate would be less than your yearly income. I think therefore that I may very properly confine myself to the uses I could make of the money due on your note, if paid. I assure you, and your experience will gain credit for my assurance that I can and for a long time could employ (in fact I have employed) money to such advantage as to exceed six per cent for every four months. It is therefore a sacrifice on my part to let the money remain where it is, and this I state because I know and take pleasure in believing, that you will desire to see my property augmented, and that it will be a motive as cogent with your friendship as any I could suggest for your taking measures to pay the balance of your note, if possible, within a month. I add to this my health and inclination oblige me to narrow the receipts from my profession very much, and unless I can immediately augment my capital to employ as I have already employed a part, I shall be embarrassed—and sometimes mortified accordingly, and unusually for me, by delaying my current payments—

It is a fact which may serve as an apology for the pushing style of this letter that I have prevented this last mortification only by borrowing small sums for a month past and have, to repay, been actually obliged to draw out of the best and most lucrative employment a considerable sum. I state this fact in strict confidence. I entreat you, use candor when you pass judgment on my repeating the request of payment. It is not by way of complaint against you, but to evince to your friendship the necessity of my affairs that I have written as I have. I pray you let me depend on your compliance—and write soon. [————] is a minute of your note which you can compute. The sum received to the credit of Moses Everett you have my letter on order for and by the date you may calculate the balance.

FISHER AMES

TO MR. [DWIGHT?] FOSTER

DEDHAM, DECEMBER 17, 1797

DEAR SIR

I THANK YOU for your obliging attention to Colonel Worthington's business, which I am persuaded he will not fail either by his own hand or Mrs. Hooker's to thank you for also— and to request such further arrangements as may be convenient. I am not informed as to the manner he would wish you to adopt for the remittance of the money.

It was very obliging to enclose Bache at the same time, as I seldom read the *Chronicle* into which, at second hand, all the venom of the former passes as through an alembic.

Our friend George Thacher used to excuse his reading the *Chronicle* on the ground that any one would be curious to know what was going on in hell without alleging precisely that reason. I own it is pleasant to know what the foes of all political good say against the President, the government, etc. I am persuaded New England is very well disposed towards both, and as ready as any people ever was in a *tranquil* state to submit to taxes and any really necessary measures of self defense. Should the crisis become more alarming their zeal would rise with the danger. If you can conquer Jacobinism in Congress, I vouch for it there is not enough out of your walls to make much trouble for you.

Wishing you health and happiness and an agreeable session, fruitful in good works, I am dear sir

Your very humble servant

FISHER AMES

1 7 9 8

TO JOHN WORTHINGTON

DEDHAM, JANUARY 27, 1798

DEAR SIR,

I LOSE no time to acquaint you that the last post brought me intelligence of my being appointed a commissioner, with two other persons, to settle the disputes in Tennessee, which concern that new state, the Spaniards, and the Cherokees. I expect to know more on the subject, of the duty, length of service & emoluments and when the journey must begin. I went yesterday to see my friend Mr. Cabot—he advises me to accept, if the pay should be adequate to the labor & the sacrifice of business. He and my Philadelphia correspondents think my health would be restored by the journey. To leave the estate of the late Doctor Sprague unsettled will be difficult and call for some exertions & arrangements of prudence and caution. To leave the quiet of my domestic life for the labor & responsibility of a public mission will be unpleasant—to no one more than to me. Mrs. Ames is now very well and reconciled to my going, if on more information it shall appear eligible. I shall not greatly regret the withdrawing myself from the law courts for a time, as the task is in fact too hard for me.

We have neither seen Mr. Hooker nor heard from him— we hope he has letters. We have sent in for him [by] the stage to pass Sunday with us. If Col. Dwight is at home please to communicate this letter to him.

Mr. Gray wrote to me lately that he had daily expectation of the arrival of the vessels with your adventures. If they should come safe, the profit will be handsome. Wishing you health & happiness,

I am dear sir yours

FISHER AMES

[P.S.] Mr. Appleton says your interest on stock being un-claimed is gone to Philada. where you may get it by forwarding a power to some friend. The power Mr. Ap says should run thus

> "To receive at the Treasury of the U. S. any Interest and Dividend unclaimed within the time limited by law on stock standing in my name on the Books of the Loan office in Massachusetts."

Mrs. Ames wishes Sophy to know that there is a plenty of Italian silks and very pretty in Boston. We also join in asking her to write by post as the expense of postage is less regarded than so long a delay in hearing from Springfield. Nat is in the finest health & the best boy in the world. Still we admit John is the best and love him accordingly.

TO OLIVER WOLCOTT

DEAR SIR,

I ENTERTAIN too just a sense of the duty and respect that I owe to the President and to the government, to delay communicating the result of my reflections, on the question of accepting the appointment to the Cherokee mission. I confess my first sentiments were favourable to it. With my habits and sentiments, the first thought was, of course, to obey. Since, however, I cannot but anticipate embarrassment and difficulty in arranging my affairs so as to leave them; an absence from my professional engagements, only for a few months, would render me a very uncertain man, in the opinion of clients, to employ. Thus some immediate sacrifice, and more in anticipation, combine to detain me in a situation which affords me a moderate provision for my family. The allowance heretofore made to Indian commissioners will be, and I perceive is a rule, in this case. It is very probable many persons, more competent to the duty than I can pretend to be, will be found, whose situations will permit them to serve. But I will not conceal from you my opinion, that it would be attended with a greater pecuniary sacrifice than I conceive I ought to make. Indeed, what would remain of the compensation would not maintain my family in my absence, unless I make very erroneous calculations. I know that more important offices are holden under the government, notwithstanding similar discouragements exist.

My motive for an early suggestion of my probable decision, is grounded on the importance of an early and punctual attendance of the Commissioners. This letter will call the attendance of the heads of departments to the selection of some other person in my stead. It is, however, intended as confidential. While you are engaged in the *ardua regni*, I am sensible my reasons for declining wear an ill face. If I had good health and no family, I might be liable to be called upon as a patriot, however feeble my pretentions to that character may be.

I am very sincerely yours

FISHER AMES

TO DWIGHT FOSTER

DEDHAM, FEBRUARY 18, 1798

DEAR SIR,

CRAIK'S SPEECH is extensively read and much admired. It puts arguments into the mouths of those who wanted them, and corrects many errors in regard to the character and views of the Demos. I am impatient to know the issue. When will the House vote the Senate useless, and the President dangerous? I give full credit to many who say they intend no such thing. The work of mischief never stops, because the instinct that executes it is blind. The fear of the executive power is still as lively as if the President were a king. The fear of church establishments is nearly as strong among the same set. They do not see that the tendency to certain evils is counteracted in one case by ample political precautions, in the other by the spirit of the age in addition. Our executive is no match for the representative body in a contest for his being. Suppose a war, the executive power must be used, and perhaps would be abused; but the constitutional depositary would not hold it. The use must be obtained by usurpation, sanctioned by the necessity of the case. What is to keep armies subordinate to the civil power, especially after or during a war, but the interest and the means of the executive to govern according to his functions by law instead of being controlled by usurped power? These Demos are just such friends to liberty as they would be to the bank, if they forbid guards, locks, and keys for the safety of their vault. They are just such friends as have ever betrayed it when it has been lost. The country, I really believe, is more correct in opinion, and better disposed in point of feeling than they.

Is Lyon[78] still in your cage, or turned into the woods? I owe you more thanks for your attentions, so often repeated, than I have offered—not more than prompt me at this moment to subscribe myself

Your friend.

TO JAMES McHENRY, SECRETARY OF WAR

––––––

DEDHAM, FEBRUARY 18, 1798

SIR,

I WAS honored by the last mail with your letter, and I lose no time to communicate the result of my most mature reflections upon the subject of it.

––––––

[78] *The* rencontre *between Lyon and Griswold, being the first case of the kind on the floor of Congress, excited more sensation than similar events do at the present time.* [S. AMES]

Though I want neither a sense of duty and attachment to the government, nor of grateful respect for the President, (from whom any mark of confidence is really an honor,) and though I am much affected and flattered by believing, as I do, that the expectation of good effects upon my health from the journey has contributed to my nomination as commissioner to hold a treaty with the Cherokees,—yet these considerations, powerful as they certainly are, yield, nevertheless, to others still more cogent, which compel me to decline the appointment. This I very respectfully beg leave to do.

My health is feeble; though it requires exercise, it is unequal to hardship and fatigue. The time of departure, the place of meeting, and most of the circumstances from which I might calculate the competency of my strength to the journey, are unknown to me.

I think myself bound in sincerity to disclose another obstacle to my acceptance.

The emoluments of my practice of the law are not very considerable. Such as they are, however, they are too essential to the support of my family to be neglected. It is sufficiently obvious that an absence of several months from the bar would reduce my part from little to less.

I cannot but hope the weight of my reasons will appear to justify the conclusion to which they have led me.

With sentiments of great respect, I have the honor to be,

Sir, your obedient, humble servant.

TO HON. BENJAMIN GOODHUE

DEDHAM, FEBRUARY 18, 1798

MY DEAR SIR

I saw our good friend Mr. Gray a few days ago in Boston. He thinks we had better *not* arm unless *insults* compel us to self defense. He thinks *injuries,* such as we suffer at present less than the charge of a war, that our trade is yet profitable— profitable enough, that our vessels could not afford to arm if permitted etc.

He is a very uncommon clear and right headed man, worth all the democrats (for sense as well as merit) that yet escape the gallows. But I do not subscribe to his opinions.

He says France is a distracted country not to be brought to its senses by anything but time and patience. Perhaps as he corresponds with you, the ideas I impute will be found inaccurate. You know my respect for him and will not misunderstand my comment upon his opinion.

France though crazy is systematic in pursuit of aggrandizement. The French (though divided) agree in that passion. It is therefore as rational a business as that of Britain was in 1794 and to be resisted by our nation. Nor is it true that the attacks of a *distracted* people are not to be repelled. And though our small vessels might not afford to arm the larger would. The public must arm for them and provide convoys. The calculation that our trade is gainful though disturbed by force is too mercantile for my notions. Our honor, safety, and even the profits of the trade for any length of time depend on different maxims.

By arming, by reprisals *sub modo* and condemning vessels attempting to capture ours France will be made to see that she will get blows with prizes and her prudence may even yet incline her to retreat—if not peace must be despaired of as the preparations of self defense afford the best and now the only chance to preserve it.

Pray let me hear from you.

I am much engaged. The Supreme Court being soon to sit in Boston. Pray offer my regards to Sedgwick and [Frary].

Yours etc.

FISHER AMES

TO CHRISTOPHER GORE

FEBRUARY 25, 1798

MY DEAR FRIEND,

PAINE SAYS this may go by a vessel to Ireland. I am not sure the postage on so large a packet will be compensated by the contents.

Mrs. A. left me on the 13th, and is at her father's. My solitary state will continue, I fear, a fortnight longer. It is no offset that I am to enjoy Judge Paine's company a part of this time. The Georgia cause is to be *broke* on demurrer to-morrow. The points will engage the zeal of counsel on both sides, and the anxious attention of the town of Boston. I hope for our friend, but I have my fears also.

The Attorney-General[79] and Chief Justice[80] are at open war. A committee of new trials received from the former a

---

[79] *James Sullivan.* [S. AMES]

[80] *Francis Dana, Chief Justice of the Supreme Court.* [S. AMES]

letter, in answer to their application for information respecting a cause, (The Commonwealth *vs.* Little,) in Maine, in which he says a new trial was granted by the Court, and that any other verdict of any other jury might as well be set aside. This roused the ire of the Chief Justice, who wrote to the General Court demanding a hearing on the floor, in exculpation of himself and associates. A committee is to report on this request, and it is expected will deny it; and the Chief Justice will not be so put off. How it will terminate, is matter of conjecture. A contest between these law chiefs amuses the town. The battle in Congress excites more wonder. Most persons justify Griswold for beating Lyon on their floor, where the latter spat in his face. That the whole affair will disgrace our country, all agree; but why, say they, should G. be more nice of the honor of the House, than the House itself? The disgrace was, they add, complete before, when they refused to expel Lyon for this unspeakable brutality, committed on Griswold while they were sitting. You brag of our country like a patriot. What will you say to spitting, caning, and cuffing, on the floor of Congress? The southern men of honor voted against the expulsion, and our three Massachusetts *antis*, Skinner, Varnum, and Freeman. The duellists, rather inconsistently, protect the aggressor in such a case. Is it not strange that Blount, who challenged Thacher for almost nothing, and . . . . , who was glad to be protected by the House against Gunn, should now vote in favor of Lyon? No! it is not strange.

On Thursday last, the 22d, the ex-President's birthday was celebrated in Concert Hall. The Governor and Judges were there, and your humble servant. The spirit and feelings of the day were exceedingly different from the timid and divided policy of our government. The people are as willing to follow good measures as they can be. They wish for peace; but they are impressible by appealing to their sense of duty and interest. The General Court have taxed dogs, and are about encouraging justices. A bill has passed the House to give exclusive cognizance of all causes under one hundred dollars to these Solomons. The attempted judiciary bill, which contemplated a respectable County Court, is lost; and a scheme is pushing to erect a separate supreme court for Maine, *imperium in imperio.*

All eyes will soon turn to the event of the French preparations to invade England or Ireland. The threat may be of use to them, but the execution must be very difficult. To land is no easy matter; to establish themselves and to subdue a nation, fighting at home for their household gods, is still more difficult. But the French say therefore they will succeed; that victory is chained to their car. The attempt, if made without success, will greatly change the face of affairs. I should think the ascendency of England would, in that case, become very decided. You, on the spot, can judge of appearances better than any one at this distance. Heaven forbid that they should land and triumph! The world would have to wear chains.

Congress is so divided, and faction has so debased and alienated the *amor patriæ,* I almost despair of any right measures. A letter from Murray, at the Hague, says, unofficially, that there is no prospect of the success of our Envoys.[81] This he infers from a letter to him from General Marshall. You will favor me by as full information as you can find time to give, of the state and prospect of affairs. Excuse my illegible pages. All that you cannot decipher means, that I am affectionately

Yours, &c.

P.S. The Spaniards, we hear, are actually engaged in giving up the Natchez, &c., to the United States; and the cloud in

[81] *At Paris.* [S. AMES]

that quarter is believed to be dispersed before this day. This looks as if France intended to be sweeter than her treatment of our commissioners foreboded. Gerry, we hear by a Salem vessel from Bordeaux, is used much better than his colleagues. What means that?

Griswold, after beating Lyon on the floor, I this moment read, has, with Lyon, promised to keep the peace the remainder of the session. The affair is again committed.

TO JEREMIAH SMITH

BOSTON, MARCH 13, 1798

MY DEAR FRIEND,

Do NOT wrong me so much as to suppose that my long delay in answering your letter (so full of wit and friendship) arose from any decline of my regard. I had resolved to write before I had yours. I have been busy, sick, and stupid for four weeks. I have been stupefying in the Supreme Court in this place, abusing the health I have acquired, and marring the prospect of its future improvement. No experience has been so decisive of my incompetence to any thing that excites or requires much engagement of mind, as that which I have lately had. Yet I am not dead, and hope to inhale health with the air and repose that next week offers at Dedham. Fate is heedless of my prayers, which are, to be in a situation to rear pigs and calves, and feed chickens at Dedham—the world forgetting, by the world forgot. Saving always, I would not forget my friends, nor have them forget me;—saving also the right, at all times, to rise into a rage against the politics of Congress, and a few more savings, all equally moderate and reasonable. In serious sadness, I wish to rest from all labor of the mind that wears out the body, and I would do it if I could eat Indian pudding without drudging in Court. You, I hope, enjoy good fees, *cum dignitate*—happy you certainly are, and you know it. I have heard that Mrs. Smith had a long illness when she was confined. I have not been able to learn how she is of late, and I will thank you to offer to her my best wishes and regards. I salute my daughter-in-law,[82] whose merits and accomplishments are so rare and excellent. My eldest son[83] is at Springfield, and has there cast his eyes on a young lady of that town, but my second son is at present unengaged, and is offered to you as the party to the treaty.

Apropos of treaty, I am not going to see the Cherokees, the Tennessees, nor Sacs. I dare not, vain as I am, undertake to persuade the aborigines of any thing so difficult as the task allotted for an experiment of my powers, in your facetious letter. The journey is long, and would subject me to fatigues and hardship—the duty is complicated and difficult, and would expose me to responsibility which I should choose to shun; and the absence of four, five, or six months from my office would spoil my business, which I would not consent to for the public pay proposed. The decided hostility of these back settlers to the government, fomented by party, and protected by so many in the House, (where a majority votes against the stamp act,) is formidable, and will soon bring on a crisis. The Vermont liberty-pole men have now a banner to rally under. What anarchical notions we find prevailing! What other government finds the elements of discord and dissolution so powerful within its very bosom! Everywhere, out of the United States, the government, good or bad, has

---

[82] *At this time, six months old.* [S. AMES]

[83] *About five years old.* [S. AMES]

the power to act or forbear acting. Its difficulties, and the menaced resistance to its action lie without; here, they appear within. The machinery of our government, as understood by Gallatin and Co., is made to stand still, not to go. I hope New Hampshire keeps all its federal fires alive.

A letter left at Henry Vose's, *ci-devant* Brackett's, School street, would reach me duly. Pray remember you have such a place in my esteem, that it will be always acceptable to me to know how you do, &c., &c.

Yours truly.

TO OLIVER WOLCOTT

DEDHAM, 22D APRIL, 1798

DEAR SIR,

I AM flattered, and I pray you to believe that I am thankful, for your repeated favours. I have not written till I am, I find, very much in your debt, for a reason which I also desire you to be persuaded is the only one; that I have not thought it right to force upon a busy man the correspondence of a recluse one. My sick chamber has enfeebled and impoverished the ideas, that my situation in the country might otherwise have obtained. Do not, I pray you, think I flatter or that I am too civil, when I assure you my clearest knowledge of public affairs is derived from your letters.

I am far, very far from sanguine as to our going on well; I often say, but I never say it as I feel, that the discrimination between our government and every other is this: other governments find opposition after they have resolved, ours before. Anarchy has a vote, or rather its veto on the volition, the first movement of the intellect, and of the affections of our system. For when a right measure is decided on by the government, the people will obey; all difficulties are over before those of other countries can exist. This I submit to your thoughtful mind. The venom of the old serpent, the evil one of anti-federalism, is shed upon the *prima via*, the very first concoction of our ailment. Part of our diet is poison, and the whole system is feverish and acrimonious. The English Hercules is in his full strength, and contends with a serpent; our government is in its cradle, and tastes aqua fortis, or corrosive sublimate, in the milk that it sucks. Is any civil polity in the world like ours? Would it not be a great point to postpone the action of the resisting powers till the measures of the government are laws? For we seem to exhibit the practice, as we hear in the Congress debates— the theory, of anarchy.

That I may not seem to give a too speculative cast to these observations, I will add, that the time requires the government to do what I know it cannot and will not, that is, give a strong impulse to the public mind; that it should lead, and the people would cheerfully follow. Instead of that I see, and I dread your difficulties. Cowardice will cry peace; it has been the popular cry. The elections are approaching, and he must take some responsibility on himself who says, wage an active defensive war; but the time requires that it should be said, and that the merchants should give a tone to the government, not in general terms, but explicitly; that the people should be told they must put their hands into their pockets. They are more willing to do and suffer anything than their leaders, because an influence with them is a property too precious, for even federal men to expose to loss. The people are open to right impressions, but they are not yet enough roused to give them to government. Government is paralyzed by faction, the nation by avarice; like two dead bodies they must lie and putrify side by side, till the French tiger comes to devour them, or the hydra of anarchy digs them out of the grave. Gloomy as these ideas are, I do really confide in the better disposition of our citizens. The chance of our future state is improved; government may fall, but the phenix from its ashes will be better. Still I deprecate any change, and I agree that all our good men should join their best efforts to keep this system from sinking. I do not even despair of success. But the crisis is to be decisive—I see it clearly. Experience will teach truths that sophistry will not deny; that folly will not overlook. Among our wants is that of a good newspaper; Ben. Russell's is one of the best, but he prefers a joke to an argument, and is often injudicious and always lazy. Hopkinson is clever as a writer, but extensive information and solid reasoning, are as requisite as brilliant declamation. N. Webster and Jo Dennie, at Walpole, should be kept supplied, and kept correct too; any hints you may think it material to transmit to me shall be wrought up. I am in very poor health, but recruiting. I shall ride about, and mind business but little. Scribbling is not more of a labour than backgammon. Does Gerry by his quiddities keep the envoys at Paris? I wish they were at home.

Yours, truly,

FISHER AMES

P.S.—I saw G. Cabot two days ago; he talks of you with affection and respect, and is disposed to use his exertions in Boston to promote a right conduct; he is not sure that the well disposed will say in an address, all that they ought. The *truth*, many—most will say; the *whole truth*, nobody dare. No man is good, who is not now firm. Passive virtues are little better than treachery. Zeal is now better than logic.

TO H. G. OTIS

DEDHAM, APRIL 23, 1798

DEAR SIR,

I HAVE yours of the 16th, and besides the pleasure I derive from your political remarks, I am much pleased with your half page of egotism—first as a mark of your confidence, second as an opening to be free with you.

The reputation you carried with you was well earned and deserved, but, let me tell you, it was too good, and especially too brilliant, for Congress. Expectation in such cases is extravagant, and requires that to be accomplished which discretion forbids should be attempted. Unless a man could out-thunder Jove, he would disappoint folks. Now it is my creed that reputation will not grow up in Congress with the heat of one day, and the dew of one night, like lettuce. The basis on which it stands and strikes down its root, is confidence—confidence in the experienced ability and fairness of the man. It takes time, and a good deal of time, for the weak to know, with absolute certainty, who is strong enough to lean upon—who can bear his own weight and theirs. Those who grope in the dark, naturally seek those who can guide and enlighten their path;—but their first steps in the light are hesitating. Dropping metaphor, Congress is no place for sudden character, because most of the members are above blockheadship, if they fall below the sphere of genius. I do not forget the respectable exceptions that are to be made in favor of some of the worthies. I am therefore not only satisfied, but pleased with your discretion and reserve of yourself. Your place, for the reasons before stated, will not be lost by non-claim. I go on to observe, that I do not rank you lower on the list, that the members assign to each other and the public to all, than I used to predict.

Your speech was good, but your letter to General H. better than good; it is excellent—useful to the public, reputable to you; and the strokes *ad captandum* are so blended with irony, that Roxbury vanity must be flattered and humbled at the same time. I write in confidence, and I should despise the thought of flattery. Rely on it, your friends exult on the perusal of the letter. You must not talk of fees, nor of being weary of well doing. The enlistment is such, you cannot return to private life yet, without desertion. I hope and trust your task will be in future less irksome, and more will help you. Folly has nearly burnt out its fuel, I mean the French passion; and the zeal of good men must be warmer and more active than it has been or we sink. It is too late to preach peace, and to say we do not think of war; a defensive war must be waged, whether it is formally proclaimed or not. That, or submission, is before us.

The President and his ministers are decidedly popular, and if a strong impulse should be given to the people, by the measures of government, the disorganizers would fall. But, when fallen, they would gnash their teeth. The late communications have only smothered their rage; it is now a coal-pit, lately it was an open fire. Thacher would say, the effect of the despatches is only like a sermon in hell to awaken conscience in those whose day of probation is over, to sharpen pangs which cannot be soothed by hope.

I am getting bitter; but to-morrow is our Common Pleas, and with *molliter manus imposuit,* a case or two of bastardy, and a writ of entry on disseisin, &c., &c., I shall be sick. God bless you.

Yours.

[P.S.] Surely you will not rise till you have done something efficient.[84] We, the people, wait to take our tone from you. Strong, energetic measures are more likely to be supported cheerfully, than half way things that presuppose discord and lukewarmness towards the cause and the government.

---

[84] *A very brief explanation of the position of our relations with France may be convenient at this point.*

That government saw fit to consider the British treaty negotiated by Mr. Jay (that "fatal treaty," as Jefferson called it) as a violation of the rights of France, and to resent it accordingly. Our minister, Mr. Pinckney, was not received at Paris, and the Directory expressly declared that no American minister would be received, "until after that redress of grievances which France had a right to expect from the United States." While the door was thus closed against diplomatic intercourse, the seas were swarming with French privateers, and the most audacious and piratical plundering of our commerce was systematically carried on, on a very large scale, under the sanction of that government. A new mission, composed of Messrs. Pinckney, Marshall, and Gerry, was despatched by our government, and arrived at Paris in October, 1797. These gentlemen, with much patience and discretion, occupied themselves, for many weeks, in a fruitless endeavor to be received in their official capacity. While dancing attendance in this ineffectual manner, certain informal negotiators made great efforts to induce them to buy a favorable reception by large presents in money to influential members of the French government. They were also given to understand that a large loan of money from our own treasury to France, "our ancient ally," would be an indispensable condition to the making of any treaty whatever. Rejecting these delicate overtures, our commissioners were at last constrained to take their departure without ever having been received at all in their official character.

The despatches of our commissioners very naturally produced no little excitement, and very active and vigorous defensive preparations were made. A slight exertion of our actual naval strength was sufficient to clear the West India seas of the privateers, and to reduce the spoliations to comparatively narrow limits. The reluctance manifested in Congress to do even so much, appears at this day not a little remarkable.

TO TIMOTHY PICKERING

DEDHAM, JUNE 4, 1798

DEAR SIR,

I HAVE NOT seen any time when I thought the government stood as strong as at present. The malcontents never had any efficiency, and have lost at present even the appearance of strength. The Feds have at all times possessed a power which was inactive, but would have been irresistible, if occasion had called it forth. The occasion has happened, and the confidence in government, and zeal for it, appears to me great enough to encourage every attempt for good measures, and to sustain them when adopted. But as I know, and every mail brings proof, that Congress is yet far behind the people, I fear the occasion will pass over, and yield less fruit than it might and ought. The members still talk too much of peace, as if we had our choice, and as if we ought to choose it now. They are too much afraid of measures of self-defense, as if the French or our own citizens would think them crimes. They narrow the extent of those measures, and restrict the little they grant, to an excess. All, *all* we can do is little enough, but I really believe it would prove enough to keep the French in check. To be more explicit, I am sorry more force is not raised immediately; more, and a great deal more, revenue; the employment of the ships more like war; the obligation of our treaty with France legislatively declared null; the discretion vested in the President to embargo the trade to the French West Indies; a sedition bill; and generally more decision and more despatch in passing such acts as the urgent necessity of affairs demands. No good man desires more than the security of true liberty and independence; and no good citizen will now wince at measures tending to that point. The number of Jacobins is not too great. The contrast between the sentiments in doors and out should be strongly marked to be perceived, and to induce and almost to compel the southern electors to reform their representation. Such a mass of opposition as they combine must fall, or the government will; and it is against all good sense to imagine that evidence has convinced, and that conviction will convert them. At first it confounds, and next it will enrage them. They will soon rise from the mire, where they now lie, and attach themselves to any set of honest men, who in every question shall be for doing the least and the latest. Thus a new party may be formed to paralyze and distract our measures and our counsels, and the public, relapsing into its habitual apathy, will not again give the tone to government it has lately given. I repeat it, therefore, the moments are precious, and the friends of the government ought to act under that impression. Not one Jacobin is changed, though many are dumb. The light that guides others, makes their eyeballs ache. It is indeed very necessary that the thinking federalists should note well, that the causes of opposition to free republican systems are in the heart of man and not to be eradicated. Truth has lately mown them down, but in six weeks they will sprout again, as unconquerable as the weeds. I will add that half measures are much harder to carry, and to support, than such as great perils call for. Half the debaters admit that to preserve peace is a duty, and therefore defensive measures are to be justified on ground so narrow and metaphysical, that all the weak federalists stagger or slide from it. No people can long keep steady in such a half state; and therefore a full state of *war*, waged but not *declared*, and limited cautiously to the existence of their vile acts, seems to me necessary to be passed by Congress with acclamation, and we the people will echo it. To annul the French treaty is also indispensable. Every day's delay is perilous. Everybody asks, shall we have war? My answer is, we have war, and the man who now wishes for peace holds his country's honor and safety too cheap. Cardinal de Retz, who well understood human nature, has shown the danger and folly of keeping multitudes long in suspense. Keep them in action, and shift the scenes, and you may succeed; but this state of passive obedience, this devout prayer for peace, when it is shameful for Congress-men to be caught at their prayers, will quench that fire which, like every other, will expire the sooner for burning briskly. In the actual state of things, government may give any proper tone to the people, and when once given it may be continued. I confess Congress has done better than I feared, but, I must not conceal, fall very far short of my wishes. Their beggarly system of starving their chief officers, and the committee system, must be changed. In their appropriations, they go into details on the pretence of vigilance, which transfer too much of the ministerial duty to the members. Congress should prescribe rules, the departments should apply them to the particular cases.

I did not foresee the course this letter would take, which is all the excuse I can offer for it.

The legislature of Massachusetts is good. Judge of its federalism by one fact. Levi Lincoln, of Worcester, was not chosen representative by his town, and was only a candidate for the Senate, in which body he served the last year. The two houses in convention gave him only seventeen votes out of one hundred and seventy-six, although his competitor was confessedly his inferior in every thing, but federalism. Other vacancies in the Senate have been filled up in a manner to indicate an equal preponderance of the anti-Gallic sentiment. Lincoln was obnoxious only as a Frenchman. Governor Sumner is rechosen by seventeen twentieths of the votes, and will address the two houses in language of decision, after which the Feds will vote a strong address to the President. It is only for the speech that they are waiting. I almost fear that the *antis* are down too low in our General Court to produce warmth by collision. Among other pointings of the public opinion, I mark with pleasure that the necessity of an efficient naval force is acknowledged, and it will be an easy thing to animate New England to insist upon it as a local right. I fear, however, that it will be difficult to prevent bad economy in the construction, and bad conduct in the first operations, of our ships. I should regret this the more, as it might disgust our citizens against naval protection. I cannot be insensible to the difficulty of selecting the best characters for the navy secretaryship, as the compensation is inadequate. Some of your countrymen know the weight of the services and toils which the heads of the departments have to sustain. The good will offer, as a partial reward, their thanks and esteem, and the bad will add the honorable testimony of their calumny. Thus far you may be very sure of your reward. I am, with unfeigned esteem,

Your most obedient, humble servant.

TO OLIVER WOLCOTT

DEDHAM, JUNE 8, 1798

DEAR SIR,

THERE seems to be a power in Congress to do the needful, but it meets with too much resistance, and its movement is too slow. I am impatient to see the French treaty nationally annulled. Reconciliation with France is still sighed for, and if the evil one had counselled them to offer everything, and to ask of us everything but money, we should have seen a worse state of things than the useful profligacy of the French has produced for us. Although I rely on their arrogance and rapacity to prevent their coaxing, yet I should be disposed to guard against the insidious policy which their late discovery of the spirit of the country may put them upon resorting to. Peace is a word, a vain word, that would still deceive and divide, and the spirit of Congress is so much lower than that of the nation, and the latter is so ready to sink into apathy, that I consider the middle state we are in as peculiarly awkward and without object. Why not annul the treaty? Why not authorise captures of privateers, commissioned to cruise against us, in any seas? Why not proceed at once to reprisals and letters of marque for the sufferers by their depredations? You will answer, "Congress will not do it!" and the answer stops my mouth; but that affords us reason for using temporizing language in Congress. Our friends should not make quite so much merit as they do of their desire for peace. The provisional army might have been raised, I should think, or part of it, immediately, and the more efficient [the] force the less the danger of commotion among the ultra montanes, who never yet respected the government or obeyed it. In brief, my fears, or my belief is, that the strong impulse on the public is temporary, and if left to itself, its reflux will be embarrassing. I admit, more has been done than I expected, and I am willing to hope that enough is done to give the proper direction to measures and opinions, and that the consequences will follow almost spontaneously as we desire. Yet I know the substratum of the sentiments of all our citizens is peace; and as I dread the art of France, even after detection, I wish to have our political thraldom legislatively terminated. Nor do I see why attempts should not be made to go every proper length in Congress, as no time seems to promise such success to rendering the Jacobin members obnoxious before another election. However necessary any further members may be, I will not pretend to judge so well as you who are on the spot, and at the fountain head of information. But my wishes to improve the moments, which seem to be so unexpectedly propitious to government, may have misled me as to their necessity. I wrote three days ago to Col. Pickering in a like strain, and possibly he may wonder at my doing it. I had half resolved to address it, when I had done, to you.

Among other grounds of my concern, the stay of the envoys in Paris is strange, and fills people's heads with delusive expectations of a reconciliation, which ought not to be; for though I do not wish Congress to *declare* war, I long to see them wage it. Then the country would be in a situation to sustain and to employ its present energies. Does Gerry, by his quiddities, detain his colleagues?

Sincerely yours,

FISHER AMES

TO DWIGHT FOSTER

DEDHAM, JUNE 24, 1798

DEAR SIR,

COLONEL DWIGHT is with me, and speaks of you in a manner that revives my sense of your obliging attentions. I wish your body was half as federal as that he belongs to. I am a state-government man, you know, and I am half willing Congress should order, assign, and endorse its powers to our General Court. The timid, doubting spirit of the former, that seems yet undecided whether to serve God or Mammon, would do for Switzerland, for the *Bullocks* of Europe, whose necks are patient of the yoke, but ill suits the Yankee stiffness. The impulse given by the Despatches[85] to the people is excellent, and is yet strong; but it is too much to expect that any popular impulse will last long, and not only go right, but keep government right. Yet, as your body is using *dampers*, that last duty is needful. Rely on it, trimming will expose the members to a severe account. Bullock is spoken of as a doubtful man. S. Lyman wrote some letters home, condemning long speeches and warm zeal, which ill accord with the decided spirit of his district.

Senator Dexter called, the instant I wrote the last word, on his return from Newport. His election is a good proof of the excellent disposition of our General Court. His talents will prop our federal temple; and, as war is evidently unavoidable, the employment of such talents is important.

The French will try arts and arms to trouble our politics, more than to subdue our strength; and, therefore, timid, temporizing measures will be out of season, and out of credit. Is Bullock turning *anti?* Is Coit incurable? The policy of the French is never so blind as ours. They discern and they seize all advantages at the very critical moment. How does Fenno succeed? He is a good man and true, and merits success. Porcupine is patronized, and I hope Fenno is not neglected. Will Virginia amend its delegation, that is, make a new one?

Yours, truly.

---

[85] *From the commissioners at Paris, giving an account of the attempts to obtain bribes from them. It was deemed prudent, in their despatches, to suppress the names of the persons by whom the propositions were urged, and they were described as X, Y, and Z.*

TO TIMOTHY PICKERING

DEDHAM, JULY [6,] 1798

MY DEAR SIR,

FINDING the minds of our people in Dedham and its vicinity well prepared, I recommended to some very capable young men an oration, dinner, patriotic song, &c., &c. A week only remained for preparation before the 4th instant. But antifederal and Gallic as our people have been, the proposition took exceedingly well. I am happy to announce to you, that it has succeeded; and, inconsiderable as the politics of a village may be, yet, as an indication of the progress of right opinions, and as a proof of the rapid decline of Gallicism where it was lately strongest, and is still perhaps the most malevolent in spirit that exists, it will not be deemed quite unimportant.

The company at dinner was about sixty. The number of men of education was unusually great. Five clergymen attended, whose hearts are with us. Three signed the address, two others retired before it was proposed, a sixth was invited, and, like the rest of his valuable order, was federal, but could not attend. Among the signers are magistrates, men of influence in their several circles, enlightened farmers, and mechanics. On the whole, I may say, with truth, no meeting has been held in this part of the country, within my memory, equally respectable. It was not attempted to get subscribers to the address out of the number of those who were present on the occasion, and, as you see, it was nearly unanimous. As our representative in the General Court did not vote for the address of that body, we conceived it right and proper to signify for ourselves that we are not of his antifederal sect.

I am persuaded the effect of the meeting will be salutary, and will rally the friends of government to their posts. Our representative was at the dinner, but declined signing, as consistency required that he should.

On the whole, I am confident that vigor in Congress would electrify this part of the country, and mount their zeal up to the old revolutionary pitch. I wish Congress may not take another nap so long and benumbing to their patriotism as the last. I am, dear sir, with great respect,

Your very humble servant.

[P.S.] The address will be sent to you under another cover. If you think these particulars worthy of the President's notice, please to let him read this.

TO OLIVER WOLCOTT

DEDHAM, JULY 6, 1798

DEAR SIR,

AT LAST the seeds of federalism which have slept so long in our Dedham ground seem to be sprouting. I have long wished some opportunity to favour the appearance of good sentiments: the 4th of July afforded it. A proposition from me to a young man for an oration, dinner, &c., took very well, and though only a week remained for preparation, it has passed off very well. About sixty clergymen, gentlemen, mechanics and farmers of Dedham and its vicinity exceeding in point of influence and respectability, any public meeting I have seen in Dedham, met and dined and drank federal toasts as you will see by the enclosed Gazette. The temper of the company was excellent, and the progress of federalism seems to have begun. Our representative in the general court did not vote for the address, and very properly declined signing that which the company agreed to; but he perceives the strength of the current against his conduct, and would change it, if pride would let him, which it will not. The company almost unanimously signed the address; the extension of the subscription to persons who were not present was not thought proper, and would have occasioned delay.

The detail of a village dinner and its petty politics will not seem wholly trivial to you, as the retired scene affords as good evidence of the working of opinion as the larger, in which the causes of influence are more complicated, and besides it is the first fruits of political conversion in a part of the country which has been exceedingly misled. The vicinity of Boston, the Chronicle, and other causes, have produced Gallicism in abundance. I shall, by the post of to-morrow, send on the address to Col. Pickering.

Yours, &c.,

FISHER AMES

TO TIMOTHY PICKERING

DEDHAM, JULY 10, 1798

DEAR SIR,

YOUR obliging letter, besides the pleasure it afforded on other accounts, relieved me from the stings of a bad conscience, which had continually reproved me for writing *that* to which yours was an answer. I had really feared mine was an unwarranted intrusion upon the time of a man so oppressed with the weight of correspondence as you are. To avoid the sin of augmenting this burden, I will add, that I do not expect you will answer this. You have intimated that I may communicate my thoughts, which is as much as I ought to engross of your time.

The burden of my former letter was, that the people could not be kept up at the height of zeal where they are, if Congress should finally bind us all up in the frost of that Platonism they so much affect. Half measures are seldom generally intelligible, and almost never safe, in the crisis of great affairs. The answers of the President have elevated the spirit, and cleared the filmy eyes, of the many. The people have risen *gradatim;* every answer was a step up stairs. But Congress follows too slowly, and unless they make haste to overtake the people, the latter, I fear, will begin to descend. I should be absolutely certain of this collapsing and sinking of the public, if I did not depend on the friendly profligacy of the French. They will kick us into courage. Their plan allows us no retreat. The southern Congress men will be obliged, at last, to feel French blows, with some pain, through their thick skins, although hitherto what has wounded others only tickles them. To us, the wrongs of France are whips and scorpions; to them, the strokes of a feather. As France aims at empire, and will exact compliances unexpected even by democrats; as she wants cash, and will insist on more than they will freely give,—I calculate on her doing for us, at last, that which Congress seems resolved shall not be attributable to the energy and wisdom of our counsels. If, in the interim of our infatuated torpor and indecision, she should condescend to resort to fraud and flattery, we should even yet be lost. But as her violence and arrogance happily lessen our fears on that head, I calculate on the eventual resort of Congress to measures of force. Internal foes can do us twice as much harm as they could in an open war. The hope of peace is yet strong enough to furnish the means of popular influence and delusion; at any rate, it chills the spirit of the citizens, and distracts them in the exercise of duty. I wish therefore, impatiently, to see Congress urged to proceed to steps which will have no such ambiguity in them. A declaration of war would be such a step. But it is the very one that their imbecility would reluct at; it is the very one that demands something like unanimity. I think this very reluctance might be used to advantage. Instead of *declaring* war in form, could they not be persuaded, even some of the Demos, to *enact* penal laws, *as if* it was war? To do something short of duty, something tamer than energy, suits the foible of the weak, temporizing, trimming members.

I should imagine a number, who would flinch from a *declaration of war,* would urge the enacting, one by one, the effects of a state of war. Not being on the spot, I can judge only from my knowledge of some characters, and the color of their conduct and speeches; with such materials I may be deceived in my conclusion. I think it probable, however, that several votes could be gained for strong measures, from the dread of being urged to adopt still stronger. Energy is a word of comparison, and to vote *as if* we were in war, might seem a half-way business, compared with a *declaration* of war. In this way they may authorize the burning, sinking, and destroying French ships and property *gradatim,* till no case is left which is to shelter them from hostility. As every armed French vessel takes our vessels, every armed French vessel should be prize, every one on board a prisoner; correspondence with the French, adhering to our enemies, &c., &c. I need not detail the consequences of this idea, as they will occur to you, nor discriminate the odds between a formed declaration of war, which would instantly draw after it all the consequences of a state of war, and a series of acts of Congress, which would annex to our state of peace all those consequences, one by one.

The difference of effect on the public mind is also worth computation and deliberation.

To declare is to choose war; it is voluntarily changing our condition, which however urgent the reasons and motives of the change may be, leaves a door open for blame on the government; it is, no doubt, a change at all times involving a high responsibility. Disasters in the conduct of a war would aggravate first ill impressions, and give a malcontent party a specific text of sedition. Ripe as the citizens are for self-defence, they reluct at offence; they would yield much, far too much, for peace; and this hope would delude them, if proud France would condescend to hold it out. Now why should not we play off against our foe a part of their own policy? Wage war, and call it self-defence; forbear to call it war; on the contrary, let it be said that we deprecate war, and will desist from arms, as soon as her acts shall be repealed, &c., &c., grounding all we do on the necessity of self-preservation, &c. We should need no negotiation to restore peace; at least we should act, as the *salus reipublicæ* demands we should, instantly, and there would be little balancing among the citizens, and the spirit would grow warmer in its progress. But a formal declaration would perhaps engender discords; all the thinking would come first, the action after. I would reverse this order. Not that I would conceal from the country its duties or its dangers. No, they should be fully stated and enforced. I would, however, oppose art to art, and employ, in self-defense against French intrigue, some of those means of influence which we may lawfully use, and which her party will so much abuse if we do not first possess them.

My long letter amounts to this: we must make haste to *wage war*, or we shall be lost. But in doing it, and, I might premise, to induce Congress to do it, and that without its ordinary slowness, we had better begin at the tail of the business, and go on enacting the consequences of war, instead of declaring it at once. The latter might be the bolder measure; its adaptedness to the temper of Congress, and even of the country, is not equally clear. Something energetic and decisive must be done soon. Congress fiddles while Rome is burning. America, if just to her own character, and not too frugal of her means, can interdict France the ocean. Great Britain will keep her close in her European ports; we can clear our coasts, and, before long, the West Indian seas. My faith is that we are born to high destinies. The length of this letter, and the fear of being too officious, restrains me from descanting on our prospects, as to our government, and as to any alliance with England. As to the former idea, governments are generally lost from bashfulness. Great occasions, like the present, either overturn or establish them.

I am ashamed to begin a third sheet. I have written very rapidly, as you will have already observed, and with less revisal and care than I ought. I am so earnestly engaged in thought on the state of our country, and so anxious to see its measures answer the noble style of the President's replies to addresses, as well as correspond with the peril arising from the power and insidious art of our foe, that I cannot forbear pouring myself forth in this way. Congress is willing to do little, at a time when less than all we can do is treachery. We halt apparently between two opinions, at a time when the alternative is war or subjugation.

I inclosed our address lately to you. Jacobinism, in the vicinity of Boston, is not yet dead, it sleepeth.

I am, respectfully, &c.,
Your most obedient servant.

TO CHRISTOPHER GORE

JULY 28, 1798

MY DEAR FRIEND,

You ASK for letters from America with such earnestness, I am half persuaded to think mine may be worth rather more in the London market than at home in the factory. I do not pick a quarrel with you because it is so long, so very long, since the date of your last. I lay it all to the French, or if that should be an error, I will charge it to hurry, to the supposed allowance of letters to other friends, such as George Cabot, *as if* they were addressed to me. I will never tease a real friend on this account, as I know there is no danger of your forgetting me, and for any other reason I care not a pin.

Your last was, I think, dated in February. I have written in folio since, like a Dutch civilian. I know not what I write, as I keep no copies, premeditate nothing, and say to myself, it is only for my Gore. I would be very wise if I could on the subject of our government, but the weather is too warm. Congress is up, and has *middled* its measures without being *tutissimus*. The last measure, a bounty per gun captured, was negatived by Harper's perverseness. Did Lord Grenville and Mr. Dundas know that their eulogium on his book would help the French by marring a good thing of Congress? Yet so it was. H. is a fine fellow, but praise has half spoiled him, and made him sometimes cold and sometimes opposed towards right things originated by others. George Cabot thinks the act not so very material. I do not concur with him. It would have weakened the privateering spirit, cut out work for the active, warmed the frigid, and placed our safety beyond the dreaded stroke of French coaxing. I own my hope is that we are beyond it. But as the trade of France affords no prizes, something was needed to give a spur, instead of the usual one. A bounty per gun was that spur. I am afraid of inertness, of languor, of the collapsing of the national spirit; an event always to be feared when there is much to apprehend and little to do. France will not forgive us for doing so much, and I am in a patriotic rage because we do so little. Should they fly into a passion, as their manner is, and wage an open war, we shall know what to do. There will be no puzzle about measures, and little ground to fear the event. For surely we can beat Frenchmen. The Austrian men think the French devils. Our Marblehead boys shall thrash them at the rate of two to three. The President will be in a hurry to see Congress speedily together again, sooner, I think, than December.

Mr. Gerry's return is earnestly desired. He will reap the harvest he has sowed. His stay was well calculated to spoil every good act of our government, but it has not. I do not rail at Congress for *not declaring* war, but then they ought to have gone the farther in *waging* it. Nothing doubtful in the situation of the United States, or in the duty of citizens should have been left. The donations to build ships is noble, and will soon form a decent naval force. *Hone,* and the Chronicle wretches, are despised and abhorred; but their malace is unchanged, and I dread of all things a revolution in Paris or a change of system, that would try art in place of force against us. For the fallen Jacobins would rise recruited, from bathing in the mud where they now lie, and the impressions in favor of a delusive, fatal peace would be perhaps irresistible. God forbid! I hate war as much as anybody, but nothing else can save us from France. Many supposed good men showed great weakness in Congress.

The President has turned out three Portsmouth Jacobins from office. One Whipple has sued Ben Russell for a paragraph, which, he says, lost him the office. I admit it is actionable and slanderous to call a man democrat; but this W. passed for such for years, and if he bore it quietly, let him sit down with the consequence. . . . Are we not, on the whole, a very incorrect people—not more than half in earnest in our best principles. Our very political righteous are to be saved only from free grace, as their theory is almost ever visionary or pernicious. It is true they seldom long stand to it, but are led by good affections and by the impulse of events to act beyond the squeamish mediocrity of their whims. The federal government would have been years ago in its grave, and in oblivion, if the providence of man had alone watched over it. Events supply the place of wisdom and of habit. I do not say this to detract from Washington, Adams, &c., God bless them, but to reiterate my conviction, that we are democrats playing republicanism. I love and reverence the latter. I do really think it practicable, and monarchy, though excellent in England, impracticable here. But it will require great efforts to procure a fair chance for the former in the United States. I do this justice, however, to our citizens. They receive strong impressions of political truth very readily, and are as much affected by it as any people ever known; witness the late Despatches: they really electrified all classes. To open the cabinet, to play government as it were in the street, and to affect the merit of introducing the sovereign people into negotiations, is a concession and a precedent from the event. In future we may find we have done some evil that great good might come of it. I see that Great Britain (and even the Emperor) talks democracy to the nation. So the world is changed.

Will there be a new coalition against France? Is Prussia to be paid for duplicity, by the gift of French principles? Is Russia to be always seeming to act, and never acting? Is the Emperor so thrashed, that he can only wait till the scabs fall off from his old wounds? Is his new territory to be kept under only by force, which, employing a part of his troops, weakens him, while Belgium, &c., adds much to the power of France? Is Spain to be revolutionized, demoralized, and minted by France, or to rejoin Great Britain? Is the Toulon fleet to catch the King of Naples and his little navy, or to dig a canal through Egypt into the Red Sea, or to help the Irish liberty boys? Is Great Britain to be better or worse by the state of things between the United States and France? A little squadron cruising on our coast, and a larger, duly active, in the West India seas, would keep all pirates close.

Yours, once more.

[P.S.] My question above relates to spoliations. Will Great Britain act rightly, or rely on our being obliged to fight her foe, and be tolerably civil to her, whether she does our folks justice or not? Woe be to her greatness if she plays such a dirty game. Rufus King will tell the great ones that tricks of that sort will not answer.

God bless Mrs. G., so says and prays my wife, and I say, Amen.

TO THOMAS DWIGHT

DEDHAM, SEPTEMBER 25, 1798

MY DEAR FRIEND,

BOSTON has been worse afflicted, for a few days past, than its inhabitants, jealous of its fame for salubrity, would own, as long as they could help it.[86] My creed is, that the fever

---

[86] *The yellow fever prevailed at this time in Boston and Philadelphia.* [S. AMES]

is yet either an unknown malady, or so rapid in its march that remedies come too late. This is certain, all the systems of care have been equally disgraced by the event. This town is perfectly healthy. . . .

My own health is much mended, since a cold, got at the Supreme Court, went off. Like an evil spirit, it threw me down before it was cast out, and produced a fainting turn, which, however, was not followed by the great prostration of strength I have generally experienced in like cases. . . . I am bound fast in chains of darkness in the Common Pleas, for the week, and hope to survive some few ten-dollar causes which are intrusted to my care.

.   .   .   .

Philadelphia has sipped the bitter dregs from the cup of affliction. If legislative bounty to our cities, to supply water to wash the streets, would afford security against the return of this curse, which is becoming almost annual, I should rejoice to see it granted, and liberally. The reputation of our country is impaired, which is some evil in commerce. I agree with you, the probable check of *patriotic* emigrants would be no matter of grief. Perhaps the overgrowth of cities may not be desirable, as they render the operations of our government rather more problematical for a length of years. These speculative ideas are no counterpoise to the evil of the fever, and if a remedy could be had for money, it would be cheap.

Report says Mr. Gerry is to return, with a Frenchman as an envoy, to coax, and lie, and sow division. For every purpose that demands negotiation, they might proceed at Paris, and Mr. Gerry was not disliked as a diplomatic man. The project, therefore, is on its very face unfair and insidious. But many will be deluded, and the mock converts among the democrats would take the occasion to go back to their old cause and companions. Nicholson's capture of the twenty-gun ship is a good thing as an antidote to French *diplomatic skill*. I have never thought France would be angry with any thing we do, but to supplicate and kneel. *Our* spirit is sure to mollify *hers*. Hypocrisy is her only weapon. Without ships, she cannot much annoy us; and she will not, by declaring war in form, deprive herself of the means of carrying it on by lies and intrigues—her only means.

Your friend.

Alas, poor John Fenno,[87] a worthy man, a true federalist, always firm in his principles, mild in maintaining them, and bitter against foes and persecutors. No printer was ever so *correct* in his politics. . . . . .

TO JEREMIAH SMITH

BOSTON, NOVEMBER 22, 1798

MY DEAR FRIEND,

SEEING Mr. Conner in an office, I steal a moment from the din of the Supreme Court, sitting here, to tell you I am alive, pretty well, very glad to hear from you and your better half, as I do by Mr. Conner. Write to me, and kiss my daughter-in-law, the princess. Her future spouse is a fine fat boy, as ragged and saucy as any democrat in Portsmouth. You have none in Exeter. They abound in Dedham, though the liberty-pole is down. Nelson has beaten the French fleet. Do not grieve for that. What are we to do? The devil of sedition is

---

[87] *Editor of the Gazette of the United States. His death had recently been announced.* [S. AMES]

immortal, and we, the saints, have endless struggle to maintain with him. Your state is free enough from his imps and influence, to give joy and courage to the two Langdons.[88] I really wish to see you and Mrs. Smith. God bless you.

Yours.

TO TIMOTHY PICKERING

DEDHAM, NOVEMBER 22, 1798

DEAR SIR,

I WAS at Albany when I first saw the letter you addressed to the democrat Johnston, and which, on my return, I found you had obligingly inclosed to me. I was gratified to perceive that its spirit was felt, and its reasoning duly apprehended, by most persons. Few publications in favor of government appear to me to have been so generally well received. The public mind is as near right as it can be, and nearer than it can be long kept, if Congress should flinch from spirited measures. I had, six months ago, some hopes, but they were then faint, that the pride of France would prevail over her artful policy. It is, however, apparent that the proud are the lowest stoopers, and that their palaver, as the tars call it, will be more *outré* than even their former insolence. Great care seems necessary, that the answer of the House to the President's speech should be in unison with the voice of America. The faction is not changed, nor like to be; and the

---

[88] *Governor John Langdon, and Judge Woodbury Langdon.* [S. AMES]

Chronicle has been puffing the votes for Heath as a muster of their strength. They are overjoyed to find they yet have any, and that the resources afforded to their cause by popular credulity, envy, and levity, are not soon to be exhausted. If the elections should go very badly, (and I fear it,) our danger will be, perhaps, greater than ever, unless the fate of France should be so far decided, in the interim, as to take away from our perverseness the option of public ruin.

It is very important that Congress should not retrograde any thing, in its approaching short session; and yet that body has manifested, on most critical occasions, so much imbecility to act, and so much energy within itself to oppose acting, that no great advance in the measures of defence can be expected, if it should be necessary to make any. The Gallatins will argue publicly, or, more probably, will whisper to the members whose votes they influence, that even if France is deceitful, her hypocrisy may be a good reason for jealousy and vigilance, but is none for our hostility; that events show that the force we begin to prepare will not be wanted, and that our country, once at war, will be more exposed to its chances and reverses, and still more to the insidious and enslaving friendship of Great Britain, than to the apprehended deceit and ambition of the Directory. Noah Webster, I perceive, says we must have a fleet, and, *therefore*, we do *not* want an army. It is also an even chance that the men, who deprecated measures of self-defense, because France is omnipotent, and would resent any thing but the raising our hands suppliant and unarmed, will change their tune, and insist that Nelson has so reduced that omnipotence, that our resistance is not necessary to shield us from her domination. Thus the power of that restless state is at one time to be an excuse for our timidity, and at another for our supineness or instability of counsels. I hope our good men in Congress will take due pains to animate the public spirit, which is high enough to second the government, but cannot be expected to keep up its own tone long, and to impart one to Congress. Even Mr. Gerry, I hear, says that nothing is to be expected from negotiation; that harmony of opinion and energy in measures must be inculcated; that Congress has done well in the latter concern, and if it has failed, it is that enough was not done; that France has no liberty, the people no voice, and the government no integrity; that its objects are all temporary, &c. How he can reconcile such ideas, with such conduct as his mission led him to follow, I know not.

The liberty-pole in this town was cut down by some federal young men of Dedham, who were attacked by the seditious, and one of their number seized. To get his liberty, he very indiscreetly paid the mob guard, of five, twenty dollars. One of the persons concerned in raising the pole, an opulent farmer, has been arrested and bound over. The deluded are awed by this measure, but the effect is not so great as their intemperance and folly merit. The powers of the law must be used moderately, but with spirit and decision, otherwise great risk of disorders will be incurred. I hope you are, with your family, safe in Philadelphia from fever, and not disquieted by the dread of it. I am, dear sir, with great esteem, &c.

Your very humble servant.

TO THOMAS DWIGHT

DEDHAM, DECEMBER 7, 1798.—FRIDAY EVENING

DEAR FRIEND,

. . . I HAVE also made a new hen-house for my pullets to roost, and all these projects nearly addle me with joy.

Nelson's victory pleases other people, and is a good thing;— next to my stove and coal-house, a very good thing, as it reduces the pride and the power of the evil *one*, and the more evil *five*.[89] Our wise fools will cry peace, and hope a revolution in Paris. I do not wish it. These rogues, being known as such, are to be preferred to any new set yet to be found out.

Congress will soon manifest its disposition to persevere in well-doing to the end, or to flinch from it. I fear the latter, as their courage was, the last summer, when it was the most extolled, a mere *make believe*. Rely on it, our teaching is to cost something. We are to feel birch, before we learn political wisdom. Our *antis* will at last take arms against the laws. Their folly, their want of spirit, and the course of events, have checked their malice. The crisis, so often delayed, will come. I will not proceed any further with the dismal prophecies my fixed and habitual creed would dictate. Vigor in our government would delay their accomplishment, and perhaps finally prevent them from happening at all. But the parsimony that will starve talents out of office, or forbid their acceptance of it, will, I fear, greatly lessen the chances of such an administration, for the next ten or twenty years, as would impart strength to our federal system. My decided belief is, our federal men are very incorrect, and more than half democrats in their doctrines. They act right indeed, from hatred and dread of the democrats. Their theory is yet to be settled by severer experience than our kind fates have called us to suffer. Precept is thrown away on mankind. The stripes of adversity, while they tingle, print political instruction more than skin deep. We must smart for all the knowledge that will abide.

Dedham thrives in house and business, and our tradesmen are growing richer. I do not think we grow worse in sin and

---

[89] *The French Directory.* [S. AMES]

jacobinism. Thacher's parish is confessedly the worst. The south (Chickering's) is decidedly federal; and the old parish, were I live, is divided—the old are half Demos, the young chiefly Feds. The tone of Hampshire and Berkshire is excellent. . . . . . .

With my best regards to Mrs. D., and at Col. Worthington's,

I am truly yours.

TO CHRISTOPHER GORE

DECEMBER 18, 1798

MY DEAR FRIEND,

YOUR LETTERS would be valuable if they were not scarce, as they are; and mine would be cheap if I did not labor so much to make them plenty. The scene you survey, and your place near the point or fulcrum of the British power, make me greedy for the news you send, or the comments that explain it. My seat in my chimney-corner compels me to generalize my ideas, and to bore you with essays, instead of amusing you with intelligence. All that I can write about is already pretty familiar to you. I know little of European events, and the characters of their drama. Expect, therefore, to be weary of the task assigned you, of satisfying my curiosity, and of the epistolary good works, on which I found my claim to your compliance.

The struggle with our Jabobins is like the good Christian's with the evil one. It is no amusement to the bystander, and is barren of events for description. Besides, one cannot tell how much others have gone into detail in their letters to you, nor what parts of our drama excite your curiosity, and to write every thing is impossible.

These are my apologies for being dull. When the despatches from our envoys were published here, the Jacobins were confounded, and the trimmers dropt off from the party, like windfalls from an apple-tree in September, the worst of the fruit—vapid in cider and soon vinegar. The wretches looked round, like Milton's devils when first recovering from the stunning force of their fall from Heaven, to see what new ground they could take. The alien and sedition bills, and the land tax, were chosen as affording topics of discontent, and, of course, a renewal of the popularity of the party. The meditated vengeance and the wrongs of France done by our treaty, were less spouted on. And the implacable foes of the Constitution—foes before it was made, while it was making, and since,—became full of tender fears lest it should be violated by the alien and sedition laws. You know that federalists are forever hazarding the cause by needless and rash concessions. John Marshall, with all his honors in blossom and bearing fruit, answers some newspaper queries unfavorably to these laws. George Cabot says that Otis, our representative, condemns him *ore rotundo*, yet, inconsistently enough, sedulously declares his dislike of those laws. G. C. vindicates J. M., and stoutly asserts his soundness of federalism. I deny it. No correct man,—no incorrect man even,—whose affections and feelings are wedded to the government, would give his name to the base opposers of law, as a means for its annoyance. This he has done. Excuses may palliate,—future zeal in the cause may partially atone,— but his character is done for. *Hæret lateri lethalis* Virginia newspaper. Like a man who in battle receives an ounce ball in his body—it may heal, it lies too deep to be extracted; but, on every change of weather, it will be apt to fester and twinge. There let it lie. False federalists, or such as act wrong from false fears, should be dealt hardly by, if I were Jupiter Tonans.[90] The theory of the Feds is worse than that of the *antis*, in one respect. They help the government at a pinch, and then shout victory for two seconds,—after which, they coax and try to gain the *antis*, by yielding the very principles in dispute. The moderates are the meanest of cowards, the falsest of hypocrites. The other side has none of them, though it abounds in every other kind of baseness. Their Guy Fauxes are no triflers. They have energy enough to vindicate the French, and, if opportunity favored, to imitate them. They stick to the cause, and never yield any thing that can be contested, nor even then, without a more than equivalent concession. They beat us in industry, audacity, and perseverance; and will at last meet us in the field, where they will be beaten.

There is no describing the impulse they have given their party to decry these acts. They have sent runners everywhere to blow the trumpet of sedition. One David Brown, a vagabond ragged fellow, has lurked about in Dedham, telling everybody the sins and enormities of the government. He had been, he said, in all the offices in all the states, and knew my speculating connection with you, and how I made my immense wealth. I was not in this part of the country, otherwise I should have noticed his lies,—not to preserve my reputation, but to disarm his wickedness. Before I returned from my trip to the westward, he had fled, and a warrant to apprehend him for sedition was not served. He had, however, poisoned Mr. Thacher's parish, and got them ready to set up a liberty-pole, which was soon after actually done. This insult on the law, was the cause of sending out the marshal with his warrant; but the Feds of Mr. Chickering's parish had previously cut down the pole. One of the Fed party was, however,

---

[90] *This spleen at John Marshall was by no means the writer's deliberate or permanent sentiment.* [S. AMES]

seized by the mobbers, and twenty dollars extorted from him before he got free. There is at least the appearance of tardiness and apathy, on the part of government, in avenging this insult on law. But the judge and attorney think all is done right. The government must display its power *in terrorem*, or, if that be neglected or delayed, in earnest. So much irritable folly and credulity, managed by so much villainy, will explode at last; and the issue will be tried, like the ancient suits, by wager of battle.

I think the clamor against the alien law, a proof that the party has chosen to make one, and that it makes no odds on what the choice falls, an equal clamor being excitable on one as much as on another subject. The *salus Reipub.* so plainly requires the power of expelling or refusing admission to aliens, and the rebel Irish, and negroes of the West Indies so much augment the danger, that reason, one would think, was disregarded by the Jacobins, too much even to be perverted. Kentucky is all alien; and we learn that the Governor Gerard has made a most intemperate address to the legislature of that state, little short of a manifesto. This is said to be echoed by the legislature. In that case, the issue must be tendered and tried. The gazettes will, no doubt, explain the fact to you more fully than I can at present.

I hear that one of our *trio* says, that he could not, with *any safety*, refuse compliance with the demand to disclose the X, Y, Z of the Paris business. Can any words express the *merit* of the man, who can now plead his fears as his apology? Were I intrusted by a great nation, and called to act on a great stage, I should pray God to give me courage to defy a thousand deaths in such a case,—or, if that should fail me, that I might have the discretion to let others find out some better excuse for my conduct than that I was *afraid*. Will not Europeans note such facts, and, if they feel a spirit of candor, say for us, that we are yet new in our independence, and that the notions of shame and honor, though not factitious in their origin, are so in their application? Our public men, they will say, will learn when they ought to lose life sooner than honor.

My wife joins with me in offering our united regards to you and Mrs. G.

Yours.

1 7 9 9

TO CHRISTOPHER GORE

JANUARY 11, 1799

DEAR FRIEND,

I PASSED two or three hours of the last evening with Paine, at your house in town, and while he was making himself up as a beau to dance, we chatted about your farm.

. . . Can you bear with me? Do I *bore* you with the subject of husbandry? or is it still enough your hobby to revive your old sensibilities? If you still like the theme, it will be wholesome to give you these two pages, as the smell of the clods of fresh earth is said to abate the virulence of the sea scurvy. If you are crammed with politics as we are, any change, even to less delicate fare, will be a feast.

By looking at Congress you will see that the French faction there is no better than formerly. Gallatin and Nicholas vindicate Logan's mission[91] very boldly. The country, where such abominations as they utter can be even tolerated, is to be tried and purified in the furnace of affliction. Are Englishmen, even the malcontents, in the habit of prating as perversely as our Demos?

Virginia, excited by crazy Taylor, is fulminating its manifesto against the federal government, as we hear. But the papers as yet only state that the *antis* prevailed on the decision of Taylor's motion. The precise nature of their proceedings is not fully known. The more absurd and violent the better. The less will it be in the power of government to forbear proper measures, or to adopt them by halves, and the more will the spirit of the Virginia Feds rise; for Feds there are even in Virginia.

General Heath's memoirs are said to be a strange farrago of egotism and pompous inanity. The wits are hacking the author and his book. He is not a firm subject enough for their dissecting knives.

The General Court is convened, and are not in the humor of falling in with the rage of Virginia. The insult to the American flag, by impressing seamen from the sloop of war *Baltimore*, rouses all the tongue-valor of Congress. It is indeed too outrageous for that government to avow; and yet the liableness of Britons to serve their king and country will not be abandoned.

I am in better health than I was a year ago, and hope, by great care and a good regimen, to be fit to stay at home and

---

[91] *Dr. Logan, of Philadelphia, visited France in August, 1798, as a sort of volunteer ambassador. He was provided with letters of introduction from Jefferson, and was received with great eclat, after the departure of the commissioners, the more authentic representatives of our government. He was very coldly received by the Administration, on his return, and his mission gave very great offence to the federal party. Congress, soon after, passed an act, prohibiting, under severe penalties, this sort of interference with the foreign diplomacy of the government.* [S. AMES.] [*The act bears the title* "The Logan Act." Ed.]

do nothing before your return. Slight deviations from my usual carefulness of diet, &c., still derange my health.

Health and fraternity.[92]

Yours.

TO THOMAS DWIGHT

BOSTON, FEBRUARY 27, 1799

DEAR SIR,

·   ·   ·   ·   ·   ·   ·   ·   ·

THE new embassy to France, however qualified and guarded by the President, disgusts most men here.[93] Peace with France they think an evil, and holding out the hope of it another,

---

[92] *A few extracts from a letter of Mr. Gore to Mr. Ames, dated London, 7th September, 1798, are subjoined.*

MY DEAR FRIEND,
Logan arrived at Hamburg, had passports, it is said, from Jefferson and McKean, was extremely desirous of reaching Paris before Gerry's departure, in which, however, he did not succeed. The French newspapers say, he is an American envoy. A paper, Le Surveillant, of the 13th Fructidor, (for your information, who, I suppose, are not conversant in the French calendar, that is 30th August,) has the following paragraph, "Le nouvel envoyé Americain, venu a Paris au nom du parti patriote des Etats Unis, est le docteur Logan. C'est lui qui a obtenu la levée de l'embargo en faveur de la plupart des bâtimens de sa nation." You will have seen that the United Irishmen have had an accredited minister at Paris, a long time. The raising of the embargo from the vessels is false, in my belief. There is not the smallest paragraph in any of the papers to support the idea, that they have or intend to release the vessels or their cargoes. [S. AMES]

[93] *While the quarrel with France was at its height, the President, without consulting or even notifying his Cabinet, astonished all parties*

as it tends to chill the public fervor. *Inter nos*, I like it little on its outside appearance, yet I believe the President will exact more terms to secure respect, and if a negotiation should be begun, will urge indemnity further than French arrogance and poverty can or will go. What good he sees in it, I know not. I rely on his good judgment as much as I ought, and his patriotism is undoubted. The step, however, ought to have been known, if not approved, by the chief officers and supporters of government in Congress, which fame whispers it was not. The *antis* raise their fallen crests upon the news, and promise the renewal of our first love.

TO TIMOTHY PICKERING

DEDHAM, MARCH 12, 1799

DEAR SIR,

I COULD make long excuses for my long neglect of writing to you. You have been so very obliging, I will not stand mute on the occasion, though I will not defend myself at full length. The courts have kept me very busy. I have also thought my silence a merit, as I do not think I have a right to impose on you the burden of answering. I am really very thankful for the seeds, and I will give part to some friends, who will attend to their culture, and who keep a gardener. Seeds from a rank democratic soil would not thrive in my garden, but the south of France is, I suppose, far from

---

by nominating a new Minister to that country. This unexpected coup d'etat *was a blow from which the federal party did not recover. It produced a schism among the friends of the administration which could not be healed.* [S. AMES]

democratic. Besides, the Aurora would maintain, that they are the seeds of aristocracy which *you* delight to spread.

Had the President acted only half as wonderfully, the defense of his conduct would have been harder to the few who vindicate the nomination of Mr. Murray. The reasons, though weak, might have been accessible, and their weight determined by the scales. But the thing was so totally contrary to his conduct, his speeches, and the expectations of all men, that reasons, though sought for, could not be found, and must therefore be imagined; and when that failed, they must be referred further on to mysteries of state locked up in his cabinet. That even that plea, so paramount to all others, fails in this instance, because negotiation can be vindicated only as the mean to an end—peace with France; the end being a bad one, all means are unwise and indefensible. I could say much on the subject, though nothing that you have not anticipated. Two remarks occur, and there is consolation in both—that there is some energy in our counsels, for they skilfully parried the measure, and prevented all the bad effects of it, except its disgrace; and secondly, that our nation has some energy, as all men condemn the thing in its appearance; and some put their wits to the task, to fancy that information is possessed by the President, to call for the measure.

Public opinion is the real sovereign of our country, and not a very capricious one neither. France is neither loved nor trusted. War is not desired for its own sake, as it should not be; but peace, as France would give it, is not desired, as it should not be. We begin to feel a little patriotism, and the capture of the *Insurgente* cherishes it. But if the next Congress should be democratic, and the intrigues for the chair of state should proceed with as much heat as internal faction and foreign influence can engender, we shall see trouble. You who watch for us, have a hard task, and if its weight and irksomeness are to be aggravated, by your being ostensibly excluded from participating in advising measures, your magnanimity and sense of duty must be your present reward. Your country will add to it, and so will posterity. I am, dear sir,

Yours, truly.

[P.S.] I hope the President will not doubt that the public is averse to all delusive negotiations. In his answer to the Dedham address, he says—echoing the words of it—"For delaying counsels, the Constitution has not made me responsible; but, while I hold my present place, there shall be no more delusive negotiations." Evidently, our public connects shame with feeble and receding measures. Fortunately our fate has not been always, if ever, at the disposal of our folly. England fights our battles with her own, and the momentum of European politics is imparted to ours, and carries us on, even when we stop, or would go backward.

What I write, you will, of course, consider as strictly confidential. No one respects more sincerely the talents and virtues of our chief, but few know better than I do, the singularities that too frequently discredit his prudence.

TO JOHN WORTHINGTON

DEDHAM, MARCH 30, 1799

DEAR SIR,

I FOUND lately at the bank deposited to my credit the seven hundred dollars you sent (I think) by the mail, out of which I shall take the sum of $198 and hold the remainder subject yr order. $198 is the Balance due me when Col. Dwight left me, and which it did not incommode me in the smallest degree to advance.

By the last mail I have inclosed from Col. Dwight the order on Mr. Ste. Higginson $741.69 which I will call for as soon as I can go to town, and hold it when received as the former sum to be disposed of as you may direct. Mr. Gray's ship, Capt. Ward, will soon sail or is gone already to sea— so that this mode of investment of the property will be out of the question. I have placed $2500 more in his hand for this voyage which I had not funds of my own to command, but have run the venture to borrow. I shall insure it against every risk, and am advised by my best friends to borrow and place it as before mentioned. As it is my only debt and I have enough to face it in case of the worst. I have not thought it prudent to lose the chance altho' I felt some reluctance to avail myself of it by a loan. I am glad you adventure again, but I hope you will not allow yourself to be disquieted by it, as you have no occasion to be. The danger of French cruisers is less than ever and the profit will be good if the vessel arrives safely.

Mrs. Ames is below stairs and doing well. Her nurse is very careful and joins with me in urging every precaution against taking cold that her situation in a season so inclement requires. The little Hannah grows as fat as a pig and is as quiet as one that is well fed.

My mother has been ill and is yet confined to her chamber. A fall on the hearth hurt her hip and the rheumatism seated itself there and has caused her uncommon pain and some danger of a sore ————. We hope she is recovering.

I wrote lately by Mr. Ashman that I thought of visiting Springfield in April. Since then, I hear that Sophy and Master John propose a visit to Dedham. I shall therefore probably dismiss the thought of it to some future and I hope not very distant day. I am attracted to Springfield by strong feelings as well as duties and shall not of choice very long delay my visit.

Dedham and the adjoining towns is not decreasing in *patriotic* zeal, as the mistaken folks term it. The Boston market the Chronicle and some Demogogues who have twice as much ambition as sens[e or] principle will not let our people get ———— Heath I fear will be supported by great ———— with my very best regard to Mrs. Worthington.

Dear Sir

Yours truly

FISHER AMES

TO RUFUS KING

BOSTON, JUNE 12TH, 1799

MY DEAR SIR:

I WOULD BE or seem to be, *too civil by half*, if I were to tell you that it is the fashion to think we are strong in England; which however was the phrase of Genl. Washington. Now if any thing goes wrong in regard to the *amiable dispositions* which the Chronicle accused me of crediting G. B. for, you are to expect to be holden to answer. If the Emperor fights faint, if the K. of Prussia will not fight at all, or if Buonaparte fights too long or too hardly in Egypt we must look to some one in office to lay the blame upon. For your sake, I wish that Trowbridge may glean some laurels in Nelson's field &c, &c, &c. We shall never turn our eyes on ourselves and see how much we expect from others, how little we do for ourselves. Gore and our friends in London are mortified and sadly disappointed in the events of our politics. I admit you have reason to be so. The mission of new envoys was strange indeed, and though I am less surprised, I am no better pleased than I was at first. Yet, after all, I am not clear that our ground could have been by other, and I admit more sound measures, essentially better than it is. France is to be fought with till she is fought down, till her power is moderate, and her ambition, which never will be moderate, will then be harmless. But as fighting for some years, building great ships and spending millions is not to our Dutch taste, and the most resentful of the enemies of France among us dare not say half as much as I do, the Public Spirit is yet a mere braggart, and spends itself in addresses. I think we ought to be and ought long ago to have been in open war. Even then a treaty offered by France, rich in promise, soothing to our pride, and an excuse for our parsimony that grudges the charges of self defence, would nearly as much paralise our energies as it wd. at present, if La Fayette should come with one. It is however due to our citizens to say they have outrun the govt. with their purses and their zeal which was more precious. In March and April I saw clouds and thick darkness in our horizon. The antis were buzzing with their work of sedition and electioneering and seemed sure of getting the state govts. into their hands to play them like batteries on the U. S. govt. They have been successfully counteracted, old Masstts. stands firm—a few more antis say 5 or 10 at most in the house, the rest firmer and warmer on that very acct. In N. York all is going right as we hear. Burr is out of credit, tho' his water or bank scrip has turned reputation into the ready. Virginia sends say ten federalists (so called) and N. Carolina another set. Congress will be impressible, if public opinion should point to measures of energy. But I scarcely know what in our awkward posture ought to be proposed. To be active in planning and urging such measures is not to be expected in any govt. except from the high responsible officers, who unfortunately are excluded from our

Congress. Events must be waited for, and if you take care that the Arch Duke is not beaten, we shall I think jog on as well as we have done till Jeff. becomes again the candidate for the chair. Then *clamorque virorum clangorque tubarum;* I mean in the newspapers.

The merchants say our trade flourishes, is well protected, little loss by captures: our navy is of course very popular and prodigiously so among the farmers. The land and house tax progresses and will yield something; it may be made a great resource.

Mr. Warren will inform you of the death and pompous funeral of Gov. Summer. Lt. Governor Gill, whom you know, proceeds to the chair for the year.

Yrs. truly

FISHER AMES

TO CHRISTOPHER GORE

DEDHAM, OCTOBER 9, 1799

MY DEAR FRIEND,

I HAVE your favor, of the 4th August. In a former letter you invite me to London to recover my health. I should like the trip very much, especially if I had no other object than amusement to command a six or eight months' expatriation. Business, the *res angustæ domi,* and the ties that hold me fast with my family, forbid the idea. My health might profit by it, but does not exact such a step. The proposition deserves two reflections: that I have a friend with the heart to make it; and a heart of my own to estimate its value rightly.

Thank God, I am better. Clients came in at the Dedham

August Supreme Court, and overpowered me with application to stakes and stones, and plots of land in ejectment. My mind was not excited with zeal, but my spirits were exhausted by continued attention. The second day of the Court, after a night of disturbed sleep, I fainted at 5, A.M., and was kept from fainting, for three hours, only by water dashed into my face, and volatiles; during all which time I was swimming off into insensibility. That day clients came into my chamber per force; and the next, I went into Court to enjoy the soothing civilities of Judge *Ursa Major* R. T. Paine.[94] I did not die from weariness or vexation. The next week I went to Boston, and Paine's caresses were continued *per curiam.* The robbery of the Nantucket Bank, charged on the prime men of the Island, employed me five days, and kept me afterwards very low for six more with a cold procured in a court-house, crowded with unusual numbers. I was also hoarse, by four hours' bawling to a jury.

At Dedham Common Pleas, last Tuesday of September, the work was small, and the law laborers many. A writ of right for a pigsty, in which I am for the defendant, continued to April. Old Doctor S. is dead intestate; the heirs have contested the administration, and at length your friend, by consent of all, is the administrator. Thus I am in business, you see, and must demand payment for boluses and pills to the last generation, as well as this. In spite of all these cares, and some relapses, I progress in health, and am now unusually well. It is my time to fatten. . . .

Excuse my long-winded egotism. What can I fill these long pages with else? I observe every word you write; but politics are forbidden, since our vessels are liable to be prizes. . . . . . .

---

[94] *Judge Paine was somewhat deaf, and not at all distinguished for suavity of manners. After an uncomfortable scene in his Court, Mr. Ames said that "no man could get on there, unless he came with a club in one hand and a speaking-trumpet in the other."* [S. AMES]

My wife forbids my writing further than to offer her very best regards to you and Mrs. G., with those of

Yours, &c.

TO TIMOTHY PICKERING

DEDHAM, OCTOBER 19, 1799

DEAR SIR,

I WROTE to you, months ago, with great freedom and little discretion, on the subject of the new mission of envoys. I then endeavored to account for this astonishing measure, on the ground of personal weakness, as I found no reason for it in public principles. If my imprudence has restrained you from making any answer, I will thank you to burn my letter, as it is not proper to be trusted to the chances of falling into other hands. But, while I acknowledge my indiscretion, I will repeat it. I cannot yet compose myself, when I think of the consequences of this error, or notice its existing evil. Federal men already begin to divide upon it. Already the Jacobins raise their disgraced heads from the mire of contempt. Attachment to the person of the President, or to the singleness of the executive power, is the plea of two different sets of men, once called federal, for palliating (none justify) this miraculous caprice. I hear that the envoys are not to go at present. But the measure is only suspended, not abandoned; and until it is, the schism among the friends of government cannot be healed. The measure has not even the merit of imposture;—not even plausible vindications of it are offered;—not even the shadow of any good is exhibited. The hatred of Great Britain is to be courted, and excited to do as much mischief and to embroil our affairs, as much as love of France once did: and I own I fear that, while all good men *una voce* condemn the business, the multitude are to be addressed for favor, in a style that will obtain it for a time. France is our foe, and so is Britain. We must depend on ourselves. This is true in a degree, and the inference would be right, if it were not made to sustain a policy that threatens to bring on a war with England, and to revive the Jacobin faction in our bosom. The state of things is very gloomy and embarrassing; and I fear that the good men at helm will feel intolerable disgust, and perhaps meet with it, to induce them to quit their principles or their places. But I hope the opportunity to do good will be too much valued, to be lost or neglected by them. Two resources occur to my impaired hopes: one, in the real virtue and discernment of the President; the other, in the clear views our public has taken of the policy and character of the French. How the influence on the former can be impressed, so as to soothe, without shocking, his feelings, I know not. I fear it is too difficult and too late. The latter is not to be neglected. Never was there a time when our public ought to be made to see the truth more clearly. Those who seek office, and who court power, will flinch at the meeting of Congress, and the Jacobins will join them. The public is right, and ought to make its good sense and honest zeal intelligible, so that the members, who incline to act right, shall feel incited and supported.

I will disclose to you, that Governor Gill, in his proclamation, had a clause to thank God for this mission of envoys. This was got out, and our Thanksgiving may be as free as usual from hypocrisy and nonsense. . . . . .

The temporizing, weak federal members of Congress will be tampered with, and I do not see how any thing, but a very strong impression of public sentiment, can prevent a division of the federal party. The despised and the detested already are Jacobins. Any new assortment of our citizens must, of necessity, give that bad cause better men. Perseverance in the first error may embroil the peace of the nation with England, and I greatly fear it will; and if it should, evils within and without will be numberless. But the event will be no less fatal to the peace and reputation of the author of the measure. This will be poor consolation to me, for I wish him honor and permanence in office, as much as any one.

I again request that your discretion to burn this, will supply my want of it. I am, dear sir, with great esteem,

Yours, truly

[P.S.] I perceive that the Jacobins, and the half federalists, are ripe for attacking the permanent force, as expensive, and unnecessary, and dangerous to liberty. By disbanding the troops, Congress would create many malcontents and disarm authority.

TO THOMAS DWIGHT

DEDHAM, OCTOBER 20, 1799

MY DEAR FRIEND,

FROM PIGS to politics:[95] How do you like the Thanksgiving proclamation? I did not write it. It was, when I first saw it,

---

[95] *In the beginning of this letter, he had given some information about his farm.* [S. AMES]

a Janus, looking sweet at the mission of envoys, and affectedly sour at the French, whom it denominated our foes. This is confidential.

Alas, that mission, though suspended, blasts the character and the hopes of our country. Either it will bring on a war with England, or humiliation to avoid it. It has not even the gloss of an imposture, not even a show of advantage, to cheat with. . . . . There is every thing to excite your wonder, your vexation, and your fears. Take these scraps and place them in order, to make sentences to your liking. The Jacobins will rise in consequence of this blunder. Trouble with them and with Britain will follow. McKean will be Governor of Pennsylvania. It is all the better. Every good man will feel shocked and roused to action, by so scandalous an event. Had Ross been chosen, they would have gone to sleep, expecting him to keep all the wild Irish who vote for McKean in good order. The Feds will have a proper stimulus for the next three years. The things that have happened against our wishes, for the last seven years, have, ultimately, more promoted them than the events called, at the time, prosperous. *Ne cede malis, sed contra audentior ito.*

The defeats of the French will do good on both sides the Atlantic. Nothing less than severe, and, I maintain, nothing less than bloody, experience will cure our people of some of their prejudices, and impress some truths that concern our peace, so that we can get along. We are democrats; we pretend to be republicans. Experience will punish and teach. I am, dear sir,

Your affectionate friend.

TO TIMOTHY PICKERING

DEDHAM, NOVEMBER 5, 1799

MY DEAR SIR,

YOUR apology for the delay of an answer to a former letter of mine, was not necessary, nor expected by me. It is more than I think my correspondence entitled to. You have much to communicate, both of facts and remarks, and I have little more than complaints and forebodings to give in return.

The mission to France has not been vindicated by even one reason offered to the public. The unfriendliness of Great Britain affords none, as it will aggravate *that*, and provide no resource against it. On the contrary, internal union will be less, and foreign help worse than nothing. It is a measure to *make* dangers, and to nullify resources; to make the navy without object; the army an object of popular terror,—which, for Hamilton's sake, will be artfully prosecuted. Government will be weakened by the friends it loses, and betrayed by those it will gain. It will lose, and it rejects, the friendship of the sense, and worth, and property of the United States, and get in exchange the prejudice, vice, and bankruptcy of the nation: a faction who honor government by their hostility, as that shows it is no patron of their views, not the dupe of their prejudices, not the instrument of their passions. The Jacobins, too, serve the good cause by the violence of their attack, which makes good men enough afraid of their success, to rouse their own energies, and to oppose passion to passion. In this way, as our government is ever in danger of falling by party, it is fated to be saved and to live, if it shall live, by party. Its bane must be its diet. But this measure threatens to stop its breath suddenly. Our system never could stand alone, and scarcely with holding up; and if the men who hold the property and respect the principles that will protect it, are compelled to even a passive silence, and a desponding neutrality, (and at this moment it requires some virtue to stop there,) the Jacobins will break in, and get possession of the public authority, and, in six months, make the man who holds it their captive, their tool, their trophy. He will not long be permitted to figure even in that under character. The first seat in their synagogue is full, and they will not displace the occupant for another, whose vanity makes him intractable, even with the associates of his own cause, and his own principles; and as he *has* principles, he will, from them and his weakness both, soon become doubly intractable to his new allies. This, they well know; and their friendship, which he seeks for himself, will prove like that of France, which he no less blindly seeks for his country, a snare; not peace, but a sword. They will not prop up his fame, nor his power; and, finally, he will see his mistake, and wish himself back again. Perhaps his return may be possible; and things may demand great sacrifices of feeling and interest to occasions. Therefore, I incline *at present* to think he must be spared, and not driven quite over to the foe. While measures are under discussion, it is proper to paint the probable evils strongly. After they are adopted, it is right to hope for success, that such a hope may inspire wisdom and spirit in the choice of the means of precaution and safety.

I rely on Mr. E.[96] as much as any one can, to watch the foe, and to parry the stroke of her dagger. But the measure is so deadly in its nature, I do not see how even he can do much to preserve us; a treaty ready made, in which nothing is refused, would be hard to evade. Pledges of security for its performance are not to be asked, if exorbitant, and, if moderate, possibly they would not be denied. *I* would require

---

[96] *Mr. Ellsworth, one of the envoys.* [S. AMES]

the delivery of ships, or islands, or money, as pledges, so that, in case of a breach of faith, we should start anew with a part of our enemy's force. That, however, I know, is chimerical. The spirit that sends envoys, asks no indemnities.

France is proud, and may find it harder to stoop in her adversity than ever. It may be, too, that the care her rulers may be taking (at the time of negotiating) of their lives and plunder, may spoil the game of their policy. I notice that, in the charges against the ex-Directors, the vile usage of the United States is not an article, though less wrongs done the Cisalpines and Dutch are inserted and exaggerated. This denotes a perseverance in the old system, in regard to us. I do not see how the late measure can be made popular, without promoting that French system. The friendship of that nation must be made to appear worth something in its effects, and worthy of some trust. The fear of British hostility must be magnified in proportion, and it will be easy to make that chimera real. Popular feelings will coöperate with executive acts, and will be resistless *at the beginning*.

No passion should be attacked in its strength; in its ebb, or when some new one runs counter, it may be overcome. Thus I conclude that public discussion would not be discreet at present, farther than to suggest that the mission has its dangers, though it may have wise reasons, yet to be disclosed, for its vindication. The splitting of the friends of government, and the revival of a French faction, are those dangers; and writers may urge, without much alarm to the friends of the President, the mischiefs to be apprehended from both. When the business is more advanced, something lucky may turn up to save us for the hundredth time.

The French may expose some vile trick, that will again exasperate our nation. The treaty may be such, as to afford good grounds of objection. The sense and virtue, and the fears and feelings of the country, may be again brought to act together. In a word, the present moment seems to me to call for this kind of conduct, to keep the public mind excitable, as before mentioned, to a sense of the two dangers; but not to excite it against the late measure, nor its author, till events afford the means and the excuse. Our people really distrust France, but they hate Great Britain; and yet they are vexed that their government does not return us love for hatred, and show to us the partiality our government, at least, still shows to France, or seems to show.

On the whole, new aspects of affairs present themselves; new parties will arise, and new evils with them. Our citizens are rather democrats than republicans; and nothing short of experience, that cuts the flesh, and dresses the wounds with caustics, will cure the errors of public opinion. The biggest fools we have are our sensible fools, whose theories are more pestilent than popular prejudices. They are more stubborn, are more tinctured with fanaticism, and with the rage of making proselytes. It would greatly improve such theories to dash them strongly with stupidity. Of this sort I reckon the dreams of all the philosophers who think the people angels, rulers devils; information will keep all right, quell riots and rebellions, and save the expense of armies; the people always mean right, and if the government do not oppress, the citizens will not resist; that man is a perfectible animal, and all governments are obstacles to his apotheosis. This nonsense is inhaled with every breath. It gives a bias to the opinions of those who are no philosophers, or who, at least, do not imagine they are such. Errors so deep, so hostile to order, so far out of the reach of all cures, except the killing one of experience, are to be mitigated and palliated by truth, perhaps delayed from exploding for some years. But they will have vent, and then all will shake to the Alleghany ridge.

I have written thus far as fast as I could make my pen go—too fast, perhaps, for my discretion to follow. I confide the letter to your friendship and prudence, not unwilling, however, that Mr. Wolcott should see it, under the like securities. I am, dear sir,

Yours, with perfect regard and esteem.

P.S. While I think it unwise to provoke a discussion of the mission at present, I fear we shall not be allowed to choose our time for it, or to adopt any plan that we may believe suitable to the sad state of affairs. A war with Great Britain will be, somehow or other, begun, and it will then be said, the hostility of that government justifies the step, and glorifies the foresight of the President. The war might have been avoided. If Great Britain will search our men of war, it is plain she means to understand the temper of our cabinet unfavorably, and to strike the first blow. Our commercial capital will melt away, and perhaps Jefferson and other patriots may see with joy the republican sky cleared of the corrupt vapors and clouds that the northern *funded* and other capital throws up. It will also make the northern states so much the lighter in the scale. Philosophers can enjoy the future good of great evils, and call those changes cheap, that beggar the aristocratic merchants and stockholders, but cannot cost the patriots any thing. British influence Baldwin will see decline, as our wealth takes wing and flies away.

2d P.S. The order of the British king to detain and search our ships of war, as well as the vessels under their convoy, denotes a resolution to go to war with us. If it be so in fact, perhaps, all we have to do is to exert our best force and courage in the war. But, if any alternative be yet left to us, peace with that power is to be sought most earnestly, as all our floating capital would soon fall a sacrifice, and the anti-funding party might rejoice that their northern antagonists were so much the weaker. To hold up a war with Great Britain as a triumph of the Jacobins, as the ruin of commerce, as the source of new evils, new taxes, endless confusion, &c., would be right, in case it is not too late. I have felt restrained, by the sense of propriety, from plainly stating to you the usefulness of some prudent course of conduct being considered by you and Mr. Wolcott, and intimated to some discreet person here. The newspapers are venal, servile, base, and stupid. But they would, for the last reason, publish a good deal very freely, because they would not understand it. I am very deeply distressed and anxious about the state of our affairs. No one would reject desponding and trimming counsels, however, with more disdain than I. This letter being strictly confidential, and the urgency of the occasion being great, I will not scruple to signify my hope that Mr. Cabot, or I, should have such sentiments furnished to us, as the public ought to comprehend. Any very elaborate or detailed argument, or series of essays, would do less good than light paragraphs and incidental remarks. In that way something, I hope, may yet be done to keep our friends and regain our deserters. I will only add my entreaties that you will excuse my loose method of writing; and be assured that I am greatly honored and obliged by your expressions of friendship and regard.

TO CHRISTOPHER GORE

NOVEMBER 10TH, 1799–SUNDAY

DEAR FRIEND,

I WISH, by the safe hands of Mr. Paine, to write all that you would wish to read. My last was so stuffed with croakings about the envoys, that I have left it to Paine, after all, to tell you *viva voce* all that I could write.

Since the Despatches were published, the trimmers among the Jacobins have pretended to be converted. The town of Boston has been so decidedly anti-French, that the Sullivans, and the Winthrops, and the Master Vinals, the leaders of fifties and hundreds, joined the *vox populi,* as it was natural they should; but the captains of thousands, the Honesti, Jarvis, and old S. Adams, remain unchanged.

If any point is really conceded by that party, it is that of a navy, which they admit to be wise and right, perhaps with the sole view of insisting the more on the uselessness and danger of armies, which, besides, can go after rebels by *land,* which ships cannot. In the heart of even the proselytes the same rancor still lurks. The mission is the darling measure of them all. The Jacobins in the vicinity of Boston are as openly bitter as ever, though rather less clamorous, and, on the whole, the *rabies canina* of jacobinism has gradually spread, of late years, from the cities, where it was confined to docks and mob, to the country. I think it is still spreading silently, and why should it not? All that is base is of course Jacobin, and all that is prejudice, and jealousy, and rancor, in good hearts, (and even they have a taint of every evil propensity,) is susceptible of their impressions. Envy, fear, and cupidity, will renew the generations of factious men to the world's end. I smile at the shallow hopes expressed in conversation, of talking or writing folly and prejudice down, and of dosing the citizens with *information,* till they cannot take the contagion of faction. As well might we hope, by keeping people on a milk diet, to starve out the contagion of the smallpox.

Our good men feel better towards the government than they talk or reason. They really believe seven eighths of the democratic lying theories invented and propagated to subvert all government. They really think paper constitutions adamantine walls about liberty. Their creed, in short, would damn the government as surely as the passions of the Jacobins.

Few men, however, act up to their creed, be it what it may. Our good men, therefore, would act, on occasion, with some spirit and constancy, in support of the good cause, and I cannot but hope that events will, in future, favor our tranquility, or at least our political liberty and existence, as in times past. We shall profit, though little and slowly, by experience, and when things seem desperate, and a crisis inevitable, we have uniformly profited the most. I own I see not how this blind hope can be realized, but, like S. B., I will try to think that good will come out of evil.

Wolcott and Pickering are certainly most excellent ministers, and if they should not be turned out, or get disgusted and refuse to stay in office, they will moderate evils; they will draw to themselves a share of the confidence of the country. These are reasons for my wishing them to remain—perhaps weak reasons; for, after all, I am half of the mind, that bad measures are the longer persevered in for not being clearly understood by the citizens, and this leads me to doubt whether Ellsworth ought to have been urged to go. He goes reluctantly. Monroe and Burr would have done better, and left the case as plain and intelligible as we could wish to make it. The Envoys do not, we are told, even know to what port they are destined. Their instructions, no doubt, are, to adjust differences, to demand reperation for captures, and to make a treaty to regulate our commercial intercourse. The last part seems to me like putting up good furniture in a house that is already on fire; if it should burn, we lose our furniture; if it should be put out, the engines will spoil and soak it. As to reparation, I should hope pledges will be asked to secure the performance. Why not tell Monsieur Fiveheads,[97] Give us ships, give us an island in pawn; we trust your rogueships no further than we can see you, and that is too far, unless you are bound hand and foot. But why prattle

---

[97] *The French Directory.* [S. AMES]

about the pledges of a treaty with France? It is like Doctor Faustus's league with the devil—our soul for his services.

The soberest result of my reflections is this—that our people understand the French, but do not understand the English. They do not comprehend the interests or policy of their government any better than its structure or materials. We expect their love and friendship, yet think it a crime to have any for them. We also magnify our own importance, at the very moment we are content to forfeit all pretension to it. For we tamely take kicks and snubs from France, and fancy Great Britain full of terror, lest our cutters should grow up into a rival navy. I do not trust to that, far off as jealousy can look for a rival. With a thousand ships, she is not afraid of us. The monopoly spirit and the rage against France are more obvious and powerful springs of action. Why should we expect that nations will see, or prefer their interests to their passions, when very wise individuals every day make a sacrifice of the former to the latter? We are like the English; the comparison is to be made between us and them, and in *that*, national pride takes an interest and feels a wound. Our envy, hatred, and revenge, naturally point against England, therefore, because we resemble them, and not against France, whom we do not resemble. Like two rival beauties, we are in danger of hating each other, because both are handsome. Which is handsomest, is a question that shoots through every marrow bone, like the pains of the rheumatism. While France had so many partisans, no Frenchman here had many friends. England, on the contrary, was hated, yet every Englishman was courted, trusted, and preferred. From our love and hatred of those two nations, we took care, as often as we had opportunity, to make exception of every individual belonging to the one or the other. Soon or late, every strong popular impulse will be felt. Every stubborn national error is a root of bitterness, that tillage will not extirpate. It will appear in such a country as ours, in acts of government. Therefore I conclude that our absurd hatred of Great Britain will produce a war with that nation, and our excessive democracy, a convulsion or revolution.

. . . .

I have made, at two sittings, a very long *despatch*. I freely own it, that I am rather barren in my communications to you. I find a scarcity of materials. If I could see you, my tongue would run like a mill. I should find subjects supplied by conversation forever and ever. I need not tell you, that you are a friend to whom I am bound by ties not to be severed; and I please myself with believing, that if God, in his mercy, should spare us both to old age, we shall hobble along our downhill path the more cheerfully, for treading it together. When you are to return, you scarcely know yourself. The ill aspect of affairs between the two countries may bring you home the sooner. But as it may create subjects of adjustment, it may detain you. I scarcely wish you to return soon; yet I am not very unwilling to see you again at the bar—dear as your fame and happiness will ever be to me; for I do not believe that will degrade you, or plague you very much after the first six weeks. You would act on a respectable scale, which, in my dictionary, is synonymous with large fees. I sincerely wish, however, that your return to the professional drudgery may be most perfectly optional with you.

God bless you, and Mrs. Gore.

Yours, &c.

TO T. PICKERING

DEDHAM, NOVEMBER 23, 1799

(Private.)

DEAR SIR,

I EXPRESSED such thoughts, in my late letter, as occurred to me, in the first moments of my surprise and vexation, on finding the envoys were actually going. They were crude, and deduced from a very imperfect view of the whole case. I then thought the public had been more prepared by art, and were more strongly impressed by the authority of the President, than I now think. I then thought an indirect plan of self-defense the only one left, to diminish or escape the enormous mischiefs of that fatal measure. I still think, that a direct newspaper discussion is to be postponed. I did not, however, duly consider the probable state of things in Congress. *There*, the public sentiment will spring, as from its proper fountainhead. If the speech should be a menace to Great Britain, all will be lost, if Congress should echo, or only tacitly acquiesce.

If the President should only state facts, and give a general view of the state of affairs, and of the hopes of the effect of his mission, the question (as) to the proper conduct for federal men to pursue, in framing the *answer*, will be more difficult. I have a little turned my thoughts to the subject, and though it is but a little, I will hastily and unreservedly state them to you.

If this mission is to be a flam, to delude the French with mock friendship, they will, I fear, turn it into serious earnest.

The President, I hear, says he has no hope of its success. But why he should calculate on their being so shallow as to refuse the promise of any thing, I cannot see.

It is, apparently, a game too delicate to play with advantage, against any but novices, and these old sinners will certainly beat us at it. My own belief is, that, for certain reasons, the mission proceeds on the ground, that Great Britain is hostile, is too great, and that France and we are to lean to the same side, to make a balance. Though war is not intended, perhaps not foreseen, by the President, yet he is willing to have the multitude, and the Jacobins, give him credit, as no friend to the English, and no well-wisher to the growth of their naval power, or to the depression of their rivals. This is a prodigious merit, and will throw such a glory round any prophet's head, as may well fascinate. He may calculate that this will procure and secure popularity, not only with the multitude, but with the pretended American party, as I have heard he terms those who are not of the French or British parties; all which parties he supposes to exist distinctly.

. . . If, to the effect of these dispositions and measures on the part of the chief of the government, we should unfortunately have to add what will be produced by the acquiescence, tacit or express, of Congress, and the newspaper assent of the nation, which, as the newspapers now are, will be expressed loudly in favor of the President and his mission, will not Great Britain banish all doubt of our hostility, and act accordingly? Will not an open war, or an active one, though not declared, but ruinous to our trade, be the certain and speedy consequence? I know some wise folks insist, that she has her hands full, and that we are too good customers to quarrel with. This is plausible, but false. Armed as she is, our hostility would be nothing. With a thousand ships, *her* trade would be safe, and with a thousand privateers, which such a trade as ours would invite to scour the seas, *we* should be stript of nearly our whole commercial capital in one short season. And as to manufactures, we must have them. They would reach us (at) a dear rate, and so scantily as to ensure poverty and nakedness.

. . . .

But to return from this long digression. I have endeavored to show, that this is the worst time for us, the best for Great Britain, to go to war. Any time would be a bad one, for both countries, and would cost a great sacrifice of interest to passion. But the minister of Great Britain might argue thus: These people hate us, and would fight us, if they dared; with such animosities, they will join our foe as soon, and annoy us, even in peace, as much as possible. Better then choose war; it is our time. We are clad in armor, and invulnerable. The order to their cruisers will be rigorous; spoliation will be augmented, discontents will multiply, the Jacobins, who profit by all ill humors, will speedily triumph, and then we should have open war. Or it may be, open war will happen first, and that would bring on poverty, discontent, faction, and triumphant jacobinism.

Admitting this progress, (no matter which end it may begin at,) the petty discords among federalists, the small talk among the small politicians, about disrespect to the President, &c., &c., (which, on any other question than that of national life or death I should call important,) I say, these minor considerations lose all weight in the comparison.

If the House, by an express answer disapproving, could prevent the impression on foreign nations, that the mission was the expression of the will of all the branches of our government, the evil might yet be stopped. We might be only disgraced, not ruined—suffer some clamors, lose some federalists, and save our peace, wealth, and government.

But if the House will not speak the true language, I do not see why a few, why even *one* member should not speak it, if a second would not join him. The division of the federalists might be disclosed by such a debate, but it would not be occasioned. The public would rally; the real dangers would strike the real patriots, who now sleep ignorant of them. If Gallatin and Co. should be for the mission, Connecticut, always sound, against it, and the known friends of order and government should join the latter, even yet something might be done. . . .

But if it is a case fit, as the Catholics say, for extreme unction, good men are bound to do all they can to save the nation. If they fail in the attempt, the nation will then have to answer for its own undoing. I submit it, therefore, to you, whether every effort ought not to be made in debate, to open the eyes of the people, even if the good men were sure of being in a minority.

Perhaps some equally impressive ground may appear to you and others accessible and tenable. I wish to engage your most mature thoughts, in conjunction with the friends about you, and the friends of the country. Congress ever meets unimpressed, and ready to take a plan of conduct, if well digested and properly recommended, but never ready to frame one for itself.

I am, dear sir, with a grateful sense of your exertions for us all, and with perfect esteem,

Yours, truly.

FROM OLIVER WOLCOTT
TO FISHER AMES

PHILADELPHIA, DECEMBER 29TH, 1799

I HAVE RECEIVED your excellent letter of the 16th instant. Among the many deficiencies of which I am conscious, no one appears to my own mind more reprehensible, than the neglect with which I have treated your correspondence. Your letter of March 19th in particular, ought to have been answered. I read it with attention. I recollect its contents, and cannot sufficiently regret that the world was not seasonably acquainted with the true character of the person therein described.

Since the departure of the envoys, our political magicians have gravely employed themselves in reconciling contrarieties; their experiments would afford exquisite amusement, were there no room to apprehend mischief to the country. Very little is said by discerning men, about the state of our public affairs, except in confidence; all profess a desire to extinguish party spirit, to cultivate friendship and harmony, and at all events, to maintain union in the federal party. A few weeks ago, it was said that France was so reduced as to be unable to injure; that there would be a general peace this winter; others said that there would be no peace, but that the allies would grow insolent, and that policy required us to join the weaker party, and thus preserve the balance of power. It is now discovered that the coalition will dissolve; that France will triumph, and it is said to be wise to conciliate, and not rashly plunge into war with a victorious nation. There is, however, a class of statesmen who, from all I can collect, ought to be deemed the orthodox sect; who, with arch looks, and petrifying gravity, affect astonishment that the mission should be considered as a deviation from the system of the last Congress. They say that the French overtures were insidious, and intended to divide the country; that a treaty is not to be expected; that the Directory are infinitely mortified, that what was intended in jest, was taken in earnest; that the country is now more united than ever; that confidence in the government has been strengthened, and that the mission was a fit and indispensable preliminary to a declaration of war.

But notwithstanding this grimace and masquerade, nobody

is deceived, and all are conscious that there exists some difficulty; the confiding, unsuspicious part of the community, who have no means of acquiring accurate information, are however, deceived by appearances, and lulled into a state of security.

The anti-federalists of Virginia, who have more ability than in any other part of the Union, declared that peace with France is attainable, if right steps are taken; that the President has been forced by public opinion, to adopt a measure which he dislikes; that very unsuitable characters have been selected as envoys; that much valuable time has been lost, and they affect apprehensions that the prejudices of the President, and the inveterate malice of the officers of the government have dictated improper conditions of negotiation; they admit, however, that considering all circumstances, the President has shown such respect for the voice of the people, as justly to entitle him to an increase of their confidence; and they expect from the magnanimity of France, that great allowances will be made for the unfortunate condition of the American republicans under the present administration.

It is the nature of all political parties, to consider their opponents as invariably in the wrong. The southern federalists have of course, been induced to vindicate the mission, as a sincere, honest, and politic measure; both parties are waiting the result. The failure of the negotiation, if that should happen, will be adduced as a new and conclusive proof that the French government is hostile, and unjust; if it succeeds, the antis will infer that all the clamour heretofore raised against France, was unfounded; and if peace should not be made, the failure will be attributable to bad management, and a new, and fair experiment be demanded.

Considering the state of the House, it was necessary and proper that the answer to the speech should be prepared by Mr. Marshall; he has had a hard task to perform, and you have seen how it has been executed. The object was to unite all opinions, at least of the federalists; it was of course necessary to appear to approve the mission, and yet to express the approbation in such terms as when critically analyzed would amount to no approbation at all. No one individual was really satisfied; all were unwilling to encounter the danger and heat which a debate would produce; the address passed with silent dissent; the President doubtless understood the intention, and in his response has expressed his sense of the dubious compliment in terms inimitably obscure.

The following may be considered as a tolerably correct outline of the state of the public councils. The federal party is composed of the old members who were generally re-elected in the northern, with new members from the southern states. New York has sent an anti-federal majority; Pennsylvania has done the same; opposition principles are gaining ground in New Jersey and Maryland, and in the present Congress the votes of these states will be fluctuating and undecided. A number of distinguished men appear from the southward, who are not pledged by any act to support the system of the last Congress; these men will pay great respect to the opinions of General Marshall; he is doubtless a man of virtue and distinguished talents, but he will think much of the State of Virginia, and is too much disposed to govern the world according to rules of logic; he will read and expound the Constitution as if it were a penal statute, and will sometimes be embarassed with doubts of which his friends will not perceive the importance.

General Lee is a man of talents, address, and ambition; he is not entirely pleased with having been appointed a provisional general; but he can and will dissemble his resentments when the expression of them will not promote his interests; he will play a part, and will have, or I am mistaken, some projects, in which he will be joined by some of the anti-federalists.

The northern members can do nothing of themselves, and circumstances have imposed on them the necessity of reserve. The President will be supported by many, from personal considerations; some believe he has acted wisely; others consider it impolitic and unjust to withdraw their support, though they admit he has committed a mistake. The President's mind is in a state which renders it difficult to determine what prudence and duty require from those about him. He considers Col. Pickering, Mr. McHenry, and myself as his enemies; his resentments against General Hamilton are excessive; he declares his belief of the existence of a British faction in the United States.

In some unguarded moment he wrote a letter to Tench Coxe, attributing the appointment of Mr. Pinckney as minister to London, to British influence, and suggesting that if he (Mr. A.) were in an executive office he would watch the progress of that influence. Coxe, has perfidiously disclosed this letter, and copies are circulating among the suspicious and malignant. This state of things has greatly impaired the confidence which subsisted among men of a certain class in society; no one knows how soon his own character may be assailed. Spies and informers carry tales to the President, with the hope of producing changes in the administration. Mr. Otis, your successor, is suspected of aspiring to the office of Secretary of State. Cunning half Jacobins assure the President that he can combine the virtuous and moderate men of both parties, and that all our difficulties are owing to an oligarchy which it is in his power to crush, and thus acquire the general support of the nation. I believe that I am not mistaken in any of the facts which I have stated; it is certain that confidence is impaired, but no man can be certain that, when many are interested in promoting dissension, he may not himself be the dupe of artifice; possibly this is my own case.

Among the officers of government there is a sensation of unhappiness. I do not know whether you are acquainted with Mr. McHenry; he is a man of honour and entirely trustworthy; he is also a man of sense, and delivers correct opinions when required, but he is not skilled in the details of executive business, and he is at the head of a difficult and unpopular department. The diffidence which he feels, exposes his business to delays, and he sometimes commits mistakes which his enemies employ to impair his influence.

Mr. Lee is a sensible man, and I think a candid man, who thinks much of Virginia; he fears disorders and a dissolution of the union; he frequently dissents to what is proposed by others, and approves of the sentiments of the President, but with respect to *measures* will rarely take an active part.

Mr. Stoddert is a man of great sagacity, and conducts the business of department with success and energy; he means to be popular; he has more of the confidence of the President than any officer of the government. He professes to know less than he really knows, and to be unequal to the task of forming or understanding a political system; he will have much influence in the government, and avoid taking his share of the responsibility.

In this state of things, the country has lost her Washington. There can be no doubt that his character afforded a resource in an extreme case. The President may attempt, but he will attempt in vain to be the arbiter of contending factions.

The states of Virginia and Pennsylvania mean to carry on a legislative opposition to the government; in the latter the majority of the Senate is federal, in the House the case is different; the Senate is desirous of providing by law for the choice of electors in districts, by which mode the votes would be divided; the House is said to be inflexibly determined that the election shall be general throughout the state. It is reported, and I consider it as probably true, that the Governor has decided that he will reject a bill for a district election, and if no law is passed, that he will authorize and regulate a general election by proclamation. If this course should be pursued, and the choice of a President should depend on the votes of Pennsylvania, a civil war will not be improbable, in any event we may consider the public councils as a conclave of cardinals, intriguing for the election of a Pope; the best we can hope for is, that the passions of the parties will evaporate in slander, and every species of injustice short of the employment of actual force.

The steady men in Congress will attempt to extend the judicial department and I hope that their measures will be very decided. It is impossible, in this country, to render an army an engine of government; and there is no way to combat the state opposition but by an efficient and extended organization of judges, magistrates, and other civil officers.

The revenue fell short the last year one million of dollars, that is, the duties on imports decreased from seven millions and a half, to six and a half millions, and we are to expect great troubles from the explosion of commercial credit in Europe. The British finances have been managed with great skill, but Mr. Pitt cannot do what is impossible; he cannot support the public credit much longer. Our merchants will suffer considerably from the stock of West India goods unsold, and will not be pleased with an increase of duties; we must, however, increase our revenue in some way or other; in the meantime, we can borrow, perhaps, on better terms than heretofore, in consequence of the events which have lately occurred in Europe. But although the state of our finances is yet sound, and though we can borrow sufficient for our immediate wants, it is necessary to remember that our permanent revenues cannot be estimated higher than eight millions of dollars, and that the expense of our existing establishments, including the public annuity, amounts to thirteen millions; we must borrow five millions annually; and to provide permanent revenues of even four hundred thousand dollars for several successive years, will require much firmness in Congress. The public creditors will not long suffer the debt to be increased, without an increase of revenue at least adequate to the payment of interest.

The direct tax has been attended with as little opposition as I expected, and a considerable part will be collected during the ensuing year, but the tax is not permanent, and can only be considered as an experiment: that part which will be assessed on new and unproductive lands will come slowly into the treasury. It is not a fact that the ability of people of different states to pay taxes, is in proportion to their numbers, and it is therefore certain that direct taxes which must be apportioned to the states, will be found unequal and of course odious, except in times of war or imminent danger. A tax on houses might be so modified as to raise a considerable revenue without opposition, but many say that a house tax must be apportioned to the states: time will correct this idea, but such a tax cannot now be obtained.

The only question which will arise respecting the army, will be whether it shall be disbanded, or the present establishment continued upon condition of suspending further enlistments. The subject is attended with vast difficulties in whatever light it is considered. The generals, and I believe I may say the officers, with their connections and a great proportion of the wisest and best friends of the government, think the existing army ought to be preserved as a permanent establishment. Nothing, however, is more certain than that the army is unpopular, even in the southern states, for whose defence it was raised. Who is to defend the army if the southern members oppose the establishment, or even support it faintly? The northern people fear no invasion, or if they did, they perceive no security in a handful of troops; nobody has thought it prudent to say that the army is kept on foot to suppress or prevent rebellions; for such a purpose, the troops are worse than nothing, especially as the state of idleness to which they are necessarily condemned, tends to corrupt their principles. It was not encouraging to know that companies of federal troops shouted for Governor McKean, yet such facts have happened. In short, the army is composed of men; it has its intriguers, it has its factions, and is infected with the spirit of the times; how can it be otherwise when the President's opinion of the general is no secret? when all feel insecure, and perceive that essential changes in the administration are preparing?

I anticipate your surprise at the perusal of these observations; candour requires me to say that my opinions are singular, and have been kept in my own breast as much as possible. A year since, the army was in the power of the government, and I then freely explained my sentiments to General Washington and General Hamilton, that it ought to be the immediate object of the government to form ample arsenals, and deposit therein arms and ammunition adequate to the supply of the whole force of the country; that but few officers ought to be appointed, and the expense of supporting idle men avoided as much as possible. I stated my doubts whether the best selection of officers could be made at that time, whether the best men could be enlisted, and whether it was probable that the establishment could be maintained. The reply was, that if money could be borrowed, the army ought to be raised; and that the delay which had happened was hardly to be excused. Finding the decision against my sentiments, the money was procured, and nothing has been omitted on my part to give success to the system of government.

To reduce the army while the mission is pending, will be most humiliating; it must be supported for the present year at least. I presume that all are agreed respecting the policy of forbearing to accelerate enlistments. I hope no law will be passed requiring the suspension, as such a measure would tend still more to repress a spirit which is already at too low a point.

I beg you to believe that my observations respecting the army are not dictated by a desire of being thought wiser, even on the point in question, than General Washington and General Hamilton. My self love, if I am not deceived, carries me no further than a desire that you may understand that I have been consistent, and have not adopted a new opinion in opposition to my friends at this critical period. My sentiments are but little known. I should not disclose them at this time, did not the plan of this letter require that I should open my whole heart.

The events which have lately occurred in Europe, in my opinion diminish the probability that the envoys will negotiate a treaty with France; the Directory well consider how they can best extend their power and influence, and they will be embarrassed with opposite considerations; a treaty would, according to present appearances, procure France some supplies, and tend to embroil us with England; on the other hand, the French will wish to yield peace to a Jeffersonian administration, who would give them better terms. The expectation of uniting this country against France, which is indulged in by the friends of the mission, will be found fallacious. I shall be well pleased to find that the French do not, by uniting favourable with inadmissible terms of negotiation, furnish a new source of dissention.

Your information respecting the general state of Europe is probably equal to what I possess. Germany and the Northern nations, except Russia, are full of discord. The emperor of Germany is accused, and I believe justly, of having ruined the cause of the allies, by his rapacious ambition. In Italy he has conquered for himself and not for the old system of government. The co-operation of the Swiss was lost merely from the want of a declaration that the ancient governments should be re-established. Viewed with reference to the moral causes which will decide the fortunes of the parties in this war, there is reason to fear that the campaign has on the whole been favourable to France.

I find I have written a long and very dismal letter; perhaps it will be found that the country will really suffer but little from the events which are foreboded. I thank God that politicians have much less power than they are apt to imagine. In the worst of times, the great body of the people have been tranquil, and have fancied themselves secure; let us presume that no great national calamities await the present and a few succeeding generations of the United States.

You are sensible that I cannot often write even a short letter, and that I rarely write much with the freedom I have taken in this. It is not that I am cowardly, but because I cannot write what I do not think, and am determined not to be factious. This is intended for the eye of friendship. You have my permission to show it to Mr. Cabot, after which I request it may be destroyed, and the contents remain a secret.

1 8 0 0

===

———

BOSTON, JANUARY 6, 1800

MY DEAR FRIEND,

. . . .

Inter nos. I fear that I shall be asked to deliver an Eulogium on General Washington. I am intriguing to parry this malicious blow of the fates, for I have not time to prepare. I cannot do the thing justice. I should disappoint everybody, and mortify myself intolerably. This is not a modesty trap, but a sad prognostic of the event.

Yours, affectionately.

TO OLIVER WOLCOTT

———

DEDHAM, JANUARY 12, 1800

(Private)

MY DEAR SIR,

For my correspondence, you owe me neither punctuality nor apologies. It is not a mock modesty, for I hate affectation, and most of all among friends, but a correct sense of your situation and mine that makes me say that I cannot make you any adequate return for the favour of your correspondence. I possess no information of facts, and my sentiments are known to you before I write them down. I have, therefore, made little other excuse for writing to you, than such as I glean from my own repeated assurances that you are tax free. If you reply, it is *ex abundante;* if you forbear, still I thank you for allowing me to pour forth my bad temper and bad spirits upon you. Let this perfectly sincere explanation suffice; there is not a word of compliment in it. Let it be a treaty between us; on my part, it is a release of all demands on your pen and ink. It was in this frame of mind that I received your long letter of the 29th December. I am flattered exceedingly by your frankness; I know that it is a mark of your trust both in my friendship and discretion; you do not lavish such things. I am not behind Mr. Cabot in regard for you, and I will add in respect, too; he, alone, shall know the contents; they are a treasure which I should be unworthy to possess if I could not bring myself to destroy. I will do it after I have read the letter a hundred times more, yet, I confess, however informing, I was not quite unapprised of most of the circumstances detailed in it. My knowledge is now more perfect on each article, and much the more comprehensive for your assistance.

I have neither time nor maturity of thought to write you a long letter; yet I wish to do it. The views you have taken of our affairs are profound; they appear to me perfectly just; yet I should think two hours most agreeably spent in discussing some of your points, and as we are not soon to converse together, I will seek some leisure to put my reflections into writing. In the meantime, I would spend this sheet in suggesting my first impressions, but I scarcely know where to begin. Your observations furnish the materials for a book, which I have no fancy to write, as the readers would consign it to the hands of the hangman to burn.

The fact really is, that over and above the difficulties of sustaining a free government, and the freer, the more difficult, there is a want of accordance between our system and the state of our public opinion. THE GOVERNMENT IS REPUBLICAN; OPINION IS ESSENTIALLY DEMOCRATIC—(perhaps I have said this very thing in a former letter—no matter if I have). Either, events will raise public opinion high enough to support our government, or public opinion will pull down the government to its own level. They must equalize. The false notions of liberty are pretty general among those who read and are thought to understand, so that over and above the error into which the multitude is prone to fall from passion and prejudice, is that which is imposed upon them by authority. The guides they take, are not fools but fanatics. Political fanaticism has its run in Virginia. I give them credit for being fools in earnest, as to democracy. This admission does not hinder their being factious and knavish. The extreme sensibility of the good men in Virginia to silly principles and silly people, has ever been characteristic. Madison crept into the first Congress by some declarations in print, which made some persons say then, there was not room for him to crawl through with his principles, and therefore he was forced to crawl without them. Jefferson, in 1789, wrote some such stuff about the will of majorities, as a New Englander would lose his rank among men of sense to avow. They are not ashamed, in Virginia, of most of the disorganizing dogmas of Tom Paine, and they are afraid to contest their authority. Add to all this ordinary and extraordinary fertility of popular errors, the infinity of the product of other causes.

Our government is feeble in its structure, and therefore factions are bold and powerful. The rival state governments are organized factions, and I have long seen, are systematically levying the force to subvert their common enemy. New York will be Jacobinized; Massachusetts is threatened with Gerry, who, though a weak creature, would unite the confidence of the anarchists and would gain and abuse a portion of that of his adversaries. Within the United States, I see the great states leaguing together under democratic governors; Jefferson and Co., at the head of a stronger faction than any government can struggle with long, or prevail against at last, unless by military force; for it is obvious to me, that all other modes of decision will be spurned as soon as the antis think they have force on their side. Abroad, I see France, by the judgment of Heaven on our infatuation, put into possession of the means of wielding our government by the faction in their interests. The government, amidst all these dangers, afraid of its friends, parrying no blows but such as are not aimed at it, confident of bullying England and of outwitting France, stingy of its resources; as the danger thickens and approaches, it will certainly be more divided in affection, more confounded in counsel, more tardy in preparation or action. This dismal state of things seems to discourage the hope of doing much with effect, or of preparing anything without incurring the risk of its being seized and converted into a weapon for annoyance by the foe. But though this is a serious danger of the army, though, you justly remark, it is no engine of the government, the civil magistrate and process are better ordinary means of self-defense, yet I hesitate to admit that *therefore* the army must not be levied and relied upon. It is certainly a subject of great nicety, requiring the soundest judgment to decide on the proper choice of the means of self-preservation in the crisis which is near, as my belief is, that the appeal will be made to arms. I would have in preparation the force to decide the issue in favor of government. It is not an ordinary, it is an extreme that I contemplate, and when that happens the difficulties you so forcibly exhibit will disappear. Neither the want of revenue nor of popularity will disarm a military force at such a period. All force, all revenue is viewed by the factious as the power of a foe, and therefore they will try to strip the government of both, but it must have both or be a victim to the faction; and if our people cannot be brought to bear necessary taxes, and to maintain so small a force as our army, they are (and I am afraid they are) unfit for an independent government. The army will be democratic, factious, and perhaps treacherous when wanted; but means could be used to prevent, or, in due time, before using force, to cure this evil, and once impelled the right way they would keep on in it. Nor can I, quite so far as you seem to go, admit that our handful of troops would not much help the government at a pinch; a few thousand, or even a few hundred regular troops, well officered, would give the first advantages to government in every contest; and that, by allowing the cause of order and law to take the upper hand at the outset, would probably decide the event against faction. Besides, when things approach to extremities, a different state of things will exist. Even trimming popularity seekers, and all real patriots will ask for shelter under the force of the government. Taxes and armies would then be popular. In common times they must be unpopular, and however necessary the augmentation, it must be gradual, except when danger is seen to be near and felt to be great. But if the want of money first exists, the resources for it will be supplied, and the faster for that want. I do not much reluct at expenses when prudently chosen and assented to by Congress, because I know the country is in no want of means, though it requires time and a train of good habits to draw them forth. On the whole, the prospect is dismal, and perhaps human wisdom is too short-sighted to provide resources against the danger. To push on too fast while public sentiment lays far behind, would be rash; on the other hand, occasions must not be lost to get for the government such means of self-defense as they present. Jacobinism is certainly spreading from towns and cities into the country places. It is less watched and less warmly resisted in the latter than the former. It is, therefore, getting to be much at home in the country, and will remain till the convulsion of some great internal events shall change the whole political and moral order of our nation. Then, taught by suffering, we shall learn wisdom, when perhaps it is too late to put it in practice. I have written more than I intended, with too much haste for method or precision.

Yours truly,

FISHER AMES

FROM GEORGE CABOT
TO OLIVER WOLCOTT

———

BROOKLINE, JANUARY 16, 1800

(Private.)

MY DEAR SIR,

MR. AMES passed last evening with me. He is to pronounce the eulogy of Washington before our state legislature, three weeks hence. I hope he will weave into it as much as possible, of his own politics. They are such as Washington approved, and I hardly know what greater praise can be given him, than a display of this fact.

TO JOHN WARD FENNO, ESQ., PHILADELPHIA

DEDHAM, FEBRUARY, 1800

MY DEAR SIR,

A FRIEND in Boston had occasionally sent me your Gazette. That, joined to my being engaged in business in Boston, makes me doubtful whether I had received any of your papers, before the two that came with your esteemed favor of the 10th. I value the favor of your Gazette, as I ought. Those who *think*, are not very many, and the world's business, luckily, is not to be done by thinking. All have passions and prejudices, and these are called principles, creeds, virtues. A Gazette, conducted by a man of keen remark, and who dares to publish what he has discernment enough to comprehend, will of course have rivals and slanderers, even among his most clumsy imitators. This distinction, like all preëminence, is fascinating, and requires a variety, and at least a seeming contrariety, of qualities, to wear with grace and manage with advantage. Your father was a rare good man: my heart grows heavy as often as I revive in it the remembrance of his death. My affection for his memory, and my regard for you, would authorize me to set myself up, through one page, as your adviser, if I did not know, that of all rights, those of advisers are the most mistaken and abused. Prudence is thought to be of a mean parentage, and is often in a bad neighborhood, being reputed the offspring of dull feelings and base fears, a sort of jockey virtue, a substitute for both sense and morals. I am, I confess, at length old enough to consider it as the ripe fruit of experience, the just discernment of things as they are, and the condescension to weaknesses and prejudices.

This, I confess, is rather a grave and awkward beginning. It is not designed as the preface to a sermon of reproof. Far from it. Young men, with an honest warmth of heart, despise little condescensions. Yet there is no possibility of getting along in this world among so many little folks and little prejudices, without making a great many. It is impossible to strip off these, as they make up half or nine tenths of the whole political man. Young men of talents, also, who discern dangers far off, are impatient, that others are dull to see and slow to provide against them. This is your case, and that of the public. Sanguine hopes, of the most ridiculous kind, enable millions to extract comfort from facts that show how fallacious they are. They suffer few ills by anticipation, and reflect little on such as have happened. The mass of the nation are, of course, little affected by theories; not much by any but very great events. They communicate almost no impulse to government, and are open to all strong impressions, either of government or of the faction opposed to it. A few leading ideas are, however, deeply rooted. I hope love of the Union is one, and when the crisis arrives that will oblige them to choose, I flatter myself they will choose right, or at least stand by authority, in support of such a choice.

I admit, however, that things are gloomy enough. I lament the tame and fluctuating spirit that some of our measures indicate. I cannot deny, that many bad consequences are scarcely to be shunned. But, on the whole, I glean a good number of hopes from the same field where my fears grow so rank. The federal Constitution is at least as correct as public opinion, and as events mend the latter, the former will gain energy. A system that shall thus adapt itself to experience, will be worth a million of Abbe Sieyes's theories.

I am not of the opinion that any change or amendment would answer, that the people do not understand in some degree, and feel the want of in a greater, before it is incorporated into our Constitution. Gradually, we shall, I hope, adjust our systems to our wants, and our opinions to our systems. At any rate, we must not give up our hold on this Constitution; we must support it; we must, when necessary, amend it, and in your day it may acquire the strength that time and habit, as well as judicious alterations, will supply. These are my leading ideas of the actual state of our affairs, of what is prudence and what is duty. Allow me to proceed frankly with you. You are not obliged to assume the opinions you reprobate. But when they are adopted by great numbers, who cannot or will not reason, they are to be attacked with some caution, if you would overcome them. They are often insensible to argument, always enraged by contempt. There is scarcely any lesson that may not be taught so as to avoid disgusting. Truth ought to be made popular, if possible. Your Gazette ought to be the vehicle of such lessons, and to make it such, many hands ought to aid your labors. The style of the pieces should never be such as to separate you from the good in disposition, who are slow in understanding. Truths incessantly inculcated are not quite lost upon us, though I own the effect is not very manifest. But less experience will teach us, and we shall be the sooner taught. I should be happy, for your own sake, as well as for the public's, to see your Gazette as correct in taste, style, and sentiment, a terror to evil-doers, and a praise to such as do well, as the Leyden Gazette was formerly. Do not infer, from this mode of expression, that I would censure it. I consider the task too much for any one man to accomplish. The most able friends of the government ought to be your assistants. With such aid, and the maturing of your mind by the advantages of so great early experience, I should hope you would make the success satisfactory to yourself and to us all.

I agree with you, that the turgid bombast of our papers

has been abominable. I have heard much of Thomas's eulogium on Turenne, but know not where to find it. I will send you one of my *things*, as soon as printed. To interest people, after their impressions had all grown flat, and to play tricks with pathos, when they had buried their grief, was not to be done; therefore I attempted neither. Simplicity of thought and expression would be merit, and such merit as I would affect. It would be of a novel kind, as the public taste is formed to the Johnsonian method. An oration may, and, indeed, must be raised on stilts, or it will not be raised at all. I thank you for your attentions, and am much obliged to Mr. Dennie for his. My best wishes for the happiness and fame of you both.

Yours, &c.

TO CHRISTOPHER GORE

———

BOSTON, MARCH 5, 1800

DEAR FRIEND,

THE COURT will break up to-day, after passing several acts, of some value to the state; one for inspecting beef, much wanted, and which will make a great reform in this article; turnpike acts, to bring the produce of Vermont to this market, and which will recover to Boston a large part of the back country, which has for many years gone to New York. A turnpike is granted from the line of Connecticut to the thirty-milestone, on the road west of Dedham and Medfield, and which joins the Connecticut turnpike from Hartford ferry to the aforesaid line, adjoining this state at Douglas. This will divert the cheese, butter, &c., &c., which has gone to Providence more and more, and restore to the South End rum-and-molasses shops, the Jonathans who used to have their sweet communion with them. These regulations will really tend to raise Boston; and if your Middlesex Canal should suceed, the success will be hastened. Do I not write like a patriot? yet I sell neither rum nor molasses.

The members go home well affected to Government, but I think so many interests combine to make the members more numerous, and to change the sort, that the Jacobins will be stronger in the next House. The mode of choosing electors in this state will be to confirm or alter, and Mr. Adams will be, I think, supported by all the Feds in the United States, and opposed by all the *antis*. This was, perhaps, not expected by either his friends or his foes, but events control the men who think they control *them*. Our parties in Congress seem to regard that approaching election as the only object of attention. We expect a treaty from our envoys. The common prattle is, we shall not give heed to the promises and lies of France, and yet all, except a dozen persons, hunger and thirst and pray, without ceasing, for a batch of such promises and lies in the form of a treaty. Truxton's battle with a superior French ship, McKean's violence, and the tiresome perseverance of frigid eulogies, shall not add another sheet to my letter.

Your friend.

[P.S.] Write, I pray you. I will make compensation, if that could do it, by two letters to one from you.

TO CHAUNCEY GOODRICH

DEDHAM, JUNE 12, 1800

MY DEAR SIR,

THIS MOMENT I have received Mr. Wolcott's letter of the 7th, and am desired to send my answer to your care. It is not improper to address it to you. His letter shall go to Mr. Cabot, with that regard and attention which we both feel for the writer. I lose no time to write, and shall be brief, as I am hard pushed for time to prepare some law business in my hands.

I returned from Connecticut strongly impressed with the necessity for awakening the federalists to a sense of their danger, and persuaded that the danger was likely to be much augmented by the obstacles, [which] local and personal attachments, would create in Massachusetts, to the proper exercise of our state's right of suffrage. You will know that this state is to choose electors by the legislature; that this was intended, and was expected to secure a unanimous vote for Adams and Gen. Pinckney; that the choice must be made in November next; and it is probable, though not so certain as I wish, that all the votes will be given for those two. I believe further, that it is understood by most persons, that Pickney's chance is worse than Jefferson's, and better than Adams'. Of those who foresee the exclusion of the latter, few yet dare, and fewer think it prudent or necessary, to avow their desire, of such an event of the election. The Demos, would join in the cry to make any man opposed to the President, unpopular, and no party is yet formed, and in activity among the federalists, to vindicate and shelter him. I scorn, as much as my friends do, duplicity, or timidity in politics; yet, while I avow my opinions and expectations as much as any enquirer has a right to know them, I think myself bound to exercise that discreet reserve, [without which,] we might divide the votes, and mar the success of good measures. Many explanations must be given, and time must pass, to familiarise good minds to correct new ideas, before you can expect more than I have stated, as the expectation and object of the legislature of Massachusetts, to choose the electors themselves. An open attack, if made soon on one of the two, would, I fear, divide our force, and perhaps give some votes to Jefferson; yet, Mr. Wolcott seems to think (for on this point he is not perfectly clear) that we in this state, ought to vote for only *one* of the two intended candidates. I perceive a great fund of federal zeal and merit, such as he could wish, in the leading members of our General Court, and I also see that a *certain interest* is jealous and busy, but manifestly weak in both branches. Due care will be taken to get men of sound, independent patriotism, for electors. The difficulty of securing their election, and of their due conduct in that character, is understood. I expect a progressive alarm will be felt, as the time of election approaches, and as the strange, whimsical conduct of a certain great man is more generally comprehended. Now, I wish to know how much further you would wish us to go. I have carefully stated on all occasions, that the object is to keep an *anti* out, and get a federal President in; and that the only way to do it, is, by voting for General Pinckney, at the risk, which every one I converse with suggests, of excluding Mr. A. Many of us are willing to say all that the cause requires, and unwilling to say anything that truth forbids; but on the former point, you and Mr. W. may probably decide that Massachusetts ought to bear more than I have stated. Any strong impulse on public opinion here, could produce, at best, only a pretty general effect, whereas, we must have a unanimous vote, or have Jefferson.

I will desire Mr. Cabot to write fully, after enquiring much. I have not time for the task. After two weeks, I hope to be more at leisure.

Y'r friend,

FISHER AMES

TO OLIVER WOLCOTT

DEDHAM, JUNE 12, 1800

MY DEAR SIR,

I HAVE twice read your favour of the 7th, received by this day's mail, and have written to Mr. Goodrich a brief and hasty reply. Really I have no leisure, and am not to have any for a fortnight, but being more politician than lawyer, I cannot forbear to add another sheet. Towards the last days of the commonwealth, all our fears claim to be important. Yet I hope, while I unreservedly communicate mine, that our republic will live to wear grey hairs and green honours.

There are three parties in the United States. Men, who from mere want or folly, abhor restraint; those who from principle, habit, or property, would impose it, and the personal or interested friends of a man, whose caprices and weaknesses have been sometimes *scienter*, but often blindly used, to weaken our party and to animate the other. This man is vindictive enough at any risk or even ruin, to disappoint those who will, he thinks, *alone* disappoint him. His vanity is also soothed to exhibit his fate as proceeding from the art or force of the antis, rather than the disgust of the feds. In that event want of votes would seem more tolerable than the detected want of character. Yet do not condemn me if I say that man has talents for every thing but business, and keep him to making books, he is a great man. Precisely such men act most absurdly. The weak parts of great characters are most prominent and decisive of events. It has long been a common place axiom of my creed, that the world's wisdom has not half as much to do in its government as its weaknesses. This man fancied parties could not do without him. You must remember, though you say you did not know him till his election, that I told you at great length and most faithfully in your office, exactly what *I knew* him to be, before he was in office. This extravagant opinion of himself, this ignorance of parties and characters, this pride that wanted Jefferson to be, and to be exhibited to be his second, and that was not hurt at being in return his dupe, this caprice that was often shifting style and that forbid him ever to have a sober, reflected system. I say all this was known to Cabot and to me in kind, though we both confess, in some of the points, less in degree than the event has exhibited. So it is, however. When his strange measure was announced, and the stranger affectation of mystery as to its reasons, I did not scruple to say it to confidential persons, that when a man is lost with his party, he is irretrievably lost; that he had renounced us, and it was in vain ever to expect he would be right. The truth is, his party is feeble; doubts infest the timid, and they do not know how to get rid of old opinions, which they know were once popular, and to take new ones which they apprehend will be violently unpopular. All the influence of office, of popular prejudices, and habits, and all the effect of the arts of our political rivals are manifest at this moment, and the division of the federal people, and the augmented spirit and force of the antis are evils scarcely to be avoided. My thoughts are, that as the unanimous vote of Massachusetts must be had, the plain truth, which in other moments can alone work miracles to save, would now operate to divide us. That, instead of analyzing the measures of the man who has thus brought the cause into jeopardy, you must sound the tocsin about Jefferson; that the hopes and fears of the citizens are the only sources of influence, and surely we have enough to fear from Jefferson; by thus continually sounding our just alarms we remain united with the people, instead of separated from them, and losing at least a part of our influence. This will not exclude our suggestion of the experienced bad effects of the attempts to coin them, (i. e. by the envoys to France,) and the little cause for apprehension if General P. should be elected. This part of the business will require judgment, but it will be impossible to exclude the thoughts of political men from running in this train.

Why not then, without delay, begin a series of papers to prove the dreadful evils to be apprehended from a Jacobin President. That he would try the first year to coax and to delude, to promise to support the existing system of measures, to gain and to employ in office the known friends of those measures, and to give hopes to many more that they will in turn be employed, thus to abate the fear which federalists entertain, and which is the source of their union. When he has so far broken their force as that the fear of it no longer keeps the antis in check, and submissive to his guidance, then he must act as his party will have him, and not as his own timidity or prudence might otherwise incline him. Moderation, however he might first affect it, would be perceived to gain him no friends among the real federalists, and it would, if persevered in, like the policy of the present chief, sap the foundation of his influence with his own party. He would not rashly and absurdly desert his friends to gain his foes, and thus there would be one year of hypocrisy to divide our party, and three years of jacobinism to oppress and plunder it. For it is not easy for him to act otherwise. Either a chief must join the malcontents who hate restraint, and most of all legal restraint, the natural and unconquerable

Jacobins, or he must unite with those who respect law and order, and who would impose such restraint. In the one case or the other, his friends and his foes, his objects to choose and to shun, his reasons, pretexts, and means are all foreordained by the decrees of political fate. This Mr. Jefferson well knows, and will act accordingly. He will have, it is true, a personal object, somewhat distinct from his party; i.e. to keep his post, and that will lead him to promise, to coax, and to intrigue; but as soon as the federal men, who might happen to be in office, or who might be there on his accession to the chair, by agreement or coalition, as soon as their influence had been used and exhausted to gain apostates from us, and to blast their own fame with our party, then he would act as his party would require. They would require that the active capital of the country should not augment the over-weight of the northern scale; it is the power of an enemy, and must be lessened. A thousand ways of attacking property are plausible, popular, and fatal. Besides, however fond of power and resolute to maintain it, his situation would impose it upon him to maintain it by the energies of jacobinism, by courting, exciting, and guiding the passions of the people, a source of power, which, though disguised, is a resort to mere *force*, and accordingly as soon as experience has pointed out that such force is often wanted, and always clumsy, and sometimes taken out of the demagogue's hands by a fresher and therefore more favourite demagogue, it will lead to a more permanent and manageable force. Behold France— what is theory here, is fact there. What is here faith, is there fruition. The men, the means, the end of such a government as Jefferson must, *nolens volens*, prefer, will soon ensure war with Great Britain, a Cisalpine alliance with France, plunder and anarchy.

Such ideas exhibited with vivacity and force, would arouse the public, if the sleep of death be not already upon us. We should feel and make manifest our sympathy with it. Our power over opinion would not be wholly lost, as I think it would be by a hasty attack on the present chief. I write very hastily, and steal the moments from business, which I ought not to neglect, and make no scruple of submitting crudities to your friendly judgment. I pray you write in confidence to me or Mr. Cabot, and be assured that I am unfeignedly your friend, &c.,

FISHER AMES

FROM GEORGE CABOT
TO OLIVER WOLCOTT

PHILADELPHIA, JUNE 16, 1800

I WROTE a letter to Mr. Ames from Hartford, which I desired him to show to you. Whatever may be thought of my sentiments, I think it right to communicate them to my friends. It is probable the same opinions will be more generally entertained than avowed; but if General Pinckney is not elected, all good men will find cause to regret the present inaction of the federal party. It is at least in their power to defend their principles, and to assume a position in which, if defeated, they may avoid dishonour. It is with grief and humiliation, but at the same time with perfect confidence, that I declare that no administration of the government by President Adams can be successful. His prejudices are too violent, and the resentments of men of influence are too keen, to render it possible that he should please either party, and we all know that he does not possess, and cannot command the talents, fortitude, and constancy necessary to the formation of a new party.

The facts upon which these opinions are founded, are not generally known to the federalists, although they are well understood by our adversaries, and this circumstance constitutes our principal danger. There is nothing said in defense of the government which is understood by the people. The papers on our side are filled with toasts and nonsensical paragraphs, attributing wisdom and firmness to the President, while at the same time all confidence is destroyed by the skillful attacks of a vindictive and intelligent opposition. I am no advocate for rash measures, and know that public opinion cannot be suddenly changed; but it is clear to my mind that we shall never find ourselves in the straight road of federalism while Mr. Adams is President. If, however, sensible men think otherwise, he will be supported, for I shall certainly admit that a *change* ought not to be attempted except upon the clearest evidence. . . .

TO RUFUS KING
(TO WILLIAM PAYNE)

BOSTON, 15TH JULY, 1800

MY GOOD FRIEND:

. . . IT IS getting to be the fashion here again to call the federalists the British faction. Nothing can be more false, for though such men respect the laws and courts and government of Britain and detest the arbitrary tyrants of France yet they allow no country any kind of competition in point of respect & affection with our own. You will be surprised to hear that the P. of the U. S lately at the Faneuil Hall dinner on the visitation of the schools gave as a volunteer toast "The proscribed Patriots Hancock & Adams." This was well understood by the Jacobins whom it will not gain, and begins to be comprehended by a small number of correct thinkers whom it will not embolden to speak out. Never was there a more singular and mysterious state of parties. The plot of an old Spanish play is not more complicated with underplot. I scarcely trust myself with the attempt to unfold it.

There is no doubt that the legislature of this state determined to choose electors by the legisle. (instead of the district mode as formerly) with the view to secure the votes for *two* federal candidates. The friends of a certain great man manifested at the time a strong dislike of the measure and the Jacobin Gazettes poured forth accusations agt. the federalists as intriguers agt. *that man* whose re-election they had secretly resolved to defeat by art & management, though they did not dare to confess it. Since his return to the state the new position of parties begins to be perceived. Gen. H. came this way and spoke in most companies without reserve. You know he is the most frank of men. A real or affected alarm is attempted to be spread & the Massachusetts feelings are to be called up to defend their own state born patriot. The great man has been south as far as Alexandria, making his addressers acquainted with his revolutionary merits, and claiming, almost in plain words at New London, office as the only reward. Whether these answers and toasts are to be considered as the first steps towds. reviving the revolutionary spirit you must judge for yourself; his language is bitter even to outrage and swearing and calling names against many who once were and I believe still are thought as good as any men in the country. He inveighs against the British faction and the Essex Junto like one possessed. I have not seen him and from the reception given to one person I do not anticipate any pleasure in a visit. It would be embarrassing to know what to say or how to behave in case of rudeness & insult which I have reason to believe wd. not fail to be thrown in the faces of some persons unaccustomed to such things. In the mean time, every exertion is making to spread the passions that enrage and almost madden him, and it seems to be expected that the ferment of the people awe the Genl. Court in Nov. next to choose electors who will vote for Mr A & *throw away* the votes for the other candidate. This game will be played in Connecticut, N. Hampshire and R. Island, and no measures will be too intemperate that tend to make the citizens revolutionary enough to make the man of 1775 the man of 1800. Whether this fervor will melt the tender hearts of the Jacobins is not clear. At present it seems they are not disposed to give up their old favorite and chief for a new one whose repentance and conversion are rather late. But I think it probable that his sincerity will be made more & more manifest till they perceive that he is no longer the supporter of, or supported by, the federalists. Then perhaps they will take him, if they find they cannot carry their own candidate. This ultimate resort to him is the more a matter of fair calculation in this political jumble, as it may then appear to be the best thing they can do for their own cause & the most fatal to that of their adversaries, as it would insure their division & their discomfiture. Their chief also might be satisfied with a place which would confer the first power and the second rank, but without any responsibility. Thus the party and its' head might severally find their interests in such an arrangement. Col. B. of New York also is at market and may give his influence to the highest bidder. Thus you see no affair can be more involved in doubt or more dependent on intrigue, caprice or accident. I have not half disclosed the thoughts that hurry along through my brain and leave as they pass some very unpleasant marks.

There is also another consequence to be apprehended. Those who have need of the aid that popular impulse can lend to their designs probably will know that to command that impulse and to have all its force it is necessary to agitate the popular passions. A cold multitude like a cold iron is too hard for the hammers—red hot, they are ductile to the pincers. How shall this heat, this welding heat, be imparted, and kept up? no way is so sure and obvious as re-exciting the rage against G. B. A war, or measures leading to war will heat every body red hot. Whether these steps are to be taken in all events, and of choice, or whether they are to be only the expedients of necessity and are to be adopted as occasions call for them, I will not say. But when a man thinks no cause good or safe *without him,* he may possibly act with as much blindness as extravagance when he resolves rather to hazard the ships than his captaincy.

Yr friend.

FISHER AMES

TO OLIVER WOLCOTT

DEDHAM, JULY 22D, 1800

MY DEAR FRIEND,

By THIS mail I enclose two *Centinels* and a *Commercial Gazette.* In that of the 5th July (a *Centinel*) you will read the *Massachusetts Federalist,* the object and full interpretation of which you will instantly see. In that of the 12th, is an answer reprinted from the *Chronicle,* addressed to me by name. In yesterday's *Gazette* is *Junius Americanus.* I beg your attention to them all, to discern and judge for yourself the temper and conduct of parties. I think you will see a design on one side to establish a system of terror, to appeal to the people against the high flying feds, to use local and personal influences to the utmost, and even to resort to pity for forgotten services, sacrifices great and unrewarded, insults unmerited and base. All this, too, in a scene where whispers have been low, for fear of raising a clamour that the whisperers are foes to. Now these questions occur, will the sort of feeling that is in Boston and its vicinity, no matter whether art or prejudices raised it, spread in the state? Will not the members of the General Court, half afraid of having done too much by taking the election from the people, be afraid to do the very thing they did the first to bring about? Will they dare to choose electors who will not throw away votes? I am not able to conjecture. They *were* right, but art and industry will be exerted to make them wrong in November. As the bold tone of these folks intimidates *trimming* feds, (if such creatures can be); as sober, good men cannot see how the cause can be separated from the man, and as the attacks of those writers indicate a violent war, will not prudence, will not self defence, call for a change of conduct on our part? Will not an exposure of such things as would surprise and mortify, become necessary to prevent the public from being deceived, and in consequence entirely separated from its best friends, friends whom ambition or resentment have not made the opposers of the person in question? These inquiries may seem to militate very much with the sentiments of my letter to Mr. Goodrich. I take no pains to appear consistent; as things appear when I write, I represent them to you. On execution, the decision of the point in this state would be less favourable to discussion than Jersey or Connecticut. Yet I will not pretend that I have made up my opinion as to the most successful mode of avoiding the great evils with which our country is certainly threatened.

I wish you health and happiness, and am, with sincere esteem, yours, &c.,

FISHER AMES

TO OLIVER WOLCOTT

DEDHAM, AUGUST 3D, 1800

(Private)

MY DEAR SIR,

YOU WILL at length, clearly discern in the gazettes, the whole plan of a certain great man. It is, by prating about impartiality, Americanism, liberty, and equality, to gull the weak among the feds. Half the wealthy can be made to repine that talents without wealth, take the right hand of them. Purse pride works in Boston. They are vexed that an Essex Junto should be more regarded, than the men whose credit in money matters so far outweighs them. The virulent invectives of————, against the British partisans, will please the silly feds, and the cunning Jacobins. These latter well know that such things divide only the former; themselves are as fixed as vice. The federalists scarcely deserve the name of party. Their association is a loose one—formed by accident, and shaken by every prospect of labour or hazard. Such appeals, therefore, to the shallow, the timorous, the envious, the credulous, are always made with some effect. *This man,* I hear, says that the Jacobins will not vote for him. It is therefore, he says, absurd to charge him with courting, or intending to join them. But it is evident from Junius, and other essays, (all of them ill written) that his friends rely on making a third party, neither French nor English—neither federalist nor anti, but *constitutionalist*. This will not form a third party, but it may baffle the federal party. Perhaps a party, whenever it thinks itself strong, naturally splits; nothing but dread of its rival, will bind it firmly enough together.

What is to be done in Massachusetts?—what in other States? Already B. Hichborn gives J. A. the first toast at his table; and no doubt he thinks to get the popularity that the Essex Junto will lose, and rejoices in the good luck the crisis seems to bring him, or being in better company than formerly; but I think the Jacobins will not take the offered alliance. They stick to Jefferson, and will not attach themselves to any man suspected of sticking to right principles, though he may in the hour of his necessity, seem to renounce them. It is not impossible, when they see him too far advanced, to go back, when they see him engaged in a war of offence against the friends of the federal cause, that they will take him up as a tool. Jefferson, the first in power, second in place. Is this possible?

Y'r friend,

FISHER AMES

It seems as if Burr would have little chance, unless by forcing a vote from the Jacobins; that would put Jefferson too much at risk. Foreseeing this, will he not wish to join some other candidate who may need him, and whose friends could make him stand a better chance of being second? He is like Lord Stanley at the battle of Bosworth, ready to act according to circumstances.

TO THOMAS DWIGHT

DEDHAM, AUGUST 15, 1800

MY DEAR FRIEND,

. . . .

I WAS at Newport last Sunday, where I went on law business, and no showers blessed them. They do not count every vote of their state federal, unless they should change the mode of appointing electors, from districts, to a choice by the legislature. Their Governor will be one by the former mode, and not by the latter, and he would probably vote for Adams and Jefferson. Maryland will not alter its mode; it will be seven federal, three *anti*. South Carolina will be all Adams and Pinckney, if they should get a federal legislature chosen, for which an effort is now making. I fear it will fail; then it will be all Jefferson and Burr. On the whole, Mr. Jefferson will surely be elected, unless all New England will unite for Adams and Pinckney. The friends of the President resolve that it shall not be so. They will not have this union, which if they prevent, they will oust Mr. Adams. This, if not victory, will be revenge, because it will oust, or rather prevent the election of, Pinckney. The Feds, in the south, fully rely on our coöperation faithfully and fairly for both, leaving it, as the Constitution has unfortunately left it, to chance, to decide the issue. If South Carolina should be *anti*, I think Jefferson will stand a chance to be chosen, in spite of the *united* opposition of all the Feds throughout the United States. Indeed, I can make no computation how he should fail. If that state should be federal, as there is some hope, then no federal candidate can be elected without their coöperation. How, then, the Adamites can make up a face to charge the

Essex Junto with opposing Adams, and how they can hope to carry his election against the friends of Pinckney in the south, is to me inconceivable. When they fail, they will charge their failure on the Essex Junto, who recommend union for Adams and Pinckney, and not on the Jacobins, who will bring about the event. Will the General Court meet in the same temper they separated, that is, to combine the federal votes for Adams and Pinckney?

MONDAY MORNING

(Private)

I SHOULD NOT be surprised if the Feds, at New York or further south, should be so much provoked by the conduct of the Adamites here, as to attack and expose the capricious, strange excesses of temper, language, and conduct, which have so much distinguished the *Great Man.* What would be the effect?

Yours.

TO RUFUS KING

AUGUST 19, 1800

I PUT myself prodigiously at my ease in writing to you, and as I have a knack of flattering myself, I make it out that you will not dispute my claim. It is exceedingly convenient to me to ascertain my footing—for I struggle with my indolence before I can undertake to write at all, and I believe never fail to write so lackadaysically as to convince my correspondent that I have *not* gained the victory.

I had some thoughts of writing to Gore, but perhaps he is taken and at this moment professing to love soup maigre better than roast beef. I ought and intended to write to Paine to whom I owe every sentiment that belongs of right to a prodigiously clever fellow. But I am sure he w'd curse my politics and wish from his soul I could write the news from Boston. He must excuse me. The Boston fair are not communicative to me and for my life I could not fill a single page with anecdote or scandal, which latter I know he abominates. Therefore it is, excuse me, Hopson's choice to write to you, which I mention as an excuse for obtruding a letter so unlike, as I foresee this will be, to any other that a statesman will receive. Our affairs are so much influenced by tattle and vulgar prejudice that nothing w'd more surely mislead you than the position of correct political principles and the proper inferences from them. Therefore your very wise political correspondents will tell you anything sooner than the truth. For not one of them will look for anything but profound reasons of state at the bottom of the odd superstructure of parties here. There is nothing of the kind at the bottom. There is indeed a good deal of it on the *outside*. In other words, no such reasons are motives, they are pretexts. Calculations of prudence and almost the gift of prophetic foresight are offered as a vindication by some apologists for the mission to France, now established and glorified by Buonaparte's victories. Others pretend that the exorbitant naval power of G. B. is an evil, & a close alliance with France the remedy. Never was there a time when such shallow reasons were imagined to vindicate a thing that did not originate from any reason, but sudden *impulse*, caprice & prejudice. You are no stranger to multitudes, nor to the things that give them their creeds & their passions. Judge how difficult it is for men who never once suspected that they are not of *the multitude* to analyse principles, measures and characters, and who cannot perceive that they ought not to stir when their leader has deserted them. It is incomprehensible to them that any federalists should pretend that the *new* ground he has taken is not the *same* he occupied before he openly accused his friends and awkwardly tried to win his adversaries. They never knew *where* they were, they only knew who was *with* them and *before* them. This confusion of ideas, so natural to those who have but few of them, has animated the State street patriots of our metropolis. I mean nothing disrespectful to them in the observation, for I think them clever & well informed. But though abundantly capable of reasoning, they are like seven eighths of mankind, too much at ease to submit to so irksome a task. Opinions that lie on the surface are better than such as are in the mine, and are to be had only by hard digging. Popular opinions too defend themselves and give fees to their advocates. But such as are sound and profound require labor to find and Courage, Patience and Talent to maintain. Boston, like the rest of the world, is impressible and is impressed.

There is no doubt that our Legislature was strongly disposed to choose electors to vote for Adams & P. But since a certain Great Man returned from the seat of gov't, the clamor has been loud that he is to be sacrificed and tricked out of his place. The Essex Junto is cursed and lampooned. Now, what is to be the consequence? apparently this. Unless South Carolina should be federal, (and an effort is making to elect a federal state legislature,) Jefferson will have a majority and be chosen. Unless the federalists unite and run the *two* federal candidates, Jeff: will have more than either of them, though perhaps not a majority. On the whole it is highly probable that Jeff: will be elected. Every thing smoaks with political fermentation in the U. S. You must watch and pray for the country, that we may not have a war with G. B. which would augment the danger of revolution exceedingly, both to

G. B. & the U. S. The former may be again in a state to dread this danger more than it does at present. The U. S. have yet to learn almost all that experience can teach. Our govt. is republican, our opinions democratic. The latter must rise or the former will sink.

Yrs. truly,

INCOG. [FISHER AMES]

AUGUST 26, 1800

2d Sheet

THE FRIENDS of a certain great man are trying to rouse the revolutionary spirit, to awaken personal local party and national prejudices to secure for him the concentration of all the chances of the political game. It is obvious that wd. make the chance of the federal cause the worse and *his* not the better unless by some miracle people who do not prefer him wd. act just as if they did. Inclinations are not to be thus put in requisition, and so many from their souls dislike and dread the caprices, prejudices and resentments which seem to have acquired a despotic power over him, that it is impossible to extort a vote from them in favor of such a man unless by faithfully complying with the *agreement* fairly and equally to vote for the other. No doubt you will have read Harper's letter to his constituents. In that is stated the vote to be given by the federalists. But every intrigue and probably rage enough to spoil it will be practised to gain over our legislature which is to meet on the first of November to choose electors who will vote for Mr. A. and throw away their votes for some other person than General P. This will be known beforehand and will inevitably divert some southern votes from Mr. A. which wd. otherwise be given to him. Thus Mr. Jeff's election seems to be almost certain unless the electors will stand to the agreement made at Philadelphia to vote for *both*. If Gov. McKean and Dallas shd. effect their design of sacking a legislature, all Pennsylvania will be thrown into that scale. Mr. Jeff. will have nearly 70 on the best calculation that we can make, and any dependence on So. Carolina is very precarious. If the coast should be as bad as we apprehend, all hopes of seeing the country safe in the enjoyment of property or Constitution must ultimately rest in the spirit and union of men of principle. The measures pursued by the friends of Mr. A. tend to dissipate this last hope. On the contrary the compromise to vote for Gen. P. and Mr. A. affords a good ground for harmony now, acquiescence hereafter in the success of either Mr. P. or Mr. A., and energy and zeal if Mr. J. shd. be elected. Therefore on the whole I cannot but think that a truth so obvious so deeply important will extort respect and obedience from our legislature and that they will choose electors who will vote for both. Even Mr. A.'s friends wd. see, if rage would let them see anything, that by pursuing the object of throwing away P.'s votes they will infallibly exclude Mr. A. It is intended that the race shall be a fair one, all the federal electors voting for *both*, thus leaving it to chance and to Congress to decide which shall be President. But if one of the two will persist in playing foul, the consequence must be that his chance will be made as bad as it ought for that reason to be. Whether Mr. A. is willing to be Vice under Jeff is a problem and opinions in respect to its solution are various. He acts as if he did not hate nor dread Jeff—and it is clear that his friends pursue a course in conversation and in the papers which can help nobody's cause but Jefferson's. Indeed the Adams writers offer to fraternise with Jacobins whom they denominate old friends, and openly rail agt. the "exclusive federalists," "Hamiltonians," "Essex Junto," "Royalists,"

"British partizans," as they affect to call the men who stick to the good old principles and old cause. These facts, some queer toasts and a number of whisper'd anecdotes corroborate but fall short of fully proving the opinion that a *coalition* has been made and that if Mr. A. shd. be only Vice it wd. be revenge if not victory.

The tendency of our politics to intestine troubles is obvious. These wd. spring from the same causes that lead to a British War. Good Lord defend us from both. Buonaparte's successes are believed here to produce coldness towds. promising our envoys compensation. Very good. Will Austria make peace? If the minister shd. be inquisitive to know my opinion, which may possibly be the case, you may tell him not to be afraid, but to fight on alone till France is exhausted, weary and humbled. That the cause of the war was the exorbitant power of France, that her increase of territory, the subjugation of Spain, Italy, Holland, Belgium and Switzerland and the exclusion of all spirit from her people but the military and the enthusiastic exaltation of *that*, are so many aggravations of the original evil, and that of course it is foolish to consider the remedy as springing out of the monstrous growth of the evil; that a state of danger shd. become a state of security merely by the augmentation of the danger. Therefore he must war till peace is safe and tell his Englishmen to pay and fight on till that time comes without ever stopping to think or enquire when that will be.

Yours truly,

INCOG. [FISHER AMES]

TO ALEXANDER HAMILTON

DEDHAM, AUGUST 26, 1800

DEAR SIR,

I HAVE communicated your letter by Mr. Coolidge to Mr. Cabot and two or three friends. I have desired him, and he has promised, to write to you on the subject. Since its reception, I have had a long, profoundly sensible and interesting letter from Mr. Wolcott. The same friends have also considered that, and we all agree in the result.

We understand that, at the close of the late session, the federalists consulted on the measures proper to be taken by the friends of order and true liberty, to keep the chair from being occupied by an enemy of both. This was the principal object, to which all inferior considerations must be made to yield. It was known and allowed that Mr. A[dams] had conducted strangely and unaccountably, and that his reëlection would be very inauspicious to the United States. But, great as that evil appeared, it was thought indispensably necessary to run the risk of it, and to agree fairly to vote for him and General P[inckney], because chance might exclude the former, and because any other arrangement would, by dividing the party, inevitably exclude both, and absolutely secure the success of Mr. Jefferson; and because, also, many, perhaps most, of the federalists will believe, it is better to have him, Mr. A[dams], again, than Mr. Jefferson. The question being, not what opinion we must have of the candidates, but what conduct we are to pursue, I do not see cause to arraign the policy of the result of that meeting.

For, in the first place, it is manifestly impossible to get votes enough for General P. to prevent the choice of Mr.

Jefferson, in case he should be supported in open hostility to Mr. A. The sixteen votes of this State, and four of Rhode Island, may be counted as adhering, in all events, to Mr. A. Then why should we ground any plan of conduct on a known impracticability of its execution? By taking that course of open hostility, generous as it may seem, we are at issue with all the federalists who would not join us, and whose vexation and despair would ascribe the certain ill success of the party to us, and not to the Jacobins. They would say *we* make Mr. J[efferson] President, and the vindictive friends of Mr. A. would join in the accusation. The federalists would be defeated, which is bad, and disjointed and enraged against one another, which would be worse. Now it seems to me, that the great object of duty and prudence is, to keep the party strong, by its union and spirit. For I see almost no chance of preventing the election of Mr. Jefferson. Pennsylvania will be managed eventually by Governor McKean and Governor Dallas, to throw its whole weight into that scale. The question is not, I fear, how we shall fight, but how we and all federalists shall fall, that we may fall, like Antæus, the stronger for our fall.

It is, I confess, awkward and embarrassing, to act under the constraints that we do. But sincerity will do much to extricate us. Where is the inconsistency of saying, President A. has not our approbation of some of his measures, nor do we desire his reëlection: but many federalists do, and the only chance to prevent the triumph of the Jacobins, is to unite, and vote according to the compromise made at Philadelphia, for the *two* candidates? That this gives an equal chance, and a better than we would freely give to one of them. But, strong as our objections are, and strongly as we could, and are willing to, urge them to the public, we refrain, because the effect of urging them would be to split the federalists, and absolutely to insure Mr. Jefferson's success. That, however, if the rancorous and absurd attacks of Mr.

A.'s personal friends, and the meditated intrigues with our legislature, should make it necessary, we shall not fail to prevent the effect of that compromise which they thus abuse, and turn against the avowed design of those who made it; and that we shall not sit still, but resort to such measures as they will render necessary. That this compromise not only exhibits the condescension and pliancy of Mr. A.'s opposers, but is the only good basis of the success of either Mr. A.'s or General P.'s friends in the event, as it engages beforehand for the acquiescence of the disappointed part of the federalists, and also as it is the only step that can unite them to oppose the election of a Jacobin, and, in that sad event, it can keep them united as a party, without whose union, oppression and revolution will ensue.

Where is the absurdity or inconsistency of this language? It is, besides, that which we have held for some time, and it is difficult now to change it.

I am therefore clear, that *you* ought not, with your name, nor, if practicable, in any way that will be traced to *you*, to execute your purpose of exposing the reasons for a change of the executive. But a strong appeal to the sense and principles of the real federalists would not, or need not, contradict or discredit the language above stated. I have tried to compress as much as I can into one sheet. But I have much more I wish to suggest to you. I have no occasion to say how highly I respect your judgment, but I exceedingly desire to discuss with you the point of the changes which the Jacobins may force the nation to make, in the plan of the government.[98]

Yours, truly.

---

[98] *It is proper to say that the above is printed from a copy, and that the Editor only conjectures, from the evidence of its contents, that it was addressed to Hamilton.* [S. AMES] [*The present version has been corrected from the manuscript.* ED.]

TO THOMAS DWIGHT

BOSTON, AUGUST 29, 1800.—FRIDAY

MY DEAR FRIEND,

. . . .

THE *antis* rise in hopes and insolence, on the bad result of the Essex election, and that still worse in Worcester. A bad House of Representatives, and a Jacobin President, would be too much.

Mr. Adams's friends do not know, but they ought to know, that the loss of any federal votes will certainly prevent his election; that the only ground on which they can or ought to expect them, is the *agreement* made at Philadelphia, honorably and fairly to run General Pinckney with Mr. Adams, and that, if they show an intention to fall from that agreement, Mr. Adams will have no federal votes in Jersey, Delaware, or Carolina. Whether the labor I have been at to display this consequence to *some* of them, will stop the current of their rash and silly newspaper eloquence, I know not. *Quem Deus vult perdere, prius dementat.*

Yours.

TO ALEXANDER HAMILTON

DEAR SIR,

THE situation we are in, though not unexpected by a few, has filled the public with equal surprise and terror. The votes, Rhode Island excepted, have been given in a manner to take away that sort of reproach from the *Hamiltonians*, that momentary interests and the petulance of disappointment would otherwise have naturally thrown upon us. I discern symptoms of general wish to pass an act of oblivion, and to unite in self-defense against oppression, the danger of which folly persisted in refusing to discover, so long as there was, in reference to the election, any utility in thinking right, and acting together.

While we had a real or reputed federal head, weak men could see no danger, except in *over* federalism. Supposing the government to have, intrinsically, ample means of self-defense, and it being in federal hands, all, they thought, was safe, unless the men in power should govern too much and carry things too far. True patriots ought to lean against the administration, according to their opinions and feelings. This political hypercriticism is soothing to the weak, who happen to be vain, and are not yet found out, or do not know that they are. It passes for independence of spirit, for superior sense and virtue. This sort of vanity makes bad federalists as well as many democrats; it has inspirited the assault, and dispirited the defence, of the cause. It is only at times when people are very heartily afraid of their adversary, that they are well united to their party. That time has come: and all the talent, patriotism, and worth, and weight of character, in the country, ought now to be in requisition to save it. You are no stranger to my just estimate of the importance of your services and talents, and of the like importance of the country's relying on them and claiming them. I will not say that you could have delayed or suppressed your book, or that its ultimate effects will not be salutary. But, though I think it one of your best written performances, there existed more unlucky momentary causes to make it unacceptable to federal men, than any thing you ever wrote. In political affairs, few speak so much from respect for truth as for *stage effect*. In the sphere of politics,

"All would be gods and rush into the skies."

The disclosure of truth implies previous ignorance. Few dwell on faults that they do not claim to have discovered, and those they exaggerate. Your book told less than *we* knew, because you would not charge, I suppose, more than you could prove. It told more than others would admit they had to learn, and especially those who extol the man who is the subject of your writing. Yet it is amusing to hear many begin thus: Mr. Adams has his faults, we know; then conceding ten or twenty, such as are fatal to his political reputation,—yet why should General H. come out now with his pamphlet, to divide and distract the federal councils? It was insidious, unfair, and deeply, rancorously hostile. You well know there is no such thing as persuading people to believe or doubt, against their inclinations. It has, therefore, been the opinion of your friends, that the facts stated must be left to operate on the public mind; and that the rage of those whom they wound, will give them currency. At no very distant day, every right impression will be made; and it is not clear that it would be made the sooner for our sustaining, in the *newspapers,* the results that ought to be drawn from your facts. In conversation, we have been explicit enough, and our legislature was pretty extensively impressed with our sentiments. Mr. Cabot and I would readily say or write any proper thing in vindication of your character, if it were necessary. But we justly deem it superior to the prejudices against you, which have been spread with much art and some success. You know the cause and most of the pretexts. The Jacobins admit that you are their most dreaded adversary, and they greatly enjoy it, that the station unanimously assigned to you by your enemies, should torment and distract *their* enemies. These, however, are, I trust and hope, only temporary prejudices, which, with their author and the occasion, are already on the wane.

It is exceedingly important that the federalists should unite. The soundness of their councils, and their success in impressing the public, will probably depend upon you as much in future as in time past.[99]

TO HON. BENJAMIN GOODHUE

DEDHAM, SEPTEMBER 13TH, 1800

DEAR SIR

YOUR OFFER to act for me in the insuring business has great influence [on] my judgment in favor of it. The great profit derived from it of late will no doubt increase the competition and reduce the premiums. Nevertheless, knowing your experience and good judgment and relying as I do on your friendship, I request you to underwrite in my name at the insurance office kept by Mr. King on such risks as you do for yourself. By following your steps or Mr. Norris's I shall be sure that there is no want either of due caution or discernment. Therefore when you or he underwrite I shall not fear to do it. But I would not have more than five hundred dollars underwritten on any one risk, nor in the whole beyond fifteen thousand dollars at risk at the same time. I have some habits and like most other men rather more maxims of caution and prudence, and I have sometimes a little flinched from the purpose of trusting it to fortune, in her worst temper, to

---

[99] *This letter is taken from a sheet marked "Copy of my letter." It is apparently incomplete.* [S. AMES]

strip me. Within the limits I have prescribed, I shall not do it, and if my risks are small and of course greatly multiplies I do not see how fortune, unless she should have both eyes and malice, and then she would be no longer fortune, can subject me to very great losses, or with such caution on my part allow me very great profits. As Mr. Norris underwrites for you when you are absent, I hope he will also then do it for me, conforming to the principles I have laid down.

It is unnecessary to assure you that I accept your proposal as an obliging proof of your regard and that I shall be grateful whatever the event may prove.

I am dear sir, yours truly

FISHER AMES

TO RUFUS KING

SEPTEMBER 24, 1800

MY DEAR SIR:

YOU WILL be anxious to hear from the U. S. at this eventful crisis. You will have other letters than mine, and I do not know whether the light I may shed will lessen your anxiety or curiosity. I am so much plagued with my prudence when I write that I always make out to be stupid, though I generally miss of being cautious. It is indeed running a risk to send free thoughts in a letter so far and across the sea where so many pirates may happen to furnish so much entertainment to as many pimps if they shd. intercept this. It is ten to one you will not thank me for addressing such letters as I must, if I express the thoughts of my heart to you, as the receiver may be inculpated as well as the author. Perhaps you may not think as I do, but I will try to be communicative and hope that this will reach you safely.

It is not easy to describe our political state nor perhaps to do it with any clearness, unless by some delineation of character and a bold exposure of weaknesses. The classification of parties is not to be made out in any other way— especially as they appear in this scene.

Whether there is any ground, (and if any whether there is much) for the coalition charged upon the two heads of parties I will not decide. I think there is rather too much complacency on the part of our man towards his antagonist, and too little towds. the intended second of the former. This proceeds from several causes—but chiefly from the lofty idea he entertains of his own superior wisdom and greatness which disdains to have either for a second or a successor any less personage than the *first* of the other side. He has also a strong revolutionary taint in his mind, admires the characters, principles and means which that revolutionary system exacts and for a short period seems to legitimate, and as you know holds cheap any reputation that was not *then* founded and top'd off. Accordingly he respects his rival and the Gazette here, absolutely devoted to him and in the hands of his personal friends exclusively, is silent and has been for some months in respect to that rival. His irreligion, wild philosophy and gimcrackery in politics are never mentioned. On the contrary the great man has been known to speak of him with much regard, and an affected indignation at the charge of irreligion, asking what has that to do with the public and adding that he is a good patriot, citizen and father. The good lady his wife has been often talkative in a similar strain, and she is as complete a politician as any lady in the old French court.

Besides these motives, vindictive feelings will concur to disappoint those who would disappoint him, and to be excluded by his own party would be justly more mortifying than to be ousted by a majority on the side of his rival. How much character is expected to be patched up by a little courtship of the other party you may infer from his saying that the measure which has so much afflicted us all is the most glorious act of his life and he will order it engraven on his tomb stone. His partizans boast of its popularity and that only a very few like Hamilton and the Essex Junto condemn it. It is also true that the Jacobins allow that the act was good, though they intimate that it's motive was to gain them, and not a sincere right principle.

The man I allude to is too much the creature of *impulse* or freakish humour—he is a revolutionist from temperament, habit and lately what he thinks policy—he is too much irritated against many if not most of the principal sound men of the country ever to bestow on them *his* confidence or to retrieve *theirs*. In particular he is implacable against a certain great little man whom we mutually respect. With so much less than the old & requisite harmony with the best friends of the country, he has certain antipathies and prejudices connected with them that are equally strange, stubborn & pernicious. He really thinks it a light matter to have a war with G. B. as he hates that governt. in every thing but it's theory, believes it corrupt and affects to believe it possesses *influence* here; he can scarcely refrain and he seldom tries to refrain from inveighing against British influence, and to conciliate to himself the mob honors that cant will obtain. He does not hesitate to say that public debt wd. go down and paper money come up in that case. But he loves to bluster and vapor about the courage he once displayed when *he* was not afraid of that great power when we had not half our present force. He has the *os magne soniturum* and with all the ignorance of men & business that must belong to the possessor of the before mentioned tenets, he indulges the vanity, so much his favorite & his master.

The effect of having him at our head is for you and everyone to consider. The Jacobins plainly say they prefer him to his intended second. It is plain they choose we should be without a head or with one that will not fit the shoulders.

Accordingly I have long thought it probable that the leader of the Jacobins willing to hide behind his rival's back will not be sorry to see him prefer'd, believing that he will be only nominal chief, that the ruin of the Feds by discord & inefficiency will be safely and securely procured, while he, the second, would be safe not responsible, yet actually the ruler, and that by flattery the other might be inclined and by blowing up his resentments against his federal supporters, *driven* to may acts of jacobinism. Policy so refined will not prevent this man from ousting the present occupant if he can. But if he can discern beforehand that his own chance is desperate, I am almost sure the Jacobins will vote for the present rather than to let Gen. P. be chosen. The votes, as we now count them, will be nearly equally divided. South Carolina is yet uncertain as the legislature is not elected and many adverse contingencies may lessen our number. On the whole, it is probable that J. will be elected; if he cannot be, that A. will be voted for by many Jacobins and therefore his chance is the next best. People differ much on this subject and few believe as I do that the Jacobins will act as I have settled in case of their despairing of their first object.

J's election will greatly endanger our peace abroad, and order at home. The prejudices of another will perhaps with an equally bad tendency towards war dispose him to neglect every proper & reasonable step to secure peace and to take affront & sound the tocsin on the first cause of irritation given by B. Take care of our peace. I should think the present desponding crisis in B. affairs a good moment for adjusting matters of difference with them.

My former letters have probably stated my conjectures respecting the votes in New England. Some foolish writers in the Gazettes have tried their talents to divide the Feds and with some success at first. The better knowledge of the subject which has been spread more by conversation than in print has mended public opinion a good deal and I now have hopes, though I am less sanguine than most others, that our Legislature will act right.

Newspaper essays have not been much resorted to and it is thought would irritate. We have been and still are placed in a difficult pass. You will not get half as much information as you desire, because probably not one of your correspondents will be "so loose of thought" as I have been. I take no thought beforehand what I shall write and will thank you to burn this immediately after perusal.

SEPTEMBER 26

I have just seen a gentleman of South Carolina who says that his intelligence from there is very recent & very encouraging, that a federal legislature is confidently expected to be chosen in October and that the votes will be fairly, liberally and faithfully given to the two federal candidates.

FISHER AMES

TO JOHN RUTLEDGE

———

DEDHAM, OCTOBER 16TH, 1800

MY DEAR SIR

THINGS remain here as they were when you left us, and I do not know that any event has since occurred materially to vary the conjectures we then formed. I understood that very illiberal, and as we know very indiscreet essays have issued from the Commercial Gazette, but my professional business has hindered my reading the sixth part of them. They at least evince that the writing and their [practices] are no more worse or patriotic than formerly.

Every exertion will be made by the friends of the country to produce in our legislature the only result of their meeting that can be useful. I expect success. You understand our position and you will of course make it understood where it ought to be. The negotiation at Paris "like a needless [headless?] Alexand[rine]" still drags its slow length along.

The man is a fool who expects from it effective compensation, and few doubt or deny that the delay is a finesse to influence our great election. Our maiden republican honor has a skin thicker than a sea cow's hide. Like the behemoth it laughs at the arrows of insult. This callousness is called by some philosophy, by others prudent policy. I believe that if a nation will not guard its honor, it will not keep it, and that after having lost it will not retrieve it. Whether anything can be done will appear when Congress meets. I have no doubt public opinion is far from being correct, and that will ever be the case when the government gives little tone or a bad one to it. This I am persuaded of that our motley policy takes from our counsels almost all power over events and exposes us to the action of the most [audacious]. I also believe that it does almost every thing to excite faction within to assail public order, and disarm gov't of quite all its means of self defense. As you are better informed on this said subject than I pretend to be, I forbear going into any details.

Spirited speeches might do a good deal towards correcting and rousing public sentiment; whether enough is very doubtful. I pray God that we may have four years of a truly federal presidency to delay the crisis of the public evils, now impending, and to apply remedies. The correction of federal opinion and the excitement of federal zeal ought to be attempted. Some gentlemen here and in Connecticut contemplate the establishment of a very able federal gazette in Boston. The decision is now maturing and ought to be effected. But whether a gazette will be the oracle or the dupe of its readers is not hard to conjecture. Their prejudices, as soon as known, will be courted, vindicated and enforced. Like a thermometer, it will show what the weather is, but will not make it better. Printers are dependent for bread, writers for popularity—neither will dare to tell any truth that readers will not like to hear. I like the design however and will not make these remarks where they will damp it. My paper is out. & may you let me hear from you.

Yours most sincerely,

FISHER AMES

TO JOHN RUTLEDGE (WRITTEN ON BEHALF OF AMES BY GEORGE CABOT)

BROOKLINE NEAR BOSTON,
OCTOBER 22, 1800

DEAR SIR—

MR. AMES being engrossed at this moment by his professional business in the circuit court has put into my hands your letter of the 16th with an injunction to answer your enquiry respecting the probable result of the presidential election in New England.

I have been informed by gentlemen who have conversed on the subject with some of the most influential men in New Hampshire that the vote of that state will be unanimous for Adams & Pinckney; in this state (Massachusetts) you know the opposition to a united vote which has been unremittingly kept up from the moment it was proposed. I think however the language of that party has changed a little & that many of them now admit that inasmuch as Mr. Adams's election is not absolutely certain we ought for the sake of the federal cause to avail ourselves of this double chance. I have ever believed that our legislature would appoint such electors as would vote for Mr. Pinckney as well as for Mr. Adams—this belief is founded principally upon a view of the manifest propriety of the measure which can hardly be mistaken by unprejudiced men, such as compose a good majority of that body.—great pains will be taken no doubt—great pains will be taken to infuse into them a portion of that spirit which Mr. Adams's personal friends, or rather some of them have exhibited in this vicinity;—the success of these attempts cannot be calculated with anything like certainty until the legislature meets, but as far as my information goes it incourages the expectation that the majority will be uninfluenced by personal predilections & will act upon true national principles.—every sensible man I think will be easily convinced that the obligation to act in concert with the friends of gov't. thro' the Union, tho' not absolute, is very strong.— in our wide extended country a constant regard to this principle is essential to give efficasy to the will of the wise & good if they are a majority, & to give them any thing like security if they are not.—on the whole I calculate that our votes will be certainly all for Adams & probably all for Pinckney—if this shou'd appear when the electors are named I think you may consider the votes of Connecticut as certainly all for Pinckney & probably all for Adams but if it should appear that Massachusetts hesitates to support Pinckney Connecticut may be expected to withhold votes from Adams.—I am assured in the most unequivocal manner by the best informed man in Connecticut that their discontents with Mr. Adams are deep & very extensive—the leading men in that state have according to their old maxims made it a point to illustrate the merits which they supposed Mr. Adams to possess, in such a manner as to fix his popularity upon a firm basis—they think now Mr. Adams's conduct does not correspond to the ideas which they themselves had formed of him & upon patriotic principles had propagated among the people—they feel themselves deserted by him & are extremely chagrined—if they support him it will be with reluctance & under the apprehension that if he is re-elected the administration of our national affairs will be less safe & less stable than ever.—

You know everything of Rhode Island that is at present known to anyone & I am altogether uninformed of the state of parties in Vermont except that the general impression here is that the vote will be for Adams & Pinckney.—

With sentiments of great esteem &
[unfeigned] respects I am Dear sir
your most obed. svt.

GEORGE CABOT

TO JOHN RUTLEDGE

DEDHAM, DECEMBER 15TH, 1800

(in confidence)

MY DEAR SIR

I HAVE MADE all the use of your letters that the seasonableness and value of their contents enabled me to do. I have been justly sensible of the distinction conferred upon me by your confidence involving that of other federalists anxious with you to preserve the public order at this crisis. I have been,

I may assure you, discreet as well as active. The legislature of Mass'tts entered fully into the views of those who recommended the *joint* vote for Gen'l. P. with Mr. A., although it is said, and I do not know that it is denied, that the Jacobins acted with *a certain set* to recommend a very different list of electors. General Knox was deemed irresistible on that list but, on trial, his supporters were few, except the Jeffersonians. As you understand the subject I will not tire you with the explanation, though it would seem to persons, wholly ignorant of our political state here, so much a paradox as to need a good deal of solution. Probably it will be necessary to explain and [impress] the wisdom and fairness of the federal manner of proceeding so as to soothe the federalists who have been made angry and to satisfy those who are puzzled with the complexity and obscurity of the reasons on which we acted. It is extremely necessary to keep the public with us and above all things persuaded that we give them our true principles and grounds of conduct. In that view, Gen. Hamilton's pamphlet appears to me not without its uses. We had been charged as constrained pretending to approve Mr. A's administration, yet really preferring Gen. P. Explanations, though unpleasant, are generally less so than remnants of suspicion. The worst of the former comes first; the latter sours the subject and spoils it. If Mr. A should be chosen, which I take for a thing certain, it will be highly proper and useful that the Feds should preserve their identity as well as power, and that their principles should not be discredited nor overpowered. As a party they may have to save the country from a British war and the evils to our commerce, credit & finances which would follow that disaster. Believing it as unnecessary as formidable, I wish that good men may be on their guard against the irritations which the unfortunate propensities of a certain great man permit him as little to soften *after* they occur as to prevent by foresight & wisdom *before*. Why the spoliation & debt business sleeps so quietly

I cannot pretend to say. To one, "who know little of diplomacy," it appears that more than one period has occurred to favor the settlement of the dispute. Our country is said to be in G.B. under the reproach of bad faith, while the bad aspect of British affairs wd. so much enforce any moderate attempts on our part to adjust matters.

I will not scruple to add, as you already know my whole course of thinking on the main subject, that in case Gen. P. should be elected vice prsd't., as I expect, great prudence will be needed by the federalists. The assurance was generally enough given here that another election wd. not be expected by Mr. ———. This I well know goes for nothing but good men must look about them and decide with wisdom and caution on the language they adopt. Gen. P. is not wanting in prudence. I believe those who say that with a soldiery worth, honor, & frankness he is eminently gifted in *prudence*. To steer clear of blame in his place without changing his principles or making them suspected will be important. If for four years we can prevent an explosion by a Jacobin rebellion and keep the true friends of the country vigilant & firm, we may do well afterwards.

In the union, energy, and resistance of the federalists resides the strength that is to save all. These have been impaired and dissipated, but may be retrieved. The attempt must be made and never abandoned. To influence opinion that rules everything, we must be alert in availing ourselves of those engines that rule *it*. Speeches, newspapers & pamphlets are powerful means. I much commend the skill and spirit of your pamphlet makers at Charlestown. The success evinces my observation of the efficacy of writings. The Boston Mercury is to be enlarged and used as a federal paper not much unlike the Antijacobin. I doubt however whether as much industry and talent will appear to support it as the pamphlets you so kindly sent to me evince. They are all handsome performances. While you grow better in S.

Carolina I fear we degenerate. But the election of a president is a time to bring out all the bad humors of the political body and to spoil such as are sweet and kindly. After this agitation has subsided, I try to flatter myself with the hope of a few months of public tranquillity. I hope you will extend the judiciary power and widen the basis of the gov't before the end of the session.

I assure you that I do not attempt to express any thanks for your obliging letters because I cannot do it as I ought without enlarging inconveniently on the good they have done by my communication of the substance of them.

(remainder of ms. missing)

TO OLIVER WOLCOTT

DEDHAM, DECEMBER 15, 1800

MY DEAR SIR,

IT GRIEVES every thoughtful friend of the country that you should be placed in a situation which you think you ought to renounce. If the fault was generally known to lie where I suppose it does lie, it would greatly increase the displeasure that is already felt. Who will succeed you, or how our affairs are to proceed in future, when a man born in office with the government, so attached to it, and as familiarly acquainted with it as you are, receives from the head of the government such uncomfortable and discouraging treatment, though not personally affrontive, I know not. The very Jacobins abuse you with measured moderation, and allow me to say (it really is my opinion, and I would not insult you with flattery) that those whose good opinion you would value were progressively raising their esteem and respect for your character. The success of governments depends on the selection of the men who administer them. It seems as if the ruling system would rob the country of all chance, by excluding the only classes proper to make the selection from.

I wish to use the liberty of writing to you more fully than I now have time to do. If Mr. A. and P. should fill the two first places, the conduct and language of the federalists will demand much thought and prudence. To keep the party unbroken, while the head has interests and feelings separate from and hostile to it, and will be angry for the risks he has run of losing his election, will be a hard task and yet a necessary one.

The newspaper to be established in Boston will be a craving thing on my time and industry, and I shall desire from you and others at the seat of government, occasionally, any hints for filling up the part which I shall take in it; it will be a small part, but by a right manner of managing that paper some good may be done.

I am, dear sir, with great esteem,
yours truly,

FISHER AMES

TO HON. BENJAMIN GOODHUE

DEDHAM, DECEMBER 16, 1800

MY DEAR SIR

I HAVE a thousand dollars I would invest in the new ship for India Captain Birchmore, if you think the chance such as you would recommend to a friend and I would add another thousand in case Mr. Gray should be perfectly willing to advance so much of the effects belonging to me in his hands. You may in my name ask him if you think it no way improper and receive it of him for which this letter may be shown to him as an order. Please to advise me on the whole subject, and whether the storms of the elements or of our politics have threatened the insurance office with loss. My money lies in the branch bank ready for you when you signify that you have occasion for it. Dollars are not to be had in Boston without a premium, and are scarce.

Mr. Adams is I think elected. How will matters go—will the Jacobins withdraw all their praises, and abuse him till he thinks his old friends better than his new ones? Will the federalists remain divided as of late, or join if the foe should be very formidable and try the chance of war after losing that of suffrages?

Will you write to Dwight Foster and sound him whether he would accept the chief justiceship of the Common Pleas and the probacy in case the latter should be vacant, as I am told it certainly will be. Mr. Foster is the fittest man, yet I am not authorized by the Governor to ask this question. I have indeed told him that I thought Mr. Foster ought to be the man. It would not be necessary for him to resign his place as Senator unless the probate commission were also given him. All this in confidence.

I smile sometimes to hear Hamilton and his book condemned by men who go on to find fault with the President at least as heartily. They seem to admit the weight of no objections except such as they make themselves. I sincerely desire to hear of Mrs. Goodhue's better health. Please to offer to her Mrs. Ames's best wishes with my own.

Your friend etc.

FISHER AMES

TO THOMAS DWIGHT

DEDHAM, DECEMBER 27, 1800

MY DEAR FRIEND,

.   .   .   .

Our General Court has, and merits, the praise of well doing; and due care ought to be taken to prevent the sons of Belial from turning the good men out next spring. It will be attempted; and probably, nay, certainly, Governor Strong will be violently assailed. Hampshire must do as well as it has done. . . . . .

. . . The weather is mild since Jefferson was elected; but it is an unwholesome and treacherous softness, that seizes the windpipe like an assassin. Storms will succeed, and find us relaxed. Is not this an emblem of the smooth hypocrisy with which his reign will begin, as well as of its inevitable rigor and agitation?

TO CHRISTOPHER GORE

DECEMBER 29, 1800

MY DEAR FRIEND,

You will hear, with surprise and grief, the event of the election. While evils are in prospect, it is right to aggravate their magnitude and our apprehensions; after they are arrived, to make the best of them. Bad is the best. At the distance you are placed from the scene and the actors here, you will be ready to find more fault with us than you would had you been here. One, at least, of your correspondents has his reasons for thinking *we* were unconciliating and violent. The truth is, we were assaulted, rashly and unaccountably, by the head of the party, and we stood in our own defence with as much temper, forecast, and spirit, as men could. Scarcely any political transaction has seemed to me, on a retrospect, so little liable to the reproach of bad play. Judge whether the utter ruin of the federal cause, and of all federalists, was not in train, when the accusations against them were such as you heard with your own ears. He now denies it all; and a young man, his secretary, told General Marshall, he was *authorized* to deny it. This was in reply to what General M. said, that the hardest thing for federalists to bear was the charge of British influence. You will make your own comments on the contradiction. How he will act in his retirement, whether he will approve attacks on the muck heap of finance, on the impostures and swindling of banks; whether he will recommend paper money, and a war with Great Britain; whether he will permit himself to be made governor, or nominated as minister to France or Great Britain, you may amuse yourself with conjecturing. The plan of jointly and equally supporting Adams and Pinckney, met with all the opposition from him and his personal friends, and from the Commercial Gazette, that could be made, and with all the virulence that could give an edge to their passions. Now it appears that South Carolina would willingly have voted for Jefferson and Pinckney; but General and Major P., with singular good faith and honor, adhered to the compact, and rejected the offer. This forms a strong contrast with the conduct of Rhode Island, where, it is believed, *two* votes were thrown away from P. Such a fact will discredit New England; will check any future alliances with South Carolina;

will tend to make Rhode Island separate itself from federalism, especially as Governor Fenner is *anti*, and the *novus ordo seclôrum* will augment Jacobin propensities. The folly, levity, and bad faith of the two electors, who thus threw away their votes, are now conspicuous. For had not the honor and probity of the Pinckneys prevented the vote of South Carolina from being as above, Pinckney and Jefferson would have been equal, 73 and 73, and Congress would make P. President.

The excellent conduct of the Pinckneys will be long and warmly applauded in New England, and, I hope, make the basis of true federalism broader than ever. While the eastern states have grown worse, I verily believe the southern have grown better, and even the *antis* here feel a little sore that the eastern states have lost the Presidency. To support and commend even Jefferson, will be against their old malcontent habits and feelings. It remains also to be seen, whether, if Burr and Jefferson are equal, the former will not be preferred by Congress. It is the subject of discourse. It is said he is preferable, has the more energy of the two, and will keep the government together, if he can wield it. I consider it, however, as bravado, and that the Feds will not contest, if the equality of the votes should furnish the occasion, Jefferson's presidency. Madison is agreed on as Secretary of State among the *antis*. But other places are said to be undecided on. Gallatin pants for Wolcott's place, now or soon to be vacant. Stoddert will go out, and, probably enough, the navy and the department be abolished together. Dexter is not expected to quit *voluntarily*, and I think he will not be turned out. Monroe will, if he likes, return to France to embrace liberty again. To go on as formerly in measures, will not suit many of the dominant faction; the anarchists and Jacobins want the government to whirl like a top; the *antis* would amend it to death; the *democrats* would get on by temporizing and coaxing. Jefferson and Madison are, probably, of the latter. The four sorts are now melted together, and seem to be homogeneous; but, as the metal cools, I think all the four ingredients will, in some degree, separate, and appear distinctly. The Lord knows how the interior will be; and the exterior relations will be bad, or we shall try to make them bad.

Formerly, pretty good men thought the government party was rather too violent, and fond of governing too much. It seemed to such blinkers a duty to lean back from the government, and to lend a little countenance to the opposition. Now, the same jockeys will fear the new administration. They will fear for the safety of property and government, and have reason. If these should be attacked, the spirit of the new opposition will be undivided and energetic; and it is very possible that we may find ourselves fitter and more united for the work than for sustaining, as heretofore, the men and measures of our choice. All fears now will be for the safety of all that government has yet erected. Stocks have fallen, and rich men have begun to find out that they ought to bestir themselves. The late discord among federalists will probably subside. The occasion for a civil war between us is past, and there is discretion enough to hold our tongues. We see, however, that much of Jefferson's work is ready done to his hand. We are, by treaty, to embrace France, and Frenchmen will swarm in our porridgepots. Jefferson will say he only supports the friendly system of his predecessor. Had he found things as they were in 1798, it would have been a great and palpable innovation to bring them to the point where he finds them. The federalists are already stigmatized as an oligarchy, a British faction. Hamilton is obnoxious and persecuted by popular clamors, in which federalists, to their shame, join. A war with Great Britain is said to be a cowardly fear, and quite improbable; no matter if it happens. Banks, funding systems, are muck; paper money, a good revolutionary resource; Hancock and Adams forever! These are great advantages for the new administration to start with. Perhaps they are such as pretty naturally flowed from the dominancy of the federal party in 1798. Then they were very strong; and is it not the nature of every party to split, as soon as it becomes greatly superior to its antagonist? On that hypothesis, we may, perhaps, soon profit by the discord of the Jacobins. It is clear that some of them want *no* government, and are anarchists. Some plot for a revolutionary Robespierrism; they are Jacobins, thirsting for blood and plunder. The antifederalists prefer state aristocracies *allied*, not bound closely together. The democrats would trust to the rights of man and chopping logic. Locke and Paine are authorities to direct and enlighten us, and that is all that *citizens* need. Eustis[100] will have a difficult game to play. If he spiritedly supports revenue, navy, and credit, what becomes of Jacobinism?— If he joins in demolishing them, what becomes of his Boston support? On the whole, I hope that, as the elements of the new administration are discordant, they will feel their weakness; and that, when federalists have nothing to do but to *defend*, they will feel and make manifest their strength. I trust they will do it very differently from the Jacobins, and as patriots and good men should. The Palladium, or Massachusetts Mercury, is to be the federal gazette. I pray you send me sometimes pamphlets or papers, to give me just ideas of European politics.

Yours.

---

[100] *Representative in Congress from Boston.* [S. AMES]

1 8 0 1

===

DEDHAM, JANUARY 1, 1801

MY DEAR FRIEND,

. . . .

THEY TALK strongly of preferring Burr to Jefferson. It is said the Feds can decide which shall reign. The Mercury or Palladium is to be the federal paper, and pains must be taken to spread it, and gain readers and patrons in all parts of New England. It languishes hitherto for pecuniary funds. But literary help will be considerable in the beginning, and unless (this in confidence) K., J. L., and F. A., will work for it, the tug will soon become hard. One of the three is very lazy; but as he can and will write when he is, and because he is, there is a chance he will yawn over pieces that will set the readers yawning. All well here.

Yours, with love to friends, &c.

1403

TO JOHN RUTLEDGE

DEDHAM, JANUARY 26TH, 1801

MY DEAR SIR

THE PLEASURE you take in pleasing has led you to state the effect of the little publication inclosed in your last esteemed favor in the manner the most seductive to my vanity. I hope it is not too late to wrench the name *republican* from those who have unworthily usurped it. By doing so, we should augment our strength, which is ever the effect of a [fruitful] display of it. Names and appearances are in party warfare arms and ammunition. It is particularly necessary to contest this name with them now as ardently as the Greeks fought for the body of Patroclus—The *novus ordo seclôrum* must not begin with an impression on the popular mind that we are a disgraced if we are a disappointed party. We must court popular favor, we must study public opinion, and accommodate measures to what it is, and still more to what it ought to be. For that last will remain and uphold us. Spleen, caprice, and vindictive feelings are below our party now and the great duties that devolve upon its leaders.

To oppose has been an easy task. Nobody was answerable for measures, and few cared about the petite guerre of debates and newspaper invectives. Lately we had a man at our head who deserted the cause and assailed his friends & the friends of the country. The state of the federal party has been for the last six or eight months unspeakably imbarrassing and without precedent. If the Jacobins should step into power and act according to their own evil disposition, they would take our burdens and disadvantages on themselves. We should enjoy their late advantages or at least so much of them as our better principles would permit us to avail ourselves of. By exposing the innovations and hostile designs of the Jacobins we should hold forth with the propriety, virtue and sense of the nation—and I trust make it appear that though we had lost the nation we had not lost power over those who hold it. We should appear as strong as ever and stronger than when our strength was paralised as of late. This hope, the only one left us, is inestimable and worth ten times as much as the odds between Jeff. and Burr or on the odds in point of comfort between the frying pan and the fire. Now the Jacobins are free to become answerable for Jeff. but not for Burr. They disclaim this latter and in case he should be elected by Congress and while the surprise of some & the disappointment of others would be lively, they would deeply impress the idea that they were willing to be answerable for B. as vice and only as such, that his preference to J. was a federal trick—a corrupt bargain between B. and the Feds. They wd. ring all the charges on it the old bills, the power, the will, the vengeance of the people and would not the nation acquit them of the liableness for the man they opposed and when he comes to act as much like Clodius as Cato shall we wholly escape the blame[?] I know well the argument that is to be framed in reply. Its truth is one thing—its effect another. Would not Burr array the vagabonds & sans culottes and play the desperado when poverty or ambition or France sh'd invite[?] I shrink from any alliance with Burr. Resentment, the pleasure of revenge, the joke of disappointing the antis is nothing. Jeff. is perhaps not too good, and a French philosophist is bad enough, as bad in principle one would think as it is impossible to be. But B. separated from all party and acting as the occasions wd. prompt might be worse. Therefore if Jeff. wd. provide or only encourage you to expect that he wd. not countenance democratic amendmts., dependence on France, a wrangle or war with G. Britain, plunder of the banks and friends, or Madison's empiricism in regard to trade & navy, wd. it not be safer to take him[?] [Perhaps], if the proud perfidious wd. help our cause his fidelity would leave us free to fortify ourselves in the good will of the people. I think B. is generally purposed here. Yet on the whole I no longer think him preferable. You on the spot can judge best and we shall acquiesce. Will thank you to present my regards to Mr. Mason.

Yrs with perfect regards &c.

FISHER AMES

[P.S.] Suppose the states divided and no election by Congress, are we the gainers? On the contrary, those who seek confusion wd. in that state of things find it. Is not that event so puzzling, so fruitful of intrigue, the best for them, the worst for us— and therefore of all issues of this great business the most to be guarded against[?]

TO DWIGHT FOSTER

DEDHAM, FEBRUARY 9, 1801

(Private)

DEAR SIR,

You HAVE a difficult task to perform on the 11th,[101] and though I hesitate and am undecided in a degree that is not, I think, often my custom in political matters, I leave all to

[101] *At this period the Constitution required that each presidential elector should vote for two persons, without designating which should be President, and which should be Vice-President. The person having the*

the Feds, who, on the spot, will act for the best. I doubt whether Burr will be federal, if chosen by Feds, and he would reconcile himself to his old friends as soon as he can. You will, I fear, become weary of well-doing in Congress, and resolve to quit your post sooner than we shall be willing to release you from it. Will Dexter be allowed to hold *his*, or the office of State, if royal grace should remove him to it? Will Madison go to France if Jeff. reigns? Will Gallatin get an office? Will Jeff. forget or forgive your efforts to bring in Burr, if they should fail of success? Will resentment, or the sense of increased dependence on his party, precipitate him to adopt violent counsels, to attack the funds, to restrict British commerce, to hug France close, &c.? It is very important that the Feds should adopt some *plan* of conduct, suited to the state we shall soon be placed in. We must keep united, and keep the public with us. Great efforts will be made to jacobinize Massachusetts, and to elect Gerry, though many think Mr. A. will be the Jacobin candidate. The members of the General Court will go home full of zeal to reëlect Strong. The Jacobins are full of confidence that they shall triumph in Boston, and throughout the State. Accept my best wishes.

Yours, truly.

---

largest number of electoral votes was to be President, and the one having the next largest was to be Vice-President. At this time there was a tie between Jefferson and Burr, each having seventy-three votes, and the decision between them devolved upon the House of Representatives, voting by States. The balloting began on the 11th of February, 1801, and was protracted to the 17th of that month. [S. AMES]

TO JEREMIAH SMITH

DEDHAM, FEBRUARY 16, 1801

MY GOOD FRIEND,

It is bold in you, sinner as you are, to ask any thing of me. You did not answer my letter about writing to Ben Bourne, nor a former letter, nor those letters I did not write, but which you knew I had regard enough for you to write. I have your judge letter;—and with all these demerits unatoned, I wrote for you to Dexter, requesting him to show it to Marshall, and to do all that he can possibly do for you. I heap coals of fire on your unworthy head. But I will not allow my rage to proceed any further; on the contrary, thank you for early asking my influence, which, as one of the Essex Junto, you know is great, in favor of your appointment. I did not write to Mr. Adams, which piece of neglect he will excuse, and I hope you will. I have read, and I admire, his book. And if you will write a great book on tenures, as you promised, I will buy it, and, if possible, read it. I am your friend, and will exert myself, you see, to serve you. Seriously, I wish you a judge, though you have not gravity. I wish to see you, to give you pudding in my house, and to tell you, with the warmth of feeling of 1796, that I am, Court sitting, very busy.

Your friend, &c.

TO THEODORE DWIGHT

DEDHAM, MARCH 19, 1801

SIR,

THERE ARE many federalists who think that nothing can be done, and others who think it is *too soon* to do any thing, to prevent the subversion of property and right of every kind. Some even say that Mr. Jefferson will be a federalist, and, of course, there is no need that any thing should be done. As I happen to entertain a very different opinion on all these three points, I ask leave to state, as briefly as I must in a letter, my sentiments to you. I will crowd the paper that I may do it the more fully. I conceive that the Virginia politics are violent, according to the temper of her Taylors, Monroes, and Gileses, and I may add Jeffersons. They are vindictive, because that state owes much, and the commercial states have gained, and now possess, much; and this newly accumulated moneyed interest, so corrupt and corrupting, is considered a rival interest, that baffles Virginia in her claim of ruling the public counsels. The *great* state has the ambition to be the *great nation*. Philosophism and jacobinism add vigor to the passions that spring from the sources before mentioned. As political power is to be wholly in their hands; as even the senate will apparently be Jacobin; and as the popular current is setting in favor of the extremest use of this power,—it seems strange that any federalist of good sense can see matter of consolation in the prospect before us.

Party is an association of honest men for honest purposes, and, when the state falls into bad hands, is the only efficient defence; a champion who never flinches, a watchman who never sleeps. But the federalists are scarcely associated.

Their confidence is so blind, and they are yet acted upon so little by their fears, their trust in the *sinless* perfection of a democracy is so entire, that perhaps suffering severely is the only mode for teaching. Others, who foresee and foretell the danger, must suffer with them. Is it not, therefore, proper, and indispensably necessary, to be active, in order to prevent the dissolution of the feeble ties by which the federal party is held together? Is it not practicable to rouse a part of the good men, and to stay the contagion of jacobinism within, at least, its present ample limits? It would be wrong to assail the new administration with invective. Even when bad measures occur, much temperance will be requisite. To encourage Mr. Jefferson to act right, and to aid him against his violent Jacobin adherents, we must make it manifest that we act on principle, and that we are deeply alarmed for the public good; that we are identified with the public. We must speak in the name and with the voice of the good and the wise, the lovers of liberty and the owners of property. By early impressing the preciousness, if I may use the word, of certain principles, and of the credit, commerce, and arts, that depend on adhering to them, and by pointing out the utter ruin of the commercial states by a Virginia or democratic system, may we not consolidate the federalists, and check the licentiousness of the Jacobin administration? I do not believe that the eastern states, if roused effectually, would be assailed in their great interests; I believe as little that if they are suffered to sleep supinely, confiding, instead of watching, they will escape ruin. Smooth promises, and a tinsel called conciliation, are to be used to break their coherence, to invite deserters from their corps, and, after thinning their ranks, the breach of those promises would be safe. Violence would enjoy impunity. It will be too late to alarm after the contagious principles of jacobinism have made New England as rotten as Pennsylvania.

The newspapers are an overmatch for any government.

They will first overawe and then usurp it. This has been done; and the Jacobins owe their triumph to the unceasing use of this engine; not so much to skill in the use of it, as by repetition. *Fas est et ab hoste doceri.* We must use, but honestly, and without lying, an engine that wit and good sense would make powerful and safe. To this end, the talents of Connecticut must be put in requisition. The Palladium might be made a great auxiliary to true liberty, and the endangered cause of good order. Its circulation, however, must be greatly increased. Any paper, to be useful at this crisis, must spread ten times as much as any will or can, unless the federal party, by a common concert, join to make it, like the London Gazette, *the* Gazette of the party. Could not your clergy, your legislators, your good men, be impressed with the zeal to diffuse it at once through your state? The attempt is making here; but, I confess, many think it a folly to be alarmed. Many others are alarmed. An active spirit must be roused in every town to check the incessant proselytizing arts of the Jacobins, who will soon or late subvert Connecticut, as surely as other states, unless resisted with a spirit as ardent as their own. If such a spirit could be roused, we should certainly preserve all that we have not yet lost. We should save property, credit, and commerce. We should, I am sanguine enough to believe, throw upon our antagonists the burdens of supporting and vindicating government, and enjoy their late advantages of finding fault, which popular prejudice is ever prone to listen to. We should soon stand on high ground, and be ready to resume the reins of government with advantage. You will suppose that I still bear in mind, that we are not to revile or abuse magistrates, or lie even for a good cause. We must act as good citizens, using only truth, and argument, and zeal to impress them.

The success of this design depends on the diffusion of like ideas among all the federalists, and the exertion of the first talents of the party. I think myself entitled to call upon you, and to ask you to call upon the mighty Trumbull, who must not slumber, like Achilles in his tent, while the camp is in danger of being forced. Mr. Wolcott must be summoned to give his counsels, as well as to mend his excellent pen. Connecticut is the lifeguard of liberty and federalism. I am trying to sound the tocsin. Mr. Dutton, the editor of the Palladium, has talents, learning, and taste; what is no less essential, he has discretion. It is intended that every clergyman in Massachusetts, New Hampshire, and Vermont shall have a paper one year by a subscription.

I write as much, in confidence, to you as the nature of the subject requires. I am, sir, with great respect, &c.

Yours.

TO HON. BENJAMIN GOODHUE

———

DEDHAM, MARCH 23D, 1801

MY DEAR SIR

THIS day's mail brought your esteemed favor of the 20th, in which you state the balance of six months insurance at two hundred and sixteen dollars 70/100 against me, and desire me to remit the amount to you. This I do by a check or order on the Boston branch, on the other side.

I am duly sensible of your friendship in the business and I know that you have exercised all the vigilance and zeal for my interest that you would for your own. I thank you for it, and I am not afraid to stand in the way of fortune hereafter if she chooses to be kind. That must however be risked.

Taking a length of time and the best risks, as Mr. Prescott thinks those to India are, I cannot hesitate to go on, carefully adhering to the principles of my first letter or power to you. I beg you would consult with Mr. Prescott or Mr. Norris when you think it necessary and act as your judgment may direct, within the limits however of my first plan.

The West India premiums seem to me very low, as the nest of pirates in the Islands and the principles of the trade are so much worse than any other. I confess that I am no adequate judge of the proper plan of underwriting. Too much caution is often as dangerous as rashness. I will thank you to keep me advised of the business.

I have great fears of Gerry's election. The spirit, industry, and exertion of the Jacobins exceed credibility. I am fully persuaded that every effort must be made by the newspapers to counteract them, to detect their lies and to explain. This is rowing against the stream—but discouraging as the resort to fact and argument against lies and prejudice, we must try it. The *Palladium* must be made to concenter the talents and patronage of the federalists or all will be lost. The *Aurora* is in no want of readers or writers.

With perfect regard I am, dear sir,
yours truly

FISHER AMES

TO THOMAS DWIGHT

DEDHAM, APRIL 28, 1801

MY DEAR FRIEND,

I AM very glad you are Senator once more, first for my own sake, as I shall see you the sooner and the longer; next for the public's. If we can stave off the evil for a year, we shall rise again—New York may vote right. Massachusetts may appear as well in the next General Court as ever. A less number, more sensible of the danger, more vigilant and spirited to repel it, will be a gainful substitute for a large majority, trusting where no trust ought to be placed. If from New Jersey eastward, all should look federal, a correspondent of mine observes, Jefferson will stand in his place, a monument of despair—popular without power, the head of the Virginia body, which is languid and impotent. Virginia is a giant in a palsy; when you would lift him he is more than your load; when you would assail him, he is less than your match.

.   .   .   .

Your friend.

TO JOHN RUTLEDGE

DEDHAM, JULY 30TH, 1801

DEAR SIR

I HAVE some knowledge of Mr. [Crofts] and rather more of his connexions. I know that some of my friends esteem him, and as he had your recommendation there was an accumulation of reasons for my attending to him. But he did not call on me, and I have not had leisure to call on him at Boston as I will as soon as my professional calls, now very urgent, will permit.

Mr. Jefferson's removals and appointments afford proof enough of the *quo amino* he administers the gov't. They present a most singular confutation of the puritanism with which his party sought office, and a noiseless efficient instrument of exposing the party to the world. A prevailing party should forbid their chief pen & ink, especially if he is a scribbler by trade and vain of his writing. Tom Payne has said that nobody could write a man *down* who was *up* but himself. The two Toms are strong illustrations that the fellow, so often in the wrong, was for once in the right. But I agree with you that great [. . .] as well as skill is necessary to the right management of the federal cause.

There is nothing forbidden by truth or virtue that is permitted to us. For the federal cause is really that of common honesty as well as of patriotism. But as the only agents in political affairs are popular passions, it is difficult to abstain from an unfair resort to these. We must abstain—we must reason. We must exhort to duty, and we must wait till the intemperance of the victors has recruited our force with the passions which grow up under a system of political intolerance and persecution. Mr. Jeff. has used his pen & ink to the New Haven remonstrants in a manner to afford much advantage to his adversaries. But to seize our advantages, we must keep a little *behind* the public feeling—we must state facts and keep a record of the memoranda you mention. But we next wait for time before we try to impress them. I am more than ever convinced that philosophism is a poor thing in the chair. Those who spin cobweb are poor spinners of common thread and as an inefficient empirical plan of governing will be a disappointment to those who have looked for the Millenium, and a subject of ridicule to all the laughers, I think our time will come—and when it comes, we shall want a paper as national, as able, as much in credit, as widely diffused as our united labors and patronage can make it. Till that day, we oppose our foe as the Mexicans did Cortes: with clubs against gunpowder and grape shot. The Palladium is a candidate for the yet vacant place of such a paper. It will take time to make it occupy that place. It will call Gen. Hamilton, great always when he errs (if he does err), and such master spirits to support and enliven its columns. Its position is good, as the seat of federalism must for the present be in N. England[.] A few long pieces must be inserted when dry abstract points are to be reasoned out for the conviction of half a hundred sound thinkers in the U.S. But I agree with you that the prevailing cast of the paper must be lighter and more adapted to general reading. The stile must be quaint, the subjects must be chosen for popular impression, and treated in the way to furnish flippant federalists with themes of eloquence in discourse. I object however to disputations. I think our party should not be *disputants* in the country. They should *explain* to good men, but not engage in controversy with Jacobins. The Palladium ought to be the national paper, but other good papers ought to enjoy all their present credit and patronage. The former must therefore be a *political* paper. To effect this, its circulation must be greatly extended, and partizans must be engaged in every quarter to puff it. Wm. Hunter has taste and talents and I advise the printer to send a subscription paper to him. The like could be done in other scenes.

It will be difficult to use the passions of the citizens without suffering by their excess and intemperance. At present therefore I conceive we should act on this plan you suggest[.] Keep and diffuse memoranda of facts, but reserve comments on them to the time when the effect could be turned to more account. Our union, government as it is, and our public liberty are to be in every event sound. Some already despair of these, and many would be brought to chuse new evils as new remedies. We must take care not to be discredited by the conduct of our too zealous friends. On the other hand, we must be active and provident, [. . .] or our party will lose its identity and its existence. Its very name is attempted to be made odious. An active correspondence and a general excitement of the zeal and talents of the federalists must be kept up till they are needed in self defense.

I think you will perceive that we are entirely agreed in these leading points, which I assure you is very flattering to me. I thank you unfeignedly for the expression of your regard—it is reciprocal—for I am, dear sir, with entire esteem,

Yrs &c

FISHER AMES

[P.S.] Mr. Isaac Davis has promised to call for this. He you know is a true man and has the worth and spirit of the federal character. I wish we had more as good as he.

TO RUFUS KING

BOSTON, OCTOBER 27TH, 1801

DEAR SIR:

WHILE Mr. Gore[102] is on the Continent, I may be allowed to address a letter to you, and if I could give either clear or comforting information about our affairs I might hope that my letters wd. be acceptable to you without that excuse. But democracy rides the high horse. Bradley is chosen a Vermont Senator, yet they say the assembly of that state is federal. Others say that all goes there by barter and that offices are trucked off to Feds & Jacobins without much discrimination, provided the high-contracting parties find their individual amount in it. Royal Tyler is a Judge of their Supreme Court,

[102] *During the suspension of the sitting of the Commission under the Seventh Article of the Treaty with Great Britain, Mr. Gore, a member of the Committee, made a visit to the Continent of Europe.* [Life and Correspondence of Rufus King.]

Israel Smith Ch. Justice. A motley bench which ought to try *per mediatatem.*

N. Jersey is said to be democratic. Delaware has a demo. governor chosen by the people. Connecticut still shews a bold face, and vaunts of its federalism which I fear is losing ground—yet so slowly that the pendulum may swing back again before the Demos get the majority. N. Hampshire still chuses Gilman, yet their "intriguans" intend to run Langdon as soon as the fullness of time has come—which is expected to be next spring. Here, Govr. Strong will be rechosen, but the most zealously federal parts of the state are leavening and souring with the same fermentation that in other parts has passed beyond the vinous almost to the putrid. Where jacobinism triumphs, it is probable, it's numbers do not increase—but it's insolence does,—and the Feds in those places yield the ground to them with less contest than formerly. So that on a fair calculation of force, we are weak indeed. New England ought to be roused and all our efforts ought to be directed to saving the remnants of federalism; our life and being would be lost, if the skill of our masters had been equal to the felicity of the conjuncture when they conquered us. They had only to promise well—indeed they did—and to keep on promising smoothly, which they have not done, easy as the task was. Instead of it, they write foolish letters of excuse for themselves and inculpating the Feds as a sect. There is hardly anything that a skilful statesman may not *do,* but there is very little, he can *say.* This prating vain letter[103] has certainly alarmed the Feds, who consider it as a manifesto announcing a violent Jacobin administration. And the knowing ones among the Jaco', think it stiff. Already they whisper that little B. alone has the needed energy of character, and party for him will be form'd

---

[103] *Probably Jefferson's New Haven letter.* [Life and Correspondence of Rufus King.]

whenever it can be employed with effect. In the mean time he will push his captain forward to do obnoxious things, and when resentments are concentered on him, then perhaps he will think the Feds despairing of victory will only seek revenge. To secure which, *he* will be wanted. It is indeed evident that a govt. too democratic in it's structure, or a people too democratic in their notions to support any energetic form, will breed endless factions. We have hoped that our system was, as Mr. Jefferson says very sagely, the *strongest* in the world and that we are the people the fittest in it for such a system. I presume not to decide so grave a question. I think however our experience soon will. In New York the rights & the property of the city and state are subject to the vice and folly and poverty of the society. The like will be brought about in every other state as in Pennsylvania unless the quill shall be found a weapon of power enough to counteract the progress we have commenced. Even that weapon will be wielded by champions who do not think all is at hazard. The popular consolation still is as much as ever that all goes well—Prosperity smiles on everybody—Wealth increases, and the New men promise to make great savings. The displacing a few exasperates a few hundreds, who soon forget their anger and the circumstances and occasion of it. Those who affect great concern for the people will be the men to have popular power committed to them and newspaper writers will fail as formerly in the attempt to make the understanding of those who will not reason an overmatch for the blind impulses of those who can only feel. Accordingly as I see the propensities of things, as I estimate the feebleness of the means to hinder their further and fatal decline, judge whether I am sanguine as to the effect of Federal Gazettes. Yet I think despair ought not to be confessed—still less circulated. Soon if the evil apprehended should be deemed inevitable, which is rather more than my belief—yet a certain manner of meeting it is necessary—otherwise it will come with aggravation. We must openly and zealously and with all our skill labor to prevent it. We must honestly and faithfully cling to the Govt. and Constitution and to the rules of virtue and real patriotism to the last; so that our fall, if fate decrees it, shall be incontestably due to our political adversaries, not to ourselves. As what is best and what is practicable are points depending on events, and not to be foreseen or decided before they happen, we shall thus stand ready to act as may be proper—we shall keep ourselves united with the public sentiment and when danger is obvious, the good and able will feel an impulse as strong as we vainly wish to inspire beforehand. Therefore the Gazettes are now of importance and the Feds are preparing this kind of ammunition in Pennsylvania, N. York & Boston. Such gazettes will keep alive all the yet surviving respect for principles, and if the Jacos. in Congress are not callous may check their most outrageous designs. It is however obvious to me that charges of violating the Constitution affect the Jacos. very little, while you know that the Feds when in power were exceeding affected by them—even when palpably false and frivolous— as if the Feds were rather cowards who feared to be indicted for breaking the Constitution, not really lovers of it who will not suffer any others to do it. The bold liberties taken with the power of displacing and appointing are *abuses* if not infractions—yet as the Jacos. care little for principles and as the Feds are averse to making a great clamor for what to most persons will appear a little thing, I do not expect much check from that source. On the contrary, I expect a repeal of the late Judicial Law and an ousting of the new circuit judges will be received with patience by all, and with approbation with some federalists. If repealing a law will deprive a judge of his office and salary, there will be no independence of the judiciary on the legislature.

As to the views and plan of politics of the ruling party in respect to foreign nations and to their own ultimate objects all is but conjecture. Probably one great man is a democrat and thinks the extremes of democratic principles are wise principles.

Madison certainly knows better and yet there ever was a strange vein of absurdity in his head. But the *second* has no such nonsense, jacobinism now uses and urges democracy, as it did in France—We are now in the Roland & Condorcet act of our Comedy—Whether we go on to the Danton and Robespierre acts depends on time and accident and not on the discernment energy or force of the Feds. This I sometimes hope; Jacobins will not hold power contentedly only for fair honest purposes and they cannot proceed to use it to any very profitable extent for any other, without rousing a late opposition that would delay if not prevent the crisis—They cannot oppress and rob without our knowing; and the oppressed will not be coaxed. Excuse my running on thus into infinite space. I stand again on old firm ground when I assure you of my cordial regard with best respects to Mrs. King—

Yours &c.

FISHER AMES

TO THOMAS DWIGHT

DEDHAM, DECEMBER 7, 1801

MY DEAR FRIEND,

. . . .

THE great evil of our school law is, that the towns, when unwilling to maintain schools, may render themselves unable by splitting up their districts. . . . . Pray take the matter into your senatorial consideration, and your petitioner as in duty bound, shall &c.; which is, ever vote for your honor as long as you live, and longer. It is strange, that with my thoughts so turned to legislation, I cannot be chosen; but the people know no better than to neglect me.

I divide my cares for my country with those for my farm, and I have the pleasure to inform you that I carried my pigs to a good market, the peace notwithstanding. Ten cents a pound in September indemnified me for all the grain consumed for my horse, oxen, cows, calves, poultry and family, and a handsome balance in cash. I make no secret of the way to get rich. If corn could be bought on the river to advantage, I would wish to place cash in your hands for the purpose. I have more than sixty pigs, who are pretty expensive boarders. My cows produce only in butter and calves nearly thirty-six dollars each. Keep that to yourself till the valuation is settled. To be serious, I think my farm is approaching the period when it will be profitable. If I did not think it would be, it would not be an amusement. It would be a mere piece of ostentation on any other prospect—an expensive folly, a toilsome disappointment. The peace will reduce labor and produce and lands. Its effects are not to be foreseen, and on the whole, I incline to believe, though I scarcely know why, they are overrated.

France will be busy with her intrigues in all countries. She has made peace as a conqueror, and annexed to her empire a great territory. Her arrogance will be great, and I suppose that the British minister, seeing [that] Europe, so far from being willing to combine and fight against France, was not willing to let Great Britain fight alone and save them all; that Russia, Prussia, and the Emperor were more or less jealous of the naval greatness of England, and not enough jealous of the Roman greatness of France; I say, I suppose that he was willing, and almost forced, to make a peace,— and such a peace, as by exhibiting and augmenting the arrogance of France, would rouse a jealousy of her in all Europe. The territory ceded was not of much value to keep, not worth the impression supposed upon all other nations. The schemes of Russia, and the discords in France will be probably the points on which the question of the peace lasting or not lasting will turn. As weatherwise folks tell you on being asked of the weather, I will let you know more hereafter.

Yours &c.

TO RUFUS KING

DECEMBER 20TH, 1801

MY DEAR SIR:

THE new president's speech is out, he calls it a message. This difference is pretended to be important to save time, money and ceremony. Is not this philosophy, dignity &c &c. The message announces the downfall of the late revision of the judiciary; economy, the patriotism of the shallow and the trick of the ambitious—It proposes that Congress shall legislate in every case to the very rim and outside edge of its power—lest executive discretion should take its place and usurp its powers. Therefore the items for appropriation are to be designated specifically. Instead of laying down rules of conduct, Congress is to apply these rules in detail and is to be president, as to army, navy and taxes, the U. S. gov't has little to do, and is to be dismantled like an old ship. For it is evident that the state gov'ts are to be exhibited as alone safe and salutary. Thus Congress is to do everything instead of the heads of departments. Committees instead of

Cong. The sovereign people are to be excited to control these and Virginia is to be as strong as the union is made weak.

I am full of commentary on this ample text, but you will not need my help to make your own. Those who lean for support on one state, and on exciting the passions of the people to weaken every obstacle to the domination of that state, will understand their part. You will see a broad hint about the *carrying Trade*. Expect Madison's resolutions over again and the pretty plan of the Report on the privileges and restrictions of our Commerce.

You will see perhaps by some of the Mass'tts papers that the Farmer, alias Atty General U. S., alias Lincoln is outrageously agt. the federalists and the whole body of the clergy and denounces the wrath of The People unless they abstain from their evil ways. The peace (between France and England) will not calm the agitations of this country: its terms present France as an object both of terror & admiration. Unless Buonaparte shd. die, her exorbitant power will be consolidated so as to overturn Europe first, then the world. But his life is precarious. I am surprised at the kind of admiration lavished by wise men on this adventurer; allow him heroism—allow him genius—yet his admirers invest him with qualities which he has given little evidence that he possesses. Political sagacity is ascribed to him as if he excelled Pitt and Thugut and all the old statesmen of old govts. The *vis major* requires very little of it. . . . I cannot conceive of a long duration of peace, when all that exists is prodigious and out of nature. Ambition sees no obstacles and it's victims can have no shelter. Is not Europe as much a prey as Italy was to Rome after the war with Pyrrhus? Spain, Portugal, Holland and Italy are so many provinces of France.

This state affords no matter of news. It is quiet, but soon to be agitated by the intrigues to bring in Gerry governor. The National Egis, a paper at Worcester, is set up for that end. Lincoln is said to have formed, as well as promoted, the plan, but when there was a call for money, he was off. It is hoped by printing frothy nonsense in that county to revolutionize the state. What sense we have is no match for our prejudice and nonsense, and soon or late, the contest will turn against us. I omitted to say that the Farmer in his Egis modestly and consistently rails agt. the Palladium as a gazette that is supported by the federalists, and the clergy.

Yrs &c

FISHER AMES

1 8 0 2

===

TO RUFUS KING

———

BOSTON, FEBRUARY 23, 1802

MY DEAR SIR:

... *That*, the ascendancy of France, we are told, is to be displayed on our borders, and that in exchange for ½ St. Domingo, she is to have Louisiana. Our Southern brethren are expected to wince when this happens. I deduce no hopes from the event. Factions always hate & dread their domestic rivals more than foreign enemies. Virginia has the spirit of domestic restlessness and arrogance that abhors restraint, and of state ambition that wd. impose it, of laziness that will not earn, of luxury that will not retrench, of a debtor that will not pay. Great states are strong factions, and a feeble govt. is of course their victim and their instrument—at present their trophy.

To repeal the Judicial Law to save a small sum shocks many who could swallow the claim of a constitutional right to repeat it. It is understood to be the declaration of the *bellum internecionum* agt. the best institutions of the late administrations. Gouv. Morris's speeches are justly admired and have had effect on thinking men—i. e. on 600 of 6 millions.

Truth however filters through the stone & reaches the folks standing below, drop by drop. The mint is voted out. Govt. seems to be clearing the ships for action, by throwing every thing of value overboard—

Our General Court has rejected a motion in one house by Hichborn, in the other by Morton, for an address of the President. The majority was so small it shows an unsound state of the public opinion in this state. Still as it clearly proves the Jacobins to be a minority, this disclosure of their weakness tends to keep them weak. On inquiry I cannot find that they are gaining ground. Still it is to be supposed that those who address the popular passions will in the end prevail against those who presume on their sense & virtue. Gov. Strong's re-election is probable, though of course the virtuous Gerry will contest it. Robbins is the most conspicuous candidate for the Lt. Governor's place, vacant by the death of Mr. Phillips. We make turnpikes and busy ourselves with local objects. Virginia rides the great horse.

No doubt you are a watchful and anxious spectator of our affairs. It is beyond human foresight to predict the events that await us. We are hastening towards changes, which forebode other changes and so on to the end of the chapter. We are not at present under a Theocracy, and if we were, our propensity to worship strange Gods would involve us in trouble.

I am with esteem & affection
Yrs

FISHER AMES

TO RUFUS KING

DEDHAM, APRIL 13, 1802

DEAR SIR:

. . . I do not despair of G. B. and of course I trust somewhat in the chances of the world's escaping from the fangs of french domination. The ambitious project of getting Louisiana can do nothing but good. We need as all nations do the compression on the outside of our circle of a formidable neighbor—whose presence shall at all times excite stronger fears than demagogues can inspire the people with towards their govt. The object of popular aversion and dread has been only govt. France if she could float here and anchor on our coast has no terrors equal to our near prospect of anarchy first and then Jacobin despotism. We ought to rejoice in a new position of things in which courage toil and suffering might avail to extricate us from imminent evils—instead of that smooth and swift descent down the precipice that we have been making for a year past. . . .

Great joy is felt here on occasion of the adjustment made with G. Britain of the spoliation and treaty debts. It is well known and truly felt and acknowledged that your and Mr Gore's residence in London has been infinitely serviceable to the U. S. This consideration ought to keep you both quiet a little longer in a situation that the newspapers have said you were weary of and about to quit. God bless you when you return with the sight of a country grateful, free and secure of it's freedom on fixed principles.

With great regard &c
Yrs

FISHER AMES

TO THOMAS DWIGHT

DEDHAM, APRIL 16, 1802

MY DEAR FRIEND,

. . . .

OUR POLITICS go swimmingly, as there is need they should, for the angels of destruction at Washington are making haste, as if they knew their time is short. It is now their part to vindicate, and stand on their defense when attacked; a post hard to keep, and yet they must keep it, or part with their power. Like the first National Assembly, they or two thirds of their gang have been silly enough to suppose they could go on with the Constitution by the will of the people—that is, by indulging their own passions. The French from 1789 to 1792 in like manner established a democracy of the wildest and wickedest sort, and thought they could have a king at the head of it. A monarchical mobocracy was their philosophical plan. It answered just as we might expect from joining contradictions together. A like issue must attend our democrats, and the next thing will be, as in France, anarchy, then jacobinism organized with energy enough to plunder and shed blood. The only chance of safety lies in the revival of the energy of the federalists, who alone will or can preserve liberty, property or Constitution. This revival is most encouragingly indicated by the late election. It is a victory which we ought to reap the fruits of. We ought to exert ourselves throughout New England to counteract the Jacobins, by understanding what their topics of declamation are, and then confuting them in the newspapers, in pamphlets and discourse.

. . . .

Your affectionate friend.

TO HON. BENJAMIN GOODHUE

DEDHAM, MAY 29, 1802

DEAR FRIEND,

I SUBSCRIBED sixty shares in the Norfolk of Bristol Turnpike stock for you, which at $50 each is the amount you limited. It is not expected that more will be assessed than $50 each. If however we get the road to Boston it will be clearly our interest to make no new shares, as the stock will rise above par. The late survey shortens the road more than two miles hence to the neck. The ground is good in every sense. Indeed the most singular and unexpected good fortune attends the operation. Almost without any loss in distance, say 27 rods in as many miles, we avoid the hills and swamps. The like happens in the route to Boston to our joy and surprise. The clerk is absent, otherwise I would send your certificate. I will advance for your payments, if agreeable and advise you of it. Perhaps 60 or 80 shares are yet unsubscribed; it is easy to procure adventurers. If any Salem friends wish to take more please to let me know it. I wish to leave the stock on the sea coast that the object may be promoted by those who know its importance.

Yours truly

FISHER AMES

NB. 30 of the within are to be for Captain Forrester
20 for Captain Wheatland
10 for myself

TO HON. BENJAMIN GOODHUE

BOSTON, JUNE 10, 1802

MY DEAR FRIEND,

I AM favored with your letter on the subject of the Dedham Turnpike. I do not send your certificates for the sixty shares, as you desire, because the clerk and the printed blanks being at Dedham the business must be done there. I will see to it however, and your sixty shares shall be made out accordingly. As to the residue, I believe the whole number and a surplus is subscribed for. The names of those who wish to take shares shall be kept, and in case we obtain the extension of our road to Boston, it is be very probable they may then have their number. I think the stock promises fair, and will be productive after the first year or two of rivalry with the old road has elapsed. Twelve dollars on each share is now due. To accommodate you and Salem friends subscribers, I propose that you should deposit to my credit in the branch bank here the amount due, and advise me of it by the mail. I will see it applied, and your discharges shall be forwarded to you. I shall be understood to speak of the sixty shares.

It is expected that only 14 miles of the road will be made this year, which may require ten or fifteen dollars more. This you will receive as I offer it only as conjecture. If the road should be granted to Dedham from Boston line, the property will be good and even if it is not granted, I think it cannot be very bad. You will know in a few days whether we prevail. Mr. Marsh the Senator is one of the Turnpike Commissioners and if he should be in our favor, there will be a report to grant the prayer of our petition. This will aid us very much.

Your friend etc.

FISHER AMES

TO HON. BENJAMIN GOODHUE

DEDHAM, AUGUST 14, 1802

MY DEAR FRIEND,

THE certificates for the sixty shares subscribed for you in the Pawtucket Turnpike will be forwarded to you whenever you direct, or I will keep them till I go to Salem. Thirty of them are for Mr. Simon Forrester, twenty for Mr. Richard Wheatland, and ten for you. The Payment of twelve dollars on each share has been made.

I think it inevitable that we increase our shares beyond 800, the number intended, so as to include an excess of 100 or 120 subscribed for. It is not easy to say positively in what order the subscribers claim, nor who is prior. We shall certainly obtain the extension of our road from Dedham to Boston line, if the General Court act at the next session with as much good sense and public spirit as we are to expect from that body. Then we shall want the extra subscription money. The stock will be worth more, as the road to Boston must be productive. Therefore after reflection on the matter, and consulting several of the proprietors, I have concluded to offer to the persons named in your letter of the 7th June who desire shares the number expressed in that letter. They are

    10 Richard Wheatland
    10 Nathaniel Fisher
    12 Charles Cleveland
    10 William S. Gray
    12 John Dabney
    10 Jacob Ashton

In case they incline to take the shares as above, I beg you would inform them of this letter. I have put down their names on the list. Twelve dollars each share are assessed and it is probable a third assessment will be called for this year which I estimate not to exceed ten dollars more.

I am sanguine—perhaps blindly so—that the Norfolk and Bristol Turnpike property will prove profitable. The intercourse is great and growing, and the Directors who superintend the work are good men who neither neglect it nor suffer the money to be wasted. We have no job work—no contracts which ensure a bad road to the corporation unless the bargain be a hard one against it as to price. Please to advise me a line.

your friend etc.

FISHER AMES

TO HON. BENJAMIN GOODHUE

DEDHAM, SEPTEMBER 17, 1802

DEAR SIR,

THIS will be handed to you by Mr. James Richardson, late my pupil in the law, now in practice in this town. He is respectable, and in heart and politics as right as any man.

I ask leave to introduce him to you. He goes on our Turnpike business and will hand the certificates of the 124 shares to the several gentlemen named in your last favor. I subscribed Mr. Gray 100 shares, and wish to know whether he takes them. I freely hazard my opinion that I know no stock fitter for a capitalist than our turnpike. Mr. Richardson will state to him and to others concerned the manner of executing the work, which for goodness and economy promises as well as any undertaking of the kind in the state.

I will thank you to give any assistance to Mr. Richardson that he may need. By calling on Mr. B. Pickman, junior and Mr. Gray I have supposed he would accommodate them in respect to transacting the business of their shares, instead of their having any trouble to do it for themselves.

I do not expect to attend the Court at Newbury Port, and therefore I shall not see you at Salem so soon as I expected. Wishing you and your family a great deal of happiness, I am, dear sir,

your friend etc

FISHER AMES

TO CHRISTOPHER GORE

DEDHAM, OCTOBER 5, 1802

MY DEAR FRIEND,

SINCE I have sought pleasure and profit among my trees and cows and pigs, and since the cares of a little law business and a large family have engrossed my time and thoughts, I am no longer so desperate a scribbler to my friends as I was while in Congress. Then I gave you little respite. I confess that I find an increasing indisposition to letter-writing, which I regret and will resist. Besides you read the Boston papers, and I cast about to find matter not taken up in them; and, uncertain what you know and what you are ignorant of, I write under the discouragement that I give you nothing but what is stale. Your reproof that I write you too seldom and too short, is flattering yet painful, and the sensibility, with which your letter of the 29th July bemoans your apprehended estrangement from country and friends, is conveyed in a manner very much to sharpen my remorse that I have given you occasion, as I confess I have, for your regrets and remonstrances. I promise reformation. Repentance is strongest while it is new and fresh, and I will avail myself of its earliest impulse to write a letter as long and as lively as any thing ever written, and *not* for publication—excepting only General Heath's orders when he detached a party. In that case the commander of the detachment seldom found the task to be performed so laborious, as the reading of a quire of instructions. I pray you do not interpret this engagement of mine to write a great deal, as a threat. For I have something to add that I would not intimidate you from reading.

You ask my advice about your resuming the law business. I cheerfully undertake the office, only premising that in deciding the most momentous concerns of life, a man is not only his best, but almost solely, his own adviser. He has exclusively that instinctive perception of what he prefers, and of what he can do, that the most discerning friend must only suppose, and may, and indeed must, in a great measure mistake. Nevertheless, friends ought to advise, because they bring this power of *self* judging into operation *precisely*, and with ample materials. All I will pretend to do is to frame a special verdict, and then humbly submit it to your honor's judgment.

1435

Great law knowledge is sure to gain business and emolument. The splendid eloquence that displays its treasures may hasten the popular judgment to decide that a man posesses them, but ultimately the learning of the lawyer decides the measure of his fame. Now, I pronounce that you are well fitted by nature and study, as well as practice for such eminence, and by a practice that evinces your extensive learning and sound judgment as a lawyer, I cannot conceive that you will submit to an unfavorable test of character, or that you will be degraded from the place your friends wish to see you take.

I will therefore assume it as a point proved, that by practice in great causes, and where law learning will be chiefly sought for, you will not impair the dignity of your standing by resorting to the bar. But you will reply, that by returning to open shop you cannot choose your customers, nor refuse to sell ordinary wares;—to harangue a jury about the flogging given to a sailor, or to mingle in the snipsnap war about admitting a witness or a deposition, will often vex and humble the liberal mind;—business of small value will not lie in your way. I reply, your share will be made up by insurance cases, and questions which our bankrupt law is sowing for the harvest of 1804. I observe that the little contests and litigations are engrossed by the junior class of the profession and by those who never advance beyond mediocrity. This is, I think, a different position of things from what existed in 1786. You will not calculate on the small fees, nor the vexatious litigation which concern sixpenny interests and sixpenny passions. Mr. Parsons practises on this large scale that I recommend; and I will add, fees are infinitely better than they were in 1786.

Who are the rivals for this business with whom you must divide the booty? Parsons stands first, but he is growing older, less industrious, and wealth, or the hypo, may stop his practice. Otis is eager in the chase of fame and wealth, and, with a great deal of eloquence, is really a good lawyer, and improving. He however sighs for political office—he knows not what; and he will file off the moment an opportunity offers.

Dexter is very able, and will be an Ajax at the bar as long as he stays. You know, however, that his aversion to reading and to practice are avowed, and I believe sincere. His head aches on reading a few hours, and if he did not love money very well, he would not pursue the law. Sullivan, who seems immortal, is admonished of his decay by a fit every three months, and will not be in your way.

I, your humble servant, never was qualified by nature or inclination for the bar, and this I always well knew. Want of health, and the possession of a small competence will stop my mouth, if fate should not stop my breath before your return. I have reckoned all the persons who pretend to be considerable. John Lowell's health is wretched. . . . A number of eminent lawyers will be wanted in Boston, and though the place is overstocked, I think the prospect for 1804 not unhopeful. I know of no very dashing young men coming forward.

Yet truth requires that I should, after all, state my expectation, that your share of the business will not be as great as it would have been if you had not left the country. It takes time to form connections and to resume the old set of clients. You are no chicken, and ought not to calculate on a very long period of drudgery at the bar. You will, and you ought to, enjoy the *otium cum amicis et libris et dignitate*, for many years before you die. I will not conceal from you my opinion, that you ought not to expect, or to take into your plan, the receipt of a great many great bags of money from your practice. I do not found this moderate calculation on your want of merit and talent, or on the refusal of the public to admit your title to both; I only insist that, from circumstances connected with you, with rivals in practice, and with the state of business, you are not to look for a very large income.

Suppose, however, instead of six, eight or ten thousand dollars a year, which Hamilton and some others are said to derive from practice, you get only fifteen hundred or two thousand dollars, ought you to decline practice on that account, or to feel mortified, as if the public had rejected and degraded you? I am interested to insist that this estimate of reputation is not fair, for I am not entitled to boast of a lucrative practice. The truth is, other considerations deserve weight, and the public will give it to them.

To be engaged on great law points, and to acquit yourself as you will, surely cannot fail to vindicate you with everybody. Your time of life, your reputation, property, and moderation as to the passion for gain, will be assigned as reasons, even before you can assign them yourself, for your declining the toil of promiscuous business. It will be said, you would not be idle, nor will you be a drudge. This line of practice, the only one in your choice, will shelter you from the ungentlemanly wrangles of the bar, and the Court have of late years set about learning some manners.

Then the question is fairly before you, whether you will open your shop on such terms, and with such prospects as I have stated. Why not? I ask. You will, or some friends rather of yours will reply, why should Mr. Gore descend to this not very respectable, not very comfortable, not very lucrative fagging at the bar? I urge that it is better to keep up your style of living by some business, than to change it for an idle life, and a style observably lower than that you have been accustomed to. A man may make some retrenchments and savings, but he cannot greatly alter his expense without *descending*, which I should be sorry you should have forced upon you. A man may not incline to take a certain degree on the scale of genteel living, but having once taken it he must maintain it. Still I think that law in Boston will keep you out of the way of spending fifteen hundred or two thousand dollars, that a retirement of idle luxury would impose upon you at Waltham. Every southern visitor must see your improvements, show them to his wife, and eat and drink you ten guineas' worth. $2000 saved, and $2000 got is $4000, enough to meet all the demands on your treasury, over and above the resources drawn from your property. Perhaps the superior cheapness of living in Boston may not strike you. I reply, a busy man may make savings and reputably, if he will; and indeed he must renounce business, or be moderate in his pleasures. He must often draw a special plea and refuse a feast. This is not all. Make the comparison between business and no business. Farming at Waltham will be some resource, but I have no idea that it will afford that steady occupation which is essential to keep life from being a heavy burden. Books, you will say, afford that resource. In some degree they do, but they need auxiliary resources. In case you should be at Waltham, unemployed by the public, you will be in some danger of being forgotten by the great multitude—out of sight out of mind, is their maxim. By practice you will be in sight, and ready, in every one's mind, for such public employment as your friends will say ought to seek you. Therefore the bar is in my judgment the best place for you to occupy, whether you aim at economy in expense, tranquil enjoyment of friends, or the resumption of any public station. Your social affections will find objects and exercise; you will be kept busy, and of course cheerful; you will not appear to be laid by or thrown away, but to have chosen your old post. Even if you should do little business, the extent of your sacrifice will be the more apparent. You will return, not with a raging thirst of gain, but with a resolution to study your cases and to merit confidence and reputation.

Hence I conclude you ought to "open shop" again. On conversing with Mr. Cabot, I confess he instantly decided the point against me; on further discussion he came over to

my opinion. Indeed it seems to me not merely the best
course, but the only one left to you. All which is humbly
submitted.

FISHER AMES, *Foreman.*

TO CHRISTOPHER GORE

———

DEDHAM, NOVEMBER 7, 1802

MY DEAR FRIEND,

THE very hour and minute that I received and was reading
your letter about Mr. Salisbury's experiments on my orchard
grass-seed, pronouncing it, on philosophical authority, to be
coarse and unfit for pasture, my cows were in my house-lot,
eating it with the voracious appetite of ignorance. The
Encyclopædia, I find, says it is liked by sheep and horses,
but is *refused* by cows. The poor things did not know that it
was the *dactylis glomeratus,* and was *refused* by cows. It is
a shame to the very cattle to be so ignorant. It was natural
to expect dreadful consequences from this apparently fatal
mistake. The arts and sciences, who had spoken so plainly
in their Encyclopædia, one would think, would send a witch
to give my cows the colic. There was no temptation and very
little excuse for the blunder, for in the lot were other grasses
in abundance,—the honey-suckle, or white clover, the May
or spear grass, and the other various sorts, or *gramina,* as
we the learned, choose to term them. Yet, rejecting what
was good and lawful, and preferring that which it turns out,
though I must insist they did not know it, was prohibited,
they did prefer the aforesaid *dactylis glomeratus,* against the
dignity of the Royal Society, and their Botanical Garden,

and in contempt of the common law, and of the Encyclopædia, as before recited, and in very evil example to sundry other cows, who looked over my fence, desiring to offend in like manner. I will not wholly vindicate this enormity—it is too bad for that; but I urge, in palliation, that probably the *dactylis glomeratus* is as sweet as any grass that grows so rank; probably somewhat sweeter, for the hay is preferred by my cattle. But I can scarcely doubt, that the white clover, and other small grasses, are better pasture. But as the orchard grass grows very fast, while the others stand still, and often forms a tuft, or hassock, in rich land, as large as a peck measure, unless the cattle love it much better, they will not keep it down so close; for in an equal space of time it will be ranker than other grasses, and, being the rankest, will of course be left. Yet this very inconsiderable difference, supposing it to exist, in favor of other grasses, which is, however, mere hypothesis, is an affair of trivial account. As the orchard grass is succulent and juicy, and cattle will eat it, their preference or taste is of no great importance to your own cows. If, indeed, you invite your neighbor's cows to push down your fence and breakfast in your lot, you should entertain them on the best. The grass and hay are highly nourishing; they are abundant, and, with manure, bring better crops on dry lands than any other grass, perhaps not excepting clover.

The last spring I remarked my orchard grass grew thick, and formed hassocks, while the dry cold weather kept all other sorts back. On the whole, this species of grass is with me beyond the grade of experiment. It has tried excellence, and I will stick to it.

I have a great deal more to say to you. I am full of zeal about farming. Cattle and fruit trees are my themes, in prose. Poetry, if I had any, I would devote to my pigsty and politics—two scurvy subjects, that should be coupled together. I wish exceedingly to get such cows as, being well fed on the *dactylis glomeratus,* will give more milk than any other cows. The Alderney breed is said to be of that description, but, being English, I make no doubt they would refuse the *dactylis.* Expect to hear from me again very soon.

Your affectionate friend.

P.S. . . . I will add a word on *breeding* cattle, and on *feeding* them.

Breeding.—I see, in my experience, full proof that certain fine properties are transmissible. As much care should be had for the bull as the cow; and this care, continued for two or three generations of the cattle, will banish those instances of a degenerate progeny which sometimes appear. A calf will resemble a distant relation of the family, more than the sire or dam, and the properties may be as different as the shape and color. But, admitting these exceptions to exist, which prove the rule, not detract from it, an improved race, and a peculiar race, having certain excellences to distinguish them, will be formed. It is a folly very much in fashion to breed horses, and great dependence is placed on the invariable excellence of the colts from the sires and dams. The race of gamblers and spendthrifts is indubitably propagated, and is not in the least inferior to the gamblers and spendthrifts of any former age. Why, then, should not cattle be produced like their sires, as certainly as coxcombs? *Omne majus in se continet minus.*

Feeding.—In our red hot climate, the grass dries up every year exactly on the 20th of July, and remains brown till the 1st of September. The cows, half starved, are pinched, and when the grass grows, their milk returns no more. Nature very prudently applies her energies to cover their ribs. Hence the loss of milk is great. To prevent this loss, I plant corn, and cut it up close to the ground, for my cows to eat it while the ears are green. I plant pumpkins without corn to shade them; these ripen early. I slice them once a day for their supper or breakfast. Item, I sow carrots and give them tops and all. Thus I keep them full of milk and full of flesh. But a cow will not easily gain more flesh in the barn. She comes out in the spring as lean as she goes in. Therefore, besides good hay, currying and great care in often feeding, I give some meal daily, say one or two quarts to each cow, from January to June, increasing it as the days lengthen and the calves lug their dams more and more. My calves weigh thirty pounds a quarter at seven or eight weeks old. I choose to continue the meal two or three weeks after the cows go to grass, then the green feed will not drench them. They will hold their flesh; they will immediately give out great messes; a short drought will not pinch their bags; the milk will yield more cream and butter; whereas the cows that are poorly fed, do not give full messes for fifteen or twenty days after being turned out to grass. Being weak in health, dry weather reduces their milk and it is poor in quality.

You will say, such expense in meal exceeds the profit. I reply, my cows pay nearly ten pounds a year each. The meal is food, and of course less hay will answer. Moreover, cows in good flesh eat less food than such as are very lean. They are even less dainty, and reject meadow or bog hay less fastidiously than other cows. In case of an accident, a broken limb, for instance, or an unforseen necessity to dry a cow, she is easily turned into beef.

I admire to visit my barn, and see the cows as happy as the being well born and well fed can make them. I recollect an expression of a French traveller in England. Speaking of the cows in a gentleman's lawn, I believe you call it, he says of the cows, *de qui l'embonpoint annonceroit leur maitre.* I should be very proud of such a description given of my cows, and, after a year or two, I hope to deserve it for them. But that honor depends on the progress of my English mowing. I manure my best lands, and, after having made a lot very good, I think it fitted for manure. Thus I prefer the aristocracy of grounds: the best will make the best returns.

.   .   .   .

Take only one crop from such lands, and feed off the after growth. Your cows will pay for it better than the rowen or after crop would; an acre of fine mowing to each cow will keep her full fed, and thus a dairy always urged by the best food, winter and summer, and never pinched, will be all that a dairy can be. How important, then, is it to have cows that will give a pailful, say ten wine quarts, instead of six? that will give it a month longer than other cows, and milk of a better quality?

I wish a fair trial of the Alderney race, or any other good race in England, but I hope more from selecting the very best Yankees.

Not a word of the foregoing was written to be published, but if you think the materials of any value to Arthur Young, or such very wise folks, I care not what use you make of them, provided you excuse me from the glory of appearing, *nominatim,* in print.

TO CHRISTOPHER GORE

————

BOSTON, DECEMBER 13, 1802

MY DEAR FRIEND,

OUR ruin advances like a ship-launch, very slow at first, so that you can scarcely see motion, then quicker, and then so quick as to fire the ways. Congress is sitting, and we are expecting the gracious message from the throne. Its nature I will not pretend to say I can conjecture. It will, no doubt, address the popular passions, and try to excite or to gratify them. The hopes and fears of the people are two windlasses, which the political machine obeys, as implicitly as any machine can. Those who turn the windlass, are as blind as the French revolutionists to the ruin that is sure to reach them. For revolution is merciless towards those of her own household; like some other loathsome existences, she is sure to eat up her own litter. They will probably change the places of doing the financial business of the government from the United States Bank to the state banks. They will thus hope to organize a faction in each state, devoted to themselves; to divide, by such means, the moneyed interest of the state, and to attach a part to themselves; and, after having thus secured an influence in each state, to throw back the government, by amendments, into the hands of their partisans in the several states: Virginia being not first among equals, but such a head to the confederacy as Rome was to the confederacy of the Latins, or Tuscans, the more a mistress for affecting to hide her power. All this will not be done at this session; the mob must be trained, and kept as ferocious as a Spanish bull, first teased by little darts stuck into his hide, before he is turned out to toss men and dogs.

To prevent this utter destruction of all that is worth saving, we must animate the federalists. We must try to raise their zeal high enough to defend, on principle, what the others would seize by violence. The federalists must entrench themselves in the state governments, and endeavor to make state justice and state power a shelter of the wise, and good, and rich, from the wild destroying rage of the southern Jacobins. Such a post will be a high one, from which to combine in our favor the honest sentiments of New England at least. Public opinion must be addressed; must be purified from the dangerous errors with which it is infected; and, above all, must be roused from the prevailing apathy, the still more absurd and perilous trust in the moderation of the violent, and the tendency of revolution itself to liberty. These latter expect order as the only thing that can ensue from confusion. Liberty, they think, gets rid of a fever by bleeding at the throat; her winding-sheet is so much wholesome clean linen. Her assassins say (and these dupes will believe they are her champions) she is a goddess, and cannot die.

It is indispensably necessary;—it is, I believe, though most of my friends say not—it is practicable to rouse our sleeping patriotism—sleeping, like a drunkard in the snow, to wake no more. It is possible to rouse the able men to action with pen and ink, and by their support of one newspaper—not a dozen newspapers, as at present—federalism would take the ascendant; the sense of the country would be nearly unanimous; jacobinism would sneak back into dirty lanes and yellow fever courts; vice and ignorance would march under their own banners, and, though we may be overpowered, we should not be deluded. Such an exertion, as I allude to, has not yet been made. The newspapers have been left to the lazy or the ill-informed, or to those who undertook singly work enough for six.

But, as I have written a long letter to Mr. Wolcott on this subject, I will not enlarge upon it here. Expect to see it, without a name, as soon as I can find courage to copy four sheets. This is certain, our revolution cannot be stopped, provided our rich and able men remain as inactive as they now are, or prove as great dupes as those of France did. No resources but those of the mind need be employed. Let wealth lie snug in its iron chest, and let its defense be committed to the wit, learning, and talent of a few, then it will be safer than armies could make it. But where are the few? A puzzling question. But England did not need an *anti-Jacobin* half as much as we do; yet a few were found there, who did as much as Lord Duncan or Lord Nelson.

TO CHRISTOPHER GORE

MY DEAR FRIEND,

YOUNG Warren has just called at the Council Chamber, (the Council is now adjourned till January next,) with your letter of October 15. I shall be happy to notice him for your, his father's, and his own sake. Colonel Dwight's seal came rather later than August, when you say mine was dated, and your letter. He, Colonel D., is pleased with it. He is member elect to Congress, and a good fellow; grateful for little favors from those to whom he ascribes great merit. I have also received seven volumes of books—Suetonius, Herodotus, Demosthenes; as to any others, I will employ James White, if I have occasion, though, I confess, I am very willing to ask any such service from you. Books claim and deserve more of my attention than fees. I am, in health, a man of straw; my declamation is not of the bar sort; and the clients are rather dull that I am not more out of credit with them than I am, which, however, is pretty generally. I hate the sort of application that needs drudgery. Impulses command me; I cannot command them; and the bar requires that they should be bespoke a month beforehand. Absolute poverty exacted of me, four years ago, that I should go to the bar and truck off reputation for cash. I am now, with the aid of Mrs. A.'s portion, and my own good management, which is better than you think it, rather better off. My farm will be soon productive; my India adventures turn out well; and though it pleases God to fill my house with children, (a son born in October, which makes my census four sons, one daughter,) yet beef and pork abound, and bread, and milk, and butter. I will not, therefore, work hard at the bar. *You* may, if you like it, yet I think you ought, but that you will *not* contract your expenses, in case you should get less than you expect in an office. I have written you at great length on the subject. You will soon have it. Though a nobleman, you ought to resume the practice. Joe Hall laughs at the project.

I have written a four-sheet letter to Mr. Wolcott, and one to you, yesterday, in the Council Chamber, which I have asked a friend to copy, on the state of affairs, and the need of exerting the best and utmost power of the pen, before the time comes (it is coming) to see the power of the sword. Your own I intend you shall have by this vessel, and a copy of that to Wolcott, and also of one I wrote, this day, to Jere Smith. The whole will show you nearly all my thoughts on paper. I am alone and unaided; you would impel things here with a force beyond all the rest. Revolution might be hindered: it will not be; for alone I cannot do it, and not a soul will help me. They sometimes yield to, but oftener stare at, my zeal, and, oftener still, laugh at my means. In the Palladium you will see an imitation of an ode of Horace, *ad navem qua Virgilius vehebatur.* You will suspect the author, from the *notes.* He is unsuspected here, and is supposed to be from Connecticut. Much may be done, and something more than the former lazy effusions shall be; but others are surprisingly inert.

Your friend, &c.

Bonaparte will surely flinch, if England does not. Democracy is a bully, fierce towards those who are afraid, conceding to those who defy. B. is no democrat, but he will not fight when England is ready and willing.

TO JEREMIAH SMITH

BOSTON, DECEMBER 14, 1802

MY DEAR FRIEND,

THE second French and first American Revolution is now commencing, or rather has advanced two sessions of the National Assembly almost, for the message will decide and do the work of the pending session. To demolish banks and funds, not directly, but under plausible pretexts, all false and cheating, all founded on experienced state policy, will be the first act, though the death-blow may not be given to either of them till the fifth, which will be three or five years later. To amend the Constitution, and give to Virginia the power to reign over us, is the next step. To do this, new activity will be used to raise and to strengthen the factions in each state, and to drill and equip them as *subs* to Virginia. The newspapers will lie and declaim as usual, and more than usual. Unprinted lies will be spread abroad, carefully steering off from post-roads and offices, as pedlars carry their packs, far out of the way of large shops. Emissaries, such as David Brown was, will be pedestrian and equestrian carriers of the *people's mail*. This is doing in all the obscure parts of New England; and the spirit of New England will be as much perverted soon, as it is flattered now. Even Connecticut, so ardent in federalism, will decline from her high station, and learn politics of Abraham Bishop. I am serious. A party inactive, is half conquered. The Feds maintain twenty opinions, the best of which is quite enough to ruin any party. "Let the people run themselves out of breath; all will come right; there is no occasion for us to do any thing." Others say, "We despair; nothing can be done with effect." Not unfrequently the same persons maintain both these opinions.

Let us be precise in deciding our object. First, negatively, it is not the regaining of the supreme power. The end is, security against the approaching danger, or the best security, if not perfect, that is attainable. What are the means? Not indispensably that we should again have a majority. It is enough to have a strong minority. That minority need not be very numerous; but it should be powerful in talents, union, energy, and zeal. It should see far, and act soon.

At this moment, we actually hold sway in three of the New England States. Vermont has a good governor, and many good Feds, almost one half the legislature. Rhode Island should be wrong, and lend the dirty mantle of its infamy to the nakedness of *sans-culottism*. New Jersey and New York are not hopeless. Delaware and Maryland are not yet as much emptied of federalism as Pennsylvania is,—say little of the more southern states, though federalism sprouts in all of them. It is, I own, however, with such a sickly, yellow vegetation as the potatoes show in winter, in a too warm cellar.

Now sum up the forces, and surely we are not to despair. We have a strong minority in numbers; of talents enough; of zeal little, but more may be excited, and the approaching danger, if duly represented, would excite it all. Self-defence exacts from us a union closer than ever, and supplies to our party the energy that party alone possesses—an energy that is inconsistent with languor or inaction in the chief men who inspire and guide it.

As the newspapers greatly influence public opinion, and that controls every thing else, it is not only important, but absolutely essential, that these should be used with more effect than ever. Let all the federal papers be kept up as high as at present; but let a combination of the able men throughout New England be made, to supply some one gazette with such materials of wit, learning, and good sense, as will make that superior to any thing ever known in our country, or in any other, except the English Anti-Jacobin in 1797 and 1798. To pretend to supply, with such materials, twenty federal papers, is absurd and impracticable. But, instead of uneducated printers, shop-boys, and raw schoolmasters being, as at present, the chief instructors in politics, let the interests of the country be explained and asserted by the able men, who have had concern in the transaction of affairs, who understand those interests, and who will, and ever will, when they try, produce a deep national impression. The pen will govern, till the resort is to the sword, and even then, ink is of some importance, and every nation at war thinks it needful to shed a great deal of it. As matters are actually arranged, the Palladium must be that paper. It must have, it must have by requisition, the contributions of the mind from those who are rich in that sort of treasure. One or two of that gazette ought to be crowded into every small town, and more into larger towns, throughout New England. It must be so supplied, as to need no helps in money, but to force its own progressively increasing circulation. It should clearly and aptly state the merits of every question; tell every inquirer exactly what he wants to know about the public business, and in the manner that will impress him—in the manner that will confound and disarm jacobin liars. The principles, the circumstances, the effects of measures should be unfolded, summarily, for the most part, but often by profound investigation and close argument. Business paragraphs should be short, clear, and frequent. Occasional essays should appear to examine speculative democratic notions, which yet prevail, and almost all of which are either false or pernicious, but often mischievous conclusions from admitted principles.

Wit and satire should flash like the electrical fire; but the Palladium should be fastidiously polite and well-bred. It should whip Jacobins as a gentleman would a chimney-sweeper, at arm's length, and keeping aloof from his soot. By avoiding coarse, vulgar phrases, it would conciliate esteem, and appear with an unusual dignity for a newspaper being. Foreign news should be skilfully exhibited, not in the jumbled mass that is usual. Literature demands the review of books, and especially of all newspapers, so far as their general scope, or any remarkable performances, require it. Agriculture should have a share, once a week at least, of the paper. Morals, manners, schools, and such disquisitions as general knowledge would supply, should be furnished with regularity. And for all these labors, various classes of able men should be engaged to supply these various departments. But for the superintendence and principal conduct of the paper, only a few should be selected, and the others should hold themselves as a body of reserve, to step in fresh when the front rank grows weary.

Only six able men in the different branches of this undertaking—I mean six men in the whole—would secure its success. McFingal Trumbull, I hope, would be one, as he is *Hermes redivivus*.

Will you think of these things? Will you make these ideas known, in confidence, to Governor Gilman and Mr. Peabody? Will you contribute, with your pen, to such discussions of law or constitution, or such pleasantries as you can easily forward to Warren Dutton, Esq.? Will you spread these opinions among your leading good men, and hasten their deliberate judgment on the only means to save our country? All this being done, and well done, in every state, then let the building up the state governments be considered an important federal object. Let state justice be made stable and effective, to shelter the wise and rich from the proscriptions, and decrees to make emigrants, that the progress of the American Revolution will produce. Let the first men be persuaded to take places in the state assemblies. Let a system of conciliation and courting of the people—I mean such as are yet undecided—be pursued; let it be a system of proselytism. Let the popular and wealthy Feds take commissions in the militia, and try to win the men. All this must be done, or all will be in confusion, and that speedily. Federalism cannot be lost, or decline much lower, without losing all; for though new parties would succeed federal and Jacobin, yet the extinction of federalism would be followed by the ruin of the wise, rich, and good. The only parties that would rise up afterwards will be the subdivisions of the victors—the robbers quarrelling about their plunder—all wicked.

Despondency, inaction, democratic sanguine notions, or federal despair, are to be renounced. I write as fast as I can, and am in a hurry to get done.

Now *you* may talk, for I require no more of your attention.

Your affectionate friend.

1 8 0 3 – 1 8 0 5

TO DWIGHT FOSTER

DEDHAM, FEBRUARY 6, 1803

MY DEAR SIR,

I AM at home, after passing the week in Boston. You will have learned that the struggle of the choice of senator is over, at least, supposing the Senate should concur in the election of John Q. Adams.[104] The Democrats exult because Colonel Pickering had not a majority, and because Skinner had a plurality of seventy-one votes. Jacobinism is full of ardor, and is proud of its power in the government. It boasts that all the south is democratic, and I confess I see little

---

[104] *Adams and Pickering were chosen senators from Massachusetts. Pickering had been a candidate for the House of Representatives, but had failed of election, though the majority against him was but small.* [S. AMES]

cause to expect that the southern state governments will be in federal hands. Louisiana is a subject of popular irritation, and of temporary embarrassment to the powers that be. But I foretell the acquiescence of public opinion in the measures of forbearance and disgrace. We shall sit down, as Junius says, as a nation infamous and contented. We shall preserve peace and lose character. We shall part with our rights, and with armies and taxes. The rogue, who has his ears cropped for forgery, may say, "Ears bring in nothing; I can hear as well as ever." What is national character but a phantom that delights in blood? Such is philosophy, on the pillory and in the chair.

Yet Kentucky may possibly break its bridle, and rush into business. How would our philosopher[105] tame the infuriate man of the mountains? Perish, he would not; coöperate, he dare not; tax, he dare not; raise troops, he dare not. Your surly Davis seems to understand the Quaker character of our government, that when one cheek of Kentucky is smitten, requires them to turn the other. I will not say that war ought to be chosen; it is a great evil. But it ought to be prepared for, and the best mean to avert it is by preparation. I leave to Mr. Jefferson to write pretty nonsense about peace and universal philanthropy.

The work of destruction seems to be retarded, and your democrats seem to wait for the next year's crop of ruin. I own I expected mint and debt would go this year. They go the next, and soon the workers of iniquity will follow their work, and worse destroyers will follow them. I hope nothing from time and truth, who tell, like gravestones, where the body rots. Passion and prejudice will slay, before they are chiselled and placed as memorials over the grave. Much

[105] *Jefferson. The Spanish authorities in Louisiana had recently refused to permit the deposit of American merchandise at New Orleans; an event which occasioned much excitement in the western states, and particularly in Kentucky.* [S. AMES]

might be done by writing; nothing will be. Federalism takes opium; Jacobinism gunpowder and rum.

We are told you are to resign. This I do not wish, and, all things considered, I am not sure I should advise. Your resolution will be taken before this will reach you, and your family will rejoice in it. I cannot, therefore, urge a reconsideration. Indeed Washington is not paradise but purgatory, where, I fear, sinners are made worse.

With the prevalence of southern politics, we have southern winters, rain in torrents, little snow, roads like harrowteeth when it freezes, and like swamps when it thaws. I am, dear sir,

Your friend, &c.

TO CHRISTOPHER GORE

———

BOSTON, FEBRUARY 24, 1803

MY DEAR FRIEND,

I BEGIN to wish, with more than usual impatience, for your return to Boston. Life is wasting away; and all that part of it that passes without enjoying our friends is time lost. Besides I am almost separated from all my federal friends. They are lazy or in despair, and they urge, with wonderful eagerness, the futility of all exertions to retrieve the public mind from its errors, or to prevent their consequences. I will not bore you with my side of the argument, which I still think as sound as I did before I began to be teased and vexed with any opposition to it. I still believe the talents of a nation might sway its opinions, if not its sceptre of elective power. The pen will rule till the sword is drawn; and no matter which side draws it or finally holds it, the sword alone will rule. Liberty will be lost, and a military government, not a whit the better or the milder for the victory having been gained by the good men, if that should happen, will be established.

Hence I maintain that all the energies, of the wise and good should be summoned into action, and strained to their *ne plus*, while this state of probation, this salvable interval shall continue. For when the progress of faction has reached violence, we go to our future state—to that region from whose bourne no republic can return. Fully impressed with the idea that we are making this progress; that for want of a strong impulse on the public mind, our federal strength is wasting, some part is lost by timidity, some by sloth, some by apathy, and much more by the envy and mean spirit of competition, which are sure to divide a party when no impulse, stronger than these petty passions, combines it,—I have, over and over again, made the offer to almost every considerable man in Connecticut and New Hampshire, as well as Massachusetts, to form a phalanx to write, &c.

My offers have produced some ridicule, more disgust, no coöperation. Weary and disgusted myself, despairing, as well I may, of any good effect from my single efforts, I now claim the quiet repose that, like a fool, I have so long refused to enjoy, and that I have so fruitlessly offered to renounce. I have done. And even if to-morrow the combination of able and industrious writers were made, I think I should persist in preferring my ease to the labor and obloquy of scribbling. I begin to relish the apathy that benumbs my friends. Zeal is a bad sleeper, and I will try opium with the rest of them. Expect me then, in future, to write about pruning apple trees, or breeding cattle. Let the federalists who are made for slaves, although their driver will be at great charge for whips, reap where they have sown; their harvest is ripening, and it will be all tares.

I hear that the debates of Parliament denote a risen spirit in England. I rejoice in it—as they have the power, I am glad they have the spunk to resist the new Romans. But Bonaparte will not accept the challenge. As long as he can avoid war with John Bull, he will, and any nation that is willing and prepared to fight him, he will not fight. The French heroes seek no foes, but such as their own fears or the arts of France have already conquered. If, however, Russia will join England, I expect to see the war renewed *nolente* Bonaparte. As to Louisiana we shall sit down infamous and contented. Prayers and missions are our arms. If Victor should arrive at New Orleans, he will coax, bribe, and terrify; he will grant; by way of indulgence to the friends of liberty, what he will refuse as of right to the nation. Kentucky will be pacified to sell its produce, and lose the title to the navigation of the river; and when a war breaks out between France and England, the latter will block up the mouth, and the French will use the American flag to protect their own French cargoes, and the exercise of the rights of search and capture will be used with success, as a subject of complaint against the English. Thus we shall be useful tools to France, and she will have an influence to make us her associates in the war, if she has occasion for it. Yet I expect that France will see impending dangers from Great Britain so near and great as to delay the expedition to Louisiana, till a more convenient season, which may not soon arrive. At any rate our government dare not go to war, nor lay a tax for one hundred pounds, nor raise a battalion. The claims of Kentucky are embarrassing to them, and some pretext is wanted, that will pacify the wild men of the mountains for the present. France will furnish some pretext, and then we shall hear boasts enough of the wisdom that has saved our peace, and the spirit that has vindicated our honor. Is there any point on the scale of disgrace lower than that to which we have descended?

Massachusetts has yet a show of federalism. It may last a year longer. In the mean time, all that can be corrupted is corrupting, and all that cannot be perverted is nodding into a lethargy. The Jacobin mode of waging war resembles the expedition of Diomed into the Trojan camp. There is to be seen only a quick destruction, that provokes no resistance—the victims die without waking. At Worcester, the son of Levi Lincoln is to pronounce an oration on the accession of Mr. Jefferson to the Consulate, and a great feast is to be made, that the ignorant may eat and drink themselves into jacobinism. This pretty business is to be transacted also on a great scale at New Haven. Connecticut stands, but its good men should say incessantly, Take heed lest we fall. The race for governor here will probably be uncontested; no symptoms yet appear of his Excellency Governor Gerry, being run. The General Court is busy making banks and turnpikes. A great bank in Boston, of twelve hundred thousand dollars, is now in debate in the Senate, having passed the House. It is supported by the principal moneyed men in this town, and opposed by John Q. Adams, whose popularity is lessened by it. They say also he is too unmanageable. Yet he is chosen Senator to Congress in consequence of a caucus compact, that if Col. Pickering should not be elected on two trials, then the Feds would combine and vote for J. Q. A. This happened accordingly.

A bill reducing our seven judges to five, as soon as two vacancies shall happen, altering their terms, and allowing at one of the two terms in a county, one judge to be a quorum, and raising their salaries to $2000 when such reduction shall take place, has passed the House. Its fate in the Senate is dubious. It is a proof of melioration that a competent salary is voted. We may need the state tribunals as sanctuaries, when jacobinism comes to rob or slay. I pray you write often, for nothing is more acceptable than news from you. I pray you offer my best compliments, &c. to Mrs. Gore, in which my wife always most sincerely joins.

Yours, &c.

TO CHRISTOPHER GORE

OCTOBER 3, 1803

MY DEAR FRIEND,

YOUR welcome favor of the 15th of August by the Galen, received this moment, reminds me that I must write by the John Adams, nearly ready to sail, in which Mr. Lowell and family are to be passengers. By him, you will of course expect to get news of me. Yet he has not lately seen me, and knows only from report how I am.

Many months ago, I believed my health in danger of a downfall. A series of colds half the winter, and all the spring, and through summer a bad stomach, and a laxity and irritation of the lower viscera, announced a crisis not far distant. Accordingly in August, I had a severe fainting fit, followed, as it was caused, by that complaint. For four days, my life was apprehended in instant danger. I sent, *in extremis,* for Dr. Jeffries, and have since taken other advice. I have renounced wine, butter, tea, and almost cider, and I think my change of regimen has produced a small, but progressive improvement of my condition. . . . I creep slowly and often sliding back, along the steep side of that hill from which I leaped headlong in August last. These details will not be

uninteresting to you. I will only add, the visceral irritation
has diminished, and my decline of strength is arrested at
least. I have yet exuberant spirits, and should talk myself to
death if I yielded to ten dollar clients, who urge me to go
into Court, to keep my wits and my fibres, only half an hour
for each of them, on the grindstone. This I have had the
sense and the fortitude to refuse doing. I ride five miles in
a chaise and return weak and weary, but daily stronger. Oh,
if I could step on board the Adams, pass the winter in
London, and return with you in May, how delightful! yet I
am a fool to add, how painful! I am seriously advised, and
importunately urged, to take a voyage to Calcutta, and I have
offered, in that event, to use my endeavors with the British
government to ransom one of Tippoo's sons for a king, whose
color and hereditary principles qualify him excellently to
reign over the Jacobins. I hope that I can recruit by staying
at home. It is a problem whether the sea air, seasickness,
and the *et cœteras*, which on shipboard must be borne, if I
could not bear them, would not give me to the sharks. My
health, now it seems to be worth so little care, engrosses all
I can bestow. The object of my life is to live, and to ascertain
which answers best, boiled rice, or a dry rusk. Thus my
friend, I am an outside passenger in the journey of the
political folks. I take my part of the jolts and the dust, but
am not to touch the reins with one of my fingers.

As to Louisiana, I agree with you in almost all your
opinions. I cannot conceive that our Monroe and Livingston
were ignorant (they ought not when the convention was signed
to be ignorant) that the war between the First Consul and
Great Britain would be renewed. I also say that the acquiring
of territory with money is mean and despicable. For as to
the right of navigating, &c. the Mississippi, *that* was our
own before; and the nation that will put its rights into
negotiation, is deserving of shame and chains. The least
show of spirit, the least array of force, the slightest proof

that any measure of shame, however ample, might find at last even *our* cowardice would reject, this would certainly have brought the Consul to terms—to any terms. As to the money we are to pay, I care not for it. As to the territory, the less of it the better. But the abject spirit of our administration is below all scorn. In such a state of things as we see, the rulers have the lowest of all personal and private views to answer. Their popularity is their all. Even that vile trinket is at risk. I do not believe that in New England, and especially with the yeomanry, they have gained applause. The merchants at the southward look with eyes of favor to the opening of the port of New Orleans. The western settlers also like the thing, and care not what mean compliances, nor how many millions it costs. The Mississippi was a boundary somewhat like Governor Bowdoin's whimsical all-surrounding orb—we were confined within some limits. Now, by adding an unmeasured world beyond that river, we rush like a comet into infinite space. In our wild career, we may jostle some other world out of its orbit, but we shall, in every event, quench the light of our own.

Two causes might make a government free in principle, tranquil in operation, and stable in its existence: Separate orders in the state, each possessing much and therefore pledged to preserve all; or, secondly, the pressure of an external foe. The latter would produce the most exalted patriotism—the former would provide the most adequate substitute for it. But a democracy is only the isthmus of a middle state; it is nothing of itself. Like death it is only the dismal passport to a more dismal hereafter. Such is our state. Yet we have so few rabble, power centres so much in the hands of, say, three hundred thousand small landholders, and our state governments, rankly teeming with poison, so naturally sprout with the antidotes—because every separate mass of power breeds fear and hostility towards every other preponderant mass, that I have hopes blended with my anxiety, and I say that the crisis of our evils is probably more remote than my day or probably than yours, or even my children's. A safer conclusion is, that a case so anomalous as ours, so unlike every thing European in its ingredients, its action, and thus far in its operation, will baffle, for a long time, all the conjectures and prognostics that are drawn from other scenes. Not that I fancy other republics were ruled by men inferior to our heaven-born administation, or that our citizens are *angeli implumes*, as flattery has already made them believe,—but the means for faction to work with, and the means for good men to resist faction, are essentially different here from what they were in Greece or Rome, or even in pure France. Quiet is forbidden to us. Hope is not, chiefly because we can discern some impediments to our ruin, though scarcely any practicable path to our liberty. Monarchy is no path to liberty, offers no hopes. It could not stand, and would, if tried, lead to more agitation and revolution than any thing else. Our political soil must be seeded, like the earth after Noah's flood. Some of the seeds are winged and float at random; some swim in the flood, and no one can foretell whether they will strike root, or where; others are swallowed by birds, and dropped in the regions to which they may migrate; others lie buried deep in the ground, covered with an oily coat, sealed up for posterity, when the plough may by some chance bring them up to the surface. How many ages it will take, for the right plants to get established in the right places, I know not. I leave that problem to Thucydides the second to decide, in his new History of the American Peloponnesian War, and whether that war will be between Virginia and New England, or between the Atlantic and Tramontane States, or whether Chaos and old Night will jumble together the elements of society, as in France, the poor against the rich, and the vile against the worthy, I say not. No muse has told me, and uninspired I cannot tell you.

I dismount from my Pegasus, as an invalid should not ride too far at a time, and observe, in prose, that I think Congress will ratify the Convention,[106] and provide the needful to carry it into effect. But I hope the orators on the federal side will fully develop the subject, start all the fair objections and no others; and impress on the public every topic that will hold the administration responsible for this great affair, as their measure, which, without approving or aiding, the Feds will not obstruct by their votes;—they will make it intelligible; they will call for explanations and answers to objections, so that the whole force of their reasons shall be left to operate with the nation. This contrast would signalize federalism. For in the case of the British Treaty, since proved to be a good one, the Jacobins opposed *con furore*. Now the Feds show their regard for principles by their forbearance, and resort only to truth and argument. I will not be sparing of any means in my power to urge the grant of your outfit. But I have not confidence enough in the powers that be to expect that such hearts will devise liberal things.

I observe that the valiant printers of London threaten to invade France, with royalists under the command of Pichegru and Dumourier and the Princes. I hope not yet. It is too soon. If the invasion be laid aside, and the arms of the Consul should be in disgrace, the coward spirit of Europe may be roused, the weight of their new chains may make the nations weary; and after two or three years, an insurrection, once begun in Brittany, the Low Countries, Italy or Holland, may be furnished with officers, money and continental aid, with some effect. But until the British nation has become really martial in spirit, and confident in discipline, it is too soon to think of encountering France in her interior or in her dependencies. It would be putting too much at risk, and with too little chance of success. A failure would prove a sad

---

[106] *With France.* [S. AMES]

disaster, as it would remove, to an indefinite distance, the reduction of the gigantic power of the Consul.

The brilliant success of your Commission ought to crown Mr. Jay with glory,[107] and wreathe very green honors about your head, my friend. For I know very well your perseverance, and your being so much *au fait* on all the many questions that have occurred, has contributed essentially to the success. Your own mind and your friends will bestow the due praise; perhaps the body of the merchants will allow as much per cent. as they pay when bankrupt. But the Jacobins and the administration will not forgive you the success that puts them so much in the wrong.

OCTOBER 7

Mr. CABOT was here at my house yesterday, and had much to say about you. He almost advises me to take a trip to England. But while I hope I shall do well at home, I doubt extremely whether I could bear the hardships even of a favorable voyage. But should it please God to give a little addition to my strength before spring, I may then contemplate, with some seriousness, the project of visiting London. At present I should be barely able to get as far as Boston.

I shall be very happy to see you here in May next, because, among other reasons, I calculate that I must then have better health, if I do see you. Be that as it may, I shall be, as long as I am any thing,

Your affectionate friend, &c.

Mrs. A. joins with me in best regards to you and Mrs. Gore.

---

[107] *The indemnities awarded to American merchants by the Commission amounted to about six millions of dollars.* [S. AMES]

TO THOMAS DWIGHT

DEDHAM, OCTOBER 26, 1803

MY DEAR FRIEND,

I HAD resolved to write to you, before I received any letter from you. For a week this scheme of merit has been formed and postponed, till by your esteemed favor, with the printed copy of the message, it has this day failed entirely.

I am glad to hear of your safe, though weary, arrival at the heaven of other men's ambition, your purgatory, where indeed you will see good spirits, with *other* spirits conjured by democracy from the vasty deep. Remember what I have often told you, that the scene you are entering upon will form the best characters, and display them to the greatest advantage. The furnace of political adversity will separate the dross, but purify the gold. You will have the best society, under circumstances to endear it to you and you to them. To serve the people successfully, will be out of your power; the attempt to do it will be unpopular. To flatter, inflame, and betray them, will be the applauded work of demagogues, who will dig graves for themselves, and erect thrones for their victors, as in France.

The principles of democracy are everywhere what they have been in France; the materials for them to work upon are not in all places equally favorable. The fire of revolution burnt in Paris like our New England rum, quick to kindle, not to be quenched, and leaving only a bitter, nauseous, spiritless mass. Our country would burn like its own swamps, only after a long drought, with much smoke, and little flame; but when once kindled, it would burrow deep into the soil, search out and consume the roots, and leave, after one crop,

1466

a *caput mortuum*, black and barren, for ages. If it should rain blessings, and keep our soil wet and soaking, it might not take fire in our day.

Our country is too big for union, too sordid for patriotism, too democratic for liberty. What is to become of it, he who made it best knows. Its vice will govern it, by practising upon its folly. This is ordained for democracies; and if morals as pure as Mr. Fauchet ascribes to the French republic, did not inspire the present administration, it would have been our lot at this day.

But on reading the message I am edified, as much as if I had heard a Methodist sermon in a barn. The men who have the best principles, and those who act from the worst, will talk alike, except only that the latter will exceed the former in fervor. But the language of deceit, though stale and exposed to detection, will deceive as long as the multitude love flattery better than restraints, as long as truth has only charms for the blind, and eloquence for the deaf. Suppose a missionary should go to the Indians and recommend self-denial and the ten commandments, and another should exhort them to drink rum, which would first convert the heathen? Yet we are told, the *vox populi* is the *vox dei;* and our demagogues claim a right divine to reign over us, deduced no doubt from the pure source I have indicated.

.   .   .   .

Your truly affectionate friend, &c.

TO THOMAS DWIGHT

DEDHAM, OCTOBER 31, 1803

MY DEAR FRIEND,

I HAVE this morning received by post your delightful treaty,[108] and S. H. Smith's paper, and your esteemed favor, in which you give me a particular account of yourself and your accommodations. This latter is really more interesting to my curiosity and feelings than the rest of the contents under cover.

There is little room for hope, almost none for satisfaction, in the contemplation of public affairs. When *somebody* (a Jacobin too) drives, we must go; and we shall go the old and broad road, so smooth, so much travelled, but without any half-way house.

Having bought an empire, who is to be emperor? The sovereign people? and what people? all, or only the people of the dominant states, and the dominant demagogues in those states, who call themselves the people? As in old Rome, Marius or Sylla, or Cæsar, Pompey, Antony, or Lepidus will vote themselves provinces and triumphs.

I have as loyal and respectful an opinion as possible of the sincerity in folly of our rulers. But surely it exceeds all my credulity and candor on that head, to suppose even they can contemplate a republican form as practicable, honest, or free, if applied when it is so manifestly inapplicable to the government of the third of God's earth. It could not, I think, even maintain forms; and as to principles, the otters would as soon obey and give them effect, as the *Gallo-*

---

[108] *A copy of the Convention with France. Mr. Dwight was at this time a representative in Congress.* [S. AMES]

Hispano-Indian omnium gatherum of savages and adventurers, whose pure morals are expected to sustain and glorify our republic. Never before was it attempted to play the fool on so great a scale. The game will not however be half played; may, it will not be begun, before it is changed into another, where the knave will turn up trumps and win the odd trick.

Property at public disposal is sure to corrupt. Here, to make this result equally inevitable and inveterate, power is also to be for some ages within the *arbitrium* of a house of representatives. Before that period, Botany Bay will be a bettering-house for our public men. Our morals, forever sunning and flyblown, like fresh meat hung up in the election market, will taint the air like a pestilence. Liberty, if she is not a goddess that delights in carnage, will choke in such an atmosphere, fouler than the vapor of death in a mine.

Yet I see, that the multitude are told, and it is plain they are told because they will believe it, that liberty will be a gainer by the purchase. They are deceived on their weak side; they think the purchase a great bargain. We are to be rich by selling lands. If the multitude was not blind before, their sordid avarice, thus addressed, would blind them.

But what say your wise ones? Is the payment of so many millions to a belligerent no breach of neutrality, especially under the existing circumstances of the case, when Great Britain is fighting our battles and the battles of mankind, and France is combating for the power to enslave and plunder us and all the world? Is not the twelve years reserve of a right to navigate, &c. a contravention of our treaty with Great Britain, as all other nations are for twelve years excluded from a participation of this privilege, especially too as the increase of the French and Spanish navigation is avowedly the object of the stipulation?

I have not yet read the treaty. I have only glanced my eye over the seventh article. I am weary and sick of my subject.

My health is bad, and is to be bad through the winter. I sleep poorly, digest poorly, and often take cold. I persevere in riding on horseback, and shall saw wood in bad weather when I cannot ride. I live like an ostrich or man-monkey, imported from a foreign climate, and pining amidst plenty for want of the native food that would suit his stomach. Mine is as fastidious as a fine lady's, who is afraid of butter on her potatoes, lest it should tinge her complexion.

I intend soon to try the lukewarm bath in the evening, not often, but occasionally. A bad digestion is an evil not to be removed. Its effects I hope may be parried by finding something that I can better digest than my usual food.

My wife and I join in saying, God bless you.

Being yours, &c.

TO CHRISTOPHER GORE

————

DEDHAM, NOVEMBER 16, 1803

MY DEAR FRIEND,

You will soon see Edmund Dwight, who sailed in the ship John Adams, and hear from his mouth all that relates to my health. The care of this object is all that occupies me. In good weather, and in bad, I find exercise to ride in the one, and saw wood in the other; and, on the whole, I have some strength, though not much new flesh to boast of. I am confined to my house and six miles round it, and have seen Boston but once in the last three months. Being thus out of the world, you will not expect much from my correspondence, and this must be my excuse, if I write seldom and short.

Our own politics are unworthy comment. We are in the hands of the philosophers of Lilliput. I have lately read Randolph's and Nicholson's speeches in reply to R. Griswold's call for papers,[109] and I protest that the Court of Sessions, in old Justice Gardner's day, produced as good sense and as good logic. What can be expected from a country where Tom Paine is invited to come by the chief man, as Plato was by Dionysius; where the whiskey secretary is Secretary of the Treasury; and where such men as the English laws confine in gaol for sedition, make the laws, and unmake the judges? The purchase of Louisiana is said to begin to make trouble for these poor creatures. The Don blusters, in the person of the Marquis Irujo, and swears we shall not have it; and the majority seem to be ready and willing to send General Wilkinson to serve an *habere facias possessionem* at New Orleans. Our people care not much for these things. To get money is our business; the measures of government and political events, are only our amusements. To be told of our sovereignty, our rights, &c., &c., only gives zest to that entertainment; it does not change its nature, nor our nature.

In England I behold a real people, patriotism broad awake, and holding authority over all the passions and prejudices of the nation. This, at least, is the outside look of the thing. I well know how deceptive this often is. You are behind the scenes, and, probably enough, discern the meanness of those who seem to play the great parts so well. We expect a great *fête* for Bonaparte, as soon as the dark nights admit of his passage. I confess I am not quite free from inquietude in respect to the invasion. I suppose his passage possible; if he should land an army on English ground, his first victories probable, and his ultimate defeat certain. Great Britain is not to be conquered; but I place little reliance on the tailors

---

[109] *This call was for a copy of the treaty between France and Spain, under which France claimed a title to Louisiana.* [S. AMES]

and men-milliners in regimentals; they would be beaten. Pray let me hear from you often.

I am more than ever engrossed by my farm. *Hic libertas, hic patria.* It is liberty to have one hundred acres, and that is emphatically *my* country. How much my swine weigh, how much milk my cows give, what bright hopes I have in my trees, I will not tell you; yes, I will, when you come here to eat my pork and Indian pudding.

Mrs. Ames enjoins it upon me, to offer to you and Mrs. Gore her best regards with my own.

Your friend, &c.

TO THOMAS DWIGHT

DEDHAM, NOVEMBER 29, 1803

YOUR LETTERS, my dear friend, afford me so much pleasure and information, that I cannot forbear writing without ingratitude, nor write without making very barren returns. Whether bad health has abated my ardor in every thing, or that the inevitable consequence of having nothing to do with our politics is, that I cease to care who has, or how the work is done, the fact is certain, I am almost at home expatriated from the concerns that once exclusively ingrossed my thoughts. In this philosophic, lackadaisical temper, I really think my fellow sovereigns participate. Congress-hall is a stage, and by shifting the scenes, or treading the boards in comedy or farce, (for, since the repeal of the judiciary, you do not get up tragedy,) you amuse our lazy mornings or evenings as much, or nearly as much, as the other theatres. But, in sober truth, the affair is as much theatrical on our part as on that of the honorable members on the floor. You personate the patriot, and we, the people, affect the sovereign. We beg you to believe, on the evidence of the newspapers, that we watch you closely, and lie awake a-nights with our fears for the public safety. No such thing. We talk over our drink as much in earnest as we possibly can, and among ourselves, when nobody is a looker-on whose opinion we dread, we laugh in the midst of our counterfeit rage. The fact is, our folks are ten times more weary of their politics, than anxious about their results. Touch our pockets directly, or our pleasures ever so indirectly, then see our spirit. We flame, we soar on eagles' wings, as high as barn-door fowl, and, like them, we light to scratch again in the muckheap. Alter the Constitution; amend it, till it is good for nothing; amend it again and again, till it is worse than nothing; violate without altering its letter, it is your sport, not ours. Our apathy is a match for your party spirit. The dead flesh defies your stimulants. We sleep under the operation of your knife, as the Dutchman is said to have gnawed a roasted fowl, while the surgeon cut off his leg. There is no greater imposture than to pretend our people watch, understand, or care a sixpence for these cheap sins, or the distant damnation they will draw down on our heads. If honest men could associate for honest purposes, if we had, in short, a party, which I think federalists have not, or have not had the stuff to make, their steady opposition to the progress of a faction towards tyranny, revolutionary tyranny, might be checked. I waive the subject, however, on which I have a thousand times vented my vexations to no purpose. Peace to the dead!

Louisiana excites less interest than our Thanksgiving. It is an old story. I am half of Talleyrand's opinion, when he says we are phlegmatic, and without any passion except that for money-getting.

Mr. Huger, in his speech on the alteration of the clause respecting the votes for President and Vice-President, pays compliments to the candor and sincerity of the amendment-mongers, when they protest and swear, that they want no other amendment. This compliment is not worth much to the receivers, but is a costly one to the bestower. Roland and Condorcet always protested that they would stop. But is a revolution or the lightning to be stopped in midway? Mr. E. has libelled the Constitution in a newspaper. The Virginia Assembly has voted amendments of the most abominable sort. All the noble lords of Virginia and the south are as much for rotation in office as the senators of Venice. It is the genuine spirit of an oligarchy, eager to divide power among themselves, and jealous of the preëminence of any one even of their own order.

Mr. R., in his speech on the constitutionality of acquiring territory, has risen again in my opinion. I cannot readily assent to the federal argument, that our government is a mere affair of special pleading, and to be interpreted in every case as if every thing was written down in a book. Are not certain powers inseparable from the fact of a society's being formed? are they not incident to its being? Besides, as party interprets and amends the Constitution, and as we the people care not a pin's point for it, all arguments from that source, however solid, would avail nothing.

One of two things will, I confess, take place: either the advances of the faction will create a federal party, or their unobstructed progress will embolden them to use their power, as all such gentry will if they dare, in acts of violence on property. In the former case, a federal party, with the spirit which, in every other free country, political divisions impart to a minority, will retard and obstruct the course of the ruling faction towards revolution; and if they do not move quick, they will not, perhaps, be able long to move at all. In case of a strong opposition, (I use the term in a qualified and guarded sense,) the federalists could preserve some portion of right, though they might not have strength to reassume power, which, I confess, I do not look for.

Suppose an attack on property, I calculate on the "sensibilities" of our nation. There is our sensorium. Like a negro's shins, there our patriotism would feel the kicks, and twinge with agonies that we should not be able so much as to conceive of, if we only have our faces spit in. In this case, we could wipe off the ignominy, and think no more of the matter. He that robs me of my good name, takes trash. What is it but a little foul breath, tainted from every sot's lungs? But he who takes my purse, robs me of that which enriches him, instead of me, and therefore I will have vengeance.

Hence I am far from despairing of our commonwealth. It is true, our notions are pestilent and silly. But we have been cured already in fourteen years of more of them than a civil war and ten pitched battles would have eradicated from France. The remainder are, indeed, enough to ensure our destruction; and we should be destroyed, if these silly democratic opinions, which once governed us all, were not now so exclusively claimed and carried to extremes by those whom we so dread and despise, that we in New England are, in a great measure, driven out of them. The fool's cap has been snatched from our heads by the southern Demos, who say this Olympic crown was won by them. Let them wear it.

Connecticut is sound enough perhaps; for if democracy were less in that state, federalism would sink with them as in the other states. But their first men are compelled to come forward in self-defence. They are in the federal army what the immortals were in the Persian, or the sacred band under Pelopidas. I will not mention Vermont. Rhode Island is not to be spoken of by any body. But New Hampshire, old Massachusetts, and Connecticut are too important to be forced into a revolution; and, at present, appearances do not indicate that they will join in hastening it on willingly.

For these and other reasons, I think our condition may not soon be changed so essentially as, in like critical circumstances, it would be in any other country. We shall lose indeed almost every thing; but my hope is, that we shall save something, and preserve it long.

Thus we may, like a wounded snake, drag our slow length along for twenty years; and time will in that period have more to do in fixing our future destiny than our administration. Events govern us; and probably those of Europe will, as heretofore, communicate an unforeseen and irresistible impulse to our politics. We are in a gulf stream, which has hitherto swept us along with more force than our sails and oars. I think the government will last my time. For that reason, I will fatten my pigs, and prune my trees; nor will I any longer be at the trouble to govern this country. I am no Atlas, and my shoulders ache. No, that irksome task I devolve upon Mr. . . . ., and Mr. . . . ., of the House, and Mr. . . . ., of the Senate. You federalists are only lookers-on.

You are a polite man, otherwise you would say I have tired you. In that respect I have used you as well as I do myself. In mercy to both, I this moment assure you of the affectionate regard with which I am, dear friend,

Yours, truly.

TO THOMAS DWIGHT

DEDHAM, JANUARY 25, 1804

MY DEAR FRIEND,

THE VIOLENCE of Randolph and Co. against the judges somewhat exceeds my estimate of the man and the party.[110] Democracy is a troubled spirit, fated never to rest, and whose dreams, if it sleeps, present only visions of hell. I have long thought justice one of the most refined luxuries of the most refined society; that ours is too gross, too nearly barbarous, to have it. Justice, to be any thing, must be stronger than government, or at least stronger than the popular passions. Nothing in the United States is half so strong as these passions; indeed the government itself has no other strength. I have contemplated an essay, to show that democracy and justice are incompatible; but Randolph's tongue outruns my wits, and proves before I could discuss.

I am very early in life arrived at the still water, where all is contemplative, and nothing is action. I live, the ambitious would say I stay, but it is for my friends and my family. My health is bad enough; but, on the whole, very good for a bad sort. God give you health, long life, and patience.

Yours, ever.

---

[110] *The Judge of the United States District Court for New Hampshire, had recently been impeached and removed. Articles of impeachment were voted also against Judge Chase, who was tried and acquitted. Randolph afterwards, in his mortification at this failure, proposed to*

TO COLONEL DWIGHT

DEDHAM, JANUARY 10TH, 1805
THURSDAY EVE

MY DEAR FRIEND,

I HOPE Judge Chase has good advisers. The declining a trial may be right, but whether it will make impression as right is a grave matter of consideration which I am not competent to decide. I cannot but remark how J. Randolph denies the constitutional power of Congress to legislate over a drop of Virginia water, and seems ready to claim the recession to that state of the part of the federal territory that lies west of the Potomac, while no doubt exists of the right to abolish courts or buy wild land *out* of the Union for new states. The doubting faculties of these gentlemen of the *Dominion*, a word no longer to be used jocosely, seem to be well trained. I enjoy it to see Clairborne so much at home in debating on the *mud* of the river—and a Mr. Jackson is no believer in the doctrine that *the people may be their own enemies*. Of course I must be permitted to be a doubter of his sense or spirit of independence. Either a man must be as ignorant as most of his constituents, or basely servile to their prejudices, to avow his belief of the contrary doctrine.

When a man mistakes his own talents, he generally leads other people to underrate them. That I candidly think is the case with Levi Lincoln. He will return richer, but more

---

amend the Constitution, so as to make the judges removable by joint resolution of the two Houses. He also prevailed upon the House to refuse to pay the respondent's witnesses. The violence spoken of in the text was displayed in a debate in the House on the adoption of the articles of impeachment against Judge Chase. [S. AMES]

disappointed with his lot in life than if he had not been tempted by the political devil to change it. Will our demos, when they begin their reign with power and glory, make him a lieutenant governor or a judge—or will Mr. Jefferson make him a judge when another vacancy is made by death, resignation, or removal—which last vacancy maker seems to be more efficient than his good brother death.

The making of a president by election goes on as smoothly as the making of a justice of the peace by commission of the governor and council. All this time, the people imagine they elect. And as the name and the bustle of election is all that pride and levity desire to have, the mistake will last possibly half a century. I do not see any reason to suppose there will be any discontent from any violations of right or Constitution that the ruling faction may perpetuate. Any people will bear wrongs because they may be blinded by their authors.—But insults by which tyrants get nothing must be forborne. Tarquin was a tyrant many years before he was an exile, but when his son raped Lucretia every father in Rome felt the sense of his degradation. Then and not till then, the people or rather the aristocracy took fire and resorted to arms.

Nat continues to walk better, but still limps. The Doctor has no fears of a remaining lameness. Little Jeremiah is also better then he was when you left us. Worthington is still at home, and for the present goes to the town school. Mrs. Ames is often complaining, but advances unusually well for her. May heaven in its mercy take care of her. As my domestic treasures multiply, I am exposed to more alarms and perils.

It is snowing briskly and bodes a deep snow.

Yours affectionately

FISHER AMES

TO THOMAS DWIGHT

DEDHAM, JANUARY 20, 1805

MY DEAR FRIEND,

IF I write often, as I like to write, you must be content to accept very little at a time. My stock of merchantable ideas will not bear any thing beyond a small retail trade. There was a time when I was foolish enough to think the examination of a public question of some public importance; but since party reasons are the only ones sought for and regarded, I am duly and humbly sensible of the impertinence of urging any other. Congress may restrict the trade to Saint Domingo, and hang the traders, or permit the French to do it. Our public, I engage, will be as tame as Mr. Randolph can desire. You may broil Judge Chase and eat him, or eat him raw; it shall stir up less anger or pity, than the Six Nations would show, if Cornplanter or Red Jacket were refused a belt of wampum. The boast of a love of liberty, so often repeated, like a coward's boast how he would fight when once he gets hotly engaged, is all bluster. Perhaps Connecticut has some spunk. The rest of the Yankees have none; and will part with their plaything, liberty, with less of the pouts than your or my children would yield to any boy big enough to be president, their gingerbread chariot. Virginia has nothing to fear from us, and we have nothing to hope from her.

. . . . Governor Caleb's speech is a calm defiance of the votes of next April. For once I think his preaching on principles in the abstract seasonable, and because such preaching is now as effectual as any other.

. . . .

TO JOSIAH QUINCY

DEDHAM, NOVEMBER 27, 1805

MY DEAR SIR,

THE late condemnations in England have filled men's minds with anxiety, and not a little eagerness of expectation of the measures of Congress.[111] It is a misfortune for a man, who has nothing to do with public affairs but to talk about them, to have his doubts on popular questions. This is my case. I am very willing the British should turn out exceedingly in the wrong, in regard to condemning our vessels when laden with colony produce. If they are not in the wrong, I see not the policy or fitness of hazarding our commerce, peace, and prosperity, on an untenable point. Force of guns is on their side. I would not voluntarily have the force of argument against us also. In case a candid examination should create many doubts of our assumed principles, as I think it will, why should we make the retracting of the contrary principles by England a *sine qua non* of our measures? You will see many members very willing to kindle and blaze, because England is in question. Others, I think, will in their hearts feel hostility to eastern commerce, and act from that hostility. Some more will be ignorant, and will be made to believe all the blustering tales our vanity has to tell, about the dependence of England on the United States. Confiscation of British debts is a measure very like war. There can be no other

---

[111] *Several American vessels had recently been condemned by the Admiralty Courts in Great Britain, for reasons that were considered new and strange, and to be justified only by a forced construction of maritime law. Their neutrality had been declared to be fraudulent and evasive, on grounds that produced great alarm among our merchants.* [S. AMES]

ground for it, than as reprisals for losses by their unjust condemnations. When angry nations resort to reprisals, they ought to expect war, and prepare for it. A non-intercourse act, so much commended in the Chronicle, is little better. Unless the administration intend war, they are, except their dishonor and folly, measures of no avail.

I cannot believe our administration intend to fight England. I cannot think of any way Mr. Jefferson has to extricate himself and the country from out this scrape, so eligible as to remonstrate to that court, and to spin out the affair into length, till he feels bold enough to make a British Treaty, if he can, and perhaps the new coalition will be dissipated, and John Bull will be in another year more pliant. My hopes of that coalition are slender, as you know. Austria is hearty in the cause, but wants power. Russia has power, but is not hearty. To reduce France within moderate limits will require an age of battles, and England alone is possessed of the means, and forced to display the courage, to fight them with the necessary perseverance. I expect reverses and disasters, and that Great Britain, now on the high horse, will dismount again. The time will come, therefore, when negotiation may effect much. Menace and the base hostility of confiscation will surely prevent its being effected. I could fill a dozen sheets with speculations, because I should deal in conjectures. I will spare you. Why should one Yankee help another to guess?

The session portends much bustle and debate. I confess I see no prospect of any auspicious issue to it, either as it respects the prosperity or rather security of commerce, or the effect on our public in favor of the old Washington system. Among your friends I shall feel not the coldest, in regard to the impression your public labors may make, being, with unfeigned regard,

Your friend, &c.

TO THOMAS DWIGHT

DEDHAM, NOVEMBER 29, 1805
THANKSGIVING EVENING

MY DEAR FRIEND,

N. IS BETTER. His leg is yet much swelled, but nearly free from pain, and the doctor hopes no suppuration will ensue. You will rejoice with us, for our revived hopes make a truly joyful Thanksgiving. In every other respect, it is dull enough.

M. and H. are at my mother's, in search of something more cheerful than my house affords. They have fine spirits, and improve, I make no doubt, by their Medford school. My John W. sits by me at his book, "the world forgetting," and enjoying a Thanksgiving feast for his mind. It is true, he reads on such occasions for amusement, but I indulge him, for I hope something will stick to him. The habit of literary labor may be ingrafted on the free stock of literary curiosity. I will not defend my metaphor, but I believe my meaning is expressed clearly by it. A passion for books is never inspired, I believe, *late,* in the breasts of those who, having access to books, do not feel it young. But to apply, to investigate closely, to study, to make the mind work, is a very different thing from a passionate fondness for battles and romances. It is by performing tasks, not by choosing books for their amusement, that boys obtain this power to fix and detain attention.

But is there encouragement in our country to educate boys for any great degree of usefulness? While faction is forging our fetters, the specious talents are more in demand than the solid. But after a tyranny is settled, perhaps our Augustus will have a fancy, that learning is an essential thing to his glory. Nero pretends to be an artist himself, and would feel himself eclipsed by the excellence of another.

Every popular despotism is, I believe, in its inception, base and tasteless. As great geniuses snatch the sceptre from the hands of great little rascals, the government rises, though liberty rises no more. Ours is gone, never to return. To mitigate a tyranny, is all that is left for our hopes. We cannot maintain justice by the force of our Constitution; yet, I think, the spirit of commerce, which cannot be separated from the Yankee mind, is favorable to justice. To guard property by some good rules, is a necessary of life in every commercial state.

But it is foolish, or rather it is presumptuous, to speculate on the untried state of being that our degraded country has to pass through.

> Vestibulum ante ipsum, primoque in limine Ditis
> Luctus et ultrices posuere cubilia Curæ.

I quote from memory of Virgil's sixth book, perhaps not correctly.[112] The application seems to me fearfully correct. At the threshold of our new state of being, we are to meet the *Luctus et ultrices Curæ.*

I will leave my letter open till morning, to inform you more of N.

Your affectionate friend.

---

[112] *Virgil's words are:*
> *Vestibulum ante ipsum, primisque in faucibus Orci*
> *Luctus et ultrices posuere cubilia Curæ.* [S. AMES]

TO TIMOTHY PICKERING

DEDHAM, DECEMBER 2, 1805

MY DEAR SIR,

I HAVE just returned from Boston, where I find the merchants have had a meeting on Mr. Fitzsimmons's letter, and appointed a committee of seven.[113] Our friend Cabot is much—too much, mortified that he is one of them. He hates hypocrisy, and respects principles, and he dreads lest the popular feeling should impel the committee to deny what he believes to be true, or to ask for what he knows to be mischievous. I confess I have rather approved the meetings of merchants. Losers will feel and complain; and capricious and fickle as passions are, when they possess a multitude, interest will keep the merchants as steady as the anchors do their own ships. Besides, this body is not loved nor cherished by our government, and I like to see them claim and take their place as a part of the people. I expect more good than evil from their interposition, especially if such men as Cabot will consent to appear among them. I hope they will be prevailed on soon or late to depute such men as James Lloyd and Thomas H. Perkins to the government, as their committee, who could not fail to impose respect on the Sam Smiths[114] among you.

If party considerations may be admitted, it seems to me a time when the probable hostility and undeniable negligence of our administration, in respect to our commerce, may be

---

[113] *On the subject of the condemnations in admiralty in England.* [S. AMES]

[114] *Mr. Smith was a senator from Maryland.* [S. AMES]

made appear. The very hatred of Great Britain, which generally locks up men's minds against argument, will now rouse them to attention. I have not the least doubt, that an early attempt at negotiation would have been successful; and why the attempt was not made, when the British instructions of June, 1803, plainly denounced the now experienced evil, I cannot comprehend on any grounds, but the want of good will or good sense, in regard to the hated and dreaded moneyed or trading interest of the United States. In 1803, Great Britain was alone, and wished help or countenance from any quarter. Then she would have been comparatively pliant. Now she is arrogant, or at least elated with her new allies, who, I think, will not help her long or much. Even yet the chance of negotiation is worth something, and as we can only humbly pray, while others fight, it is worth every thing to us. Negotiation seems to me the object we ought to propose to ourselves. The administration, probably, does not wish to fight, and, least of all, to fight for commerce and for Yankees. Their ignorance may choose hostile measures, supposing them to be equally safe and efficacious. Their malice towards trade may be delighted to hear the *vox populi* calling for its poison. The influence of Bonaparte, whose resentment they dare not rouse, whose aid they still court, whose friends are their friends, may hurry them on to sequester, and other violences. The popular rage may be easily roused against Great Britain; but, if I mistake not the temper of the country, they love their gain more than they hate England, and therefore peace, and the measures of peace, and a negotiation to preserve it, may be supported on popular grounds. The attempt ought to be made, as it will be right in itself, and is the best defense against the furious rashness of the faction of revolutionists. I know that government possesses the power to move, or to stop moving, in this business. But I think public expectation ought to be steadily and strongly directed to this end. It would not be policy to concede, at once, all that Great Britain claims, even if we should think her claim plausibly well grounded. It seems to me that her practice, during the late war, ought to be urged as her own exposition of her rights; and if she would adjust the matter on that footing, I believe it would be satisfactory to the merchants. I wrote lately to Mr. Quincy on the subject; and I find Mr. Cabot has forwarded by mail my long letter to you. I omitted, to both of you, one remark, which, though perhaps quite unnecessary, I will now subjoin.

The conduct of Great Britain is undoubtedly unpopular, which, in our country, is the test of right and wrong. Inquiry usually stops at that point. I hope the federalists will be very shy, therefore, and cautious how they come out as the avowed apologists for England. It is for our own best interest that we ought to provide; and, that we may be permitted to do it in any degree, I hope the Feds will not needlessly make themselves unpopular, by vindicating the British principles. Waiving such discussion, is it not clear that Mr. Monroe, or the government, neglected all reasonable care of our commercial concerns? And is it not the point for prudence now to ascertain, how our embarrassed trade can be most effectually relieved from the effects of their unexpected operation? I am not to lecture you on these matters; but I well know you hate all evasion and duplicity.

My letter would have been shorter, and much more to the purpose, if I had bestowed more time and meditation upon it.

The *message* is expected, as the raising of the curtain of our political playhouse. With respect and esteem,

Yours, unfeignedly.

TO JOSIAH QUINCY

DEDHAM, DECEMBER 16, 1805

MY DEAR SIR,

I RECEIVED this day, and have read with pleasure, your favor of the 6th. The message seems to me ill written, and liable to endless criticism as to its matter. Mr. Jefferson seems to take his ground, that the British principle is wrong, and is to be resisted in every event. When Spain violated a treaty, without any pretext for the violation, then he was for negotiating, pimping, begging, and buying; any thing but fighting. What a difference! How does he know that the British Cabinet claim the principle, as they exercise it of late by their Admiralty Courts? Answer: By their Instructions of June, 1803. Why then did he not long ago remonstrate or negotiate in London? A grain of prevention, say the wise, is worth a ton of remedy.

Suppose the British doctrine right, is it to be met in arms, in "the bloody arena"? Suppose it wrong, is its error not to be exposed by Mr. Monroe's able and spirited notes, before we make resort to measures of compulsion? And do nations undertake to compel other nations, more proud and powerful than themselves, without expecting the game to be shifted from acts of Congress to broadsides? Be it that Great Britain is unjust, yet all men will say the object of our patriots is to preserve our peace and commerce, if they can be preserved with due regard to the dignity of the nation. Angry measures of commercial restriction, in the first resort, seem to throw away both these objects. Why does our Solomon, in the first instance, put down his foot, that Great Britain is unwarranted in her doctrine, unless he means to appeal to the *ultima ratio regum*, and to make that appeal absolutely necessary?

Negotiation is the measure that I should think he would adopt, if even party wisdom guided him. Our federal few ought not, I am sure, to be the advocates of Great Britain, nor yet flinchers from the truth of principles. There are ways of stating the British reasoning, so as to check and confound the Jacobin declaimers, without becoming responsible for its conclusions. Yet, I am clear, the folly of prohibitions, sequestration, &c., ought to be strongly exposed; and I verily believe our multitude will not fail to applaud the side of peace and moderation. Our merchants are not thought to be so sanguine now in condemning the British doctrine, as they were three weeks ago. It would be madness to assume, as a *sine qua non* of peace with England, a doctrine that we could not sustain any better in argument than in arms. The federalists not being the responsible men, ought to expose the mischiefs of the measures proposed by the dominant party; and in case such as are recommended by the Jacobin gazettes should be brought forward, the task would not be hard.

As to your part, my friend, I wish you to reserve yourself to act as circumstances may require, after the progress of debate has afforded you all the means of being decided. I shall take great pleasure in observing the rise of your reputation; and as I know you love your country with passion, the increase of your influence with your parliamentary experience will be a good omen.

The symptoms of discord among the bad deserve notice. By dividing, their power to destroy will be diminished.

I pray you offer my best wishes to Mrs. Quincy, for herself and the children.

Yours, with unfeigned regard, &c.

1 8 0 6

===

TO ELIPHALET PEARSON, LL.D

DEDHAM, JANUARY 6, 1806

SIR,

I HAVE RECEIVED notice through a friendly and authentic, though unofficial, channel, that the Corporation of Harvard College, at a meeting on the 11th December last, unanimously elected me President of that University.

However I may have been accustomed to rate my claim to reputation, I could not fail to perceive the influence of this event to extend and confirm it. I can say, with gratitude, as well as with unfeigned sincerity, and on due reflection, that, situated as I am in life, and with my habits of thinking, there is no testimonial of public approbation that could be more soothing to my self-love, or, in my conception, more substantially honorable to me, than the suffrages of the learned and truly respectable members of the Corporation.

On the first information I had of the choice, I perceived instantly that it was due to the Corporation, as well as to the members individually,—to the public, as well as to myself,—that I should bestow my most careful thoughts upon the subject; that I should delay my determination till I had revolved every consideration of propriety and duty that ought to influence it; and that as soon as possible after I had thus matured my final decision, and without permitting its disclosure to the public, I should hasten, with equal frankness and respect, to lay it before the Corporation.

. . . .

My first and only difficult inquiry was to ascertain what is my duty in this case. I should be unworthy of your very flattering approbation, and should certainly impair my own, if I could resolve to decline the office of President against a clear sense of moral obligation to accept it. Two considerations have, nevertheless, appeared to me to allow that I should decide the question with a perfect liberty of choice. In this widely extended and not unfruitful field of the sciences, it will not be thought an excess, or an affectation of modesty, if I believe, and assume it to be certain, that there is ample room for the selection of a candidate, at least as well qualified for this important office as I can pretend, or even imagine I am thought, to be. While I view the University as one of the brightest lights and ornaments of our quarter of the globe, I rejoice that its interests are committed to gentlemen whose zeal for their advancement is no less ardent than pure. Am I not, then, warranted to act on the supposition, that such a selection will, of course, be made? To this I can truly add, that the slender health which I have but very recently enjoyed, and which almost every week's experience admonishes me I hold by an unusually frail tenure, has, by God's blessing, slowly accrued by my persisting to renounce almost all the cares, even more apprehensively than the labors, of life. However by your indulgence the labors of the office, if

I should enter upon it, might be diminished, the high responsibility, the anxious solicitude, the strenuous exertion inseparable from its duties, would remain, and to these, it is my entire belief, my health would prove inadequate.

As considerations of duty, therefore, are so far from exacting my acceptance of the appointment, that they actually deter me from it, I might, very properly, desist from alleging any further reasons for my decision. I have none of equal force. But I think it will readily occur to every discerning mind, that a man, so far advanced in life as I am, ought to dread as fatal, or at least perilous, to its happiness, so complete a change of all its habits as I must make, if I should be transferred from the position I now occupy, to that more distinguished one which you are pleased to offer me.

I should submit these considerations to you, sir, and to the gentlemen of the Corporation, with no little pain of mind, if I did not anticipate from your known candor and good sense a ready acquiescence in the result to which they have impelled me. Being, therefore, not only permitted, but, as I conceive, constrained, to decline the appointment, to which you have proposed to raise me, I wish it to be explicitly understood, that I do decline it; and may the great Source of wisdom enlighten you in the future election of a President.

I must beg you to communicate this letter, with the expressions of my most grateful respect, to the gentlemen of the Corporation; and allow me to add, that I am, with sentiments of entire esteem,

Sir, yours.

TO JOSIAH QUINCY

DEDHAM, JANUARY 20, 1806

MY DEAR SIR,

You will find no want of correspondents, and the greater number will exact from you more, in point both of frequency and length of letters, than comports with my notion either of justice or liberty. To write as much as business or common civility requires, is no small task for the representative of the capital of Massachusetts. And I consider too, how unreasonable it is to expect a Congress-man can fill letter after letter with important matter, when your wise body actually brings nothing to pass; and if any thing be intended to be done, you forlorn Feds, who are not allowed to attend the legislative caucus, can know nothing about it. A wanderer on the deserts of Barca, can call no variety of fruits or flowers. *Apropos*, I liked your amendment of Barca for Lybia. Classical names, when laid aside, are no more to be used than *quidnunc* names never yet adopted, as Doctor Mitchell's Fredonia. I hate Columbia too, because it is not *our* name, nor can all the efforts of all our literary fops bring it into vogue. I wish Congress may learn that giving swords and medals lothly, and by bare majorities, is not conferring honor. In stable governments, usages become laws. Things wear a certain channel for themselves; and if they bear along some abuses in their current, they do not stagnate for want of current. Without a metaphor, habits, if not principles, then govern; whereas, in democracies, prejudices not only subvert every thing that is sacred, but disfigure every thing that is decent. The discussion of the question of *"Thank you, General Eaton,"* is both rudeness and ingratitude. Is Eaton a hearty federalist? Is he, on that account, obnoxious to the ruling Virginians? Is Lear a favorite with them?

Mr. Jefferson's message indicates that he looks to Congress as the fountain of power. He says and unsays, and seems to be willing to stand to any thing that the two houses will signify they would have him say. This is the natural course for the head of a party; he evades responsibility. When the seal of secrecy is broken, we expect to know what Congress, acting in the diplomatic line, will do. If confiscation, non-importation, &c., should be agreed to, the seventh seal will be broken—the seventh vial poured out; and as the woes denounced in that event will reach the workers of iniquity, I cannot think our rulers will be passionately fond of the project. When the time allowed by fate arrives, I, as one of the people, shall be glad to know what is to be done, and who are the agents of the great political work. Is Randolph really in discredit, as the gazettes allege? Is Bidwell viewed by this grand seignior as a brother too near the throne? Who is Clinton? not De Witt. Is Brown, of Delaware, as fine a fellow as Bayard? While you are seeing the play, I, who have no ticket, should like to know the *dramatis personæ* a little better. If you should think fit to send a page or two of "federal scurrility," I will put it into the fire. I must be allowed to read it first, to know that it is scurrility.

The answers to my questions may not fill more than a quire or two of paper; and as federal members have not the least concern with the deliberative business of Congress, the work of filling those quires may keep you busy, but cannot interrupt your discharge of duty. Without banter, I claim nothing from you as a correspondent, neither punctuality, nor frequency, nor quantity, nor labor; but observe, as a friend, I am not willing to abate any of my pretensions to your remembrance and regard. In the full exercise of them, I beg leave to assure you of the esteem with which I am, dear sir,

Yours, truly.

TO TIMOTHY PICKERING

DEDHAM, JANUARY 28, 1806

MY DEAR SIR,

I HAVE had it in my thoughts to examine the question of our right to trade with the revolted part of Saint Domingo, as it is laid down in books. And I well know, that to meddle with it in a loose way is peculiarly improper in a letter to you, who spare no pains to get at truth, and hold every substitute for it in contempt. Nevertheless, as I perceive I shall be occupied on some turnpike business, and hindered from reading writers on the law of nations, I feel a desire to communicate such thoughts as rise uppermost.

Nations very properly abstain from assuming the decision of questions of right between any two contending powers. Facts alone are regarded. When, therefore, one state claims from another subjection and obedience, which that other refuses to yield, and maintains its refusal by successful arms, no third power will constitute itself the judge of the legitimacy of its reasons for so refusing. The actual possession of independence is ground enough for holding a state independent of right, as far as third parties are concerned nationally. I mean, that the trade to such a self-made new state, is not a national offence against the power claiming sovereignty over the revolted country. This intercourse is at the peril of the private individuals concerned, whose cargoes may be seized and confiscated by the cruisers of the offended nation. But their so continuing to trade, seems not obviously to implicate the nation to which the traders belong, unless that nation, or its government, should do some act, whereby such responsibility is assumed. For the greater clearness, I will put a case. The Dutch assumed independence in 1570 or '80. While this event was recent, and the contest depending, the Dutch cities suffering sieges, and the armies of Spain superior in the field in Holland, the supply of arms by Queen Elizabeth was, of course, an act of aggression. But for a London merchant to send flour or sugar at the risk of capture by the Spaniards, it seems to me, would not amount to an act of intermeddling by the English government; especially, I will add, if the queen had, by proclamation, apprised her subjects, that a civil war raged in Holland, in which she would take no part; and that she forbade her subjects trading with the Dutch, on the peril of capture, as aforesaid, by the Spaniards, in which case she would not claim restitution, nor afford protection to the captured. The war would then proceed by Spain against English traders; and the supplies poured into Holland would afford no ground for hostilities against England. But after the Spanish armies were beaten out of the country, and the lapse of near thirty years without any effort to subdue the Dutch, the capture of such vessels would be apparently unjust.

Whether the suspension of the efforts of France to recover Saint Domingo, merely because of the war with England, amounts to an abandonment of the colony, is questionable. There is, in fact, no doubt she intends to resume the business, as soon as the *mare clausum* becomes once more a *mare liberum*, by a peace with Great Britain. *Ad interim*, any national act of intermeddling, on the part of the United

States, in favor of Dessalines, would be an aggression. Permitting the use of force against French captures may possibly be unwarrantable. But the declaring, by Mr. Jefferson's proclamation, that traders taken in such commerce will not be protected; in other words, that they traffic with Dessalines at their peril,—that is, the peril of capture by the French,—I should think, would exculpate our government and nation, on principle.

For Congress to legislate, seems to me quite another thing. It is *ex abundantia*, it is more than France can properly require. If Mr. Jefferson should issue a proclamation, declaring the trade unauthorized, and at the peril of the concerned, it would be left to the French to enforce the law as it now exists, by capturing the vessels, if they can. But for us to extend, or create rights and remedies for them; to say, you cannot catch these wrongdoers, but we can and will, seems to be journey-work for Bonaparte. As I premised, it quits the ground of matter of fact for perplexing theories. If the power of France is not adequate to exclude Saint Domingo from the exercise of its independence, it has just the same right, the right of the strongest, to independence, that other nations found their exercise of it upon. It is already *de facto*, and of course *de jure*, independent.

On the other hand, if France has means to cut off the trade of that island, and to capture the vessels concerned in it, let her use those means. We abandon our traders to capture.

Thus the question is left to work its own peaceable decision, without compromitting the tranquillity, dignity, or rights of either the United States or France. Has the latter any right beyond the foregoing, that is, to a public disclaimer by proclamation of all protection to those concerned in trading, and to a faithful forbearance to form treaties, or afford any aid, as a government, to the black emperor? Is not the request, or rather insolent claim, of more than this, an admission that Saint Domingo is lost to France, and that the United States must turn the war into a blockade to starve the blacks into submission? Is it not saying to us, We do not merely ask your forbearance, we insist on your coöperation; you must meddle, but only on our side?

If my ideas are made intelligible, they seem to me of some use to discriminate the line of right and duty in the case, which line, perhaps, is to admit, that the French have rights, and leave them to exercise them as they now exist, but to refuse legislating for extending those rights or enforcing them by our power.

As to the line of policy, I can scarcely doubt, that we ought to shun a quarrel with France upon the point, if France contents herself with claiming no more than an existing right, and the enforcing it by capturing the vessels in the trade. If she claims more from the United States as a vassal, our dignity should be temperately asserted, and her demand civilly but firmly refused. We ought by no means to commit ourselves to the discredit of a treaty with Dessalines, or in any way to intermeddle as a government. But we ought to wish most earnestly, that Hayti may maintain its independence; and so much the more, as the colonial systems of all nations may be expected on a peace to abridge our intercourse with the dependent islands.

I have run the risk to write these crude conceptions as fast as I can drive my quill, and I can assure you, I shall feel no mortification, if it should turn out, that I commit several mistakes in the argument. I am, dear sir, with unfeigned esteem,

Yours, &c.

P.S. It occurs to me to add, that there is some, though I am aware, not a close analogy between the case of our trade with Hayti and the revenue laws of foreign nations. To enforce these, one state never asks legislative or any other aid from another. Yet smuggling is an evil. I know it has been said, that the reason for this mutual forbearance is, that revenue laws are merely municipal, and create neither right nor obligation out of the territory for which they were made.

But, as a matter of right, we equally abstain from the question depending in arms between the two emperors, Dessalines and Napoleon. The fact that Saint Domingo once acknowledged, and now refuses to acknowledge, the supreme authority of France, is all that we know, or will, if we are wise, concern ourselves to know. The rights claimed by France are merely, that we shall not intermeddle in the contest; not that we shall help her.

Justice requires that I should make it understood, that I claim from you no answers to my communications. I would sooner suppress such of my letters, than have them operate to impose a task on you.

TO THOMAS DWIGHT

DEDHAM, FEBRUARY 1, 1806, SATURDAY

MY DEAR FRIEND,

ALL habits grow stronger as we grow older; and I am sorry to find that the bad habit of neglecting to write to you becomes more inveterate by indulgence. I condemn myself for it, and go round the beaten circle of resolving to do better in future. But what avail wise *saws* against foolish propensities?

Happening to be in the office, pen and ink before me, and expecting your brother J. this evening, I say to myself, nick the moment, and write, or you will persist in your sins, and aggravate them by your fruitless repentance. Conscience, which will sometimes meddle against old sinners, speaks out, contrary to custom, with some authority, and I obey.

These few lines come to let you know, that I am very well, sickness excepted, as I hope you are, without exception, at this present writing. Want of exercise brings want of appetite that furs my tongue and dulls my wits. I sleep worse, and yet am a sleepy fellow; and, on the whole, have ground for two dozen complaints about my health, and not one new apprehension.

Why did you not invite me to visit Springfield? That omission, some care of our ever-depending turnpike, the depth of the snow, and its faithless appearance in this thawy weather, banish or retard the project I wish to ripen and execute of going with my one-horse cutter to your town. Why should I not? Do I not want some of your large pepper seed? The dry season forbade mine to ripen. Do I not want to see your great bridge? Do I not want to drink your cider, which article is scarce here? How reasons thicken in my catalogue. Yet as they govern me just as little as they do the rest of this stubborn, unreasonable world, I think it probable I shall not go; and that, on the aforesaid grounds, it is much more proper that you and your good wife should come here, although you could not find one of the reasons for it that I have urged in my own case.

As you would not come for pepper seed, nor to drink cider, nor to see the Dedham canal up Charles river, which is not to be seen, I will readily admit that you both come to see Mrs. A. and your humble servant. I will not enlarge on the weight these last motives would have with any other good people, but my vanity stiffly maintains that they have influence with you. Indeed it founds itself a good deal on such kind of pretensions.

Sir, I was elected President—not of the United States; and do you know why I did not accept? I had no inclination for it. The health I have, would have been used up at Cambridge in a year. My old habits are my dear comforts, and these must have been violently changed.

How much I was in a scrape in consequence of the offer, and with what three weeks' mystery and address I extricated myself, are themes for conversation when we meet. I have extricated myself, and feel like a truck or stage horse, who is once more allowed to roll in the dirt without his harness. Everybody has heard of Mrs. A.'s proposing that I should take H. A., if I went to Cambridge, as *she* would neither go nor learn Greek.

Apropos of Hannah Adams. Her abridgment of her History of New England, for the use of schools, has, I believe, superior merit. I have read a chapter, and, after reading more, shall put my name to the recommendation of the work. Young . . . . , and others, friends to modest merit, have bought the whole of her first edition, and a second is preparing. I wish to see it in use.

Are you sharp-shooters of Hampshire ready to get the bounty for Englishmen's scalps? . . . . .'s intemperate folly shows the temper of the ruling party. If a step should be stirred onward in that path, we are plump in a war. I have hoped that the sacred shield of cowardice, as Junius calls it, would protect our peace. I still hope. Yet this tongue-courage is a bad omen. If we assert rights that we cannot maintain by argument, and that we will not enforce by arms, what follows from our so early putting down our foot—so positively stating that Britain usurps our rights, and that we never will abandon them? What, I say, but an increased and a very unnecessary propensity on both sides to war; an indisposition to negotiation, "the only umpire between just nations;" and a tenfold disgrace, if we tamely forbear to enforce our claims, or explicitly renounce them? In point of true dignity or common prudence, this preliminary engagement of our government to be inflexible seems singularly absurd. Mr. Madison's great pamphlet on the maritime principle of Great Britain, however plausible and ingenious, is an indiscreet pledge of the government, and of the public opinion, to maintain what we know England will not concede, and we will not enforce.

I could subjoin, that the chief labor of Madison is to show that Great Britain has no right from old treaties nor from old writers. He might as well show that neither Aristotle nor the laws of Solon make any mention of such a principle. A new state of things exists, and a new case requires a new application of old principles. Here, I strongly apprehend, the decision will be against us at "the bar of reason," where Mr. Jefferson, like the crier, summons Mr. Pitt to appear and answer. How is it possible for Great Britain to defend herself, without the utmost use of her navy? And how can she use her navy with any effect against her deadly enemy, if she leaves his colony trade free to neutrals, and thereby makes that immense fund of wealth cheaply accessible to France? I confess, I know not. But why do I bore you with a prize question?

N. continues to mend. We are all well. Thank you for more of Doctor Lathrop. Remember me to all friends, especially to those of your household. A kiss for little Bess.

Yours, &c.

TO TIMOTHY PICKERING

DEDHAM, FEBRUARY 1, 1806

MY DEAR SIR,

THE proprietors of the stage through Dedham to Hartford have procured a list of subscribers to a petition to Congress, that the Postmaster-General may be required, by law, to cause a mail to be carried, three times a week, on that road. Being a Dedham and a turnpike man, I premise that I am an interested witness. Still I come forward to testify, that reasons exist to recommend their petition, which others will allow to have force.

This great extent of country is destitute of information, except by a slow creeping mail on horseback once a week; and as all information is admitted by our rules to come through newspapers, the people may be supposed to be in a benighted condition, being too, for half the distance, Connecticut folks. The request may possibly awaken the town patriotism of Mr. Granger, and the Worcester men may feel as if their preëminence, as to the mail, would be attacked. You know the middle road; it is the nearest. The stage is supported with spirit, and in excellent order; and I should think the expense of a mail need not be very great to our economical government, as the stage runs without it. While it is better for the public that the mail should go in the stage, I suppose it is nearly essential to the future success of the proprietors of the line, that they should get the contract. They promise great expedition. A turnpike is made, or granted, the whole distance, and the due improvement of the road, where it wants any, depends on the arrangement in question, as without it, the want of enterprise and want of means, which so long obstruct improvements, will retard this.

I shall be informed by getting my Boston newspaper with my breakfast; and yet I cannot suppose that accommodation, singly taken, would induce our loving administration to spend many dollars on the contract. Be this as it may, I have made a promise to Messrs. Trask and Wheelock, the stage owners, in Boston, that I will use my influence in promoting this project. This influence I was obliged to leave them at liberty to believe very considerable, otherwise I could not have resisted their importunate request to put my name to their petition.

They did not seem to comprehend why my name would create them opposition. I did comprehend it, as I believe you will. Will you then allow me to assign over these men and their affair to your attention and friendly patronage. Having been at the head of the department, you ought to have more influence than I claim. I am, with esteem, &c.

Yours, truly.

TO JOSIAH QUINCY

DEDHAM, FEBRUARY 1, 1806

MY DEAR SIR,

MESSRS. Trask and Wheelock, two knights of the currycomb in Bromfield lane, and proprietors of the stage through Dedham to Hartford, from a sheer love to the public, are willing to use and abuse their horses to expedite the mail in eighteen hours in summer, provided that Congress will order the Postmaster-General to make a contract with them to carry it three times a week. Even love, you know, grows faint if unrequited. Here we sit in darkness; and instead of having the light of the newspapers, the only light men can see to think by, shed dingy and streaked every morning, like Aurora, we often have to wait, as they do in Greenland, for the weather and the northern lights. The town stage is often stopped by rain or snow; the driver forgets to bring the newspapers, or loses them out of his box. This is our bad condition here. How much worse it is ten miles farther from Boston, you may conceive. The darkness might be felt. Now, as the government alone possesses information, and as the stage-horses alone are the pipes for its transmission to the printers, who are the issuing commissaries to the people, we, the people, the rank-and-file men, ask our officers, through Trask and Wheelock, to provide for our accommodation. Let us have food for the mind every other day.

The middle road is the nearest, by twenty or twenty-five miles; besides Mr. Dowse lives upon it, and as it is now all turnpike, in fact or on paper, and as fifty miles of it through Connecticut, without granting the petition, might not in any season, if at all, get knowledge of Mr. Wright's bill, and his bounty for shooting Englishmen, the public reasons are the strongest imaginable for ordering the Postmaster-General to make such a contract. It would not cost much; and as the increase of mails increases letter-writing, who will say that ultimately it will cost any thing? The only sensible economy in farming is to spend money; it may be so in government matters.

To be serious, there can be no doubt the public good requires the arrangement in question, as Sam Brown, George Blake, and Dr. Eustis subscribe the petition. The Worcester road may seem to be attacked, by the conferring the high prerogative of a mail three times a week on a parallel road; and Granger's bowels may yearn for his imperial city of feathers and wooden trays, which is situated on the route through Springfield. Pray do what you can for these folks, and get others to help you. Even Mr. Randolph ought to promote these views, as it will, no doubt, increase the number of the readers of his speeches.

Yours, truly, &c.

TO JOSIAH QUINCY

DEDHAM, FEBRUARY 12, 1806

MY DEAR SIR,

YOUR highly esteemed favor, of 27th January, reached me on the 8th, and that of the 30th January, on the 10th February. Shall I say they give me pleasure? I had curiosity to pry into the books of the fates, and your answers are like those of the ancient interpreters of those books, to inquirers predestined to ruin,—a terrible satisfaction of curiosity. I had hoped our feeble chief would have done nothing, and left time and chance to work for our country. But Gregg,[115] or the evil one, will not let us profit by events. Our folly must meddle, and hasten our destruction. Non-intercourse surely needs no exposure as a folly. Admit its inefficacy, it is proved. Admit its efficacy, will Great Britain wait to have it manifested? She can bear a war as well as we; non-intercourse, say they, worse. The option is for her to make, which she will bear. Park exposes it well in his Repertory. I sit at home, and mope, ignorant of any effects of Congress's extravagance on prices. I have not seen George Cabot, to whom I will show your favors.

The conquest of Europe seems already achieved by Bonaparte, if we may believe French accounts. I do not believe them without great allowances, yet, truly, I see little means and less spirit of resistance left there. England would merit ruin, if she accepted peace, and took it quietly. Russia surely has force enough untouched; but distance, want of

---

[115] *Mr. Gregg, of Pennsylvania, had proposed resolutions for the non-importation of goods of British production.* [S. AMES]

money, and blockheads in the cabinet, for they glide in through every keyhole, may incline her (I can scarcely think it) to quit "the bloody arena." In case Europe accepts peace and chains, we, of the United States, are ripe and rotten for servitude and tribute. Bonaparte would have no need to pull trigger. Disguise the name, and we shall furnish our quota as cheerfully as Italy or Spain. If Burr goes and finds Bonaparte triumphant, Jefferson has a master, and the United States a prefect. In point of military preparation, we are scarcely a match for the Mamelukes, or even the cooks of the world's emperor; and our one hundred thousand militia would do little more in the field than the tailors that make their uniforms. Prussia has probably fallen like a forest tree, not by cutting it down, or prying up its roots, but by felling the neighboring trees that sheltered and propped it. The backwoodsmen will tell you that such trees fall, because the very zephyrs that fan their leafy tops loosen their foundations. Yet these woodsmen are our legislators, and make our commerce not the object to contend for, but the weapon to contend with. This is certain, if England cannot save Europe, we cannot save ourselves. The spirit that would buy rights when Spain violates them, would pay tribute when France offers land to disguise it. I have long thought a democracy incapable of liberty. It seems now almost impossible that we should long enjoy the honor and happiness of a tyrant of our own.

Company interrupts, and I will finish my croakings. Please to offer my best wishes and respects to Mrs. Quincy.

Yours, truly.

TO TIMOTHY PICKERING

DEDHAM, FEBRUARY 14, 1806

MY DEAR SIR,

I HAVE sent your letters to Mr. Cabot, who, I am sure, will think their contents as interesting as I do. Indeed, "they suit the gloomy habit of my soul," as Young says in his Zanga. I am infinitely dejected with the view of Europe, as well as of our own country; and I begin to consider the utmost extreme of public evils as more dreadfully imminent than ever I did before in my life. I have long consoled myself with believing that the germs of political evil, as well as of good, lie long, like the unnumbered seeds of every species of plants, in the ground without sprouting; and that it was unnecessary and unwise to contemplate the possibilities of national servitude, and, more properly, of universal convulsion and ruin under a French empire, as either very near or very probable. Late events, I confess, lessen my confidence in the military capacity of resistance of all the foes of France, England not excepted. A fate seems to sweep the prostrate world along that is not to be averted by submission, nor retarded by arms. The British navy stands like Briareus, parrying the thunderbolts, but can hurl none back again; and if Bonaparte effects his conquest of the dry land, the empire of the sea must in the end belong to him. That he will reign supreme and alone on the Continent is to be disputed by nobody but Russia; and if pride, poverty, distance, false ambition, or fools in his cabinet persuade the Emperor Alexander to make a separate peace, France must be Rome, and Russia, Parthia, invincible and insignificant. The second Punic war must terminate in that case, for aught I can see, in the ruin of England; and the world must bow its base neck to the yoke. It will sweat in servitude and grope in darkness, perhaps another thousand years; for the emulation of the European states, extinguished by the establishment of one empire, will no longer sustain the arts. They and the sciences will soon become the corrupters of society. It is already doubtful whether the press is not their enemy.

I make no doubt, Bonaparte will offer almost *carte blanche* to Russia and Austria, saving only his rights as master; and I greatly fear that Russia will be lured, as Austria will be forced, to abandon Great Britain. Another peace makes Bonaparte master of Europe.

Russia has soldiers, and they are brave enough; and I should think so vast an augmentation of the French empire would seem to Alexander to demand the exertion of all his vast energies. Without Pitt's gold, this will be a slow and inadequate exertion; and how Pitt is to get money, if neutrals take this generous opportunity to quarrel with him, I cannot see.

If we intend to quarrel and to assert our rights in arms, it may be wise and right to take up our cause as we do; for if England will not recede, we cannot honorably,—which last word, I well know, is a mere expletive, of no more import than a semicolon, or rather an interjection. If we resolve that Great Britain shall fight or yield, and that the United States will sooner fight than yield, it is all; of a piece to argue and bluster as we do. But on the hypothesis, that we mean peace in every event, the folly of this prompt assumption of our ultimatum is strange. I am the more ready to think it so, because I expect to hear John Bull say, he is as little convinced as afraid. Like a good citizen, I am silent while our side is argued; but I am far from thinking it impossible that the question should appear to the candid and intelligent to have another side. If it has, I abstain from all insult and reproach, and from all feelings of indignation against Great

Britain for her alleged "interpolations." On one point, her condemning without notice, I think her culpable, and that if an envoy like Mr. King were sent, she would refund.

It is ever a misfortune for a man to differ from the political or religious creed of his countrymen. You will not fail to perceive, that I am worse than a lingerer in my faith in the conclusiveness of the reasoning of Mr. Madison & Co. This, however, I keep to myself and less than half a dozen friends. As you seem to be more orthodox than I am on this article, I am the more ready to applaud your generous and just sentiments in favor of the British cause against France.

It has never happened, I believe, for any great length of time, that our American politics have been much governed either by our policy or blunders. Events abroad have imposed both their character and result; and I see no reason to doubt that this is to be the case more than ever. If France dictates by land and sea, we fall without an effort. The wind of the cannon-ball that smashes John Bull's brains out, will lay us on our backs with all our tinsel honors in the dirt. Therefore I think I may, and feel that I must, return to European affairs.

Two obstacles, and only two, impede the establishment of universal monarchy: Russia and the British navy. The military means of the former are vast, her troops numerous and brave. Of money she has little, but a little goes a great way, for every thing is cheap. This is owing to the barbarism of her inhabitants. Now, for revenue, a highly civilized state is most favorable; but for arms, I beg leave to doubt whether men half savage are not best. Not because rude nations have more courage than those that are polished, but because they have not such an invincible aversion to a military life as the sons of luxury and pleasure, and the sons of labor too, in the latter. As society refines, greater freedom of the choice of life is progressively allowed; and the endless variety of employments and arts of life attaches men, and almost all the men, to the occupations of peace. To bring soldiers into the field, the prince must overbid the allurements of these occupations. He exhausts his treasury without filling his camp.

But in Russia men are yet cheap, as well as provisions. Little is left to the peasantry to choose, whether they will stand in the ranks or at a work-bench; and though the emperor may not incline absolutely to force men into the army, a sum of money, that John Bull would disdain to accept, would allure them in crowds. Russia in Asia is thinly settled; but Russia in Europe is the seat of five sixths of the inhabitants of the empire, and not very deficient in populousness, if we consider the extent of unimprovable lands, and the little demand for manufacturing labor. With thirty millions in Europe, Russia is surely able to withstand Bonaparte; and the latter will not long forbear to say to *ci-devant* Poland, "shake off your chains, rise to liberty and fraternity." Prussia and Austria could say nothing against this; but Russia could not and would not acquiesce in it.

I amuse myself with inquiring into the existence of physical means to resist France. I seem to forget, though in truth I do not forget, that means twice as great once existed in the hands of the fallen nations. They were divided in counsel, and taken unprepared. Russia being a single power, and untainted with revolution mania, and plainly seeing her danger, ought to do more than all the rest. Yet, after all, I well know that if small minds preside on great occasions, they are sure to temporize when the worst of all things is to do nothing; and very possibly the Russian cabinet sages partake of this fatal blockheadship.

It also seems to me that the science, or at least the practice, of war has greatly changed since Marlborough's days. In 1702 to 1709, or 1710, he fought a great battle on a plain of six miles extent. On gaining the victory, he besieged a fortress as big as an Indian trading post, mined, scaled, battered, and fought six weeks to take it, and then went into winter quarters. Thus the war went on campaign after campaign, as slowly as the Middlesex canal, which in eight years has been dug thirty miles.

The French have done with sieges and field-battles. Posts are occupied along the whole frontier line of a country. If the line of defence be less extensive, they pass round it; if weakened by extent, through it. An immense artillery, light, yet powerful, rains such a horrible tempest on any part that is to be forced, that the defenders are driven back before the charge of the bayonet is resorted to. The lines once forced, the defending army falls back, takes new positions, and again loses them as before. Thus a country is taken possession of without a battle, and a brave people wonder and blush to find they are slaves.

Is not this invariable and yet always surprising result owing to the number, spirit, and discipline of the French, and to their almost irresistible superiority of artillery? No arts being regarded, every Frenchman is a soldier, if his master chooses to call him into the ranks. Military means are, therefore, infinite. Success and the national character have supplied the spirit to animate this mass. The opposers of France can have no such means. Men enjoying liberty will not march as if they were soldiers without their consent. They are to be bought and paid for at a dear rate before they will march. Of course government can command means to buy only a few of them;—a scanty force is collected, impatient of discipline, pining for their return to their homes, easily discouraged and dispersed. Why then should we wonder to see France mistress of Europe?

On these grounds of advantage on the side of France, I have long deemed the fate of Europe fixed irreversibly, unless other nations can be made almost as military as she is; and I confide less than ever in the possibility of this change, or at least, within the term when it could avail for resistance.

I have never believed the volunteers of England worth a

day's rations of beef to the island, if invaded. With you, I have assumed it, as a thing absolutely certain, that they would be beaten and dispersed by one hundred thousand invading Frenchmen. Improved as the military art now is, and, as I have supposed, far beyond what it was in the Duke of Marlborough's days, it is folly at all times, and infatuation in time of danger, to consider militia as capable of defending a country. My hope has been that England would array two hundred and fifty thousand regulars, and perfect their discipline without delay. Without a great land force, I now think with you, she is in extreme danger.

After her fall, ours would not cost Bonaparte a blow. We are prostrate already, and of all men on earth the fittest to be slaves. Even our darling avarice would not make a week's resistance to tribute, if the name were disguised; and I much doubt whether, if France were lord of the navies of Europe, we should reluct at that, or even at the appellation and condition of Helots.

I write too fast to avoid mistakes, or to correct them. You, I know, will overlook them, inasmuch as you permit me to subscribe myself

Your unfeigned friend, &c.

TO TIMOTHY PICKERING

DEDHAM, MARCH 3, 1806

MY DEAR SIR,

WHEN I wrote to you, not long since, on the affairs of Europe, I was under more political dejection than I remember ever to have felt before in my life. The news then was that the Russian army had capitulated, and was to be sent home; that Austria had made a separate peace, and of course that Europe, England excepted, was conquered. Assuming those facts, universal monarchy would be no thing of speculation. It would be as real at Washington, as at Berlin, Madrid, or Amsterdam. Thank kind Heaven, still the protector of this spiritless country, the Russian bayonets are long, and the French had four inches of them in their vitals before they could reach their antagonists. Still I fear that the Lisbon story of the French victory on the 9th December, will turn out true.[116] Even if true, I do not despair; for so many rumors concur in announcing the accession of Prussia to the coalition, that I more than half believe it. If the military powers still contend, the loss or gain of a battle is nothing in my eyes. The longer they contend, the better will be the exercise for all the virtues that sprout and blossom and bear fruit in the emulation of states, and that wither and rot when one subdues the rest.

The morbid cause of the French Revolution lies deep; it is not a rash on the skin; it is a plague that makes the bones brittle and cankers the marrow. The disease is not medicable. The world must wait for a sound generation to be born, and war must educate them in all the ancient manly virtues, before there can be peace or security. As to liberty we are to have none—democracy will kindle its own hell, and consume in it. Our independence may be, and I now begin to think it will be, preserved, by the French being rendered as incapable of usurping as we are of defending it. In a democracy, factions hate none but rival factions. A foreign enemy may happen to be, indeed must be, the friend of one of them. We are capable of resisting, but we should no more be permitted to resist, than Switzerland was. With these

---

[116] *The Russian bayonets did not prove quite long enough. The Lisbon story was the first rumor of the battle of Austerlitz, and was true in all but the date.* [S. AMES]

conceptions, I am ready to believe our folly is as impotent as our spirit or our wisdom, and that we shall not enjoy the honor and happiness of being able to undo ourselves. We shall try, and in the work of ruin, no men are more efficient than the weak men. Yet with all these advantages and dispositions, I think we shall have a chance to be saved if Europe is. I smile, therefore, at the drawn dagger, and defy the point of Sam Smith's and Crowninshield's resolutions.[117] They may have some stage effect upon our mob. But John Bull, though he may be nettled, will scorn to let the world see he is angry, with their playhouse thunder. I can scarcely be justified in noticing the reported intention of buying Florida after what I have intimated of the insignificance of our domestic politics. If the multitude ever paid any regard to merit in the choice of a favorite, I should expect that the exposure of the folly of our land bargains would shake their First Consul out of his triumphal car into the mire. All that can be done by displaying the truth, which is very little, ought to be done as soon as the facts may be used for the purpose. Such a display might, and I think would, influence some votes on our approaching election for governor, &c. Much exertion will be used on both sides. If Sullivan should be chosen, what can we say more than that vice and folly have taken their natural ascendant?

The terms of our correspondence are, I know, exceedingly in my favor; for I am a rustic, and you a statesman forced to be a spectator, if not allowed to be an actor, in the political drama. I write because I would not be ungrateful, and your obliging acceptance of my letters is a fresh obligation. I refrain, however, from what some would think compliments, as I know you do not like such light commodities.

I am, with entire esteem and regard,
dear sir, Yours, truly.

---

[117] *Resolutions proposing commercial restrictions, by way of retaliation, against the aggressions of Great Britain.* [S. AMES]

TO TIMOTHY PICKERING

DEDHAM, MARCH 10, 1806

MY DEAR SIR,

I RECEIVE your letters so often and in such a series, that there is not the least doubt of their all reaching me. How undeserving am I, that I have left you in doubt on this head! It is, however, some consolation, if not excuse to me, that Mr. Cabot is as negligent as I have been. He has repeatedly shown me your letters, and that in particular to which you allude with some concern lest it should have miscarried. They are full of matter, valuable and interesting; and if I had been an admirer of the administration, your well-drawn pictures of their poverty of intellect and spirit, would oblige me to despise them as ordinary knaves, who happen to be in a situation to do more than ordinary mischief. With power, they are base and abject; and with cowardice and ignorance, they are odious. If any one should doubt the exact justice of this character, their unspeakable servility in the St. Domingo business would fully establish it. In case the Russians arrive in season to check Bonaparte, and the King of Prussia really joins the coalition, all these condescensions will appear as unwise as dastardly.

Towards Great Britain, it seems, we have courage enough to swagger. Wright's motion, so worthy of a Mohawk, will convince Europeans, that we are savages, and perhaps revolutionists. I lament the disgrace of the Senate in so far allowing it countenance. There was a time when John Bull would strike, because we make such mouths at him. He, poor fellow, is bound to keep the peace, and, I feared six weeks ago, to sit in the stocks. Sending Burr will not alienate the people from the administration. They need not fear the moral sense, or sense of honor, or any other sense of our people, except their nonsense, which they will take special good care to keep on their side.

The discords of your democratic leaders will raise hopes of good, for the federalists are stubborn hopers. Randolph, no longer the guest of the great man's private board, no longer his earwig, will not be his antagonist. If he is, he will lose his party and his influence. These people may disagree about the manner or even the extent of doing mischief, but to do good they have neither inclination nor understanding. Our disease is democracy. It is not the skin that festers— our very bones are carious, and their marrow blackens with gangrene. Which rogues shall be first, is of no moment—our republicanism must die, and I am sorry for it. But why should we care what sexton happens to be in office at our funeral. Nevertheless, though I indulge no hopes, I derive much entertainment from the squabbles in Madam Liberty's family. After so many liberties have been taken with her, I presume she is no longer a *miss* and a virgin, though she may still be a goddess.

It is a mark of a little mind in a great man, to get such people about him for favorites as our chief is said to prefer. Hancock thought himself a Jupiter, and filled his Olympus with buffoons, sots, and blockheads. Is our Jupiter to reign another term of four years? I am at a loss to comprehend his ardent passion for buying territory. Is he land-mad, or is he afflicted with a gunpowder-phobia? Admitting that we must either buy the Spanish right or take it, reasons of the day may decide in favor of buying; but a million mischiefs will grow out of this enlargement of our territory, and some of them at no great distance.

I am flattered agreeably by finding, that you and Mr. Bayard approve my opinions respecting St. Domingo. I have never seen that gentleman, but I have, as everybody here has, a very high respect for his merit and talents: I lament, that they are so much lost to our country, which, you know, is destined to the grasp of all its vice and ambition, the ambition of its low tyrants.

You will read that Professor Webber is chosen President of the College, and I hear that it is in print that Mr. Pearson has resigned.

Our election will excite at least as much zeal and bustle as ever. We live in the island of Lemnos, and in Vulcan's own shop; it seems as if we had no business but to forge party thunderbolts. We maintain, that there is as much honor as noise in this happy situation, but surely we cannot deceive ourselves so far as to suppose there ever will be any tranquillity.

The District of Maine, I fear, grows yearly worse and worse. If that part of the state could stand neuter, Massachusetts proper would be right some years longer. Either we ought to dismember that territory, reserving perhaps the extreme part of it, where the state lands, yet unsold, chiefly lie, for a second state, or we should make the most unremitted exertions to federalize it. I have some faith in at least the partial success of the latter, if the expense of pamphlets and newspapers could be amply supplied. I believe Strong will be chosen, because I wish it, and because I think great industry will be exerted to effect it.

Mason's strange scheme of the portraits of the three Presidents, is, I suppose, left to die. Your comment is very just.

How numerous are the foes of order, and how incorrect as well as faint-hearted are its friends! With respect and unfeigned regard, I am, dear sir,

Yours, truly.

TO JOSIAH QUINCY

DEDHAM, MARCH 19, 1806

MY DEAR SIR,

THE NEWS from Europe is truly distressing.[118] The death of Mr. Pitt fills me with grief and terror,—with grief, that so great a statesman and patriot should sink under his labors— and with terror, that Fox, Erskine, and Sheridan should come into power. A neighbor of mine, well known to you as a good-hearted man, is overjoyed that Billy Pitt is dead. He also exults in the prospect of Sullivan's election, whose morals, he says, are purity itself. You will not be at a loss to conjecture who it is I mean. When a man of so much real worth is so deluded, as to rejoice that Pitt is dead, and that Sullivan lives to be Governor, as he believes, what reason have we to think the people will see their error when they commit any and return to the right path? I wish to learn from you, how our Congress patriots are affected, by the successes of Bonaparte, and the peace he has dictated. Are they silly or base enough to believe his success is our success? The newspapers inform us that Mr. Randolph has denounced the administration and Bonaparte. But I have read no speech, or part of a speech, from that gentleman, nor have I lately had a line from any correspondent, on the state of Congress business. I am therefore quite in the dark about your politics. The discords of your Randolphs and Bidwells can do no harm to their betters, or the cause of good order. But I can scarcely believe they will part so widely, as not to come together, and unite again heartily, when any signal mischief

---

[118] *The victory of Austerlitz, and its immediate consequences.* [S. AMES]

is to be done. Of all descriptions of political men, I most profoundly dread the fools. Randolph is immature in judgment as a statesman, and perhaps has too much impetuosity and fancy, ever to ripen into one. But he is no fool, and if he ever consents to promote mischief, he will know what he is doing. I am far from sure that I rightly comprehend his character, and for that reason I the more freely disclose to you my opinion of it. It will be a topic of conversation, when I shall again be so happy as to see you.

You have often mentioned, in your letters, the subject of the election of a President of Harvard College. I have no reserves with my friends, but I can communicate very little, as to the reasons that determined me not to accept it, that you will not anticipate; I want health for it. I also want the most indispensable of all talents, inclination for it. Mr. Webber is chosen. He has, it is said, great learning in the mathematics, and great modesty.

Is Iruco's refusal to quit the United States deemed a correct thing in point of diplomatic principle?[119] It is indeed singular that a foreign minister should thus take post in a country, and intrench himself as a citizen. I have never looked at a book, nor revolved the matter enough to form any conclusion.

Yours, truly.

Breaking with the self-imposed decision generally to publish only Ames's own letters in this edition, the following letter has been included both because it responds directly to Ames's last letter and because it so well provides a solid context in the light of

---

[119] *The Spanish government had been requested to recall Irujo, the minister from that nation to this country. He somewhat cavalierly refused to go, although notified by Mr. Madison that his presence at Washington "was dissatisfactory to the President."* [S. AMES] *A similar event occurred under Washington's Administration when attempt was made to recall the French minister, Genet, in 1793.* [ED.]

which the reader may judge how far Ames's apparent brooding in his last years was merely idiosyncratic and how far it participated in certain generally shared forebodings.

TO FISHER AMES

CITY OF WASHINGTON, MARCH 24, 1806

DEAR SIR,

A LETTER from Mr. King now before me, dated the 20th, enclosed a newspaper containing details of European events to some time in February. Whatever Mr. K. says of England, I consider as our authority; and therefore transcribe for your information the following passage:

"As no nation is more reasonable, more docile, more loyal than England, when wisely governed, so none has greater firmness, longer patience, nor higher courage than our ancestors; *(our ancestors:* I like that phrase: our mother country: "England, with all thy faults I love thee still;") and notwithstanding it has pleased the almighty to take from them, almost at the same moment, their first statesman, their most fortunate admiral, and their ablest general, I feel a strong presentiment and hope that the high spirit and ancient glory of the nation will enable them to contend against and finally to triumph over their gigantic adversary."—"The new ministry united the strength and talents, as it does the parties and confidence of the nation."

The reading of that passage led me to express my own sentiments on British affairs, in an answer to Mr. King, which I have just written, and which, as I can say nothing better—and you "endure" my scribbling—I will here simply copy.

"We had heard of the death of Mr. Pitt. It did not alarm me. For though I consider the independence of the United States as absolutely dependent on the ability of England to maintain *hers*, against all the efforts of Napoleon; yet I have at no time entertained an exalted opinion of Mr. Pitt as a statesman *to plan and direct great military enterprises* and *to select*, and *in defiance of all opposition, to call forth the requisite talents to execute them.* With an eloquence powerful perhaps as his father's, did he not want much of that *vigor* which enabled the latter successfully to execute the bold projects he conceived? With great talents, I expect more *efficiency* in Lord Grenville. Perfectly relying on your judgment of their pre-eminent talents, strength and popularity (founded on a personal knowledge of the men) I rejoice that such a ministry [has] been formed. It furnished just ground for the [con]fident hope you express (in which I cordia[lly] join) "that the high spirit and ancient glory of the nation will [en]able them to contend against and finally triumph over their (and the world's) gigantic adversary".

"But what will be the effect on our commerce? It is said (by way of Bordeaux) that the British are releasing all American vessels. Will this relaxation continue? I trust not. It commenced prior to Mr. Pitt's decease, probably influenced by the catastrophe of the continental war. The captures and condemnations may not instantly be renewed. Lord Grenville[120] and his associates will deeply consider the subject as essentially connected with the continuance of the war. Doubtless their measures may be influenced very much by those of Bonaparte. If the latter commands the ports of the continent, from the Baltic to the Adriatic, to be shut against the commerce of Britain (and he has only to command, to be obeyed)—doubtless the British will interdict the commerce

---

[120] *You will recollect his Lordship's decided sentiments on neutral commerce, in his celebrated speech on the treaty with Russia in 1801.* [PICKERING]

of neutrals, at least with all the belligerent nations. *Necessity* will be declared to be the ground of the interdiction. And will it not be an adequate plea? It will be done openly, frankly, boldly; and such time given, that neutrals shall not complain of being taken by surprise. In a word, the principles of war in disguise will be adopted. And if we feel no wish to succour our parent state, when fighting for her liberty and her existence; shall we not 'at least desist from wrongs [or measures] which augment her dangers, and frustrate her defensive efforts'? I, for one, shall bid her Godspeed. When she is spending, liberally spending, her blood and treasure, *in fact* for our safety and independence, shall we be restive, because she denies us an *accumulation* of *profit* beyond that which arises from our regular, permanent course of trade?— If we had an administration that regarded anything in comparison with its own immediate, personal interest and popularity, and the indulgence of its hateful passions,— satisfactory arrangements, I am fully persuaded, might be made with Great Britain. But I do not believe these will be attempted through any other agent than the miserable minister now at that court. Would you believe it? A very few days only had elapsed, after Mr. Pitt's death, and when the new ministers had scarcely taken their seats in their offices, before Mr. Monroe applied for an answer to his letter (or remonstrance) to Lord Mulgrave!—Such is the out-door information.—Yet this is the [man likely] to be the next President of the United States . . . next President;—the actual President is exploring the wilds of Louisiana;—its salt plains—its rock, or mineral salt—its immense prairies—in which he has discovered the earthly "paradise"—its numerous tribes and remnants of tribes of Indians, and how many *original* languages they speak—the hot-springs, and the warm mudpuddles in their vicinity—and the wonderful phenomena, in one, of a small or "very minute shell-fish," in shape resembling a muscle, but having four legs; and in another "a vermes about half an inch long, moving with a serpentine or vermicular motion!"

"Should Monroe be our next President Randolph I presume must be his prime minister—and Nicholson Secretary of the Navy. Gallatin (whom Randolph lately eulogized) must remain Secretary of the Treasury; for they have no southern man of ability and industry to fill his place. They would not be much embarrassed to find a successor to Mr. Dearborn.

"*Confidential* at present. On Saturday, while the doors were closed, Mr. Randolph said that about the middle of December, he called on Mr. Madison, who told him that the French government had forbidden our negotiating directly with Spain: that we must negotiate through the medium of the French government which wanted money; and that we must give it.—Randolph added—"I had not much confidence in him (Madison) before, and from that time I have had none;" at that moment, with an indignant motion, throwing his hat across the hall!—You will connect this anecdote with the secret appropriation of 2 millions."

Thus far my letter to Mr. King.—I think I have already told you that Armstrong has been approved, together with Boudoin, to be Commissioners extraordinary to negotiate on all our disputes with Spain.

Colonel Smith (Mr. Adams's son-in-law) was with much difficulty, and by means not very honorable, appointed by his father-in-law, to be surveyor of the port of New York. His concern with Miranda has caused Mr. Jefferson to remove him. A Mr. Schenck is appointed in his place.

Always and very sincerely yours,

T. PICKERING

P.M. The out-of-door information proves incorrect. Mr. Monroe's letter of January 28 was sent today to the two houses (doors closed) in which he said he should soon apply to the new ministry. Nothing very material in the contents.

TO TIMOTHY PICKERING

DEDHAM, MARCH 24, 1806, MONDAY

MY DEAR SIR,

I HAD three days ago your favor of the 11th inst. The mail this morning brought your precious communications of the same date, the four sheets no date, the letter of the 13th, and Mr. White's speech. In that of the 11th, first received, I had the pamphlet of Nicklin and Griffith, to which you have added the United States Gazette, containing additional documents in that case.

It is a violent snow storm, equal to any that has happened this winter. I am quite at leisure to enjoy my feast. It has had one hasty reading, and I am going to give the whole another, more deliberately. A lad who draws the highest prize in a lottery feels no richer than I do, with my secret hoard. As to my discretion in the use of it, I will, as soon as it clears up, go to Boston, and with our excellent friend George Cabot, who is the keeper of my conscience and judgment, endeavor to frame a mature plan of conduct. I abstain now from all comment.

As Randolph is no federalist, is too Virginian, and perhaps too ambitious to be any sooner trusted than the other Jacobin competitors for power, why, I ask, should the federal orators be silent? It is no doubt right to let them, the Jacobins, get by the ears. Too prompt a declaration on any question might be a cause for some weak democrats to vote worse than they otherwise would. Yet I confess I have strong doubts whether the Feds do not carry their reserve to an extreme. A party exists by acting, and dies by wholly forbearing to act. Feeble as the Feds are in numbers, they are strong in talents, formidable by their virtues, and chance now arms them with the weapons of John Randolph & Co. I decide nothing on the point, but I hope and trust it is considered by our worthy friends, in both houses, that the crisis is favorable to popular impression; that Quincy, Dana, and Broom in the House, you, Mr. Bayard, &c., in the Senate, by stating facts with their just inferences, can make that impression. I see not why the Feds should not let the nation know that they still exist, and that they are still faithful to their old principles. They may take their own peculiar federal ground, and if converts should not be made from democracy, let them bear it in mind, federalism in New England needs exhortation, consolation, and encouragement incessantly. I would not be impertinent with Mr. Bayard, but I have no objection to your suggesting these ideas to him. With my old friend Tracy I need no apologies for hinting what comes uppermost.

Fit and proper as I think it to use exertions, I nevertheless concede the point, that the splitting of the Jacobin party bodes no good to our cause. There is no return, in political affairs, from vice to virtue, from the wrangles of jacobinism to the peace of federal order. Worse men, if they are to be found, will succeed Jefferson; meaner I think will not. If rogues must rule us, it is luck to obey knowing ones. I will write to you soon, but I have little to export to pay for my late valuable imports.

Yours with unfeigned esteem, &c.

TO [UNKNOWN,
PERHAPS DWIGHT FOSTER]

DEDHAM, JUNE 2, 1806

Confidential

MY DEAR FRIEND,

MR. William Sullivan, whom I know to be high in your esteem, wrote to me on Sunday requesting that I would sketch a draft of a *Protest*[121] in case the H. of R. should vote an address to Jefferson.

I replied instantly that I could not do it, being engaged with friends etc. This is true. It is also true that I feel the difficulty of such a performance in a degree that few will comprehend. To execute it well, would require meditation, ample materials, time to write and reject perhaps twenty drafts, and finally to strike out something unlike them all. As I am a ready writer when I write at all, this alleged incapacity will not be believed. To write for the people and not the best informed, is not my usual employment. Yet as I feel guilty when I play shy towards my friends, and W. Sullivan is a man of too much worth and talent to be refused almost anything, I will ask you to consider the plan on which such a draft should be made. Is it not, first, to gain the attention and good will of the people by exhibiting the value of republican liberty and the impediments to its enjoyment. The faction, Jefferson's faction, creates those impediments or aggravates them—and that we foresee the fall of liberty in case the Jeffersonian system should be persisted in. The people love the republican cause. Jefferson really makes that

---

[121] *The draft of Ames's effort immediately follows this letter.* [ED.]

cause desperate. Their love and hate, their hopes and fears are only to be addressed. Logic is not worth chopping.

I began a sketch of the protest on this plan, but I liked it so little that I forsook the task. I send it to you that you may comprehend my design, and if you think it of any use, be so obliging as to communicate with Mr. Sullivan on the subject. I think he will not condemn me for this disclosure to you of his wishes and intentions. No doubt he knows our intimacy and will not consider it a breach of confidence. I really regret it that I cannot make anything of the business, for I think a good protest would make impression. I can sometimes use the power to write, but you know I cannot always command it.

Your friend etc.

[P.S.] Mr. Sullivan expects to hear from me Tuesday afternoon at the latest—

[The Protest]

IF WE did not perceive or could not suppress the most urgent considerations both of private honour and of public duty, we should want neither reasons nor inducements for submitting without remonstrance to the vote of the House. As republics are founded on virtue and cannot subsist (?) without morals, the elevation of bad men to office has ever been deemed the sign and instrument of their fall. When from the successful intrigue of faction this happens to be the case, it is our duty to obey their authority; but our virtuous constituents would be no less stigmatised than astonished, if as representatives and on their behalf we should presume to concur in bestowing applause on their incapacity and it is not yet, as in the tyranny that supplants a republic it need be, a necessary condition of our disgrace that we should as little dare to withhold our flattery as to express our abhorrence to our enlightened constituents[.] [A]t a time, as we believe, of the utmost peril to their liberty, we proceed to oppose the reasons for our dissent from the vote.

Every plan of govt though it may spring from the highest exertion of the wisdom of man must necessarily partake of his imperfections and frailty. And of all the various forms, there is not one that has not some peculiar propensity to mark its character, some inbred malady that preys upon its vitals. No political theory can be more fascinating, no principles more pure, than those of a republic, which seems to be a plan devised by wisdom to give power to virtue that virtue may impart security to innocence. But history and experience blend their light to demonstrate that the prevailing, and as yet with the single exception of the United States the *fatal* vice of republics is licentiousness. The most exalted political condition is no doubt the hardest to maintain, for our own republic is now the only one that persists in the attempt to maintain it. The success of that attempt we have anxiously contemplated as depending on the election of the best men and preserving unimpaired our best institutions. While Washington ruled, who derived no less authority from his fame and his virtues than from his office, while the principal departments were executed by great men of his appointment whose reputations have passed unhurt [through] the ordeal of time and of enemies, while we had an independent judiciary and before the Constitution was *amended* to secure Mr. Jefferson's reelection, we have been told that our govt was "in the full tide of successful experiment." Before that time it appears however that the grossest and most unfounded calumnies were vented by Mr. Jefferson[122] against General Washington and the principles of the Con-

[122] *Letter to Mazzei.* [F. AMES]

stitution. No comment is necessary to exhibit all the turpitude of this duplicity. We cannot refrain from viewing Mr. Jefferson at that time as the head of a faction insidiously engaged in fomenting the spirit of licentiousness. In the midst of public and private prosperity that spirit was dangerously fomented and a faction under the influence of a foreign minister audaciously defied the laws and equipped armed rebels to cruise against a nation in amity with the United States. That minister publicly accused Mr. Jefferson with having "initiated him in the mysteries of our govt." When we consider his avowed partiality for the worst revolutionary men and principles, and his employment of the two most infamous libellers of any age or country, one of whom he invited after praising his useful labours to return to this country, the other he rewarded with money, we cannot think it uncandid to charge him with a participation in the guilt and infamy of those men. Stronger reasons for abhorrence and detestation it is not in our power to imagine.

From these facts and many others in corroboration it was impossible that we should not consider Mr. Jefferson as guided by an inordinate and unprincipled ambition. That has been called the vice/infirmity of noble minds. It might have been expected that he would seek its gratification in the prosperity and aggrandisement of the nation, and that it might consist with national honour though not with virtue. Even this hope, if any but the blind dupes of party entertained it, has been disappointed. His ambition has been as much without dignity as moderation. Within the United States it was his policy and apparently his passion to break down every fence that the wisdom of Constitution had erected against an unbridled spirit of licence. He recommended to Congress that the Judiciary Law should be abolished, and by the fatal compliance of that body with his recommendation, change in our constitutional system has been accomplished which in all the republics that ever subsisted has been the first forerunner of their degeneracy and the last artificer of their ruin. If a republic could maintain justice, justice would maintain the republic. But licentiousness/faction has never failed to break this most obnoxious of its fetters. In 1774, our first patriots considered an independent judiciary as the most precious of our rights. In 1804, it has been represented as the most burdensome and degrading of our incumbrances.

The removal of federal officers, with a formulary of approbation of their conduct, has been considered the proof of a vindictive and implacable spirit. Under royal government we believe no such sweeping removals are made, nor can we conceive that any government can expect to be faithfully served, if continuance in office is avowedly made to depend not on perseverance in faithful services, but on the predominance of a faction. Hence we cannot but view the measures as tending and as designed to signalize and extend the influence of executive patronage and to make all public officers the servants of the president and not the public.

TO HON. BENJAMIN GOODHUE

DEDHAM, JULY 30TH, 1806

MY DEAR FRIEND,

You MAY call it negligence or tardiness, and I will compound with you, but I cannot allow it to be called ingratitude that I have so long delayed to thank you for your kind letter respecting my insurance concerns, and for your very friendly attention to those concerns. I am very sensible of my obligations to you, and I trust, perhaps too much, to your ancient knowledge of my regard and esteem for you as an excuse for my want of punctuality in answering your letter. A man in business is carried strait along by the current of that business, but I am idle and lazy, and though it is impossible for me to lose my attachment to my old friends, I perceive it is daily growing a harder task to assure them of it by writing. I have neglected a letter from our excellent friend Rundle till I am too much ashamed to write one. I will however repent late rather than not at all. This very act of writing to you is the sign of a good beginning and it encourages me.

I left a receit [sic] with Mr. J. Pierce, for the balance stated in your's of which he no doubt with mercantile punctuality has apprised you. As soon as it may be practicable I could wish the whole account closed. I see I was too late in the business. When every brook had sands of gold, you and I were at Congress helping to make a statute book.

How far it is now possible to save our sinking state is a problem. While there is life there is hope. Instead of depending on long essays in the newspapers I have been for years of the opinion that influence should be used more directly. Six or eight per cent, say, of the voters are yet waken[ed] enough to take impression, not from everybody, but from some particular persons and at some times and in very skillful and indirect ways. This is all that can be done, and *all this should be done in every town.*

I hear that you are, with great reason too, very happy in your domestic connection. From my heart I rejoice in it. Long may you enjoy this happiness.

I am, my dear friend, yours truly

FISHER AMES

TO JOSIAH QUINCY

DEDHAM, DECEMBER 5, 1806

MY DEAR SIR,

I HOPE you and good Mrs. Quincy were snug and safe at Washington, before the snow storm of the 3d. The wind was violent, but so much rain followed, and so warm weather, that we have little snow on the ground.

I have just read the second number of Decius, ascribed to Mr. Randolph, and I am deceived if he will not find that he writes himself down. His attack on the Feds is not only illiberal, not only unworthy of a man of sense, for it gives vent to vulgar prejudices, but I confess it sinks him exceedingly as a man of spirit. It attacks the foes of Jefferson, as a propitiatory merit to beg his own acquittal. He even praises Fox for being the friend of the illustrious American Chief Magistrate. No enemy of Mr. Randolph can desire to see him sink lower than to crawl at the foot of Jefferson's throne, and to flatter the man he has offended, and still despises. Thus it is that Burr disgraced himself, that Callender drowned himself, and Bonaparte went to war again, just at the time when Jefferson needed exactly such good luck to escape disgrace. And now Randolph, his enemy, voluntarily becomes, nay publicly petitions to become, his footstool. I always doubted his judgment, and never could get so far as to have a doubt about his wild, irregular ambition. But I did suppose he had spirit, that often felt when it should not, and always when it should. As I take his word for his sentiments and intentions, I am obliged to put him back again, for the present, on the list of ordinary demagogues, where he placed himself, and the public placed him, on the trial of Judge

Chase. He rose by brevet last winter—(that is not the right phrase)—he acted as a commander in chief, but his commission must be made out as ensign, unless he displays more independence in every sense of the word. I greatly desire to know how the play will open, on the Washington boards, and what part Mr. R. will take.

I do not hesitate to give you my first impressions, because I do not cherish my claim to wisdom in foretelling what Congress will do, believing as I do with all imaginable civism and duty, that Congress knows as little of its own plans as I do.

Lord Lauderdale will eat his Christmas pie in London; but whether Bonaparte will eat his in Berlin, is not so certain. He brags as if he felt a little afraid to play the risky game of war once more, and the King of Prussia is no doubt ten times as much afraid as he. He has more reason.

Your friend, &c.

[P.S.] Please show the other side to Colonel Pickering.

TO JOSIAH QUINCY

DEDHAM, THURSDAY, DECEMBER 11, 1806

DEAR MR. QUINCY,

I RECEIVED by the mail from Boston the favor of yours, covering the message. It had appeared in the Boston paper of Tuesday, which I have not seen; and unless the mail be corrected, I must ask you to send me the Boston news. We have here three mails a week, called the great mail, Mondays,

Wednesdays, and Fridays, which do not stop at our little office, and on each of the other days, a little mail, which regularly fails to bring the papers in season. If my dear Seaver did but know how the poor people's bowels yearn in vain for the Chronicle, he would pity our case, and would use his influence with Granger to get "the procedure corrected." So much for the grievances of Lilliput.

The message is insipid. It is pompous inanity. While he thinks gunboats will do instead of a navy, and that a little more in the way of doing nothing to fortify our harbors will answer for the seaports, where God's chosen people are not to be found, and five hundred cavalry instead of an army, he gravely pronounces that the liberation of our revenue is "of all objects the most desirable." There is something as despicable as unsound in this sentiment. One would imagine the message was a report from George Deblois to the town of Boston, about the management and expenditures of the almshouse. The scale of his message is graduated below the politics of Sancho's government of Barataria, and is really below it. For Mr. Jefferson only takes care of his popularity, which forbids him to govern at all. The day of judgment for nations comes while sinners live. Experience will yet whip out of our flesh what folly has bred in our bone. All our notions, our prejudices, our very vanity that makes other nations fight, are unsocial and make us base and sordid. If we remain so, we cannot defend our liberty, and if we get a master, he will try to raise our spirit, because with such slaves he could not maintain his usurpation.

I make these remarks because I seem to see the John Winthrops and Deacon Tudors as the men chiefly relied on to applaud the sentiments of our illustrious Cæsar. While it (the message) boasts of our overflowing treasury, the political horizon is allowed to be overcast and threatening; and, to make amends for unwelcome tidings, he doubles his usual dose of slang.

Let us, however, be just to this man. Is he not a very good chief for us? Would any man, who was free from the lowest passions and prejudices of the lowest mob, manage our affairs with success? Our nation must act out its character, or rather act without one, till forty years of adversity have taught all those who can learn, and exterminated those who will not. Colonel Burr is not, I suppose, formidable, but his designs show the presumption of democratic reliance on our cobweb ties for lions.

I restrain my propensity to preach. I am one of your congregation, and dutifully wait for information, which you know the southern members biennially distribute in circulars.

Yours, &c.

TO RICHARD PETERS, PHILADELPHIA

DEDHAM, DECEMBER 14, 1806

MY DEAR SIR,

A CONSCIENCE is a plague to a man—and yet a man is the worse for having none. I read your letter with pleasure. I thought it kind and friendly, and richly full of good matter. I could make a book upon it, if I had a pen like General Heath, whose orders, I have been told, were very voluminous. But though a ready scribbler, I am no author—I shall never rise to the honor of being bound in calf or sheepskin. There is so much matter in your letter I could not in ten days decide which of its topics first claims an answer.

I am no royalist, Anglo-American, nor tory. I only ask

how our government is to be supported;—and I answer by miracle. The miracle of virtue, that loves others first, then one's-self.

All this I admire, and I am willing to say, when the proof comes, *ecce signum*. It will never come. Our mistake is in supposing men better than they are. They are bad, and will act their bad character out. The federalists are good for nothing to govern—worth every thing to check those who do. Behold, here is my political creed! I like the pretty business of hoping, but I see very little foundation for it. The rogues may fall out, but the honest men will never come by their right in consequence.

I now resume my first position: a conscience is a plague to a man—for I liked your letter very much. I thought it kind and friendly, deserving my grateful and speedy acknowledgment. It furnished, too, the most copious theme for scribbling, and that is another thing I like. Nevertheless I have shamefully delayed acknowledging my obligation; and, say what you will on the subject, I say beforehand I deserve reproof, and my impertinent, officious conscience is very forward to make it.

You wish to see a navy; but are you not satisfied with gunboats, which candid judges, I presume, would pronounce not to be much worse than good for nothing? The system of our rulers is anti-commercial, and yet their noisiest supporters are in cities.

I pray you offer my ever affectionate regards to my friend Mr. Rundle. Mrs. R. will readily know a geranium from an oleander; but I have been afraid my sagacious friend would make some mistakes about his potatoes and cucumbers. I have heard of a city farmer who turned his beans down again when he thought they sprouted wrong end uppermost.

With sentiments of respect and esteem,
I am, dear sir, yours.

TO JOSIAH QUINCY

DEDHAM, DECEMBER 20, 1806

MY DEAR SIR,

FROM you and Colonel Pickering I have the message and the Spanish papers. The message plainly tells us we are not to have protection. I am ignorant what gunboats are good for. Yet they are now most clearly adopted in lieu of a navy; and troops are not to be raised, because they are never to be employed while an overflowing treasury will afford tribute, and tribute upon tribute. Your non-importation act is, I perceive, suspended by the House, and no doubt by the Senate. The occasions will recur to expose the folly and impotence of that measure. It appears to me right for the Feds to seek or make the occasions, and use them. Efforts are not lost, though baffled. Our people argue badly, but they feel, and the baseness of the policy of [the] administration ought to be exposed. The repeal of the salt tax is an abominable proposal. Of all our taxes, it is the easiest collected, the article very cheap, of universal consumption, great bulk, and capable of yielding, in times of urgency, a great supply to government. It ought to be resisted by the most forcible, yet temperate appeal, to the boasted good sense of the country.

Burr is still the theme of conversation. Eaton's narrative creates surprise, and though I am far from thinking it false, I can scarcely allow it to be accurate. Burr was in no condition for such a project, and if he had been, would he have opened himself so indiscreetly to Eaton? Does the disclosure awaken no fears of the future politics of the transalpine states? Will not our imperial mistress Virginia allow that her chicken[123] will one day peck her eyes out? If Bonaparte demolishes the King of Prussia, Mr. Jefferson must redouble his assiduities, to please our future master.

You will have with you our excellent friends. Pray give my regards to J. P. Davis and the rest.

I am, dear sir, yours, truly.

TO TIMOTHY PICKERING

DEDHAM, DECEMBER 22, 1806

MY DEAR SIR,

THIS being our Forefathers' day, I could wish I was in good plight to celebrate it with many of the worthies at Vila's, in Boston. I hope the day will be ever memorable with a posterity worthy of such ancestors. Still, I confess, it is matter of regret that the celebration has been used for high party purposes, and has been charged with degenerating into a bacchanalian feast. Our excellent friend, Isaac P. Davis, has exerted himself much to give it *eclat*. By separating this celebration from party, and giving it, as it deserves, a serious and even religious turn, it might be diffused over New England. If, in the course of events, a second Burr should divide our empire by the Alleghany, (the present Burr will not succeed in it,) the nationality of New England will be a security against the disasters of such a convulsion. When peace opens the door for foreign intrigue, and the growth of

---

[123] *Kentucky.* [S. AMES]

the tramontane states shall make them "feel power and forget right," (it may be ten years for this progress to be completed,) another Burr would probably succeed, and our fifteen-million paradise would go with the mountaineers. Would not Virginia tremble at such a foresight of things? Her cheap defense of the nation would then seem to be no defense.

I perceive by the message, which you was kind enough to inclose in a pamphlet, (date of your letter, 3d December,) that Mr. Jefferson's system is now fixed. The sea is to have no defense but gunboats and non-importation acts; and our territory is to be made safe by paying tribute. He would not arm on seeing a speck of war in the horizon. What a trap for popularity with the basest of our vulgar! If force is not to be prepared before it is wanted, when can it be prepared? To be always prepared, is the surest way to be long at peace. To free our treasury from claims upon it, is "of all things the most desirable," says Mr. Jefferson. To be free within, enjoying justice, and respected without our limits, so as to have liberty and justice with the greatest possible degree of security for their lasting long, seems to me a more desirable object.

No matter for the trading cities—"the great sores"— provided God's chosen people, many of whom have renounced him, or are ignorant of his government and revealed will, are protected and paid five or six times as much for riding into the woods and scalping some old squaws, as a regular force would cost. This is economy; this is equality. I see no reason for the forbearance of the federalists. Why should they not expose, in speeches, the tricks of [the] administration?

I am flattered by your letter, because it says, a little unexpectedly I confess, that my correspondence would not be irksome. Our commerce is quite unequal, as I have almost nothing to export of any value, in comparison with what I receive.

I am an invalid, moping obscurely in the country, and grieving that the King of Prussia is probably unkinged before this date.

Isaac P. Davis and some other very good men of Boston, are with you, and will often see you. They will come back fuller than all the newspapers with the secret history of our American St. Cloud.

Yours, with the highest regard, &c.

1 8 0 7

==

DEDHAM, JANUARY 1, 1807

MY DEAR SIR,

THE PRESIDENT, by delaying the recommendation of the suspension of Nicholson's act[124] till the world had been edified with his message, seems to have chosen, on plan, that the molasses for the mob should be unmingled with acid. The fools in Congress seem too to be instructed to boast that Great Britain has yielded to the mere show of this tremendous weapon of non-intercourse. How far that nation consults her dignity, or feels herself pressed by her situation as a belligerent, to permit this mistake to be made, I know not. I should think she would insist, as a preliminary, that the act be repealed, or, better yet for her, leave the United States

---

[124] *The non-importation act.* [S. AMES]

to the sad and shameful experience of its operation. As matters now are, party will teach, and fools will believe, on the evidence of experience, that we have bullied her into concessions. Whether Tracy's motion for papers be perfectly correct, pending a negotiation, I have not considered. Great Britain, I should imagine from the little that I know, is more afraid of our hostility than she need be. The United States could not be forced into war with her, until Bonaparte has so nearly conquered this great rival, that there would be no danger in it for the United States to coalesce with him. Now Fox is dead, and Lord Grenville resumes, I suppose, the control he had in Pitt's day, I should calculate on a greater degree of indifference for a treaty with the United States. Fortune seems to be almost as much a friend to Jefferson as to Bonaparte. The depressed fortunes of Great Britain keep her surprisingly tame under insult, and eager to coax us into a reconciliation. The sad fate of Prussia will still more subdue her pride, and the sagacious ignorance of our country will cry, Behold the fruit of Jefferson's vigorous counsels? Behold what means the Feds always possessed but never dared to use!

No strong impression can be made on national opinion. There is apathy enough to blunt the edge of Demosthenes' rhetoric. He would be so far from changing our faith, he would not command our attention. But though great strokes are not to be struck, I still rely on the effect of repetition. Our lazy ignorance would yield to an assault perpetually renewed. I cannot, therefore, see why the Feds should be so very shy, as they are, about speaking out. I cannot see why a strong yet temperate manner, like that of the best sort of English parliamentary opposition in 1773 and 1774, should not be tried, and tried over again, with an incessant repetition. Why should not Dana move in the House to expose abuses, and to tear, if possible, the veil with which [the] administration choose to hide their doings? It might fail of effect. It would not make power change hands, nor, if I may use a low expression, make power wash its hands, but it would help to retard its progress. It would fortify that declining power of control that the Feds throughout the Union yet possess, and which cannot be lost without losing the last hope of mitigating the despotism to which we are devoted. All former reasons for forbearance are now at an end. Randolph yields to a master whom he finds too firm in his seat to be lifted out of it; and it is clear that his success would be no triumph for our party. Efforts are not lost, and I wish the Feds would make them. The discords of our masters can only charge our masters not to restore our power. Why then suppress the voice of truth and patriotism in Congress.

If Burr has the ambition of a Lord Clive, I think it full as likely, as his, to take the road to speculation as insurrection. I cannot believe that Burr is going to set up the standard of civil war. Has not he some land scheme beyond the Mississippi? If I understand the papers from Wilkinson, it is not the Spaniards that flinch. They are to patrol the disputed ground, &c. With great regard and esteem,

Yours, truly.

[P.S.] I am afraid Russia will be reduced to nullity, so that Bonaparte will conquer alone, or take her into partnership with him to share the Ottoman Empire.

TO JOSIAH QUINCY

MY DEAR SIR,

IT would be a violation of the rules of evidence to deny that V . . . . ., S . . . . ., and C . . . . . are as great fools as they pretend to be, in regard to the bullying effect of our non-intercourse law. This sort of candor would, however, be excessive towards B . . . . .; for, if I mistake not the character of the man, it would take him a whole age of probation, and perhaps purgatory, to rise in the scale of reformation so high as sincerity in vice. I make no doubt the folly of that impotent measure will be hid from the eyes of our wise multitude, who have eyes, but see not. How Great Britain can, and why she would, concede the question of neutral rights, is incomprehensible. It seems as if that point would be to be settled with France yet; for, if Prussia falls, and Russia is disarmed, how long will it be before Great Britain will be done for? I expect yet to see Mr. Jefferson a prefect of Bonaparte. He is one of his Legion of Honor already. Is that permitted by our Constitution? I cannot imagine that Burr has means for any thing great as a public enemy. Neither France, Spain, nor Great Britain would furnish those means; and the western country will not be ripe for such a man as Burr these ten years.

To repeal any existing tax is absurd enough. Certainly we want ships and fortifications, and lessening our treasure must delay the extinction of our debt. "To free the revenue is, of all objects, the most desirable!" How loose, how incorrect is Mr. Jefferson! The salt tax is one of the best, the least felt, and most unexceptionable. Is it not pledged for the public debt? Why should not such schemes to get popularity be exposed? Who fitter for that task than you? And why not seize that occasion to urge the necessity of a navy, and the fitness of applying as much as the salt revenue yearly to the construction of ships of the line, (especially as, in case of the neutrality of the British navy, our only mode of resistance would be to meet an invading foe half seas over,) that we might equip ships enough to destroy such expeditions? A navy is popular, and the public is not quite blind to its danger, if Great Britain should cease to fight Bonaparte. The employment it would create in our seaports, the call for timber, &c., &c., in those parts of the country where the salt tax is felt, or pretended to be felt, would afford good heads of discourse; and as the ground is solid, as true patriotism calls for a navy, as Mr. Jefferson means to get taxes from us to spend in the woods, the public attention might be a little engaged.

I am delighted with yours of the 21st, just received. It delineates character in a most interesting manner. I shall read it over till I am sure I lose no part of the portrait you have drawn.

What do you think of the frequent observations in the Repertory, in reference to their effect, good or bad, or no effect, on the once expected division of the party? Will the man alluded to be made better or worse by them? I do not believe that vanity ever wears so thick a mail as to be unwounded by merited sarcasm, however invariably this may be pretended. I see, too, that Bidwell begins to crow again like a dunghill cock, as if he had forgotten his former beating. Will R.[125] let him crow?

I pray you offer my most respectful compliments to Mrs. Quincy, and believe me, with regard and esteem,

Yours, &c.

---

[125] *Randolph*. [S. AMES]

TO TIMOTHY PICKERING

DEDHAM, JANUARY 12, 1807

MY DEAR SIR,

THE MAN who never flatters cannot avoid furnishing the occasions for his friends to flatter themselves. Indeed their being his friends will furnish one. Your kind wishes for my health, in your favor of New Year's day, will afford another. I was much gratified by the perusal of the other parts of your letter, but that part was not the least pleasing. In return, I will wish that fortune may serve you as well as you serve your country, and that one of your rewards and enjoyments may be, to see our country escape from the perils to which it is blind, and the administration to which it is now partial.

You describe our dangers and disgraces with so just a discernment of their causes, and with so much feeling for the public evils that will be their consequences, that I am ready to acquit former republics from a good deal of the reproach that has survived their ruin—the reproach of wanting sense to see it, when it was obvious and near. Probably, however, we shall yet find evidence enough in the works of their great writers, to prove that the wise and good among their citizens did foresee their fate, and would have resisted it, if they could; but that a republic tends, experience says, irresistibly towards licentiousness, and that a licentious republic, or democracy, is of all governments that very one in which the wise and good are most completely reduced to impotence. Such men no more deserve the reproach that their republics fall, than the ships are cast away at sea; or, if I may drop all high metaphor and speak like a farmer, that a fence falls when it is supported by nothing but white birch stakes. It is the nature of these to fail in two years;

and a republic wears out its morals almost as soon as the sap of a white birch rots the wood.

And are we not fated to have our present chief the longer on account of his inefficiency? His whole care is to be where he is, and to do nothing to risk his place. Unless great public disasters get the multitude angry with this do-nothing policy, they will like it exceedingly. The chiefs of party, of course, cannot get a handle to turn him out; and their inducement to do it is always least, when the squad of the party that is secretly opposed to him is the most clearly convinced of his imbecility. It is not contempt, it is the dread of a really able man at the head of a hostile party that rouses all the fierceness of political competition.

It is natural to ask, whether we are not hastening to the time when public disasters will make him obnoxious. It seems to me probable, his election will happen first. Of course our country must remain unprepared, and be ruined, if it please God to permit the British navy to belong to Bonaparte. The Assyrian will tread us down like the mire of the streets. I have read the tenth chapter of Isaiah, to which you refer me, and I think it strikingly applicable to the French and to the United States. As, however, the British navy may resist for several years, we may be permitted, without interruption, to finish our destruction ourselves. When I note Crowninshield's anti-bank scheme, Gallatin's report to refund, or unfund, the debt, and the schemes for amending the Constitution to death, I am ready to suppose that our Jacobins will be in at the death before our French conquerors.

I am a little less disposed than most persons to throw all the blame, of delaying to resist France, on the king of Prussia. Last fall I stated, that unless the coalition would consent to make him great, they had no right to expect to make him hostile to Bonaparte; that small powers could not now exist in Europe independent; that Prussia would be ruined by France, if he joined against her, and the coalition failed of its object; that he would as certainly be ruined by his allies, if the coalition succeeded, for he would be little and they great; and that the foresight of this manifest danger would justify him, if he insisted, as a *sine qua non,* to be made as potent at least as Austria; that he ought to have Hanover, Saxony, Hesse, and Holland added to his kingdom, indemnifying in money, or other territory, the ousted princes; and thus he would be placed to fight France with only the Rhine for a barrier; but I added, that probably neither of the parties to the coalition would agree to his aggrandizement.

It was not long after the disasters of Austria before the king of England, as elector of Hanover, declared to the king of Prussia, that in no possible event would he alienate his German dominions. Such narrow views, such stiffness at a time which required yielding to a friend, lest he should have to yield to a foe, still appear to me to merit the reproach of ruining the coalition, and excluding the king of Prussia when he was willing to reënforce it. His late manifesto alludes darkly to some of these facts. His gallant conduct to meet Bonaparte in the field of battle was probably well and maturely considered beforehand; yet it has turned out wrong; for if he had led his army to join the Russians, the battle would have been yet to fight, and the event might be different. It seems as if Frederick thought a defensive system a poor one against the French. In that, no doubt, he was right; still I wish he had waited for the Russians.

I think I have formerly communicated to you some reflections I had made, on the causes of the steady superiority maintained in war by the French armies, and that I ascribed them to their superiority in numbers, in cavalry, and in artillery. From hence it ensues that fortified towns are of little significance, and small arms of much less than formerly. On each of these heads I could dilate, but I think it needless to you. But the consequence of this real superiority is, that the defensive system is no longer to be trusted. Nations could formerly spin out a war, and tire down a foe. To conquer was, of course, next to impossible. Since, however, the experience of the French system has evinced that absolute conquest is no longer an improbable event of a contest with France, it becomes obvious that nations, who would be safe, must get the sort of force that gives to France this tremendous superiority. Relying no longer on a frontier of fortified towns with strong garrisons, and a weak army of observation in the field, they must now have numbers, cavalry, and artillery superior to the invader, or make up their minds to submit to him. A navy, if we had one, might hinder this invader from coming over. But if he comes, he will be our master, if we have nothing but militia with small arms to oppose his march. Indeed his march would be a quiet procession, through the centre of the States, from Norfolk to New York, little disturbed, and not at all obstructed by myriads of popping militia. Such an enemy could get horses by stripping Long Island, the eastern shore, and the coast of South Carolina and Georgia. Our patriots too would, no doubt, supply them for a good price. The light artillery they would bring with them; and as the French stow men as thick in their ships as the Guinea traders do their negro slaves, they could bring over fifty thousand troops and twenty thousand dismounted dragoons. What could we do but join Duane in lamenting that we had so long suffered anglo-federal presses to provoke the great nation? *Apropos* of Duane, how audaciously insolent he is on that subject!

These are my grounds for showing that, unless we prepare, and on a great scale, we must submit when our English defenders give out.

I really wish you would examine this perhaps obscure sketch of the grounds of my military notions, to convince Mr. Giles how defenceless we are, and how fallacious are his popular ideas. The sing-song of Bunker Hill Yankee heroes will not do against the French. They understand their trade. An inferior army, even of regulars, would be exposed, would be sure to have its flank turned; and thus a victory would be won without a chance to fight. With a numerous cavalry, there would be no chance for running away. Is any country, then, more conquerable than the United States, from New York southward? Even our Yankee land, though abounding in strong posts, would be destitute of men and means to occupy and maintain them. My idea would be, that the utmost energies of the United States should be called forth to equip a powerful fleet of ships of the line, and that salt duties, interior and direct house taxes should be resumed or augmented, to array a considerable body of artillerists, and a military school of engineers, &c., and regiments enough to suppply officers; the complement of men to be small. On the whole, a less number than twelve thousand I should think unsafe to trust to. If any fears of the danger to liberty should arise from such an army, have a select militia, three times as numerous, of yeomanry, encamped yearly in such numbers as would teach discipline, and let that be perfect. To that end, there must be martial law in the camp.

I well know that all this is moonshine, and that embarrassments in executing so great a plan would arise. The people would think it madness; the federalists would be as much afraid of arming as the democrats. I know too, as a consequence of all this, that we fall when the navy of our unthanked champion is withdrawn. Fifty thousand real soldiers might make us safe; and we might have, and ought to have, a navy to block up Cadiz, Brest, and Toulon, whenever England makes peace, and our danger from France should make it necessary.

I will ask of Mr. Cabot the perusal of your letter to him.

Yours, &c.

TO JOSIAH QUINCY

DEDHAM, JANUARY 27, 1807

DEAR MR. QUINCY,

You great men in Congress love to banter us poor farmers. The style of the court, we have always heard, is very flattering; otherwise I should say, you are too civil by half, when you profess yourself my pupil.

Abstract truths still appear to us at home to be truths; but their application depends upon circumstances, which we cannot know at all, or not in season for advising you, who are on the spot. I am ready therefore, with, I believe, nine tenths of the men whom you too modestly think well informed on the subjects that pass before your honorable body, to approve whatever you do and say, because you think fit to do and say it. I really felt impressed with the judicious manner of your opposition to the repeal of the salt tax; and I not only honored your spirit, which so small a minority renders the more conspicuous, but I thought it politic, if you had only cared for reputation, to brave such a majority. The spirit of the country is not very high, but it is higher than the administration.

What you do and say is very right, for we, the people, yield to every strong impression upon our minds. Therefore, what your party neglects to do and say seems to me very wrong, for it leaves us to the impression of the clumsy arts of your adversaries. They do what ought not to be done, they neglect what ought to be done, and all seems right to us, the people, so long as you good men in Congress forbear to expose the facts. In Great Britain, opposition is methodical in its way. Every thing is done on plan, and that plan is to show the incapacity and tricks of administration. Why is this task left, and left exclusively, to Randolph? Why should not the Feds speak out, *quasi* Feds? Why should they permit their name and prnciples, and the memory of both, to perish? Either Bonaparte must kill our liberty, or faction will kill it. But states have an hereafter in this world. In our future state, which may not be five years off, perhaps not two, the influence of the Feds to mitigate a tyranny may be great, though it is found little to prevent its occurrence. The peculiar federal ground should be forever notorious with our citizens. As matters are, the Feds seem to me too much merged in the other parties. Popular topics are ever at hand with those who find fault. Your own good speech on fortifications is an example. It made an impression, and the impression yet remains. The objects of the administration are mean and personal. The people want some of the advantages of good government; and when there is no question about the burden of taxes, the denial of those advantages affords aliment to that malcontent spirit, which is unappeasable in all republics. But the silence of the federalists as a party, and as a peculiar party, still adhering to *Washington* principles, nearly loses all the influence arising from all these various sources. I will thank you to offer my respectful salutations to Mr. Theodore Dwight, and ask his reflections on the plan of the campaign for the Feds. He is a man of resource, and well knows the avenues to New England minds.

It is certainly better that Randolph should expose the wretched policy of our Solomons, than that it should be left unnoticed. But while his course should be left free, why should not the Feds fastidiously pursue their own, taking care to let it appear that it is different from his? You good men in Washington are not to be lectured by anybody, and I feel as little disposed to take the chair of lecturer as any man alive. You will not do me the injustice to interpret my suggestions otherwise than I wish you should. The entertaining matter and vivacity of manner in your letters extort from me the prosing returns I make you. I wish to see the federal grounds displayed, and become as public as the public roads. All eyes are turned to Washington. There federalism concentres its deputies, and thence should emanate the facts, documents, and arguments for us all. It is true you are a minority, and what you ask for will be refused; but it will nevertheless remain a notorious fact that you ask, and you are not tongue-tied, but you can surely make the reasons why you ask universally known. Great caution, no doubt, great concert and great ability are necessary; and a few able men can furnish all these requisites. I declare to you, I fear federalism will not only die, but all remembrance of it be lost. As a party, it is still good for every thing it ever was good for; that is to say, to cry "fire" and "stop thief," when jacobinism attempts to burn and rob. It never had the power to put out the fire, or to seize the thief.

Nor should too much maiden modesty be affected about causing your speeches to be carefully corrected and printed. It is respectful towards the public to expose reasons, as if we could comprehend or would regard them. S. H. Smith is too partial to be trusted with that business.

I am glad Randolph's mouth is at last open.

Your friend.

TO JOSIAH QUINCY

———

DEDHAM, FEBRUARY 3, 1807

MY DEAR SIR,

As soon as I learned where your salt speech could be found in print with any correctness, I took measures to get it republished. It is in the Repertory of this day, and is, I say it without compliment, an ornament to its columns. I am as well satisfied with what you do not say, but only hint, as if you had said it in form. Your argument is sound, and the subject is presented in the right point of view. No man seldomer says flattering things to his friends than I do; and if I had waited a week after reading your speech, I should have been more stingy of praise. Having just read it, I cannot wholly suppress my warmth of approbation. Let me repeat that you should not be too modest about getting your speeches into print correctly. It is the public that is argued with; that public that always pronounces its judgment, and seldom condescends to give its attention; that is almost always wrong in the hour of deliberation, and right in the day of repentance. Federalism is allowed to have little to do with deliberation; and I am far from certain that popular repentance is often accompanied with saving grace. We are not so truly sorry for the sin, as for its bad success. To get people to think right therefore, either first or last, is not the most hopeful undertaking in the world. But federal good sense is never to guide measures. Archimedes might calculate the force of the wind, but could not prevent its blowing. Now, though argument will never turn the weathercock, it may prove how it points. That power, which your adversary can use in spite of you, is checked by your efforts. If he exerts all his force, and you all yours, his force is reduced to the degree in which he surpasses you, and in that degree you may not be liable to very serious injury. Federalism is not a sword, nor a gun; it is not wings, but a parachute. In this sense, the good men in Congress should be on the alert.

I feel assured that we are to be subjugated by Bonaparte; and I have a curiosity to know how Randolph and the knowing ones can sit as easy as the fools do, and see him hastening to snatch from their hands the power they are so ready to contend among themselves about. I saw in the Repertory, of last week, a long piece, of five or six columns, on the causes of the French military superiority, and on the facility of their conquest of the United States, unless we prepare on a great scale. Whether such discussions produce any effect, I know not; but if they do not produce any, it must be because our noisy liberty-men are eager for power, and perfectly indifferent about the fall of the country from its boasted independence. J. R.'s boast, that he never reads the newspapers, is a shrewd sign that he studies them. I hope his real politics are better than Varnum's, whose ignorance blinds him, or than Jefferson's, whose fears make him a slave. But if J. R. was disposed ever so heartily to urge preparations, he could not prevail to have any made. The force of primary popular notions would control Lord Chatham, if he was our premier. I often dare to think our nation began self-government without education for it. Like negroes, freed after having grown up to man's estate, we are incapable of learning and practising the great art of taking care of ourselves. We must be put to school again, I fear, and whipped into wisdom.

Nobody here seems to care a cent about Burr's plan. They think him desperate and profligate; but they concern themselves very little about his managing his own affairs in his own way, without too much of Mr. Jefferson's regulation. The riots on account of Selfridge are over, but the effect on the popular mind is not obliterated. Our General Court seems to be nearly as ready for revolution as that in Pennsylvania, which McKean lately resisted with success.

On the whole, if Bonaparte should not come soon, we shall ruin ourselves before he gets here; and if he comes, he will ruin us. I like usurpation better than conquest. It is better to lie in purgatory than in hell.

It was my design to write you a short letter, but I cannot stop my pen when I would, and if I have tired you two pages back, charge it, I pray you, to my infirmity.

Your friend, &c.

TO TIMOTHY PICKERING

DEDHAM, FEBRUARY 4, 1807

MY DEAR SIR,

THE immeasurable ambition, and equal profligacy of Colonel Burr, have created no surprise, nor have I doubted that his desperate situation would urge him upon desperate measures, if any chance of success in any such should offer. But my surprise still continues, because I cannot see that any chance of success could have flattered him. Burr I supposed shrewd and intelligent, of all men the least likely to mistake peevish discontents among the western people for deep disaffection, or to take other men, like Truxton, for instance, to be Aaron Burrs. I supposed he might err in daring too much; I little thought he would hazard every thing by trusting too soon, and opening his designs to men who, everybody could have sworn, would reject his proposals. The men who are destitute of any virtue, are generally too much in want of character, to have influence;—and to mislead the men of virtue, two things must, I think, concur. The prospect must be such as to enable him to corrupt them, by their virtues, which is as sure a way to corrupt *them*, as to tempt bad men by their passions. There was nothing in Burr's scheme but rebellion, without plausible pretexts. The next way to gain men is so to contrive the project, that the total loss of character should not be the penalty. It is too much to expect that the chance of power or land should reconcile Truxton, or even Wilkinson, to live execrated by all men in the United States at least. Instant disgrace is a condition that would spoil any offer with all the ordinary rogues, who as seldom act steadily upon bad principles, as good men upon those of virtue.

However, nobody cares for Burr or his conspiracy. I am struck with it, to see how little the hopes and fears of our part of the public are interested. Curiosity is hungry, but our patriotism seems unconcerned. The separation of the western country has not appeared to me a probable event. Democracy acts by the physical force of the many, and the *vis major* will keep the whole territory indivisible. Insurrection will either conquer or be conquered, and division will thus end in unity. Foreign events may work great interior changes. We approach the term when they will begin. France is gaining the dominion over us as well as Europe, and Bonaparte may hinder licentiousness from undoing us, by acquiring the mastery here first. He will not then allow anybody to play the oppressor but himself and his subs. My heart sinks at the prospect. We are abject and base, people as well as government, and nothing could save us but energy and magnanimity. We have none of these. Our great democracy cannot remain as it is. *Ipsa moles nocet.* It must ferment, if Bonaparte should let it alone, and fermentation is an agent that must change and may destroy the mass. Indeed I consider the whole civilized world as metal thrown back into the furnace, to be melted over again. If we should lose our dross, our negro population, and our licentious spirit, we shall come out of the furnace much less in bulk than we go in with. Futurity, however, like the blue ether of the sky, is impenetrable without seeming to be so. There appears to be nothing to stop our vision, but there is nothing to guide it. Indeed, I think in both cases we can see most, by shutting our eyes. Providence will dispose of us, and if our destiny should be no better than our deserts, we shall have no great consolation in the prospect.

Supposing that you see the Repertory regularly, I have not sent it to you. The last week a long essay of five columns appeared in it, to show the causes of the French superiority, and the facility with which they could get the upperhand over our militia. You will see other pieces in that paper, written apparently in the hope of rousing the people, and alarming the administration, which you will say is no great proof of the writer's discernment. I remember Tracy used to say of the Jacobins, they were hell-hardened sinners. If the government saw the danger, the people would not let them provide against it. But I have a curiosity to know whether Giles, Randolph, and Jefferson himself are blind to it. Whether the latter confides in Bonaparte, or, if he should attempt invasion, whether he thinks a militia any defence. All these men are talkers, and I should suppose open themselves frequently on every subject. Mr. Quincy's speech on the salt tax is a good one, and is much approved. I did not greatly mistake Mr. Dana's character, but somebody must come forward in the House; and for a great speech or two, Mr. D., I should hope, would be found adequate. He is sprightly and witty, though I apprehend, not a great lover of business and drudgery. Your idea of the dejection of Great Britain agrees with mine, though I think not exactly with Mr. Cabot's. He has suggested that they act on a refined plan of policy, to evade rather than to yield the points in dispute. So much evasion, however, looks like real timidity. Our cowards appear to think themselves entitled to brag about the non-intercourse law. When Bonaparte has all Europe, from the Baltic round to the Euxine, in his dominion, I really fear Great Britain will find it difficult, or at least useless, to contend longer. Then we must yield. The insolent threat of the young Frenchman could be executed. We should take monarchy, despotism, fetters, and ignominy better than any people, not excepting the Dutch, that Bonaparte has yet conquered. I ought to have said sooner, that yours of 23d January is received. I make no doubt Truxton is brave and honest.

With esteem and regard, yours, &c.

TO TIMOTH PICKERING

DEDHAM, NOVEMBER 6, 1807

MY DEAR SIR,

YOUR FAVOR of the 28th October, covering the message and documents referred to, reached me yesterday somewhat unexpectedly. I had supposed you would not go on to Washington till November. Besides, shut up half my time in a sick chamber, and the other half in my parlor, I am unaffectedly sensible of my insignificance. If, however, you and my worthy friend Mr. Quincy think fit sometimes to send me intelligence, I shall be grateful. I am in the habit of thinking your comments better than the text.

I was disgusted about a fortnight since, on reading, in Ben Russell, a short piece tending to show that Great Britain had the empire of the sea and Bonaparte of the land; that both obtained it by force, which gives them all the rights they have, the one to subjugate the nations, and the other to make and expound the laws of nations. When federal newspapers publish such stuff, are we to wonder at the folly of our people? Have we any security, as long as that folly or worse reigns? I am ready to believe that we, as great boasters as the ancient Greeks, are the most ignorant nation in the world, because we have had the least experience. Fresh from the hands of a political mother, who would not let us fall, we now think it impossible that we should fall. Bonaparte will cure us of our presumption; or, if that task should be left to some other rough teacher, we shall learn at last the art, that is, the habits, manners, and prejudices of a nation, especially the prejudices which are worth more than philosophy, without which I venture to consider our playing government as a sort of free negro attempt. It is probably necessary, that we should endure slavery for some ages, till every drop of democratic blood has been got rid of by fermentation or bleeding. I dread to look forward to the dismal scenes, through which my children are to pass. As every nation has been trodden under foot, ground in a mill, and purged in the fire of adversity, I know not why we should hope for all fair weather and sunshine, for peace and gainful commerce and an everlasting futurity of elysium, before we have lived and suffered as others have done. We seem to expect a state of felicity before a state of probation. Of our six millions of people there are scarcely six hundred who yet look for liberty anywhere except on paper. Excuse me—I am teasing you with a theme as trite and as tragical as the Children in the Wood.

. . . .

Dear sir, your friend, &c.

TO JOSIAH QUINCY

DEDHAM, NOVEMBER 11, 1807

MY DEAR SIR,

I AM amused to see the embarrassment that your motion for a select committee to state the facts in the affair of the Chesapeake, produced among the governing party. Facts could not be stated truly without exposing the unneutral omissions and commissions of the administration. I may err in my views of things as they pass at such a distance. But I think I see clearly that the Jeffersonians rely on the vague but violent impressions of the people, and will by no means descend to particulars. In this their policy is skilful, for I confess I can discern but little excuse for our government, if the whole truth be laid open. But the speculative opinion, who is in the right or who in the wrong, will be of no account in the final result. We hate Great Britain, and would fight her if we dared. She would resent our aggressions, if it were not so very inconvenient to herself as it is actually at this time. Her whole soul is engaged in a struggle that concerns us, and we should confess it, if we had any soul. We are, however, either blind to the common danger, or resolved to seek our safety by helping to hasten the worst. Yet is seems to me, that little as Congress affairs look like true wisdom, they look still less like war. I hear no motion for a declaration of war, for bills to confiscate, or to put the non-intercourse law into operation. War does not come from cold blood, and the salamanders have not yet appeared among you. What will J. Randolph do? Will the coming election of a new king keep him in the background?

I cannot write five words worth your reading, but I get all the information worth attending to, from you and Colonel Pickering. Why then should I not contrive to extort replies from you that will furnish it?

Yours, &c.

TO JOSIAH QUINCY

DEDHAM, NOVEMBER 19, 1807

DEAR SIR,

I CONSIDER familiar letters as a substitute for conversation, and that when writing to you, I may pour out my careless effusions to a friend without premeditation on my part, or disappointment on yours. Your letter of the 7th to Mr. Cabot seems to be a graver cast, and to demand a well-examined answer. Even then, however, when we pretend to think deeply, (I speak for one,) we do but skim off from the surface the old thoughts that have long floated there;—and it is in truth no little proof of their being right, that neither experience nor disputation have expelled them from their post. I make this confession, because I am willing to lay open the source of my opinion on your question, "Whether the federalists should make motions and speeches, or should wait in silence for the effect of the civil wars that are ready to break out among the Jacobins?" The federal party, which I consider as that of all honest men, would wish to do some things, and to hinder others from being done. Your means for both are not in your votes, but in the influence you may produce on public opinion. That is wrong, but it is not weak. It is blinded in error, but not disarmed by power. Here I observe, that your address to public opinion is not to get power yourselves, but to hinder or control its exercise in the hands of others. You would have the people see what exists, or is impending, not make them choose what they dread, or love those they hate. You would make them love liberty, not you. You cannot make the people federal, because you cannot change their hearts and affections. You could sooner sink the Alleghany to a lake. Though they have partialities and aversions which you cannot control, they have also hopes and fears which you can. They are incurably timorous. They see tempests in every cloud, and goblins in every shadow. Hence I draw this result: Do not disturb the people in their love and hatred, but confine your energies to the display of the public embarrassments and apprehensions. Leave Jefferson to Randolph. Be patient and mild when misrepresented in the House. I shall be sooner at my point, if I say at once, do not irritate;— expose public dangers, and refrain as much as possible from recriminations and individual misconduct in office, Wilkinson, perhaps, excepted. In his case, the popular ground may be taken. I will not pretend to say that you may not be forced to act occasionally in opposition to every one of the ideas I have ventured to suggest. Still, I presume to think your plan, as a party, ought to rest upon them. It is, in a word, that you should do what can be done, not waste your force in trying to do what you cannot. You really love liberty, but the people do not love you, and they never hate you more than when you attack their favorites. These they cherish the more for their disgraces, which they call persecutions for their sakes.

The people dread war, and they will allow you to point out remedies—at least this is what I hope. Even suppose the majority will not receive the truth when you exhibit it, at least the federalists will. You are chosen to do what you can, and if after all, it is unavailing, the party will applaud you, and gather zeal from your arguments. Suppose you sit silent, will it long be possible to hinder the apathy of despair, indeed the chills of dissolution, from pervading the federal body? Will men eagerly vote for others who sit sullen, and will not speak? Feeble as the federal party is, it is inestimable to the public. It is "*Spes ultima Romœ.*" Can liberty have any chance, when it no longer has any friends? Even now, federalism checks, though it cannot govern. It is fitter to check than to rule. And it is all the check we want, when it deters faction from eating us alive. All we ask is, that they would let us exist. It is better to suffer the fatigue of pumping, than to sit sullen till the ship sinks. It is despair that raises among you these doubts as to your exertions. Will not your feelings be contagious, and induce your constituents to dissolve the party? Will not they refuse to make efforts in a cause that you abandon? A party out of action is out of existence. It is a salamander that dies if you refuse fresh fuel, and, what is no less essential, the breath of the bellows. This last, I am afraid you will say, means speeches: I disclaim all evil meanings, and am quite serious. I repeat it, that the chance of liberty will be the worse, probably worse than nothing, if our party be dissolved. How has party subsisted in England? Certainly not by long inaction. Incessantly baffled, yet still assailing, and at last in power for a short time. This is what federalism is not to expect—I think not to desire. By the flight of the emigrants, France instantly fell into the extremes of revolution. Besides, your cautious but ever-vigilant spirit will find or make the opportunities to be useful. A war, if it is hindered, will be hindered by you. If it happens, the first danger will be that the rage of the people will persecute or sacrifice the federalists. It may oppress them in a thousand ways, all intolerable, unless you preserve to us an independent existence. When the people suffer much, (as they will,) if they do not tear us to pieces, (which I confess I think not improbable,) there will be times when they will hear you.

There will yet be many new organizations of party, many overwhelming changes. In resettling affairs, the federalists should be in some force, that is, in credit. They deserve credit for wisdom and patriotism; and in times of fearful adversity, the wise and good are sometimes allowed to advise. It is this eventual employment of party that I would have in view. For instance, if France should propose an alliance, would you wish to have federalism extinct? Would you leave it to John Randolph to awaken New England? I shall be told, that what you all say goes for nothing. Consider whether this is true. If Junius should write in our papers, and genius should sparkle like phosphorus in every column, the pride of every other federal editor would reluct at republishing the performances, and as to the Chronicle, Egis, and Aurora, their readers would never hear of the publication. It is otherwise with speeches in Congress. They are printed in Jacobin papers, as well as federal, and all the nation, soon or late, gets the substance of a great debate. By all means renounce that false pride that leaves your argument to be stated by the tools of faction. Write yourselves. It will not, unless too long, be refused by S. H. Smith. Here alone (in Congress) the candle of federal truth shines outside of the bushel, and I think you should see that it is kept lighted, and snuffed on every great dark question. I am far from recommending that you should be verbose, or forever spouting. Quite the reverse. Leave the *petite guerre* to others. Let John Randolph and Smilie have the amusement of the cockpit to themselves. Turn your backs on the combats of the wild beasts in the Amphitheatre, but take your places as Senators in the Forum. In zeal for liberty, no men are your rivals. Show that zeal in its temperance and wisdom. There is not likely to be a want of occasions.

Nothing is to be expected from the civil wars of the faction. You will not hinder their fighting, but you will never profit by their victories. They will conquer for themselves, not you, and the views of the victor, whether Randolph or Varnum, are to be always at variance with yours. Do as our nation ought, and place trust only in yourselves. There is scarcely any great national question in which you would make efforts in vain. I confess great prudence and many forbearances are necessary. In almost every case, a popular, or, at least, inoffensive aspect can be given to your argument. Invincible popular notions may be let alone, or touched without wounding them. For, I repeat, the skill of the business is to attempt only what is practicable, and some of the popular tenets are false yet sacred, and therefore respectable. I keep writing on, I find, because I did not stop at first to make an exact division of my subject. I hope, however, I have not omitted any thing that I deem material. The illustration and detail of my principal ideas would lead me a great way, but to experienced and able men I have suggested more than enough. I readily allow that you on the spot are the best judges, and I am in the habit of thinking what you do and say is right, because you have said and done it. Yet your question was so general, that I have not thought myself incompetent to discuss it, on account of my distance from the scene of your debates. Brevity, and not a spirit of dogmatism, has made me use the imperative style, which I pray you to excuse. I have scarcely a doubt that I should, if I had a seat in Congress, agree with the majority of the federalists, on any plan of conduct they may adopt. I truly rejoice in the acquisition of talents from Maryland, New York, and Kentucky. I say of you all, *"melioribus utere fatis."* The very time has come that should make able men active.

From the beginning of my letter, you would expect from me the result of profound meditation. On the contrary, I have written as fast as I could, but not crude new thoughts. I cannot write in any other manner, unless I would submit to a more rigorous toil of thinking than you would expect from a lazy volunteer.

I am, my dear sir, with great esteem and regard,

Yours, most sincerely.

TO JOSIAH QUINCY

———

DEDHAM, DECEMBER 6, 1807, SUNDAY

MY DEAR SIR,

I OWE YOU many thanks for your letter of the 26th, because, by writing it, you must have aggravated your nervous headache, because the contents were very interesting, and because I, confined closer than a debtor, am not worth a statesman's correspondence. In this last, I assure you, I have no mock modesty, for I feel and know, that a man out of the world has no right to any account from those who are doing its business. I shall have no miffs if I am left to glean all I can from the occasional bounty of our mutual friends in Boston. Yours to J. P. Davis was in this way communicated to me, to my great satisfaction. But that to Thomas H. Perkins has not been sent out to me.

I have no doubt that Great Britain will forbear to begin war. Yet unwilling as your men of cotton may be to do any thing to make one, it happens that by doing nothing, your wise non-importation law will soon go into effect, and that, we are told, will be taken for war by Great Britain. How correctly this is rumored, of course I know not. Nevertheless from the high tone of your folks, from Mr. Adams's bill, and from the majority against committing the Philadelphia petition, I should draw the inference that Varnum and Co. will not allow that act to be repealed. Although I cannot suppose that Congress wishes for a war, yet nobody but the federalists, and perhaps not all of them, seems to be willing to take, or as yet to urge, the measures that will prevent one. Your dark, but encouraging assurances about the federalists, come very seasonably, just as I am ready to despair of peace. If a British envoy should come, will he negotiate, while war measures are permitted to go into operation? And how can your Solons find a pretext for repealing it now, after having done so much to bind themselves to its support? Great Britain deplores already the shame of the Foxites, whose treaty was made *pendente lege*.[126] Will that shame be endured by the Pittites, who then said it was intolerable? As the Boston Exchange is, I am told, pretty calm, I suppose I am ignorant of the grounds of their pacific hopes. The *Revenge* going and returning *via* France looks like our administration asking leave to negotiate, or assistance to fight. Which is it? or an alliance to draw closer the fraternal bands.

Of your Randolph's sentiments or designs, I know nothing. Yet I expect to see him in a minority. Here I believe there is great dread of a war, yet great apathy about the men or the measures that will bring it about. The repugnance of the southern men to a war appears to me an incompetent security against that dire event. Great resolutions are always brought to maturity unexpectedly to the many. These men of cotton have the same passions with the war party. Their confidence

---

[126] *During the short administration of Mr. Fox, a treaty was agreed upon by the negotiators of the two nations at London, substantially like Mr. Jay's treaty. The question of impressment was not disposed of by it, but arrangements were made for the suspension or mitigation of that obnoxious claim. Unfortunately President Jefferson rejected it* instanter, *and thereby threw away the last chance of avoiding war.* [S. AMES]

is reposed in the same leading men. They will cheerfully act out any anti-British scheme of policy, which can still be called peace. For to act hostilely was called pacific, when the non-importation law passed. I shall look, therefore, with some apprehension to the 14th December, when the suspension is to expire.

Ever since independence, we have cherished our vanity and nourished our passions. These last have been the fiercer, for being impotent. We have hated those most who oftenest make us feel their impotence. The British have done this, by their searches of our vessels, even while our trade became a monopoly in consequence of the British naval triumphs, as it would be easy to demonstrate. Our cargoes sold well, because the enemies of Great Britain could not sell at all, and we have grown year by year more enraged, because we ascribe to the British vexations the disappointment of our hopes that they would sell still better. We met nobody at sea but Englishmen, and they never failed to exact from us submission, and sometimes sacrifices. Our pride was mortified, and our avarice stript. We cursed their navy, and their maritime law, and wished success to France, and a free sea, that is, that neutrals in every future war should have nothing to do, but take a few hundred dollars freight, instead of fifty per cent. profit on the cargoes. This last item shows how blind we are in our rage, and how little our passions are curbed by our government. On the contrary, the business of the administration has been to find fagots for the bonfire. Thus opinionated and inflamed, our democracy has got loose from every restraint but fear. Our cabinet takes counsel of the mob; and it is now a question, whether the hatred of Great Britain, and the reproach fixed even upon violent men, if they will not proceed in their violence, will not overcome the fears of the maritime States, and of the planters in Congress. The usual levity of a democracy has not appeared in regard to Great Britain. We have been steady in our hatred of her, and when popular passions are not worn out by time, but augment, they must, I should think, explode in war. You are in a situation to judge much better than your eastern friends. I shall rejoice in the success of your efforts, and if, as I expect, your particular merits should be distinguished, I shall rejoice in it with the warmth of a friend.

Yours, truly.

INDEX

"anonymous slanderer" view of, 300–302
British influence on federalists and, 270, 276, 281, 282
characterized, 19
in Congress, 313, 315, 1215–1217
creed of, 307–310
equality as viewed by, 238–242, 244
and equality in New England, 267–268
French Revolution and, 251–253, 258, 259
and inequality in Virginia, 265–266
and power of branches of government, 249–250
rabble's right to power included in, 242–243, 245–247, 250
and rights of aliens, 267
sovereignty of the people and, see Sovereignty of the people
France and
dangers of French power, 338, 340, 344, 366, 369
Franco-British war and, 468, 469, 495
French conquests and, 494
undeclared war with France and, 1287, 1288
government as viewed by, 20, 1215–1217
Jacobins using, 10
See also Jacobinism and Jacobins
Jay treaty and, 1112n, 1120
in Jefferson administration, 220–221
Jefferson's electoral victory and, 1400
politics of, attacked, 311–317
and trade with Britain, 472
Virginia, 130–131
Demodocus, 30
Demosthenes, 515, 1447, 1543
Denmark, 448, 456, 457, 482
Dennie, Jo, 1273, 1354
Despotism, see Tyranny and despotism
Dessalines, Jean Jacques, 348, 1497, 1499

Dexter, Samuel (Sam), 583, 735, 1029, 1039, 1040, 1101, 1112, 1193, 1283, 1407, 1408, 1437
Dickinson, T., 1034
Diomed, 24, 1459
Dionysius, 1471
Dionysius of Halicarnassus, 421
Discrimination resolutions, 279–280, 463, 468, 476, 819, 1424, 1515
correspondence on, 1028–1037, 1041–1042, 1048–1051, 1078–1079
speeches on, 989–1028
Dodd, 40
Dorchester, Lord, 1034, 1050, 1158n
Dorians, 101
Dowse, 1505
Duane, William, 218, 226n, 306, 1550
Dublin (Ireland), 245
Duilius, 402
Dumourier, Charles François, 1464
Duncan, Lord, 1446
Dundas, Sir, 1194n, 1291
Dunkirk (France), 1003
Duties, see Funding system; Taxation
Dutton, Warren, 1412, 1452
Dwight, Edmund, 1470
Dwight, Josiah, 1116
Dwight, Theodore, 1553
Dwight, Thomas, 634, 866, 1260, 1282, 1312, 1447
correspondence with, 837–838, 865–866, 874–875, 937–940, 946–951, 1089, 1116–1119, 1184–1185, 1206–1208, 1299–1301, 1413–1414, 1480
on assumption of debt, 831–834, 836–837, 839–840, 950, 954, 958, 960–961
on British condemnation of U.S. ships, 1501–1502
on character of Congressional activities, 891, 942–943, 958–959, 1183
on *The Chronicle*, 1044–1045
on Dedham, 1043–1044
(*continued*)

Gallatin, Albert (*continued*)
  in Jefferson's Cabinet, 1407
  and mission to France, 1306,
    1334
  undeclared war with France and,
    1334
Ganges (river), 451
Gardiner, 831
Gardner, 1479
Gaul, 165, 166, 467, 477, 499,
    500
Gazette (newspaper), 568, 714,
    1051, 1351, 1353, 1385
Gazette of the United States (news-
    paper), 682n, 694n
Genet, Edmund, 985, 987, 1049,
    1142
  exposed, 1051, 1064, 1112n
  as minister to France, 1158n
    actions of, criticized, 207,
      282, 326, 331, 338, 451,
      1196
    recalled, 207n, 964, 1520n
  planned expedition against New
    Orleans by, 1033n
Geneva (Switzerland), 465
Gengis Khan (Mongol chieftain),
    479
Genoa (Italy), 465
George I (King of England), 791
George III (King of England), 380,
    408, 1159, 1165, 1167
Georgetown, 710
Georgia, 469, 549, 605, 1220,
    1266, 1550
  apportionment of representation
    and, 935, 936
  assumption of debt of, 783, 847
  Congress as viewed in, 881
  Jay treaty and, 1157
  land speculation in, 1104
  reactions to Hamilton's death in,
    512
Gerard, 1304
German Empire (Germany), 406,
    466
  in European balance of power,
    456–457
  France and
    France defeats, 366, 444, 453,
      476, 1343
    French military character com-

pared with that of Germany,
    504
  and new coalition against
    France, 487–488
Greece compared with, 502
property ownership and education
    in, 1072
Russian aspirations on, 480
size of armies of, 422
U.S. trade restrictions and, 1015
See also Austria; Prussia
Germanicus (Roman emperor), 510
Gerry, Elbridge, 191n, 276, 319–
    320, 420, 568, 840, 1269,
    1273, 1348, 1459
  election of, feared, 1407, 1413,
    1424
  as envoy to France, 1282, 1292,
    1295, 1308n
  funding system and, 835
  seat of government and, 827
Geyer, 581
Gibbon, Edward, 35, 502
Gibson, Colonel, 886
Giles, William Branch, 645, 943,
    1027, 1073, 1077, 1115,
    1207n, 1559
  bounties on cod fisheries and,
    893, 900
  establishment of National Bank
    and, 862
  Jay treaty and, 1137, 1139, 1141
  military preparedness and, 1238,
    1550
  naturalization of alien nobles
    and, 1093
  propriety of replies to presidential
    speeches and, 1053
  resolutions presented by, 674–
    676
  1796 elections and, 1209
Gill, 1315, 1318
Gilman, John Taylor, 1452
Gloucester, Duke of, 379
Goodrich, 1367
Goodhue, Benjamin, 568, 599,
    828, 1194n
  correspondence with, 1251–1252
  on investments, 1383–1384,
    1396–1397, 1430–1434,
    1531–1532
  on need to resist jacobins,
    1413

Independent Chronicle, The (newspaper), 38, 45, 49, 56, 63, 69, 73, 81, 583*n*
India, 348, 406
    British control of, 414, 460, 477
    French designs on, 408, 417, 459
Indians (Native Americans), 950, 954, 981, 1086, 1523
    prospect of peace with, 1086
    war against, 886, 889–890, 892, 944, 1102, 1173–1174, 1178, 1239
        military preparedness for, 1237–1243
Individual liberty
    sovereignty of the people versus, 174–177
    See also Liberty
Industry, *see* Fisheries; Manufactures
Ionian Sea, 101
Insurgente (ship), 1310
Ireland, 275, 290, 417, 455, 473, 1268
Irujo, Marquis, 1254*n*, 1421, 1520*n*
Isthmian Games, 80
Italian (Cisalpine) republics, 399, 409, 464, 496, 1017, 1323
Italy, 206, 223, 334, 411, 813, 1464
    in European balance of power, 458
    French conquest of, 348, 405, 410, 411, 417, 419, 421, 429, 444, 446, 453, 465, 466, 471, 476, 482, 485, 487, 496, 1188, 1196, 1376, 1424, 1507
    and new coalition against France, 488
    Roman conquest of, 421, 477, 502
Ithurial, Spear of, 62
Izard, Ralph, 1097, 1127

Jackson, James, 835, 838, 846, 879
Jacobins and Jacobinism, 10, 80, 160, 247, 248, 382, 891, 1106, 1428

assumption of debt and, 981
avoiding controversy with, 1416
in Boston, 1290, 1407
British condemnation of U.S. ships and, 1489
British influence on federalists and, 271, 272, 274, 277, 280, 282, 292
Carthaginian, 79
characterized, 10, 19, 192–193, 200–203
in check (1793), 965
concept of equality of, 241
    See also Sovereignty of the people
Constitution defied by, 91
correspondence on, 1409–1411
1800 elections and, 1364, 1368, 1369, 1371, 1378, 1386, 1387, 1397
1804 elections and, 89, 305
essay attacking, 974–985
federalists and
    comparison between, 7–8
    See also Federalism and federalists, need to resist Jacobins by; Federalism and federalists, the press and
France and, 213, 416–420, 424, 981
France as model for, 982, 983
French politics and, 398–399, 407
and Jacobins as French faction, 195–200, 202–205, 208, 215, 257
and French Revolution, 532–533
quarrel with France and, 1247–1250, 1278, 1281, 1292, 1317–1319, 1321–1322, 1327, 1332
Franco-British war and, 354, 404, 407, 408, 451–452, 468, 469
French, 21, 193, 334, 338, 438, 441–444, 532–533, 1063
Gerry's election and, 1413
goal of, 976–978
Gore commission and, 1465
government power strengthened by, 189
        (*continued*)

Lee, Richard Henry, 558, 564, 806
Legislative power, *see* Congress
Lemnos, island of, 1518
Leonidas, 100, 535
Lepidus, 1468
Lethe, stream of, 25
Leuctra, battle of, 107
Levant, 1018
Lexington (Massachusetts), 772
Leyden Gazette (newspaper), 1353
Liberty, 47, 82, 86, 87, 89–90,
    358, 528
  as birthright, 62
  and biennial elections, 545–546
  breeding vanity, 323–324
  commerce and, 413–414
  Constitution as guarantor of, 146,
    147, 652
    See also United States Consti-
      tution
  cost of preserving, 188
  democrats' view of, 307, 315,
    324
  education and, 1072–1074
  in France, 132, 155, 159
    destroyed, 118, 119, 189–
      191, 198–199, 227, 254,
      259, 262, 263, 341, 359,
      434–437, 531, 532, 1299;
      see also French Revolution
    equality and, 252
    in monarchic France, 253–257
  government viewed as impedi-
    ment to, 19
  in Great Britain, 72, 122, 124,
    241
    basis of, 273
    English Revolution and, 379
    and opposition to conquest,
      414
    and safeguard of property,
      412–413
  in Greece, 127–129, 1058
  Hamilton's policy opposed in
    name of, 967–968
  human nature and, 527
    See also Human nature
  literature and, 34
  and maintenance of the Union,
    525
  monarchy and, 1463
  of nature, 64, 543–544
  need for constraints on, 5

  property and, 358, 1072, 1073
  public opinion and false notions
    of, 1347
  and right to power, 247
  in Rome, 225–226
  Spartan, 115
  threats to
    democracy as, *see* Democracy,
      as threat to liberty
    democratic clubs as threat to,
      1062
    factions as, 123, 124, 130,
      137, 138, 140, 144–149,
      151–156, 160, 162, 168,
      180, 181, 189, 1553; *see
      also* Factions
    free press as, 185; *see also*
      Free press
    Jacobins as, 130, 172, 189–
      190, 194, 247, 248, 976,
      978; *see also* Jacobins and
      jacobinism
    France as, *see* France
    Shays's Rebellion as, 61, 68,
      71, 73
    sovereignty of the people as,
      130, 137, 174–177; *see also*
      Sovereignty of the people
    Virginia as, 129–131, 143; *see
      also* Virginia
  Washington's warning on, 529
  See also Elections; Rights
Licentiousness, 1531
  guarding against, in framing of
    Constitution, 126
  law and order versus, 1060
  of the rabble, 1073
  in Virginia, 130, 131
  See also Anarchy; Democracy;
    Factions *and specific exam-
    ples of licentiousness; for ex-
    ample:* Shays's Rebellion
Lilliput and Lilliputians, 88, 1471
Lincoln, Levi, 631, 696, 831,
    1052, 1279, 1424–1425,
    1459, 1478–1479
Linus, 25
Lisbon (Portugal), 413
Literature, *see* Arts and literature
Livermore, Samuel, 658, 714, 732,
    737, 1237
Livingston, Edward, 1089, 1122
Livingston, Robert R., 21, 569

on funding system, 829, 1100
on impost debate, 624–627,
629–630, 636, 640, 643
on Indian wars, 944
on Jay treaty, 1050–1057,
1140–1141
on judicial system, 714–715,
717
on Madison, 569, 636–638
on National Bank, 863
on *National Gazette*, 962
on need to develop national
sentiment, 913–914
on need to protect government,
1099–1100
on seat of government, 714,
716, 830
on 1792 elections, 951–952
on smallpox epidemic, 985–
987
on Washington, 567
Mississippi (river), 382, 383, 469,
681, 710, 776, 1033n,
1461, 1462
Missouri (river), 370
Mithridates (King of Pontus), 164,
336, 348, 417, 441, 442,
478
Mixed government, 124, 125, 168–
173, 233–234, 1167, 1293
Mohawk Indians, 1042
Monarchy, 143, 168–170, 1067
"anonymous slanderer" and, 302
call for, following Shays's Rebellion, 83–84
federalist view of, 123, 170,
233–236
French, 25, 72, 233, 253–257
government by consent and, 173,
233
liberty versus, 1463
mixed, 25, 125, 168–173, 233–
234, 1167, 1293
Napoleonic conquests and universal, 1514
republic versus, *see* Republican
government (and republi-
cans)
threat of, 291–292
viewed as impractical in U.S.,
1293
See also Aristocracy
Monongahela (river), 383

Monroe, James, 210, 276, 374,
1104, 1328, 1400, 1487,
1488, 1523, 1524
Montezuma, Washington character-
ized as, 1138
Monticello, 335, 463
Moreau, General, 343, 1205
Morehead, 1110–1111
Morfontaine, Treaty of (1800;
French treaty), 248–249,
475n, 1104, 1169, 1277,
1278, 1280–1281, 1464,
1468–1469
Morgan, Daniel, 1186
Morris, Gouverneur, 714, 827,
1029, 1427
Morris, Robert (Bobby), 827, 830,
832, 839, 846, 1051
Morse, Jedediah, 957
Morton, Thomas, 1065, 1427
Moses, 98, 374
Mounier, 971
Mount Vernon, 524, 1114, 1142
Muhlenburg, Frederic, A., 562,
1082n, 1189
Mulgrave, Lord, 1523
Murray, William Vans, 957, 1268,
1310
Musaeus, 25

Nabis (King of Lacedaemon), 80
Nantes (France), 253, 239, 407
Naples (Italy), 238, 283, 333, 494,
504, 847, 1072, 1294
Napoleon I (Emperor of the
French), 93, 118, 119, 131,
224, 227, 258, 280, 391,
460, 494
as conqueror, 429
consequences of victories of,
481, 494–496
Roman conquests compared
with, 7, 467
See also Great Britain, war between France and; *specific
European countries*
fear of U.S. invasion by, 1556–
1559
Fox and, 350, 351
French Jacobins and, 442, 443
(*continued*)

Revenue, *see* Funding system; Taxation

Revolutionary War (War of Independence), 253, 365–366, 470, 522–524, 575–579, 739, 742, 772–773, 781, 1157

Revolutions, 6–10, 1445, 1448
  causes of, 6
  in defense of property rights, 17
  favorite work of, 356
  nature of, 117–118, 179–182
  violence of, 178–179
  See also specific revolutions and insurrections

Rhine (river), 164, 427, 474, 488, 494, 1549

Rhode Island, 54, 220, 549, 570, 1113–1115
  adoption of Constitution by, 687, 694–695, 970
  apportionment of representation and, 926, 929, 935, 936
  assumption of debt and, 220, 233, 961
  duties and, 640
  1800 elections and, 1365, 1381, 1392, 1400
  federalism in, 1400, 1450, 1475
  military preparedness, 1238
  and seat of government, 701, 828

Rhodians, 493

Rice, Major, 629

Richardson, James, 1433–1434

Right(s), 8, 17, 19
  to annual elections, 67–68
    See also Elections
  in democracy, violations of, 126
  derived from social contract, 66
  1800 elections and protection of, 212
  equality of, 240–242
  people's disrespect for, 123
  to petition Congress, debates on, 571–581
  restraint on state power to protect, 18–19
  in Rome, 223–225
  state government and protection of, 548
  See also Liberty *and specific rights*

Rights of Man, Declaration of the, 118, 174, 209, 245, 400

Rittenhouse, 117

Robertson (*History of Scotland*), 1210

Robespierre, Maximilien de, 182, 204, 259, 344, 407, 432, 1402, 1421

Robin Hood, 73, 642

Robbins, 1427

Roland, 155, 218, 257, 259, 1421, 1474

Rome, 15, 114, 169, 523
  checks and balances in, 163
  democracy in, 163–168
  elections in, 545
  factions in, 226
  laws of, 159
  liberty destroyed in, 132–133
  literature of, 25, 32
  as military power, 114, 166, 333–336, 338, 346, 348, 366, 410, 477, 502
    France compared with, 65, 77–80, 206, 259, 264, 333–334, 401, 403, 416–418, 420–441, 451, 464, 466, 468, 477–489, 495, 500–502, 531
  military service in, 156
  patriotism in, 114, 334, 425
  people's tribunes in, 113
  as republic, 24, 223–227, 384–385, 425, 498–504
  superstitions of, 15
  Virginia compared with, 1445
  virtue in, 114, 223, 225, 507

Romulus, 114

Ross, James, 1189, 1320

Rule-of-Three, 917, 925

Rule of the War (1756), 472*n*

Rundle, 1537

Rush, 987

Russell, Benjamin, 570, 624, 643, 952, 987, 1251, 1273, 1292, 1560

Russia, 334, 343, 346, 406, 454–459, 466, 467, 494, 1422, 1423, 1506, 1545, 1549
  Austerlitz and, 335, 345–347, 1514

(*continued*)

This book was set in Bodoni Book,
a typeface derived from the designs of
Giambattista Bodoni, who worked in Parma
in the early nineteenth century. His designs broke
with the old traditions by eliminating ornament and
emphasizing thick and thin contrasts. A member
of the Bodoni type family, Bodoni Book is
a refined and elegant face particularly
appropriate for books.

———

Book design by Betty Binns Graphics, New York, New York
Editorial service by Harkavy Publishing Service, New York, New York
Typography by Monotype Composition Co., Inc.,
Baltimore, Maryland
Soft-covers printed by Phoenix Color Corp.,
Long Island City, New York
Printed and bound by R. R. Donnelley and Sons,
Crawfordsville, Indiana